DATE DUE			

NORTH and SOUTH CAROLINA
MARRIAGE RECORDS

By the same author

AMERICAN MARRIAGE RECORDS BEFORE 1699

E. P. DUTTON & COMPANY

NORTH AND SOUTH CAROLINA MARRIAGE RECORDS

FROM THE EARLIEST COLONIAL DAYS TO THE CIVIL WAR

Compiled and Edited By

WILLIAM MONTGOMERY CLEMENS

Editor of

Genealogy Magazine

E. P. DUTTON & COMPANY

681 FIFTH AVENUE   NEW YORK

INTRODUCTION

HISTORY has dealt sparingly with the early settlements in the Carolinas. No doubt the first white man to explore the coastline from Maryland southward was Giovanni Verrazano, an Italian voyager, who visited the shores of what is now called North and South Carolina in the year 1524. The Carolinas originally were included in the territory designated as South Virginia. The first settlement in what is now North Carolina was in the county named Albermarle, which was divided in the three precincts of Carteret, Berkeley and Shaftesbury. Here were among the first English settlements made in America.

In the year 1663 a land patent and grant was made to Lord Clarendon by Charles the Second of England. Nine years later Charleston was founded and about this time a more ample charter was obtained and the government passed into the hands of the proprietors. This Proprietary Government continued for about fifty years.

In 1728 Carolina which at this period meant the North and South sections combined, contained three counties, Albemarle, Bath, and Clarendon. Albemarle was divided into the precincts of Currituck, Pasquetank, Perquimans, Chowan, Bertie, and Tyrrell. In Bath County there were four precincts, Beaufort, Hyde, Craven, and Carteret. Clarendon had the single precinct of Hanover. At the end of the Proprietary Government these counties and precincts were abolished and became counties of North and South Carolina.

NORTH CAROLINA

THE first straggling settlements in North Carolina after the Clarendon grant of 1663 were gradually broken up. While North Carolina was not a separate province until 1729, the country had been settled about the year 1710 by a colony of Palatines from Germany who had fled from the north after a disastrous war with the Indians, and seeking a retreat they settled in the Carolina wilderness. They had scarcely taken possession of their asylum in Albemarle and Bath precincts when again they fell a prey to the savages. The colony was nearly destroyed, over a hundred settlers having been massacred.

Help came from the South Carolina settlements and the Indians were defeated, about the year 1712. The colony remained in peace under the

Proprietary Government until 1729 when seven of the proprietors, for a valuable consideration, vested their property and jurisdiction in the crown and the colony was erected under the name of North Carolina. The present limits of the colony were established by an order of King George the Second, the Governor and Council being appointed by His Majesty.

By a regal act of 1770 the large county of Rowan was divided into three counties. Wake County in which the capital of North Carolina was situated was formed in 1771 from portions of Cumberland, Orange, and Johnston, chiefly from the latter. Cumberland County had been chartered May 21, 1757, and with Orange County had been formed from Bladen. Tyrrell County which had been created out of Albemarle in 1729 was abolished and then re-established in 1755.

In 1771 there was an insurrection of a small body of the inhabitants. They complained of oppression, called themselves regulators, and endeavored to prostrate the government. Governor Tryon marched against them and they were defeated leaving three hundred dead on the field. At the commencement of the Revolution the regulators espoused the cause of the British and were again defeated by Colonel Caswell in February, 1776. North Carolina ratified the Constitution of the United States November 21, 1789. Her three signers to the Declaration of Independence were William Hooper, Joseph Hughes, and John Penn. North Carolina has given three presidents to the country, Andrew Jackson, James K. Polk, and Andrew Johnston, and one vice-president, William R. King.

Prominent among the early colonists who figured largely in the history of North Carolina were William Davidson, who removed to Rowan County in 1750 from Pennsylvania; Davidson County is named in his honor. Davie County is named for William Richardson Davie who was a famous soldier of the Revolution. Caswell County is named for Richard Caswell distinguished as a governor of the state who was appointed a member of the First Congress in 1774.

Another governor for whom a county was named was Nathaniel Alexander and from a perusal of the Alexander marriages in this volume the reader will discover that the Alexanders outnumber all other names in this book. Iredell County received its name from James Iradell, a North Carolina judge who was made a judge of the United States Supreme Court in 1790. Samuel Ashe, chief justice in 1777 and governor in 1796 gives the name to Ashe County.

Under the conditions existing in North Carolina it is not surprising to find very few marriages on record prior to 1700, as there were no authentic records available and the marriages recorded in this book before the year 1699 were discovered only after the most careful and patient research.

As an example of incomplete marriage records we give certain data found in court and other county records. These marriages, not included in the regular alphabetical arrangement, will show the reader how difficult the work of making complete records has become and will well illustrate the lack of early data, especially before 1700.

William Badham married about 1735 Martha Mooney at Edenton.

Thomas Blount married the widow of Joseph Scott before February 5, 1686. Recorded at Edenton, Chowan Precinct.

Thomas Burnby married Hannah, daughter of Edmund Chancy, before 1686. Recorded at Edenton.

William Duckinfield married Susannah —— who married (2) —— Hartley. Before 1695 at Edenton.

Ann Durant (born 1719) married Thomas Corpreu who married (2) Sarah Vail. (Apparently recorded at Perquimans District.)

James Harlve married (by 1684) "ye relict of Hugh Barlow."

Governor Thomas Harvey of North Carolina (from Warwickshire, England), married (1) on April 13, 1682, Joannah Jenkins "ye relict of Hon Jenkins"; married (2) Sarah, daughter of Benjamin Laker, Perquimans, N. C.

John Hecklefield had married Elizabeth, widow of Jonathan Godfrey by 1697. Edenton, N. C.

Major John Hinton (moved to Wake County, N. C., about the middle of the 18th Century; son of John Hinton; died 1784) married Grizella Kimbrough.

Thomas Keele married Mary —— who married (2) —— Relfe, before 1684. Recorded at Edenton.

Joseph Lane married, 1730, Patience, daughter of Barnabas McKinne, Sr.

Paul Latham married the widow of William Leary, before February 5, 1686, at Edenton.

John Lynch married (before 1756) Elizabeth, widow of Hugh Allen. Chowan Precinct.

William Mara married Mary, daughter of William Therrill, before February 5, 1686, at Edenton.

George Matthews married Elizabeth, daughter of Richard Williams, before 1693.

Benjamin Messenge had married Anne, daughter of Thomas and Elizabeth Waller, before 1694.

Isaac Rowden married Sarah, daughter of George and Ann Durant, before February 5, 1686.

John Simpson married (before 1732) Mary Brinn.

John Stamps married Joannah —— who married (2) before March, 1684, Edward Wells.

Samuel Sutton married (before 1746) Mary Buncombe, daughter of Joseph Buncombe and wife, Ann Durant.

Hester Sweetman (of Maryland; died 1716) married (1) John Harris (2) Colonel William Wilkinson (3) Thomas Pollock.

Thomas Waller had married Miss Durant, the sister of Thomas Durant, before 1697.

Dorothy St. M. Wellsmar married before October, 1684 ——— Minsy.
Arthur Workman married Mary ——— and (by 1707) ——— Clark.

SOUTH CAROLINA

BEFORE the Clarendon grant in 1663, a plantation had for some years been in operation within the boundaries of the patent. In fact South Carolina was inhabited by a small colony of whites before there was a settlement in North Carolina. James Colleton, from whom a county is named, was appointed governor by the king and served from 1686 to 1690. He came from the Barbadoes and was a proprietor and landgrave. He was one of the first to build a large residence, which was located on the bank of Cooper River. Many disputes arose concerning tenures of land and quit-rents, and the Colleton government became very unpopular. In 1687 Colleton assembled a parliament and changed some of the fundamental laws. But he had offended members of the high church party and in the end the governor was driven from the province.

Meanwhile in addition to perpetual quarrels among the inhabitants, the colony was harassed by the Indians, frequently visited by pirates and invaded by French and Spanish fleets. Charles Craven, who had been secretary to the proprietors, was governor of the colony, from 1712 to 1716. He explored Port Royal River and is supposed to have built the town of Beaufort. Following Craven, Robert Johnson became governor in 1719. In 1729, as previously stated, the Carolinas were divided into the two distinct governments. One of the most distinguished men of this period was Mark Catesby, an eminent naturalist who coming from England to Virginia in 1712 took up his residence in South Carolina in 1722. He lived for a time at Fort Moore from which place he made several visits to the Indians and made researches in the uninhabited mountain country.

In 1730 Robert Johnson was again made governor and continued in office until his death in Charleston, May 3, 1735. In 1731, he negotiated a treaty with the Cherokee Indians. He proved himself an efficient friend of Oglethorpe and others who first settled the country to the south known as Georgia, and upon the arrival of the party at Charleston, the assembly at the suggestion of Governor Johnson, furnished them with cattle, hogs and provisions, and gave them ten mounted horse-men for their protection. It was during Governor Johnson's administration that the settlement of Purrysburgh was made by 600 Swiss under Colonel Peter Purry.

South Carolina prior to the Revolution had probably more distinguished men than any other colony in the new world. Among these was William Drayton, Judge of the Federal Court, who was born in the province in 1733 and afterwards in 1768 became Chief Justice of East Florida. Christopher Gadsden, Lieutenant Governor, born in Charleston in 1724, was one of the delegates to New York in 1765 to petition against the Stamp Act. Arthur Middleton, the Signer, was born on the banks of Ashley River in 1743, his grandfather Arthur being the first royal governor of South Carolina. He married the daughter of Walter Izard. Charles C. Pinckney was born in 1746, the son of Chief Justice Pinckney and was to become a famous soldier of the Revolution. His brother Thomas was a distinguished patriot. Thomas Heyward, judge and patriot, was born in St. Lukes Parish in 1746, his father being a wealthy planter. William Bull who died in 1755, was the first native physician of South Carolina, and probably the first American, to obtain a degree in medicine. Henry Laurens was president of the Provincial Congress of Carolina in 1755. In the Revolution he was captured by the British and taken as a state prisoner charged with high treason and was confined in the Tower. Thomas Lynch, another patriot, was born in Prince George Parish in 1749. John Lining, an eminent physician and philosopher, practised his profession in Charleston for thirty years and died in 1760. Stephen Elliott, a famous botanist, was born in Beaufort in 1771. William Moultrie, one of the governors of the state served in the Cherokee war and was a famous soldier of the Revolution. Other names famous in the early history of South Carolina, are those of Isaac Hayne, Andrew Pickens, Daniel McCalla, John Matthews, Aedanus Burke, William Butler, David Ramsey, Gabriel Manigault and John Gaillard.

South Carolina ratified the constitution of the United States, May 23, 1788, and her signers to the Declaration of Independence were Edward Rutledge, Thomas Heyward, Jr., Thomas Lynch, Jr., and Arthur Middleton. Vice President John C. Calhoun was a native of South Carolina.

The marriage records to be found in this volume, include the descendents of the men made famous in the early history of South Carolina and it will be discovered that the Middletons, the Izards, the Laurens, and other famous families continue prominent to the present day, the early families having continually intermarried, leaving many descendants. The records of churches, parishes and court houses have been carefully examined for the data contained in this volume, and naturally through the long periods of war and rebellions, many of these records have been lost and destroyed. Consequently the reader must expect disappointment occasionally in not finding the particular name of ancestors supposed to have been married in South Carolina. This applies also to North Carolina. The variations in the spelling of family names, is due not always to the ancestors themselves, but largely through the carelessness and ignorance of parish clerks and court officials, who inscribed the names of parties contracting marriages, by sound, without regard to the actual spelling. It will be interesting to note fanciful nick-names of some of the daughters of the Carolinas whose marriages are recorded, with first names such as, Dovey, Hasky, Sukey, Dicey, Tarsy, Owny, Ludy, Minty, Tully, Hanny, Penny and in one instance the name of the young lady was Athenatious.

The editor of this volume desires to express his heart-felt thanks to the following prominent sons and daughters of the Carolinas, for their valuable

assistance in the compilation of this work: Frank H. Covington, of Bennettsville, N. C.; Samuel M. Carothers, of Sumter, S. C.; C. D. Kenny, of Warrens-
ville, S. C.; Miss Edna H. White, of Oxford, N. C.; Miss Lilly Cooper, of
Denmark, S. C.; Miss Gladys Gieger, of Swansea, S. C.; and Mrs. Susan B.
Hill, of Edgefield, S. C.

W. M. C.

Pompton Lakes, New Jersey, June 1927.

NORTH and SOUTH CAROLINA MARRIAGE RECORDS

NORTH AND SOUTH CAROLINA
MARRIAGE RECORDS

A

AARONS, Rachel and Joseph Tobias, 2 November 1785, Charleston, S. C.

ABBETS, Samuel and Catherine Winchester, 11 December 1802, Mecklenburg Co., N. C.

ABBEY, Daniel and Elizabeth Pressly, 16 February 1843, Edgefield District, S. C.

ABBOTT, William and Barbara Dawson, 6 June 1801, Charleston, S. C.

ABECKLIN, Kilian and Maria Schwartz, 12 January 1740, Orangeburg Co., S. C.

ABERCROMBIE, John and Sarah Mitchell, 1777, Charleston, S. C.

ABERCROMBIE, Zany and Tolaver Armstrong, 7 April 1857, Laurens Co., S. C.

ABERNATHY, C. W. and Mary A. Kistler, 25 September 1856, Mecklenburg Co., N. C.

ABERNATHY, John C. and Sarah S. Hutson, 13 May 1843, Mecklenburg Co. N. C.

ABERNATHY, John W. and Martha A. Ray, 11 June 1861, Mecklenburg Co., N. C.

ABERNATHY, Lockey and Joshua T. Moore, 6 January 1830, Mecklenburg Co., N. C.

ABERNATHY, W. D. and Isabella Cole, 27 June 1860, Mecklenburg Co., N. C.

ABINGTON, Littlebury and Sarah Moore, 4 May 1790, Bertie Co., N. C.

ABLE, A. R. and Perasday Gregory, 12 July 1855, Edgefield District, S. C.

ABNEY, James B. and Martha Livingston, 21 December 1848, Edgefield Co., S. C.

ABRAHAMS, Hannah and Samuel Levy, 1 June 1796, Charleston, S. C.

ABRAMS, Francis and Milford Motes, 23 November 1858, Laurens Co., S. C.

ABRAMS, Resess and Mercer Bailey, 20 November 1860, Laurens Co., S. C.

ABSTANCE, Eunice and Christian Faust, 1795, Barnwell District, S. C.

ACHISON, Thomas and Aurora Griffith, 17 April 1793, Mecklenburg Co., N. C.

ACOCK, Elizabeth H. and John Rea, 1 March 1823, Mecklenburg Co., N. C.

ACOCK, John N. and Susannah Caskey, 30 December 1844, Mecklenburg Co., N. C.

ACOCK, Thomas W. and Ursla Huddleston, 23 October 1814, Mecklenburg Co., N. C.

ACREE, William and Ferebee Skinner, 12 March 1791, Bertie Co., N. C.

ADAM, Mary and Abraham Groef, 3 November 1779, Rowan Co., N. C.

ADAMS, Charles W. and Esther M. Izard, 3 April 1782, Prince George Parish, S. C.

ADAMS, Cicero and Mary A. Hughes, 27 May 1856, Edgefield District, S. C.

ADAMS, Diana and Joshua Hicks, 19 September 1794, Rowan Co., N. C.

ADAMS, Elizabeth (Mrs.) and Daniel J. Greene, 22 April 1784, Beaufort, S. C.

ADAMS, Ellen and Iredel Jones, 4 November 1869, Live Oak, S. C.

ADAMS, James P. and Margaret Kerney, 20 January 1852, Mecklenburg Co., N. C.

ADAMS, Joel F. and Isabella McKenzie, 9 January 1861, Mecklenburg Co., N. C.

ADAMS, John and Margaret Young, 15 November 1788, Orange Co., N. C.

ADAMS, John and Mahaleth Atkins, 2 October 1816, Newberry, S. C.

ADAMS, Jonathan and Martha Combs, 8 February 1783, Tyrrell Co., N. C.

ADAMS, Leroy and Mary Grier, 14 July 1847, Mecklenburg Co., N. C.

ADAMS, Lewis and Elizabeth Sanders, 25 May 1834, Mecklenburg Co., N. C.

ADAMS, Margaret and Joseph Atkins, 1 January 1824, Edgefield, S. C.

ADAMS, Martha and Henry Romering, 29 December 1800, Charleston, S. C.

ADAMS, Mary and William Ervin, 13 October 1788, Rowan Co., N. C.

ADAMS, Mary Goodwyn and J. Hampton Brooks, 24 January 1856, Edgefield District, S. C.

ADAMS, Miss and William Saunders, 1725, Orange Co., N. C.

ADAMS, Peter and (Mrs.) Sarah Smith, 3 June 1745, Chowan Co., N. C.

ADAMS, Providence and John Cape, 10 May 1796, Charleston, S. C.

ADAMS, Samuel and Matheze Givens, 24 January 1799, Mecklenburg Co., N. C.

ADAMS, Sarah (widow) and Micajah Bunch, 10 August 1747, Chowan Co., N. C.

ADAMS, Susannah and Samuel Estep, 3 November 1789, Rowan Co., N. C.

ADAMS, Thomas and Esther Rogers, 12 October 1785, Tyrrell Co., N. C.

ADAMSON, William and Amelia Alexander, 23 October 1800, Camden, S. C.

ADDISON, John and Tamson Ralph, May 1784, Charleston, S. C.

ADDISON, Joseph (Dr.), and Emma Louise Brown, 27 February 1850, Barnwell Co., S. C.

ADDISON, Kezia and James McKnight, May 1784, St. Thomas Parish, S. C.

ADDISON, Mary (widow) and Ezekial Mills, January 1784, St. Thomas Parish, S. C.

ADELY, Frances A. and Benjamin Pearson, 26 October 1800, Charleston, S. C.

ADGER, Anna E. and Thomas H. Law, 16 March 1860, Charleston, S. C.

ADKINS, Jackson and Lucretia J. Wilson, 19 December 1847, Mecklenburg Co., N. C.

ADKINS, James and Mary Carson, 18 February 1790, Orange Co., N. C.

ADKINS, Lucretia and James Ashley, 3 July 1851, Mecklenburg Co., N. C.

ADKINSON, Lucy and Elias Fort, 7 March 1764, Edgecombe Co., N. C.

AGENOR, Margaret and George Frailey, 15 June 1796, Rowan Co., N. C.

AHORN, Margaret and Eli Alexander, 21 December 1804, Mecklenburg Co., N. C.

AHRENS, F. W. and (Miss) L. A. Henderson, 10 December 1857, Mecklenburg Co., N. C.

AIKEN, Eliza J. and William Black, 19 March 1861, Mecklenburg Co., N. C.

AIKEN, Isabell and William McClain, 4 January 1800, Guilford Co., N. C.

AIKEN, Serena and Thomas G. Simons, 11 November 1879, Charleston, S. C.

AIKENS, Ann and John, 3 September 1798, Mecklenburg Co., N. C.

AIKENS, John and Ann, 3 September 1798, Mecklenburg Co., N. C.

AINESLEY, Amelia and Joshua Alexander, 1782, Tyrrell Co., N. C.

AINESLEY, Elizabeth and William Tarkinton, 6 April 1785, Tyrrell Co., N. C.

AINESLEY, Joseph (Jr.) and Mary Swain, 15 March 1786, Tyrrell Co., N. C.

AINGER, Edward and Elizabeth Shaw, 26 October 1799, Charleston, S. C.

AINSLIE, John and Mary Child, 18 January 1750, Charleston, S. C.

AINSLIE, John and Mary Drayton (widow), 17 June 1762, Charleston, S. C.

AIR, Elizabeth and Isaac Holmes, 5 January 1779, Charleston, S. C.

AIR, William and Polly Stephenson, 2 August 1770, Charleston, S. C.

AIRS, Elizabeth and John Cummings, 8 October 1801, Charleston, S. C.

AIRS, Zilpa and John Griffin, 26 December 1775, Tyrrell Co., N. C.

AKIN, William and Henrietta Wyatt, 12 November 1801, Charleston, S. C.

ALBERSON, John and Mary Warren, 7 January 1778, Chowan Co., N. C.

ALBRIGHT, Sarah and William Montgomery, 13 November 1817, Guilford Co., N. C.

ALCOCK, Mary and Godfrey Spruill, 1780, Tyrrell Co., N. C.

ALCORN, Sarah and William Nance, 18 December 1814, Mecklenburg Co., N. C.

ALDER, Conrad and Anna Rickenbacker, (nee Burgin, widow) 1 January 1740, Orangeburg Co., S. C.

ALDERSON, Armistead and Peggy Hutchinson, 14 January 1803, Mecklenburg Co., N. C.

ALDERSON, Robert and Nancy Smith, 20 February 1804, Mecklenburg Co., N. C.

ALDRICH, Hanna and Thomas Felps, 20 April 1792, Rowan Co., N. C.

ALDRICH, John and Drady Owen, 18 August 1822, Edgefield District, S. C.

ALEXANDER, Abdon and Martha J. Sloan, 27 August 1860, Mecklenburg Co., N. C.

ALEXANDER, Abel A. and Angeline Davis, 13 October 1835, Mecklenburg Co., N. C.

ALEXANDER, Abigail B. and Samuel C. Caldwell, 8 May 1793, Mecklenburg Co., N. C.

ALEXANDER, Abijah F. and Esther A. Ross, 10 September 1851, Mecklenburg Co., N. C.

ALEXANDER, Abisba and Abigail McFarlin, 23 August 1798, Mecklenburg Co., N. C.

ALEXANDER, Adley L. and Nancy Robinson, 1 January 1817, Mecklenburg Co., N. C.

ALEXANDER, Albert and Susan Alexander, 19 December 1846, Mecklenburg Co., N. C.

ALEXANDER, Alexander and Mary Willis, 24 September 1851, Laurens Co., S. C.

ALEXANDER, Alexi and Rachel Anderson, 22 October 1767, Charleston, S. C.

ALEXANDER, Alexi and Elizabeth Murray, 1 February 1774, Charleston, S. C.

ALEXANDER, Alice A. and Samuel H. Blankenship, 3 December 1859, Mecklenburg Co., N. C.

ALEXANDER, Alley and Nancy Robison, 1 January 1817, Mecklenburg Co., N. C.

ALEXANDER, Allison and Harriet C. Shelly, 17 December 1823, Mecklenburg Co., N. C.

ALEXANDER, Amelia and William Adamson, 23 October 1800, Camden, S. C.

ALEXANDER, Amelia S. and James T. Orr, 26 March 1831, Mecklenburg Co. N. C.

ALEXANDER, Amos and Mildred Orr, 23 December 1797, Mecklenburg Co., N. C.

ALEXANDER, Ann and John Alexander, 1780, Tyrrell Co., N. C.

ALEXANDER, Ann and James Alexander, 7 July 1802, Mecklenburg Co., N. C.

ALEXANDER, Ann and James Clark, 31 March 1818, Mecklenburg Co., N. C.

ALEXANDER, Anthony and Keziah Blount, 1781, Tyrrell Co., N. C.

ALEXANDER, Augustus and Sally Glass, 13 February 1839, Mecklenburg Co., N. C.

ALEXANDER, Azni and Martha Robison, 16 April 1806, Mecklenburg Co., N. C.

ALEXANDER, Azariah and Fanny Alexander, 16 November 1802, Mecklenburg Co., N. C.

ALEXANDER, A. H. (Miss) and William K. Reid, 15 January 1841, Mecklenburg Co., N. C.

ALEXANDER, Benjamin F. and Hannah K. Wilson, 23 July 1823, Mecklenburg Co., N. C.

ALEXANDER, C. L. and Margaret Moore, 5 April 1845, Mecklenburg Co., N. C.

ALEXANDER, Calvin G. and Nancy Kirk, 27 March 1833, Mecklenburg Co., N. C.

ALEXANDER, Caroline and Milton Blair, 31 March 1831, Mecklenburg Co., N. C.

ALEXANDER, Caroline and Nathaniel Alexander, 27 October 1823, Mecklenburg Co., N. C.

ALEXANDER, Cassa and James Houston, 1 January 1803, Mecklenburg Co., N. C.

ALEXANDER, Charles W. and Margaret A. Flow, 26 December 1861, Mecklenburg Co., N. C.

ALEXANDER, Christian and Joseph Pledger, 8 May 1783, Tyrrell Co., N. C.

ALEXANDER, Clarisa and Alexander Robison, 16 August 1815, Mecklenburg Co., N. C.

ALEXANDER, Cornelius and Mary E. Caldwell, 26 November 1856, Mecklenburg Co., N. C.

ALEXANDER, Cynthia and Jonathan Orr, 18 April 1835, Mecklenburg Co., N. C.

ALEXANDER, Cyrus and Rebecca Arthur, 20 March 1797, Mecklenburg Co., N. C.

ALEXANDER, Cyrus J. and Elizabeth E. Sloan, 17 September 1814, Mecklenburg Co., N. C.

ALEXANDER, Cyrus M. and Martha Cole, 23 February 1836, Mecklenburg Co., N. C.

ALEXANDER, Cyrus W. and Nancy Lawring, 23 June 1835, Mecklenburg Co., N. C.

ALEXANDER, Dan and Susannah Shelby, 11 June 1800, Mecklenburg Co., N. C.

ALEXANDER, Daniel and Sarah Alexander, 14 August 1800, Mecklenburg Co., N. C.

ALEXANDER, David and Rebecca Doherty, 17 Sept. 1814, Mecklenburg Co., N. C.

ALEXANDER, Dionisius and Harriet C. Harris, 31 December 1846, Mecklenburg Co., N. C.

ALEXANDER, Dorcas and Eli Collins, 10 December 1829, Mecklenburg Co., N. C.

ALEXANDER, Dorcas and Ira Alexander, 11 December 1842, Mecklenburg Co., N. C.

ALEXANDER, Edward and Elizabeth Gardner, 1784, Tyrrell Co., N. C.

ALEXANDER, Elam E. and Mary P. Hartgrove, 2 January 1844, Mecklenburg Co., N. C.

ALEXANDER, Eli and Margaret Ahorn, 21 December 1804, Mecklenburg Co., N. C.

ALEXANDER, Eli and Margaret Orr, 1 April 1806, Mecklenburg Co., N. C.

ALEXANDER, Elias and Patsy Garrison, 7 July 1810, Mecklenburg Co., N. C.

ALEXANDER, Elinor and John S. Rankin, 28 August 1835, Mecklenburg Co., N. C.

ALEXANDER, Eliza and Samuel Blair, 26 November 1823, Mecklenburg Co., N. C.

ALEXANDER, Eliza and James Coffey, 23 May 1827, Mecklenburg Co., N. C.

ALEXANDER, Eliza and H. R. Reid, 21 November 1865, Mecklenburg Co., N. C.

ALEXANDER, Elizabeth and Stephen Davenport, 28 December 1778, Tyrrell Co., N. C.

ALEXANDER, Elizabeth and Wells Cooper, 1780, Tyrrell Co., N. C.

ALEXANDER, Elizabeth and John D. Vale, 1788, St. Johns Parish, S. C.

ALEXANDER, Elizabeth C. and John Johnson, 18 December 1833, Mecklenburg Co., N. C.

ALEXANDER, Elizabeth and Gerard Alexander, 14 March 1837, Chowan Co., N. C.

ALEXANDER, Elizabeth and John R. Rodgers, 17 February 1859, Mecklenburg Co., N. C.

ALEXANDER, Ellen M. and William M. Bailey, 13 December 1850, Mecklenburg Co., N. C.

ALEXANDER, Emily and Thomas P. Rodgers, 26 September 1848, Mecklenburg Co., N. C.

ALEXANDER, Evan and Agness Moore, 2 November 1818, Mecklenburg Co., N. C.

ALEXANDER, Ezekiel and Patsey Robison, 8 March 1806, Mecklenburg Co., N. C.

ALEXANDER, Ezekiel and Rachel Price, 25 March 1811, Mecklenburg Co., N. C.

ALEXANDER, Evan P. and Elizabeth Berryhill, 24 February 1824, Mecklenburg Co., N. C.

ALEXANDER, Ezekial and Catherine C. Houston, 20 December 1836, Mecklenburg Co., N. C.

ALEXANDER, Fanny and Azariah Alexander, 16 November 1802, Mecklenburg Co., N. C.

ALEXANDER, Francis and Margaret Alexander, 1 April 1789, Mecklenburg Co., N. C.

ALEXANDER, Francis and Jane McCorkle, 5 November 1815, Mecklenburg Co., N. C.

ALEXANDER, G. W. and Sarah S. Yetton, 28 February 1855, Mecklenburg Co., N. C.

ALEXANDER, George W. and Wilmuth A. Christenberry, 31 March 1857, Mecklenburg Co., N. C.

ALEXANDER, Gerard and Elizabeth Alexander, 14 March 1837, Chowan Co., N. C.

ALEXANDER, Hannah and William Neal, 23 November 1819, Mecklenburg Co., N. C.

ALEXANDER, Hannah and Laird H. Harris, 23 June 1840, Mecklenburg Co., N. C.

ALEXANDER, Hannah E. and James H. Brown, 3 December 1857, Mecklenburg Co., N. C.

ALEXANDER, Harmon and Frances Bateman, 14 December 1865, Chowan Co., N. C.

ALEXANDER, Harriet C. and Daniel G. Caldwell, 28 February 1861, Mecklenburg Co., N. C.

ALEXANDER, Helena and Hugh Moore, 19 March 1824, Mecklenburg Co., N. C.

ALEXANDER, Ira and Dorcas Alexander, 11 December 1842, Mecklenburg Co., N. C.

ALEXANDER, Isaac and Caroline Morrison, 8 August 1845, Mecklenburg Co., N. C.

ALEXANDER, Isaac F. and Lydia Campbell, 1 September 1830, Mecklenburg Co., N. C.

ALEXANDER, Isabella L. and William S. Alexander, 26 December 1842, Mecklenburg Co., N. C.

ALEXANDER, J. S. (Miss)) and C. E. Moss, 21 April 1845, Mecklenburg Co., N. C.

ALEXANDER, James and Rhoda Cunningham, 1782, Rowan Co., N. C.

ALEXANDER, James and Hannah Clark, 16 October 1798, Mecklenburg Co., N. C.

ALEXANDER, James and Ann Alexander, 7 July 1802, Mecklenburg Co., N. C.

ALEXANDER, James and Martha Rodgers, 14 November 1806, Mecklenburg Co., N. C.

ALEXANDER, James and Isabella Maxwell, 14 January 1831, Mecklenburg Co., N. C.

ALEXANDER, James and Elizabeth Stringfellow, 26 May 1834, Mecklenburg Co., N. C.

ALEXANDER, James Addison and Margaret C. Alexander, 29 June 1816, Mecklenburg Co., N. C.

ALEXANDER, James C. and Catherine Thomason, 24 February 1831, Mecklenburg Co., N. C.

ALEXANDER, James F. and Martha McGinness, 16 May 1859, Mecklenburg Co., N. C.

ALEXANDER, James H. and M. E. Beaty, 27 May 1862, Mecklenburg Co., N. C.

ALEXANDER, James L. and Rosanna Blanchard, 23 August 1842, Mecklenburg Co., N. C.

ALEXANDER, James L. and Catherine E. McGee, 14 December 1854, Mecklenburg Co., N. C.

ALEXANDER, James M. and Nancy Forster, 1814, Buncombe Co., N. C.

ALEXANDER, James M. and Mary L. Wilson, 9 July 1844, Mecklenburg Co., N. C.

ALEXANDER, James N. and Mary M. Caldwell, 4 March 1858, Mecklenburg Co., N. C.

ALEXANDER, James P. and Sarah Bentley, 18 January 1830, Mecklenburg Co., N. C.

ALEXANDER, James R. and Harriet Baker, 8 December 1836, Mecklenburg Co., N. C.

ALEXANDER, James S. and Mary Allen, 16 February 1836, Mecklenburg Co., N. C.

ALEXANDER, James Scott and Matilda McLean, 14 December 1814, Mecklenburg Co., N. C.

ALEXANDER, James W. and Mary McCartney, 24 December 1835, Abbeville District, S. C.

ALEXANDER, James W. and Margaret L. Reid, 17 December 1850, Mecklenburg Co., N. C.

ALEXANDER, Jane and David Reed, 7 April 1795, Mecklenburg Co., N. C.

ALEXANDER, Jane E. and Isaiah D. Irwin, 25 August 1859, Mecklenburg Co., N. C.

ALEXANDER, Jane F. and Andrew McConnell, 26 February 1822, Mecklenburg Co., N. C.

ALEXANDER, James R. and William C. Bigham, 8 May 1845, Mecklenburg Co., N. C.

ALEXANDER, Jefferson and Malinda Johnson, 29 January 1843, Laurens Co., S. C.

ALEXANDER, Jennet and Ozy Strickland, 7 January 1828, Mecklenburg Co., N. C.

ALEXANDER, Joel B. and Cynthia Morrison, 16 August 1815, Mecklenburg Co., N. C.

ALEXANDER, John and Mary Spruill, (widow) 23 February 1763, Tyrrell Co., N. C.

ALEXANDER, John and Ann Barnes, 11 August 1768, Tyrrell Co., N. C.

ALEXANDER, John and Ann Alexander, 1780, Tyrrell Co., N. C.

ALEXANDER, John and Sarah Shilly, 15 August 1798, Mecklenburg Co., N. C.

ALEXANDER, John and Susanah Alexander, 18 October 1830, Mecklenburg Co., N. C.

ALEXANDER, John G. and Elizabeth Lemmond, 3 April 1811, Mecklenburg Co., N. C.

ALEXANDER, John M. and Jane F. Harris, 2 January 1814, Mecklenburg Co., N. C.

ALEXANDER, John M. and Cynthia M. Todd, 27 December 1854, Mecklenburg Co., N. C.

ALEXANDER, John O. and Jane E. Lee, 17 February 1857, Mecklenburg Co., N. C.

ALEXANDER, John R. and Harriet Henderson, 14 December 1823, Mecklenburg Co., N. C.

ALEXANDER, Joshua and Amelia Ainesley, 1782, Tyrrell Co., N. C.

ALEXANDER, Lawson and Jenny Berry Elliot, 6 May 1828, Mecklenburg Co., N. C.

ALEXANDER, Leander D. and Margaret Parks, 31 July 1843, Mecklenburg Co., N. C.

ALEXANDER, M. E. (Miss) and G. W. Caldwell, 1 February 1866, Mecklenburg Co., N. C.

ALEXANDER, M. S. (Miss) and E. A. McAuley, 19 December 1849, Mecklenburg Co., N. C.

ALEXANDER, Maggie C. and S. I. Nessler, 28 April 1864, Mecklenburg Co., N. C.

ALEXANDER, Marcus and Malinda McClure, 21 August 1811, Mecklenburg Co., N. C.

ALEXANDER, Marcus and Martha Gilmore, 13 April 1822, Mecklenburg Co., N. C.

ALEXANDER, Marcus F. and Mary Johnston, 30 January 1844, Mecklenburg Co., N. C.

ALEXANDER, Margaret and Francis Alexander, 1 April 1789, Mecklenburg Co., N. C.

ALEXANDER, Margaret and Robert Wilson, 3 December 1816, Mecklenburg Co., N. C.

ALEXANDER, Margaret and Samuel Berryhill, 10 February 1823, Mecklenburg Co., N. C.

ALEXANDER, Margaret and Alexander Irvin, 14 October 1833, Mecklenburg Co., N. C.

ALEXANDER, Margaret C. and James Addison Alexander, 29 June 1816, Mecklenburg Co., N. C.

ALEXANDER, Margaret M. and Moses W. Alexander, 6 December 1830, Mecklenburg Co., N. C.

ALEXANDER, Martha and Aaron Askew, 7 May 1805, Bertie Co., N. C.

ALEXANDER, Martha and John Montieth, 29 January 1833, Mecklenburg Co., N. C.

ALEXANDER, Martha and Robert Irvin, 4 August 1838, Mecklenburg Co., N. C.

ALEXANDER, Martha and James Boatwright, 4 September 1845, Mecklenburg Co., N. C.

ALEXANDER, Mary and Asa Hill, 1784, Tyrrell Co., N. C.

ALEXANDER, Mary A. and C. H. Robison, 11 March 1844, Mecklenburg Co., N. C.

ALEXANDER, Mary A. and Wilson Montgomery, 15 April 1846, Mecklenburg Co., N. C.

ALEXANDER, Mary C. and William P. Jennings, 16 July 1836, Mecklenburg Co., N. C.

ALEXANDER, Mary R. and L. F. Brown, 7 September 1765, Mecklenburg Co., N. C.

ALEXANDER, Mary S. and John K. Rea, 15 March 1860, Mecklenburg Co., N. C.

ALEXANDER, Mary W. and Nicholson R. Morgan, 29 November 1820, Mecklenburg Co., N. C.

ALEXANDER, Mathew and Jenny Martin, 27 September 1810, Mecklenburg Co., N. C.

ALEXANDER, Matthew and Margaret McCorkle, 5 October 1824, Mecklenburg Co., N. C.

ALEXANDER, Matthew A. and Abby W. Barnett, 20 December 1860. Mecklenburg Co., N. C.

ALEXANDER, Matilda C. and William Burnett, 10 December 1811, Mecklenburg Co., N. C.

ALEXANDER, Moses and Elizabeth Orr, 28 January 1800, Mecklenburg Co., N. C.

ALEXANDER, Moses and Margaret H. Allen, 14 December 1836. Mecklenburg Co., N. C.

ALEXANDER, Moses Mc. and Margaret M. Boales, 24 July 1830, Mecklenburg Co., N. C.

ALEXANDER, Moses W. and Margaret M. Alexander, 6 December 1830, Mecklenburg Co., N. C.

ALEXANDER, Milly and Ulysses Alexander, 6 June 1838, Mecklenburg Co., N. C.

ALEXANDER, Nancy D. and Hugh McCauley, 13 May 1822, Mecklenburg Co., N. C.

ALEXANDER, Nancy H. and Ezekial Black, 18 July 1834, Mecklenburg Co., N. C.

ALEXANDER, Nathaniel and Caroline Alexander, 27 October 1823, Mecklenburg Co., N. C.

ALEXANDER, Oswald and Hannah Park, 20 March 1809, Mecklenburg Co., N. C.

ALEXANDER, Oswald and Mary Moore, 17 October 1826, Mecklenburg Co., N. C.

ALEXANDER, Polly and John Bain, 3 June 1819, Mecklenburg Co., N. C.

ALEXANDER, Prudence and Daniel McAuley, 7 February 1802, Mecklenburg Co., N. C.

ALEXANDER, R. B. and Cornelia A. Wilson, 19 September 1860, Mecklenburg Co., N. C.

ALEXANDER, Rachel and Joshua Outlaw, 26 March 1805, Bertie Co., N. C.

ALEXANDER, Robert D. and Abigail B. Caldwell, 9 February 1829, Mecklenburg Co., N. C.

ALEXANDER, Rufus L. and Milisa N. Montgomery, 22 May 1844, Mecklenburg Co., N. C.

ALEXANDER, Ruth and Nathaniel Morrison, 20 January 1827, Mecklenburg Co., N. C.

ALEXANDER, Ruth Jane and John N. Caldwell, 27 January 1857, Mecklenburg Co., N. C.

ALEXANDER, S. C. and Mary Brown, 21 May 1857, Mecklenburg Co., N. C.

ALEXANDER, Sample and Betsy McCracken, 21 March 1809, Mecklenburg Co., N. C.

ALEXANDER, Samuel C. and Nannie R. Price, 25 March 1863, Mecklenburg Co., N. C.

ALEXANDER, Sarah and Hezekiah Norman, 3 January 1786, Tyrrell Co., N. C.

ALEXANDER, Sarah and Daniel Alexander, 14 August 1800, Mecklenburg Co., N. C.

ALEXANDER, Sarah J. and Drury M. Culp, 24 July 1841, Mecklenburg Co., N. C.

ALEXANDER, Silas and Nancy Brown, 8 May 1846, Mecklenburg Co., N. C.

ALEXANDER, Sinai and Dorcas Hartgrove, 6 January 1843, Mecklenburg Co., N. C.

ALEXANDER, Sinai and Clementine Hartgrove, 14 April 1853, Mecklenburg Co., N. C.

ALEXANDER, Sophia and James J. Orr, 2 April 1834, Mecklenburg Co., N. C.

ALEXANDER, Stanhope W. and Dorcas H. Hunter, 24 September 1851, Mecklenburg Co., N. C.

ALEXANDER, Stephen and Isabella Shelby, 22 November 1797, Mecklenburg Co., N. C.

ALEXANDER, Stephen and Martha Montgomery, 8 September 1819, Mecklenburg Co., N. C.

ALEXANDER, Susan and William Allison, 2 November 1814, Mecklenburg Co., N. C.

ALEXANDER, Susan and James Osborne, 28 October 1816, Mecklenburg Co., N. C.

ALEXANDER, Susan and Albert Alexander, 19 December 1846, Mecklenburg Co., N. C.

ALEXANDER, Susan M. and Thomas McDonald, 20 July 1825, Mecklenburg Co., N. C.

ALEXANDER, Susan M. and John A. Campbell, 3 March 1841, Mecklenburg Co., N. C.

ALEXANDER, Susannah and John Alexander, 18 October 1830, Mecklenburg Co., N. C.

ALEXANDER, Terza and William B. W. Reed, 22 January 1839, Mecklenburg Co., N. C.

ALEXANDER, Thomas and Nancy Lilien, 24 January 1845, Mecklenburg Co., N. C.

ALEXANDER, Thomas R. and Adline I. Howell, 30 June 1861, Mecklenburg Co., N. C.

ALEXANDER, Ulysses and Jane Hunter, 12 January 1831, Mecklenburg Co., N. C.

ALEXANDER, Ulysses and Milly Alexander, 6 June 1838, Mecklenburg Co., N. C.

ALEXANDER, W. J. and Sarah A. Reid, 22 February 1860, Mecklenburg Co., N. C.

ALEXANDER, William and Mary Witter, 30 January 1801, Charleston, S. C.

ALEXANDER, William and Parmelia Ferguson, 4 January 1844, Mecklenburg Co., N. C.

ALEXANDER, William A. and Margaret E. Hayes, 15 October 1835, Mecklenburg Co., N. C.

ALEXANDER, William B. and Violet Davidson, 21 August 1791, Mecklenburg Co., N. C.

ALEXANDER, William J. and Elvira C. Wilson, 2 December 1824, Mecklenburg Co., N. C.

ALEXANDER, William L. and Margaret Cochran, 31 July 1846, Mecklenburg Co., N. C.

ALEXANDER, William L. D. and Catherine J. C. Johnston, 21 April 1859, Mecklenburg Co., N. C.

ALEXANDER, William W. and Sarah L. White, 29 October, 1855, Mecklenburg Co., N. C.

ALEXANDER, William P. and Susan P. Griffith, 3 November 1857, Mecklenburg Co., N. C.

ALEXANDER, William S. and Isabella L. Alexander, 26 December 1842, Mecklenburg Co., N. C.

ALEXANDER, William S and Nancy Gray, 7 March 1835, Mecklenburg Co., N. C.

ALEXANDER, Zadick and Fanny Darnell, 4 March 1820, Mecklenburg Co., N. C.

ALEXANDER, Zilpha and John McCleese, 28 March 1778, Tyrrell Co., N. C.

ALFORD, M. A. E. and W. A. McLeod, 24 February 1848, Marlboro Co., S. C.

ALGEA, Robert and Jane Hayes, 5 January 1811, Mecklenburg Co., N. C.

ALKINS, Abby and George Gunter, 3 August 1774, Rowan Co., N. C.

ALLAN, James and Amy Hobcraft, 13 August 1856, Charleston, S. C.

ALLAN, Mary A. and Israel G. Collins, 5 October 1801, Sullivans Island, S. C.

ALLAN, William and Sarah Haig, 18 April 1801, Charleston, S. C.

ALLEN, Agnes and William Foster, 2 August 1779, Rowan Co., N. C.

ALLEN, Ambrose and Nancy S. Cooper, 30 October 1854, Mecklenburg Co., N. C.

ALLEN, Ann and Joshua Harris, 10 September 1811, Mecklenburg Co., N. C.

ALLEN, Ann and Edward Hall, 23 June 1813, Mecklenburg Co., N. C.

ALLEN, Arthur and Jemima Reed, (widow), 20 October 1750, Chowan Co., N. C.

ALLEN, Benjamin and Ann Lawring, 14 January 1797, Mecklenburg Co., N. C.

ALLEN, David and Mary Mitchell, 14 February 1720, Charleston, S. C.

ALLEN, David and Margaret L. Wier, 10 January 1826, Mecklenburg Co., N. C.

ALLEN, Eliza and (Capt.) Thomas Thomson, September 1839, Edgefield District, S. C.

ALLEN, Elizabeth and Samuel Cannady, 18 January 1763, Edgecombe Co., N. C.

ALLEN, Elizabeth and George Blythe, 5 December 1865, Mecklenburg Co., N. C.

ALLEN, Elizabeth E. and John W. Tompkins, 24 November 1848, Edgefield District, S. C.

ALLEN, Jane and Robert Pringle, 18 July 1734, Charleston, S. C.

ALLEN, Jean and Richard Bond, 25 November 1763, Edgecombe Co., N. C.

ALLEN, John and Dorcas M. Cochran, 17 December 1836, Mecklenburg Co., N. C.

ALLEN, John S. and C. Simmons, 9 February 1840, Edgefield District, S. C.

ALLEN, John N. and Nancy Mahon, 1 November 1836, Mecklenburg Co., N. C.

ALLEN, Josiah and Elizabeth Baker, 18 May 1818, Mecklenburg Co., N. C.

ALLEN, Margaret and Austin Cook, 22 September 1819, Mecklenburg Co., N. C.

ALLEN, Margaret H. and Moses Alexander, 14 December 1836, Mecklenburg Co., N. C.

ALLEN, Mary and James S. Alexander, 16 Feburary 1836, Mecklenburg Co., N. C.

ALLEN, Nancy and James Latta, 24 August 1790, Orange Co., N. C.

ALLEN, Rachael and Joshua White, 7 January 1805, Granville Co., N. C.

ALLEN, Rebecca and William Johnson, 11 December 1811, Mecklenburg Co., N. C.

ALLEN, Robert and Jenny Green, 13 February 1806, Mecklenburg Co., N. C.

ALLEN, Robert M. and Margaret M. Cook, 23 February 1836, Mecklenburg Co., N. C.

ALLEN, Samuel and Nancy Hester, 27 August 1782, Orange Co., N. C.

ALLEN, Samuel and Polly Mathews, 30 January 1821, Mecklenburg Co., N. C.

ALLEN, Sarah and John McClure, 18 December 1792, Mecklenburg Co., N. C.

ALLEN, Sarah and Miles Moliva, 20 July 1836, Mecklenburg Co., N. C.

ALLEN, Thomas and Katherine Pittman, 31 March 1813, Mecklenburg Co., N. C.

ALLEN, Thomas P. and Sarah P. Bell, 1834, Charleston, S. C.

ALLEN, Widow and John Savage, 18 April 1749, Charleston, S. C.

ALLEN, William and Charlotte Robinson, 25 September 1834, Mecklenburg Co., N. C.

ALLCOCK, Mary and Nickolas Hoskins, 19 February 1786, Tyrrell Co., N. C.

ALLISON, Ann and Charles Overman, 6 April 1837, Mecklenburg Co., N. C.

ALLISON, Elizabeth R. and A. H. Cochran, 8 February 1851, Mecklenburg Co., N. C.

ALLISON, Henry and Elizabeth Clark, 10 September 1834, Mecklenburg Co., N. C.

ALLISON, Hugh (Rev.) and Dolly Smiser, 11 January 1770, Charleston, S. C.

ALLISON, Isaac A. and Mary N. Robinson 10 December 1855, Mecklenburg Co., N. C.

ALLISON, James and Elizabeth Augeton, April 1785, Charleston, S. C.

ALLISON, Jane E. and Henry C. Owens, 18 December 1832, Mecklenburg Co., N. C.

ALLISON, Jasper and Margaret Cunningham, 23 October 1856, Laurens Co., S. C.

ALLISON, John and Eleanor Buchanan, 17 July 1799, Mecklenburg Co., N. C.

ALLISON, John and Nancy M. Lemons, 28 January 1822, Mecklenburg Co., N. C.

ALLISON, Margaret and James Finley, 1844, Laurens Co., S. C.

ALLISON, Mary and Robert Culberson, December 1851, Laurens Co., S. C.

ALLISON, Moses G. and Mary E. Rigler, 22 December 1853, Mecklenburg Co., N. C.

ALLISON, Rebecca L. and William Irwin, 8 February 1826, Mecklenburg Co., N. C.

ALLISON, Sarah M. and John I. Erwin, 12 January 1825, Mecklenburg Co., N. C.

ALLISON, Saxton and Susan Wilcut, 26 February 1857, Laurens Co., S. C.

ALLISON, Susan and William Bolt, 14 December 1858, Laurens Co., S. C.

ALLISON, William and Susan Alexander, 2 November 1814, Mecklenburg Co., N. C.

ALLISON, Thomas C. and Mary A. Irvin, 11 June 1859, Mecklenburg Co., N. C.

ALLISON, William (Jr.) and Rachel Moore, February 1775, Charleston, S. C.

ALLSTON, Elizabeth and Henry Gibbes, 29 August 1782, Charleston, S. C.

ALLSTON, Hannah and Joseph La Bruce, 3 February 1780, Santee, S. C.

ALLSTON, Mary and Thomas Allston, 21 July 1785, Charleston, S. C.

ALLSTON, Mrs. and (Dr.) Henry C. Flagg, 5 December 1784, Charleston, S. C.

ALLSTON, Nancy and Francis Deliesseline, 15 December 1785, Charleston, S. C.

ALLSTON, Thomas and Mary Allston, 21 July 1785, Charleston, S. C.

ALSOBROOK, James and Phebe Wall, 20 March 1764, Edgecombe Co., N. C.

ALSTON, Elizabeth and Thomas Lynch, 5 September 1745, Georgetown, S. C.

ALSTON, John and Sarah McPherson, 26 March 1801, Prince William Parish, S. C.

ALSTON. Jonathan and Barbara Smith, 18 April 1791, Rowan Co., N. C.

ALSTON, Martha and Lemuel Wilson, 29 January 1752, Chowan Co., N. C.

ALSTON, Sarah and John I. Middleton, 28 March 1828, Georgetown Co., S. C.

ALSTON, William (Dr.), and Mary Pyatt, 4 February 1800, Waccamaw, S. C.

ALTON, Caroline and John Williams, 8 May 1856, Edgefield District, S. C.

ALVES, Walter and Amelia Johnson, 11 May 1787, Orange Co., N. C.

AMACHER, Anna and Gotlieb Ebert, 27 December 1751, Orangeburg Co., S. C.

AMBROSE, James and Ruth Hare, 1784, Tyrrell Co., N. C.

AMBROSE, Mary and Stephen Bateman, 7 April 1783, Tyrrell Co., N. C.

AMBROSE, Susannah and Lewis Jones, 6 August 1752, Chowan Co., N. C.

AMEY, Lewsy and Benjamin Bell, 20 November 1768, Edgecombe Co., N. C.

ANCRUM, George and Catherine Porcher, 26 November 1769, Charleston, S. C.

ANCRUM, James H. and Jane Washington, 16 November 1801, Sandy Hill, S. C.

ANDERSON, Agnes and Hugh Micklin, 22 November 1785, Guilford Co., N. C.

ANDERSON, Annie M. and (Rev.) William A Rogers, 22 March 1876, Anderson Co., S. C.

ANDERSON, Elizabeth and William Bell, 8 May 1765, Santee, S. C.

ANDERSON, Enos and Elizabeth Price, 16 April 1804, Chowan Co., N. C.

ANDERSON, George and Eliza Garrett, 21 February 1850, Edgefield District, S. C.

ANDERSON, Hugh and Anne Robinson, 28 March 1745, Charleson, S. C.

ANDERSON, James and Rachel Johnson, 3 December 1778, Tyrrell Co., N. C.

ANDERSON, James E. and Susan Fowler, 18 April 1860, Laurens Co., S. C.

ANDERSON, J. M. and Margaret A. Real, 11 August 1841, Mecklenburg Co., N. C.

ANDERSON, Jean and James Bell, 14 February 1764, Santee, S. C.

ANDERSON, John and Miriam Spruill, 4 December 1778, Tyrrell Co., N. C.

ANDERSON, John and Martha White, 5 December 1805, Union District, S. C.

ANDERSON, John (2nd. Marriage) and Susan Coleman, 11 April 1822, Union District, S. C.

ANDERSON, John and Sarah Irwin, 14 September 1811, Mecklenburg Co., N. C.

ANDERSON, Joseph and Elizabeth Fitch, 21 February 1760, Santee, S. C.

ANDERSON, Milly and Abraham Noales, 30 August 1822, Mecklenburg Co., N. C.

ANDERSON, Mrs. and George Nettles, 6 August 1797, Charleston, S. C.

ANDERSON, Rachel and Alexander Alexander, 22 October 1767, Charleston, S. C.

ANDERSON, Sally and John Woodberry, 26 May 1772, Charleston, S. C.

ANDERSON, Sarah and John Hall, 2 March 1796, Rowan Co., N. C.

ANDERSON, Thomas and Susanna Warner, 9 May 1795, Chowan Co., N. C.

ANDERSON, Thomas and Anne White, 25 July 1812, Union District, S. C.

ANDERSON, Thomas F. and Margaret Box, 1803, Burke Co., N. C.

ANDERSON, William and Catherine Lane, 6 November 1733, Charleston, S. C.

ANDERSON, William and Ann McDonald, 2 November 1762, Edgecombe Co., N. C.

ANDERSON, William and Mourning Price, 21 July 1763, Edgecombe Co., N. C.

ANDERSON, William and Catherine Sullivan, 11 April 1840, Hamburg, S. C.

ANDERSON, William P. and Catherine Askew, 2 May 1843, Union District, S. C.

ANDERSON, William W. and Jane Capps, 19 April 1841, Mecklenburg Co., N. C.

ANDING, John and Margaret Brunner, 2 February 1756, Orangeburg Co., S. C.

ANDRE, Polly and Demsey Gay, 6 February 1800, Edgecombe Co., N. C.

ANDREW, Abnit and Mary Nagely, 1740, Orangeburg Co., S. C.

ANDREW, Hannah and William Grey, 11 July 1721, St. Andrews Parish, S. C.

ANDREW, Margaret and John Haynes, 29 April 1783, Rowan Co., N. C.

ANDREWS, Clary and James T. Ennis, 3 December 1799, Edgecombe Co., N. C.

ANDREWS, C. A. and Sarah A. Bolton, 16 September 1845, Mecklenburg Co., N. C.

ANDREWS, Deborah and William Maxwell, 10 October 1790, Guilford Co., N. C.

ANDREWS, Elizabeth and Thomas L. Blanchard, 15 March 1841, Mecklenburg Co., N. C.

ANDREWS, Etheldred and Dinah Wallis, 30 January 1771, Tyrrell Co., N. C.

ANDREWS, Jennet and James Erwin, 10 October 1766, Rowan Co., N. C.

ANDREWS, Micajah and Elizabeth Jamerson, 26 January 1763, Edgecombe Co., N. C.

ANDREWS, Robert and Mary Carney, 11 July 1750, Orangeburg Co., S. C.

ANDREWS, Sarah (Mrs.) and Samuel Redman, 25 December 1801, Charleston, S. C.

ANDREWS, William and Barbara Caldwell, 16 April 1792, Mecklenburg Co., N. C.

ANDREWS, William and Peggy Houston, 30 March 1821, Mecklenburg Co., N. C.

APPLETON, Thomas and Mrs. Mary Piercy, 11 December 1801, Charleston, S. C.

ARCHER, Alma and Julius A. Mood, 13 January 1876, Spartanburg, S. C.

ARCHER, Frances and Pinckney Massey, 8 October 1839, Guilford Co., N. C.

ARCHER, Wilson and Violet Worsham, 29 October 1853, Mecklenburg Co., N. C.

ARDERY, John White and Mary Massey, 27 October 1866, York Co., S. C.

ARDRY, Mary J. and Robert C. Bell, 22 August 1854, Mecklenburg Co., N. C.

ARKILL, William and Elizabeth Steward, 15 February 1748, Chowan Co., N. C.

ARMISTEAD, Anthony and Milly Rhodes, 5 December 1758, Chowan Co., N. C.

ARMOUR, Samuel I. and Elizabeth E. Deweese, 21 January 1843, Mecklenburg Co., N. C.

ARMS, Sylvester and Elizabeth Oliver, 22 November 1800, Charleston, S. C.

ARMSTRONG, Cynthia and William Beaty, 25 July 1839, Mecklenburg Co., N. C.

ARMSTRONG, Elliott and William Curry, 30 August 1866, Laurens Co., S. C.

ARMSTRONG, Fanny and Melmoth Willis, 24 September 1850, Laurens Co., S. C.

ARMSTRONG, Tolaver and Zany Abercrombie, 7 April 1857, Laurens Co., S. C.

ARNHART, Mary and George Hartline, 9 August 1793, Rowan Co., N. C.

ARNOLD, George H. and Susanna Esngler, 5 August 1812, Mecklenburg Co., N. C.

ARNOLD, John and Margaret Grier, 14 March 1835, Mecklenburg Co., N. C.

ARNOLD, Mary and Jesse Spruell, 23 December 1785, Tyrrell Co., N. C.

ARNOLD, Robert and Eliza Kerr, 13 February 1832, Mecklenburg Co., N. C.

ARNOLL, John and Lidia Reynolds, 18 November 1722, Charleston, S. C.

ARONHART, Christian and Michael Fisher, 20 November 1778, Rowan Co., N. C.

ARRATON, Sarah and Littleton Bennett, 1 January 1808, Mecklenburg Co., N. C.

ARTHUR, James and Jamina Gallman, 14 December 1834, Edgefield District, S. C.

ARTHUR, Mary (Mrs.) and Richard Withers, April 1786, Christ Church Parish, S. C.

ARTHUR, Nathaniel and Mary Simmons, 3 December 1772, Santee, S. C.

ARTHUR, Rebecca and Cyrus Alexander, 20 March 1797, Mecklenburg Co., N. C.

ASBELL, Nannie and William Mitchell, 22 August 1797, Chowan Co., N. C.

ASBILL, Pauline and Washington Timmerman, June 1856, Edgefield Co., S. C.

ASH, Ann and John Berwick, 2 January 1774, Charleston, S. C.

ASH, Margaret and Hezekiah Singleton, 6 March 1745, Chowan Co., N. C.

ASH, Mary (Mrs.) and Joseph Brown, 29 January 1795, Charleston, S. C.

ASH, Samuel and Catherine Clements, 24 February 1726, Charleston, S. C.

ASH, Samuel and Hannah Deveaux, July 1785, Beaufort, S. C.

ASHBY, Anthony and Charlotte Marion, August 1783, Charleston, S. C.

ASHBY, Charlotte (widow) and Theodore S. Marion, April 1786, Charleston, S. C.

ASHBY, Elizabeth and (Rev.) Thomas Hasell, 21 January 1714, Charleston, S. C.

ASHE, John and Elizabeth Legare, 23 October 1783, Christ Church Parish, S. C.

ASHLEY, Elizabeth and Jesse Mitchell, 28 September 1802, Chowan Co., N. C.

ASHLEY, James and Lucretia Adkins, 3 July 1851, Mecklenburg Co., N. C.

ASHLEY, Rachel and John Finney, 6 October 1772, Rowan Co., N. C.

ASHLEY, Sarah and John Mitchell, 23 December 1797, Chowan Co., N. C.

ASKEW, Aaron and Martha Alexander, 7 May 1805, Bertie Co., N. C.

ASKEW, Catherine and William P. Anderson, 2 May 1843, Union District, S. C.

ASKEW, John and Mary Dunning, 17 August 1790, Bertie Co., N. C.

ASKEW, Lemuel B. (Dr.) and Elizabeth Sanders, 5 February 1807, Union District, S. C.

ATCHISON, William and Dury Byrom, 3 May 1823, Mecklenburg Co., N. C.

ATKINS, Benjamin and Martha Buchanan, 27 May 1844, Mecklenburg Co., N. C.

ATKINS, Francis and Sarah Cobb, December 1820, Newberry, S. C.

ATKINS, James and Rosa Bowman, 28 December 1816, Newberry, S. C.

ATKINS, Jane and Abraham Lites, 5 September 1816, Newberry, S. C.

ATKINS, Joseph and Margaret Adams, 1 January 1824, Edgefield, S. C.

ATKINS, Lady Anne and (Dr.) John Murray, 16 February 1764, Charleston, S. C.

ATKINS, Mahaleth and John Adams, 2 October 1816, Newberry, S. C.

ATKINS, Rachel and Elias Teague, October 1814, Newberry, S. C.

ATKINS, Robert and Jane Barnett, 19 September 1793, Newberry, S. C.

ATKINSON, George and Grace Stackpole, April 1832, Charleston, S. C.

ATKINSON, Hannah and Thomas Boone (Jr.), 14 September 1769, Santee, S. C.

ATKINSON, John and Sarah Carter, 6 September 1741, Orangeburg Co., S. C.

ATKINSON, Joseph and Polly Burrows, 13 October 1774, Charleston, S. C.

ATKINSON, Polly and John McQuinn, 17 November 1827, Mecklenburg Co., N. C.

ATKINSON, Priscilla and Joseph Moore, 29 October 1790, Bertie Co., N. C.

ATKINSON, Sarah and John Barnecastle, 2 August 1822, Mecklenburg Co., N. C. N. C.

ATTMORE, Elizabeth and Isaac Singletary, April 1786, Charleston, S. C.

AUGUST, John and Polly Cook, August 1773, Camden, S. C.

AUSTEN, Elizabeth (Mrs.) and Elias Jennings, 21 June 1800, Charleston, S. C.

AUSTEN, Jane S. and Lewis Strobel, 15 January 1801, Charleston, S. C.

AUSTIN, Henrietta and Minyard Sanders, July 1865, Laurens Co., S. C.

AUSTIN, Jonathan and Parmela Star, 14 December 1809, Mecklenburg Co., N. C.

AUSTIN, Moses and Mary Williams, 23 March 1790, Orange Co., N. C.

AUSTIN, Nathaniel and Laura Barksdale, 25 April 1859, Laurens Co., S. C.

AUTEN, Anthony and Rachel Christenberry, 9 March 1833, Mecklenburg Co., N. C.

AUTEN, Isaac and Jemima P. Peoples, 2 January 1841, Mecklenburg Co., N. C.

AUTEN, Isaac W. and Margaret McRee, 1 September 1857, Mecklenburg Co., N. C.

AUTEN, Jane and Robert Barnhill, 24 February 1824, Mecklenburg Co., N. C.

AUTEN, Josiah and Margaret Berryhill, 20 February 1800, Mecklenburg Co., N. C.

AUTEN, Margaret H. and George F. Read, 17 July 1856, Mecklenburg Co., N. C.

AUTEN, Paul and Emily Burns, 15 March 1838, Mecklenburg Co., N. C.

AUTON, John and Betsy Barnhill, 18 February 1819, Mecklenburg Co., N. C.

AUTON, John W. and Isabelle McLeary, 18 May 1847, Mecklenburg Co., N. C.

AUTON, Samuel and Eliza J. Jamison, 25 October 1859, Mecklenburg Co., N. C.

AUTON, Thomas J. and Sarah Watts, 3 April 1862, Mecklenburg Co., N. C.

AUTON, William M. and Louisa Hutchison, 27 December 1860, Mecklenburg Co., N. C.

AUTRY, Augusta and Richard Ripley, 1 February 1827, Edgefield District, S. C.

AUTRY, Elizabeth and Felix Smith, 6 January 1842, Edgefield District, S. C.

AUTRY, John and Tabitha Bush, 4 November 1841, Edgefield District, S. C.

AUTRY, Polly and Stephen Sutton, 17 December 1822, Edgefield District, S. C.

AUTRY, Rebecca and Joseph Grice, 28 January 1836, Edgefield District, S. C.

AVERIT, Henry and Sarah Montgomery, 9 May 1792, Bertie Co., N. C.

AVERY, Isabella and John Hosley, 13 February 1801, Charleston, S. C.

AXSON, Elizabeth and Arthur Simmons, December 1783, Charleston, S. C.

AXSON, Esther and Stephen Sullivant, 11 October 1770, Santee, S. C.

AXSON, Jacob and Ann Bee, 7 January 1800, Charleston, S. C.

AXSON, James and Esther Champanare, 3 June 1760, Santee, S. C.

AXSON, Thomas and Esther Forgartie, December 1783, Charleston, S. C.

AYDLETT, Rhody and Isaac McRoney, 15 February 1797, Guilford Co., N. C.

AYER, Hattie and James B. Black, 1 August 1872, Colleton Co., S. C.

AYERS, David W. and Mary Ann Jones, 25 April 1854, Marlboro Co., S. C.

AYERS, Elizabeth Bethea and J. B. Breeden, 20 December 1854, Marlboro Co., S. C.

AYERS, Hartwell and Mary Bethea, 2 February 1815, Marlboro Co., S. C.

AYERS, Mary Ann Jane and William B. Long, 24 March 1840, Marlboro Co., S. C.

AYERS, Sarah Hicks and Thomas S. Marshall, 27 November 1855, Marlboro Co., S. C.

B

BABB, Joseph and Huldy Ball, 10 January 1867, Laurens Co., S. C.

BABB, Liza and Richardson Riddle, 5 October 1865, Laurens Co., S. C.

BABB, Newton and Ann Pinson, 17 January 1852, Laurens Co., S. C.

BACCHUS, James and Ann Mitchell, 17 October 1811, Chowan Co., N. C.

BACKUS, Thomas and Catherine Means, 24 October 1786, Chowan Co., N. C.

BACON, Berrisford and Sarah Montgomerie, 26 June 1738, Charleston, S. C.

BACON, J. L. and Mary E. Chapman, December 1854, Edgefield District, S. C.

BACOT, Elizabeth and John Smith, 11 February 1768, Santee, S. C.

BACOT, Peter and Elizabeth Harramond, 11 November 1764, Charleston, S. C.

BADDELEY, John and Ann Golden, 9 November 1784, Charleston, S. C.

BADGER, James and Elizabeth Swint, September 1786, Charleston, S. C.

BADGER, Samuel J. W. and Jane V. C. Collins, 25 March 1844, Mecklenburg Co. N. C.

BAGET, Margaret and John Montgomery, 26 February 1802, Mecklenburg Co., N. C.

BAGETT, Thomas and Susan Cannady, 15 June 1849, Laurens Co., S. C.

BADHAM, William and Mary Luten, (widow) 13 November 1758, Chowan Co., N. C.

BAGOT, Irwin and Judy Rodden, 11 June 1818, Mecklenburg Co., N. C.

BAILEY, Dorothy and Tandy Walker, 20 March 1856, Laurens Co., S. C.

BAILEY, Franklin and Fannie Walker, 4 April 1866, Laurens Co., S. C.

BAILEY, Hester and Robert Dealey, 22 February 1780, Santee, S. C.

BAILEY, Hugh and Jane Todd, 11 April 1807, Mecklenburg Co., N. C.

BAILEY, James R. and Nancy C. Partlin, 2 January 1842, Mecklenburg Co., N. C.

BAILEY, Joanna and John Foster, 3 March 1797, Rowan Co., N. C.

BAILEY, Mary and Joseph Halde, 30 November 1789, Rowan Co., N. C.

BAILEY, Melton and Lucinda Chandler, 3 February 1856, Laurens Co., S. C.

BAILEY, Mercer and Resess Abrams, 20 November 1860, Laurens Co., S. C.

BAILEY, Rebecca and Ebenezer Frost, 12 April 1796, Rowan Co., N. C.

BAILEY, Silas and Fanny Bolt, 23 December 1858, Laurens Co., S. C.

BAILEY, Thomas and Elizabeth Baker, 24 June 1790, Orange Co., N. C.

BAILEY, William M. and Ellen M. Alexander, 13 December 1850, Mecklenburg Co., N. C.

BALEY, Tabitha and Nichol W. Gaither, 18 September 1792, Rowan Co., N. C.

BAIN, Daniel and Margaret—————24 October 1788, Mecklenburg Co., N. C.

BAIN, David and Rachel G. Robison, 4 April 1841, Mecklenburg Co., N. C.

BAIN, James N. and Elizabeth B. Doherty, 29 March 1825, Mecklenburg Co., N. C.

BAIN, Jane H. and Andrew Jones, 5 August 1837, Mecklenburg Co., N. C.

BAIN, John and Polly Alexander, 3 June 1819, Mecklenburg Co., N. C.

BAIN, Samuel and Jane Hood, 20 January 1820, Mecklenburg Co., N. C.

BAINS, John C. and Katherine Wilkins, 29 March 1757, Chowan Co., N. C.

BAIRD, James and Margaret Bonner, 24 January 1801, Charleston, S. C.

BAKER, Aaron and Jean Davis, 23 February 1805, Mecklenburg Co., N. C.

BAKER, Abel and Susanna Dow, 4 January 1816, Mecklenburg Co., N. C.

BAKER, Charles M. and Cynthia Hanks, 28 June 1836, Mecklenburg Co., N. C.

BAKER, Elijah and Mary Wiley, 15 November 1798, Mecklenburg Co., N. C.

BAKER, Elijah, (Jr.) and Jane C. Baker, 15 January 1838, Mecklenburg Co., N. C.

BAKER, Elizabeth and James Manning, 7 January 1757, Chowan Co., N. C.

BAKER, Elizabeth and Thomas Bailey, 24 June 1790, Orange Co., N. C.

BAKER, Elizabeth and Josiah Allen, 18 May 1818, Mecklenburg Co., N. C.

BAKER, Elizabeth and William Elliott, 13 December 1721, St. Andrews Parish, S. C.

BAKER, Elizabeth and Benjamin Rodden, 16 September 1829, Mecklenburg Co., N. C.

BAKER, George and Elizabeth Cook, 28 July 1817, Mecklenburg Co., N. C.

BAKER, Griffith and Susanna Todd, 22 May 1819, Mecklenburg Co., N. C.

BAKER, Harriet and George Evans, October 1784, Charleston, S. C.

BAKER, Harriet and James R. Alexander, 8 December 1836, Mecklenburg Co., N. C.

BAKER, Hilery and Ann Ewen, 4 July 1786, Tyrrell Co., N. C.

BAKER, Isaac and Elizabeth Hooks, 15 December 1830, Mecklenburg Co., N. C.

BAKER, Jacob and Hannah C. Pelt, 21 December 1825, Mecklenburg Co., N. C.

BAKER, Jacob and Emeline Duese, 10 January 1832, Mecklenburg Co., N. C.

BAKER, James W. and Lavina Richmond, 20 May 1835, Mecklenburg Co., N. C.

BAKER, Jane C. and Elijah Baker, Jr., 15 January 1838, Mecklenburg Co., N. C.

BAKER, Jeptha and Elizabeth Pitman, 11 March 1797, Mecklenburg Co., N. C.

BAKER, Jeptha and Rebecca R. Henderson, 18 December 1860, Mecklenburg Co., N. C.

BAKER, Jesse and Mary Wallace, 27 August 1857, Mecklenburg Co., N. C.

BAKER, J. E., (Miss) and Harry T. Russell, 19 July 1860, Mecklenburg Co., N. C.

BAKER, John and Amy Legare, 13 October 1767, Charleston, S. C.

BAKER, John and Martha Cherry, 17 September 1790, Bertie Co., N. C.

BAKER, Jonathan and Damson Roddin, 16 September 1801, Mecklenburg Co., N. C.

BAKER, Laura L. and Joseph H. Saunders, 28 April 1833, Warrenton, N. C.

BAKER, Mary and Henry Toomer, 23 June 1719, St. Andrews Parish, S. C.

BAKER, Mary and John Williams, 16 June 1720, St. Andrews Parish, S. C.

BAKER, Mary and Andrew Cuming, February 1775, Charleston, S. C.

BAKER, Matilda and Valentine W. Rice, 15 October 1853, Mecklenburg Co., N. C.

BAKER, Michael and Rachel Griffith, 13 May 1812, Mecklenburg Co., N. C.

BAKER, Priscilla and Caleb Holbrooke, 1 April 1780, Rowan Co., N. C.

BAKER, Rachel and Ezekial W. Clark, 20 April 1825, Mecklenburg Co., N. C.

BAKER, Rebecca and John Mitchell, 31 January 1797, Mecklenburg Co., N. C.

BAKER, Sally and David Dott, 13 February 1768, Charleston, S. C.

BAKER, Samuel and Rebecca Davis, 16 December 1804, Mecklenburg Co., N. C.

BAKER, Sarah and James Espey, 2 January 1786, Orange Co., N. C.

BAKER, Sarah and John Harkey, 1 August 1822, Mecklenburg Co., N. C.

BAKER, Sarah H. and John G. Maxwell, 18 November 1856, Mecklenburg Co., N. C.

BAKER, Susannah and Samuel Rogers, 3 July 1794, Charleston, S. C.

BAKER, Susannah and John Marr, 16 July 1833, Mecklenburg Co., N. C.

BAKER, Thomas and Penelope Williams, 12 January 1763, Edgecombe Co., N. C.

BAKER, Thomas and Frances Withers, 13 July 1800, Charleston, S. C.

BAKER, William and Martha Screven, 18 July 1763, James Island, S. C.

BAKER, William and Polly Bowen, 7 December 1805, Bertie Co., N. C.

BAKER, William H. and Martha A. Stephens, 2 February 1842, Mecklenburg Co., N. C.

BAKER, William S. and Isabella Kerr, 3 May 1860, Mecklenburg Co., N. C.

BALDRIGE, Elizabeth and William Steele Henderson, 18 September 1804, Mecklenburg Co., N. C.

BALDWIN, Allen and Elizabeth Henderson, 3 June 1818, Mecklenburg Co., N. C.

BALDWIN, Mary C. and (Rev.) John Robinson, 9 April 1795, Mecklenburg Co., N. C.

BALDWIN, Peter and Sarah Jones, 25 January 1855, Laurens Co., S. C.

BALDWIN, Sarah and Peter Ford, 1 November 1774, Rowan Co., N. C.

BALDY, Cicely and Henry Dexter, 19 November 1761, Santee, S. C.

BALEY, Tabitha and Nichol W. Gaither, 18 September 1792, Rowan Co., N. C.

BALFOUR, Margaret and Hudson Hughes, 8 September 1796, Rowan Co., N. C.

BALL, Archibald S. and Mary St. John, 13 February 1800, Charleston, S. C.

BALL, Charity, (widow) and Richard Lushington, 9 July 1774, Charleston, S. C.

BALL, Elias and Catherine Gaillard, 14 May 1765, Santee, S. C.

BALL, Elizabeth and Henry Smith, 13 December 1764, Berkley Co., S. C.

BALL, Huldy and Joseph Babb, 10 January 1867, Laurens Co., S. C.

BALL, John and Huldy Martin, 8 May 1855, Laurens Co., S. C.

BALL, Katherine and Benjamin Smith, 9 April 1773, St. Johns Parish, S. C.

BALL, Lydia and Edward Simons, 17 October 1771, Charleston, S. C.

BALL, Nancy and Johnston Jones, 24 August 1790, Orange Co., N. C.

BALL, Sarah and Anderson McDole, 10 February 1848, Laurens Co., S. C.

BALL, Simeon and Malinda Bramlet, 24 July 1866, Laurens Co., S. C.

BALL, Y. J. and Nancy Mary Putman, 30 December 1846, Laurens Co., S. C.

BALLARD, James and Mary Gribble, 15 September 1795, Mecklenburg Co., N. C.

BALLARD, Jesse and Nancy Boyd, 27 December 1806, Mecklenburg Co., N. C.

BALLARD, Jethro and Elizabeth Sumner, 30 December 1774, Chowan Co., N. C.

BALLARD, Milley and Timothy Murphy, 4 January 1774, Guilford Co., N. C.

BALLARD, William H. and Margaret A. Reid, 2 April 1861, Mecklenburg Co., N. C.

BALLENTINE, James and Sally Buchanan, 10 March 1772, Charleston, S. C.

BALLEW, Thomas and Ann Cox, 10 April 1753, Orangeburg Co., S. C.

BANKER, Jacob L. and Nancy C. Irwin, 7 October 1844, Mecklenburg Co., N. C.

BANKER, Jacob L. and Mary E. Cook, 8 December 1865, Mecklenburg Co., N. C.

BANKER, John and Elizabeth Goforth, 7 January 1813, Mecklenburg Co., N. C.

BANKS, Ralph and Rachel Jones, 1788, Wake Co., N. C.

BANKS, William and Mary Liverman, 3 January 1786, Tyrrell Co., N. C.

BANNATYNE, Thomas and Susanna Rose, 8 May 1801, Charleston, S. C.

BANNER, Elizabeth and John M. Mitchell, 9 July 1850, Guilford Co., N. C.

BANNISTER, Ann and John Frierson, 28 April 1785, Charleston, S. C.

BARBEE, Dolly and John George, 1866, Orange Co., N. C.

BARBER, John and Esther Herndon, 20 March 1790, Orange Co., N. C.

BARBER, Mary Ann and Green E. Herndon, 20 December 1842, Orange Co., N. C.

BARE, Sarah (widow) and Edward Jinkes, 11 October 1777, Chowan Co., N. C.

BARFIELD, Anne and Pomphrett Herndon, 28 October 1812, Orange Co., N. C.

BARHAM, William A. and Martha E. Buchanan, 22 September 1843, Mecklenburg Co., N. C.

BARKER, Bailey and Charity Phifer, 7 September 1839, Mecklenburg Co., N. C.

BARKER, Mary and Boswell Newell, 11 December 1845, Mecklenburg Co., N. C.

BARKER, Thomas and Margaret Reddin, 22 November 1846, Mecklenburg Co., N. C.

BARKLEY, Ann and John Fleming, 7 October 1784, Rowan Co., N. C.

BARKLEY, Eleanor and David Houston, 20 March 1788, Mecklenburg Co., N. C.

BARKSDALE, Downs and Lucinda Dial, 7 September 1843, Laurens Co., S. C.

BARKSDALE, Elizabeth and Jeremiah Glenn, (widower), 30 March 1854, Laurens Co., S. C.

BARKSDALE, Ethalinda and Asa Forgy, 29 November 1849, Laurens Co., S. C.

BARKSDALE, George and Cornelia Downs, 15 October 1846, Laurens Co., S. C.

BARKSDALE, Jane and James Parks, 28 November 1844, Laurens Co., S. C.

BARKSDALE, John A. and Martha Nance, 7 October 1852, Newberry, S. C.

BARKSDALE, John and Amanda Coleman, 8 November 1855, Laurens Co., S. C.

BARKSDALE, Laura and Nathainel Austin, 25 April 1859, Laurens Co., S. C.

BARKSDALE, Louis and Allen Dial, 8 May 1856, Laurens Co., S. C.

BARKSDALE, Mary and Barksdale Franks, 2 January 1866, Laurens Co., S. C.

BARKSDALE, Nathaniel and Mary Burns, 18 November 1856, Laurens Co., S. C.

BARKSDALE, Polly and John Edwards (Jr.), 1 December 1773, Charleston, S. C.

BARKSDALE, Rebecca and Albert Dial, 2 December 1847, Laurens Co., S. C.

BARKSDALE, Susannah F. and Edward Phelon, February 1789, Charleston, S. C.

BARKSDALE, William and Christian Sumner, 7 April 1788, Bertie Co., N. C.

BARLOW, Ruth and John Wallace, 1797, Iredell Co., N. C.

BARNARD, Clinton and Melissa Brever, 12 November 1856, Surrey Co., N. C.

BARNARD, James and Esther Joudon, 3 December 1761, Santee, S. C.

BARNARD, Nelson and Mary Lumpkin, 2 February 1851, Surrey Co., N. C.

BARNARD, Oliver W. and Mary Williams, 4 March 1850, Surrey Co., N. C.

BARNARD, Uriah and Elizabeth Macy, 21 February 1782, Center, N. C.

BARNARD, William and Sally Williams, 20 October 1827, Surrey Co., N. C.

BARNECASTLE, John and Sarah Atkinson, 2 August 1822, Mecklenburg Co., N. C.

BARNECASTLE, Martha and Nathan Bowen, 29 August 1797, Bertie Co., N. C.

BARNES, Amelia and John B. Turner, 29 December 1789, Bertie Co., N. C.

BARNES, Ann and John Alexander, 11 August 1768, Tyrrell Co., N. C.

BARNES, Elizabeth and John Bentley, 17 February 1800, Edgecombe Co., N. C.

BARNES, Jesse and Orpah Fort, 2 February 1761, Edgecombe Co., N. C.

BARNES, Malachi and Ony Tisdale, 22 February 1800, Edgecombe Co., N. C.

BARNES, Mary and Isaac Hill, 12 January 1788, Rowan Co., N. C.

BARNES, Merica and Lewis Jones, 1764, Edgecombe Co., N. C.

BARNES, Miss and Benjamin Wilkins, 6 December 1767, Charleston, S. C.

BARNES, Mourning and David Bradley, (Jr.), 2 December 1810, Edgecombe Co., N. C.

BARNES, Reddick and Patsy Simms, 20 December 1799, Edgecombe Co., N. C.

BARNES, Wesley and Susan Gray, 19 December 1838, Edgefield District, S. C.

BARNES, William and Keziah Cunningham, 17 November 1819, Mecklenburg Co., N. C.

BARNETT, Abby W. and Matthew A. Alexander, 20 December 1860, Mecklenburg Co., N. C.

BARNETT, Abigail and Archibald Robison, 16 February 1820, Mecklenburg Co., N. C.

BARNETT, Amos and Catherine Porter, 25 December 1819, Mecklenburg Co., N. C.

BARNETT, Ann and George Safford, 22 April 1785, Tyrrell Co., N. C.

BARNETT, Anna and B. F. Brown, 10 October 1865, Mecklenburg Co., N. C.

BARNETT, Catherine and Isaac Henry, 30 May 1800, Mecklenburg Co., N. C.

BARNETT, David E. and Rebekah Montgomery, 7 February 1827, Mecklenburg Co., N. C.

BARNETT, D. W. and Mary E. Thomason, 22 September 1859, Mecklenburg Co., N. C.

BARNETT, Elizabeth and William Rice, 14 July 1803, Mecklenburg Co., N. C.

BARNETT, Hugh M. and Patsy Johnston, 4 January 1819, Mecklenburg Co., N. C.

BARNETT, James G. and Deborah Montgomery, 24 January 1827, Mecklenburg Co., N. C.

BARNETT, Jane and Robert Atkins, 19 September 1793, Newberry, S. C.

BARNETT, John and Ann Bochett, 2 December 1762, Santee, S. C.

BARNETT, John and Jane Gaston, 22 July 1795, Mecklenburg Co., N. C.

BARNETT, John W. and Mary A. Lee, 18 November 1752, Mecklenburg Co., N. C.

BARNETT, Marcus and Cinthy Frazier, 27 March 1826, Mecklenburg Co., N. C.

BARNETT, Moses and Frances Robinson, 16 August 1794, Mecklenburg Co., N. C.

BARNETT, Robert and Jennett Todd, 7 May 1789, Mecklenburg Co., N. C.

BARNETT, Robert C. and Margaret Weeks, 27 November 1827, Mecklenburg Co., N. C.

BARNETT, Robert F. and Mary T. Sample, 9 December 1828, Mecklenburg Co., N. C.

BARNETT, Thomas G. and Margaret Brown, 12 December 1826, Mecklenburg Co., N. C.

BARNETT, Thomas G. and Elizabeth Ewart, 15 December 1838, Mecklenburg Co., N. C.

BARNETT, Vincent and Lucinda Potts, 6 February 1828, Mecklenburg Co., N. C.

BARNETT, William and Janny Davis, 24 October 1812, Mecklenburg Co., N. C.

BARNETT, William and Rebecca Hanner, 9 December 1865, Laurens Co., S. C.

BARNETT, William G. and Margaret M. Dewese, 17 January 1846, Mecklenburg Co., N. C.

BARNHARDT, Daniel C. and Mary E. Berryhill, 26 February 1852, Mecklenburg Co., N. C.

BARNHILL, Betsy and John Auten, 18 February 1819, Mecklenburg Co., N. C.

BARNHILL, John and Nancy Jameson, 28 February 1816, Mecklenburg Co., N. C.

BARNHILL, John H. and Mary Jameson, 20 August 1840, Mecklenburg Co., N. C.

BARNHILL, Robert and Jane Auten, 24 February 1824, Mecklenburg Co., N. C.

BARNHILL, Scarrett and Miles D. Cashon, 19 April 1849, Mecklenburg Co., N. C.

BARNHILL, Thomas and Mary Phillips, 18 December 1849, Mecklenburg Co., N. C.

BARNHILL, William and Elizabeth Conner, 31 October 1810, Mecklenburg Co., N. C.

BARNS, Harriett Pope and David Stuart Harllee, 3 February 1819, Roberson Co., N. C.

BARNWELL, Anne and Thomas Stanyarne, 29 March 1726, Beaufort, S. C.

BARNWELL, Anne and Stephen Bull, 24 May 1772, Sheldon, S. C.

BARNWELL, Bridget and Robert Sams, 18 April 1741, St. Johns Island, S. C.

BARNWELL, Catherine and Hugh Bryan, 2 January 1734, St. Johns Island, S. C.

BARNWELL, Catherine and William H. W. Barnwell, 26 November 1829, Charleston, S. C.

BARNWELL, Edward and Mary Williamson, 8 June 1783, St. Johns Island, S. C.

BARNWELL, Edward and Mary Hutson, 29 July 1790, St. Johns Island, S. C.

BARNWELL, Edward H. and Harriet Hayne, 20 November 1860, Charleston, S. C.

BARNWELL, Eliza and Robert Barnwell, 9 August 1827, Beaufort, S. C.

BARNWELL, John and Martha Chaplin, 31 October 1737, Beaufort, S. C.

BARNWELL, John (Jr.) and Anne Hutson, 7 May 1777, Charleston, S. C.

BARNWELL, Joseph W. and Harriet Cheves, 23 January 1883, Charleston, S. C.

BARNWELL, Martha and David Guerard, 23 September 1770, Port Royal, S. C.

BARNWELL, Mary and John Heywood, (Jr.), 1788, Beaufort, S. C.

BARNWELL, Nathaniel and Mary Gibbes, 7 April 1738, St. Johns Island, S. C.

BARNWELL, Nathaniel and Elizabeth Waight, 1 December 1768, St. Johns Island, S. C.

BARNWELL, Robert W. and Eliza Barnwell, 9 August 1827, Beaufort, S. C.

BARNWELL, Sarah and James Cuthbert, 5 May 1784, Beaufort, S. C.

BARNWELL, William H. W. and Catherine Barnwell, 26 November 1829, Charleston, S. C.

BARNWELL, William W. and Sarah R. Gibbes, 11 January 1816, Charleston, S. C.

BARON, Alexander (Dr.) and Sally Cleiland, 1 January 1773, Charleston, S. C.

BARON, Anne, (widow) and John Burn, 25 October 1767, Charleston, S. C.

BARON, Sarah and Hugh Campbell, 12 June 1766, Charleston, S. C.

BARR, John C. and Eliza Orr, 13 February 1819, Mecklenburg Co., N. C.

BARRETT, Mary and Griffith Edwards, 19 October 1774, Rowan Co., N. C.

BARRETT, Polly and Ezekial Eades, 12 January 1799, Rowan Co., N. C.

BARRETT, William and Anne Carter, 3 March 1767, Edgecombe Co., N. C.

BARRIE, Elizabeth (widow) and James Taylor, 20 August 1754, Orangeburg Co., S. C.

BARRIN, Eva C. and John George Hayner, 24 August 1755, Orangeburg Co., S. C.

BARRINGER, Caleb A. and Mary G. L. Caldwell, 16 February 1842, Mecklenburg Co., N. C.

BARRON, John and Abey Pitman, 5 November 1799, Edgecombe Co., N. C.

BARRY, Andrew and Jemima Sample, 15 March 1796, Mecklenburg Co., N. C.

BARRY, Eleanor R. and Balto Irwin, 2 December 1833, Mecklenburg Co., N. C.

BARRY, Violet and William Montieth, 4 September 1807, Mecklenburg Co., N. C.

BARTLETT, Rebecca and Jesse Blount, 28 February 1788, Bertie Co., N. C.

BARTON, Eliza and John S. Rose, 16 September 1799, Charleston, S. C.

BARTON, Hanna and Anthony White, 30 August 1770, Santee, S. C.

BARTON, John and Elizabeth Pearcey, 9 July 1778, Santee, S. C.

BARTON, Leonard and Eliza Nephew, 31 January 1812, Beaufort, S. C.

BARTON, Mary S. and William E. Holliday, 30 April 1845, Mecklenburg Co., N. C.

BARTON, Richard and Sarah Strain, 2 June 1801, Mecklenburg Co., N. C.

BARTON, Sarah and Stephen Ford, 25 January 1761, Santee, S. C.

BARTON, William and Jane Thompson, 24 September 1773, Santee, S. C.

BARUS, John H. and Mary E. Lake, 19 January 1852, Edgefield District, S. C.

BASNIGHT, William and Ann Sivels, 1781, Tyrrell Co., N. C.

BASONAN, John and Mary Weston, 17 January 1789, Bertie Co., N. C.

BASS, Addizer C. and James E. Coxe, 20 December 1854, St. Pauls Parish, N. C.

BASS, Ann and Ezra P. Coxe, 17 May 1821, Marlboro Co., S. C.

BASS, H. E. and M. Will Smith, 10 January 1850, Marlboro Co., S. C.

BASS, Jacob and Mary Lassiter, 8 September 1789, Bertie Co., N. C.

BASS, Martha Louisa and John S. Page, 10 January 1847, Marlboro Co., S. C.

BASSETT, Widow and John Dart, 16 April 1744, Charleston, S. C.

BASTENOT, Benjamin and Mary Beard, 20 February 1719, St. Andrews Parish, S. C.

BASTISLE, Mary and Joseph Norfleet Meredith, 15 May 1800, Oxford, N. C.

BATEMAN, Ann and Edward Moseley, 16 January 1795, Chowan Co., N. C.

BATEMAN, Cassandra and Isaac K. Hopkins, 8 September 1836, Chowan Co., N. C.

BATEMAN, Frances and Harmon Alexander, 14 December 1865, Chowan Co., N. C.

BATEMAN, Jere and Mary Oliver, 1781, Tyrrell Co., N. C.

BATEMAN, Jeremiah and Sarah Phelps, 28 January 1762, Tyrrell Co., N. C.

BATEMAN, Jonathan and Catharine Ray, 20 January 1766, Tyrrell Co., N. C.

BATEMAN, Mary and John Davis, 1780, Tyrrell Co., N. C.

BATEMAN, Nehemiah and Sarah Streator, 22 March 1779, Chowan Co., N. C.

BATEMAN, Rachel and William Call, October 1783, Tyrrell Co., N. C.

BATEMAN, Sarah and William Bilding, 5 October 1785, Tyrrell Co., N. C.

BATEMAN, Sarah and Ezra Davenport, 27 December 1785, Tyrrell Co., N. C.

BATEMAN, Stephen and Mary Ambrose, 7 April 1783, Tyrrell Co., N. C.

BATEMAN, Will and Mary Bunch, 5 June 1767, Chowan Co., N. C.

BATES, Harriet A. and Francis A. Cash, 18 November 1822, Mecklenburg Co., N. C.

BATTEN, Mary and George Evans, 1781, Tyrrell Co., N. C.

BATTIN, Dorcas and John O'Neal, 25 September 1778, Tyrrell Co., N. C.

BATTLE, Elizabeth and Josiah Crudup, 28 November 1767, Edgecombe Co., N. C.

BATTLE, Joel and Mary P. Johnston, 9 April 1801, Edgecombe Co., N. C.

BATTLE, Kemp P. and Martha A. Battle, 25 November 1855, Franklin Co., N. C.

BATTLE, Martha A. and Kemp P. Battle, 25 November 1855, Franklin Co., N. C.

BATTLE, Nancy and Lewis Fort, 28 May 1800, Edgecombe Co., N. C.

BATTLE, William and Charity Horn, 1742, Edgecombe Co., N. C.

BAUGNIET, Charles and (Mrs.) Wilhemina Beyerly, 13 July 1800, Charleston, S. C.

BAXTER, Daniel and Isabella Stewart, 10 February 1807, Mecklenburg Co., N. C.

BAXTER, Frances and John Hovey, 22 October 1788, Mecklenburg Co., N. C.

BAYNARD, Thomas and Sally Calder, 6 July 1784, Edisto, S. C.

BAZEMORE, Lovenand and Elizabeth Huff, 13 July 1785, Tyrrell Co., N. C.

BEAGLES, Robertson and Lucinda Watson, 17 March 1859, Laurens Co., S. C.

BEAM, Dorothy and Joshua Hawkins, 8 April 1780, Rowan Co., N. C.

BEAMORE, John and Judith Stewart, 29 November 1719, St. Andrews Parish, S. C.

BEAN, Daniel and Sarah Ross, 29 December 1789, Mecklenburg Co., N. C.

BEAN, Hugh and Elizabeth Hood, 3 November 1809, Mecklenburg Co., N. C.

BEAN, John and Elizabeth Wilson, 7 March 1797, Mecklenburg Co., N. C.

BEAN, William and Margaret McCracken, 12 September 1791, Mecklenburg Co., N. C.

BEAR, John and Sarah Howell, 1 December 1865, Mecklenburg Co., N. C.

BEAR, William and Leah Bouknight, 19 December 1839, Edgefield District, S. C.

BEARD, Catherine and Thomas Gillespie, 24 August 1796, Rowan Co., N. C.

BEARD, Duanna and Abel Hunt, 17 February 1787, Rowan Co., N. C.

BEARD, Joseph H. and Rebecca C. Caldwell, 30 December 1859, Mecklenburg Co., N. C.

BEARD, Lenora and William B. Osborn, 7 October 1858, Mecklenburg Co., N. C.

BEARD, Margaret and George Hoover, 4 May 1784, Rowan Co., N. C.

BEARD, Mary and Benjamin Bastenot, 20 February 1719, St. Andrews Parish, S. C.

BEARD, Robert and Mary Colles, 6 December 1767, Charleston, S. C.

BEARD, Robert and Elizabeth Higgins (widow) 16 July 1796, Charleston, S. C.

BEARD, Robert and Mary Knox, 15 February 1838 Mecklenburg Co., N. C.

BEARD, William L. and Frances Brown, 26 March 1834, Mecklenburg Co., N. C.

BEARMAN, Ann and Richard Blake, (Jr.), 23 July 1772, Santee, S. C.

BEASLEY, John and Sarah Lilse, 30 September 1752, Chowan Co., N. C.

BEASLEY, Mary and Peter Payne, 18 October 1751, Chowan Co., N. C.

BEASLEY, Mary and Simeon Long, 4 June 1773, Chowan Co., N. C.

BEATEY, Henry L. and Margaret E. Smith, 6 October 1857, Mecklenburg Co., N. C.

BEATTIE, William E. and Kittie Marshall, 17 December 1885, Greenville, S. C.

BEATTY, Eleanor and Samuel Gingles, 14 December 1782, Rowan Co., N. C.

BEATTY, John and Martha Hill, 21 August 1798, Mecklenburg Co., N. C.

BEATTY, Milly and John Rodden, 1 March 1842, Mecklenburg Co., N. C.

BEATTY, Salina and Thomas M. Rodden, 8 April 1834, Mecklenburg Co., N. C.

BEATTY, William and Matha Dunn, 6 October 1807, Mecklenburg Co., N. C.

BEATY, Andrew and Clarissa Robinson, 2 February 1843, Mecklenburg Co., N. C.

BEATY, Clarissa O. and John H. McCoy, 8 February 1826, Mecklenburg Co., N. C.

BEATY, Cynthia C. and Hugh P. McCorkle, 20 February 1843, Mecklenburg Co., N. C.

BEATY, Eleanor and Drury Clanton, 8 May 1828, Mecklenburg Co., N. C.

BEATY, Esther and William Owens, 25 February 1799, Mecklenburg Co., N. C.

BEATY, Ezekial and Lilly Hipp, 9 June 1847, Mecklenburg Co., N. C.

BEATY, Frances and Hugh A. McCoy, 5 September 1838, Mecklenburg Co., N. C.

BEATY, Francis and Jane Waddell, 3 January 1806, Mecklenburg Co., N. C.

BEATY, Isabella and Nathan Beaty, 10 December 1801, Mecklenburg Co., N. C.

BEATY, James and Esther Owen, 25 August 1803, Mecklenburg Co., N. C.

BEATY, James and Ellen Lentile, 14 November 1831, Mecklenburg Co., N. C.

BEATY, John and Polly Wilson, 20 May 1806, Mecklenburg Co., N. C.

BEATY, John and Esther Sadler, 24 January 1817, Mecklenburg Co., N. C.

BEATY, John and Isabella Clark, 12 April 1837, Mecklenburg Co., N. C.

BEATY, John D. and Mary J. Clark, 26 December 1838, Mecklenburg Co., N. C.

BEATY, Joseph and Susanna McRea, 14 August 1798, Mecklenburg Co., N. C.

BEATY, Levina and Joseph Haynes, 25 April 1800, Mecklenburg Co., N. C.

BEATY, Moses and Martha Campbell, 4 November 1794, Mecklenburg Co., N. C.

BEATY, Moses and Nancy Weathers, 1 December 1800, Mecklenburg Co., N. C.

BEATY, M. E. (Miss) and James H. Alexander, 27 May 1862, Mecklenburg Co., N. C.

BEATY, Nancy and Robert F. Clark, 26 September 1839, Mecklenburg Co., N. C.

BEATY, Nathan and Isabella Beaty, 10 December 1801, Mecklenburg Co., N. C.

BEATY, Robert M. and Mary Jamieson, 7 November 1836, Mecklenburg Co., N. C.

BEATY, Samson and Mary E. McClure, 20 November 1833, Mecklenburg Co., N. C.

BEATY, Samuel W. and Elizabeth Johnston, 17 December 1823, Mecklenburg Co., N. C.

BEATY, William and Isabella McCorkle, 21 April 1791, Mecklenburg Co., N. C.

BEATY, William and Margaret Byram, 16 March 1825, Mecklenburg Co., N. C.

BEATY, William and Cynthia Armstrong, 25 July 1839, Mecklenburg Co., N. C.

BEATY, William and Caroline Rea, 1 April 1841, Mecklenburg Co., N. C.

BEATY, William and Mira E. McGee, 22 November 1852, Mecklenburg Co., N. C.

BEAVER, John M. and Margaret E. White, 16 January 1862, Mecklenburg Co., N. C.

BEAVER, Mary and Jona Hartsile, 5 March 1792, Rowan Co., N. C.

BEAVER, William and Margaret Young, 25 July 1813, Mecklenburg Co., N. C.

BECK, Jacob and Brigitta Smith, 19 February 1754, Orangeburg Co., S. C.

BECKET, James and Elizabeth Osborn, 30 January 1794, Mecklenburg Co., N. C.

BECKET, Samuel and Susanna Osborn, 27 July 1801, Mecklenburg Co., N. C.

BECKLER, H. N. and Miss A. M. Hill, 14 February 1866, Mecklenburg Co., N. C.

BEDELL, Hepsibah and Richard Ralton, 22 February 1722, St. Andrews Parish, S. C.

BEDON, Elizabeth and John Gibbes, 25 August 1748, St. Andrews Parish, S. C.

BEDON, John (Jr.) and Elizabeth Massey (widow), 29 July 1736, Charleston, S. C.

BEDON, Stephen and Ruth Nicholls, 11 August 1743, Charleston, S. C.

BEE, Ann and Jacob Axson, 7 January 1800, Charleston, S. C.

BEE, John and Martha Miller, 7 June 1731, Charleston, S. C.

BEE, John S. and Mary Warnock, 21 May 1796, Charleston, S. C.

BEE, Joseph and Susanna Duboise, (widow) 13 November 1783, Charleston, S. C.

BEE, Rachel and Jonah Rivers, 2 March 1786, Charleston, S. C.

BEE, Rebecca and Isaac Holmes, 8 May 1759, Charleston, S. C.

BEE, Thomas and Susannah Holmes, 5 May 1761, Charleston, S. C.

BEE, Thomas and Susana Shubrick (widow) May 1786, Charleston, S. C.

BEECHAM, Catherine and Evan Ellis, 17 December 1791, Rowan Co., N. C.

BEECHAM, Sarah and Michael Hinkle, 26 November 1787, Rowan Co., N. C.

BEEKMAN, Bernard and Elizabeth Scott (widow) 14 December 1769, Charleston, S. C.

BEGETT, (or Buhet) Margaret and John Montgomery, 26 February 1802, Mecklenburg Co., N. C.

BELSH, Thusey and Solomon Miller, 17 January 1842, Chowan Co., N. C.

BELK, Samson D. and Mary Richardson, 3 December 1834, Mecklenburg Co., N. C.

BELL, Alexander and Betsy Geiger, December 1785, Charleston, S. C.

BELL, Andrew and Anne Murray, 3 December 1767, Charleston, S. C.

BELL, Benjamin and Lewsy Amey, 20 November 1768, Edgecombe Co., N. C.

BELL, Bright and Mourning Cobb, 22 February 1800, Bertie Co., N. C.

BELL, Charity and John Ingraham, 1807, Sampson Co., N. C.

BELL, Chordy and Nathan Jones, 1 January 1763, Edgecombe Co., N. C.

BELL, James and Jean Anderson, 14 February 1764, Santee, S. C.

BELL, James and Esther Chovin, 23 May 1768, Santee, S. C.

BELL, John and Rachel Price, 18 December 1792, Mecklenburg Co., N. C.

BELL, John and Esther Davis, 12 February 1798, Mecklenburg Co., N. C.

BELL, John and Alice Watson, 26 April 1865, Mecklenburg Co., N. C.

BELL, Joseph (Capt.) and Miss Langstaff, January 1786, Charleston, S. C.

BELL, Joseph D. and (Mrs.) Hannah Mitchell, 18 January 1800, Charleston, S. C.

BELL, Margaret and James S. McCubbins, 18 October 1860, Statesville, N. C.

BELL, Robert and Dolly Dillard, 26 April 1808, Mecklenburg Co., N. C.

BELL, Robert C. and Mary J. Ardry, 22 August 1854, Mecklenburg Co., N. C.

BELL, Sarah P. and Thomas P. Allen, 1834, Charleston, S. C.

BELL, Selah and Moses Medearis, 12 August 1800, Guilford Co., N. C.

BELL, William and Elizabeth Anderson, 8 May 1765, Santee, S. C.

BELLAMY, Sally and Mr. Crawford, 17 May 1732, Charleston, S. C.

BELLINGER, Eliza and————————Tallifer, 21 March 1769, Charleston, S. C.

BELLINGER, George D. and Fannie J. O'Bannon, 7 June 1881, Barnwell Co., S. C.

BELLINGER, John Rice and Martha C. Rice, 23 October 1872, Blackville, S. C.

BELLINGER, Lucia and Miles B. Pinckney, 14 June 1796, Charleston, S. C.

BELLINGER, Lucy and Thomas Skottowe, 22 December 1766, St. Andrews Parish, S. C.

BELLINGER, William and Elizabeth Pinckney, February 1784, Charleston, S. C.

BENBURY, Bridget and John Garrett, 19 October 1756, Chowan Co., N. C.

BENBURY, John and Ann Boyd, (widow) 14 August 1752, Chowan Co., N. C.

BENBURY, Sarah and William Luten, 23 December 1756, Chowan Co., N. C.

BENFIELD, Amanda and William Russ, 2 October 1856, Mecklenburg Co., N. C.

BENNERMAN, William and Elizabeth Davis, 17 November 1794, Mecklenburg Co., N. C.

BENNETT, Abraham and Hannah Williams, 24 December 1805, Mecklenburg Co., N. C.

BENNETT, Ealies and David Black, 24 October 1798, Chowan Co., N. C.

BENNETT, John and Sarah Clark, 21 May 1776, Chowan Co., N. C.

BENNETT, Littleton and Sarah Arraton, 1 January 1808, Mecklenburg Co., N. C.

BENNETT, Luke and Melia Garrett, 12 May 1766, Tyrrell Co., N. C.

BENNETT, Thomas (Jr.) and Mary L. Stone, 19 February 1801, Charleston, S. C.

BENNETT, Sarah and Adam Lanier, 7 June 1766, Tyrrell Co., N. C.

BENNETT, William and Sarah Wheatley, 5 September 1766, Tyrrell Co., N. C.

BENNISON, Mary and William Gibbs, 7 February 1743, Charleston, S. C.

BENSON, Elizabeth and Philip Foil, 20 April 1792, Rowan Co., N. C.

BENSON, John Kerr and Jenny Finch, 21 October 1796, Mecklenburg Co., N. C.

BENT, Thomas and Elizabeth Forbes, 1784, Tyrrell Co., N. C.

BENTHALL, Azal and Mary Carter, 24 December 1764, Edgecombe Co., N. C.

BENTHAM, Harriet S. and Benjamin Leefe, 6 January 1801, Charleston, S. C.

BENTHAM, James and Eleanor Phillips (widow) 5 May 1773, Charleston, S. C.

BENTHAM, Mary and Nicholas Boylston, 7 December 1794, Charleston, S. C.

BENTLEY, Ann and John Norcom, 2 June 1741, Chowan Co., N. C.

BENTLEY, Francis and Drury Malone, 19 July 1788, Bertie Co., N. C.

BENTLEY, John and Elizabeth Barnes, 17 February 1800, Edgecombe Co., N. C.

BENTLEY, Mary and Aaron Freeman, 17 December 1769, Rowan Co., N. C.

BENTLEY, Penelope and George P. B. Hasell, 20 September 1802, St. Thomas Parish S. C.

BENTLEY, Sarah and James P. Alexander, 18 January 1830, Mecklenburg Co., N. C.

BENTLEY, Zilphia and Samuel Halsey, 12 July 1770, Chowan Co., N. C.

BENTON, John and Mary Puckett, 15 March 1825, Mecklenburg Co., N. C.

BENTON, John and Patsy Roach, 8 May 1827, Mecklenburg Co., N. C.

BENTON, Judith and Adam Raby, 30 September 1748, Chowan Co., N. C.

BENTON, Mary and Thomas Gregory, 4 July 1767, Chowan Co., N. C.

BENTON, Susannah and John Exum, 18 July 1766, Edgecombe Co., N. C.

BERKLEY, Eliza and John Grimball, 25 April 1797, Beaufort Co., S. C.

BERNARD, Esther and William Leigh, 27 August 1778, Santee, S. C.

BERNARD, Judith and Jacob Bonpost, 26 November 1761, Santee, S. C.

BERNARD, Penelope and John Hays, 8 March 1779, Santee, S. C.

BERONNEAU, Martha and John Witherston, 11 August 1743, Charleston, S. C.

BERRESFORD, Elizabeth and Peter Delancy, 1 October 1770, Charleston, S. C.

BERRY, Abigail and David Hunter, 14 June 1775, Rowan Co., N. C.

BERRY, Ann A. and David Harry, 6 December 1828, Mecklenburg Co., N. C.

BERRY, Eliza and Vinson Bledsoe, 19 November 1854, Edgefield District, S. C.

BERRY, Elizabeth and Bryant Jones, 10 March 1836, Marion Co., S. C.

BERRY, Elizabeth and John Hendrickson, 20 December 1784, Rowan Co., N. C.

BERRY, May and Robert Irwin, 26 March 1798, Mecklenburg Co., N. C.

BERRY, Susan and Allen Little, 12 December 1839, Edgefield District, S. C.

BERRY, William and Mary King, (widow) 21 May 1750, Orangeburg Co., S. C.

BERRY, William P. and Aramenta S. Sample, 28 December 1831, Mecklenburg Co., N. C.

BERRYHILL, Allison and Peggy A. Berryhill, 11 January 1820, Mecklenburg Co., N. C.

BERRYHILL, Andrew A. and Matilda Roddin, 17 December 1833, Mecklenburg Co., N. C.

BERRYHILL, Betsy and William Berryhill, 23 August 1820, Mecklenburg Co., N. C.

BERRYHILL, David F. and Elizabeth Cathcart, 8 April 1816, Mecklenburg Co., N. C.

BERRYHILL, David W. and Minton H. Rowdon, 26 September 1839, Mecklenburg Co., N. C.

BERRYHILL, Dorris and Lawson H. McCoy, 3 January 1820, Mecklenburg Co., N. C.

BERRYHILL, Elizabeth and William Boyley, 31 January 1820, Mecklenburg Co., N. C.

BERRYHILL, Elizabeth and Evan P. Alexander, 24 February 1824, Mecklenburg Co., N. C.

BERRYHILL, Hannah and William Rea, 23 March 1814, Mecklenburg Co., N. C.

BERRYHILL, James McRea and Elizabeth Quincy, 2 August 1802, Mecklenburg Co., N. C.

BERRYHILL, James S. and Elizabeth J. Warwick, 22 March 1866, Mecklenburg Co., N. C.

BERRYHILL, John and Catherine S. Reed (or Rudd), 30 March 1836, Mecklenburg Co., N. C.

BERRYHILL, Joseph J. and Harriet Todd, 15 June 1825, Mecklenburg Co., N. C.

BERRYHILL, Joseph R. and Peggy A. Freeman, 9 April 1840, Mecklenburg Co., N. C.

BERRYHILL, Margaret and Josiah Auten, 20 February 1800, Mecklenburg Co., N. C.

BERRYHILL, Margaret and William K. Read, 3 February 1830, Mecklenburg Co., N. C.

BERRYHILL, Margaret E. and James Rodden, 28 January 1847, Mecklenburg Co., N. C.

BERRYHILL, Margaret B. and Robert M. Bigham, 14 April 1847, Mecklenburg Co., N. C.

BERRYHILL, Mary E. and Daniel C. Barnhart, 26 February 1852, Mecklenburg Co., N. C.

BERRYHILL, Michael W. and Mary Pelt, 6 October 1824, Mecklenburg Co., N. C.

BERRYHILL, Peggy A. and Allison Berryhill, 11 January 1820, Mecklenburg Co., N. C.

BERRYHILL, Sam and Sarah Bigham, 6 January 1802, Mecklenburg Co., N. C.

BERRYHILL, Samuel and Elizabeth Rodden, 16 August 1825, Mecklenburg Co., N. C.

BERRYHILL, Samuel and Margaret Alexander, 10 February 1823, Mecklenburg Co., N. C.

BERRYHILL, Sarah and William M. Read, 7 March 1854, Mecklenburg Co., N. C.

BERRYHILL, Taylor H. and Margaret E. Rea, 15 May 1832, Mecklenburg Co., N. C.

BERRYHILL, Thomas P. and Cynthia M. Todd, 3 March 1821, Mecklenburg Co., N. C.

BERRYHILL, Willliam and Betsy Berryhill, 23 August 1820, Mecklenburg Co., N. C.

BERRYHILL, William A. and Mary E. Roddin, 13 January 1858, Mecklenburg Co., N. C.

BERRYHILL, William R. and Mary L. Reed, 11 December 1837, Mecklenburg Co., N. C.

BERWICK, John and Ann Ash (widow) 2 January 1774, Charleston, S. C.

BESSELLEU, Johanna and Joseph Purdie, 6 June 1800, Charleston, S. C.

BEST, Henry and Mickey Morris, 17 January 1789, Bertie Co., N. C.

BESWICKE, John and Mary Hill, 16 November 1742, Charleston, S. C.

BETHEA, Mary and Richard Tatum, 18 June 1857, Marlboro Co., S. C.

BETHEA, Mary and Hartwell Ayers, 2 February 1815, Marlboro Co., S. C.

BETHUNE, Angus and Margaret Willeman, 14 January 1801, Charleston, S. C.

BEVAN, Moses and Sally Cochran, 20 January 1820, Mecklenburg Co., N. C.

BEVANHAM, Chloe and Richard Swinson, 1782, Tyrrell Co., N.C.

BEVANS, Thomas and Elizabeth King, 18 August 1751, Chowan Co., N. C.

BEVINS, Abraham and Polly Cochran, 6 October 1818, Mecklenburg Co., N. C.

BEVINS, Hannah and Ezra Cochran, 17 February 1824, Mecklenburg Co., N. C.

BEVINS, Union and Patrick McCorkle, 15 September 1815, Mecklenburg Co., N. C.

BEYERLY, Wilhemina (Mrs.) and Charles Baugniet, 13 July 1800, Charleston, S. C.

BIBB, Nancy and Heziah Ingram, 22 April 1819, Mecklenburg Co., N. C.

BIBB, William and Rachel Simons, 3 December 1818, Mecklenburg Co., N. C.

BIBBS, Mathew and Ester Mons, 23 March 1818, Mecklenburg Co., N. C.

BIBBY, Elizabeth and Levi Cochran, 14 February 1822, Mecklenburg Co., N. C.

BICKLY, Lucy and John S. Newby, 18 June 1801, Charleston, S. C.

BIDDYS, M. and Lewis Montier, 1740, Orangeburg Co., S. C.

BIGGART, James and Jane Rea, 8 June 1836, Mecklenburg Co., N. C.

BIGELOW, Martha and Patrick Mair, 17 November 1801, Charleston, S. C.

BIGELOW, Norman and Rebekah Whithead, 17 January 1787, Orange Co., N. C.

BIGGER, John W. H. and Mary Simpson, 13 October 1732, Mecklenburg Co., N. C.

BIGGER, Mary C. and David C. Robinson, 27 June 1849, Mecklenburg Co., N. C.

BIGGER, Robert and Catherine Thompson, 1 January 1788, Mecklenburg Co., N. C.

BIGGER, Robert and Rebecca Robison, 31 July 1826, Mecklenburg Co., N. C.

BIGGER, William B. and Mary A. Snell, 10 September 1827, Mecklenburg Co., N. C.

BIGGERS, Allison H. and Catherine M. Smith, 24 May 1860, Mecklenburg Co., N. C.

BIGGERS, Francis A. and Lucinda S. Miller, 22 February 1853, Mecklenburg Co., N. C.

BIGGERS, Joseph and Sarah Snell, 23 February 1811, Mecklenburg Co., N. C.

BIGGERS, Robert H. M. and Sarah H. Biggers, 14 March 1839, Mecklenburg Co., N. C.

BIGGERS, Sarah H. and Robert H. M. Biggers, 14 March 1839, Mecklenburg Co., N. C.

BIGGERS, Susannah J. and John S. Hooks, 6 April 1858, Mecklenburg Co., N. C.

BIGGS, Davis and Annie Morris, 1781, Camden, N. C.

BIGHAM, Elizabeth and William Roan, 25 April 1822, Mecklenburg Co., N. C.

BIGHAM, Green L. and Mary A. Harry, 11 February 1846, Mecklenburg Co., N. C.

BIGHAM, Hugh and Sarah Bigham, 15 July 1795, Mecklenburg Co., N. C.

BIGHAM, James and Sarah Walker, 19 July 1803, Mecklenburg Co., N. C.

BIGHAM, James and Mary W. Hunter, 14 February 1831, Mecklenburg Co., N. C.

BIGHAM, James and Isabella E. Neely, 4 May 1837, Mecklenburg Co., N. C.

BIGHAM, Jane and Hugh Nelson, 28 August 1794, Mecklenburg Co., N. C.

BIGHAM, John and Agnes Ross, 4 September 1799, Mecklenburg Co., N. C.

BIGHAM, L. S. and Jane E. Harris, 2 February 1849, Mecklenburg Co., N. C.

BIGHAM, Margaret E. and John Read, 6 March 1844, Mecklenburg Co., N. C.

BIGHAM, Mary and Robert Hunter, 14 November 1837, Mecklenburg Co., N. C.

BIGHAM, Mathies, and Tabitha Green, 27 September 1808, Mecklenburg Co., N. C.

BIGHAM, Robert and Martha Young Reed, 31 December 1799, Mecklenburg Co., N. C.

BIGHAM, Robert and Jane Matthews, 31 December 1813, Mecklenburg Co., N. C.

BIGHAM, Robert and Polly Jackson, 4 January 1815, Mecklenburg Co., N. C.

BIGHAM, Robert and Jane Hunter, 23 December 1829, Mecklenburg Co., N. C.

BIGHAM, Robert M. and Margaret B. Berryhill, 14 April 1847, Mecklenburg Co., N. C.

BIGHAM, Samuel and Nancy McKnight, 29 April 1818, Mecklenburg Co., N. C.

BIGHAM, Sarah and Hugh Bigham, 15 July 1795, Mecklenburg Co., N. C.

BIGHAM, Sarah and Samuel Berryhill, 6 January 1802, Mecklenburg Co., N. C.

BIGHAM, William C. and Jane R. Alexander, 8 May 1845, Mecklenburg Co., N. C.

BIGHAM, William M. and Sarah L. Rea, 6 June 1844, Mecklenburg Co., N. C.

BILBROWE, James and Margaret Kelly, 19 February 1766, Edgecombe Co., N. C.

BILDING, William and Sarah Bateman, 5 October 1785, Tyrrell Co., N. C.

BILL, Sarah and Charles McClure, 15 January 1793, Mecklenburg Co., N. C.

BILLING, Rebecca and Jacob Goss, 24 September 1791, Rowan Co., N. C.

BILLINGER, Lucy and William Rose, 10 December 1743, Charleston, S. C.

BILLOPS, Frances and Robert Boggs, 5 June 1778, Chowan Co., N. C.

BIRD, Charles and Betsy Lansing, 15 December 1834, Mecklenburg Co., N. C.

BIRD, James and Polly Hull, 7 January 1811, Mecklenburg Co., N. C.

BIRD, John and Jane Duffy, 9 January 1810, Mecklenburg Co., N. C.

BIRD, Lucy and James Clark, 18 September 1805, Mecklenburg Co., N. C.

BIRD, Mary and Eli B. Revells, 8 February 1837, Mecklenburg Co., N. C.

BIRD, Nelson and Polly McCullough, 21 May 1816, Mecklenburg Co., N. C.

BIRD, Rachel and Solomon Braswell, 24 December 1765, Edgecombe Co., N. C.

BIRD, Sally and James Richardson, 11 December 1817, Mecklenburg Co., N. C.

BIRNEY, Catherine and David McLean, 5 June 1790, Guilford Co., N. C.

BIRTCH, Elizabeth and William Hassell, 1784, Tyrrell Co., N. C.

BISANER, Isabel and R. M. Crocker, 15 April 1864, Lincoln, N. C.

BISHOP, Ann and Alexander Harden, 16 February 1773, Rowan Co., N. C.

BISHOP, Samuel N. and Harriet J. King, 8 January 1821, Charleston, S. C.

BISHOP, Thomas and Ann Sullivan, 26 February 1763, Chowan Co., N. C.

BISSET, Susanna and James Marsh, 10 January 1743, Charleston, S. C.

BIZE, Daniel and Joana S. Rechon, 3 November 1799, Charleston, S. C.

BLACK, Abraham and Jane Quiry, 29 June 1818, Mecklenburg Co., N. C.

BLACK, Abner L. and Catherine Smith, 7 August 1845, Mecklenburg Co., N. C.

BLACK, Amelia and William Black, 26 January 1807, Mecklenburg Co., N. C.

BLACK, A. M. (Miss) and N. Alexander F. Brewer, 1 August 1842, Mecklenburg Co., N. C.

BLACK, Betsy and Thomas G. Caldwell, 2 May 1801, Mecklenburg Co., N. C.

BLACK, Caroline and Henry Hunter, 29 August 1810, Mecklenburg Co., N. C.

BLACK, Cyrus and Mary Irvin, 7 October 1828, Mecklenburg Co., N. C.

BLACK, Cyrus and Elizabeth Harkey, 31 May 1831 Mecklenburg Co., N. C.

BLACK, David and Ealies Bennett, 24 October 1798, Chowan Co., N. C.

BLACK, David L. and Isabella Patton, 24 August 1836, Mecklenburg Co., N. C.

BLACK, Eli O. and Lydia C. Maxwell, 8 March 1830, Mecklenburg Co., N. C.

BLACK, Elizabeth and John Leacroft, 25 October 1784, Beaufort, S. C.

BLACK, Elizabeth and Thomas McCall, 8 April 1812, Mecklenburg Co., N. C.

BLACK, Elizabeth and John Maxwell, 19 February 1831, Mecklenburg Co., N. C.

BLACK, Ezekial and Sarah McEwen, 26 October 1807, Mecklenburg Co., N. C.

BLACK, Ezekial and Delila Saunders, 30 December 1839, Mecklenburg Co., N. C.

BLACK, Ezekial and Nancy H. Alexander, 18 July 1843, Mecklenburg Co., N. C.

BLACK, George and Agnes Osborne, 25 March 1800, Mecklenburg Co., N. C.

BLACK, H. W. and Alvira McComb, 8 October 1841, Mecklenburg Co., N. C.

BLACK, Isabelle and Peter Tomplet, 17 April 1732, Berkeley Co., S. C.

BLACK, James and Elizabeth Shanks, 24 March 1801, Mecklenburg Co., N. C.

BLACK, James and Peggy Black, 2 February 1814, Mecklenburg Co., N. C.

BLACK, James and Sally McComb, 12 March 1817, Mecklenburg Co., N. C.

BLACK, James B. and Hattie Ayer, 1 August 1872, Colleton Co., S. C.

BLACK, James M. and Elizabeth Johnston, 19 November 1836, Mecklenburg Co., N. C.

BLACK, Jane and John Thomas, 1740, Fair Forest, S. C.

BLACK, Jane and John Ennis, 30 January 1767, Rowan Co., N. C.

BLACK, Jane and Jamus Elder, 1 March 1773, Chowan Co., N. C.

BLACK, Jensey and William Hays, 2 April 1805, Mecklenburg Co., N. C.

BLACK, John and Miss Carrell, 15 August 1765, Chowan Co., N. C.

BLACK, John and Mary Walker, 1 September 1790, Mecklenburg Co., N. C.

BLACK, John and Agnes Weir, 10 August 1792, Mecklenburg Co., N. C.

BLACK, John and Lydia Hood, 25 August 1802, Mecklenburg Co., N. C.

BLACK, John and Peggy Meek, 9 March 1803, Mecklenburg Co., N. C.

BLACK, Joseph and Martha L. Morrow, 17 August 1737, Mecklenburg Co., N. C.

BLACK, Joseph B. and Jane A. Quay, 16 December 1842, Mecklenburg Co., N. C.

BLACK, Julie and John Irwin, 5 October 1820, Mecklenburg Co., N. C.

BLACK, J. C. and Margaret K. Black, 26 September 1861, Mecklenburg Co., N. C.

BLACK, Margaret and Roderick McCauley, 22 March 1803, Mecklenburg Co., N. C.

BLACK, Margaret K. and J. C. Black, 26 September 1861, Mecklenburg Co., N. C.

BLACK, Margaret T. and John C. Johnston, 16 April 1833, Mecklenburg Co., N. C.

BLACK, Mary and William Hanseman, 9 February 1790, Rowan Co., N. C.

BLACK, Mary and John Mariegu, 25 May 1795, Guilford Co., N. C.

BLACK, Mary and William Johnston, 6 October 1807, Mecklenburg Co., N. C.

BLACK, Mary A. and John W. Brown, 23 September 1851, Mecklenburg Co., N. C.

BLACK, Nelson L. and Sarah B. Lawson, 6 December 1839, Mecklenburg Co., N. C.

BLACK, Peggy and David Hart, 29 May 1789, Rowan Co., N. C.

BLACK, Peggy and James Black, 21 February 1814, Mecklenburg Co., N. C.

BLACK, Richard and Elizabeth Partlow, 1 January 1805, Mecklenburg Co., N. C.

BLACK, Robert and Dovey Harth, 4 April 1808, Mecklenburg Co., N. C.

BLACK, Samuel and Elizabeth Hardy, 10 October 1765, Bertie Co., N. C.

BLACK, Samuel and Margaret Robinett, 23 October 1810, Mecklenburg Co., N. C.

BLACK, Samuel and Rachel Green (or Greer), 24 August 1819, Mecklenburg Co., N. C.

BLACK, Samuel and Elizabeth McAuley, 26 January 1822, Mecklenburg Co., N. C.

BLACK, Thomas O. and Frances Greble, 7 March 1823, Mecklenburg Co., N. C.

BLACK, Thomas M. and Amanda E. McCauley, 11 March 1858, Mecklenburg Co., N. C.

BLACK, Thomas O. and Celia Irwin, 2 January 1828, Mecklenburg Co., N. C.

BLACK, William and Mary Ann Johnston, 13 July 1792, Mecklenburg Co., N. C.

BLACK, William and Mary Irwin, 20 February 1793, Mecklenburg Co., N. C.

BLACK, William and Elizabeth Meachand, 22 July 1801, Mecklenburg Co., N. C.

BLACK, William and Margaret Neil, 22 September 1801, Mecklenburg Co., N. C.

BLACK, William and Amelia Black, 26 January 1807, Mecklenburg Co., N. C.

BLACK, William and Eliza J. Aiken, 19 March 1861, Mecklenburg Co., N. C.

BLACK, William J. and Matilda Flow, 30 December 1824, Mecklenburg Co., N. C.

BLACK, William L. and Rachel M. Wentz, 22 January 1841, Mecklenburg Co., N. C.

BLACK, William M. and E. M. Harmon, 11 May 1865, Mecklenburg Co., N. C.

BLACK, Willis and Tabitha Darnell, 29 December 1806, Mecklenburg Co., N. C.

BLACKWELDER, David M. and Lucy Hagler, 23 December 1857, Mecklenburg Co., N. C.

BLACKBURN, Hugh and Margaret Boyd, 9 March 1808, Mecklenburg Co., N. C.

BLACKBURN, Louisa and Thomas Read, 5 February 1830, Mecklenburg Co., N. C.

BLACKLEY, Thomas H. and Mary H. Morrow, 20 September 1836, Mecklenburg Co., N. C.

BLACKSTON, Thomas and Sarah Blount, 20 October 1777, Tyrrell Co., N. C.

BLACKWELDER, Isaac W. and Nelly Hagler, 6 September 1856, Mecklenburg Co., N. C.

BLACKWOOD, Ann and Gideon Blackwood, 14 November 1811, Mecklenburg Co., N. C.

BLACKWOOD, Gideon and Ann Blackwood, 14 November 1811, Mecklenburg, Co., N. C.

BLACKWOOD, Joseph and Peggy Haynes, 17 April 1824, Mecklenburg Co., N. C.

BLACKWOOD, Mary and William Boyle, 15 November 1797, Mecklenburg Co., N. C.

BLACKWOOD, Susannah and John Holmes, 9 December 1793, Rowan Co., N. C.

BLACKWOOD, Thomas and Harriet Quelch, 23 April 1801, Charleston, S. C.

BLAIN, Clarinda J. and John H. Houston, 2 February 1829, Mecklenburg Co., N. C.

BLAIR, Ann and Robert L. McLin, 20 June 1816, Guilford, N. C.

BLAIR, David and Mary A. Wilson, 20 August 1828, Mecklenburg Co., N. C.

BLAIR, Elizabeth and William Mitchell, 2 December 1828, Guilford, N. C.

BLAIR, Isabel and Josiah McCall, 12 March 1833, Mecklenburg Co., N. C.

BLAIR, James and Mary Cantzon, 15 May 1792, Williamsburg, S. C.

BLAIR, James G. and Piety Hooks, 27 November 1819, Mecklenburg Co., N. C.

BLAIR, James J. and Martha C. Ray, 5 November 1822, Camden, S. C.

BLAIR, John and Jane Gamble, 9 February 1771, Guilford Co., N. C.

BLAIR, John and Agnes Smith, 8 October 1799, Mecklenburg, N. C.

BLAIR, John and Elizabeth Snell, 26 March 1800, Mecklenburg Co., N. C.

BLAIR, John and Nancy Eakes, 3 November 1808, Mecklenburg Co., N. C.

BLAIR, John M. and Susan I. Crowell, 9 April 1861, Mecklenburg Co., N. C.

BLAIR, Laird and Margaret C. Orr, 24 July 1833, Mecklenburg Co., N. C.

BLAIR, Martha and Robert Johnston, 29 July 1865, Mecklenburg Co., N. C.

BLAIR, Mary H. and John A. Dunlap, 1820, Lancaster Co., S. C.

BLAIR, Milton and Caroline Alexander, 31 March 1831, Mecklenburg Co., N. C.

BLAIR, Robert L. and Martha R. Cunningham, 1 November 1838, Guilford, N. C.

BLAIR, Samuel and Eliza Alexander, 26 November 1823, Mecklenburg Co., N. C.

BLAIR, Sarah and James McCandly, 19 March 1793, Guilford Co., N. C.

BLAKE, Daniel and Elizabeth Izard, 21 March 1762, Pawlets, S. C.

BLAKE, Daniel and Anna L. Middleton, 2 February 1800, Charleston, S. C.

BLAKE, Daniel and Helen Craig, 21 July 1856, Newington, S. C.

BLAKE, James H. and Margaret A. Davidson, 13 September 1820, Mecklenburg Co., N. C.

BLAKE, Joseph and Elizabeth Turgis (widow), December 1698, Pawlets, S. C.

BLAKE, Joseph and Sarah Lindrey, 16 June 1720, Newington, S. C.

BLAKE, Mary and Thomas Rose, 13 October 1774, Berkeley Co., S. C.

BLAKE, Rebecca and George Smith, 9 March 1717, Plainfield, S. C.

BLAKE, Richard (Jr.) and Ann Bearman, 23 July 1772, Santee, S. C.

BLAKE, Walter and Anna S. Izard, 16 June 1837, Schevening, S. C.

BLAKE, William and Anne Izard, 11 February 1759, Pawlets, S. C.

BLAKELEY, Hugh and Rebecca Peoples, 21 December 1843, Mecklenburg Co., N. C.

BLAKELY, Daniel A. and Margaret C. Montieth, 25 March 1837, Mecklenburg Co., N. C.

BLAKELY, Dock and Miss Hudgens, 18 October 1864, Laurens Co., S. C.

BLAKELY, Thomas and Teresa Hunter, 8 October 1812, Mecklenburg Co., N. C.

BLAKELY, Thomas H. and Jane Gilden, 31 March 1862, Mecklenburg Co., N. C.

BLAKELY, William J. and Mary J. Cook, 5 January 1866, Mecklenburg Co., N. C.

BLAKEY, George and Elizabeth Roffe, (widow) 22 November 1767, Charleston, S. C.

BLAKLEY, I. A. and E. J. Solomon (Miss) 26 March 1863, Mecklenburg Co., N. C.

BLAKLEY, James and Martha Walker, 29 May 1793, Mecklenburg Co., N. C.

BLALOCK, William and Louisa Shepard, 6 July 1840, Mecklenburg Co., N. C.

BLANCHARD, Millerson (Mrs.) and Nathaniel Jones, 12 June 1772, Chowan Co., N. C.

BLANCHARD, Rachel and Jesse Garrett, 30 January 1756, Chowan Co., N. C.

BLANCHARD, Rachel and Demsey Bond, 16 March 1774, Chowan Co., N. C.

BLANCHARD, Rosanna ad James L. Alexander, 23 August 1842, Mecklenburg Co., N. C.

BLANCHARD, Thomas L. and Elizabeth Andrews, 15 March 1841, Mecklenburg Co., N. C.

BLANCHARD, Zilpha and WilliamWynns, 2 January 1752, Chowan Co., N. C.

BLANCHETTE, Thomas and Rosanna Roddin, 8 September 1805, Mecklenburg Co., N. C.

BLAND, E. M. and Elizabeth Cochran, 26 January 1840, Edgefield District, S. C.

BLAND, John P. and Eliza Singleterry, 11 November 1857, Edgefield District, S. C.

BLAND, Peggy and Casper Donaldson, 23 January 1823, Edgefield District, S. C.

BLAND, Talton and Polly Carter, 23 January 1823, Edgefield District, S. C.

BLAND, Theodoric J. and Georgiana Lamb, 8 October 1829, Chowan Co., N. C.

BLANKENSHIP, Polly and Wiley Roberts, 27 January 1808, Mecklenburg Co., N. C.

BLANKENSHIP, Samuel H. and Adaline Hoover, 10 August 1854, Mecklenburg Co., N. C.

BLANKENSHIP, Samuel H. and Alice A. Alexander, 3 December 1859, Mecklenburg Co., N. C.

BLAYLOCK, Isom and Margaret Wilson, 21 May 1839, Mecklenburg Co., N. C.

BLEASE, Horatio and Eliza Mooney, 23 October 1835, Edgefield District, S. C.

BLEDSOE, Lewis and Elizabeth Mackmanus, 21 February 1850, Edgefield District, S. C.

BLEDSOE, Vinson and Eliza Berry, 19 November 1854, Edgefield District, S. C.

BLESS, Kelly and John Ettleman, 5 January 1789, Rowan Co., N. C.

BLOOM, Andrew and Mary Rowe, 22 January 1797, Charleston, S. C.

BLOUNT, Asia and Henry Hunter, 24 March 1783, Tyrrell Co., N. C.
BLOUNT, Billah and Thomas Brown, 10 March 1780, Tyrrell Co., N. C.
BLOUNT, Edmund and Mary Hoskins, 26 February 1765, Chowan Co., N. C.
BLOUNT, Edmond and Judeth Rhodes, 30 December 1777, Tyrrell Co., N. C.
BLOUNT, Elizabeth and Joshua Swain, 1 March 1753, Chowan Co., N. C.
BLOUNT, Elizabeth and Andrew Miller, February 1763, Perquimans Co., N. C.
BLOUNT, Esther and Timothy Cunningham, 1784, Tyrrell Co., N. C.
BLOUNT, Hannah and Thomas Bog, 3 November 1770, Tyrrell Co., N. C.
BLOUNT, Jacob and Esther Jordan, 24 March 1768, Tyrrell Co., N. C.
BLOUNT, James and Louise A. Narment, 17 May 1826, Mecklenburg Co., N. C.
BLOUNT, Jane and Robert L. McKibben, 13 July 1840, Mecklenburg Co., N. C.
BLOUNT, Jesse and Rebecca Bartlett, 28 February 1788, Bertie Co., N. C.
BLOUNT, Joana (widow) and John Long, 23 December 1766, Tyrrell Co., N. C.
BLOUNT, John and Elizabeth Milburn, 13 January 1790, Bertie Co., N. C.
BLOUNT, John and Jane L. Crump, 14 September 1864, Mecklenburg Co., N. C.
BLOUNT, Joseph and Sarah Hoskins (widow), 15 May 1771, Chowan Co., N. C.
BLOUNT, Joseph (Jr.) and Lydia Bonner, 15 July 1775, Chowan Co., N. C.
BLOUNT, Keziah and Anthony Alexander, 1781, Tyrrel Co., N. C.
BLOUNT, Lydia and John Swain, 19 February 1780, Tyrrell Co., N. C.
BLOUNT, Margaret and Joseph L. Crisman, 17 April 1785, Chowan Co., N. C.
BLOUNT, Mary and Charles Pettigrew, 28 October 1778, Chowan Co., N. C.
BLOUNT, Matilda and Nelson McCorkle, 28 October 1839, Mecklenburg Co., N. C.
BLOUNT, Sarah and Thomas Blackston, 20 October 1777, Tyrrell Co., N. C.
BLUE, Margaret and David Hays, 10 October 1788, Rowan Co., N. C.
BLUM, Eliza Corbett and Asbury Coward, 25 December 1856, Yorkville, S. C.
BLUMANDER, Elizabeth and Robert Mitchell, 13 November 1839, Guilford Co., N. C.
BLYTHE, Ann and Thomas Martin, 17 October 1786, Mecklenburg Co., N. C.
BLYTHE, George and Elizabeth Allen, 5 December 1865, Mecklenburg Co., N. C.
BLYTHE, Robert and Mary Crenshaw, 12 October 1865, Mecklenburg Co., N. C.
BLYTHE, Samuel and Isabella Nance, 8 January 1822, Mecklenburg Co., N. C.
BLYTHE, Samuel and Patsy Bond, 9 May 1803, Mecklenburg Co., N. C.
BLYTHEWOOD, Benjamin R. and Sarah J. Fickling, 14 January 1813, Beaufort, S. C.
BLYTHEWOOD, Daniel and Elizabeth Taylor, 17 April 1792, Charleston, S. C.
BLYTHEWOOD, Thomas and Sarah Mallery, 14 December 1794, Charleston, S. C.
BOAL, Margaret and John McGinn, 3 November 1796, Mecklenburg Co., N. C.
BOALES, Margaret M. and Moses M. Alexander, 24 July 1830, Mecklenburg Co., N. C.
BOALS, Addison P. and Jane Irwin, 1 March 1825, Mecklenburg Co., N. C.
BOALS, Thomas and Abigail Orr, 27 February 1799, Mecklenburg Co., N. C.
BOATWRIGHT, James and Martha Alexander, 4 September 1845, Mecklenburg Co., N. C.
BOATWRIGHT, James and Rebecca Kennedy, 5 March 1857, Edgefield District, S. C.
BOATWRIGHT, John and Margaret A. Porter, 26 May 1832, Mecklenburg Co., N. C.
BOATWRIGHT, Samuel and Nancy Weathers, 1 August 1792, Mecklenburg Co., N. C.

BOATWRIGHT, Samuel W. and Mary Porter, 8 January 1846, Mecklenburg Co., N. C.

BOATWRIGHT, S. Washington and Cynthia Robison, 10 April 1834, Mecklenburg Co., N. C.

BOBBETT, Elizabeth and Conrad Crump, 26 November 1840, Mecklenburg Co., N. C.

BOBO, Burwell and Sue Drummond, 29 September 1859, Laurens Co., S. C.

BOBO, Elizabeth Harper and Benjamin Franklin, 28 July 1839, Union District, S. C.

BOBO, J. William and Macilda G. Nance, 11 November 1847, Union District, S. C.

BOBO, Robert and Ann P. Gorden, 6 May 1858, Union District, S. C.

BOBO, Young and Nancy Browning, 4 April 1819, Union District, S. C.

BOCHETT, Ann and John Barnett, 2 December 1762, Santee, S. C.

BODKIN, John and Polly Sandford, 25 September 1828, Mecklenburg Co., N. C.

BOG, Thomas and Hannah Blount, 3 November 1770, Tyrrell Co., N. C.

BOGER, Betsy and Jacob File, 24 October 1797, Rowan Co., N. C.

BOGGS, Asahel and Esther McCoy, 25 January 1792, Mecklenburg Co., N. C.

BOGGS, Robert and Frances Billops, 5 June 1778, Chowan Co., N. C.

BOGLE, Jonathan and Mary Easter, 7 September 1801, Charleston, S. C.

BOHANNON, Mary and David Murdock, 12 August 1788, Orange Co., N. C.

BOILLAT, Peter and Jane E. Dupont, 14 October 1784, Charleston, S. C.

BOILSTON, Elizabeth and Samuel Reed, 31 December 1823, Barnwell District, S. C.

BOINEAU, Magdeline and John Monk, 20 October 1767, Santee, S. C.

BOINEAU, Mary and John Dutart, 1 March 1764, Santee, S. C.

BOLT, Elizabeth and Milton Moore, 18 November 1866, Laurens Co., S. C.

BOLT, Emily and Mr. Burnside, 13 November 1859, Laurens Co., S. C.

BOLT, Fanny and Silas Bailey, 23 December 1858, Laurens Co., S. C.

BOLT, John L. and Louvenia Walker, 11 August 1859, Laurens Co., S. C.

BOLT, Martha and Edward Boyd, 24 November 1857, Laurens Co., S. C.

BOLT, Samuel and Elline Cannady, 9 February 1848, Laurens Co., S. C.

BOLT, Sarah J. and Calvin Hellams, 22 December 1859, Laurens Co., S. C.

BOLT, William and Susan Allison, 14 December 1858, Laurens Co., S. C.

BOLTENHAMER, Ann and Andrew Mandring, 22 March 1789, Guilford Co., N. C.

BOLTON, Abner and Mary Raiborn, 14 December 1856, Edgefield District, S. C.

BOLTON, Richard and Sarah Langston, 1 January 1770, Edgecombe Co., N. C.

BOLTON, Sarah A. and C. A. Andrews, 16 September 1845, Mecklenburg Co., N. C.

BOMMER, Miss and Richard Cole, 29 May 1777, Charleston, S. C.

BOND, Catherine and (Dr.) Samuel Carne, 18 February 1759, Christ Parish, S. C.

BOND, Catherine and Charles Gee, 24 April 1770, Santee, S. C.

BOND, Demsey and Rachel Blanchard, 16 March 1774, Chowan Co., N. C.

BOND, Eleanor (widow) and Joseph Speight, 11 January 1775, Chowan Co., N. C.

BOND, John and Mary Mathias, 27 April 1776, Chowan Co., N. C.

BOND, Mary and Job Milner, May 1759, Charleston, S. C.

BOND, Mary and Arthur Jernagan, 25 February 1790, Bertie Co., N. C.

BOND, Nathaniel and Nancy Miller, 4 July 1831, Chowan Co., N. C.

BOND, Patsy and Samuel Blythe, 9 May 1803, Mecklenburg Co., N. C.

BOND, Rhoda and Thomas Bond, 30 December 1790, Bertie Co., N. C.

BOND, Richard and Jean Allen, 25 November 1763, Edgecombe Co., N. C.

BOND, Sally and Allen Morris, 30 October 1805, Mecklenburg Co., N. C.

BOND, Teresa and Bond Jameson, 9 February 1785, Chowan Co., N. C.

BOND, Thomas and Rhoda Bond, 30 December 1790, Bertie Co., N. C.

BONDS, James and Peggy Morrow, (or McCulloch) 27 April 1802, Mecklenburg Co., N. C.

BONHOST, Joseph and Rebecca Vereen, 25 April 1770, Santee, S. C.

BONHOSTE, Jacob and Hannah Sullivan, 21 April 1768, Santee, S. C.

BONNEAU, Floride and John E. Calhoun, 8 October 1786, St. Johns Parish, S. C.

BONNEAU, Jane (Mrs.) and Robert Ewing, September 1785, Charleston, S. C.

BONNEAU, Josiah and Susannah Eberson, 13 September 1774, Ponpon, S. C.

BONNER, Elizabeth (widow) and William Roberts, 21 February 1767, Chowan Co., N. C.

BONNER, Henry and Esther Worley, 5 November 1753, Chowan Co., N. C.

BONNER, Henry and Elizabeth Hardy, 4 January 1758, Chowan Co., N. C.

BONNER, Henry and Elizabeth Williams, 14 June 1779, Chowan Co., N. C.

BONNER, Lydia and Joseph Blount (Jr.), 15 July 1775, Chowan Co., N. C.

BONNER, Margaret and James Baird, 24 January 1801, Charleston, S. C.

BONNER, Mrs. and John Williams, January 1786, Charleston, S. C.

BONNER, Penelope and Frederick Dorsey, 16 July 1764, Tyrrell Co., N. C.

BONNER, Sarah and Henry Norman, 1784, Tyrrell Co., N. C.

BONNER, Thomas and Mary Standing, February 1752, Chowan Co., N. C.

BONNER, Thomas and Margaret Jones, 6 May 1767, Chowan Co., N. C.

BONNER, William and Sarah Luten, 21 August 1744, Chowan Co., N. C.

BONNEY, Ann and William Hull, 1 May 1745, St. Thomas Parish, S. C.

BONPOST, Jacob and Judith Bernard, 26 November 1761, Santee, S. C.

BOOE, Elizabeth and George Graves, 18 December 1792, Rowan Co., N. C.

BOOE, Rebecca and John Frost, 21 August 1793, Rowan Co., N. C.

BOONER, Arabella (Mrs.) and John H. Kahnle, 18 September 1794, Charleston, S. C.

BOOMER, John and Elizabeth Cleator (widow) 9 July 1774, Charleston, S. C.

BOOKER, Eleanor and William Martin, 2 November 1808, Mecklenburg Co., N. C.

BOONE, Capers and Mary Smith, 16 July 1767, Santee, S. C.

BOONE, James and Rebecca Bryan, 14 August 1756, Yadkin River, N. C.

BOONE, John and Elizabeth Jordan, 19 January 1762, Santee, S. C.

BOONE, Mary and George Ford, 13 October 1778, Santee, S. C.

BOONE, Rebecca and John Lloyd, 25 November 1752, Charleston, S. C.

BOONE, Rebecca and Arthur Smith, 1788, Black River, S. C.

BOONE, Squire and Jane Van Cleft, 11 July 1765, Rowan Co., N. C.

BOONE, Susan and John Gaillard, 10 November 1768, Santee, S. C.

BOONE, Susan and Henry White, 5 December 1771, Santee, S. C.

BOONE, Thomas (Jr.) and Hannah Atkinson, 14 September 1769, Santee, S. C.

BOOTH, Benjamin and Isabella Cropton, 20 April 1797, Charleston, S. C.

BOOTH, Catherine and Roger Heriot, 24 March 1801, Charleston, S. C.

BOOTH, Elizabeth and Enoch Green, 9 September 1794, Rowan Co., N. C.

BOOTH, John and Selveah Spell, 24 December 1799, Edgecombe Co., N. C.

BOOTH, Mary and Isaac Green, 21 December 1793, Rowan Co., N. C.

BOOTH, Mary and Henry Martin, 29 May 1795, Guilford Co., N. C.

BOOTH, Milly and Brinkley George, 1810, Orange Co., N. C.

BOOTH, Termehia and Bartlett Herndon, 27 April 1853, Orange Co., N. C.

BOOWER, Jeremiah and Christina Miller, 6 September 1774, Charleston, S. C.

BOOZER, Pauline and Godfrey Harman, 24 November 1864, Lexington, S. C.

BORY, John H. and Mary Randall, 22 July 1778, Chowan Co., N. C.

BOSOMWORTH, Abraham and Susanna Seabrook, 2 November 1749, Ashley Ferry, S. C.

BOSS, Elizabeth and David Goss, 24 March 1794, Rowan Co., N. C.

BOST, John M. and Ann H. King, 17 March 1855, Mecklenburg Co., N. C.

BOSTWICK, William M. and Caroline Graham, 21 February 1817, Mecklenburg Co., N. C.

BOSWELL, Charles and Margaret Soward, 7 October 1790, Bertie Co., N. C.

BOSWELL, Thomas and Hannah M. Peters, 23 September 1835, Mecklenburg Co., N. C.

BOSWELL, William and Margery McMath, 5 November 1761, Chowan Co., N. C.

BOSWELL, Winifred and Lamb Hardy, 23 August 1790, Bertie Co., N. C.

BOSWOOD, Mary and Thomas Mell, 23 December 1718, St. Andrews Parish, S. C.

BOUD, Sallie and Madison Martin, 18 February 1866, Laurens Co., S. C.

BOUKNIGHT, Leah and William Bear, 19 December 1839, Edgefield District, S. C.

BOULNARE, Andrew and Ann D. Rutherford, 16 July 1835, Edgefield District, S. C.

BOULTON, Jonathan and Fanny Williams, (widow) 8 April 1773, Chowan Co., N. C.

BOULTON, Thomas and Elizabeth Miller, 25 July 1724, Charleston, S. C.

BOURDEAUX, Daniel and Patty Smith, 11 January 1770, Charleston, S. C.

BOURLIN, Martha and James Gibbons, 16 September 1794, Rowan Co., N. C.

BOUQUET, Rachel and Edward Trescott, May 1777, Charleston, S. C.

BOURQUIN, Elizabeth and Blakley White, 2 March 1772, Charleston, S. C.

BOUYSSON, Rosena and Thomas Gyles, 11 January 1800, Charleston, S. C.

BOWDEN, Arthur and Elizabeth Smith, 31 March 1832, Mecklenburg Co., N. C.

BOWDON, John and Margaret Randolph, 6 November 1817, Mecklenburg Co., N. C.

BOWEN, Eleanor and Edmondson Smithwick, 1 September 1768, Tyrrell Co., N. C.

BOWEN, J. W. S. and Lucretia Reynolds, 13 January 1857, Edgefield District, S. C.

BOWEN, Margaret and Teenan Moore, 15 June 1797, Guilford Co., N. C.

BOWEN, Nathaniel and Martha Barnecastle, 29 August 1797, Bertie Co., N. C.

BOWEN, Polly and William Baker, 7 December 1805, Bertie Co., N. C.

BOWEN, Robert E. and Martha A. Oliver, 15 October 1857, Pickens Co., S. C.

BOWEN, Sarah and Nathan McKoney, 10 November 1790, Guilford Co., N. C.

BOWEN, William and Margaret Skinner, 1 August 1771, Santee, S. C.

BOWERS, David and Jane Riley, 29 October 1800, Mecklenburg Co., N. C.

BOWIE, Benjamin and Elenor Moore, 25 October 1827, Mecklenburg Co., N. C.

BOWLES, Tobias and Miss Drayton, 12 March 1795, Charleston, S. C.

BOWMAN, Anne and David Moorer, 1789, Orangeburg Co., S. C.

BOWMAN, Elinor and David Robison, 12 January 1813, Mecklenburg Co., N. C.

BOWMAN, James and Margaret Green, December 1785, Beaufort, S. C.

BOWMAN, Rosa and James Atkins, 28 December 1816, Newberry, S. C.

BOWMAN, Samuel (Major) and (Mrs.) Mary Wilson, 12 July 1801, Mecklenburg Co., N. C.

BOWMAN, Zachariah and Nancy Goodman, 27 August 1801, Vienna, S. C.

BOX, Margaret and Thomas F. Anderson, 1803, Burke Co., N. C.

BOY, John and Sally Miles, 9 November 1784, Ashepoo, S. C.

BOYCE, Caroline and Samuel C. Read, 9 December 1847, Mecklenburg Co., N. C.

BOYCE, Elizabeth and Charles Dunning, 8 December 1783, Bertie Co., N. C.

BOYCE, Hardy and Mary Hubbard, 13 August 1790, Bertie Co., N. C.

BOYCE, Jacob and Agnes Eccleston, (widow) 7 March 1775, Chowan Co., N. C.

BOYCE, John and Isabella Kirkpatrick, 27 December 1800, Mecklenburg Co., N. C.

BOYCE, John and Sarah Mitchell, 4 August 1834, Chowan Co., N. C.

BOYCE, Lucy and Robert Johnston, 26 January 1866, Mecklenburg Co., N. C.

BOYCE, Thomas and Susan Mitchell, 12 January 1838, Chowan Co., N. C.

BOYCE, William and Judith Lamb, 3 May 1787, Bertie Co., N. C.

BOYCE, William and Emeline Walkup, 8 January 1852, Mecklenburg Co., N. C.

BOYD, Andrew and Sarah Dunbar, 12 December 1793, Mecklenburg Co., N. C.

BOYD, Ann (widow) and John Benbury, 14 August 1752, Chowan Co., N. C.

BOYD, Anne (widow) and John Delahowe, 23 April 1767, Charleston, S. C.

BOYD, Benjamin P. and Terza Rea, 11 November 1839, Mecklenburg Co., N. C.

BOYD, Daniel and Patsy Parish, 15 September 1812, Mecklenburg Co., N. C.

BOYD, David and Elizabeth Simonds, 1 June 1822, Mecklenburg Co., N. C.

BOYD, Edward and Martha Bolt, 24 November 1857, Laurens Co., S. C.

BOYD, Elender and James McCann, 15 October 1799, Mecklenburg Co., N. C.

BOYD, Elizabeth and Thomas Lesesne, December 1785, Charleston, S. C.

BOYD, Elizabeth and Colon Halsey, 16 December 1785, Chowan Co., N. C.

BOYD, Elizabeth and James McLeary, 27 February 1822, Mecklenburg Co., N. C.

BOYD, H. B. and Margaret E. Helms, 4 October 1865, Mecklenburg Co., N. C.

BOYD, James and Elizabeth J. Smith, 10 October 1831, Mecklenburg Co., N. C.

BOYD, John and Jane Henderson, 20 January 1853, Laurens Co., S. C.

BOYD, Joshua D. and Altona L. Smith, 28 December 1826, Mecklenburg Co., N. C.

BOYD, Josiah and Mary Segel, 4 July 1839, Mecklenburg Co., N. C.

BOYD, Lucy A. and John Taylor, 27 September 1815, Granville Co., N. C.

BOYD, Lydia (widow) and Joseph Harron, 10 April 1742, Chowan Co., N. C.

BOYD, Margaret and Hugh Blackburn, 9 March 1808, Mecklenburg Co., N. C.

BOYD, Marian and (Dr.) George Wells, 3 February 1767, Chowan Co., N. C.

BOYD, Mary and Wesley Fowler, 11 March 1852, Laurens Co., S. C.

BOYD, Nancy and Jesse Ballard, 27 December 1806, Mecklenburg Co., N. C.

BOYD, Panthia Burwell and William W. White, 12 October 1848, Warren Co., N. C.

BOYD, Susan and Thomas Hill, 13 December 1860, Laurens Co., S. C.

BOYD, Susan and Allen Robison, 25 August 1830, Mecklenburg Co., N. C.

BOYD, Thomas and Susanna Darnell, 19 December 1796, Mecklenburg Co., N. C.

BOYD, William B. (Rev.) and Lucinda Paine, 22 April 1858, Laurens Co., S. C.

BOYDEN, Daniel and Martha Stent, 25 May 1797, James Island, S. C.

BOYER, Elam B. and Sarah A. Hunter, 26 September 1841, Mecklenburg Co., N. C.

BOYES, William and Nancy Scott, 4 October 1833, Mecklenburg Co., N. C.

BOYKIN, Edward and Esther Williams, 2 April 1799, Edgecombe Co., N. C.

BOYLE, Daniel and (Mrs.) Jane Slann, 10 November 1800, Charleston, S. C.

BOYLE, William and Mary Blackwood, 15 November 1797, Mecklenburg Co., N. C.

BOYLESTON, Nicholas and Mary Bentham, 7 December 1794, Charleston, S. C.

BOYLEY, William and Elizabeth Berryhill, 31 January 1820, Mecklenburg Co., N. C.

BOZZELL, Polly and James Rea, 13 March 1809, Mecklenburg Co., N. C.

BOZZLE, Sarah S. and Robert A. Martin, 4 December 1838, Mecklenburg Co., N. C.

BRACKEN, Jesse and Jean Cantril, 20 March 1790, Orange Co., N. C.

BRACKETT, Benjamin and Margaret I. Wilson, 25 January 1837, Mecklenburg Co., N. C.

BRADFIELD, Emiline and Edward Walsh, 28 December 1852, Edgefield District, S. C.

BRADFORD, James and Malinda Wallace, 12 December 1835, Mecklenburg Co., N. C.

BRADFORD, Selah and Coleman Read White, 13 March 1786, Granville Co., N. C.

BRADFORD, Susanna and John Humphrey, 7 January 1793, Rowan Co., N. C.

BRADFORD, Thomas and Christiana George, 1788, Charleston, S. C.

BRADHAM, Daniel and Sarah F. Hodge, 13 October 1859, Clarendon Co., S. C.

BRADLEY, David (Jr.) and Mourning Barnes, 2 December 1810, Edgecombe Co., N. C.

BRADLEY, David F. and Mary Breazeale, 3 November 1865, Pickens Co., S. C.

BRADLEY, Elizabeth and Green Dixon, 12 November 1799, Edgecombe Co., N. C.

BRADLEY, Evan B. and Elizabeth ———, 12 February 1799, Mecklenburg Co., N. C.

BRADLEY, Francis A. and Martha Henderson, 12 August 1836, Mecklenburg Co., N. C.

BRADLEY, James A. and Elizabeth Houston, 30 October 1810, Mecklenburg Co., N. C.

BRADLEY, John McK. and Jean Mitchell, 13 February 1796, Mecklenburg Co., N. C.

BRADLEY, Mary and George D. Row, 8 December 1799, Charleston, S. C.

BRADLEY, Mary and William Carter, 10 August 1838, Mecklenburg Co., N. C.

BRADLEY, Mary E. and James G. Brawley, 22 November 1858, Mecklenburg Co., N. C.

BRADLEY, Robert F. and Martha R. Wideman, 11 September 1871, Abbeville Co., S. C.

BRADLEY, Susan and Joshua G. Wright, 1780, Wilmington, N. C.

BRADSHAW, Jane and John Morrison, 5 April 1791, Mecklenburg Co., N. C.

BRADSHAW, Solomon and Elizabeth Givens, 1 August 1797, Mecklenburg Co., N. C.

BRADSHAW, William and Ann Winchester, 8 August 1800, Mecklenburg Co., N. C.

BRADWELL, John and Betsy Lloyd, 30 March 1775, Charleston, S. C.

BRADY, Alice and William Grice, 2 April 1780, Rowan Co., N. C.

BRADY, Edward and Rachael Whiteford, 27 September 1753, Orangeburg Co., S. C.

BRAILSFORD, John and Polly Moncrief, 6 December 1769, Charleston, S. C.

BRAILSFORD, Morton and Mary Stanyarne, 25 October 1753, Charleston, S. C.

BRAILSFORD, Samuel and Elizabeth Holmes, 7 April 1750, Charleston, S. C.

BRAILSFORD, Sarah and William Scott, October 1765, Charleston, S. C.

BRAILSFORD, William and Maria Heyward, June 1786, Charleston, S. C.

BRAINER, Ann and J. Straits, 1784, Tyrrell Co., N. C.

BRALEY, Martha and John Montgomery, 16 May 1786, Guilford Co., N. C.

BRAMLET, Henry and Rebecca Burns, 2 November 1847, Laurens Co., S. C.

BRAMLET, Malinda and Simeon Ball, 24 July 1866, Laurens Co., S. C.

BRAMLET, Reuben and Milly Robertson, 8 November 1842, Laurens Co., S. C.

BRANCH, Armistead and Sarah Dinkins, 18 March 1824, Mecklenburg Co., N. C.

BRANCH, Burwell and Nancy Morgan, 15 October 1788, Bertie Co., N. C.

BRANCH, Elizabeth and Edward Underhill, 9 April 1755, Chowan Co., N. C.

BRANDON, Alee and John Erwin, 28 July 1779, Rowan Co., N. C.

BRANDON, James A. and Mary C. Carothers, 15 January 1841, Mecklenburg Co., N. C.

BRANDON, John and Jane M. Carothers, 20 November 1840, Mecklenburg Co., N. C.

BRANDON, Polly and John Gillespie, 14 March 1790, Rowan Co., N. C.

BRANDFORD, Elizabeth and Elias Horry, (Jr.), 15 November 1770, Charleston, S. C.

BRANDFORD, Martha and Hugh Bryan, 19 October 1721, St. Andrews Parish, S. C.

BRANFORD, Nancy and Thomas Horry, 13 June 1772, Charleston, S. C.

BRANFORD, William and Ann Creighton, 23 March 1721, St. Andrews Parish, S. C.

BRANFORD, William and Elizabeth Savage, 24 April 1751, Charleston, S. C.

BRASWELL, David and Nancy Ritterford, 14 September 1762, Edgecombe Co., N. C.

BRASWELL, Mary and Lewis Griffis, 28 June 1764, Edgecombe Co., N. C.

BRASWELL, Sampson and Miss Moore, 31 May 1762, Edgecombe Co., N. C.

BRASWELL, Samuel and Mary Williams, 30 November 1762, Edgecombe Co., N. C.

BRASWELL, Simon and Mary Turner, 25 February 1764, Edgecombe Co., N. C.

BRASWELL, Solomon and Rachel Bird, 24 December 1765, Edgecombe Co., N. C.

BRASWELL, Zadock and Sally Howell, 27 January 1800, Edgecombe Co., N. C.

BRATTEN, Benjamin and Nancy Clements, 17 April 1817, Chowan Co., N. C.

BRATTON, S. E. and Letitia A. Torrence, 7 September 1847, Mecklenburg Co., N. C.

BRAWLEY, James G. and Mary E. Brawley, 22 November 1858, Mecklenburg Co., N. C.

BREAZEALE, Mary and David F. Bradley, 3 November 1865, Pickens Co., S. C.

BREEDEN, J. B. and Elizabeth Bethea Ayers, 20 December 1854, Marlboro Co., S. C.

BREM, Cynthia and S. E. Johnston, 19 September 1865, Mecklenburg Co., N. C.

BRETT, Elizabeth and Cotton M. Stevens, 28 November 1784, Charleston, S. C.

BREVARD, Asenath and James Huston, 24 September 1774, Rowan Co., N. C.

BREVARD, Eloise and Edward William Hayne, 28 January 1806, Colleton, S. C.

BREVARD, John F. and Margaret J. Conner, 15 August 1720, Mecklenburg Co., N. C.

BREVARD, Mary and James Huggins, 21 March 1785, Rowan Co., N. C.

BREVER, Melissa and Clinton Barnard, 12 November 1756, Surrey Co., N. C.

BREWER, N. Alexander F. and (Miss) A. M. Black, 1 August 1842, Mecklenburg Co., N. C.

BREWER, Thomas F. and Harriet E. Oekler, 24 February 1856, Mecklenburg Co., N. C.

BREWTON, Frances and Charles Pinckney, January 1753, Charleston, S. C.

BREWTON, John and Polly Weyman, 1 January 1771, Charleston, S. C.

BREWTON, Mary (Mrs.) and (Dr.) Thomas Dale, 28 March 1733, Charleston, S. C.

BREWTON, Mary (widow) and Thomas Foster, 19 June 1784, Charleston, S. C.

BREWTON, Miles and Widow Paine, March 1743, Charleston, S. C.

BREWTON, Miles and Polly Izard, 26 May 1759, Charleston, S. C.

BRIAN, James and Sarah A. Robison, 6 November 1850, Mecklenburg Co., N. C.

BRICE, Margaret Jane and James Henry Carlisle, 12 December 1848, Columbia, S. C.

BRICE, Robert Wilson and Anna M. Steele, 4 March 1850, Chester Co., S. C.

BRICK, Margaret (widow) and Daniel Geltzer, 1748, Orangeburg Co., S. C.

BRICKELL, Mathias and Rachel Noaille, 6 November 1849, Charleston, S. C.

BRIDE, John and (Mrs.) Elizabeth Sargeant, 27 April 1801, Charleston, S. C.

BRIDGER, Robert and Margaret Montgomery, 2 November 1786, Bertie Co., N. C.

BRIDGERS, Elizabeth and William Hudnall, 21 February 1766, Edgecombe Co., N. C.

BRIDGES, Benjamin and Nancy Coburn, 27 February 1816, Mecklenburg Co., N. C.

BRIDWELL, Pleasant and Sarah Harris, 1 April 1832, Edgefield District, S. C.

BRIGGS, Elias and Miriam Turner, 14 August 1779, Perquimans Co., N. C.

BRIGGS, Margaret (widow) and John Vanderslice, 17 November 1752, Chowan Co., N. C.

BRIGMAN, George M. and Martha Ann Neil, 15 March 1866, Mecklenburg Co., N. C.

BRIMSTONE, Jonathan and Martha Pickings, 1748, Orangeburg Co., S. C.

BRINKLEY, Eli and Sally Gaskins, 26 November 1788, Bertie Co., N. C.

BRINKLEY, Mary (Mrs.) and John Reid, 12 October 1799, Charleston, S. C.

BRINKLEY, Thomas and Sarah J. Lancaster, 25 June 1861, Mecklenburg Co., N. C.

BRINKLEY, William and Clarissa Stuart, 15 January 1828, Mecklenburg Co., N. C.

BRINN, Lydia and John Robinson, 30 March 1778, Chowan Co., N. C.

BRINN, Richard and Mary Cahoon, 1781, Tyrrell Co., N. C.

BRISBANE, Catherine and Joseph Elliott, 24 March 1763, Berkeley Co., S. C.

BRISBANE, James and Sally Stanyarne, 25 May 1772, Charleston, S. C.

BRISBANE, Widow and Alexander Hogg, 18 July 1773, Charleston, S. C.

BRISBANE, William S. and Maria Hall, 19 March 1795, Charleston, S. C.

BRISBANE, William and Mary Deveaux, 22 January 1795, St. Pauls Parish, S .C.

BRISTOW, C. and B. F. McGilbery, 23 January 1850, Marlboro Co., S. C.

BRISTOW, F. C. and E. Weatherly, 24 January 1850, Marlboro Co., S. C.

BRITT, Ann and Absalom Wilder, 8 July 1779, Bertie Co., N. C.

BRITT, Betsy and Seth Lawrence, 8 February 1796, Bertie Co., N. C.

BRITT, Jesse and Sarah Cook, 30 July 1793, Bertie Co., N. C.

BRITT, Josiah and Priscilla Floyd, 1 February 1797, Bertie Co., N. C.

RRITT, Loving and James Morris, 7 November 1791, Bertie Co., N. C.

BRITT, Martha and King White, 22 January 1788, Bertie Co., N. C.

BRITT, Patience and Stephen White, 13 February 1795, Bertie Co., N. C.

BRITT, Sarah and John Thomas, 26 November 1800, Bertie Co., N. C.

BRITT, Thomas and Martha King, 2 March 1793, Bertie Co., N. C.

BRITAIN, Daniel and Sarah Outlaw, 3 May 1803, Bertie Co., N. C.

BRITAIN, Nancy and Hezekial Mizell, 8 May 1805, Bertie C., N. C.

BRITAIN, Thomas and Elizabeth Wilson, 1 April 1777, Chowan Co., N. C.

BRITTON, Elizabeth (widow) and Shadrick Simons, August 1785, Pedee, S. C.

BRITTON, Richard O. and Margaret E. Spivey, 10 November 1830, Bertie Co., N. C.

BROGDON, Timothy and Sarah McHenry, 18 August 1791, Bertie Co., N. C.

BROMLY, Elizabeth and Dr. Rees, December 1784, Georgetown, S. C.

BRONSON, Edward M. and Sarah A. Orr, 6 March 1813, Mecklenburg Co., N. C.

BRONZON, Barbara (widow) and Robert Lammon, 28 May 1751, Orangeburg Co., S. C.

BROOKS, Hetty (of Norwalk, Conn.) and William Jackson, (of N. Y.), 9 August 1800, Charleston, S. C.

BROOKS, James C. and Sarah C. Robert, 20 November 1843, Edgefield, S. C.

BROOKS, John and Patsy Cuthbertson, 26 November 1825, Mecklenburg Co., N. C.

BROOKS, John H. (2nd., M.) and Jane M. Gist, 30 December 1858, Edgefield, S. C.

BROOKS, J. Hampton and Mary Goodwyn Adams, 24 January 1856, Edgefield District S. C.

BROOKS, William and Catherine M. Kloutz, 21 November 1833, Mecklenburg Co.,

BROOKSHIRE, Betsy and Jacob Hagey, 28 December 1799, Rowan Co., N. C.

BROOM, Abe and Elizabeth Kanaugh, 13 August 1840, Mecklenburg Co., N. C.

BROUGHTON, Charlotte and Alexander Mazyck, 15 November 1770, Charleston, S. C.

BROUGHTON, Christiana and Rev. Dwight, January 1732, Charleston, S. C.

BROUGHTON, Johannah and Thomas Monk, 13 January 1732, Charleston, S. C.

BROUGHTON, Mary E. and John Wilkins, 6 January 1801, Prince William Parish, S. C.

BROUGHTON, Susannah and William Doughty, October 1783, Charleston, S. C.

BROUGHTON, Thomas and Widow Izard, 5 March 1746, Charleston, S. C.

BROUN, Margaret and John Lord, 19 February 1767, Charleston, S. C.

BROWER, Jeremiah and Christina Miller, 6 September 1774, Charleston, S. C.

BROWN, Adams, and Jenny Morrow, 28 April 1801, Mecklenburg Co., N. C.

BROWN, Alfred and Lydia Smith, 14 November 1865, Mecklenburg Co., N. C.

BROWN, Allen H. and Nancy C. Jameson, 22 August 1838, Mecklenburg Co., N. C.

BROWN, Ann (Mrs.) and John Ward, 21 November 1801, Charleston, S. C.

BROWN, Annie and James Cusack, 30 April 1773, Charleston, S. C.

BROWN, Ann G. and William Veitch, 4 December 1800, Charleston, S. C.

BROWN, Armistead (Capt.) and Mary Ann R. Meredith, 30 December 1824, Oxford, N. C.

BROWN, A. F. and Lucretia Hall , 13 December 1860, Mecklenburg Co., N. C.

BROWN, Benjamin and Jane Herron, 9 June 1809, Mecklenburg Co., N. C.

BROWN, Benjamin and Erexly McCarty, 7 January 1828, Mecklenburg Co., N. C.

BROWN, Benjamin F. and Mary Jameson, 20 May 1843, Mecklenburg Co., N. C.

BROWN, B. F. and Anna Barnett, 10 October 1865, Mecklenburg Co., N. C.

BROWN, Berreman and Mary Knight, 10 March 1858, Laurens Co., S. C.

BROWN, Charles and Susanna Tennent, October 1783, Charleston, S. C.

BROWN, Charles and Sarah Chitty, 25 December 1799, Charleston, S. C.

BROWN, Charles and Mary S. Kirkpatrick, 4 September 1848, Mecklenburg Co., N. C.

BROWN, Daniel and Mary Polk, 24 December 1794, Mecklenburg Co., N. C.

BROWN, David and Mary Gibbons, 25 October 1804, Mecklenburg Co., N. C.

BROWN, Eli and Nancy P. Freeman, 5 November 1832, Mecklenburg Co., N. C.

BROWN, Elizabeth and Samuel Coxe, 14 February 1782, Marlboro Co., S. C.

BROWN, Elizabeth and James McMurray, 14 April 1774, Guilford Co., N. C.

BROWN, Elizabeth and Conrad Fight, 14 February 1788, Rowan Co., N. C.

BROWN, Elizabeth and Jacob Fraley, 22 July 1793, Rowan Co., N. C.

BROWN, Elizabeth and Moses Maxwell, 1 December 1802, Mecklenburg Co., N. C.

BROWN, Elizabeth R. and Alexander Robinson, 3 December 1831, Mecklenburg Co., N. C.

BROWN, Ellen and Marion Nelson, 23 November 1865, Laurens Co., S. C.

BROWN, Emma Louise and (Dr.) Joseph Addison, 27 February 1850, Barnwell Co., S. C.

BROWN, Enoch and Patsy Wilson, 18 March 1813, Mecklenburg Co., N. C.

BROWN, Ester and Michael Robison, 5 January 1828, Mecklenburg Co., N. C.

BROWN, Euphemia and John Ready, 5 April 1774, Chowan Co., N. C.

BROWN, E. A. and A. F. Montgomery, 15 June 1865, Mecklenburg Co., N. C.

BROWN, Fanny and (Dr.) Peter Spence, 8 April 1771, Charleston, S. C.

BROWN, Frances and William L. Beard, 26 March 1834, Mecklenburg Co., N. C.

BROWN, Gabriel and Polly Ferrill, 22 December 1813, Mecklenburg Co., N. C.

BROWN, George and Ann Liebert, 5 August 1797, Charleston, S. C.

BROWN, Hannah and Joseph Elliott, 4 June 1767, Rowan Co., N. C.

BROWN, Isabella and William Erwin, 10 February 1775, Rowan Co., N. C.

BROWN, James and Agnes Walker, 7 October 1795, Mecklenburg Co., N. C.

BROWN, James and Jean Jamison, 10 February 1797, Mecklenburg Co., N. C.

BROWN, James and Nancy Smith, 28 February 1804, Mecklenburg Co., N. C.

BROWN, James G. and Mary J. Hall, 4 September 1860, Mecklenburg Co., N. C.

BROWN, James H. and Sarah J. Freeman, 28 July 1828, Mecklenburg Co., N. C.

BROWN, James H. and Hannah E. Alexander, 3 December 1857, Mecklenburg Co., N. C.

BROWN, James J. and Amelia E. Edwards, 8 January 1857, Mecklenburg Co., N. C.

BROWN, James T. and Sarah A. Norham, 30 July 1861, Mecklenburg Co., N. C.

BROWN, James W. and Miranda E. Ray, 19 October 1848, Mecklenburg Co., N. C.

BROWN, Jane and John Erwin, 19 October 1772, Rowan Co., N. C.

BROWN, Jane E. and William J. Jameson, 18 March 1884, Mecklenburg Co., N. C.

BROWN, John and Elizabeth Graves, 7 February 1771, Charleston, S. C.

BROWN, John and Martha Maxwell, 17 December 1792, Mecklenburg Co., N. C.

BROWN, John and Betsy Sharpe, 22 February 1802, Mecklenburg Co., N. C.

BROWN, John C. and Sarah A. Patterson, 14 December 1854, Mecklenburg Co., N. C.

BROWN, John G. and Eliza Merchant, 2 April 1833, Mecklenburg Co., N. C.

BROWN, John M. and Nanica Kerr, 7 April 1832, Mecklenburg Co., N. C.

BROWN, John W. and Mary Huron, (or Huson) 5 February 1828, Mecklenburg Co., N. C.

BROWN, John W. and Mary A. Black, 23 September 1851, Mecklenburg Co., N. C.

BROWN, John W. and Ann E. Griffith, 13 January 1853, Mecklenburg Co., N. C.

BROWN, Joseph and Harriet Lowndes, 25 November 1784, Charleston, S. C.

BROWN, Joseph and (Mrs.) Mary Ash, 29 January 1795, Charleston, S. C.

BROWN, Joseph Newton and Lizzie Bruce, 28 February 1866, Anderson, S. C.

BROWN, Josiah and Levina Frazer, 19 June 1814, Mecklenburg Co., N. C.

BROWN, Josiah and Sarah A. Smith, 4 October 1825, Mecklenburg Co., N. C.

BROWN, Leander and Miss Snow, 21 September 1844, Laurens Co., S. C.

BROWN, L. F. and Mary R. Alexander, 7 September 1865, Mecklenburg Co., N. C.

BROWN, Margaret and Thomas G. Barnett, 12 December 1826, Mecklenburg Co., N. C.

BROWN, Margaret I. and Joseph C. Nicholson, 4 October 1837, Mecklenburg Co., N. C.

BROWN, Martha and Amos Minot, May 1786, Charleston, S. C.

MROWN, Martha and Young Owins, 29 October 1865, Laurens Co., S. C.

BROWN, Martha and William Elroy, 28 January 1801, Mecklenburg Co., N. C.

BROWN, Martha J. and John K. Rea, 18 January 1848, Mecklenburg Co., N. C.

BROWN, Mary and James Long, 20 June 1768, Chowan Co., N. C.

BROWN, Mary and Alexander McLeod, 9 December 1826, Mecklenburg Co., N. C.

BROWN, Mary and Wallace Robinson, 5 March 1831, Mecklenburg Co., N. C.

BROWN, Mary and Bluford Putman, 28 June 1866, Laurens Co., S. C.

BROWN, Mary and S. C. Alexander, 21 May 1857, Mecklenburg Co., N. C.

BROWN, Milky and Edward Mitchell, 30 July 1823, Guilford Co., N. C.

BROWN, Moren and Alexander Hopkins, 10 February 1796, Bertie Co., N. C.

BROWN, Murrell and Margaret Luckey, 24 July 1840, Mecklenburg Co., N. C.

BROWN, Nancy and Silas Alexander, 8 May 1846, Mecklenburg Co., N. C.

BROWN, Peggy and Henry Capps, 10 July 1823, Mecklenburg Co., N. C.

BROWN, Peter and Sarah Pitman, 29 April 1800, Mecklenburg Co., N. C.

BROWN, Robert and Catherine Graham, 22 January 1800, Beaufort, S. C.

BROWN, Robert and Elizabeth Bryson, 28 March 1794, Mecklenburg Co., N. C.

BROWN, Samantha and John Edwards, 24 December 1850, Laurens Co., S. C.

BROWN, Samuel and Katherine Jameson, 31 March 1801, Mecklenburg Co., N. C.

BROWN, Samuel C. and Sarah J. Sun, 29 August 1859, Mecklenburg Co., N. C.

BROWN, Silas and Jean Ormond, 19 March 1816, Mecklenburg Co., N. C.

BROWN, Stephen and Eliza Radford, 8 August 1841, Edgefield District, S. C.

BROWN, Thomas and Billah Blount, 10 March 1780, Tyrrell Co., N. C.

BROWN, Troy and Selena Thompson, 6 December 1840, Mecklenburg Co., N. C.

BROWN, William and Jane Haines, 12 April 1800, Mecklenburg Co., N. C.

BROWN, William and Betsy Crittenberry, 4 December 1819, Mecklenburg Co., N. C.

BROWN, William and Martha A. Montieth, 29 October 1839, Mecklenburg Co., N. C.

BROWN, William A. and Margaret Reed, 12 October 1847, Mecklenburg Co., N. C.

BROWN, William B. and Anne Denoon, 16 January 1801, Charleston, S. C.

BROWN, William N. and Elizabeth Flanigan, 19 September 1835, Mecklenburg Co., N. C.

BROWN, William P. and Harriet C. Hevin, 28 April 1846, Mecklenburg Co., N. C.

BRAWNE, Rebecca and Michael Moore, 22 June 1797, Charleston, S. C.

BROWNING, Mary and Jackson Randall, 1 July 1841, Edgefield District, S. C.

BROWNING, Nancy and Young Bobo, 4 April 1819, Union District, S. C.

BROWNING, Sarah (widow) and David Meredith, 2 June 1773, Chowan Co., N. C.

BROWNLEE, Mary and John Simmons, 3 December 1844, Laurens Co., S. C.

BROWNLEE, Trainham and Polly Riddle, 4 February 1847, Laurens Co., S. C.

BROWNLOW, Ann and William Fowle, 22 August 1825, Crawfield, S. C.

BROWNRIGG, George and A. Hooker, 6 October 1783, Tyrrell Co., N. C.

BROYLES, O. R. and Sarah A. Taliaferro, 20 March 1823, Pendleton, S. C.

BRUCE, David and (Mrs.) Eleanor Dryden, 7 April 1765, Charleston, S. C.

BRUCE, Judey Ann and James Pearson, 4 January 1846, Marlboro, S. C.

BRUCE, Lizzie and Joseph Newton Brown, 28 February 1866, Anderson, S. C.

BRUCE, Susannah (Mrs.) and Andrew Smylie, 8 October 1801, Charleston, S. C.

BRUMBY, Sue G. and James McF. Gaston, 2 November 1852, Columbia, S. C.

BRUNET, Joseph and Jane C. Messan, (widow), 15 March 1800, Charleston, S. C.

BRUNHEAD, Jennet and James Gardner, 1 November 1797, Rowan Co., N. C.

BRUNNER, Anna M. and John Mooer, 1792, Orangeburg Co., S. C.

BRUNNER, Margaret and John Anding, 2 February 1756, Orangeburg Co., S. C.

BRUNSON, John and (Mrs.) Susannah Bryan, 6 June 1800, Charleston, S. C.

BRUTON, Ira and Rodah Rodgers, 9 October 1865, Laurens Co. S. C.

BRYAN, Aaron M. and Mary Houston, 14 February 1837, Mecklenburg Co., N. C.

BRYAN, Ann and William Grimes, 21 January 1790, Avon, N. C.

BRYAN, Arthur and (Mrs.) Anna M. Rudhall, 1788, Charleston, S. C.

BRYAN, Arthur and Helen Cumming, 6 July 1797, Port Royal Island, S. C.

BRYAN, B. C. and Ann L. Penn, 17 January 1854, Edgefield District, S. C.

BRYAN, Catherine and William Byram, 28 February 1824, Mecklenburg Co., N. C.

BRYAN, Charlotte E. and Bryan Grimes, 15 September 1863, Grimesland, N. C.

BRYAN, Elsey and Joshua Howard, 7 March 1789, Rowan Co., N. C.

BRYAN, George D. and Mary M. King, 3 August 1869, Charleston, S. C.

BRYAN, Hugh and Martha Brandford, 19 October 1721, St. Andrews Parish, S. C.

BRYAN, Hugh and Catherine Barnwell, 2 January 1734, St. Johns Island, S. C.

BRYAN, Jacob and Sarah Webster, 10 December 1762, Edgecombe Co., N. C.

BRYAN, James and (Mrs.) Mary Sanks, 18 June 1772, Charleston, S. C.

BRYAN, James and Sarah A. Robinson, 16 November 1850, Mecklenburg Co., N. C.

BRYAN, John and Sarah Hobby, 1 July 1766, Edgecombe Co., N. C.

BRYAN, John and Rachel Simons, 24 April 1777, Charleston, S. C.

BRYAN, Margaret and John Ellis, 11 March 1779, Rowan Co., N. C.

BRYAN, Margaret and William Forbis, 13 February 1779, Rowan Co., N. C.

BRYAN, Martha and Henry Harwood, March 1792, Rowan Co., N. C.

BRYAN, Mary and David Hampton, 18 August 1786, Rowan Co., N. C.

BRYAN, Matthew and Levina Pitman, 25 July 1810, Mecklenburg Co., N. C.

BRYAN, Nancy and Thomas Enochs, 16 October 1786, Rowan Co., N. C.

BRYAN, Needham and Susannah Harell, 1732, Snowfield, N. C.

BRYAN, Nicholas and Mary Williams, 9 June 1759, Santee, S. C.

BRYAN, Phebe and James Forbis, 10 March 1779, Rowan Co., N. C.

BRYAN, Rachel and William Whitfield, 6 November 1741, Bertie Co., N. C.

BRYAN, Rebecca and James Boone, 14 August 1756, Yadkin River, N. C.

BRYAN, Samuel and Mary Hunt, 5 October 1775, Rowan Co., N. C.

BRYAN, Sarah and John Gano, 15 April 1793, Rowan Co., N. C.

BRYAN, Susannah (Mrs.) and John Brunson, 6 June 1800, Charleson, S. C.

BRYAN, William and Elizabeth Smith, 1744, Snowfield, N. C.

BRYAN, William and Jean Page, 11 December 1809, Mecklenburg Co., N. C.

BRYANT, Arthur and Rodah Hobby, 4 January 1766, Edgecombe Co., N. C.

BRYANT, Jacob and Juda Hargrove, 29 January 1800, Edgecombe Co., N. C.

BRYANT, James and Mary Hough, (dau. of Richard) 2 October 1780, Tyrrell Co., N. C.

BRYANT, Jesse and Sarah Harris, 26 January 1836, Edgefield District, S. C.

BRYANT, Mary and Thomas Hughey, 7 February 1787, Rowan Co., N. C.

BRYANT, Sydney and Amelia R. Hipp, 16 August 1860, Mecklenburg Co., N. C.

BRYSON, Elizabeth and Robert Brown, 28 March 1794, Mecklenburg Co., N. C.

BRYSON, James and Anne Doherty, 11 March 1799, Mecklenburg Co., N. C.

BRYSON, Robert and Louisa Davis, 23 March 1858, Laurens Co., S. C.

BUCHANAN, Charles and Betsy Simmons, 8 May 1821, Mecklenburg Co., N. C.

BUCHANAN, Eleanor and John Allison, 17 July 1799, Mecklenburg Co., N. C.

BUCHANAN, Hugh and Susanna Rose, 20 December 1803, Mecklenburg Co., N. C.

BUCHANAN, James and Mary Potter, 27 December 1794, Mecklenburg Co., N. C.

BUCHANAN, Martha E. and William A. Barham, 22 September 1843, Mecklenburg Co., N. C.

BUCHANAN, Martha and Benjamin Atkins, 27 May 1844, Mecklenburg Co., N. C.

BUCHANAN, Robert and Elizabeth Gloon, 1 December 1824, Mecklenburg Co. N. C.

BUCHANAN, Sally and James Ballentine, 8 March 1772, Charleston, S. C.

BUCHANAN, Susannah and Nicholas Hunter, 14 November 1777, Chowan Co., N. C.

BUCKLE, Thomas and Nancy Hare, 1788, Charleston, S. C.

BUCKLEY, Maurice and Elizabeth Deshon, 4 February 1785, Chowan Co., N. C.

BUCKLEY, Richard and Lydia Copeland, 3 February 1786, Chowan Co., N. C.

BUCKNER, Presley and Risdon Fisher, 29 June 1798, Rowan Co., N. C.

BUDD, David and Ann Kerr, 11 May 1801, Mecklenburg Co., N. C.

BUDD, Hetty and Adam Gilchrist, (of N. Y.), 10 June 1784, Charleston, S. C.

BUFORD, Benjamin and Nancy Perres, 1 March 1797, Mecklenburg Co., N. C.

BUFORD, William and Susan Stow, 20 December 1803, Mecklenburg Co., N. C.

BULL, Charlotte and John Drayton, 14 November 1742, Charleston, S. C.

BULL, Elizabeth and Thomas Drayton, 26 December 1730, Charleston, S. C.

BULL, John and Eleanor Purry, 29 March 1768, Charleston, S. C.

BULL, John and Sarah Phillips, 16 July 1769, Charleston, S. C.

BULL, Judith, (widow) and Robert Pringle, 16 April 1751, Charleston, S. C.

BULL, Stephen and Anne Middleton Barnwell, (widow), 24 May 1772, Newberry, S. C.

BULL, Stephen and Martha Godin, 27 April 1731, Newberry, S. C.

BULL, Stephen and Judith Mayrant, 2 May 1747, Newberry, S. C.

BULL, Thomas and Sarah Simpson, 12 May 1771, Charleston, S. C.

BULL, William and Elizabeth Reid, 26 August 1779, Charleston, S. C.

BULLINE, Mary and (Dr.) Matthew Irwin, (of Virginia), August 1783, Charleston, S. C.

BULLINE, Susannah and Richard Shubrick, 3 October 1772, Charleston, S. C.

BULLINGER, Abel and Harriet Patton, 12 July 1732, Mecklenburg Co., N. C.

BULLOCK, John and Mary Mitchell, 12 November 1759, Oxford, N. C.

BULLOCK, John and Elizabeth Wolf, 2 February 1789, Orange Co., N. C.

BULLOCK, Nathaniel and Mary Hawkins, 1760, Granville Co., N. C.

BULLOCK, Stephen and Winny Robinson, 24 March 1800, Edgecombe Co., N. C.

BULLOCK, Susannah and John Taylor, 16 March 1784, Granville Co., N. C.

BULLONG, Peggy and George Hess, 19 May 1798, Rowan Co., N. C.

BUNCE, Jared (of Conn.) and Mary Ann Dickinson, 23 December 1801, Charleston, S. C.

BUNCH, Cullen and Rhoda Hallowell, 27 December 1785, Chowan Co., N. C.

BUNCH, Mary and Will Bateman, 5 June 1767, Chowan Co., N. C.

BUNCH, Micajah and (Mrs.) Sarah Adams, 10 August 1747, Chowan Co., N. C.

BUNCH, Micajah and Mary Payne, 8 May 1758, Chowan Co., N. C.

BUNCH, Micajah and Levina Holden, 8 April 1791, Bertie Co., N. C.

BUNCH, Naomy and John Joyner, 23 December 1754, Orangeburg Co., S. C.

BUNCH, Nehemiah and Juda Hill, 14 February 1765, Chowan Co., N. C.

BUNCH, Paul and Amy Winigum, 1748, Orangeburg Co., S. C.

BUNCH, Sarah and John McGuire, 10 December 1778, Chowan Co., N. C.

BUNCH, Sarah and James Mitchell, 26 January 1809, Chowan Co., N. C.

BUNCH, Judy and John McDorman, 12 October 1799, Guilford Co., N. C.

BUNTING, John and Lucretia Pippen, 17 May 1806, Edgecombe Co., N. C.

BUNTON, Sarah and John Graham, 25 January 1785, Rowan Co., N. C.

BURCHELL, Lois and Mallory Rivers, 23 December 1800, James Island, S. C.

BURDETH, Elizabeth and Thomas Burton, 1851, Laurens Co., S. C.

BURDETH, John and Elizabeth Wells, 17 June 1852, Laurens Co., S. C.

BURDETH, Thomas and Caroline Peterson, 27 March 1851, Laurens Co., S. C.

BURDETT, Eliza and Ivory Curry, 23 December 1847, Laurens Co., S. C.

BURDETT, Joseph and Arinda Putman, 16 January 1851, Laurens Co., S. C.

BURDETT, Milly and Stephen Wells, 23 April 1848, Laurens Co., S. C.

BURDINE, Martin and Manima Putman, 12 November 1859, Laurens Co., S. C.

BURDINE, William and Loucinda Putman, 1 August 1859, Laurens Co., S. C.

BURGESS, Milly and Thomas Hartley, 9 October 1787, Rowan Co., N. C.

BURK, Mary and Peter Powers, 23 June 1778, Chowan Co., N. C.

BURK, Miles and Mary Powers, 10 May 1775, Chowan Co., N. C.

BURKHEAD, John and Catherine Will, August 1784, St. Johns Parish, S. C.

BURN, John and Anne Baron (widow), 25 October 1767, Charleston, S. C.

BURNETT, Alexander and Eliza Herndon, 5 January 1793, Orange Co., N. C.

BURNETT, Elizabeth and ―― Peterson, 13 November 1854, Edgefield District, S. C.

BURNETT, P. M. and Eliza Fincher, 12 October 1841, Mecklenburg Co., N. C.

BURNETT, Sarah and Samuel Henderson, 8 January 1782, Rowan Co., N. C.

BURNETT, William and Matilda C. Alexander, 10 December 1811, Mecklenburg Co., N. C.

BURNEY, E. L. and Martha H. Henderson, 1 October 1851, Mecklenburg Co., N. C.

BURNEY, Rebecca and William Mebane (Jr.), 13 December 1794, Guilford Co., N. C.

BURNS, Corra and James O. Owings, 19 July 1866, Laurens Co., S. C.

BURNS, Emily and Paul Auten, 15 March 1838, Mecklenburg Co., N. C.

BURNS, Franklin and Sophy Martin, 21 July 1849, Laurens Co., S. C.

BURNS, Laird and Jean Williams, 30 January 1801, Mecklenburg Co., N. C.

BURNS, Martha M. and John Read, 4 February 1846, Mecklenburg Co., N. C.

BURNS, Mary and Stobo Garrett, 1 November 1855, Laurens Co., S. C.

BURNS, Mary and Nathaniel Barksdale, 18 November 1856, Laurens Co., S. C.

BURNS, Rebecca and Henry Bramlet, 2 November 1847, Laurens Co., S. C.

BURNS, Robertson and Kiziah Putman, 7 December 1847, Laurens Co., S. C.

BURNS, Samuel A. and Elizabeth Harris, 27 August 1851, Mecklenburg Co., N. C.

BURNSIDE, Mr. and Emily Bolt, 13 November 1859, Laurens Co., S. C.

BURNSIDES, Allen (Col.) and Mary Wallis, 21 March 1859, Laurens Co., S. C.

BURRINGTON, Thomas and Katy Reid, 20 June 1751, Charleston, S. C.

BURRIS, Elizabeth and William Moss, 5 November 1851, Edgefield District, S. C.

BURROUGHS, J. C. and Margaret E. Spratt, 13 August 1860, Mecklenburg Co., N. C.

BURROWS, Jeremiah and Belinda Heap, 30 October 1720, St. Andrews Parish, S. C.

BURROWS, John and Margaret Piper, 3 May 1788, Orange Co., N. C.

BURROWS, Polly and Joseph Atkinson, 13 October 1774, Charleston, S. C.

BURTIS, Martha and John Hughes, 25 June 1795, Rowan Co., N. C.

BURTON, B. B. and Caroline Williams, 7 July 1857, Edgefield District, S. C.

BURTON, Isaac and Nancy Remington, February 1775, Charleston, S. C.

BURTON, John and Sarah O. Joyner, 15 January 1801, Beaufort, S. C.

BURTON, Mary and Jacob Milcham, 15 September 1795, Guilford Co., N. C.

BURTON, Robert and Martha Williams, 1775, Granville Co., N. C.

BURTON, Thomas and Elizabeth Burdeth, 1851, Laurens Co., S. C.

BURWELL, Catherine and Hugh Bryan, 1734, Laurens Co., S. C.

BUSBY, William and Mary Morrow, 5 March 1812, Mecklenburg Co., N. C.

BUSER, Ann and Hans Jacob Myer, 1 January 1740, Orangeburg Co., S. C.

BUSH, Daniel S. and Emma Templeton, 29 December 1855, Edgefield District, S. C.

BUSH, Polly and Van Swearingen, 17 November 1822, Edgefield District, S. C.

BUSH, Sarah and Henry Hurdle, 14 August 1807, Chowan Co., N. C.

BUSH, Sarah and Arthur Lott, 23 December 1841, Edgefield District, S. C.

BUSH, Tabitha and John Autry, 4 November 1841, Edgefield District, S. C.

BUSH, William and Sarah Jackson, 2 December 1793, Chowan Co., N. C.

BUSSEY, Elizabeth and John Nixon, 28 November 1854, Edgefield District, S. C.

BUSSY, Delily and George Ernest, 8 February 1793, Rowan Co., N. C.

BUSTRIN, Anna and John Jacob Meyer, 1 January 1740, Orangeburg Co., S. C.

BUTCHER, Isbell and John Robinson, 1748, Orangeburg Co., S. C.

BUTCHER, Mary and James Long, 15 July 1775, Tyrrell Co., N. C.

BUTLER, Ann and John Simons, 5 June 1742, Chowan Co., N. C.

BUTLER, Anne and Richard Christmas, 22 December 1788, Orange Co., N. C.

BUTLER, Anthony and Ann M. Moore, 15 October 1799, Charleston, S. C.

BUTLER, Elizabeth (Mrs.) and Captain Hill, December 1785, Charleston, S. C.

BUTLER, Elizabeth and Jethro Coffield, 25 April 1788, Bertie Co., N. C.

BUTLER, Ferebee and George McHenry, 9 March 1764, Tyrrell Co., N. C.

BUTLER, Francis and Ann Weston, 3 December 1764, Chowan Co., N. C.

BUTLER, Henrietta (nee Wilson) and Samuel Dunscombe, 21 December 1752, Chowan Co., N. C.

BUTLER, Hester and William Elliott, (Jr.), 24 February 1722, St. Andrews Parish, S. C.

BUTLER, Jacob and Elizabeth Penrice, 18 December 1755, Chowan Co., N. C.

BUTLER, Job and Margaret Wateridge (of Virginia), 29 January 1756, Chowan Co., N. C.

BUTLER, Lucinda and James Hunt, 1824, Granville Co., N. C.

BUTLER, Matthew C. and Maria S. Pickens, 21 February 1858, Edgefield, S. C.

BUTLER, Pierce and Polly Middleton, 10 January 1771, Charleston, S. C.

BUTT, Peter and Elizabeth Harvey, 10 July 1782, Santee, S. C.

BUTTON, Margaret E. and Thomas Marks, 28 April 1832, Mecklenburg Co., N. C.

BUZZARD, James and Ann Hart, 19 February 1856, Edgefield District, S. C.

BYERLY, Barbara and William Frank, 12 November 1796, Rowan Co., N. C.

BYERS, Elizabeth and Charles H. Pickton, 8 May 1800, Charleston, S. C.

BYERS, Mary E. and Alexander S. Douglas, 6 November 1760, Spartanburg, S. C.

BYNE, Lucy and Richard Taylor, 15 February 1775, Granville Co., N. C.

BYNUM, Abner and Milly Cooper, 13 August 1790, Bertie Co., N. C.

BYNUM, Turner and Elizabeth Miller, 13 August 1799, Charleston, S. C.

BYNUM, William and Margaret Vintz, 7 December 1797, Mecklenburg Co., N. C.

BYRAM, Beverly and Sally Williamson, 13 April 1807, Mecklenburg Co., N. C.

BYRAM, Caroline and Matthew A. Robinson, 19 January 1848, Mecklenburg Co., N. C.

BYRAM, Clarissa and Henry McBride, 26 November 1818, Mecklenburg Co., N. C.

BYRAM, Dolly and John Byram, 23 May 1791, Mecklenburg Co., N. C.

BYRAM, Drury and William Atchison, 3 May 1823, Mecklenburg Co., N. C.

BYRAM, Elizabeth and John F. Orr, 8 October 1835, Mecklenburg Co., N. C.

BYRAM, Henry and Mary Cook, 8 January 1803, Mecklenburg Co., N. C.

BYRAM, James and Hannah Williams, 26 September 1808, Mecklenburg Co., N. C.

BYRAM, James and Elizabeth E. Glover, 1 January 1839, Mecklenburg Co., N. C.

BYRAM, James and Margaret Hannore, 13 June 1844, Mecklenburg Co., N. C.

BYRAM, John and Dolly Byram, 23 May 1791, Mecklenburg Co., N. C.

BYRAM, John P. and Catherine L. Kerr, 23 March 1838, Mecklenburg Co., N. C.

BYRAM, John W. and Nancy Gullent, 4 August 1828, Mecklenburg Co., N. C.

BYRAM, Joseph and Catherine Griffith, 17 February 1818, Mecklenburg Co., N. C.

BYRAM, Margaret and William Beaty, 16 March 1825, Mecklenburg Co., N. C.

BYRAM, Robert J. and Caroline Sharp, 3 September 1829, Mecklenburg Co., N. C.

BYRAM, Upton and Dolly McDowell, 13 December 1793, Mecklenburg Co., N. C.

BYRAM, Upton and Peggy Porter, 15 June 1807, Mecklenburg Co., N. C.

BYRAM, William and Katherine Cook, 5 December 1792, Mecklenburg Co., N. C.

BYRAM, William and Nancy Watkins, 18 March 1818, Mecklenburg Co., N. C.

BYRAM, William and Catherine Bryan, 28 February 1824, Mecklenburg Co., N. C.

BYRAM, William D. and Mary Condin, 20 September 1825, Mecklenburg Co., N. C.

BYRD, Daniel and Mary E. Gardner, 18 December 1855, Edgefield District, S. C.

BYRD, Emmie and T. N. Shadrack, 14 April 1857, Edgefield District, S. C.

BYRD, Mary and John Graham, 11 October 1782, Orange Co., N. C.

C

CABBART, Elsy and Henry Garrett, 21 January 1846, Laurens Co., S. C.

CADDY, George and Sarah Clements, 21 February 1823, Chowan Co., N. C.

CADELL, Ann and Christopher Hopkins, 13 November 1736, Charleston, S. C.

CAHOON, Mary and Richard Brinn, 1781, Tyrrell Co., N. C.

CAHOON, Puss and Hezekiah Duke, 1780, Tyrrell Co., N. C.

CAIN, Alcy and Nathaniel Walker, 1762, Barnwell Co., S. C.

CAIN, Celia and Dawson Hull, 15 May 1775, Chowan Co., N. C.

CAIN, Elisha and Catherine Lewis, 6 February 1805, Mecklenburg Co., N. C.

CAIN, James and Elizabeth McKinley, 21 December 1781, Orange Co., N. C.

CAIN, Johanna and Thomas Holloway, 5 October 1782, Orange Co., N. C.

CAIN, Mary and Peter Harries, 4 June 1761, Santee, S. C.

CALDER, Margaret and Robert B. Robison, 25 April 1837, Mecklenburg Co., N. C.

CALDER, Sally and Thomas Baynard, 6 July 1784, Edisto, S. C.

CALDWELL, Abigail B. and Robert D. Alexander, 9 February 1829, Mecklenburg Co., N. C.

CALDWELL, Alice B. and William A. Owens, 24 November 1857, Mecklenburg Co., N. C.

CALDWELL, Alexander and Sarah Davidson, 9 October 1794, Mecklenburg Co., N. C.

CALDWELL, Andrew H. and Sarah A. Williamson, 26 March 1844, Mecklenburg Co., N. C.

CALDWELL, Barbara and William Andrews, 16 April 1792, Mecklenburg Co., N. C.

CALDWELL, Charles and Mary Caldwell, 23 November 1865, Mecklenburg Co., N. C.

CALDWELL, C. F. and Margaret E. Wilson, 2 December 1856, Mecklenburg Co., N. C.

CALDWELL, Daniel and Isabella Shields, 18 January 1826, Mecklenburg Co., N. C.

CALDWELL, Daniel G. and Harriet C. Alexander, 28 February 1861, Mecklenburg Co., N. C.

CALDWELL, David and Mary Smith, 29 June 1791, Mecklenburg Co., N. C.

CALDWELL, David A. and (Mrs.) Martha Caldwell, 12 December 1836, Mecklenburg Co., N. C.

CALDWELL, David T. and Harriet E. Davidson, 30 March 1826, Mecklenburg Co., N. C.

CALDWELL, Dovey and Nixon Curry, 6 September 1819, Mecklenburg Co., N. C.

CALDWELL, D. S. and (Miss) E. S. Neely, 14 May 1862, Mecklenburg Co., N. C.

CALDWELL, Edward and Ann E. Terrance, 11 August 1826, Mecklenburg Co., N. C.

CALDWELL, Franklin and Sarah Reid, 21 February 1864, Mecklenburg Co., N. C.

CALDWELL, Green W. and Jane McComb, 6 December 1832, Mecklenburg Co., N. C.

CALDWELL, G. W. and (Miss) M. E. Alexander, 1 February 1856, Mecklenburg Co., N. C.

CALDWELL, Hugh M. and Martha A. S. Kerr, 19 October 1857, Mecklenburg Co., N. C.

CALDWELL, James and Minty Parks, 12 August 1816, Mecklenburg Co., N. C.

CALDWELL, James and Mary Dixon, 23 February 1831, Mecklenburg Co., N. C.

CALDWELL, James F. and Barbara M. McCracken, 29 December 1852, Mecklenburg Co., N. C.

CALDWELL, James M. and Margaret C. Moore, 15 January 1851, Mecklenburg Co., N. C.

CALDWELL, Jane L. and James P. McGuiness, 2 March 1840, Mecklenburg Co., N. C.

CALDWELL, Jeff and Amanda Hunter, 2 January 1866, Mecklenburg Co., N. C.

CALDWELL, John and Margaret Howid, 25 February 1823, Mecklenburg Co., N. C.

CALDWELL, John D. and Martha Kerr, 6 March 1855, Mecklenburg Co., N. C.

CALDWELL, John H. and Mary Springs, 3 October 1832, Mecklenburg Co., N. C.

CALDWELL, John H. and Jane C. Query, 5 January 1860, Mecklenburg Co., N. C.

CALDWELL, John N. and Ruth Jane Alexander, 27 January 1857, Mecklenburg Co., N. C.

CALDWELL, Joshua J. and Drusilla J. Kelly, 6 October 1857, Mecklenburg Co., N. C.

CALDWELL, J. A. and Hannah C. Neely, 28 June 1841, Mecklenburg Co., N. C.

CALDWELL, J. C. and Lila A. Henderson, 1 July 1856, Mecklenburg Co., N. C.

CALDWELL, J. M. and (Miss) C. N. Cochran, 1 January 1861, Mecklenburg Co., N. C.

CALDWELL, Margaret P. S. and William L. Caldwell, 29 October 1857, Mecklenburg Co., N. C.

CALDWELL, Martha and Patrick Calhoun, 1770, Abbeville District, S. C.

CALDWELL, Martha (Mrs.) and David A. Caldwell, 12 December 1836, Mecklenburg Co., N. C.

CALDWELL, Mary E. and Cornelius Alexander, 26 November 1856, Mecklenburg Co., N. C.

CALDWELL, Mary and Charles Caldwell, 23 November 1865, Mecklenburg Co., N. C.

CALDWELL, Mary G. L. and Caleb A Barringer, 16 February 1842, Mecklenburg Co., N. C.

CALDWELL, Mary M. and James N. Alexander, 4 March 1858, Mecklenburg Co., N. C.

CALDWELL, (Miss) M. S. and H. C. Reid, 10 May 1859, Mecklenburg Co., N. C.

CALDWELL, Pinckney C. (Dr.) and Sarah R. Wilson, 12 December 1831, Mecklenburg Co., N. C.

CALDWELL, Rebecca and Samuel E. Johnston, 29 October 1842, Mecklenburg Co., N. C.

CALDWELL, Rebecca C. and Joseph H. Beard, 30 December 1859, Mecklenburg Co., N. C.

CALDWELL, Robert and Mary Shields, 20 March 1819, Mecklenburg Co., N. C.

CALDWELL, Robert and Lorina Houston, 27 December 1819, Mecklenburg Co., N. C.

CALDWELL, Robert A. and Martha Cochran, 7 February 1855, Mecklenburg Co., N. C.

CALDWELL, R. N. and Henrietta L. Harris, 2 September 1857, Mecklenburg Co., N. C.

CALDWELL, Samuel C. and Abigail B. Alexander, 8 May 1793, Mecklenburg Co., N. C.

CALDWELL, Silas and Elizabeth J. Cochran, 26 August 1864, Mecklenburg Co., N. C.

CALDWELL, Thomas G. and Betsy Black, 2 May 1801, Mecklenburg Co., N. C.

CALDWELL, William L. and Margaret P. S. Caldwell, 29 October 1857, Mecklenburg Co., N. C.

CALER, Rachel and Matthias Frick, 16 August 1794, Rowan Co., N. C.

CALHOUN, Elizabeth and John Cathay, 19 March 1800, Mecklenburg Co., N. C.

CALHOUN, Harriet and Hugh Roan, 26 May 1792, Mecklenburg Co., N. C.

CALHOUN, Henry and Ann Simons, 5 June 1796, St. Bartholomews Parish, S. C.

CALHOUN, James and Martha Monk, 5 September 1771, Santee, S. C.

CALHOUN, John and Sarah Stevens, 5 May 1801, Charleston, S. C.

CALHOUN, John and Abigail McCleary, 19 September 1803, Mecklenburg Co., N. C.

CALHOUN, John E. and Floride Bonneau, 8 October 1786, St. Johns Parish, S. C.

CALHOUN, Patrick and Martha Caldwell, June 1770, Abbeville District, S. C.

CALHOUN, Sarah and William Neal, 13 September 1800, Mecklenburg Co., N. C.

CALHOUN, William and Jane Lentile, 8 October 1825, Mecklenburg Co., N. C.

CALL, William and Rachel Bateman, October 1783, Tyrrell Co., N. C.

CALLADON, James and Martha Fleming, 29 December 1766, Santee, S. C.

CALLION, Jacobus and Margaret Waller, 9 July 1769, Santee, S. C.

CALLYHON, Mary (widow) and William Clement, 28 January 1747, Orangeburg Co., S. C.

CALTHORP, Rhoda and Joseph Hunter, 14 September 1806, Mecklenburg Co., N. C.

CAMERON, Elizabeth and John Smith, 2 October 1794, Christ Church Parish, S. C.

CAMERON, John W. and Elizabeth A. Smith, 5 October 1841, Chowan Co., N. C.

CAMERON, Mary (Mrs.) and John Grant, June 1785, Charleston, S. C.

CAMERON, Samuel and Martha Dunbar, 15 January 1797, Charleston, S. C.

CAMMELL, Jane and George Fickline, 13 May 1742, Charleston, S. C.

CAMPBELL, Agnes and John Inu, 24 April 1800, Mecklenburg Co., N. C.

CAMPBELL, Ann E. and George W. McDonald, 6 August 1834, Mecklenburg Co., N. C.

CAMPBELL, Anne and Isham Harris, 5 April 1791, Rowan Co., N. C.

CAMPBELL, Catherine and Samuel Green, 20 September 1765, S. C.

CAMPBELL, Eliza and Elam Moore, 18 January 1826, Mecklenburg Co., N. C.

CAMPBELL, Epsey and Laburn Hanner, 25 March 1848, Laurens Co., S. C.

CAMPBELL, George and Agnes Turner, (widow) 21 January 1769, Chowan Co., N. C.

CAMPBELL, George and Mary Russell, 24 January 1791, Mecklenburg Co., N. C.

CAMPBELL, George L. and Mary I. Summerville, 1 January 1845, Mecklenburg Co., N. C.

CAMPBELL, Hannah and Joseph Hall, 16 March 1796, Rowan Co., N. C.

CAMPBELL, Helen and James Fitch, 28 July 1764, Charleston, S. C.
CAMPBELL, Hugh and Catherine Delegall, 2 May 1747, Beaufort, S. C.
CAMPBELL, Hugh and Sarah Baron, 12 June 1766, Charleston, S. C.
CAMPBELL, Jennet and William Craig, 23 April 1798, Mecklenburg Co., N. C.
CAMPBELL, John and Einnefred Corry, 15 March 1770, Tyrrell Co., N. C.
CAMPBELL, John and Matilda Polk, 2 May 1792, Mecklenburg Co., N. C.
CAMPBELL, John and Nancy Spencer, 28 July 1823, Mecklenburg Co., N. C.
CAMPBELL, John A. and Susan M. Alexander, 3 March 1841, Mecklenburg Co., N. C.
CAMPBELL, Lieutenant and Betsy Smith, 6 May 1784, Charleston, S. C.
CAMPBELL, Lydia and Isaac F. Alexander, 1 September 1830, Mecklenburg Co., N. C.
CAMPBELL, Margaret and William Davis, 11 March 1775, Charleston, S. C.
CAMPBELL, Margaret and William Parke, 3 October 1798, Spartanburg Co., S. C.
CAMPBELL, Martha and Samuel Forgus, 22 July 1778, Rowan Co., N. C.
CAMPBELL, Martha and Moses Beaty, 4 November, Mecklenburg Co., N. C.
CAMPBELL, Rachel and William McCord, 19 March 1798, Mecklenburg Co., N. C.
CAMPBELL, Robert and Jane Turner, 30 March 1791, Mecklenburg Co., N. C.
CAMPBELL, Sarah and Hugh Gallagher, 4 May 1778, Rowan Co., N. C.
CAMPBELL, Sarah L. and John F. Johnston, 10 July 1844, Mecklenburg Co., N. C.
CAMPBELL, Susan and William McCleary, 6 July 1795, Mecklenburg Co., N. C.
CAMPBELL, William and Mary Times, 2 June 1749, Charleston, S. C.
CAMPBELL, William (Lord) and Sarah Izard, 17 April 1763, St. George Parish, S. C.
CAMPBELL, William and Ann Shuman, 7 July 1841, Mecklenburg Co., N. C.
CAMREN, Ann and John Kingston, 13 January 1743, Charleston, S. C.
CANE, Elizabeth and Jacob Flowers, 19 April 1760, Edgecombe Co., N. C.
CANNADY, Elline and Samuel Bolt, 9 February 1848, Laurens Co., S. C.
CANNADY, Nancy and John Franks, 12 December 1846, Laurens Co., S. C.
CANNADY, Natti O'Brian and Frances Meadows, 30 March 1847, Laurens Co., S. C.
CANNADY, Samuel and Elizabeth Allen, 18 January 1763, Edgecombe Co., N. C.
CANNADY, Sally and James Stubbs, 1780, Tyrrell Co., N. C.
CANNADY, Susan and Thomas Badgett, 15 June 1849, Laurens Co., S. C.
CANNON, Exelina and Josiah Morris, 11 August 1842, Mecklenburg Co., N. C.
CANNON, John and Polly Scot Moore, 23 December 1791, Mecklenburg Co., N. C.
CANNON, Moses H. and Eliza Houston, 5 August 1839, Mecklenburg Co., N. C.
CANNON, Sally and James Wakefield, 24 November 1771, Charleston, S. C.
CANTEY, Mary and Eli Kershaw, 19 November 1769, Camden, S. C.
CANTEY, Polly and Wade Hampton, July 1801, Santee, S. C.
CANTRIL, Jean and Jesse Bracken, 20 March 1790, Orange Co., N. C.
CANTY, Elizabeth B. (widow) and Joshua Hargreaves, 10 January 1801, Charleston, S. C.
CANTY, Martha and Charles Diston, 16 June 1719, St. Andrews Parish, S. C.
CANTZON, John and Sarah Dickey, 1765, Lancaster Co., S. C.
CANTZON, John and Rachel Foster, 18 July 1791, Lancaster Co., S. C.
CANTZON, Mary and James Blair, 15 May 1792, Williamsburg, S. C.

CAPE, Brian and Mary Hetherington (widow), 13 May 1770, Charleston, S. C.

CAPE, John and Providence Adams, 10 May 1796, Charleston, S. C.

CAPERS, Elizabeth and Thomas Ladson, 24 February 1785, Beaufort, S. C.

CAPERS, Ellison and Charlotte Palmer, 24 February 1859, Columbia, S. C.

CAPERS, William and Mary Singletary, September 1783, St. Thomas Parish, S. C.

CAPPS, Betsy and John W. Clark, 23 November 1848, Mecklenburg Co., N. C.

CAPPS, Henry and Peggy Brown, 10 July 1823, Mecklenburg Co., N. C.

CAPPS, Hiram T. and Sarah R. Williamson, 23 March 1840, Mecklenburg Co., N. C.

CAPPS, Jane and William W. Anderson, 19 April 1841, Mecklenburg Co., N. C.

CAPPS, Polly and Eli Martin, 13 May 1823, Mecklenburg Co., N. C.

CAPPS, Sarah and Robert McGee, 7 April 1831, Mecklenburg Co., N. C.

CAPPS, Thomas and Caroline Lepner, 9 October 1809, Mecklenburg Co., N. C.

CAREW, Eleanor and Alexander Douglas, 2 January 1801, Charleston, S. C.

CARLILE, Robert and Sarah Coleman, 5 January 1763, Edgecombe Co., N. C.

CARLISLE, James Henry and Margaret Jane Brice, 12 December 1848, Columbia, S. C.

CARLISLE, John E. and Emma L. Jones, 2 May 1877, Abbeville Co., S. C.

CARLISLE, John Mason and Elizabeth C. Sharpe, 30 April 1850, Fairfield Co., S. C.

CARLISLE, Robert and Sarah Snell, 10 February 1764, Chowan Co., N. C.

CARLOCK, Cornelius and Matilda Byron, 5 October 1831, Mecklenburg Co., N. C.

CARLOCK, Thomas and Hannah Stevens, 26 April 1831, Mecklenburg Co., N. C.

CARNE, Samuel (Dr.) and Catherine Bond, 18 February 1759, Christ Church Parish, S. C.

CARNEY, Josiah and Sarah Power, 19 August 1789, Bertie Co., N. C.

CARNEY, Mary and Robert Andrews, 11 July 1750, Orangeburg Co., S. C.

CAROTHERS, Betsy and John Neely, 3 January 1811, Mecklenburg Co., N. C.

CAROTHERS, Esther and James Ratchford, 14 February 1825, Mecklenburg Co., N. C.

CAROTHERS, James and Elizabeth Lovenes, 17 May 1791, Mecklenburg Co., N. C.

CAROTHERS, James and Margaret Swann Neely, 10 October 1809, Mecklenburg Co., N. C.

CAROTHERS, James Franklin and Margaret E. Harris, 28 July 1847, York Co., S. C.

CAROTHERS, James F. and Martha A. Garrison, 1852, York Co., S. C.

CAROTHERS, Jamina and James McRee, 28 March 1825, Mecklenburg Co., N. C.

CAROTHERS, Jane H. and John Brandon, 20 November 1840, Mecklenburg Co., N. C.

CAROTHERS, Margaret and Charles C. Mason, 2 October 1835, Mecklenburg Co., N. C.

CAROTHERS, Mary and James A. Brandon, 15 January 1841, Mecklenburg Co., N. C.

CAROTHERS, Margaret H. and John Starr Neely, 4 March 1841, York Co., S. C.

CAROTHERS, Martha Neely and Franklin Harris, 25 November 1836, York Co., S. C.

CAROTHERS, Nancy A. and Elisha G. Thompson, 6 October 1836, York Co., S. C.

CAROTHERS, Nancy A. and Randolph A. Enom, 1846, York Co., S. C.

CAROTHERS, Samuel D. and Zilla B. Miller, 11 February 1836, York Co., S. C.

CAROTHERS, Thomas Milton and Jane Levicia Potts, 10 June 1856, Mecklenburg Co., N. C.

CAROTHERS, William Neely and Sarah Cornelia Taylor, 1 May 1849, Mecklenburg Co., N. C.

CARR, James and Ann Jones, 5 March 1776, Chowan Co., N. C.

CARR, Jennet and John Stoutmire, November 1799, St. Matthews Parish, S. C.

CARR, Margaret and John Murphy, 5 November 1786, Guilford Co., N. C.

CARRELL, Miss and John Black, 15 August 1765, Chowan Co., N. C.

CARRELL, Thomas and Elizabeth Stubbs, 17 November 1769, Tyrrell Co., N. C.

CARRERE, Charles and Eliza Rugge, (of Philadelphia) 8 July 1797, Charleston, S. C.

CARRIGAN, James and Jane Sample, 18 April 1786, Orange Co., N. C.

CARRIGAN, William and Rebecca Mitter, 27 December 1793, Mecklenburg Co., N. C.

CARROLL, Henrietta and Alexander Michie, 9 September 1766, Charleston, S. C.

CARROLL, James and Martha Williams, 11 June 1800, Mecklenburg Co., N. C.

CARROLL, Nathan B. and Jennett Graham, 13 October 1831, Mecklenburg Co., N. C.

CARRUTH, Sarah and Barthe Haynes, 30 August 1793, Mecklenburg Co., N. C.

CARRUTHERS, John and Elizabeth Wilkins, 15 February 1745, Chowan Co., N. C.

CARSE, Eugenia and Joseph Ratford, 1740, Orangeburg Co., S. C.

CARSE, Faithy and Thomas Joyner, 1740, Orangeburg Co., S. C.

CARSON, Archibald and Elizabeth Ross, (widow) May 1784, Charleston, S. C.

CARSON, James and Elizabeth Neal, 7 May 1796, Charleston, S. C.

CARSON, Jane and Robert H. Clark, 15 July 1828, Mecklenburg Co., N. C.

CARSON, Margaret and Andrew Clark, 17 October 1823, Mecklenburg Co., N. C.

CARSON, Mary and Robert Gordon, 11 March 1773, Rowan Co., N. C.

CARSON, Mary and James Adkins, 18 February 1790, Orange Co., N. C.

CARSON, Samuel and Mary Spires, 4 March 1793, Orange Co., N. C.

CARSON, William and Rebecca Lloyd, 16 January 1770, Charleston, S. C.

CART, John and Susannah Rumph, 14 January 1785, Charleston, S. C.

CARTER, Anne and William Barrett, 3 March 1767, Edgecombe Co., N. C.

CARTER, Benjamin and Rebecca Murphy, (widow) 14 January 1740, Orangeburg Co., S. C.

CARTER, Eliza and Richard Jennings, 11 August 1825, Mecklenburg Co., N. C.

CARTER, Elizabeth and Daniel Eaton, 17 March 1798, Rowan Co., N. C.

CARTER, James and Leah Haughton, 3 June 1773, Chowan Co., N. C.

CARTER, Mary and Azal Benthall, 24 December 1764, Edgecombe Co., N. C.

CARTER, Polly and Talton Bland, 23 January 1823, Edgefield District, S. C.

CARTER, Rebecca P. and Romulus M. Saunders, 1812, Caswell Co., N. C.

CARTER, Sarah and John Atkinson, 6 September 1741, Orangeburg Co., S. C.

CARTER, Sarah and Charles Madden, 19 December 1865, Laurens Co., S. C.

CARTER, Sue A. and Charles H. Foster, 1860, Murfreesboro, N. C.

CARTER, William and Charlotte Hough, 20 June 1786, Chowan Co., N. C.

CARTER, William and Mary Bradley, 10 August 1838, Mecklenburg Co., N. C.

CARTLEDGE, John B. and Mary L. Loveless, 21 November 1854, Edgefield District, S. C.

CARTWRIGHT, Mary and Rawlins Lowndes, 31 December 1751, Charleston, S. C.

CARUTHERS, Tamer and Richard Humphries, 16 December 1785, Chowan Co., N. C.

CASEY, Benjamin and Elizabeth Strohecker, 17 December 1799, Charleston, S. C.

CASEY, Ginny and Henry Fuller, 14 September 1859, Laurens Co., S. C.

CASH, Francis A. and Harriet Ann Bates, 18 November 1822, Mecklenburg Co., N. C.

CASHIN, John and Dolly Tucker, 1 July 1801, Mecklenburg Co., N. C.

CASHON, Burwell and Catherine B. Deweese, 14 August 1839, Mecklenburg Co., N. C.

CASHON, Hannah and Britain Rea, 4 October 1802, Mecklenburg Co., N. C.

CASHON, David L. and Cynthia J. Hutchinson, 27 January 1859, Mecklenburg Co., N. C.

CASHON, Martha and Richard Jordan, 3 February 1836, Mecklenburg Co., N. C.

CASHON, Miles D. and Scarrett Barnhill, 19 April 1849, Mecklenburg Co., N. C.

CASHON, Thomas and Sarah Sloan, 18 November 1820, Mecklenburg Co., N. C.

CASKEY, Susannah and John N. Acock, 30 December 1844, Mecklenburg Co., N. C.

CASSWELL, John and Amelia Lawrence, 26 December 1785, Tyrrell Co., N. C.

CASSWELL, Sarah and John Spruell, 15 April 1766, Tyrrell Co., N. C.

CASTELLAW, William and Sarah Mitchell, 31 March 1784, Bertie Co., N. C.

CASTELAW, John and Penelope Mitchell, 30 November 1785, Bertie Co., N. C.

CASTELBURY, Paul and Nancy Gillespie, 15 February 1824, Spartanburg, S. C.

CATES, Harriet C. and Charles H. Kenney, 28 December 1844, Edgefield District, S. C.

CATHAY, Eliza Jane and R. F. Montgomery, 17 January 1849, Mecklenburg Co., N. C.

CATHAY, Mary and William Irwin, 24 March 1796, Rowan Co., N. C.

CATHAY, William A. and Sarah A. Clark, 15 January 1845, Mecklenburg Co., N. C.

CATHCART, Elizabeth and David F. Berryhill, 8 April 1816, Mecklenburg Co., N. C.

CATHCART, Harriet and David C. Haynes, 10 November 1835, Mecklenburg Co., N. C.

CATHCART, William and Sarah Lewis, 7 January 1824, Mecklenburg Co., N. C.

CATHCART, William and Cornelia Shell, 2 May 1866, Laurens Co., S. C.

CATHERINE, Emily and William Dorn, 6 December 1855, Edgefield District, S. C.

CATHEY, Alexander and Esther Waddell, 17 February 1804, Mecklenburg Co., N. C.

CATHEY, Fanny and William Clark, 23 July 1818, Mecklenburg Co., N. C.

CATHEY, George and Malinda Tew, 10 March 1842, Mecklenburg Co., N. C.

CATHEY, James F. and Eliza J. Clark, 22 August 1855, Mecklenburg Co., N. C.

CATHEY, John and Elizabeth Calhoun, 19 March 1800, Mecklenburg Co., N. C.

CATTELL, Anne and William Cattell, 16 May 1732, Charleston, S. C.

CATTELL, John and Sarah Hall, 24 April 1728, Berkeley Co., S. C.

CATTELL, Mary and Mordecai Gist, January 1784, Charleston, S. C.

CATTELL, Sarah and George Mullins, 17 June 1773, Berkeley Co., S. C.

CATTELL, William and Anne Cattell, 16 May 1732, Charleston, S. C.

CATTELL, William (Jr.) and Anne Fraser, 1 August 1746, Charleston, S. C.

CATTELL. William and Sabina Lynch, 8 March 1767, Charleston, S. C.

CAWTHORN, John and Polly Darnell, 28 December 1805, Mecklenburg Co., N. C.

CENDRON, Elizabeth and Daniel Huger, 25 January 1710, Craven Co., S. C.

CHADWICK, Betty and Joseph Murphy, 16 November 1774, Guilford Co., N. C.

CHAFFIN, Elizabeth and Enoch Hunt, 2 June 1794, Rowan Co., N. C.

CHAFFIN, Mary and Henry Etcheson, 22 November 1794, Rowan Co., N. C.

CHALEY, Thomas and M. Jenkins, 13 April 1797, Charleston, S. C.

CHALKER, Jabez, and Ann Compton, August 1783, Charleston, S. C.

CHALMERS, Ann B. (Mrs.) and Peter Sader, 17 October 1799, Charleston, S. C.

CHALMERS, Elizabeth and Isaac Huger, 14 March 1762, Craven Co., S. C.

CHALMERS, Lionel (Dr.) and Elizabeth Warden, 16 August 1766, Charleston, S. C.

CHALMERS, Nancy and James Kennedy, 7 December 1784, Charleston, S. C.

CHALMERS, Sarah and Jehu Wilson, November 1784, Charleston, S. C.

CHAMBERLAIN, Susan and Thomas Price, 1 November 1857, Edgefield District, S. C.

CHAMBERS, Jane and Charles Hatton, 31 December 1779, Rowan Co., N. C.

CHAMBERS, Mary and Britton Going, 30 April 1791, Rowan Co., N. C.

CHAMBLEN, James and Caroline Hill, 7 October 1845, Laurens Co., S. C.

CHAMPANARE, Esther and James Axson, 3 June 1760, Santee, S. C.

CHAMPION, Mary and John Lewis, 11 March 1754, Chowan Co., N. C.

CHAMPNEYS, John and Anne Livingston, 3 November 1763, Charleston, S. C.

CHAMPNEYS, Sarah (widow) and James Skirving, May 1761, Charleston, S. C.

CHANDLER, Henry and Louisa Walker, 21 August 1856, Laurens Co., S. C.

CHANDLER, Isaac and Sally White, 9 April 1771, Charleston, S. C.

CHANDLER, Lucinda and Melton Bailey, 3 February 1856, Laurens Co., S. C.

CHANDLER, Miss and William Morgan, 1 January 1770, Charleston, S. C.

CHANDLER, Isaac and (Mrs.) Catherine McCord, 20 December 1800, Charleston, S. C.

CHANDLER, Susanna and Samuel Green, 15 January 1770, Charleston, S. C.

CHANDLER, Thomas and Margaret Durham, 29 July 1838, Edgefield District, S. C.

CHAPLIN, Martha and John Barnwell, 31 October 1737, Beaufort, S. C.

CHAPMAN, Ann and James Phelps, 17 February 1779, Tyrrell Co., N. C.

CHAPMAN, Frances and James Digin, 13 May 1776, Chowan Co., N. C.

CHAPMAN, John A. and Mary A. Chapman, 1 May 1845, Newberry, S. C.

CHAPMAN, Joseph and Frances Ormond (widow) 17 June 1773, Chowan Co., N. C.

CHAPMAN, Mary and John Williams, 6 March 1801, St. Pauls Parish, S. C.

CHAPMAN, Mary A. and John A. Chapman, 1 May 1845, Newberry, S. C.

CHAPMAN, Mary E. and J. L. Bacon, December 1854, Edgefield District, S. C.

CHAPMAN, Robert P. and I. C. Johnston, 2 August 1865, Mecklenburg Co., N. C.

CHAPPEL, Isabella and John White, 8 June 1772, Santee, S. C.

CHAPPELL, Isaac B. and Eliza Mitchell, 19 February 1852, Chowan Co., N. C.

CHAPPELL, Mary and John Hudgens, 8 October 1865, Laurens Co., S. C.

CHAPPELL, Richard and Keziah Jordan, 1 May 1779, Chowan Co., N. C.

CHARDON, Isaac and Mary Woodward, 6 November 1735, Charleston, S. C.

CHARLES, Katherine and Jacob Frarly, 2 May 1768, Rowan Co., N. C.

CHARLES, Mary and John Strohecker, 22 May 1800, Charleston, S. C.

CHARLTON, Jasper and Abigail Slaughter, 14 January 1757, Chowan Co., N. C.

CHARLTON, Job and Elizabeth Stamp, 20 September 1741, Chowan Co., N. C.

CHARLTON, John and Bethiah Tucker, 25 June 1778, Chowan Co., N. C.

CHARLTON, Rachel and John Miller, 22 December 1801, Chowan Co., N. C.

CHARNERS, Hannah and Edward Colony, 21 April 1779, Santee, S. C.

CHEATHAM, J. W. and Mary E. Shibley, 15 November 1855, Edgefield District, S. C.

CHECK, Jamima and Washington Garrett, 28 October 1853, Laurens Co., S. C.

CHECK, Willis and Sarah Fowler, 27 November 1856, Laurens Co., S. C.

CHEEK, Austin and Nancy Garrett, 20 May 1852, Laurens Co., S. C.

CHEEK, James and Julia Ann Stone, February 1851, Laurens Co., S. C.

CHEEK, John and Zalister Putman, 8 June 1852, Laurens Co., S. C.

CHEEK, Rebecca A. and Henry Marks, 24 July 1823, Mecklenburg Co., N. C.

CHERRY, Bethiah and Samuel Jacobs, 3 November 1788, Bertie Co., N. C.

CHERRY, Fanny and Enoch Flood, 19 June 1801, Edgecombe Co., N. C.

CHERRY, Mary and James Warren, 21 June 1788, Bertie Co., N. C.

CHERRY, Martha and John Baker, 17 September 1790, Bertie Co., N. C.

CHESHIRE, Elizabeth and Raply Owings, 22 December 1842, Laurens Co., S. C.

CHESHIRE, Sarah H and R. G. Mitchell, 29 June 1858, Chowan Co., N. C.

CHESTON, Mary and Josiah Powers, 1780, Tyrrell Co., N. C.

CHEVES, Sophia L. and Charles T. Haskell, 1 December 1830, Charleston, S. C.

CHEVILLETTE, John and Susannah Hepperditzel, 13 January 1745, Orangeburg Co., S. C.

CHICHESTER, Dr. and Mary B. Powell, 11 November 1794, Charleston, S. C.

CHICKEN, Catherine and Noah Thomas, 5 August 1762, Santee, S. C.

CHICKEN, Dorothy and John Steel, 30 March 1773, Santee, S. C.

CHICKEN, William and Elizabeth Chovin, 14 May 1761, Santee, S. C.

CHIFFELLE, Christina and Robert Dillon, 6 October 1768, Purrysburg, S. C.

CHILD, Mary and John Ainslie, 18 January 1750, Charleston, S. C.

CHINNERS, John C. and Hortence F. Gare, 29 March 1800, Charleston, S. C.

CHISHOLM, Alexander (Jr.) and Christian Chisholm, 5 October 1766, Charleston, S. C.

CHISHOLM, Alexander and Sarah Maxwell, (widow) 10 June 1786, Charleston, S. C.

CHISHOLM, Christina and Alexander Chisholm, 5 October 1766, Charleston, S. C.

CHISHOLM, Sarah and Alston Gibbes, 31 December 1819, Charleston, S. C.

CHISHOLM, Susan and Oliver H. Middleton, 5 April 1828, Edisto Island, S. C.

CHISNELL, Margaret and Thomas Swann, 1 July 1771, Chowan Co., N. C.

CHITTY, Sarah and Charles Brown, 25 December 1799, Charleston, S. C.

CHITTY, William and Ann Cole, 9 October 1794, Charleston, S. C.

CHOPARD, Ann and John Taylor, 1 October 1770, Charleston, S. C.

CHOVIN, Alexander and Polly Tart, November 1772, Charleston, S. C.

CHOVIN, Elizabeth and William Chicken, 14 May 1761, Santee, S. C.

CHOVIN, Esther and James Bell, 23 May 1768, Santee, S. C.

CHREITZBERG, Abel and Anna E. Manns, 26 December 1839, Charleston, S. C.

CHRISTIAN, Mary S. and John B. Van Dyck, 10 March 1831, Charleston, S. C.

CHRISTENBERRY, Arminta B. and Andrew F. Moore, 20 August 1846, Mecklenburg Co., N. C.

CHRISTENBERRY, Bailey and Richard Jordan, 25 December 1843, Mecklenburg Co., N. C.

CHRISTENBERRY, Elizabeth P. and William J. Jackson, 23 February 1828, Mecklenburg Co., N. C.

CHRISTENBERRY, James T. and Mary Robison, 15 March 1828, Mecklenburg Co., N. C.

CHRISTENBERRY, Moses and Catherine Starrett, 15 March 1828, Mecklenburg Co., N. C.

CHRISTENBERRY, Rachel and Anthony Auten, 9 March 1833, Mecklenburg Co., N. C.

CHRISTENBERRY, William P. and Mary McGarrar, 24 May 1837, Mecklenburg Co., N. C.

CHRISTENBERRY, Wilmath E. and George W. Alexander, 31 March 1857, Mecklenburg Co., N. C.

CHRISTIE, Betsy and Charles Harris, 1 January 1773, Charleston, S. C.

CHRISTIE, James and Hapzibah Rose, 15 November 1768, Charleston, S. C.

CHRISTMAS, Richard and Anne Butler, 22 December 1788, Orange Co., N. C.

CIRNAL, Julia Ann and Greenbury Sanford, 25 January 1854, Laurens Co., S. C.

CLANCY, John and Esther McRachin, 5 November 1822, Mecklenburg Co., N. C.

CLANTON, Drury and Eleanor Beaty, 8 May 1828, Mecklenburg Co., N. C.

CLAP, Mary and Kenneth Michie, February 1746, Charleston, S. C.

CLARDY, James and Gerety Henderson, 4 April 1844, Laurens Co., S. C.

CLARDY, Martha and Moses Williams, 10 November 1842, Laurens Co., S. C.

CLARDY, Sarah and Jackson Rowland, 14 January 1857, Laurens Co., S. C.

CLAREY, Ann and Jesse Griffin, 18 February 1772, Rowan Co., N. C.

CLARK, Alice (Mrs.) and James Oliver, 26 June 1800, Charleston, S. C.

CLARK, Allen and Henrietta Dunscombe, 10 November 1777, Chowan Co., N. C.

CLARK, Almarine and Elizabeth Robison, 27 December 1848, Mecklenburg Co., N. C.

CLARK, Andrew and Margaret Carson, 17 October 1823, Mecklenburg Co., N. C.

CLARK, Ann and Robert Pillans, April 1785, Charleston, S. C.

CLARK, A. W. and (Miss) R. A. Todd, 17 January 1866, Mecklenburg Co., N. C.

CLARK, Christopher and Hannah Turner, 17 January 1773, Bertie Co., N. C.

CLARK, Drury and Abraham Holland, 8 October 1799, Edgecombe Co., N. C.

CLARK, Eliza and Henry Martin, 17 February 1841, Mecklenburg Co., N. C.

CLARK, Eliza J. and James F. Cathey, 22 August 1855, Mecklenburg Co., N. C.

CLARK, Elizabeth and John Harford, 8 June 1779, Chowan Co., N. C.

CLARK, Elizabeth and Henry Allison, 10 September 1834, Mecklenburg Co., N. C.

CLARK, Ezekial W. and Rachel Baker, 20 April 1825, Mecklenburg Co., N. C.

CLARK, Hannah and James Alexander, 16 October 1798, Mecklenburg Co., N. C.

CLARK, Hannah and Charles Mason, 4 November 1814, Mecklenburg Co., N. C.

CLARK, Helen M. and Sarah Dixon, 4 December 1857, Mecklenburg Co., N. C.

CLARK, Henry and Sarah Dixon, 4 December 1857, Mecklenburg Co., N. C.

CLARK, Hillery and Susannah Inabinet, 17 January 1856, Edgefield District, S. C.

CLARK, Isabella and John Beaty, 12 April 1837, Mecklenburg Co., N. C.

CLARK, James and Lucy Bird, 18 September 1805, Mecklenburg Co., N. C.

CLARK, James and Ann Alexander, 31 March 1818, Mecklenburg Co., N. C.

CLARK, James and Melissa Moore, 24 November 1829, Mecklenburg Co., N. C.

CLARK, James and Sarah M. McCorkle, 15 November 1836, Mecklenburg Co., N. C.

CLARK, James A. and Margaret I. Clark, 11 April 1849, Mecklenburg Co., N. C.

CLARK, Jane and Ebenezer Platt, 22 November 1800, Charleston, S. C.

CLARK, Jesse M. and Jane P. McGibney, 14 April 1825, Mecklenburg Co., N. C.

CLARK, John and Nancy A. Freeman, 31 March 1859, Mecklenburg Co., N. C.

CLARK, John W. and Betsy Capps, 23 November 1848, Mecklenburg Co., N. C.

CLARK, John W. and Sarah J. Robison, 2 February 1858, Mecklenburg Co., N. C.

CLARK, Jonas (Jr.) and Ann Johnston, 15 September 1824, Mecklenburg Co., N. C.

CLARK, Joshua and Charlotte Harper, 1 January 1801, Charleston, S. C.

CLARK, Mary and John Montgomery, 1 August 1795, Mecklenburg Co., N. C.

CLARK, Mary and William Cowan, 14 October 1816, Mecklenburg Co., N. C.

CLARK, Mary J. and John D. Beaty, 26 December 1838, Mecklenburg Co., N. C.

CLARK, Margaret (Mrs.) and Nicholas Silberg, 26 March 1797, Charleston, S. C.

CLARK, Margaret I. and James A. Clark, 11 April 1849, Mecklenburg Co., N. C.

CLARK, Martha and Henry Hunter, 6 October 1840, Mecklenburg Co., N. C.

CLARK, Matilda and Samuel Clark, 19 November 1829, Mecklenburg Co., N. C.

CLARK, N. Allison and Harriet S. Rockwell, 16 May 1857, Mecklenburg Co., N. C.

CLARK, Rachel and Samuel Montgomery, 28 March 1812, Mecklenburg Co., N. C.

CLARK, Rebekah and James Montgomery, 8 January 1800, Mecklenburg Co., N. C.

CLARK, Robert F. and Nancy Beaty, 26 September 1839, Mecklenburg Co., N. C.

CLARK, Robert H. and Jane Carson, 15 July 1828, Mecklenburg Co., N. C.

CLARK, Robert H. and Christina Todd, 23 December 1841, Mecklenburg Co., N. C.

CLARK, Robert M. and Margaret S. Irwin, 18 December 1838, Mecklenburg Co., N. C.

CLARK, Samuel and Matilda Clark, 19 November 1829, Mecklenburg Co., N. C.

CLARK, Sarah and John Bennett, 21 May 1776, Chowan Co., N. C.

CLARK, Sarah A. and William A. Cathay, 15 January 1845, Mecklenburg Co., N. C.

CLARK, Thomas M. and Elizabeth Philips, 13 August 1863, Mecklenburg Co., N. C.

CLARK, Thomas B. and Nancy Sing, 21 December 1836, Mecklenburg Co., N. C.

CLARK, Virginia Q. and M. W. Robison, 12 April 1849, Mecklenburg Co., N. C.

CLARK, William and Mary Donalson, 24 September 1782, Orange Co., N. C.

CLARK, William and Ann Thompson, 2 November 1796, Mecklenburg Co., N. C.

CLARK, William and Lucinda Montgomery, 27 January 1800, Mecklenburg Co., N. C.

CLARK, William and Fanny Cathey, 23 July 1818, Mecklenburg Co., N. C.

CLARK, William and Lucretia Taylor, 30 August 1845, Mecklenburg Co., N. C.

CLARK, William H. and Ann A. Todd, 14 October 1852, Mecklenburg Co., N. C.

CLARK, William P. and Maria L. Hathaway, 24 July 1816, Mecklenburg Co., N. C.

CLARKE, Archibald C. and (Mrs.) Susannah Sutter, April 1786, Beaufort, S. C.

CLARKE, Susanna and Jonas Rudesill, 19 September 1793, Mecklenburg Co., N. C.

CLARKSON, Mary M. (Mrs.) and William Reside, 3 August 1800, Charleston, S. C.

CLATWORTHY, James and Mary Rush, 15 February 1756, Orangeburg Co., S. C.

CLAVER, Susanna and John Elliot, 18 September 1787, Rowan Co., N. C.

CLAY, Mary and Philip Evans, 1719, St. Andrews Parish, S. C.

CLAYTON, Rachel and John Fawls, 2 June 1772, Rowan Co., N. C.

CLAYTON, Sarah and Timothy Laffitte, 25 September 1741, Chowan Co., N. C.

CLAYTON, William F. and Elizabeth Brown, 22 December 1869, Marion Co., S. C.

CLEATON, John and Sirrah Fuster, (widow) 1741, Orangeburg Co., N. C.

CLEATOR, Elizabeth (widow) and John Boomer, 9 July 1774, Charleston, S. C.

CLEGG, Ervin and Martha Miles, 3 December 1856, Edgefield District, S. C.

CLEILAND, Elizabeth and David Rhind, 22 December 1774, Charleston, S. C.

CLEILAND, Sally and (Dr.) Alexander Baron, 1 January 1773, Charleston, S. C.

CLEILAND, William and Hester Maybank, 2 June 1785, Christ Church Parish, S. C.

CLEILAND, William (Dr.) and Mrs. McNabney, 13 April 1732, Charleston, S. C.

CLELAND, Elizabeth and Alexander Mow, 6 January 1763, Chowan Co., N. C.

CLELAND, John C. and Rebecca Wilkins, 10 October 1752, Chowan Co., N. C.

CLELAND, Nancy and Francis Kinloch, 7 February 1751, Charleston, S. C.

CLEMENS, Thomas and Anne Morgan, 28 June 1733, Charleston, S. C.

CLEMENS, William and Abigail Lippincott, 25 November 1774, Perquimans Co., N. C.

CLEMENS, William and Mary C. Collier, 21 December 1863, Mecklenburg Co., N. C.

CLEMENT, Eleanor and David Johnston, 16 December 1800, Charleston, S. C.

CLEMENT, John and Patience Uthert, 11 April 1721, Charleston, S. C.

CLEMENT, William and Mary Callyhon, (widow) 28 January 1747, Orangeburg Co., S. C.

CLEMENT, William and Sarah Wilkinson, 13 November 1799, Charleston, S. C.

CLEMENTS, Catherine and Samuel Ash, 24 February 1726, Charleston, S. C.

CLEMENTS, Catherine and George Page, 12 November 1739, Charleston, S. C.

CLEMENTS, Elizabeth Ann and Joseph Jordan, 9 December 1845, Chowan Co., N. C.

CLEMENTS, John and Ann Perkins, 8 July 1788, Chowan Co., N. C.

CLEMENTS, Mary and John Whiteman, 22 September 1814, Chowan Co., N. C.

CLEMENTS, Nancy and Benjamin Bratten, 17 April 1817, Chowan Co., N. C.

CLEMENTS, Sarah and William Wood, 4 October 1820, Chowan Co., N. C.

CLEMENTS, Sarah and George Caddy, 21 February 1822, Chowan Co., N. C.

CLEMENTS, William and Elizabeth Cotten, 21 December 1825, Chowan Co., N. C.

CLEMENTS, William and Mary Sansbury, 11 November 1856, Chowan Co., N. C.

CLEMMER, Margaret and William M. Hancock, 1 March 1792, Rowan Co., N. C.

CLEMMONS, Deborah and John Higgins, 29 April 1823, Chowan Co., N. C.

CLEMMONS, Polly and Richard Mendenhall, 25 July 1799, Guilford Co., N. C.

CLENDENING, Joseph and Anne Webb, 20 February 1787, Orange Co., N. C.

CLENDENNING, Betsy and Andrew Hart, 25 January 1800, Mecklenburg Co., N. C.

CLERK, John and Mary Lambert, 15 September 1770, Santee, S. C.

CLERK, Mary and Richard Hunter, 8 June 1786, Rowan Co., N. C.

CLIFFORD, Elizabeth and Richard Wayne, 14 September 1769, St. Bartholomews Parish, S. C.

CLIFT, Sarah and John Perry, 8 July 1719, St. Andrews Parish, S. C.

CLIFTON, John and Sarah Farlow, 3 April 1786, Tyrrell Co., N. C.

CLIFTON, Lydia and Zachariah Herndon, 18 March 1824, Orange Co., N. C.

CLIFTON, William and Sarah Mahaffey, 26 January 1845, Laurens Co., S. C.

CLINCH, Michael and Elizabeth Stow, (widow) 6 February 1718, St. Andrews Parish, S. C.

CLINE, Esther and Frederick Getchey, 11 April 1787, Rowan Co., N. C.

CLOUD, William and Susan Kenney, 27 February 1834, Edgefield District, S. C.

COACHMAN, James and Anne Johnston, (widow) 5 May 1773, Charleston, S. C.

COACHMAN, Thomas and Jane M. Saltus, (widow) 1 June 1797, St. Lukes Parish, S. C.

COALTER, Frances M. and David H. Means, 2 January 1817, Fairfield Co., S. C.

COATES, Hannah and John Merigu, 4 March 1795, Guilford Co., N. C.

COBB, Frances and Daniel Hopkins, 20 November 1793, Bertie Co., N. C.

COBB, Happy and Smith Davis, 5 January 1790, Bertie Co., N. C.

COBB, Mourning and Bright Bell, 22 February 1800, Bertie Co., N. C.

COBB, Nathan and Winny Mitchell, 9 August 1779, Bertie Co., N. C.

COBB, Sarah and Francis Atkins, 2 December 1820, Newberry, S. C.

COBBLE, Catherine and John Ernhart, 23 May 1796, Rowan Co., N. C.

COBLEY, Jemmitt and Helen Wright, 30 July 1746, Charleston, S. C.

COBURN, Jemima and Josiah Simmons, 1782, Tyrrell Co., N. C.

COBURN, John and Ann Pendarvis, 9 October 1800, Charleston, S. C.

COBURN, Mary and Julien Henry, 7 February 1801, Charleston, S. C.

COBURN, Nancy and Benjamin Bridges, 27 February 1816, Mecklenburg Co., N. C.

COBURN, Priscilla and Elias Smerdon, 16 June 1795, Sullivans Island, S. C.

COCHRAN, A. H. and Elizabeth R. Allison, 8 February 1851, Mecklenburg Co., N. C.

COCHRAN, Catherine and James McDowell, 30 June 1799, Charleston, S. C.

COCHRAN, C. N. (Miss.) and J. M. Caldwell, 1 January 1861, Mecklenburg Co., N. C.

COCHRAN, Dorcas M. and John Allen, 17 December 1836, Mecklenburg Co., N. C.

COCHRAN, Elizabeth and E. M. Bland, 26 January 1840, Edgefield District, S. C.

COCHRAN, Elizabeth J. and Silas Caldwell, 26 August 1864, Mecklenburg Co., N. C.

COCHRAN, Ezra and Hannah Bevins, 17 February 1824, Mecklenburg Co., N. C.

COCHRAN, John and Frances McEwen, 3 August 1791, Mecklenburg Co., N. C.

COCHRAN, Joseph and Catherine C. McKnight, 8 April 1840, Mecklenburg Co., N. C.

COCHRAN, Levi and Elizabeth Bibby, 14 February 1822, Mecklenburg Co., N. C.

COCHRAN, Lucinda and William H. Morris, 25 January 1844, Mecklenburg Co., N. C.

COCHRAN, Margaret (widow) and Andrew Cunningham, 4 January 1767, Ponpon, S. C.

COCHRAN, Margaret and William L. Alexander, 31 July 1846, Mecklenburg Co., N. C.

COCHRAN, Martha and Robert A. Caldwell, 7 February 1855, Mecklenburg Co., N. C.

COCHRAN, Martha P. and Edward H. Morris, 24 October 1854, Edgefield District, S. C.

COCHRAN, Michael and Rebecca Sullivan, 11 January 1759, Santee, S. C.

COCHRAN, Nancy B. and James R. Orr, 19 November 1841, Mecklenburg Co., N. C.

COCHRAN, Polly and Abraham Bevins, 6 October 1818, Mecklenburg Co., N. C.

COCHRAN, Rachel and Edmund Richey, 28 November 1791, Mecklenburg Co., N. C.

COCHRAN, Robert and Mary Elliott, 3 February 1763, Charleston, S. C.

COCHRAN, Sally and William McCoy, 16 October 1816, Mecklenburg Co., N. C.

COCHRAN, Sally and Moses Bevan, 20 January 1820, Mecklenburg Co., N. C.

COCHRAN, Sarah E. and P. B. Hodgy, 23 September 1857, Mecklenburg Co., N. C.

COCHRAN, Thomas (Jr.) and Eliza Torrans, 18 December 1799, Charleston, S. C.

COCHRAN, Thomas and Catherine Dulin, 17 January 1816, Mecklenburg Co., N. C.

COCKFIELD, Ann and Stephen Jones, 1831, Darlington Co., S. C.

COCKFIELD, Josiah and Hannah Singletary, 1807, Darlington Co., S. C.

CODDLE, Mary and Thomas Goodman, 1 September 1797, Rowan Co., N. C.

COFFEY, James and Eliza Alexander, 23 May 1827, Mecklenburg Co., N. C.

COFFIELD, Anne and John Jones, 20 December 1766, Edgecombe Co., N. C.

COFFIELD, Jethro and Elizabeth Butler, 25 April 1788, Bertie Co., N. C.

COFFIELD, John and Elizabeth Hoskins, 8 March 1757, Chowan Co., N. C.

COFFIELD, John and Ann Thompson, 20 March 1778, Chowan Co., N. C.

COFFIELD, Josiah and Lydia Speight, 28 August 1790, Bertie Co., N. C.

COFFIELD, Lavina and Reuben Miller, 21 September 1848, Chowan Co., N. C.

COFFIELD, Penelope and Dempsey Grimes, 24 June 1760, Avon, N. C.

COGBURN, Benjamin S. and Martha Y. Kenney, 23 November 1828, Edgefield District, S. C.

COGDELL, George and Miss Stevens, 11 May 1777, Charleston, S. C.

COHEN, Cornelia and Thomas McIntire, 18 December 1799, Charleston, S. C.

COHORT, Margaret and Andrew Elder, 19 February 1787, Rowan Co., N. C.

COKER, James L. and Susan Stout, 28 March 1860, Hartsville, S. C.

COLCOCK, John and Millicent Jones, 30 October 1768, Charleston, S. C.

COLDING, Indiana Lucy and William Blanchard Flowers, 28 November 1844, Barnwell Co., S. C.

COLDIRON, Mary and John Gobel, 25 May 1793, Rowan Co., N. C.

COLE, Ann and William Chitty, 9 October 1794, Charleston, S. C.

COLE, Betsy and Daniel Hunt, 10 May 1793, Rowan Co., N. C.

COLE, Hixey (dau. of John and Susannah Cole) and John White, 30 November 1825, Granville Co., N. C.

COLE, Isabella and W. D. Abernathy, 27 June 1860, Mecklenburg Co., N. C.

COLE, John and Mary Wood, 27 May 1767, Chowan Co., N. C.

COLE, Martha and Cyrus M. Alexander, 23 February 1836, Mecklenburg Co., N. C.

COLE, Mary and Melton Craddock, 23 September 1856, Laurens Co., S. C.

COLE, (Miss) M. and C. T. Randall, 23 June 1865, Mecklenburg Co., N. C.

COLE, Polly and Coleman Read White, 26 September 1812, Granville Co., N. C.

COLE, Richard and Miss Bommer, 29 May 1777, Charleston, S. C.

COLEMAN, Alsey and Elizabeth Teague, 29 October 1846, Laurens Co., S. C.

COLEMAN, Amanda and John Barksdale, 8 November 1855, Laurens Co., S. C.

COLEMAN, Daniel and Elliner Wellwood, 23 May 1753, Chowan Co., N. C.

COLEMAN, Elizabeth and Robert Hadlock, 6 September 1793, Rowan Co., N. C.

COLEMAN, Franklin (Dr.) and Ofelia Fuller, 12 April 1860, Laurens Co., S. C.

COLEMAN, James and Lavina Teague, 23 December 1852, Laurens Co., S. C.

COLEMAN, John and Rebekah Dancy, 7 June 1799, Edgecombe Co., N. C.

COLEMAN, John and Mary Rutherford, 12 January 1830, Edgefield District, S. C.

COLEMAN, Jonathan and Keziah Price, 4 January 1763, Edgecombe Co., N. C.

COLEMAN, Kader and Susannah Stephenson, 5 April 1764, Edgecombe Co., N. C.

COLEMAN, Mary and Hargrove Miller, 22 February 1859, Laurens Co., S. C.

COLEMAN, Robert and Sarah Story, (widow) 13 August 1762, Edgecombe Co., N. C.

COLEMAN, Sarah and Robert Carlile, 5 January 1763, Edgecombe Co., N. C.

COLEMAN, Susan and John Anderson, 11 April 1822, Union District, S. C.

COLETRAINE, Mary and Lawson Predy, 27 June 1745, Chowan Co., N. C.

COLLENS, Eli and Mary Durbin, 30 August 1781, Orange Co., N. C.

COLLES, Elizabeth and George Higgins, 13 February 1769, Charleston, S. C.

COLLES, Mary and Robert Beard, 6 December 1767, Charleston, S. C.

COLLEY, Margaret and Thomas Conner, 15 February 1817, Mecklenburg Co., N. C.

COLLIER, Catherine and James Herndon, 14 June 1802, Orange Co., N. C.

COLLIER, Mary C. and William Clemens, 21 December 1863, Mecklenburg Co., N. C.

COLLIER, Mary L. and John Osment, 11 December 1855, Mecklenburg Co., N. C.

COLLINS, Caleb and Henrietta Sutton, 12 March 1786, Tyrrell Co., N. C.

COLLINS, Daniel and (Mrs.) Jane Fontain, 11 April 1801, Charleston, S. C.

COLLINS, Eli and Dorcas Alexander, 10 December 1829, Mecklenburg Co., N. C.

COLLINS, Elizabeth and George Runell, 20 July 1768, Chowan Co., N. C.

COLLINS, Israll G. and Mary A. Allan, 5 October 1801, Sullivans Island, S. C.

COLLINS, Jane and Henry Hoover, 28 December 1849, Mecklenburg Co., N. C.

COLLINS, Jane V. C. and Samuel J. W. Badger, 25 March 1844, Mecklenburg Co., N. C.

COLLINS, John and Lydia Gray, 22 October 1767, Tyrrell Co., N. C.

COLLINS, John and Sarah Hinton, 6 February 1779, Chowan Co., N. C.

COLLINS, Jonathan and Mary A. Simmous, 3 January 1743, St. Thomas Parish, S. C.

COLLINS, Martha and John Williams, 19 May 1785, Chowan Co., N. C.

COLLINS, Mary A. and Joseph Hardison, 13 November 1765, Tyrrell Co., N. C.

COLLINS, Richard and Elizabeth Worley, 17 November 1769, Tyrrell Co., N. C.

COLLINS, Sarah and Henry Robason, 25 June 1783, Tyrrell Co., N. C.

COLLINS, Thomas and Annarita Ming, 25 January 1742, Chowan Co., N. C.

COLNER, Aaron and Anne Liles, 7 July 1785, Chowan Co., N. C.

COLONY, Edward and Hannah Charners, 21 April 1779, Santee, S. C.

COLP, Hannah and John Folick, 1 December 1794, Rowan Co., N. C.

COLSON, Gilbert and Sarah Turner, 13 August 1792, Perquimans Co., N. C.

COLSTON, Polly and Joshua Turner, 25 September 1794, Perquimans Co., N. C.

COLVARD, Sallie A. and A. M. Phine, 4 August 1865, Mecklenburg Co., N. C.

COLWELL, Sarah and Thomas Davis, 28 February 1764, Edgecombe Co., N. C.

COMBS, Martha and Jonathan Adams, 8 February 1783, Tyrrell Co., N. C.

COMBS, Robert and Mille Perisho, 1782, Tyrrell Co., N. C.

COMETT, Peter and Hannah Watson, 8 July 1746, Charlestown, S. C.

COMPTON, Ann and Jabez Chalker, August 1783, Charleston, S. C.

CONDON, John and Emily Houston, 29 December 1831, Mecklenburg Co., N. C.

CONDON, Mary and William D. Byram, 20 September 1825, Mecklenburg Co., N. C.

CONKRIGHT, Nellie and Henry Goldman, 9 September 1780, Rowan Co., N. C.

CONGER, John A. and Rebecca Meek, 14 December 1822, Mecklenburg Co., N. C.

CONGHORN, James and Elizabeth Orr, 19 January 1798, Mecklenburg Co., N. C.

CONNELL, Elizabeth and Augustus N. Miles, 7 January 1815, Mecklenburg Co., N. C.

CONNER, Catherine and Robert Morris, 21 December 1811, Mecklenburg Co., N. C.

CONNER, Elizabeth and William Barnhill, 31 October 1810, Mecklenburg Co., N. C.

CONNER, James and Lilly Wilson, 13 August 1795, Mecklenburg Co., N. C.

CONNER, Margaret J. and John F. Brevard, 15 August 1820, Mecklenburg Co., N. C.

CONNER, Mary P. and Miles Giles, 26 February 1822, Mecklenburg Co., N. C.

CONNER, Penelope and John Spier, (Jr.) 13 March 1764, Tyrrell Co., N. C.

CONNER, Thomas and Margaret Colley, 15 February 1817, Mecklenburg Co., N. C.

CONWAY, Elizabeth and George Norton, 24 October 1720, St. Andrews Parish, S. C.

COOK, Anzi W. and Margaret J. McGinnes, 11 October 1845, Mecklenburg Co., N. C.

COOK, Austin and Margaret Allen, 22 September 1819, Mecklenburg Co., N. C.

COOK. Benjamin and Winnifred Hopkins, 25 April 1774, Bertie Co., N. C.

COOK, Catherine and John Rice, 30 January 1818, Mecklenburg Co., N. C.

COOK, Caroline and Gabriel Rodden, 18 October 1842, Mecklenburg Co., N. C.

COOK, Elenor C. and James W. Wilson, 23 January 1836, Mecklenburg Co., N. C.

COOK, Eliza and Joab A. L. Orr, 9 July 1839, Mecklenburg Co., N. C.

COOK, Elizabeth and George Baker, 28 July 1817, Mecklenburg Co., N. C.

COOK, George and Eleanor Wade (widow of Richard), 17 July 1777, Charleston, S. C.

COOK, James and Sarah Millhouse, 15 October 1768, Camden, S. C.

COOK, Katherine and William King, 15 June 1774, Chowan Co., N. C.

COOK, Katherine and William Byram, 5 December 1792, Mecklenburg Co., N. C.

COOK, Margaret and Jacob Hughey, 5 September 1782, Rowan Co., N. C.

COOK, Margaret and Stephen Mayfield, 20 May 1797, Mecklenburg Co., N. C.

COOK, Margaret and William Hinton, 10 January 1824, Mecklenburg Co., N. C.

COOK, Margaret C. and Robert M. Allen, 23 February 1836, Mecklenburg Co., N. C.

COOK, Martha and Bartlett H. Herndon, 23 December 1858, Orange Co., N. C.

COOK, Mathias and Charity Welch, 13 April 1763, Edgecombe Co., N. C.

COOK, Mary and Henry Hughey, 20 March 1773, Rowan Co., N. C.

COOK, Mary (Mrs.) and McCully Righton, 27 December 1794, Charleston, S. C.

COOK, Mary and Henry Byram, 8 January 1803, Mecklenburg Co., N. C.

COOK, Mary and Eli Morrow, 19 December 1838, Mecklenburg Co., N. C.

COOK, Mary and William Gibbes, 30 October 1702, Charleston, S. C.

COOK, Mary E. and Jacob L. Banker, 8 December 1865, Mecklenburg Co., N. C.

COOK, Mary J. and William J. Blakeley, 5 January 1866, Mecklenburg Co., N. C.

COOK, Polly and John August, August 1773, Camden, S. C.

COOK, Rachel and James Merliva, 27 February 1838, Mecklenburg Co., N. C.

COOK, Rachel R. and C. J. Jennings, 14 September 1865, Mecklenburg Co., N. C.

COOK, Robert and Tirza Orr, 4 August 1814, Mecklenburg Co., N. C.

COOK, Sarah and Jesse Britt, 30 July 1793, Bertie Co., N. C.

COOK, Thomas and Peggy Lowrie, 21 December 1807, Mecklenburg Co., N. C.

COOK, William and Sarah Heron, 31 July 1850, Mecklenburg Co., N. C.

COOK, W. A. and Eleanora A. Reed, 5 September 1848, Mecklenburg Co., N. C.

COOLEY, Rhodah and Richardson Garrett, 12 July 1849, Laurens Co., S. C.

COOMBS, John and Anne Shields, 1 February 1779, Santee, S. C.

COOMBS, Samuel and Mary Marks, 21 August 1811, Mecklenburg Co., N. C.

COON, Elizabeth and John Finton, 4 November 1789, Rowan Co., N. C.

COOPER, Alexander and Elizabeth Stinson, 4 March 1824, Mecklenburg Co., N. C.

COOPER, Amelia and James Moss, 15 February 1866, Laurens Co., S. C.

COOPER, Clark Columbus and Ann Alice Reed, 16 February 1842, Barnwell
   District, S. C.

COOPER, Elijah and Sicily Griffeth, 20 March 1845, Laurens Co., S. C.

COOPER, Elizabeth and Elias Vanderhorst, 12 July 1763, Charleston, S. C.

COOPER, Fleet (Rev.) and Sarah Scott, 1783, Chowan Co., N. C.

COOPER, Joseph and Mary Livingston, 30 March 1791, Mecklenburg Co., N. C.

COOPER, Milly and Abner Bynum, 13 August 1790, Bertie Co., N. C.

COOPER, (Miss) L. C. and W. W. Robison, 18 July 1865, Mecklenburg Co.,
   N. C.

COOPER, Nancy C. and Jonathan Read, 19 January 1850, Mecklenburg Co.,
   N. C.

COOPER, Nancy S. and Ambrose Allen, 30 October 1854, Mecklenburg Co., N. C.

COOPER, Patsy and Byram Main, 24 September 1810, Mecklenburg Co., N. C.

COOPER, Thomas and Ann E. Adams, 18 November 1841, Mecklenburg Co., N. C.

COOPER, Wells and Elizabeth Alexander, 1780, Tyrrell Co., N. C.

COOPER, Willam and Margaret H. Hunter, 12 June 1823, Mecklenburg Co.,
   N. C.

COOVER, Solomon and Jane Davis, 6 December 1834, Mecklenburg Co., N. C.

COPELAND, Celia and Lemuel Long, 23 September 1773, Chowan Co., N. C.

COPELAND, Esther and Malachi Halsey, 19 October 1785, Chowan Co., N. C.

COPELAND, Frances and Warren Tribble, 20 January 1859, Laurens Co., S. C.

COPELAND, Leah and Jonathan S. Miller, 24 January 1850, Chowan Co., N. C.

COPELAND, Lydia and Richard Buckley, 3 February 1786, Chowan Co., N. C.

COPELAND, Mary and Samuel Woodward, 17 September 1754, Chowan Co., N. C.

COPELAND, Penina and Joseph Scott, 12 April 1768, Chowan Co., N. C.

COPELAND, Sarah and Solomon Miller, 16 January 1838, Chowan Co., N. C.

CORBETT, Thomas and Margaret Harleston, 8 June 1769, Berkeley Co., S. C.

CORBIT, Mr. and Elizabeth Crisp, 28 February 1855, Laurens Co., S. C.

CORDES, Catherine and Samuel Prioleau, (Jr.), 4 October 1766, Charleston, S. C.

CORDES, Esther and (Rev.) Daniel Dwight, 21 April 1747, Charleston, S. C.

CORDES, John and Catherine M. Mazyck, 1788, St. Johns Parish, S. C.

CORDES, Mary and Daniel Huger, 14 May 1741, Craven Co., S. C.

CORDES, Thomas and Charlotte Evance, 21 November 1784, Santee, S. C.

COREY, Winnifred and John Campbell, 15 March 1770, Tyrrell Co., N. C.

CORKER, Thomas and Eliza Glew, 30 May 1797, Charleston, S. C.

CORPREW, Elener and Benjamin Garrett, 11 February 1783, Tyrrell Co., N. C.

CORPREW, Thomas and Sarah Gale, 31 July 1747, Chowan Co., N. C.

COSEY, (Casey) John and Lucy Hartwick, 17 February 1816, Mecklenburg Co., N. C.

COSSENS, Edmund and Miss Jones, April 1774, Charleston, S. C.

COSSLETT, Charles M. and Ann Grimke, 17 December 1772, Charleston, S. C.

COTTEN, Elizabeth and William Clements, 21 December 1825, Chowan Co., N. C.

COTTLE, William and Elizabeth Glisson, 25 August 1790, Bertie Co., N. C.

COTTNER, Malissey and Peter Fry, 2 June 1775, Rowan Co., N. C.

COTTON, Absella and Robert Cotton, 17 October 1763, Edgecombe Co., N. C.

COTTON, Amos and Zilpha Wimberley, 23 October 1760, Edgecombe Co., N. C.

COTTON, James and Sarah Luten, 5 July 1786, Chowan Co., N. C.

COTTON, Robert and Absella Cotton, 17 October 1763, Edgecombe Co., N. C.

COTTRELL, Ruth (widow) and James Garrett, 17 December 1773, Chowan Co., N. C.

COUNTZ, Felix and Margaret Herring, 15 April 1800, Charleston, S. C.

COUSINS, John and Elizabeth Shann, 4 January 1722, St. Andrews Parish, S. C.

COVAR, Sherry and Mary Redford, 28 September 1831, Edgefield District, S. C.

COVINGTON, Benjamin H. and Mary A. Harlee, 17 June 1847, Richmond Co., N. C.

COVINGTON, B. H. and Virginia Durant, 23 December 1858, Richmond Co., N. C.

COVINGTON, Benjamin H. (Jr.) and Annie M. Coxe, 14 February 1883, Marlboro Co., S. C.

COVINGTON, B. H. and Jane Wall, 7 February 1804, Richmond Co., N. C.

COVINGTON, Benjamin H. and Francis Moorman, 6 March 1780, Anson Co., N. C.

COVINGTON, C. C. and Rachel Crawford, 12 May 1836, Richmond Co., N. C.

COVINGTON, Frances J. and Thomas J. Mousey, 1 March 1849, Richmond Co., N. C.

COVINGTON, Harrison W. and Virginia Hundon, 4 June 1844, Richmond Co., N. C.

COVINGTON, J. Edmond and Carrie Crosland, 25 April 1877, Marlboro Co., S. C.

COVINGTON, John W. and Fanny Settle, 16 November 1854, Richmond Co., N. C.

COVINGTON, Thomas A. and Laura E. Durant, July 1853, Richmond Co., N. C.

COVINGTON, William C. and Alice L. Steele, 31 July 1864, Richmond Co., N. C.

COVINGTON, William and Mary Wall, 26 July 1750, Anson Co., N. C.

COWAN, Catherine and Joseph Erwin, 17 May 1792, Rowan Co., N. C.

COWAN, Charity (widow) and James Matthews, 25 January 1767, Tyrrell Co., N. C.

COWAN, David T. and Mathers Elliott, 15 March 1808, Mecklenburg Co., N. C.

COWAN, May and David Foster, 27 February 1773, Rowan Co., N. C.

COWAN, Ruth and John Harris, 30 July 1795, Rowan Co., N. C.

COWAN, Sarah and Peter Frazer, 11 June 1794, Rowan Co., N. C.

COWAN, William and Mary Clark, 14 October 1816, Mecklenburg Co., N. C.

COWAND, Catherine and William Parker, 4 June 1785, Chowan Co., N. C.

COWARD, Asbury and Eliza Corbett Blum, 25 December 1856, Yorkville, S. C.

COX, Amy and Thomas Cox, 14 May 1778, Holly Springs, N. C.

COX, Ann and Thomas Ballew, 10 April 1753, Orangeburg Co., S. C.

COX, Clayton (Dr.) and Rebecca Martin, 15 September 1857, Laurens Co., S. C.

COX, David and Martha Dunn, 6 January 1830, Mecklenburg Co., N. C.

COX, John and Priscilla Wood, 1 August 1794, St. Georges Parish, S. C.

COX, John C. W. and Eleanor Screven, 22 December 1800, Charleston, S. C.

COX, Mary and Charles Moffitt, 27 November 1772, Guilford Co., N. C.

COX, Mary and Frederick Ezell, 28 March 1780, Rowan Co., N. C.

COX, Miss J. and Thomas A. Johnson, 21 June 1865, Mecklenburg Co., N. C.

COX, Polly and John Porter, 20 June 1784, Charleston, S. C.

COX, Samuel and Sally Jamison, 10 April 1809, Mecklenburg Co., N. C.

COX, Sarah A. and Isaac M. Johnston, 23 February 1854, Mecklenburg Co., N. C.

COXE, Ezra P. and Ann Bass, 17 May 1821, Marlboro Co., S. C.

COXE, James and Jane Hubbard, 21 March 1849, Marlboro Co., S. C.

COXE, James E. and Addizer C. Bass, 20 December 1854, St. Pauls Parish, N. C.

COXE, Samuel and Elizabeth Brown, 14 February 1782, Marlboro Co., S. C.

COZART, Jesse and Elizabeth Walker, 1786, Granville Co., N. C.

CRADDOCK, Melton and Mary Cole, 23 September 1856, Laurens Co., S. C.

CRADDOCK, Martha and Stephen Hooker, 1780, Tyrrell Co., N. C.

CRAFTS, William and Margaret Tebout, April 1786, Charleston, S. C.

CRAIG, Alexander and Agnes Huey, 9 March 1804, Mecklenburg Co., N. C.

CRAIG, Helen and Daniel Blake, 21 July 1856, Newington, S. C.

CRAIG, Margaret and James Johnston, 4 March 1788, Orange Co., N. C.

CRAIG, Margaret and John Huey, 9 March 1804, Mecklenburg Co., N. C.

CRAIG, Martha and Archibald McElroy, 1799, Pendleton Co., S. C.

CRAIG, William and Jennett Campbell, 23 April 1798, Mecklenburg Co., N. C.

CRANE, Peyton and Pruda McLain, 10 March 1823, Mecklenburg Co., N. C.

CRANER, Hannah and George Manlove, 17 January 1791, Guilford Co., N. C.

CRANK, Christian and James Perisho, 16 October 1778, Tyrrell Co., N. C.

CRANK, Elizabeth and James Seay, 26 July 1788, Bertie Co., N. C.

CRANSHAW, Henry and Mary Mitchell, 26 May 1801, Mecklenburg Co., N. C.

CRANSHAW, L. Berry and Mary Kimble, 6 December 1828, Mecklenburg Co., N. C.

CRASTON, John and Julia Miller, 11 October 1742, Charleston, S. C.

CRAWFORD, Ann and Oliver Hilliard, 1 May 1800, Charleston, S. C.

CRAWFORD, Daniel and Polly Holland, February 1748, Charleston, S. C.

CRAWFORD, David and Isabella Maine, February 1748, Charleston, S. C.

CRAWFORD, George and Mary Walls, 9 December 1856, Edgefield District, S. C.

CRAWFORD, Helen and Andrew Robertson, 8 June 1761, Charleston, S. C.

CRAWFORD, James and Sally Graham, 5 September 1804, Mecklenburg Co., N. C.

CRAWFORD, John and Ann B. Phifer, 17 October 1816, Lancaster Co., S. C.

CRAWFORD, Mr. and Sally Bellamy, 17 May 1732, Charleston, S. C.

CRAWFORD, Martha and Samuel Miller, 10 August 1792, Mecklenburg Co., N. C.

CRAWFORD, Mary (widow) and James Laurens, 19 August 1761, Charleston, S. C.

CRAWFORD, Nancy and James Hibbetts, 28 December 1792, Mecklenburg Co., N. C.

CRAWFORD, Rachel and C. C. Covington, 12 May 1836, Richmond Co., N. C.

CRAWFORD, Sarah and Isaac Donnom, 2 March 1784, Waxhaw, S. C.

CREECY, Elizabeth and Charles Moore, 15 November 1785, Chowan Co., N. C.

CREECY, Levi and (Mrs.) Mary Haughton, 1 October 1750, Chowan Co., N. C.

CREIGHTON, Ann and William Brandford, 23 March 1721, St. Andrews Parish S. C.

CREIGHTON, John and Mary Murray, April 1774, Charleston, S. C.

CREIGHTON, Leslie, (widow) and Thomas Gough, August 1783, Charleston, S. C.

CRENSHAW, Mary and Robert Blythe, 12 October 1865, Mecklenburg Co., N. C.

CRESSWILL, Rebecca and Edmund Penn, 9 January 1840, Edgefield District, S. C.

CRETELOW, Christina and Philip Jordan, 30 October 1792, Rowan Co., N. C.

CREWS, Martha M. and Joseph Penn Hunt, 1829, Granville Co., N. C.

CREWS, Susan and George W. Hunt, 25 October 1848, Granville Co., N. C.

CREWS, Thomas B. and Enheina Hance, 26 October 1856, Laurens, S. C.

CRICKELL, John and Mary Nichols, 6 June 1744, Chowan Co., N. C.

CRIPPS, Mary (widow) and Alexander Gillon, 13 July 1766, Charleston, S. C.

CRISMAN, Joseph L. and Margaret Blount, 17 April 1785, Chowan Co., N. C.

CRISP, John and Isabella Davis, 31 March 1857, Laurens Co., S. C.

CRISP, Elizabeth and Mr. Corbit, 28 February 1855, Laurens Co., S. C.

CRISPO, Antonio and Milly Porter, 7 August 1828, Mecklenburg Co., N. C.

CRISTENBERRY, Betsy and William Brown, 4 December 1819, Mecklenburg Co., N. C.

CRISTENBERRY, Harriet and Josiah Harris, 21 December 1841, Mecklenburg Co., N. C.

CRITTENDEN, Stephen S. and Elija J. Lynch, 17 May 1855, Greenville, S. C.

CROCKER, R. M. and Isabel Risaner, 15 April 1864, Lincoln, N. C.

CROCKETT, Archibald and Deborah Wilson, 12 January 1792, Mecklenburg Co., N. C.

CROCKETT, Margaret and William Morrow, 17 March 1794, Mecklenburg Co., N. C.

CROCKETT, Sarah and William McClure, 13 February 1804, Mecklenburg Co., N. C.

CROFT, Childermas and Mary Simmons, 28 May 1767, Santee, S. C.

CROFT, Childermas and Ellen Rawlins, 16 August 1781, Santee, S. C.

CROFT, Elizabeth and Henry Lenud, 13 June 1782, Santee, S. C.

CROFT, George and Elizabeth Leger, 28 January 1765, Charleston, S. C.

CROFT, Judith and Peter Guerry, 30 July 1778, Santee, S. C.

CROFT, Robert and Ann Jenkins, 24 March 1763, Santee, S. C.

CROMARTEE, Thomas and Sarah Dowd, 23 July 1768, Chowan Co., N. C.

CROMARTIE, Sarah and Alexander Montgomery, 18 May 1778, Chowan Co., N. C.

CROMLIES, Owen and Catherine Rabey, 18 January 1763, Chowan Co., N. C.

CROMWELL, Esther and Jacob Micheau, 11 June 1778, Santee, S. C.

CROMWELL, Oliver and Betsey Warham, 15 July 1773, Charleston, S. C.

CROMWELL, Oliver and Sarah Johnson, 30 August 1796, Charleston, S. C.

CROOK, Anna and Joseph Keen, 29 July 1779, Santee, S. C.

CROOK, Elizabeth and Percival Dring, 18 March 1761, Santee, S. C.

CROOK, Jane and Wyatt Goolsby, 9 October 1787, Rowan Co., N. C.

CROOK, John and Ruthy White, 2 November 1819, Granville Co., N. C.

CROOKE, Clement and Sarah Lee, 6 June 1774, Tyrrell Co., N. C.

CROOKER, T. B. and Amanda Jones, 18 December 1856, Edgefield District, S. C.

CROPTON, Isabella and Benjamin Booth, 20 April 1797, Charleston, S. C.

CROSKEY, John and Elizabeth Hill, 12 August 1721, St. Andrews Parish, S. C.

CROSKEYS, Anne and Samuel Frith, 6 June 1720, St. Andrews Parish, S. C.

CROSKEYS, Elizabeth and Joseph Dill, 2 January 1719, St. Andrews Parish, S. C.

CROSMAN, Christian and Jacob Fisher, 8 September 1768, Rowan Co., N. C.

CROSS, Elizabeth and Christopher Hainline, 29 August 1786, Rowan Co., N. C.

CROSS, Mary and Thomas Davis, 5 February 1782, Santee, S. C.

CROSS, Sarah S. and Daniel Russell, August 1784, Charleston, S. C.

CROSS, Stephen and Polly Neil, 17 April 1799, Edgecombe Co., N. C.

CROSS, William and Mary Ann Jamison, 7 February 1850, Mecklenburg Co., N. C.

CROSSTHWAITE, Sarah (widow) and William Somersall, 27 January 1774, Charleston, S. C.

CROSWELL, Rachel and Zachariah Harrowood, 10 September 1793, Rowan Co., N. C.

CROUCH, Henry and Sepha Watson, 30 May 1771, Charleston, S. C.

CROUCH, Watson and Reliance Steedman, 11 November 1754, Edgefield District, S. C.

CROW, Robert and Permelia Barnett, 29 January 1867, Laurens Co., S. C.

CROW, Simpson and Martha Layton, 21 December 1865, Laurens Co., S. C.

CROWELL, Colson and Lucy Sturhl, 15 February 1849, Mecklenburg Co., N. C.

CROWELL, John and Isabel McWilliams, 2 February 1797, Mecklenburg Co., N. C.

CROWELL, Martha and Wiley Helms, 3 December 1820, Mecklenburg Co., N. C.

CROWELL, Mary and Adam Hagler, 29 March 1838, Mecklenburg Co., N. C.

CROWELL, Susan I. and John M. Blair, 9 April 1861, Mecklenburg Co., N. C.

CROWELL, William D. and Martha Purviance, 24 May 1831, Mecklenburg Co., N. C.

CRUDUP, George and Priscilla Thomas, 1761, Edgecombe Co., N. C.

CRUDUP, Josiah and Elizabeth Battle, 28 November 1767, Edgecombe Co., N. C.

CRUGER, David and Elizabeth Guerin, June 1786, Charleston, S. C.

CRUGER, Nicholas (Jr.) and (Mrs.) Ann Heyward, 2 October 1799, Charleston, S. C.

CRUMMY, Henry and Magdalene Zorn, 9 June 1752, Orangeburg Co., S. C.

CRUMP, Conrad and Elizabeth Bobbett, 26 November 1740, Mecklenburg Co., N. C.

CRUMP, Jane L. and John Blount, 14 September 1864, Mecklenburg Co., N. C.

CRUMP, Sarah and Erasmus Jordan, 13 February 1845, Mecklenburg Co., N. C.

CRUMPLER, Martha J. and Silas Livermore, 31 October 1861, Williamsburg, N. C.

CRYER, John and Ruth Noble, 1 November 1782, Santee, S. C.

CRYER, Thomas and Elizabeth Powell, 13 July 1725, Orangeburg Co., S. C.

CRYTE, Susanna and John Hess, 19 April 1790, Rowan Co., N. C.

CUDY, Mary D. and William Nelson, 29 September 1827, Mecklenburg Co., N. C.

CULBERS, Sarah and Henry Fuller, 13 November 1856, Laurens Co., S. C.

CULBERTSON, Elizabeth and James Godfrey, 13 January 1859, Laurens Co., S. C.

CULBERTSON, Moses W. and Rachel L. Russell, 25 August 1828, Mecklenburg Co., N. C.

CULBERSON, Robert and Mary Allison, December 1851, Laurens Co., S. C.

CULCHETH, Anne and William Gibbes, 8 August 1716, St. Andrews Parish, S. C.

CULLEN, Winifred and Thomas Trotman, 3 March 1788, Bertie Co., N. C.

CULLENS, Nicholas and Mary Williams 21 October 1757, Chowan Co., N. C.

CULLER, W. W. and George Anna Reed, 1 February 1848, Barnwell District, S. C.

CULLIATT, Mary and Francis Forgatt, 27 May 1784, Jacksonboro, S. C.

CULLIFER, Isaac and Elizabeth Lucas, 1784, Tyrrell Co., N. C.

CULLIFER, Nathaniel and Nelly Miller, 30 May 1834, Bertie Co., N. C.

CULP, Benjamin A. and Caroline Hood, 23 May 1848, Mecklenburg Co., N. C.

CULP, Drury M. and Sarah J. Alexander, 24 July 1841, Mecklenburg Co., N. C.

CULP, John and Milly L. Robison, 27 January 1852, Mecklenburg Co., N. C.

CULPEPPER, Erasmus and Chloe Whitehead, 17 August 1765, Edgecombe Co., N. C.

CUMING, Andrew and Mary Baker, February 1775, Charleston, S. C.

CUMMING, Helen and Arthur Bryan, 6 July 1797, Port Royal Island, S. C.

CUMMINGS, John and Ann Dutart, 13 October 1760, Santee, S. C.

CUMMINGS, John and Elizabeth Airs, 8 October 1801, Charleston, S. C.

CUMMINGS, Martha and John Hester, 28 October 1838, Edgefield District, S. C.

CUMMINGS, Mary and William McKnight, 16 January 1802, Guilford Co., N. C.

CUMMINGS, William and Lottie Evans, 2 January 1833, Edgefield District, S. C.

CUMMINS, Elizabeth and John Edgar, 8 March 1780, Rowan Co., N. C.

CUNNINGHAM, Andrew and Margaret Cochran (widow) 4 January 1767, Pon-pon, S. C.

CUNNINGHAM, Elizabeth and Henry Robinson, 15 August 1809, Mecklenburg Co., N. C.

CUNNINGHAM, Elizabeth and James Hanfield, 25 July 1852, Mecklenburg Co., N. C.

CUNNINGHAM, F. and (Miss) Sarah Dean, 25 December 1854, Edgefield District, S. C.

CUNNINGHAM, Isabel and Robert McCuistion, 23 November 1792, Guilford Co., N. C.

CUNNINGHAM, Jane H. and William Reeves, 20 July 1824, Mecklenburg Co., N. C.

CUNNINGHAM, Jannet and Alexander Robinson, 15 October 1791, Mecklenburg Co., N. C.

CUNNINGHAM, Keziah and William Barnes, 17 November 1819, Mecklenburg Co., N. C.

CUNNINGHAM, Margaret and Jasper Allison, 23 October 1856, Laurens Co., S. C.

CUNNINGHAM, Martha R. and Robert L. Blair, 1 November 1838, Guilford, N. C.

CUNNINGHAM, Matthews and Betsy Galbraith, 16 January 1793, Orange Co., N. C.

CUNNINGHAM, Rebecca and William Johnston, 20 October 1844, Mecklenburg Co., N. C.

CUNNINGHAM, Rosanna and Archibald Huston, 6 October 1784, Rowan Co., N. C.

CUNNINGHAM, Teresa and Thomas Parker, 3 October 1779, Chowan Co., N. C.

CUNNINGHAM, Timothy and Esther Bount, 1784, Tyrrell Co., N. C.

CURLEY, Mary Ann and Joseph M. Rorke, 24 January 1856, Mecklenburg Co., N. C.

CURNAL, Willis and Miss Lanford, 15 September 1859, Laurens Co., S. C.

CURRELL, William and Caroline Draper, January 1832, Washington, N. C.

CURRY, Amelia and John Houser, 8 February 1837, Mecklenburg Co., N. C.

CURRY, Butler and Perneasy Lyons, 3 December 1857, Laurens Co., S. C.

CURRY, Hugh and Elizabeth Nunn, 22 November 1790, Orange Co., N. C.

CURRY, Ivory and Eliza Burdett, 23 December 1847, Laurens Co., S. C.

CURRY, Jenny and Reuben Johnson, 17 September 1816, Mecklenburg Co., N. C.

CURRY, Mary and Ellis Mitchell, 12 February 1857, Guilford Co., N. C.

CURRY, Nixon and Davy Caldwell, 6 September 1819, Mecklenburg Co., N. C.

CURRY, Rachel and Matthew Rogers, 4 December 1851, Laurens Co., S. C.

CURRY, Robert and Sarah Taylor, 6 March 1791, Mecklenburg Co., N. C.

CURRY, William and Elliott Armstrong, 30 August 1866, Laurens Co., S. C.

CUSACK, James and Annie Brown, 30 April 1773, Charleston, S. C.

CUSTIS, John and Elizabeth S. Littledale, 11 October 1777, Chowan Co., N. C.

CUTCHENS, Tabitha and John Hopkins, 16 March 1827, Edgecombe Co., N. C.

CUTHBERT, James and Sarah Barnwell, 5 May 1784, Beaufort, S. C.

CUTHBERTSON, Patsy and John Brooks, 26 November 1825, Mecklenburg Co., N. C.

CUTTIER, Joseph and Ann Mary Sahly, 27 March 1741, Orangeburg Co., S. C.

D

DABS, J. and Mary Hutchinson, 2 January 1844, Laurens Co., S. C.

DAGNELL, Elisha and Nancy Ray, 27 December 1855, Edgefield District, S. C.

DAIGHT, Deliah (widow) and Henry Downing, 30 December 1765, Tyrrell Co., N. C.

DAIL, Elisha and Achsa Mitchell, 24 December 1841, Chowan Co., N. C.

DAIL, Julius and Sarah Mitchell, 26 November 1824, Chowan Co., N. C.

DAIL, Mary and William Miller, 31 December 1846, Chowan Co., N. C.

DAILEY, Sarah (widow) and Robert Egan, 16 March 1775, Chowan Co., N. C.

DALE, Thomas (Dr.) and (Mrs.) Mary Brewton, 28 March 1733, Charleston, S. C.

DALY, Penelope and John Stewart, 21 March 1770, Tyrrell Co., N. C.

DANCY, Rebekah and John Coleman, 7 June 1799, Edgecombe Co., N. C.

DANCY, William and Agnes Little, 20 August 1765, Edgecombe Co., N. C.

DANDRIDGE, Frances (widow) and Samuel Hopkins, 21 June 1770, Charleston, S. C.

DANIEL, Alfred and Elizabeth Shipes, 13 November 1825, Edgefield District, S. C.

DANIEL, Elizabeth and Jonathan Lawrence, May 1777, Charleston, S. C.

DANIEL, Elizabeth and David Magee, 22 November 1796, Guilford Co., N. C.

DANIEL, Hannah and Jeremiah Walker, 1775, Granville Co., N. C.

DANIEL, John and Sarah Raven, 23 January 1736, Charleston, S. C.

DANIEL, Mary and David Royster, 1775, Granville Co., N. C.

DANIEL, Mattison and Jane Watkins, 2 February 1843, Laurens Co., S. C.

DANIEL, Polly and (Dr.) Robert Hendrick, 21 May 1795, Columbia, S. C.

DANIELL, Frances and William Scott, 17 November 1784, Goose Creek, S. C.

DARBY, James and Margaret Elliott, 4 May 1773, Charleston, S. C.

DARBY, Jonathan and Keziah Purdy, 14 July 1772, Chowan Co., N. C.

DARBY, Robert A. and Rebecca Sinkler, 23 October 1800, Charleston, S. C.

DARBY, William and Margaret Evans, 18 August 1797, Charleston, S. C.

DARDEN, Elizabeth and James Griffin, 27 December 1777, Chowan Co., N. C.

DARE, Henry and Margaret Miller (widow), 26 March 1764, Chowan Co., N. C.

DARGAN, Ann and Charles Russell, 22 August 1754, Orangeburg Co., S. C.

DARNELL, Fanny and Zadick Alexander, 4 March 1820, Mecklenburg Co., N. C.

DARNELL, Polly and John Cathorn, 28 December 1805, Mecklenburg Co., N. C.

DARNELL, Sussanna and Thomas Boyd, 19 December 1796, Mecklenburg Co., N. C.

DARNELL, Tabitha and Willis Black, 29 December 1806, Mecklenburg Co., N. C.

DARRELL, Edward and Ann Smith, 15 May 1770, Charleston, S. C.

DARRELL, Frances (widow) and John Todd, 1 January 1786, Charleston, S. C.

DARRELL, Nicholas and (Mrs.) Mary McDougall, 9 August 1800, Charleston, S. C.

DART, Anne and James McCall, 4 May 1777, Charleston, S. C.

DART, Hannah and William Roper (Jr.), 5 May 1771, Charleston, S. C.

DART, Isaac M. and Arabella Rhind, 26 January 1800, Charleston, S. C.

DART, John and Widow Bassett, 16 April 1744, Charleston, S. C.

DART, John and Margaret Hext (widow), 25 April 1746, Charleston, S. C.

DART, John and Martha Motte, 22 January 1765, Charleston, S. C.

DART, John (Jr.), and Henrietta Sommers, 20 December 1772, Charleston, S. C.

DATTWYLER, Ann and Jacob Rumph, 19 May 1748, Orangeburg Co., S. C.

DAUDY, Akillis and Mary Powell, 13 May 1858, Laurens Co., S. C.

DAVENPORT, Ann and Robert Webb, 28 April 1767, Tyrrell Co., N. C.

DAVENPORT, Daniel and Sarah Nicolls, 12 March 1786, Tyrrell Co., N. C.

DAVENPORT, Elkanah and Rachel Hassell, 8 February 1778, Tyrrell Co., N. C.

DAVENPORT, Esther and James Norman, October 1783, Tyrrell Co., N. C.

DAVENPORT, Ezra and Sarah Bateman, 27 December 1785, Tyrrell Co., N. C.

DAVENPORT, Frederick and Joana Freeman, 1784, Tyrrell Co., N. C.

DAVENPORT, Jacob and Joanna Garrett, 1 February 1768, Tyrrell Co., N. C.

DAVENPORT, Jacob and Elizabeth Duncan, 17 February 1779, Tyrrell Co., N. C.

DAVENPORT, James and Ann Mariner, 4 April 1778, Tyrrell Co., N. C.

DAVENPORT, James and Hannah Stephens, 1784, Tyrrell Co., N. C.

DAVENPORT, Joana and John Davenport, 17 April 1779, Tyrrell Co., N. C.

DAVENPORT, John and Joana Davenport, 17 April 1779, Tyrrell Co., N. C.

DAVENPORT, John and Eugenia Henderson, 1 October 1865, Laurens Co., S. C.

DAVENPORT, John and Ann Godwin, July 1783, Tyrrell Co., N. C.

DAVENPORT, Mary and Zebedee Hassell, 15 February 1770, Tyrrell Co., N. C.

DAVENPORT, Rachel and Levi Rowe, 6 April 1785, Tyrrell Co., N. C.

DAVENPORT, Stephen and Elizabeth Alexander, 28 December 1778, Tyrrell Co., N. C.

DAVIDSON, David and Elenor Hinson, 25 March 1788, Bertie Co., N. C.

DAVIDSON, Elizabeth S. and Rufus Read, 24 January 1835, Mecklenburg Co., N. C.

DAVIDSON, Gilbert and Eliza Hahnbaum (widow), 14 January 1801, Charleston, S. C.

DAVIDSON, Harriet E. and David T. Caldwell, 30 March 1826, Mecklenburg Co., N. C.

DAVIDSON, Isabella S. G. and James W. Moore, 19 January 1835, Mecklenburg Co., N. C.

DAVIDSON, John and Margaret Williams, 16 December 1751, Chowan Co., N. C.

DAVIDSON, John and Sarah Dickey, 18 November 1800, Black Mingo, S. C.

DAVIDSON, Margaret and James Harris, 10 December 1813, Mecklenburg Co., N. C.

DAVIDSON, Margaret A. and James H. Blake, 13 September 1820, Mecklenburg Co., N. C.

DAVIDSON, Robert and Mary Mackey, 25 February 1776, Tyrrell Co., N. C.

DAVIDSON, Sarah and Alexander Caldwell, 9 October 1794, Mecklenburg Co., N. C.

DAVIDSON, Sarah P. I. and Thomas J. Johnston, 9 September 1824, Mecklenburg Co., N. C.

DAVIDSON, Susanna and Lewis Griffin, 5 June 1801, Charleston, S. C.

DAVIDSON, Violet and William B. Alexander, 25 August 1791, Mecklenburg Co., N. C.

DAVIS, Angeline and Albert A. Alexander, 13 October 1835, Mecklenburg Co., N. C.

DAVIS, Annis and Henry Harrell, 10 March 1788, Bertie Co., N. C.

DAVIS, Baxter and Mary E. Webb, 1 October 1801, Granville Co., N. C.

DAVIS, Eleanor and James Irwin, 12 December 1845, Mecklenburg Co., N. C.

DAVIS, Elisha and Jennison Lockhart, 1784, Tyrrell Co., N. C.
DAVIS, Eliza and Robert McClure, 24 November 1826, Mecklenburg Co., N. C.
DAVIS, Eliza and William H. McLeary, 23 January 1822, Mecklenburg Co., N. C.
DAVIS, Eliza and Evan Hayler, 24 May 1837, Mecklenburg Co., N. C.
DAVIS, Elizabeth and Thomas Jones, 19 February 1746, Orangeburg Co., S. C.
DAVIS, Elizabeth and William Bennerman, 17 November 1794, Mecklenburg Co., N. C.
DAVIS, Elizabeth and David Ellis, 2 December 1799, Rowan Co., N. C.
DAVIS, Ermenta and Isaac Yetton, 24 September 1814, Mecklenburg Co., N. C.
DAVIS, Esther and John Bell, 12 February 1798, Mecklenburg Co., N. C.
DAVIS, E. R. (Lieutenant) and Martha E. M. Mitchell, August 1812, Charleston, S. C.
DAVIS, Henry and Margaret Price, 1795, Rutherford Co., N. C.
DAVIS, Isabella and John Crisp, 31 March 1857, Laurens Co., S. C.
DAVIS, Jane and John Roberts, 10 March 1802, Mecklenburg Co., N. C.
DAVIS, Jane and Solomon Coover, 6 December 1834, Mecklenburg Co., N. C.
DAVIS, Jean and Aaron Baker, 23 February 1805, Mecklenburg Co., N. C.
DAVIS, Jemima and George Reed, 18 August 1743, Chowan Co., N. C.
DAVIS, Jenney and William Barnett, 24 October 1812, Mecklenburg Co., N. C.
DAVIS, John and Mary Bateman, 1780, Tyrrell Co., N. C.
DAVIS, Jonathan and Matilda Howard, 14 January 1766, Tyrrell Co., N. C.
DAVIS, Julia D. and Charles Petty, 12 April 1859, Spartanburg Co., S. C.
DAVIS, Louisa and Robert Bryson, 23 March 1858, Laurens Co., S. C.
DAVIS, Mary and Robert Johnston, 9 January 1806, Mecklenburg Co., N. C.
DAVIS, Rebecca and John McDowell, 2 September 1799, Mecklenburg Co., N. C.
DAVIS, Rebecca and John Oliver, 26 March 1783, Tyrrell Co., N. C.
DAVIS, Rebecca and Samuel Baker, 16 December, 1804, Mecklenburg Co., N. C.
DAVIS, Richard and Sarah Tarkinton, 26 March 1783, Tyrrell Co., N. C.
DAVIS, Samuel and Salome Fuster, 1740, Orangeburg Co., S. C.
DAVIS, Smith and Happy Cobb, 5 January 1790, Bertie Co., N. C.
DAVIS, Thomas and Sarah Colwell, 28 February 1764, Edgecombe Co., N. C.
DAVIS, Thomas and Mary Cross, 5 February 1782, Santee, S. C.
DAVIS, Thomas and Anne King, 25 December 1769, Edgecombe Co., N. C.
DAVIS, William and Elizabeth Steron, 14 November 1778, Chowan Co., N. C.
DAVIS, William and Margaret Campbell, 11 March 1775, Charleston, S. C.
DAVIS, Zephaniah and Zinah Gray, 7 February 1786, Tyrrell Co., N. C.
DAVIS, Zimmerman and Cornelia McIver, 10 November 1857, Charleston, S. C.
DAVISON, John and Felicia C. Price, 24 March 1757, Chowan Co., N. C.
DAVISON, Robert and Elizabeth Waddell, 2 June 1770, Tyrrell Co., N. C.
DAWES, William S. and Fanny Jackson, 18 July 1785, Chowan Co., N. C.
DAWS, Rosehannah and Jesse Phelps, 1781, Tyrrell Co., N. C.
DAWSON, Barbara and William Abbott, 6 June 1801, Charleston, S. C.
DAWSON, Mary and William Postell, 29 January 1786, Charleston, S. C.
DAWSON, (Miss) Hamilton and Rowland Rugeley, 16 March 1775, Charleston, S. C.
DEADMAN, Elizabeth and Thomas Hicks, 29 October 1787, Rowan Co., N. C.
DEAL, Penelope and William Mitchell, 1 December 1819, Chowan Co., N. C.
DEALE, Malachi and Elizabeth Stacey, 4 December 1786, Chowan Co., N. C.
DEALEY, Robert and Hester Bailey, 22 February 1780, Santee, S. C.

DEAN, James and Dina Even, 1747, Orangeburg Co., S. C.

DEAN, Sarah and F. Cunningham, 25 December 1854, Edgefield District, S. C.

DEAR, Sarah and James Lester, 7 March 1778, Chowan Co., N. C.

DEARMOND, Jane and Aaron Robison, 6 June 1803, Mecklenburg Co., N. C.

DEAS, Allen and Thomas Lowndes, 12 February 1828, Charleston, S. C.

DEAS, David and Widow Michie, 12 February 1751, Charleston, S. C.

DEAS, David and Mary Sommers, 18 October 1800, Charleston, S. C.

DEAS, Elizabeth and Thomas Middleton, 22 December 1778, Crowfield, S. C.

DEAS, Mrs. and (Dr.) John Ramsay, 2 March 1797, Charleston, S. C.

DEAS, Polly and Alexander Inglis, 28 April 1773, Charleston, S. C.

DE BERNIERE, (Miss) and Robert Lane, 13 July 1799, Fayetteville, S. C.

DEBOW, William and Hannah Hunt, 6 October 1800, Charleston, S. C.

DE DAUX, Isabel and Rene Ravenel, 26 February 1856, Pooshwee, S. C.

DEES, Gracy and Samuel Slate (Slade?), 29 December 1822, Edgefield District, S. C.

DE GRASSE, Adelle and John Grochan, 17 February 1801, Charleston, S. C.

DEHART, Mary and Giles Major, 2 November 1779, Rowan Co., N. C.

DE JAU, Anne and Daniel Huger, 19 October 1649, Craven Co., S. C.

DE LA HOWE, John and Anne Boyd (widow), 23 April 1767, Charleston, S. C.

DELANCEY, Alice and Ralph Izard, 1 May 1767, Charleston, S. C.

DELANCY, Peter and Elizabeth Berresford, 1 October 1770, Charleston, S. C.

DELATOUR, Susannah and Peter J. More, 14 March 1785, Charleston, S. C.

DELEGALL, Catherine and Hugh Campbell, May 1747, Beaufort, S. C.

DE LESSILINE, Elizabeth and Samuel Dupre, 12 April 1770, Santee, S. C.

DELIESSELINE, Francis and Nancy Allston, 15 December 1785, Charleston, S. C.

DELONG, John and Rebecca Hammonds, 21 November 1846, Laurens Co., S. C.

DELORA, Anthony and Elizabeth DeWeese, 17 April 1831, Edgefield District, S. C.

DELORCH, Jesse and Penelope Ruffin, 8 March 1768, Edgecombe Co., N. C.

DEMSEY, William and Ann Miller, 25 July 1781, Bertie Co., N. C.

DENDY, Daniel and Elliott Walker, 7 December 1853, Laurens Co., S. C.

DENDY, Eliza and Elijah Moore, 17 May 1866, Laurens Co., S. C.

DENER, George and Elizabeth Patrick, 15 May 1800, Charleston, S. C.

DENHOLM, George and Ann Hill, 23 July 1778, Santee, S. C.

DENKINS, Margaret and James Roberts, 3 June 1799, Mecklenburg Co., N. C.

DENKINS, Mary Ann and Washington Morrison, 15 October 1825, Mecklenburg Co., N. C.

DENNET, Mary and John McAdoo, 14 August 1782, Guilford Co., N. C.

DENNIS, William and Betsy Hawkins, 15 September 1800, Guilford Co., N. C.

DENNISON, James and Ann E. Saylor (widow), 2 September 1796, Charleston, S. C.

DENNY, Pickens and Matilda Vansant, 10 January 1856, Edgefield District, S. C.

DENNY, Thomas and Sarah Lee, 29 October 1769, Santee, S. C.

DENOON, Anne and William B. Brown, 16 January 1801, Charleston, S. C.

DENT, Ann and Risdon Moore, 5 September 1790, Guilford Co., N. C.

DEPASS, Hannah and Benjamin Milhado, 20 April 1796, Charleston, S. C.

DERAMAS, Joseph and Ann Pfund, 1742, Orangeburg Co., S. C.

DERMODY, Thomas and Ann Fleury, 6 July 1769, Chowan Co., N. C.

DERMOND, Jane and Aaron Robinson, 6 June 1803, Mecklenburg Co., N. C.

DERMOND, Martha A. and Joseph F. Hill, 12 November 1835, Mecklenburg Co., N. C.

DERURASEUX, Daniel and Olivia Wood, 14 March 1848, Orangeburg Co., S. C.

DES CHAMPS, Esther and Archibald McClelland, 3 July 1759, Santee, S. C.

DES CHAMPS, Peter and Elizabeth Simmons, 2 August 1759, Santee, S. C.

DESHON, Elizabeth and Maurice Buckley, 4 February 1785, Chowan Co., N. C.

DESHON, Lewis and Elizabeth Rodda, 25 January 1786, Chowan Co., N. C.

DEVEAUX, Hannah and Samuel Ash, July 1785, Beaufort, S. C.

DEVEAUX, Mary and William Brisbane, 22 January 1795, St. Pauls Parish, S. C.

DEW, Abraham and Elizabeth Hickman, 2 December 1763, Edgecombe Co., N. C.

DEWAR, Polly and Robert Moncrief, 2 April 1775, Charleston, S. C.

DEWAR, Sarah and James Simons, 8 January 1784, Charleston, S. C.

DEWEESE, Abigail and James L. Johnson, 24 January 1838, Mecklenburg Co., N. C.

DEWEESE, Ann and John E. Johnson, 8 January 1836, Mecklenburg Co., N. C.

DEWEESE, Catherine B. and Burwell Cashon, 14 August 1839, Mecklenburg Co., N. C.

DEWEESE, Catherine and Ephriam A. Martin, 25 December 1839, Mecklenburg Co., N. C.

DEWEESE, Elizabeth and Anthony DeLora, 17 April 1831, Edgefield District, S. C.

DEWEESE, Elizabeth E. and Samuel I. Armour, 21 January 1843, Mecklenburg Co., N. C.

DEWEESE, Eveline and Jacob Baker, 10 January 1832, Mecklenburg Co., N. C.

DEWEESE, Henrietta and John S. Hill, 5 August 1830, Mecklenburg Co., N. C.

DEWEESE, Joseph and Betty Price, 22 May 1828, Edgefield District, S. C.

DEWEESE, Margaret and James Read, 7 January 1841, Mecklenburg Co., N. C.

DEWEESE, Margaret M. and William G. Barnett, 17 January 1846, Mecklenburg Co., N. C.

DEWICK, Hannah and James Sands, 6 December 1767, Charleston, S. C.

DEXTER, Cecelia and Peter Rembert, 25 January 1782, Santee, S. C.

DEXTER, Henry and Cicely Baldy, 19 November 1761, Santee, S. C.

DE TREVILLE, Harriot L. and Robert Guerrard, 13 January 1801, Beaufort, S. C.

DIAL, Albert and Rebecca Barksdale, 2 December 1847, Laurens Co., S. C.

DIAL, Allen and Louis Barksdale, 8 May 1856, Laurens Co., S. C.

DIAL, Emily and Melmoth Woods, 8 May 1851, Laurens Co., S. C.

DIAL, Emmaline and Andrew Johnson, 9 November 1858, Laurens Co., S. C.

DIAL, Lucinda and Downs Barksdale, 7 September 1843, Laurens Co., S. C.

DIAL, Mary and Robert Stuart, May 1855, Laurens Co., S. C.

DIAL, Mary and Washington Shell, 31 July 1851, Laurens Co., S. C.

DICK, Susanna and Moses McClain, 11 April 1796, Guilford Co., N. C.

DICKENSON, James and Mourning Thomas, 19 November 1770, Edgecombe Co., N. C.

DICKERT, Eve Margaret and John Folk, 23 October 1798, Newberry District, S. C.

DICKEY, Sarah and John Cantzon, 1765, Lancaster Co., S. C.

DICKEY, Sarah and John Davidson, 18 November 1800, Black Mingo, S. C.

DICKENS, John (Rev.) and Elizabeth Gancy, April 1779, N. C.

DICKINSON, Mary Ann and Jared Bunce (of Conn.), 23 December 1801, Charleston, S. C.

DICKSON, Eliza and John M. McLean, 23 March 1831, Mecklenburg Co., N. C.

DICKSON, James and Nancy Moore, 1786, Rowan Co., N. C.

DICKSON, Jeane and Robert Mitchell, 16 September 1786, Orange Co., N. C.

DICKY, Liza and B. F. Nickles, 22 January 1846, Laurens Co., S. C.

DIEDRICH, Agnes (widow) and George Giessendanner, June 1745, Orangeburg Co., S. C.

DIEDRICK, Anne and John Jacob Wymer, 27 January 1756, Orangeburg Co., S. C.

DIEDRICK, Barbara and Richard Hasfort, 3 January 1740, Orangeburg Co., S. C.

DIEL, Ann and Henry Rickenbacher, 1742, Orangeburg Co., S. C.

DIGIN, James and Frances Chapman, 13 May 1776, Chowan Co., N. C.

DILL, Joseph and Elizabeth Croskeys, 2 January 1719, St. Andrews Parish, S. C.

DILL, Mary and David Fox, 17 September 1737, Charleston, S. C.

DILLARD, Dolly and Robert Bell, 26 April 1808, Mecklenburg Co., N. C.

DILLARD, John Alfred and Mary O. Smart, 1 April 1842, Laurens Co., S. C.

DILLARD, Mary J. and William P. Jacobs, 20 April 1865, Laurens Co., S. C.

DILLARD, Thomas J. and Mary O. Smart, 17 January 1833, Laurens Co., S. C.

DILLIARD, John and Mary Moore, 31 March 1762, Edgecombe Co., N. C.

DILLON, James W. and Harriett Jones, 2 April 1851, Marion Co., S. C.

DILLON, Robert and Christina Chiffelle, 6 October 1768, Purrysburg, S. C.

DINKENS, Sarah and Armistead Branch, 18 March 1824, Mecklenburg Co., N. C.

DINKS, Peter and Mary Sedley, 17 August 1790, Orange Co., N. C.

DIRR, Jacob and Eva C. Keyser, 22 December 1754, Orangeburg Co., S. C.

DISTON, Charles and Martha Canty, 16 June 1719, St. Andrews Parish, S. C.

DIXON, Ann and William McFateridge, 1 January 1799, Guilford Co., N. C.

DIXON, Green and Elizabeth Bradley, 12 November 1799, Edgecombe Co., N. C.

DIXON, Mary and James Caldwell, 23 February 1831, Mecklenburg Co., N. C.

DIXON, Polly and James Herndon, 3 May 1814, Orange Co., N. C.

DIXON, Sarah and Henry Clark, 4 December 1857, Mecklenburg Co., N. C.

DIXON, Sterling and (Mrs.) Mary A. Noble, 27 September 1801, Abbeville District, S. C.

DIXON, Thomas and Sarah Sellars, 15 June 1763, Edgecombe Co., N. C.

DIXON, Thomas and Anne Turner, 28 May 1793, Orange Co., N. C.

DOAK, Mary and Alexander McKeen, Jr., 22 September 1795, Guilford Co., N. C.

DOBEL, Sarah and John Paton, 1 September 1801, Charleston, S. C.

DOBEY, Mary Ann and Benajah Rambo, 22 October 1839, Edgefield District, S. C.

DOBSON, Jane and Samuel W. Newell, 5 December 1843, Mecklenburg Co., N. C.

DODD, Mary Ann and John Hall, 10 April 1774, Charleston, S. C.

DOEBER, Chrisnow (widow) and William Cowper, 15 January 1778, Chowan Co., N. C.

DOHERTY, Anne and James Bryson, 11 March 1799, Mecklenburg Co., N. C.

DOHERTY, Elizabeth and Richard Rankin, 3 June 1793, Mecklenburg Co., N. C.

DOHERTY, Elizabeth B. and James N. Bain, 29 March 1825, Mecklenburg Co., N. C.

DOHERTY, Mary and Samuel Rankin, 16 November 1791, Mecklenburg Co., N. C.

DOHERTY, Minty and Adam McKaven, 9 February 1811, Mecklenburg Co., N. C.

DOHERTY, Rebecca and David Alexander, 17 September 1814, Mecklenburg Co., N. C.

DOLLIVER, Henry and (Mrs.) Margaret Hazzard, 14 July 1799, Charleston, S. C.

DOMINIGUE, Mary and Thomas Miller, 28 November 1801, Chowan Co., N. C.

DON, Jane and William B. Elmore, 6 August 1837, Edgefield District, S. C.

DONALDSON, Casper and Peggy Bland, 23 January 1823, Edgefield District, S. C.

DONALDSON, Jeane and John Graham, 21 December 1786, Rowan Co., N. C.

DONALDSON, Milton L. and Margaret L. Ware, 23 January 1866, Greenville Co., S. C.

DONALSON, Mary and William Clark, 24 September 1782, Orange Co., N. C.

DONELSON, Mary and Josiah Phelps, 6 February 1780, Tyrrell Co., N. C.

DONNELL, Jean and Elihu McMire, 11 March 1800, Guilford Co., N. C.

DONNOM, Isaac and Sarah Crawford, 2 March 1784, Waxhaw, S. C.

DONOVAN, Sally and John Remington (Jr.), 6 April 1774, Charleston, S. C.

DONOHOE, Thomas and Keziah Saunders, 1774, Orange Co., N. C.

DORFF, Hans and Magdalene Pieren (widow), 10 December 1740, Orangeburg Co., S. C.

DORHAM, Susan and Potiller Garrett, 24 July 1851, Laurens Co., S. C.

DORN, William and Emily Catherine, 6 December 1855, Edgefield District, S. C.

DORRELL, Jane and Joseph Quinby, 23 April 1818, Charleston, S. C.

DORROH, Samuel and Margaret McCue, 26 December 1865, Laurens Co., S. C.

DORSEY, Frederick and Penelope Bonner, 16 July 1764, Tyrrell Co., N. C.

DORSEY, Nancy and Philip Howard, 20 September 1797, Rowan Co., N. C.

DOTT, David and Sally Baker, 13 February 1768, Charleston, S. C.

DOUGHTY, Polly and John Webb, 3 January 1769, Charleston, S. C.

DOUGHTY, Rebecca C. and Bartholomew Gaillard, 6 March 1800, Charleston, S. C.

DOUGHTY, Thomas and Mary Legare, 11 October 1768, Charleston, S. C.

DOUGHTY, William and Rachel Porcher, 22 February 1770, Charleston, S. C.

DOUGHTY, William and Susannah Broughton, October 1783, Charleston, S. C.

DOUGLAS, Alexander and Elizabeth Webb, 20 November 1777, Chowan Co., N. C.

DOUGLAS, Alexander and Eleanor Carew, 2 January 1801, Charleston, S. C.

DOUGLAS, Alexander S. and Mary E. Byers, 6 November 1860, Spartanburg, S. C.

DOUGLAS, James T. and Mary Jeter, 5 December 1866, Union, S. C.

DOUGLAS, Mary and John McDuffie, 20 May 1807, Robinson Co., N. C.

DOUGLAS, Sallie B. and Daniel A. Townsend, 4 November 1864, Union, S. C.

DOUXSAINT, Catherine and James Postell, 30 December 1764, Charleston, S. C.

DOUXSAINT, Jane and Samuel Thomas, 30 October 1768, Charleston, S. C.

DOW, Margaret and William S. Norment, 12 September 1812, Mecklenburg Co., N. C.

DOW, Susanah and Abel Baker, 4 January 1816, Mecklenburg Co., N. C.

DOWD, Sarah and Thomas Cromartee, 23 July 1768, Chowan Co., N. C.

DOWELL, Sarah and Abraham Hawkins, 27 October 1798, Rowan Co., N. C.

DOWNING, Henry and Deliah Daight (widow), 30 December 1765, Tyrrell Co., N. C.

DOWNS, Adalade and William Hill, 19 November 1844, Laurens Co., S. C.

DOWNS, Cornelia and George Barksdale, 15 October 1846, Laurens Co., S. C.

DOWNS, Sophy and Thomas Downs, 25 September 1845, Laurens Co., S. C.

DOWNS, Thomas and Sophy Downs, 25 September 1845, Laurens Co., S. C.

DOWNY, James and Sally Huggens, 11 February 1858, Laurens Co., S. C.

DOYEY, Daniel and Ann R. Webb, January 1784, Charleston, S. C.

DOYLEY, Nancy and Benjamin Webb, 16 March 1775, Ashepoo, S. C.

DRAKE, Edmund and Mary Mann, 3 December 1763, Edgecombe Co., N. C.

DRAKE, Elizabeth Margaret and Dougal McCormick, 29 November 1859, Roberson Co., N. C.

DRAKE, Laura (widow) and Jasper Gibbs, 7 April 1839, Pottersville, S. C.

DRAPER, Caroline and William Currell, January 1832, Washington, N. C.

DRAYTON, Charles (Dr.) and Esther Middleton, 24 February 1774, Berkeley Co., S. C.

DRAYTON, John and Charlotte Bull, 14 November 1642, Charleston, S. C.

DRAYTON, John and Miss Glen, February 1752, Charleston, S. C.

DRAYTON, John and Rebecca Perry, 16 March 1775, St. Pauls Parish, S. C.

DRAYTON, John and Mary Tiddiman, 6 November 1794, Charleston, S. C.

DRAYTON, Mary and Richard Fuller, 21 December 1721, St. Andrews Parish, S. C.

DRAYTON, Mary and Edward Fenwicke, 2 March 1753, Berkeley Co., S. C.

DRAYTON, Mary (widow) and John Ainslie, 17 June 1762, Charleston, S. C.

DRAYTON, Miss and Tobias Bowles, 12 March 1795, Charleston, S. C.

DRAYTON, Thomas and Elizabeth Bull, 26 December 1730, Charleston, S. C.

DRAYTON, William H. and Dorothy Golightly, 29 March 1764, Charleston, S. C.

DREW, Peggy and Peter Harkey, 9 December 1813, Mecklenburg Co., N. C.

DRING, Percival and Elizabeth Crook, 18 March 1761, Santee, S. C.

DRUMMOND, Angelina and P. F. Moore, 27 August 1865, Laurens Co., S. C.

DRUMMOND, Eugenie and Henry Ferguson, 24 May 1866, Laurens Co., S. C.

DRUMMOND, James and Gracey Thompson, 19 March 1800, Charleston, S. C.

DRUMMOND, Sue and Burwell Bobo, 29 September 1859, Laurens Co., S. C.

DRY, Dorothy and John Moreton, 30 July 1747, Charleston, S. C.

DRY, Sarah and Benjamin Smith (Jr.), 20 November 1777, Charleston, S. C.

DRY, William and Mary Jane Rhett, February 1746, Charleston, S. C.

DRYDEN, Eleanor (Mrs.) and David Bruce, 7 April 1765, Charleston, S. C.

DUBBERT, Elizabeth R. and J. J. Scroter, 10 November 1800, Charleston, S. C.

DUBOISE, Susanna (widow) and Joseph Bee, 13 November 1783, Charleston, S. C.

DUBOSE, Catherine and Isaac Dubose, 6 July 1797, Camden, S. C.

DUBOSE, Daniel and Frances Semans, 11 November 1766, Santee, S. C.

DUBOSE, David and Susanna Y. Moncrief, 20 February 1800, Wadmelaw Island, S. C.

DUBOSE, Isaac and Catherine Dubose, 6 July 1797, Camden, S. C.

DUBOSE, Joanna and David Gaillard, 23 September 1773, Santee, S. C.

DUBOSE, Joseph and Mary Ann Mell, 16 October 1800, Santee, S. C.

DUBOSE, Samuel and (Mrs.) Martha White, 6 December 1801, Charleston, S. C.

DUBOSQUE, Ann and Daniel Jordan, 31 May 1759, Santee, S. C.

DUCHE, Benjamin and Agnes Given, May 1784, Beaufort, S. C.

DUCKETT, James and Sarah Hunter, 4 June 1845, Laurens Co., S. C.

DUCKWORTH, Mary and William Hunter, 1816, Mecklenburg Co., N. C.

DUDLEY, Lou A. and W. McColl, 26 April 1848, Marlboro Co., S. C.

DUDLEY, M. A. and James Osgood, 16 October 1865, Mecklenburg Co., N. C.

DUEST, Mary and John A. McKibben, 31 January 1825, Mecklenburg Co., N. C.

DUFFUS, John and Ann Johnson, 2 October 1800, Charleston, S. C.

DUFFY, Elizabeth and Thomas McKibben, 1 March 1825, Mecklenburg Co., N. C.

DUFFY, Jane and John Bird, 9 January 1810, Mecklenburg Co., N. C.

DUGAN, Aaron and Susanna Swain, 28 March 1767, Tyrrell Co., N. C.

DUGAN, Elizabeth and Samuel Holladay, 14 November 1763, Tyrrell Co., N. C.

DUGGAR, Sarah and Charles Edwards, 6 February 1790, Orange Co., N. C.

DUGGAR, Shadwick and Sally Hogan, 16 October 1793, Orange Co., N. C.

DUKE, Benjamin and Rachel Higgins (widow), 30 August 1784, Charleston, S. C.

DUKE, Elizabeth and Thomas Jackson, 10 June 1784, Charleston, S. C.

DUKE, Hezekiah and Puss Cahoon, 1780, Tyrrell Co., N. C.

DULIN, Catherine and Thomas Cochran, 17 January 1816, Mecklenburg Co., N. C.

DULIN, Nancy and William C. Miller, 16 November 1849, Mecklenburg Co., N. C.

DULIN, Surena and James Hall, 6 February 1851, Mecklenburg Co., N. C.

DULLES, Joseph and Sophia Heatley, February 1785, Charleston, S. C.

DUNBAR, Martha and Samuel Cameron, 15 January 1797, Charleston, S. C.

DUNBAR, Mary (widow) and Henry Gibbew, 30 August 1791, Charleston, S. C.

DUNBAR, Robert and Elizabeth Randolph, 9 April 1840, Edgefield District, S. C.

DUNBAR, Sarah and Andrew Boyd, 12 December 1793, Mecklenburg Co., N. C.

DUNBAR, Thomas and Mary Withers, 2 September 1784, Prince George Parish, S. C.

DUNBAR, William and (Mrs.) Elizabeth Simons, 29 December 1799, Charleston, S. C.

DUNCAN, Elizabeth and Jacob Davenport, 17 February 1779, Tyrrell Co., N. C.

DUNCAN, Mary and Thomas Wade, 4 March 1774, Chowan Co., N. C.

DUNCAN, William W. and Medora Rice, 19 March 1861, Union, S. C.

DUNCOMBE, James and Delilah Walker, 17 May 1785, Tyrrell Co., N. C.

DUNLAP, Harriet K. and Edward H. Jones, 2 November 1843, Mecklenburg Co., N. C.

DUNLAP, John A. and Mary H. Blair, 1820, Lancaster Co., S. C.

DUNLAP, Robert D. and Emily Cousau, 11 February 1830, Waxhaw, S. C.

DUNN, Elizabeth and Heny Giles, 19 June 1786, Rowan Co., N. C.

DUNN, Isabella and Thomas Moore, 26 February 1793, Mecklenburg Co., N. C.

DUNN, Isabella and John McLeary, 5 February 1823, Mecklenburg Co., N. C.

DUNN, Isabella and William A. McGinn, 28 August 1825, Mecklenburg Co., N. C.

DUNN, Louisa M. and Andrew I. Essell, 17 October 1839, Mecklenburg Co., N. C.

DUNN, Martha and William Beatty, 6 October 1807, Mecklenburg Co., N. C.

DUNN, Martha and David Cox, 6 January 1830, Mecklenburg Co., N. C.

DUNN, Mary and John Harlan, 5 December 1795, Mecklenburg Co., N. C.

DUNNING, Anne and Nicholas Harman, 3 November 1802, Bertie Co., N. C.

DUNNING, Charles and Elizabeth Boyce, 8 December 1783, Bertie Co., N. C.

DUNNING, Delitha and John Stallings, 19 September 1789, Bertie Co., N. C.

DUNNING, Elizabeth and James Long, 12 April 1762, Tyrrell Co., N. C.

DUNNING, Elizabeth and John Jones, 23 January 1798, Bertie Co., N. C.

DUNNING, Mary and John Askew, 17 August 1790, Bertie Co., N. C.

DUNNING, Minnie and Shadrack Holden, 4 February 1799, Bertie Co., N. C.

DUNNING, Uriah and Ann Early, 17 May 1790, Bertie Co., N. C.

DUNSCOMBE, Charlotte and James Hinton, 23 December 1800, Charleston, S. C.

DUNSCOMBE, Henrietta and Allen Clark, 10 November 1777, Chowan Co., N. C.

DUNSCOMBE, Samuel and Henrietta Butler (nee Wilson), 21 December 1752, Chowan Co., N. C.

DUNSTAN, Elenor and Daniel Goldsmith, 20 April 1753, Chowan Co., N. C.

DUNTON, Martin and Catherine Phelps, 5 May 1779, Tyrrell Co., N. C.

DUPONT, Jane E. and Peter Boillet, 14 October 1784, Charleston, S. C.

DUPRE, Cornelius and Mary Hartley (widow), 2 December 1784, Charleston, S. C.

DUPRE, Samuel and Elizabeth DeLessiline, 12 April 1770, Santee, S. C.

DUPREE, Ann and Daniel Sinkler, 20 August 1769, Santee, S. C.

DUPREE, Ann and Charles Gaillard, 13 September 1770, Santee, S. C.

DUPREE, Daniel and Mary Normand, 8 June 1759, Santee, S. C.

DURANT, Laura E. and Thomas A. Covington, July 1853, Richmond Co., N. C.

DURANT, Virginia and B. H. Covington, 23 December 1858, Richmond Co., N. C.

DURBIN, Mary and Ehi Collens, 30 August 1781, Orange Co., N. C.

DURHAM, Elizabeth and William Hancock, 1715, Pitt Co., N. C.

DURHAM, Margaret and Thomas Chandlier, 29 July 1838, Edgefield District, S. C.

DURHAM, Sarah and Edward Garrett, 18 December 1850, Laurens Co., S. C.

DURISOE, William F. and Mary A. E. Roper, 7 March 1830, Edgefield District, S. C.

DUTARQUE, John and Lydia Gaillard, 24 August 1774, Charleston, S. C.

DUTARQUE, Martha and Benjamin Wigfall, 2 August 1771, Berkeley Co., S. C.

DUTARQUE, Mary and John Jennings, 20 January 1765, Charleston, S. C.

DUTART, Ann and John Cummings, 13 October 1760, Santee, S. C.

DUTART, John and Mary Boineau, 1 March 1764, Santee, S. C.

DUVALL, Marion and Susan Hitch, 12 January 1860, Laurens Co., S. C.

DWIGHT, Daniel (Rev.) and Esther Cordes, 21 April 1747, Charleston, S. C.

DWIGHT, Daniel (Rev.) and Christiana Broughton, January 1732, Charleston, S. C.

DWIGHT, Esther and Henry Ravenel, 19 January 1819, Pooshwee, S. C.

DWIGHT, Mary and John Middleton, 1782, Tyrrell Co., N. C.

E

EADES, Ezekial and Polly Barrett, 12 January 1799, Rowan Co., N. C.

EAGLE, Margaret and Watson Robinson, 25 June 1850, Mecklenburg Co., N. C.

EAKES, Nancy and John Blair, 3 November 1808, Mecklenburg Co., N. C.

EAKIN, Jane and Thomas McClane, 22 December 1800, Guilford Co., N. C.

EAKIN, Nancy and Robert McClain, 6 May 1791, Guilford Co., N. C.

EAREY, Catherine and Peter Edleman, 31 January 1787, Rowan Co., N. C.

EARL, Elizabeth and Charles Johnson, 10 February 1785, Chowan Co., N. C.

EARL, William and Mary Webb, 9 September 1779, Chowan Co., N. C.

EARLE, Elias and Frances Robinson, 17 September 1782, Charleston, S. C.

EARLE, Samuel and Harriet Harrison, 12 March 1793, Pendleton Co., S. C.

EARLE, Samuel L. and Eliza Harrison, 24 December 1840, Greenville, S. C.

EARLY, Ann and Uriah Dunning, 17 May 1790, Bertie Co., N. C.

EARLY, Thomas and Betsy Mitchell, 25 September 1821, Bertie Co., N. C.

EARNHARDT, Leah and James Montgomery, 4 August 1851, Rowan Co., N. C.

EASON, Jacob and Mary Walton, 1 November 1774, Chowan Co., N. C.

EASON, Reuben and Mary Holladay, 24 December 1762, Tyrrell Co., N. C.

EASOR, Obed and Frances Lester, 17 February 1800, Edgecombe Co., N. C.

EASTER, Mary and Jonathan Bogle, 7 September 1801, Charleston, S. C.

EATON, Anne and (Dr.) William Remington, 19 May 1769, Edisto, S. C.

EATON, Daniel and Elizabeth Carter, 17 March 1798, Rowan Co., N. C.

EATON, Elizabeth and Robert Erwine, 22 February 1783, Rowan Co., N. C.

EATON, George and Elizabeth Hughey, 11 June 1779, Rowan Co., N. C.

EATON, Isaac and Phebe Hall, 27 November 1768, Rowan Co., N. C.

EATON, Miss —— and Benjamin Garner, 23 July 1798, Rowan Co., N. C.

EATON, Sallie and James Taylor, 19 December 1786, Granville Co., N. C.

EATON, Thomas (Major) and Elizabeth Wallis, 27 March 1793, Orange Co., N. C.

EBERHARD, Thomas and Mary Moor, 1746, Orangeburg Co., S. C.

EBERLY, Elizabeth and Daniel Strobel, 1787, Orangeburg Co., S. C.

EBERLY, Hans and Ann Marckly, 1748, Orangeburg Co., S. C.

EBERSON, Susannah and Josiah Bonneau, 13 September 1744, Ponpon, S. C.

EBERT, Gotlieb and Anna Amacher, 27 December 1751, Orangeburg Co., S. C.

ECCLES, John and Mary Johnston, 1 March 1788, Rowan Co., N. C.

ECCLES, Jonathan and Catherine Thornton, 1805, Camden, S. C.

ECCLESTON, Agnes (widow) and Jacob Boyce, 7 March 1775, Chowan Co., N. C.

ECCLESTON, John and Mary Garrett, 22 September 1785, Chowan Co., N. C.

ECHESON, Edmond and Edith Richardson, 14 October 1779, Rowan Co., N. C.

ECKLE, Jacob and Anne M. Little, 5 January 1779, Rowan Co., N. C.

ECTOR, Samuel and Susannah Porter, 30 August 1774, Rowan Co., N. C.

EDGAR, John and Elizabeth Cummins, 8 March 1780, Rowan Co., N. C.

EDGAR, Peggy and Thomas Lambell, 14 April 1737, Ashley Ferry, S. C.

EDLEMAN, Peter and Catherine Early, 31 January 1787, Rowan Co., N. C.

EDWARDS, Abbie S. and Harry H. Wyman, May 1866, Waterboro, S. C.

EDWARDS, Amelia E. and James J. Brown, 8 January 1857, Mecklenburg Co., N. C.

EDWARDS, Catherine and Philip Gadsden, 12 November 1783, Charleston, S. C.

EDWARDS, Charles and Sarah Duggar, 6 February 1790, Orange Co., N. C.

EDWARDS, Elizabeth and Charles McCormick, 13 October 1779, Guilford Co., N. C.

EDWARDS, Elizabeth and John Bee Holmes, 12 November 1783, Charleston, S. C.

EDWARDS, Griffith and Mary Barrett, 19 October 1774, Rowan Co., N. C.

EDWARDS, James and Rachel Hassell, 1781, Tyrrell Co., N. C.

EDWARDS, John and Rebecca Holmes (widow), 30 December 1773, Charleston, S. C.

EDWARDS, John (Jr.) and Polly Barksdale, 1 December 1773, Charleston, S. C.

EDWARDS, John and Frances Patterson, August 1796, Rowan Co., N. C.

EDWARDS, John and Samantha Brown, 24 December 1850, Laurens Co., S. C.

EDWARDS, Joseph and Mary Wolpcade, 3 May 1785, Rowan Co., N. C.

EDWARDS, Mary Ann and Young Hitch, 19 January 1847, Laurens Co., S. C.

EDWARDS, Sarah and Bradly Holcomb, 27 January 1848, Laurens Co., S. C.

EDWARDS, West and Elizabeth Penn, 1749, Greene Co., N. C.

EELBECK, Joseph and Sarah Pagett, 2 September 1750, Chowan Co., N. C.

EGAN, Robert and Sarah Dailey (widow), 16 March 1775, Chowan Co., N. C.

EGGENDER, David and Margaret Wise, 18 June 1785, Rowan Co., N. C.

EGGERS, Landrine and Joana Silvers, 16 April 1779, Rowan Co., N. C.

EGGLESTON, Barbary and Michael Wiseman, 11 July 1799, Rowan Co., N. C.

EHRHARDT, Conrad and Anna D. King, 16 February 1851, Barnwell Co., S. C.

EICHOLTZ, Geore and Anne Rodecap, 13 June 1774, Rowan Co., N. C.

ELAM, Mary E. and Wyatt L. Holmes, 28 November 1854, Edgefield District, S. C.

ELBERSON, Austin and Joana Davis, 7 April 1754, Chowan Co., N. C.

ELDER, Andrew and Margaret Cohort, 19 February 1787, Rowan Co., N. C.

ELDER, Anne and Robert Gay, 2 December 1779, Rowan Co., N. C.

ELDER, James and Elizabeth Scott, 23 August 1764, Chowan Co., N. C.

ELDER, James and Sarah Stevenson, 3 March 1767, Rowan Co., N. C.

ELDER, Janus and Jane Black, 1 March 1773, Chowan Co., N. C.

ELDER, Thomas (Dr.) and Charlotte Hartley, April 1773, Charleston, S. C.

ELERSON, Elizabeth and James Elerson, 7 June 1753, Orangeburg Co., S. C.

ELERSON, James and Elizabeth Elerson, 7 June 1753, Orangeburg Co., S. C.

ELIZABETH, Mary and John Lassiter, 22 April 1790, Bertie Co., N. C.

ELLENBERGER, John F. and Catherine Motz, 28 January 1794, Rowan Co., N. C.

ELLER, Elizabeth and John Ernhart, 29 December 1795, Rowan Co., N. C.

ELLER, John and Catherine Fost, 10 August 1785, Rowan Co., N. C.

ELLER, John and Susanna Kerns, 5 November 1792, Rowan Co., N. C.

ELLER, John and Mary Ernhart, 14 December 1793, Rowan Co., N. C.

ELLER, Margaret and Joseph Groves, 4 September 1796, Rowan Co., N. C.

ELLER, Susanna and John Eller, 9 October 1782, Rowan Co., N. C.

ELLET, Isaac and Charity Howard, 25 August 1798, Rowan Co., N. C.

ELLIAS, Nancy and Lewis Mitchell, 29 November 1827, Chowan Co., N. C.

ELLIOT, Humphrey and Elizabeth Harford, 25 January 1725, Berkeley Co., S. C.

ELLIOT, Jenny B. and Lawson Alexander, 6 May 1828, Mecklenburg Co., N. C.

ELLIOT, John and Susanna Claver, 18 September 1787, Rowan Co., N. C.

ELLIOT, Martha and Andrew McKee, 28 May 1791, Mecklenburg Co., N. C.

ELLIOT, Mathers and David T. Cowan, 15 March 1808, Mecklenburg Co., N. C.

ELLIOT, Thomas and Mary Pinckney, 27 October 1785, Charleston, S. C.

ELLIOTT, Charlotte and Henry Reeves, September 1763, Charleston, S. C.

ELLIOTT, Claudia and George Inglis, 30 April 1759, Stono, S. C.

ELLIOTT, Joseph and Catherine Brisbane, 24 March 1763, Berkeley Co., S. C.

ELLIOTT, Joseph and Hannah Brown, 4 June 1767, Rowan Co., N. C.

ELLIOTT, Katherine (widow) and Andrew Hewatt, 19 June 1773, Charleston, S. C.

ELLIOTT, Keziah and John Robinson, 31 December 1774, Chowan Co., N. C.

ELLIOTT, Margaret and James Darby, 4 May 1773, Charleston, S. C.

ELLIOTT, Mary and Culcheth Golightly, 1 April 1746, Charleston, S. C.

ELLIOTT, Mary and Robert Cochran, 3 February 1763, Charleston, S. C.

ELLIOTT, Mary and William Guerin, 24 November 1763, Charleston, S. C.

ELLIOTT, Mary and Nicholas Miller, 19 September 1844, Guilford Co., N. C.

ELLIOTT, Mary and William Miles, 26 October 1769, Wappoo, S. C.

ELLIOTT, Robert and Elizabeth Scriver, 3 February 1720, St. Andrews Parish, S. C.

ELLIOTT, Sarah and Archibald Stanyarne, May 1759, Stono, S. C.

ELLIOTT, Sarah A. and Francis Ross, 3 February 1743, Berkeley Co., S. C.

ELLIOTT, William and Elizabeth Baker, 13 December 1721, St. Andrews Parish, S. C.

ELLIOTT, William (Jr.) and Hester Butler, 24 February 1722, St. Andrews Parish S. C.

ELLIS, David and Elizabeth Davis, 2 December 1799, Rowan Co., N. C.

ELLIS, Etheldred and Elizabeth McKnight, 14 July 1795, Rowan Co., N. C.

ELLIS, Evan and Catherine Beachem, 17 December 1791, Rowan Co., N. C.

ELLIS, Isaac and Elizabeth Railsback, 26 April 1791, Rowan Co., N. C.

ELLIS, James and Lucy Davis, 20 June 1788, Rowan Co., N. C.

ELLIS, John and Margaret Bryan, 11 March 1779, Rowan Co., N. C.

ELLIS, John and Rebecca Loften, 11 June 1796, Rowan Co., N. C.

ELLIS, Mowring and James Fallow, 28 February 1763, Chowan Co., N. C.

ELLIS, Radford and Elizabeth Macay, 6 May 1788, Rowan Co., N. C.

ELLIS, Rebecca and James Farmer, 27 January 1774, Santee, S. C.

ELLIS, Reuben and Lucy Johnston, 20 January 1804, Edgecombe Co., N. C.

ELLIS, Richard and Elizabeth Greene, 22 April 1784, Beaufort, S. C.

ELLIS, Sabina and (Dr.) David Ramsay, 9 February 1775, Charleston, S. C.

ELLIS, Samuel and Martha Howard, 15 July 1788, Rowan Co., N. C.

ELLIS, Richard and Polly Snell, 16 May 1785, Charleston, S. C.

ELLIS, William (Jr.) and Ann Riddle, 27 March 1792, Rowan Co., N. C.

ELLISON, Andrew and Jean Todd, 4 September 1786, Rowan Co., N. C.

ELMES, Margaret and Emanuel Smith, December 1722, St. Andrews Parish, S. C.

ELMORE, Athenatious and Susannah Penix, 5 July 1788, Orange Co., N. C.

ELMORE, Spencer and Eliza Lott, 1 December 1836, Edgefield District, S. C.

ELMORE, William and Jane Don, 6 August 1837, Edgefield District, S. C.

ELMS, Mary and John Green, 28 November 1719, St. Andrews Parish, S. C.

ELMS, William and Sarah Fields, July 1784, Chehaw, S. C.

ELSTON, Benjamin (Sr.) and Elizabeth Long, 18 November 1786, Burke Co., N. C.

ELSTON, Elias and Jean McCartney, 12 November 1796, Rowan Co., N. C.

ELSTON, Jonathan and Mary Wiatt, 9 August 1793, Rowan Co., N. C.

ELSTON, Sarah and Frederick Goss, 1 January 1787, Rowan Co., N. C.

ELSTON, William and Hab. Doty, 5 May 1797, Rowan Co., N. C.

EMBER, William and Franky Seers, 15 May 1794, Rowan Co., N. C.

EMBERSON, Sarah and Joseph S. Moore, 20 December 1826, Mecklenburg Co., N. C.

EMERSON, Daisy and George Hutchinson, 11 June 1799, Mecklenburg Co., N. C.

EMERSON, Daisy and Matthew Ormond, 4 June 1818, Mecklenburg Co., N. C.

EMMONS, Kissiah and William Welch, 7 January 1858, Laurens Co., S. C.

ENEX, Susanna and James Holstein, 14 July 1779, Rowan Co., N. C.

ENDID, Mary and John Trott, 1788, Charleston, S. C.

ENDLESS, Thomas and Mary Johnson, 9 May 1779, Chowan Co., N. C.

ENGLAND, Martha and Hill Hewitt, 30 October 1782, Santee, S. C.

ENGLAND, Thomas and Elizabeth Rembert, 12 November 1782, Santee, S. C.

ENGLISH, Mary and Austin F. Peay, 4 January 1801, Camden, S. C.

ENNIS, James T. and Clary Andrews, 3 December 1799, Edgecombe Co., N. C.

ENNIS, John and Jane Black, 30 January 1767, Rowan Co., N. C.

ENOCHS, David and Elizabeth Wilson, 29 January 1794, Rowan Co., N. C.

ENOCHS, Elizabeth and Ephriam Hampton, 28 March 1794, Rowan Co., N. C.

ENOCHS, Enoch and Alida Rumley, 30 September 1789, Rowan Co., N. C.

ENOCHS, Polly and Spencer Glascock, 12 September 1791, Rowan Co., N. C.

ENOCHS, Sally and Joseph Howard, 20 December 1796, Rowan Co., N. C.

ENOCHS, Thomas and Nancy Bryan, 16 October 1786, Rowan Co., N. C.

ENOM, Randolph A. and Nancy A. Carothers, 1846, York Co., S. C.

ENSLEY, Mary and Benjamin Hide, 9 January 1775, Rowan Co., N. C.

ENSLOW, Mary and Abraham Gellahan, 12 April 1779, Rowan Co., N. C.

ERNEST, George and Delily Bussy, 8 February 1793, Rowan Co., N. C.

ERNHART, Henry and Eve Wibell, 24 June 1791, Rowan Co., N. C.

ERNHART, John and Catherine Cobble, 23 May 1796, Rowan Co., N. C.

ERNHART, John and Elizabeth Eller, 29 December 1795, Rowan Co., N. C.

ERNHART, Mary and John Eller, 14 December 1793, Rowan Co., N. C.

ERNST, Anna Barbara (widow) and Casper Kuhn, 28 June 1750, Orangeburg Co., S. C.

ERNST, Anthony and Ann Barbara Gyger, 1740, Orangeburg Co., S. C.

ERNST, Elizabeth and John C. Hapoldt, 22 May 1795, Charleston, S. C.

ERNST, George Adam and Ann Barbara Tapp, (widow), 1740, Orangeburg Co., S. C.

ERVIN, Christopher and Mary Lyall, 26 February 1782, Rowan Co., N. C.

ERVIN, William and Mary Adams, 13 October, 1788, Rowan Co., N. C.

ERWIN, Alexi and Margaret Patton (widow) 21 January 1786, Rowan Co., N. C.

ERWIN, George and Elizabeth Lyall, 8 February 1796, Rowan Co., N. C.

ERWIN, James and Jennet Andrews, 10 October 1766, Rowan Co., N. C.

ERWIN, Jane and Richard Graham, 20 October 1779, Rowan Co., N. C.

ERWIN, John and Jane Brown, 19 October 1772, Rowan Co., N. C.

ERWIN, John and Margaret Young, 25 April 1786, Rowan Co., N. C.

ERWIN, John and Alee Brandon, 28 July 1779, Rowan Co., N. C.

ERWIN, Joseph and Catherine Cowan, 17 May 1792, Rowan Co., N. C.

ERWIN, William and Elizabeth Orde, 3 March 1766, Rowan Co., N. C.

ERWIN, William and Isabella Brown, 10 February 1775, Rowan Co., N. C.

ERWIN, William and Matilda Sharp, May 1788, Rowan Co., N. C.

ERWIN, William and Rachel Woods, 28 November 1795, Rowan Co., N. C.

ERWINE, Robert and Elizabeth Eaton, 22 February 1783, Rowan Co., N. C.

ESMOND, Margaret (widow) and John Imrie, 10 October 1774, Charleston, S. C.

ESNGLER, Susanna and George H. Arnold, 5 August 1812, Mecklenburg Co., N. C.

ESPEY, James and Sarah Baker, 2 January 1786, Orange Co., N. C.

ESPEY, Samuel and Elizabeth Sloane, 5 April 1785, Rowan Co., N. C.

ESSELL, Andrew I. and Louisa M. Dunn, 17 October 1839, Mecklenburg Co., N. C.

ESTEL, Boardman, and (Mrs.) Sarah Huff, 21 December 1800, Charleston, S. C.

ESTEP, Samuel and Susannah Adams, 3 November 1789, Rowan Co., N. C.

ESTES, Aaron and Frances Hudson, 13 July 1790, Orange Co., N. C.

ETCHESON, Henry and Mary Chaffin, 22 November 1794, Rowan Co., N. C.

ETHERIDGE, Rachel and Nathaniel Mitchell, 30 April 1787, Chowan Co., N. C.

ETTLEMAN, John and Kelly Bless, 5 January 1789, Rowan Co., N. C.

EUBANKS, Sarah and Hezekiah Wood, 4 December 1856, Edgefield District, S. C.

EUSTIS, Abraham (Gen.) and Patience W. B. Izard, 15 May 1823, St. Georges Parish, S. C.

EVANCE, Charlotte and Thomas Cordes, 21 November 1784, Santee, S. C.

EVANS, Alse and Jasper Hardison, 3 September 1763, Tyrrell Co., N. C.

EVANS, Esther and (Dr.) Thomas T. Tucker, 7 July 1774, St. Georges Parish, S. C.

EVANS, George and Mary Batten, 1781, Tyrrell Co., N. C.

EVANS, George and Harriet Baker, October 1784, Charleston, S. C.

EVANS, James and Miriam Jordan, 19 February 1785, Chowan Co., N. C.

EVANS, John and Betty Lawrence, 21 January 1782, Rowan Co., N. C.

EVANS, Josiah and Margaret Larkins, 17 February 1755, Orangeburg Co., S.C.

EVANS, Lottie and William Cummings, 2 January 1833, Edgefield District, S. C.

EVANS, Margaret and William Darby, 18 August 1797, Charleston, S. C.

EVANS, Margaret and William McNeely, 7 June 1866, Laurens Co., S. C.

EVANS, Mary and Cropley Ray, 29 April 1765, Tyrrell Co., N. C.

EVANS, Mary and William Gibbes, 26 June 1796, James Island, S. C.

EVANS, Penny and Noah Privote, 6 September 1790, Bertie Co., N. C.

EVANS, Philip and Mary Clay, 1719, St. Andrews Parish, S. C.

EVATT, James and Susan Jones, 21 June 1785, Rowan Co., N. C.

EVELEIGH, Thomas and Nancy Simmons, 23 March 1773, Charleston, S. C.

EVEN, Dina and James Dean, 1747, Orangeburg Co., S. C.

EVERETT, Joseph and Lettice Lassiter, 26 November 1775, Tyrrell Co., N. C.

EVERETT, Mary and Thomas Montigue, 17 February 1792, Guilford Co., N. C.

EVERETT, Zilpha and Richard Hoff, 15 July 1769, Tyrrell Co., N. C.

EVERHART, John and Mary Sophia, 24 August 1788, Rowan Co., N. C.

EVERIT, Martha and Zackariah Harrell, 10 September 1764, Edgecombe Co., N. C.

EVERITT, Elizabeth and Charlton Mizell, 2 August 1764, Tyrrell Co., N. C.

EVERITT, Elizabeth and George Peacock, 17 October 1786, Tyrrell Co., N. C.

EVINS, J. and Elizabeth Weatherly, 31 January 1850, Marlboro Co., S. C.

EVITTS, Katherine and Thomas McCorkle, 15 October 1807, Mecklenburg Co.,
N. C.

EWART, Elizabeth and Thomas G. Barnett, 15 December 1838, Mecklenburg Co.,
N. C.

EWEN, Ann and Hilery Baker, 4 July 1786, Tyrrell Co., N. C.

EWING, Robert and (Mrs.) Jane Bonneau, September 1785, Charleston, S. C.

EXUM, John and Susannah Benton, 18 July 1766, Edgecombe Co., N. C.

EXUM, Micajah and Martha Van Vann, 29 December 1800, Edgecombe Co., N. C.

EXUM, Thomas and Elizabeth King, 31 July 1800, Edgecombe Co., N. C.

EZELL, Frederick and Mary Cox, 28 March 1780, Rowan Co., N. C.

F

FAESCH, Arabella and William Ormond, 5 May 1796, Charleston, S. C.

FAGAN, Shadrach and Esther Middleton, 1784, Tyrrell Co., N. C.

FAGAN, William and Mary Stubbs, 29 December 1777, Tyrrell Co., N. C.

FAGGOTT, Agnes and Isaac Freeman, 19 January 1762, Rowan Co., N. C.

FAIR, Ann and Matthias Rush, 1 April 1795, Charleston, S. C.

FAIRCHILD, Sarah and Ebenezer Frost, 5 December 1769, Rowan Co., N. C.

FAIRY, John and Ann Yosenhut, 5 February 1743, Orangeburg Co., S. C.

FALCONET, Eliza and John I. Middleton, 11 June 1810, Cedar Grove, S. C.

FALKS, Mary and Alexander McClencher, 10 January 1782, Santee, S. C.

FALLON, William and Absallah Small, 12 May 1785, Chowan Co., N. C.

FALLOW, James and Mourning Ellis, 28 February 1763, Chowan Co., N. C.

FALLS, Margaret and Thomas McKnight, 30 December 1795, Mecklenburg Co., N. C.

FALLS, William and Mary Simonton, 13 March 1786, Rowan Co., N. C.

FANNING, John and Bathsheba Layden, 11 June 1778, Perquimans Co., N. C.

FARLOW, Sarah and John Clifton, 3 April 1786, Tyrrell Co., N. C.

FARMER, James and Rebecca Ellis, 27 January 1774, Santee, S. C.

FARMER, Judy and Stephen Harman, 26 October 1790, Bertie Co., N. C.

FARQUHAR, John and Miss Bisset, January 1786, Charleston, S. C.

FARQUHAR, Margaret M. and James C. Green, 16 March 1797, Charleston, S. C.

FARR, John and Elizabeth Woodside, 14 January 1773, Rowan Co., N. C.

FARR, John and Margaret Hartley, 3 October 1784, Charleston, S. C.

FARR, Thomas and Ann Waring, 18 November 1773, Charleston, S. C.

FARR, Thomas (Jr.) and Elizabeth Holmes, 23 November 1760, Charleston, S. C.

FARR, William and Elizabeth Talifarro, 1779, Union District, S. C.

FARRAR, Sarah and John Rankin, 21 September 1814, Mecklenburg Co., N. C.

FARRELL, Delilah D. and Solomon J. Jordan, 1 January 1849, Mecklenburg Co., N. C.

FARRELL, John and Catherine Goodman, 17 January 1791, Rowan Co., N. C.

FARRELL, Sally and William Miles, 15 September 1817, Mecklenburg Co., N. C.

FARRILL, Polly and Gabriel Brown, 22 December 1813, Mecklenburg Co., N. C.

FARRINGTON, Hannah and Jonathan Mills, 8 February 1817, Guilford Co., N. C.

FARROW, Frances and George Pool, 7 October 1857, Laurens Co., S. C.

FARROW, James and Penelope West, 26 December 1789, Chowan Co., N. C.

FARROW, Jane and Samuel Woodruff, 4 March 1832, Edgefield District, S. C.

FARROW, John and Sarah Glaughan, 10 March 1785, Chowan Co., N. C.

FATIO, Mary and William Gibson, 26 August 1801, Charleston, S. C.

FAUST, Christian and Eunice Abstance, 1795, Barnwell District, S. C.

FAUST, Curtis Cornelius and Annie Catherine Jennings, 21 December 1860, Orangeburg Co., S. C.

FAUST, Owen Riley and Rebecca Wroton, 13 January 1825, Barnwell Co., S. C.

FAWLS, John and Rachel Clayton, 2 June 1772, Rowan Co., N. C.

FAYSSOUX, Peter and Sully Wilson, 7 January 1772, Charleston, S. C.

FEASER, George and Christina Smith, 18 August 1787, Rowan Co., N. C.

FEASER, Mary and Conrad Graves, 9 January 1767, Rowan Co., N. C.

FEASER, Peter and Mary Fry, 6 October 1769, Rowan Co., N. C.

FEE, John and Parthena Kellon, 23 October 1779, Rowan Co., N. C.

FELDER, Henry and Mary E. Shaumloffel, 15 December 1747, Orangeburg Co., S. C.

FELL, Isabella and George Perman, 15 November 1801, Charleston, S. C.

FELPS, Aventon and Sarah Harris, 21 April 1786, Rowan Co., N. C.

FELPS, Samuel and Polly Harper, 14 October 1791, Rowan Co., N. C.

FELPS, Thomas and Hanna Aldrich, 20 April 1792, Rowan Co., N. C.

FELPS, William and Elizabeth Jones, 20 April 1768, Rowan Co., N. C.

FELTON, Polly and William Moore, 19 February 1805, Mecklenburg Co., N. C.

FEMEY, Joseph and Rebecca Wiley, 16 January 1764, Tyrrell Co., N. C.

FENWICKE, Edward and Mary Drayton, 2 March 1753, Berkeley Co., S. C.

FERGUSON, Andrew and Elizabeth McFarland, 11 May 1791, Rowan Co., N. C.

FERGUSON, Henry and Eugenie Drummond, 24 May 1866, Laurens Co., S. C.

FERGUSON, John and Elizabeth Hamilton, 25 August 1789, Rowan Co., N. C.

FERGUSON, Mary and Stephen McReam, 3 January 1819, Mecklenburg Co., N. C.

FERGUSON, Parmela and William Alexander, 4 January 1844, Mecklenburg Co., N. C.

FERGUSON, Paul and Catherine Graham, 21 November 1791, Rowan Co., N. C.

FERGUSON, Thomas and Sarah McDowell, 30 March 1776, Rowan Co., N. C.

FESTERMAN, Elizabeth and James Melton, 26 February 1833, Mecklenburg Co., N. C.

FETTERMAN, Betsy and Peter Rowe, 17 June 1852, Mecklenburg Co., N. C.

FICHTER, Elizabeth and George Frederick Knobel, 25 March 1752, Orangeburg Co., S. C.

FICHTNER, Margaret and Jacob Ott, 3 December 1754, Orangeburg Co., S. C.

FICKEN, John F. and Margaret Horlbeck, 30 March 1871, Charleston, S. C.

FICKLAND, Jane and Henry B. Stocker, 27 October 1784, Charleston, S. C.

FICKLINE, Sarah J. and Benjamin R. Bythewood, 14 January 1813, Beaufort, S. C.

FICKLINE, George and Jane Campbell, 13 May 1742, Charleston, S. C.

FIELD, Margaret and Alexander McNilago, September 1784, Charleston, S. C.

FIELDS, Sarah and William Elms, July 1784, Chehaw, S. C.

FIELDS, Sarah and Joseph Sharp, 22 September 1801, Charleston, S. C.

FIFER, George and Elizabeth Frank, 4 December 1786, Rowan Co., N. C.

FIGHT, Conrad and Elizabeth Brown, 14 February 1788, Rowan Co., N. C.

FILLIPS, Elizabeth and William Hughey, 3 July 1791, Rowan Co., N. C.

FILE, Henry and Peggy Reap, 6 December 1797, Rowan Co., N. C.

FILE, Jacob and Betsy Boger, 24 October 1797, Rowan Co., N. C.

FINCH, Eleze and Isaac M. Johnston, 31 December 1844, Mecklenburg Co., N. C.

FINCH, Jenny and John K. Benson, 21 October 1796, Mecklenburg Co., N. C.

FINCHER, Eliza and P. M. Burnett, 12 October 1841, Mecklenburg Co., N. C.

FINCHER, Hezra and David McNeely, 15 May 1798, Mecklenburg Co., N. C.

FINCHER, Jonathan and Betsy Pitman, 4 January 1797, Rowan Co., N. C.

FINCHER, Sarah and John Roper, 16 November 1797, Mecklenburg Co., N. C.

FINK, John and Mary Goodman, 4 May 1790, Rowan Co., N. C.

FINLEY, Harrison and Melissa Henry, 13 October 1842, Laurens Co., S. C.

FINLEY, James and Margaret Allison, 1844, Laurens Co., S. C.

FINLEY, James and Molly Harris, 29 November 1866, Laurens Co., S. C.

FINLEY, John and Dorcas Henry, 8 October 1844, Laurens Co., S. C.

FINLEY, John and Virginia Langston, 7 December 1865, Laurens Co., S. C.

FINLEY, Sidney and Sarah Motes, 26 January 1858, Laurens Co., S. C.

FINNEY, Elizabeth and George Harris, 3 July 1800, Mecklenburg Co., N. C.

FINNEY, James and Mary McCune, 25 March 1776, Rowan Co., N. C.

FINNEY, John and Rachel Ashley, 6 October 1772, Rowan Co., N. C.

FINTON, John and Elizabeth Coon, 4 November 1789, Rowan Co., N. C.

FIREASH, John and Jane Turner, 12 September 1786, Perquimans Co., N. C.

FISHER, Amy and John Robinson, 9 December 1820, Mecklenburg Co., N. C.

FISHER, Catherine and George Fisher, 16 March 1790, Rowan Co., N. C.

FISHER, Frederick and Barbara Tarr, 30 January 1793, Rowan Co., N. C.

FISHER, George and Catherine Fisher, 16 March 1790, Rowan Co., N. C.

FISHER, Jacob and Christian Crosman, 8 September 1768, Rowan Co., N. C.

FISHER, Jacob and Jane Sloane, 25 February 1793, Rowan Co., N. C.

FISHER, John and Lizze Seaford, 13 June 1798, Rowan Co., N. C.

FISHER, Michael and Christian Aronhart, 20 November 1778, Rowan Co., N. C.

FISHER, Risdon and Presley Buckner, 29 June 1798, Rowan Co., N. C.

FISHER, William Harrison and Ruth Ann McMillan, 11 April 1861, Sampson Co., N. C.

FITCH, Elizabeth and Joseph Anderson, 21 February 1760, Santee, S. C.

FITCH, James and Helen Campbell, 28 July 1764, Charleston, S. C.

FITCH, John and Ann Holmes, 16 January 1748, Orangeburg Co., S. C.

FITCH, Joseph and Constant Williamson, 5 March 1718, St. Andrews Parish, S. C.

FITCH, Rachel and Alexander Miote, 22 December 1763, Santee, S. C.

FITZPATRICK, John and Mabel Guston, 3 April 1787, Rowan Co., N. C.

FITZPATRICK, Nicholas and Eleanor Haley, 1 January 1801, Charleston, S. C.

FLAGG, Henry C. (Dr.) and (Mrs.) Allston, 5 December 1784, Charleston, S. C.

FLANAGAN, Mary and Davis Irwin, 7 December 1731, Mecklenburg Co., N. C.

FLANAGAN, Mary A. and (Rev.) Read, 27 November 1844, Mecklenburg Co., N. C.

FLANAGAN, Mary J. and Julius D. Rogers, 1 June 1854, Mecklenburg Co., N. C.

FLANIGAN, Elizabeth and William N. Brown, 19 December 1835, Mecklenburg Co., N. C.

FLANIGAN, Jane R. and R. R. Rea, 18 August 1851, Mecklenburg Co., N. C.

FLANNIGAN, Elizabeth and Thomas Osborn, 17 January 1805, Mecklenburg Co., N. C.

FLEMING, Beatrix and Jeremiah S. Thompson, 21 December 1794, Charleston, S. C.

FLEMING, Elizabeth and John Fleming, 13 October 1767, Rowan Co., N. C.

FLEMING, Henry and Margaret Ray, 1 August 1784, Rowan Co., N. C.

FLEMING, James and Elizabeth Mitchell, 24 January 1784, Rowan Co., N. C.

FLEMING, James and Eveline Mosely, 6 March 1848, Laurens Co., S. C.

FLEMING, John and Ann Barkley, 7 October 1784, Rowan Co., N. C.

FLEMING, John and Elizabeth Fleming, 13 October 1767, Rowan Co., N. C.

FLEMING, Martha and James Calladon, 29 December 1766, Santee, S. C.

FLEMING, Mitchell and Agnes Kennedy, 27 January 1794, Rowan Co., N. C.

FLEMING, Preston and Permelia Higgins, 25 September 1856, Laurens Co., S. C.

FLEMING, Rebecca and William Patterson, 30 October 1856, Laurens Co., S. C.

FLEMING, Sally and Robert Ladson, 18 March 1773, Charleston, S. C.

FLEMMING, Elizabeth and Alexander Henry, 5 January 1797, Charleston, S. C.

FLEMORE, Adam and Eliza Holsenback, 4 September 1841, Edgefield District, S. C.

FLETCHER, Jesse and Ann Walton, 12 August 1793, Perquimans Co., N. C.

FLETS, Elizabeth and Pickney Teague, 4 January 1866, Laurens Co., S. C.

FLEURY, Ann and Thomas Dermody, 6 July 1769, Chowan Co., N. C.

FLEURY, Margaret (widow) and Robert Miller, 27 June 1772, Chowan Co., N. C.

FLEWELLEN, John and Sarah Hobby, 24 December 1761, Edgecombe Co., N. C.

FLINN, Elizabeth C. and Batho Irwin, 18 December 1841, Mecklenburg Co., N. C.

FLINT, Mary and Peter R. Ray, 1792, Charleston Co., S. C.

FLINT, Thomas and Sarah Forshaw, 7 January 1797, Charleston, S. C.

FLOOD, Enoch and Fanny Cherry, 19 June 1801, Edgecombe Co., N. C.

FLOOD, Minerva and Robert Mitchell, 16 May 1855, Guilford Co., N. C.

FLOOD, Sarah (widow) and Jacob Frank, 14 May 1750, Orangeburg Co., S. C.

FLOURNOY, F. M. F. and C. A. Savage, 15 December 1839, Edgefield District, S. C.

FLOW, Ellen and Elam Harrison, 26 August 1847, Mecklenburg Co., N. C.

FLOW, Margaret A. and Charles W. Alexander, 26 December 1861, Mecklenburg Co., N. C.

FLOW, Matilda and William J. Black, 30 December 1824, Mecklenburg Co., N. C.

FLOW, Sarah and Robert W. Russell, 27 January 1853, Mecklenburg Co., N. C.

FLOWERS, Jacob and Elizabeth Cane, 19 April 1760, Edgecombe Co., N. C.

FLOWERS, Jacob and Mary Morgan, 28 January 1788, Orange Co., N. C.

FLOWERS, Jacob and Mary Johnson, 20 November 1764, Edgecombe Co., N. C.

FLOWERS, William Blanchard and Indiana Lucy Colding, 28 November 1844, Barnwell Co., S. C.

FLOYD, James Bell and Mary S. White, 2 November 1852, Granville Co., N. C.

FLOYD, Priscilla and Josiah Britt, 1 February 1797, Bertie Co., N. C.

FLOYD, William and Christian White, 10 March 1779, Chowan Co., N. C.

FLUD, Harriet and Wade Hampton, August 1786, Charleston, S. C.

FLUDD, Margaret and John Gibson, 19 December 1754, Orangeburg Co., S. C.

FLURY, William and Margaret Haughton, 6 May 1752, Chowan Co., N. C.

FLUTT, George and N. Pickings, 1748, Orangeburg Co., S. C.

FLY, Polly and John Moncrieff, 4 October 1766, Charleston, S. C.

FOARD, Nancy and Isaac Moore, 5 November 1800, Mecklenburg Co., N. C.

FOGARTIE, David and Mary Perdrieu, 12 June 1763, Santee, S. C.

FOGARTIE, James and Sarah B. Scott, 2 July 1799, Charleston, S. C.

FOIL, Philip and Elizabeth Benson, 20 April 1792, Rowan Co. N. C.

FOISSON, Elizabeth and Paul Trapier, 19 November 1771, Santee, S. C.

FOLEY, Catherine and Thomas Fuller, 1773, Berkeley Co., S. C.

FOLEY, Thomas and Catherine Mellichamp, 1 November 1764, Charleston, S. C.

FOLICK, John and Hannah Colp, 1 December 1794, Rowan Co., N. C.

FOLK, John and Eve Margaret Dickert, 23 October 1798, Newberry District, S. C.

FOLTS, Henry and Elizabeth Smith, 17 August 1790, Rowan Co., N. C.

FONTAIN, Jane (Mrs.) and Daniel Collins, 11 April 1801, Charleston, S. C.

FONTS, John and Mary Younce, 31 August 1769, Rowan Co., N. C.

FORBES, Elizabeth and Thomas Bent, 1784, Tyrrell Co., N. C.

FORBES, Margaret and William Montgomery, 14 June 1802, Guilford Co., N. C.

FORBIS, James and Phebe Bryan, 10 March 1779, Rowan Co., N. C.

FORBIS, William and Margaret Bryan, 13 February 1779, Rowan Co., N. C.

FORD, Ann and Meredith Hughes, 9 January 1772, Santee, S. C.

FORD, Elizabeth and Samuel Luton, 19 November 1757, Chowan Co., N. C.

FORD, Elizabeth Nash and Philip Neale, 18 July 1797, Charleston, S. C.

FORD, George and Mary Boone, 13 October 1778, Santee, S. C.

FORD, George and Kitty Wayne, May 1784, Georgetown, S. C.

FORD, Jacob and Ann Motte Perronneau, 21 January 1797, Charleston, S. C.

FORD, Mary and Samuel Harper, 26 August 1784, Rowan Co., N. C.

FORD, Peter and Sarah Baldwin, 1 November 1774, Rowan Co., N. C.

FORD, Rebecca and Calvin Spencer, 21 August 1782, Santee, S. C.

FORD, Sarah and Daniel Horrey, 20 December 1743, St. James Parish, S. C.

FORD, Stephen and Sarah Barton, 25 January 1761, Santee, S. C.

FORD, Stephen and Margaret White, 8 July 1779, Santee, S. C.

FORD, Timothy and Mary M. Prioleau, 18 November 1800, Charleston, S. C.

FORD, Widow and Henry Webster, 18 May 1769, Charleston, S. C.

FORD, William and Emma Hunt, 4 June 1791, Rowan Co., N. C.

FORD, Wyatt and Betsy Person, 2 June 1783, Rowan Co., N. C.

FOREHAND, Solomon and Rachel Hale, 24 September 1763, Edgecombe Co., N. C.

FORGARTIE, Esther and Thomas Axson, December 1783, Charleston, S. C.

FORGATT, Francis and Mary Culliatt, 27 May 1784, Jacksonboro, S. C.

FORGUS, Samuel and Martha Campbell, 22 July 1778, Rowan Co., N. C.

FORGY, Asa and Ethalinda Barksdale, 29 November 1849, Laurens Co., S. C.

FORGY, Mattison and Martha Fuller, 29 March 1864, Laurens Co., S. C.

FORGY, Virginia and Gideon O'Neal, 22 November 1857, Laurens Co., S. C.

FORGY, Wade and Ofelia Haulk, 19 October 1865, Laurens Co., S. C.

FORMAN, John and Milly Hendricks, 17 January 1794, Rowan Co., N. C.

FORNEY, Peter and Nancy Abernathy, 1783, Lincoln Co., N. C.

FORRER, Tobias and Barbara Smith, 12 August 1790, Rowan Co., N. C.

FORREST, Anne and Richard Hooper, 11 February 1786, Orange Co., N. C.

FORREST, Elzey and Mary Rogers, 18 June 1839, Edgefield District, S. C.

FORREST, Tabitha C. and Thomas J. Forrest, 27 June 1857, Edgefield District, S. C.

FORREST, Thomas J. and Tabitha C. Forrest, 27 June 1857, Edgefield District, S. C.

FORSHAW, Elizabeth and Edward Woodruff, 15 February 1800, Charleston, S. C.

FORSHAW, Sarah and Thomas Flint, 7 January 1797, Charleston, S. C.

FORST, Mary and George E. Goss, 21 February 1792, Rowan Co., N. C.

FORSTER, Betsy and Samuel House, 8 May 1843, Mecklenburg Co., N. C.

FORSTER, Evelina M. and John M. Hoppold, 14 February 1827, Mecklenburg Co., N. C.

FORT, Catherine and Matthew Williams, 1787, Edgecombe Co., N. C.

FORT, Elias and Lucy Adkinson, 7 March 1764, Edgecombe Co., N. C.

FORT, John and Martha Turner, 30 December 1774, Bertie Co., N. C.

FORT, Lewis and Nancy Battle, 28 May 1800, Edgecombe Co., N. C.

FORT, Mary and Jonathan Howell, 20 May 1766, Edgecombe Co., N. C.

FORT, Orpah and Jesse Barnes, 2 February 1761, Edgecombe Co., N. C.

FORT, Priscilla and James Jolly, 15 October 1764, Edgecombe Co., N. C.

FOST, Catherine and John Eller, 10 August 1785, Rowan Co., N. C.

FOSTER, Betsy and William McClain, 11 May 1796, Guilford Co., N. C.

FOSTER, Charles H. and Sue A. Carter, 1860, Murfreesboro, N. C.

FOSTER, David and May Cowan, 27 February 1773, Rowan Co., N. C.

FOSTER, David and Ann Kilpatrick, 27 January 1795, Rowan Co., N. C.

FOSTER, Dorcas H. and (Dr.) John M. Hapfoldt, 2 March 1837, Mecklenburg Co., N. C.

FOSTER, Edeson and Barbara Wasson, 6 June 1798, Rowan Co., N. C.

FOSTER, Elizabeth and William Garwood, 14 January 1794, Rowan Co., N. C.

FOSTER, James and Elsy Smith, 28 December 1785, Rowan Co., N. C.

FOSTER, John and Nancy Williams, 1 October 1774, Chowan Co., N. C.

FOSTER, John and Martha Morrison, 20 March 1768, Rowan Co., N. C.

FOSTER, John and Hannah Hughett, 4 November 1782, Rowan Co., N. C.

FOSTER, John and Joanna Bailey, 3 March 1797, Rowan Co., N. C.

FOSTER, Rachel and John Cantzon, 18 July 1791, Lancaster Co., S. C.

FOSTER, Robert and Louisa Gilman, 23 November 1801, Charleston, S. C.

FOSTER, Sallie and Isaac McKissick, May 1866, Spartanburg Co., S. C.

FOSTER, Samuel and Dinah Short, 28 August 1795, Rowan Co., N. C.

FOSTER, Sarah and William Knight, 31 March 1777, Chowan Co., N. C.

FOSTER, Thomas and Mary Brewton (widow) 19 June 1784, Charleston, S. C.

FOSTER, William and Agnes Allen, 2 August 1779, Rowan Co., N. C.

FOWLE, William and Ann Brownlow, 22 August 1825, Crawfield, S. C.

FOWLER, Gilly and Graden Riddle, 10 January 1850, Laurens Co., S. C.

FOWLER, Jane and Hanelland Redin, 10 August 1848, Laurens Co., S. C.

FOWLER, John P. and Sarah Henderson (widow) 1 February 1859, Laurens Co., S. C.

FOWLER, Mary and Franklin Pool, 28 September 1865, Laurens Co., S. C.

FOWLER, Sarah and Willis Check, 27 November 1856, Laurens Co., S. C.

FOWLER, Susan and James E. Anderson, 18 April 1860, Laurens Co., S. C.

FOWLER, Wesley and Mary Boyd, 11 March 1852, Laurens Co., S. C.

FOWLER, Wiley and Nancy Riddle, 10 February 1853, Laurens Co., S. C.

FOX, David and Mary Dill, 17 September 1737, Charleston, S. C.

FOX, John and Eliza Poindexter, 1 November 1832, Edgefield District, S. C.

FOX, Mary and Alfred J. Norris, 8 February 1853, Edgefield District, S. C.

FOX, Rachel and Obediah Lawrence, 1780, Tyrrell Co., N. C.

FOY, John and Harriet Rutherford, 13 December 1836, Edgefield District, S. C.

FOY, Martha and James Rutherford, 15 December 1835, Edgefield District, S. C.

FRAILEY, George and Margaret Agenor, 15 June 1796, Rowan Co., N. C.

FRALEY, Jacob and Elizabeth Brown, 22 July 1793, Rowan Co., N. C.

FRANK, Elizabeth and George Fifer, 4 December 1786, Rowan Co., N. C.

FRANK, Jacob and Sarah Flood, (widow) 14 May 1750, Orangeburg Co., S. C.

FRANK, Jacob and Susanna Roan, 4 June 1768, Rowan Co., N. C.

FRANK, William and Barbara Byerly, 12 November 1796, Rowan Co., N. C.

FRANKLAND, Thomas and Sarah Rhett, 27 May 1743, Charleston, S. C.

FRANKLIN, Aphriam and Louisa Kirkland, 19 December 1838, Edgefield District, S. C.

FRANKLIN, Benjamin and Elizabeth Harper Bobo, 28 July 1839, Union District, S. C.

FRANKLIN, Margaret and William Rowan, 6 April 1809, Mecklenburg Co., N. C.

FRANKLIN, Margaret and Joseph Read, 12 March 1811, Mecklenburg Co., N. C.

FRANKLIN, Nancy and George Sharpton, 10 January 1833, Edgefield District, S. C.

FRANKS, Barksdale and Mary Barksdale, 2 January 1866, Laurens Co., S. C.

FRANKS, Charles and Martha Landford, 31 July 1862, Laurens Co., S. C.

FRANKS, Jane and John Powers, 17 December 1857, Laurens Co., S. C.

FRANKS, John and Nancy Cannady, 12 December 1846, Laurens Co., S. C.

FRANKS, Miles and Catherine Martin, 13 April 1848, Laurens Co., S. C.

FRARLY, Jacob and Katherine Charles, 2 May 1768, Rowan Co., N. C.

FRASER, Alexander and Anne Harvey, 6 November 1749, Charleston, S. C.

FRASER, Alexander and Mary Grimke, 20 March 1755, Charleston, S. C.

FRASER, Anne and William Cattell, (Jr.) 1 August 1746, Charleston, S. C.

FRASER, Esther and John McCoy, 16 March 1799, Mecklenburg Co., N. C.

FRASER, James and Honour Seratt, 6 June 1785, Rowan Co., N. C.

FRASER, John and Polly Stobbo, 23 June 1771, Charleston, S. C.

FRASER, Mary and (Dr.) Henry Richardson, 2 November 1801, Charleston, S. C.

FRASER, Rev. and Elizabeth Clegg Porter, 31 March 1796, Black River, S. C.

FRASER, William and Sophia Miles, January 1784, St. Bartholomews Parish, S. C.

FRAZER, John and Mehitable Halsey, 21 April 1778, Chowan Co., N. C.

FRAZER, Levina and Jonah Brown, 19 June 1814, Mecklenburg Co., N. C.

FRAZER, Peter and Sarah Cowan, 11 June 1794, Rowan Co., N. C

FRAZEY, Aaron and Hannah Hobbis, 24 July 1775, Rowan Co., N. C.

FRAZIER, Cinthy and Marcus Barnett, 27 March 1826, Mecklenburg Co., N. C.

FRAZIER, Jeremiah and Penelope Gregory, 8 March 1761, Chowan Co., N. C.

FRAZIER, Sue and Sheppard Spencer, January 1857, Edgefield District, S. C.

FREDERIC, Sarah (Mrs.) and Alexander Petrie, January 1785, Charleston, S. C.

FREDERICK, Betsy and Stewart Nicholas, 1 November 1772, Charleston, S. C.

FREDERICK, Christina and Robert Knox, May 1786, Charleston, S. C.

FREEMAN, Aaron and Mary Bentley, 17 December 1769, Rowan Co., N. C.

FREEMAN, Eliza and James McCallester, 8 December 1823, Mecklenburg Co., N. C.

FREEMAN, Emily J. and Robert H. Mitchell, 9 March 1853, Guilford Co., N. C.

FREEMAN, Isaac and Agnes Faggott, 19 January 1762, Rowan Co., N. C.

FREEMAN, Joana and Frederick Davenport, 1784, Tyrrell Co., N. C.

FREEMAN, Leah and William Leary, 24 March 1778, Chowan Co., N. C.

FREEMAN, Mary (widow) and William Ward, 29 November 1773, Chowan Co., N. C.

FREEMAN, Nancy A. and John Clark, 31 March 1859, Mecklenburg Co., N. C.

FREEMAN, Nancy P. and Eli Brown, 5 November 1832, Mecklenburg Co., N. C.

FREEMAN, Peggy A. and Joseph R. Berryhill, 9 April 1840, Mecklenburg Co., N. C.

FREEMAN, Richard and Christian Hinton, 29 September 1778, Chowan Co., N. C.

FREEMAN, Russell and Celia Good, 1 September 1796, Rowan Co., N. C.

FREEMAN, Sally and John Hepworth, 9 June 1818, Mecklenburg Co., N. C.

FREEMAN, Sarah and Adam Hall, 26 March 1778, Rowan Co., N. C.

FREEMAN, Sarah J. and James H. Brown, 28 July 1828, Mecklenburg Co., N. C.

FREEMSTER, William and Mary Sharpe, 29 May 1783, Rowan Co., N. C.

FREZE, John and Mary Freze, 9 May 1785, Rowan Co., N. C.

FREZE, Mary and John Freze, 9 May 1785, Rowan Co., N. C.

FRICE, Jesse and Sally Grice, 2 December 1830, Edgefield District, S. C.

FRICHMAN, Elizabeth and John Harresperger, 30 April 1751, Orangeburg Co., S. C.

FRICK, Mathias and Rachel Caler, 16 August 1794, Rowan Co., N. C.

FRICKLING, Samuel and Ann E. Wilkie, 17 November 1801, Charleston, S. C.

FRIERSON, Ann and James Poyas, 22 April 1797, Charleston, S. C.

FRIERSON, John and Ann Bannister, 28 April 1785, Charleston, S. C.

FRIERSON, John and Kitty Williams, 1788, Charleston, S. C.

FRILEY, Rebecca and Benjamin Gaylard, 26 February 1771, Tyrrell Co., N. C.

FRIPP, Mary J. and Charles E. Tennent, 25 July 1844, St. Johns Parish, N. C.

FRIPP, Paul (Jr.) and Betsey Jenkins, October 1783, Edisto, S. C.

FRISBY, Jonah and Elizabeth Imbler, 2 November 1794, Rowan Co., N. C.

FRITCHMAN, M. and Elias Shnell, 1746, Orangeburg Co., S. C.

FRITH, Samuel and Anne Croskeys, 6 June 1720, St. Andrews Parish, S. C.

FRITZ, George and Mary Willson, 3 January 1780, Rowan Co., N. C.

FRIZZLE, Mary and James Hancock, 1796, Pitt Co., N. C.

FROST, Ebenezer and Sarah Fairchild, 5 December 1769, Rowan Co., N. C.

FROST, Ebenezer and Elizabeth Willson, 2 November 1775, Rowan Co., N. C.

FROST, Ebenezer and Rebecca Bailey, 12 April 1796, Rowan Co., N. C.

FROST, John and Rebecca Booe, 21 August 1793, Rowan Co., N. C.

FROST, Rachel and David Holeman, 8 November 1798, Rowan Co., N. C.

FRY, Catherine and Christopher Monheim, 26 December 1752, Orangeburg Co., S. C.

FRY, John and Christina Muller, 23 November 1779, Rowan Co., N. C.

FRY, Mary and Peter Feaser, 6 October 1769, Rowan Co., N. C.

FRY, Peter and Malissey Cottner, 2 June 1775, Rowan Co., N. C.

FULKERSON, Abraham and Sarah Gibson, 2 July 1788, Rowan Co., N. C.

FULLER, Ann and William Ross, 9 December 1743, Charleston, S. C.

FULLER, Ann and (Dr.) Patrick Todd, 18 October 1857, Laurens Co., S. C.

FULLER, Benjamin and Mary O'Bryan, 7 November 1785, Tyrrell Co., N. C.

FULLER, Elizabeth and Alexander McQueen, 14 January 1774, Berkeley Co., S. C.

FULLER, Franklin (Dr.) and Sarah Odell, 3 April 1845, Laurens Co., S. C.

FULLER, Henry and Sarah Culbers, 13 November 1856, Laurens Co., S. C.

FULLER, Henry and Ginny Casey, 14 September 1859, Laurens Co., S. C.

FULLER, John R. and Kitturah Walker, 16 January 1863, Laurens Co., S. C.

FULLER, Letty and Warren Walker, 15 December 1866, Laurens Co., S. C.

FULLER, Martha and Mattison Forgy, 29 March 1864, Laurens Co., S. C.

FULLER, Mary and Robert Knight, 10 June 1856, Laurens Co., S. C.

FULLER, Ofelia and (Dr.) Franklin Coleman, 12 April 1860, Laurens Co., S. C.

FULLER, Richard and Mary Drayton, 21 December 1721, St. Andrews Parish, S. C.

FULLER, Thomas and Elizabeth Miles (widow), 7 September 1766, Ashley Ferry, S. C.

FULLER, Thomas and Catherine Foley, 1773, Berkeley Co., S. C.

FULLER, Whitmarsh and Judith Simpson, 30 June 1761, Charleston, S. C.

FULLERTON, Mary and John Thompson, 4 August 1744, Chowan Co., N. C.

FULLINWID, Henry and Eleanor Leonard, 20 August 1783, Rowan Co., N. C.

FULMER, W. W. and M. C. Jennings, 10 November 1857, Edgefield District, S. C.

FULTS, Peter and Catherine Wechman, 10 August 1785, Rowan Co., N. C.

FURGURSON, Robert and Mary Leonora, 11 August 1787, Orange Co., N. C.

FURMAN, Charles M. and Fannie E. Garden, 1 February 1864, Charleston, S. C.

FURMAN, John H. and Susan E. Miller, 8 May 1853, Sumter Co., S. C.

FURMAN, Richard and Elizabeth Haynesworth, 28 November 1774, Charleston, S. C.

FURMAN, Richard and Margaret Cammer, 15 April 1841, Charleston, S. C.

FURMAN, Samuel and Eliza A. Scrimgeour, 5 May 1814, Charleston, S. C.

FURNAS, William and Rachel Wesley, 1797, Bush River, S. C.

FURR, Elizabeth L. and Henry Jordan, 14 October 1858, Mecklenburg Co., N. C.

FURR, John and Catherine Liveley, 4 August 1783, Rowan Co., N. C.

FURSE, James and Martha Wild, 1 September 1801, Barnwell District, S. C.

FUSTER, John and Sirrah Hatcher, 1741, Orangeburg Co., S. C.

FUSTER, Salome and Samuel Davis, 1740, Orangeburg Co., S. C.

FUSTER, Sirrah (widow) and John Cleaton, 1741, Orangeburg Co., S. C.

FUSTERIN, Elizabeth and Christian Schwartz, 19 November 1741, Orangeburg Co., S. C.

FUSTERS, Barbara and Jacob Pruncen, 26 January 1738, Orangeburg Co., S. C.

FYTE, Elizabeth and George Hagar, 17 January 1791, Rowan Co., N. C.

G

GABLE, Eliza C. and O. D. Smith, 24 January 1856, Edgefield District, S. C.

GADSDEN, Christopher and Jane Godfrey, 28 July 1746, Charleston, S. C.

GADSDEN, Christopher and Mary Hasell, December 1759, Charleston, S. C.

GADSDEN, Philip and Catherine Edwards, 12 November 1783, Charleston, S. C.

GADSON, Anne and Andrew Lord, 15 November 1770, Charleston, S. C.

GADSON, Christopher S. and Florida Morrall, 9 May 1861, Charleston, S. C.

GAILLARD, Ban. and Elizabeth Webb, 19 February 1769, Santee, S. C.

GAILLARD, Bartholomew and Rebecca C. Doughty, 6 March 1800, Charleston, S. C.

GAILLARD, Catherine and Elias Ball, 14 May 1765, Santee, S. C.

GAILLARD, Charles and Ann Dupree, 13 September 1770, Santee, S. C.

GAILLARD, David and Joanna Dubose, 23 September 1773, Santee, S. C.

GAILLARD, Elizabeth (widow) and Jonathan Skrine, 26 March 1718, St. Andrews Parish, S. C.

GAILLARD, Elizabeth and Theodore Gourdine, 20 October 1785, Charleston, S. C.

GAILLARD, Elizabeth and Job Marion, 14 December 1762, Santee, S. C.

GAILLARD, James and Mary Jones, 19 July 1763, Santee, S. C.

GAILLARD, John and Susan Boone, 10 November 1768, Santee, S. C.

GAILLARD, Lydia and John Dutarque, 24 August 1774, Charleston, S. C.

GAILLARD, Mary and John Jordan, 19 April 1770, Santee, S. C.

GAILLARD, Peyre and Susan M. Hall, 26 December 1799, Charleston, S. C.

GAILLARD, Theodore and Cornelia Marshall, 3 November 1799, Charleston, S. C.

GAITHER, Harriet and Thomas Howard, 29 October 1799, Rowan Co., N. C.

GAITHER, John and Susannah Johnson, 17 February 1795, Rowan Co., N. C.

GAITHER, Margaret and John Howard, 26 January 1795, Rowan Co., N. C.

GAITHER, Nicholas W. and Tabitha Baley, 18 September 1792, Rowan Co., N. C.

GALBRAITH, Betsy and Matthews Cunningham, 16 January 1793, Orange Co., N. C.

GALE, Miles and Martha Vail, 6 August 1745, Chowan Co., N. C.

GALE, Susan and Thomas Corprew, 31 July 1747, Chowan Co., N. C.

GALEY, James and Mary McClain, 6 August 1766, Rowan Co., N. C.

GALLAGHER, Hugh and Sarah Campbell, 4 May 1778, Rowan Co., N. C.

GALLAHER, Hugh and Elizabeth Martin, 26 August 1775, Rowan Co., N. C.

GALLMAN, Gasper and Fannie McLendon, 6 February 1838, Edgefield District, S. C.

GALLMAN, Jamina and James Arthur, 14 December 1834, Edgefield District, S. C.

GALLMAN, Mary and Robert Kenney, 7 November 1805, Edgefield District, S. C.

GALLMAN, Sally and John Grice, 5 October 1828, Edgefield District, S. C.

GALLOWAY, David and Mary Stocks, 12 September 1719, St. Andrews Parish, S. C.

GALLOWAY, Martha and John McConnell, 15 December 1835, Mecklenburg Co., N. C.

GALLOWAY, Mary and William Smith, 1 January 1795, Charleston, S. C.

GALLOWAY, Rebecca and James Johnson, 14 April 1846, Mecklenburg Co., N. C.

GALLUCHAT, Joseph and Rebecca M. Gill, 22 October 1846, Lancaster, S. C.

GAMBLE, Jane and John Blair, 9 February 1771, Guilford Co., N. C.

GANCEY, Elizabeth and Rev. John Dickins, April 1779, N. C.

GANDY, Samuel and Rosina Zellwegerin, 14 March 1748, Orangeburg Co., S. C.

GANES, Amina Hamutal and Conrad M. Lowrey, 4 February 1815, Edgefield District, S. C.

GANO, John and Sarah Bryan, 15 April 1793, Rowan Co., N. C.

GANT, Rebecca and William Hickey, 1746, Orangeburg Co., S. C.

GARDEN, Alexander (Dr.) and Susannah D. Wigfall, 1788, Charleston, S. C.

GARDEN, Benjamin and Amelia Godin, 17 January 1765, Prince William Parish, S. C.

GARDEN, Fannie E. and Charles M. Furman, 1 February 1864, Charleston, S. C.

GARDEN, Martha and Sampson Neyle, 12 February 1751, Charleston, S. C.

GARDNER, Benjamin and Miss Eaton, 23 July 1798, Rowan Co., N. C.

GARDNER, Elizabeth and Edward Alexander, 1784, Tyrrell Co., N. C.

GARDNER, Elizabeth and Robert Macy, 11 December 1799, Guilford Co., N. C.

GARDNER, Francis and Jennett Kerr, 18 May 1778, Rowan Co., N. C.

GARDNER, Isaac and Mary Halton, 21 January 1764, Tyrrell Co., N. C.

GARDNER, James and Jennet Brunhead, 1 November 1797, Rowan Co., N. C.

GARDNER, John and Margaret Moore, 25 July 1786, Rowan Co., N. C.

GARDNER, Mary E. and Daniel Byrd, 18 December 1855, Edgefield District, S. C.

GARDNER, Patience and Emanuel James, 19 January 1788, Bertie Co., N. C.

GARDNER, Susannah and Philip Howard, 10 October 1774, Rowan Co., N. C.

GARE, Hortence F. and John C. Chinners, 29 March 1800, Charleston, S. C.

GARLINGTON, Maria and Richard W. Simpson, 10 February 1863, Anderson Co., S. C.

GARNER, Frances and James Parkman, 27 December 1855, Edgefield District, S. C.

GARNER, Henry and Elizabeth Lopp, 10 August 1792, Rowan Co., N. C.

GARNIER, John and Ann Keen, July 1786, Georgetown, S. C.

GARRAWOOD, Jacob and Winny Glascock, 15 September 1795, Rowan Co., N. C.

GARRET, Mary and Samuel Maxwell, 1 February 1802, Guilford Co., N. C.

GARRETT, Daniel and Esther Haughton, 19 February 1756, Chowan Co., N. C.

GARRETT, Elizabeth and Cader Riddick, 18 December 1771, Chowan Co., N. C.

GARRETT, Africa and Charles Oden Martin, 10 March 1786, Tyrrell Co., N. C.

GARRETT, Archibald and Miss Edwards, 25 August 1859, Laurens Co., S. C.

GARRETT, Benjamin and Elener Corprew, 11 February 1783, Tyrrell Co., N. C.

GARRETT, Cassander and Reuben Owings, 13 March 1851, Laurens Co., S. C.

GARRETT, Charity and Robertson Owings, 29 September 1850, Laurens Co., S. C.

GARRETT, Edward and Sarah Durham, 18 December 1850, Laurens Co., S. C.

GARRETT, Eliza and George Anderson, 21 February 1850, Edgefield District, S. C.

GARRETT, Everard and Leah Speight, 30 January 1758, Chowan Co., N. C.

GARRETT, Everard and Sarah Hurdle, 3 August 1763, Chowan Co., N. C.

GARRETT, Fanny and Henry H. Martin, 8 June 1843, Laurens Co., S. C.

GARRETT, Harman and Martha Higgins (widow), 14 December 1843, Laurens Co., S. C.

GARRETT, Harris and Harriet Moore, 20 November 1844, Laurens Co., S. C.

GARRETT, Henry and Elsy Cabbart, 21 January 1846, Laurens Co., S. C.

GARRETT, Hosea and Isabella Power, March 23, 1851, Laurens Co., S. C.

GARRETT, James and Ruth Cottrell (widow), 17 December 1773, Chowan Co., N. C.

GARRETT, Jesse and Rachel Blanchard, 30 January 1756, Chowan Co., N. C.

GARRETT, Joanna and Jacob Davenport, 1 February 1768, Tyrrell Co., N. C.

GARRETT, John and Bridget Benbury, 19 October 1756, Chowan Co., N. C.

GARRETT, John and Elizabeth Stuart, 18 July 1860, Laurens Co., S. C.

GARRETT, Mancel and Miss Hughs, 27 August 1859, Laurens Co., S. C.

GARRETT, Mary and Francis Ward, 8 April 1779, Tyrrell Co., N. C.

GARRETT, Mary and John Eccleston, 22 September 1785, Chowan Co., N. C.

GARRETT, Melia and Luke Bennett, 12 May 1766, Tyrrell Co., N. C.

GARRETT, Nancy and Austin Cheek, 20 May 1852, Laurens Co., S. C.

GARRETT, Nancy E. and John Putman, 30 December 1847, Laurens Co., S. C.

GARRETT, Potiller and Susan Dorham, 24 July 1850, Laurens Co., S. C.

GARRETT, Rachel and Jacob Outlaw, 25 November 1775, Chowan Co., N. C.

GARRETT, Richardson and Rhodah Cooley, 12 July 1849, Laurens Co., S. C.

GARRETT, Sallie and Vandiver Garrett, 19 July 1866, Laurens Co., S. C.

GARRETT, Sarah and Thomas Holstead, 20 July 1762, Tyrrell Co., N. C.

GARRETT, Sarah and Stephen Moore, 14 August 1845, Laurens Co., S. C.

GARRETT, Stobo and Mary Burns, 1 November 1855, Laurens Co., S. C.

GARRETT, Thomasine and Joseph Whedbee, 27 July 1771, Chowan Co., N. C.

GARRETT, Vandiver and Sallie Garrett, 19 July 1866, Laurens Co., S. C.

GARRETT, Washington and Martha Putman, 13 November 1866, Laurens Co., S. C.

GARRETT, Washington and Jamima Cheek, 28 October 1853, Laurens Co., S. C.

GARRETT, William and Permealy Motes, 20 December 1844, Laurens Co., S. C.

GARRETT, William and Sarah Knight, 11 March 1858, Laurens Co., S. C.

GARRISON, John and Lucretia Vaune, 12 February 1772, Rowan Co., N. C.

GARRISON, Martha A. and James F. Carothers, 1852, York Co., S. C.

GARRISON, Matilda and George Moseley, 23 December 1851, Laurens Co., S. C.

GARRISON, Patsy and Elias Alexander, 7 July 1810, Mecklenburg Co., N. C.

GARROWOOD, Nancy and Harmon Glasscock, October 1792, Rowan Co., N. C.

GARTMAN, Barbara (widow) and Joseph Lyons, 31 December 1741, Orangeburg Co., S. C.

GARWOOD, William and Elizabeth Foster, 14 January 1794, Rowan Co., N. C.

GARY, Amanda and Mr. Lock, 7 May 1857, Laurens Co., S. C.

GARY, Antho and William Jones, 7 January 1862, Laurens Co., S. C.

GARY, Duff and Emma Jones, 19 February 1861, Laurens Co., S. C.

GASKINS, Bettie and James Hardy, 30 September 1788, Bertie Co., N. C.

GASKINS, Sally and Eli Brinkley, 26 November 1788, Bertie Co., N. C.

GASKINS, William and Sarah Robertson (widow), 11 April 1774, Chowan Co., N. C.

GASSER, John and Mary Hoskins, 29 October 1785, Chowan Co., N. C.

GASTON, James McF. and Sue G. Brumby, 2 November 1852, Columbia, S. C.

GASTON, Jane and John Barnett, 22 July 1795, Mecklenburg Co., N. C.

GATES, Josiah and Catherine McClain, 10 January 1764, Rowan Co., N. C.

GAY, Demsey and Polly Andre, 6 February 1800, Edgecombe Co., N. C.

GAY, Robert and Anne Elder, 2 December 1779, Rowan Co., N. C.

GAY, Sarah and Elias Horn, 26 January 1763, Edgecombe Co., N. C.

GAYLARD, Benjamin and Rebecca Friley, 26 February 1771, Tyrrell Co., N. C.

GAYLARD, James and Zilpah Wiley, 26 February 1771, Tyrrell Co., N. C.

GEAR, Anne (widow) and Francis Howard, 11 June 1745, Chowan Co., N. C.

GEE, Charles and Catherine Bond, 24 April 1770, Santee, S. C.

GEIGER, Betsy and Alexander Bell, December 1785, Charleston, S. C.

GEISELHART, Anna Margaretta and (Capt.) W. Frederick Houseal, 1772, Orangeburg Co., S. C.

GELLAHAN, Abraham and Mary Enslow, 12 April 1779, Rowan Co., N. C.

GELTZER, Daniel and Margaret Brick (widow), 1748, Orangeburg Co., S. C.

GENSEL, John and Hannah Lane, 19 June 1800, Charleston, S. C.

GENTILE, Ellen and James Beaty, 14 November 1831, Mecklenburg Co., N. C.

GEORGE, Brinkley and Milly Booth, 1810, Orange Co., N. C.

GEORGE, Christiana and Thomas Bradford, 1788, Charleston, S. C.

GEORGE, David and Betsey Trice, 18 December 1792, Orange Co., N. C.

GEORGE, David and Sylvinia Herndon, 11 December 1837, Orange Co., N. C.

GEORGE, Elizabeth and Jeremiah Irwin, 11 December 1766, Edgecombe Co., N. C.

GEORGE, Elizabeth and William H. Herndon, 23 January 1866, Orange Co., N. C.

GEORGE, Elizabeth and Harmon Herndon, 5 April 1837, Orange Co., N. C.

GEORGE, Ezekiel and Martha Herndon, 8 June 1831, Orange Co., N. C.

GEORGE, Helen and James T. Hunt, 22 May 1861, Granville Co., N. C.

GEORGE, Jonathan and Ferebee Locust, 27 January 1802, Orange Co., N. C.

GEORGE, John and Dolly Barbee, 1866, Orange Co., N. C.

GEORGE, Mary E. and Chesley Herndon, 3 February 1866, Orange Co., N. C.

GEORGE, Roxanna and James Green, 6 January 1856, Orange Co., N. C.

GEORGE, Ruthy and Zachariah Hopson, 22 December 1789, Orange Co., N. C.

GEORGE, Solomon and Sarah Rich, October 1784, Orange Co., N. C.

GEORGE, Thomas and Cynthia Herndon, 24 March 1842, Orange Co., N. C.

GEORGE, William and Matilda Herndon, 10 June 1826, Orange Co., N. C.

GERVAIS, Claudia and R. F. Turnbull, 10 January 1797, Charleston, S. C.

GETCHEY, Frederick and Esther Cline, 11 April 1787, Rowan Co., N. C.

GHEEN, James and Mary Pinxton, 7 March 1788, Rowan Co., N. C.

GHEEN, Joseph and Ann Todd, 4 April 1797, Rowan Co., N. C.

GHEEN, Thomas and Mary McBride, 17 May 1788, Rowan Co., N. C.

GIBBES, Alice and William Hort, 7 January 1772, Charleston, S. C.

GIBBES, Alston and Sarah Chisholm, 31 December 1819, Charleston, S. C.

GIBBES, Ann and Thomas How, 25 June 1829, Charleston, S. C.

GIBBES, Anne and Edward Thomas, 27 September 1767, Charleston, S. C.

GIBBES, Benjamin and Betsey Rivers, December 1785, St. Andrews Parish, S. C.

GIBBES, Edwin and Caroline Thayer, 30 November 1821, Charleston, S. C.

GIBBES, Eliza and John Wilson, 22 January 1811, Charleston, S. C.

GIBBES, Elizabeth and Charles Shepard, 1 September 1775, Charleston, S. C.

GIBBES, Elizabeth and Walter Izard, 20 November 1739, Bulls Island, S. C.

GIBBES, Henry and Elizabeth Allston, 29 August 1782, Charleston, S. C.

GIBBES, Henry and Mary Dunbar (widow), 30 August 1791, Charleston, S. C.

GIBBES, Henry and Ann Mayrant, 15 May 1820, Charleston, S. C.

GIBBES, John and Elizabeth Jennys (widow), August 1743, Charleston, S. C.

GIBBES, John and Elizabeth Bedon, 25 August 1748, St. Andrews Parish, S. C.

GIBBES, John and Elizabeth White, 6 July 1760, St. Andrews Parish, S. C.

GIBBES, John and Susanna Guerin, 26 January 1785, Charleston, S. C.

GIBBES, John and Mary Woodward, 25 July 1719, St. Andrews Parish, S. C.

GIBBES, John (Col.) and Ann Wigg (widow), 29 August 1760, Beaufort, S. C.

GIBBES, Maria A. and Joshua Jones, 6 November 1800, Charleston, S. C.

GIBBES, Mary and Nathaniel Barnwell, 7 April 1738, St. Johns Island, S. C.

GIBBES, Mary and William C. Warham, 17 July 1784, Charleston, S. C.

GIBBES, Mary and James Harvey, 23 March 1769, Ashpoo, S. C.

GIBBES, Mary and Thomas Middleton, 17 November 1774, Crowfield, S. C.

GIBBES, Mary S. and (Rev.) Robert Wilson, 22 November 1859, Charleston, S. C.

GIBBES, Robert and Elizabeth Haddrell, 2 April 1641, St. Andrews Parish, S. C.

GIBBES, Robert and Caroline Guignard, 20 December 1827, Columbia, S. C.

GIBBES, Robert and Mary How, 6 February 1855, Columbia, S. C.

GIBBES, Robert B. and Ann Smith, 30 November 1799, Charleston, S. C.

GIBBES, Sarah R. and William W. Barnwell, 11 January 1816, Charleston, S. C.

GIBBES, Sarah R. and T. R. Wilmer, 28 January 1801, Charleston, S. C.

GIBBES, Widow and Robert Williams, April 1759, Christ Church Parish, S. C.

GIBBES, William and Mary Cook, 30 October 1702, Charleston, S. C.

GIBBES, William and Anne Culcheth, 8 August 1716, St. Andrews Parish, S. C.

GIBBES, William and Mary Bennison, 7 February 1743, Charleston, S. C.

GIBBES, William and Mary Evans, 26 June 1796, James Island, S. C.

GIBBES, William and Elizabeth Hasell, 12 February 1749, St. Andrews Parish, S. C.

GIBBES, William H. and Elizabeth Allston, 29 August 1782, Santee, S. C.

GIBBES, William H. and Mary Wilson, 21 January 1808, Charleston, S. C.

GIBBONS, James and Martha Bourlin, 16 September 1794, Rowan Co., N. C.

GIBBONS, Mary and David Brown, 25 October 1804, Mecklenburg Co., N. C.

GIBBS, Jasper and Laura Drake (widow), 7 April 1839, Pottersville, S. C.

GIBBS, Robert and Mary Smith, 1788, Charleston, S. C.

GIBSON, Edward and Susanna Schwartz, 22 December 1741, Orangeburg Co., S. C.

GIBSON, Frances and John Meredith, 25 December 1771, Guilford Co., N. C.

GIBSON, Guion and Eleanor Kennedy, 8 December 1773, Pendleton, S. C.

GIBSON, James and Rebecca Robinson, 10 March 1787, Rowan Co., N. C.

GIBSON, Jane O. and Samuel Lawing, 23 September 1856, Mecklenburg Co., N. C.

GIBSON, Jesse and Mary Elizabeth Watson, 17 February 1861, Marion Co., S. C.

GIBSON, John and Margaret Fludd, 19 December 1754, Orangeburg Co., S. C.

GIBSON, John and Elizabeth Locke, 13 January 1775, Rowan Co., N. C.

GIBSON, Jonathan and Sarah Kingham, 9 September 1755, Chowan Co., N. C.

GIBSON, Joseph and Mary McCree, 16 December 1789, Rowan Co., N. C.

GIBSON, Priscilla and Robert Hawthorne, 1831, Fairfield Co., S. C.

GIBSON, Sally and Michael Moore, 5 April 1820, Edgefield District, S. C.

GIBSON, Sarah and Abraham Fulkerson, 2 July 1788, Rowan Co., N. C.

GIBSON, Sarah B. and Ezekial A. Riley, 28 December 1835, Mecklenburg Co., N. C.

GIBSON, Thomas and Anne Stocks, 30 January 1720, St. Andrews Parish, S. C.

GIBSON, Thomas and Louisa Poyas, 5 December 1799, Charleston, S. C.

GIBSON, William and Mary Fatio, 26 August 1801, Charleston, S. C.

GIEGELMAN, Hans and Ann Elizabeth Shuler, 1740, Orangeburg Co., S. C.

GIESSENDANNER, Agnes and Peter Roth, 2 February 1752, Orangeburg Co., S. C.

GIESSENDANNER, George and Agnes Diedrich (widow), June 1745, Orangeburg Co., S. C.

GIESSENDANNER, Henry and Elizabeth Rumpf, 25 February 1767, Orangeburg Co., S. C.

GIESSENDANNER, Ursula and John W. Leysath, 3 October 1752, Orangeburg Co., S. C.

GILBERT, Jesse and Sarah Green, 28 February 1764, Edgecombe Co., N. C.

GILBERT, Penelope and Jeremiah Platt, 10 March 1772, Chowan Co., N. C.

GILBERT, William and Susannah Robinson, 15 April 1775, Rowan Co., N. C.

GILBREATH, Thomas and Mary Moore, 13 February 1797, Rowan Co., N. C.

GILCHRIST, Adam (of New York) and Hetty Budd, 10 June 1784, Charleston, S. C.

GILICHRIST, Dorothy (widow) and Thomas Handy, 6 August 1799, Charleston, S. C.

GILDEN, Jane and Thomas H. Blakely, 31 March 1862, Mecklenburg Co., N. C.

GILES, Absolom and Nancy Singer, 21 August 1778, Rowan Co., N. C.

GILES, Elizabeth and George Warley, May 1786, Charleston, S. C.

GILES, Henry and Elizabeth Dunn, 19 June 1786, Rowan Co., N. C.

GILES, John and Rachel Williams, 10 January 1782, Rowan Co., N. C.

GILES, John and Mary Shipp, 3 October 1788, Rowan Co., N. C.

GILES, Miles and May P. Conner, 26 February 1822, Mecklenburg Co., N. C.

GILL, Franky and William R. White, 1830, Granville Co., N. C.

GILL, Rebecca M. and Joseph Galluchat, 22 October 1846, Lancaster, S. C.

GILLEN, Archibald and (Mrs.) Margaret Pickam, 10 December 1800, Charleston, S. C.

GILLESPEY, David and Mary Lucky, 5 April 1783, Rowan Co., N. C.

GILLESPIE, David and Mary Rogers (widow), 12 May 1770, Charleston, S. C.

GILLESPIE, Isaac and Mary Ann McGuire, 12 April 1791, Rowan Co., N. C.

GILLESPIE, James and Jane Graham, 9 January 1765, Rowan Co., N. C.

GILLESPIE, John and Margaret Kerr, 31 January 1786, Rowan Co., N. C.

GILLESPIE, John and Polly Brandon, 14 March 1790, Rowan Co., N. C.

GILLESPIE, Nancy and Paul Castelbury, 15 February 1824, Spartanburg, S. C.

GILLESPIE, Thomas and Catherine Beard, 24 August 1796, Rowan Co., N. C.

GILLEY, James and Jesebel Matshall, 5 July 1783, Rowan Co., N. C.

GILLIDEUX, Mary and Thomas Singletary, 6 January 1785, Charleston, S. C.

GILLIRD, Nicholas and Anne Hassell, 1784, Tyrrell Co., N. C.

GILLISON, Anna M. and Abraham Huguenin, 9 April 1801, St. Lukes Parish, S. C.

GILLON, Alexi and Mary Cripps (widow), 13 July 1766, Charleston, S. C.

GILMAN, Louisa and Robert Foster, 23 November 1801, Charleston, S. C.

GILMORE, Dorcas N. and Francis M. Ross, 29 December 1839, Mecklenburg Co., N. C.

GILMORE, Martha and Marcus Alexander, 13 April 1822, Mecklenburg Co., N. C.

GILPIN, James and Rebecca Potts, 29 April 1789, Rowan Co., N. C.

GINGERY, Elizabeth and Anthony Hallman, 11 July 1774, Rowan Co., N. C.

GINGLER, Rosanna and William Morrison, 9 March 1819, Mecklenburg Co., N. C.

GINGLES, Peggy and James S. Russell, 8 February 1809, Mecklenburg Co., N. C.

GINGLES, Rachel and Samuel F. Morrison, 18 April 1818, Mecklenburg Co., N. C.

GINGLES, Samuel and Eleanor Beatty, 14 December 1782, Rowan Co., N. C.

GINING, Malissa and James Landford, 10 September 1859, Laurens Co., S. C.

GINNESS, Ann and Gabriel G. R. Des Molleres, 3 June 1796, Charleston, S. C.

GIST, Jane M. and John H. Brooks (2nd. m.), 30 December 1858, Edgefield, S. C.

GIST, Joseph and Sarah McDaniel, 28 December 1800, Union Co., S. C.

GIST, Mordecai and Mary Cattell, January 1784, Charleston, S. C.

GIVEN, Agnes and Benjamin Duche, May 1784, Beaufort, S. C.

GIVENS, Elizabeth and Solomon Bradshaw, 1 August 1797, Mecklenburg Co., N. C.

GIVENS, Elizabeth (Mrs.) and Samuel Lawrence, 18 January 1801, Beaufort, S. C.

GIVENS, James and Pheby Mosier, 19 December 1792, Rowan Co., N. C.

GIVENS, Matheze and Samuel Adams, 24 January 1799, Mecklenburg Co., N. C.

GLADDING, Joseph and Martha Wilkins, 21 March 1801, Charleston, S. C.

GLASCOCK, Charnal and Mary Luckey, 25 October 1794, Rowan Co., N. C.

GLASCOCK, Harmon and Nancy Garrowood, October 1792, Rowan Co., N. C.

GLASCOCK, Henry and Peggy Glascock, 16 March 1793, Rowan Co., N. C.

GLASCOCK, Peggy and Henry Glascock, 16 March 1793, Rowan Co., N. C.

GLASCOCK, Spencer and Polly Enochs, 12 September 1791, Rowan Co., N. C.

GLASCOCK, William and Mary Hales, 4 September 1795, Rowan Co., N. C.

GLASCOCK, Winny and Jacob Garrawood, 15 September 1795, Rowan Co., N. C.

GLASS, Sally and Augustus Alexander, 13 February 1839, Mecklenburg Co., N. C.

GLASS, Sally and Jonathan Read, 4 June 1816, Mecklenburg Co., N. C.

GLAUGHAN, Sarah and John Farrow, 10 March 1785, Chowan Co., N. C.

GLEN, Charlotte and John McCall (Jr.), 9 November 1767, Charleston, S. C.

GLEN, Eliza and Thomas Corker, 31 May 1797, Charleston, S. C.

GLEN, Miss and John Drayton, February 1752, Charleston, S. C.

GLEN, William and Martha Mitchell, 5 April 1770, Charleston, S. C.

GLENN, Elizabeth and John Switzer, 25 April 1859, Laurens Co., S. C.

GLENN, Jeremiah (widower) and Elizabeth Barksdale, 30 March 1854, Laurens Co., S. C.

GLENN, John and Ann McAfee, 10 September 1848, Laurens Co., S. C.

GLENN, Lydia J. and James McPherson, 10 January 1772, Santee, S. C.

GLEW, Eliza and Thomas Corker, 30 May 1799, Charleston, S. C.

GLISSON, Elizabeth and William Cottle, 25 August 1790, Bertie Co., N. C.

GLISSON, Isaac and (Mrs.) Martha Whitfield, June 1762, Tyrrell Co., N. C.

GLOVER, Elizabeth and Willis Nixon, 27 March 1834, Mecklenburg Co., N. C.

GLOVER, Elizabeth E. and James Byram, 1 January 1839, Mecklenburg Co., N. C.

GLOVER, Joseph and Betsy Jeanerette, April 1784, Santee, S. C.

GLOVER, Mary B. and William Ratchford, 19 September 1832, Mecklenburg Co., N. C.

GLOVER, Miss and Thomas Waties, 19 January 1786, Ponpon, S. C.

GLOVER, Moses and (Mrs.) Hepburn, 12 October 1799, Charleston, S. C.

GLOVER, Sanders and Lydia Tucker, May 1784, Charleston, S. C.

GLOVER, William and Jean McBride, 4 June 1796, Rowan Co., N. C.

GOBEL, John and Mary Coldiron, 25 May 1793, Rowan Co. N. C.

GODARD, Rene and Maria Juhoan, 7 February 1795, Charleston, S. C.

GODFREY, Ann and John Hannahan (Jr.), 20 November 1800, Charleston, S. C.

GODFREY, James and Elizabeth Culbertson, 13 January 1859, Laurens Co., S. C.

GODFREY, Jane and Christopher Gadsden, 28 July 1746, Charleston, S. C.

GODFREY, Mary and John Kannady, 29 September 1747, Orangeburg Co., S. C.

GODFREY, Richard and Rebecca Guy, 22 January 1743, St. Andrews Parish, S. C.

GODFREY, Sarah and Benjamin Whitaker, 20 May 1719, St. Andrews Parish, S. C.

GODIN, Amelia and Benjamin Garden, 17 January 1765, Prince William Parish, S. C.

GODIN, Elizabeth S. and Jacques P. de Bonnesons, 10 July 1785, Charleston, S. C.

GODIN, Martha and Stephen Bull, 27 April 1731, Newberry, S. C.
GODSDEN, Elizabeth and Andrew Rutledge, 29 September 1767, Charleston, S. C.
GODWIN, Ann and John Davenport, July 1783, Tyrrell Co., N. C.
GODWIN, Joseph and Mary Phelps, 1781, Tyrrell Co., N. C.
GODWIN, —— and Sarah Townsend, 9 April 1785, Charleston, S. C.
GOELETT, James and Mary Hancock, 27 February 1743, Charleston, S. C.
GOFF, Mary Ann and James Holliday, 30 April 1855, Edgefield District, S. C.
GOFORTH, Elizabeth and John Banker, 7 January 1813, Mecklenburg Co., N. C.
GOING, Britton and Mary Chambers, 30 April 1791, Rowan Co., N. C.
GOINS, Ezekial and Sarah Gunter, 14 July 1779, Rowan Co., N. C.
GOLDEN, Ann and John Baddeley, 9 November 1784, Charleston, S. C.
GOLDMAN, Haney and Nellie Conkright, 9 September 1780, Rowan Co., N. C.
GOLDSMITH, Daniel and Elenor Dunstan, 20 April 1753, Chowan Co., N. C.
GOLIGHTLY, Culcheth and Mary Elliott, 1 April 1746, Charleston, S. C.
GOLIGHTLY, Mary and Benjamin Huger, 26 July 1767, Charleston, S. C.
GOLIGHTLY, Dorothy and William H. Drayton, 29 March 1764, Charleston, S. C.
GOLIGHTLY, Widow and Henry Hyrne, June 1759, Charleston, S. C.
GOLSEN, Lewis and Elizabeth Stehely, 19 December 1752, Orangeburg Co., S. C.
GOMILLION, John and Polly Hatcher, 6 July 1820, Edgefield District, S. C.
GOMILLION, Lovett and Mary Ann Spann, 3 January 1852, Edgefield District, S. C.
GOMILLION, Mary and Samuel F. Goode, 28 June 1840, Edgefield District, S. C.
GOOD, Celia and Russell Freeman, 1 September 1796, Rowan Co., N. C.
GOODBY, Sirrah and John Middleton, 1746, Orangeburg Co., S. C.
GOODE, Samuel F. and Mary Gomillion, 28 June 1840, Edgefield District, S. C.
GOODEN, Perthia and Joseph Hindesley, 7 November 1785, Chowan Co., N. C.
GODIN, Drury and Teresay Knight, 15 July 1763, Edgecombe Co., N. C.
GOODING, William James and Elizabeth Terry, 4 September 1856, Beaufort District, S. C.
GOODLOE, David S. and Mary Hill, May 1801, Granville Co., N. C.
GOODLOE, Mary and John Somerville, 10 August 1779, Granville Co., N. C.
GOODMAN, Catherine and John Farrell, 17 January 1791, Rowan Co., N. C.
GOODMAN, Mary and John Fink, 4 May 1790, Rowan Co., N. C.
GOODMAN, Michael and Rosanna Speak, 9 November 1785, Rowan Co., N. C.
GOODMAN, Nancy and Zachariah Bowman, 27 August 1801, Vienna, S. C.
GOODMAN, Polly and John Hawkins, 27 December 1796, Rowan Co., N. C.
GOODMAN, Thomas and Mary Coddle, 1 September 1797, Rowan Co., N. C.
GOODWIN, Charles and Elizabeth Williamson, 1788, Charleston, S. C.
GOODWIN, Isaac and Mary Mitchell, 4 January 1821, Chowan Co., N. C.
GOODWIN, John and Elizabeth Street (widow), August 1743, Ashley Ferry, S. C.
GOODWIN, John K. and Margaret Kinnard, 1814, Edgefield, S. C.
GOODWIN, William and Tabitha Merrit, 8 March 1768, Edgecombe Co., N. C.
GOODNALL, Federick and Christina Hill, 1 August 1775, Rowan Co., N. C.
GOOLSBY, Wyatt and Jane Crook, 9 October 1787, Rowan Co., N. C.
GORDEN, Ann P. and Robert Bobo, 6 May 1858, Union District, S. C.
GORDON, Frances and John Troup, 30 May 1763, Charleston, S. C.
GORDON, James and Mary Vaux, 13 February 1764, Charleston, S. C.
GORDON, James and Mary Riddle, 12 February 1779, Rowan Co., N. C.

GORDON, James and Martha Wells, 5 August 1784, St. Thomas Parish, S. C.
GORDON, James and (Mrs.) Margaret Gray, 16 January 1800, Charleston, S. C.
GORDON, Mary and William Howie, 14 August 1834, Mecklenburg Co., N. C.
GORDON, Nancy and James O'Hare, 10 February 1774, Charleston, S. C.
GORDON, Robert and Sarah Ray, 12 August 1769, Tyrrell Co., N. C.
GORDON, Robert and Mary Carson, 11 March 1773, Rowan Co., N. C.
GORDON, Sarah and James Norfleet, 1 December 1774, Chowan Co., N. C.
GOSLIN, John and Judith Davis, 10 March 1780, Rowan Co., N. C.
GOSS, David and Elizabeth Boss, 24 March 1794, Rowan Co., N. C.
GOSS, Ephriam and Anne Workman, 23 March 1795, Rowan Co., N. C.
GOSS, Frederick and Sarah Elston, 1 January 1787, Rowan Co., N. C.
GOSS, George E. and Mary Frost, 21 February 1792, Rowan Co., N. C.
GOSS, Jacob and Rebecca Billing, 24 September 1791, Rowan Co., N. C.
GOUGH, Thomas and Leslie Creighton (widow), August 1783, Charleston, S. C.
GOURDINE, Theodore and Elizabeth Gaillard, 20 October 1785, Charleston, S. C.
GRACEY, John and Jenny Lawrence, 11 February 1784, Rowan Co., N. C.
GRADEN, William and Sarah McPherson, 6 December 1855, Laurens Co., S. C.
GRAEME, David and Anne Mathews, 21 January 1759, Charleston, S. C.
GRAHAM, Ann and John Mair, 18 November 1800, Beaufort, S. C.
GRAHAM, Ann E. and William Johnston, 16 March 1846, Mecklenburg Co., N. C.
GRAHAM, Benjamin and Faithful Hall, 13 November 1782, Rowan Co., N. C.
GRAHAM, Caroline and William M. Bostwick, 21 February 1817, Mecklenburg Co., N. C.
GRAHAM, Catherine and Paul Ferguson, 21 November 1791, Rowan Co., N. C.
GRAHAM, Catherine and Robert Brown, 22 January 1800, Beaufort, S. C.
GRAHAM, David and Elizabeth Hunter, 9 January 1770, Santee, S. C.
GRAHAM, David and Margaret Parks, 3 November 1799, Rowan Co., N. C.
GRAHAM, Edward and Mary Noland, 24 February 1794, Rowan Co., N. C.
GRAHAM, Elizabeth and Christopher Hart, 24 December 1784, Charleston, S. C.
GRAHAM, James and Margaret Porter, 6 May 1786, Rowan Co., N. C.
GRAHAM, James (Jr.) and Agnes Kerr, 27 November 1771, Rowan Co., N. C.
GRAHAM, Jane and James Gillespie, 9 January 1765, Rowan Co., N. C.
GRAHAM, Jane and William McRee, 23 December 1814, Mecklenburg Co., N. C.
GRAHAM, Jennet and Nathan B. Carroll, 13 October 1831, Mecklenburg Co., N. C.
GRAHAM, John and Sarah Bunton, 25 January 1785, Rowan Co., N. C.
GRAHAM, John and Sally Stuart, 16 July 1767, Charleston, S. C.
GRAHAM, John and Jeane Donaldson, 21 December 1786, Rowan Co., N. C.
GRAHAM, John and Mary Byrd, 11 October 1782, Orange Co., N. C.
GRAHAM, John and Margaret Hall, 6 September 1791, Rowan Co., N. C.
GRAHAM, Joseph and Jane Shiles, 24 February 1796, Rowan Co., N. C.
GRAHAM, Margaret and William Graham, 2 June 1767, Rowan Co., N. C.
GRAHAM, Polly and James Crawford, 5 September 1804, Mecklenburg Co., N. C.
GRAHAM, Richard and Jane Erwin, 20 October 1779, Rowan Co., N. C.
GRAHAM, William and Margaret Graham, 2 June 1767, Rowan Co., N. C.
GRANSBERRY, James and Penelope Moore, 18 May 1790, Bertie Co., N. C.
GRANT, Frances and James Halsey, 12 July 1764, Santee, S. C.
GRANT, John and (Mrs.) Mary Cameron, June 1785, Charleston, S. C.
GRANT, Mary and John Vivine, 7 June 1771, Santee, S. C.

GRANT, Rebecca and George W. Hines, 6 February 1759, Laurens Co., S. C.

GRANT, Washington and Mary Moore, 25 November 1858, Laurens Co., S. C.

GRAVES, Conrad and Mary Feaser, 9 January 1767, Rowan Co., N. C.

GRAVES, Elizabeth and John Brown, 7 February 1771, Charleston, S. C.

GRAVES, George and Elizabeth Booe, 18 December 1792, Rowan Co., N. C.

GRAVES, Matthew D. and Esther Mann, 15 October 1768, Tyrrell Co., N. C.

GRAVES, Patsy and Peter Pedro, 14 April 1800, Charleston, S. C.

GRAY, Ann and David Gray, 8 December 1793, Rowan Co., N. C.

GRAY, Charles and Ann Green, 2 September 1841, Edgefield District, S. C.

GRAY, David and Ann Gray, 8 December 1793, Rowan Co., N. C.

GRAY, Deborah (widow) and John Wilkins, 3 January 1744, Chowan Co., N. C.

GRAY, George and Mary Stuart, 1 July 1769, Rowan Co., N. C.

GRAY, Hugh and Isabelle Moore, 31 March 1789, Rowan Co., N. C.

GRAY, Jane and Jacob Markert, 25 November 1827, Mecklenburg Co., N. C.

GRAY, Lydia and John Collins, 22 October 1767, Tyrrell Co., N. C.

GRAY, Margaret and Andrew Holmes, 22 May 1800, Charleston, S. C.

GRAY, Margaret (Mrs.) and James Gordon, 16 January 1800, Charleston, S. C.

GRAY, Martha and Joseph Hunt, May 1772, Charleston, S. C.

GRAY, Mary and William Jeffreys, 30 July 1773, Edgecombe Co., N. C.

GRAY, Mary and John Ray, 22 February 1763, Tyrrell Co., N. C.

GRAY, Mary A. and Ira A. Orr, 24 January 1831, Mecklenburg Co., N. C.

GRAY, Nancy and William S. Alexander, 7 March 1835, Mecklenburg Co., N. C.

GRAY, Robert and Liza Taylor, 7 August 1845, Laurens Co., S. C.

GRAY, Sarah H. and James Owens, 14 November 1831, Mecklenburg Co., N. C.

GRAY, Susan and Wesley Barnes, 19 December 1838, Edgefield District, S. C.

GRAY, Thomas and Jane McGahee, 1 February 1786, Rowan Co., N. C.

GRAY, Thomas and Cinthia Moseley, 23 March 1843, Laurens Co., S. C.

GRAY, William and Ann Shaw, 1748, Orangeburg Co., S. C.

GRAY, William and Susan Wiggins, 16 February 1852, Edgefield District, S. C.

GRAY, Zinah and Zephaniah Davis, 7 February 1786, Tyrrell Co., N. C.

GRAYSON, Elizabeth and John M. Verdier, 15 December 1785, Beaufort, S. C.

GREBLE, Frances and Thomas O. Black, 7 March 1823, Mecklenburg Co., N. C.

GREEN, Ann and Charles Gray, 2 September 1841, Edgefield District, S. C.

GREEN, Enoch and Elizabeth Booth, 9 September 1794, Rowan Co., N. C.

GREEN, Isaac and Mary Booth, 21 December 1793, Rowan Co., N. C.

GREEN, James C. and Margaret M. Farquhar, 16 March 1797, Charleston, S. C.

GREEN, James and Roxanna George, 6 January 1856, Orange Co., N. C.

GREEN, Jenny and Robert Allen, 13 February 1806, Mecklenburg Co., N. C.

GREEN, Jeremiah and Mary Wiseman, 3 October 1773, Rowan Co., N. C.

GREEN, Jeremiah (Jr.) and Anne Hartley, 2 April 1790, Rowan Co., N. C.

GREEN, Joana and Reuben Harkley, 6 November 1798, Rowan Co., N. C.

GREEN, John and Hannah Hunt, 16 January 1779, Rowan Co., N. C.

GREEN, John and Mary Elms, 28 November 1719, St. Andrews Parish, S. C.

GREEN, Margaret and James Bowman, December 1785, Beaufort, S. C.

GREEN, Mary and Joy Purdie, 28 August 1765, Chowan Co., N. C.

GREEN, Mary and Walter Izard, 10 October 1827, Rose Hill, S. C.

GREEN, Miss and Asa Stevens, 13 November 1854, Edgefield District, S. C.

GREEN, Rachel and Samuel Black, 24 August 1819, Mecklenburg Co., N. C.

GREEN, Samuel and Susanna Chanler, 15 January 1770, Charleston, S. C.

GREEN, Samuel and Catherine Campbell, 20 September 1765, Charleston, S. C.

GREEN, Sarah and Jesse Gilbert, 28 February 1764, Edgecombe Co., N. C.

GREEN, Tabitha and Mathers Bigham, 27 September 1808, Mecklenburg Co., N. C.

GREENAGE, Mary and William Lenox, 6 October 1794, Charleston, S. C.

GREENE, Daniel J. and (Mrs.) Elizabeth Adams, 22 April 1784, Beaufort, S. C.

GREENE, Elizabeth and Richard Ellis, 22 April 1784, Beaufort, S. C.

GREENE, Polly and (Rev.) Stephen Lewis, 1 March 1785, Beaufort, S. C.

GREENHOW, Anne and Edward Webley, 15 September 1763, Charleston, S. C.

GREENLAND, George and Patience Simmons, 10 December 1770, Santee, S. C.

GREENLAND, Mary and Peter Simmons, 30 December 1770, Santee, S. C.

GREENLAND, Samuel A. and Esther Johnston, 14 November 1799, Charleston, S. C.

GREGORY, Barbara and Wiliam Lofther, 22 April 1756, Chowan Co., N. C.

GREGORY, Charity and Thomas White, 9 December 1785, Chowan Co., N. C.

GREGORY, Deborah and Edward Haughton, 20 February 1785, Chowan Co., N. C.

GREGORY, James (Jr.) and Ann Ladson, 5 February 1801, Charleston, S. C.

GREGORY, Luke and Elizabeth Haughton, 29 November 1779, Chowan Co., N. C.

GREGORY, Penelope and Jeremiah Frazier, 8 March 1761, Chowan Co., N. C.

GREGORY, Perasday and A. R. Able, 12 July 1855, Edgefield District, S. C.

GREGORY, Sally M. and William L. Taylor, 11 January 1845, Granville Co., N. C.

GREGORY, Thomas and Mary Benton, 4 July 1767, Chowan Co., N. C.

GREY, Sophia and James Robison, 11 December 1810, Mecklenburg Co., N. C.

GREY, William and Hannah Andrew, 11 July 1721, St. Andrews Parish, S. C.

GRIBBLE, Mary and James Ballard, 15 September 1795, Mecklenburg Co., N. C.

GRICE, John and Sally Gallman, 5 October 1828, Edgefield District, S. C.

GRICE, Joseph and Rebecca Autry, 28 January 1836, Edgefield District, S. C.

GRICE, Mary and Jesse Weatherford, 7 August 1845, Edgefield District, S. C.

GRICE, Sally and Jesse Frice, 2 December 1830, Edgefield District, S. C.

GRICE, William and Alice Brady, 2 April 1780, Rowan Co., N. C.

GRIEFFOUS, Peter and Anna Otto, 25 May 1741, Orangeburg Co., S. C.

GRIER, Elizabeth and Duncan McEwen, 5 April 1820, Mecklenburg Co., N. C.

GRIER, Joseph and Rebecca Grier, August 1785, Charleston, S. C.

GRIER, Margaret and John Arnold, 14 March 1835, Mecklenburg Co., N. C.

GRIER, Mary and Peter Mullins, 19 October 1790, Mecklenburg Co., N. C.

GRIER, Mary and Leroy Adams, 14 July 1847, Mecklenburg Co., N. C.

GRIER, Mary B. and James B. Read, 14 March 1837, Mecklenburg Co., N. C.

GRIER, Mary I. and Jeremiah S. Read, 6 November 1855, Mecklenburg Co., N. C.

GRIER, Mary J. and Robert A. Ross, 31 October 1848, Mecklenburg Co., N. C.

GRIER, Rebecca and Joseph Grier, August 1785, Charleston, S. C.

GRIFFIN, Elizabeth ad John Millersey, 22 July 1793, Guilford Co., N. C.

GRIFFIN, Exum and Lavinia Mitchell, 22 November 1830, Chowan Co., N. C.

GRIFFIN, Ezekial and Catherine Thomas, 27 September 1786, Rowan Co., N. C.

GRIFFIN, James and Elizabeth Darden, 27 December 1777, Chowan Co., N. C.

GRIFFIN, Jane and Jacob Rodden, 25 January 1795, Mecklenburg Co., N. C.

GRIFFIN, Jemima and Lewis Mitchell, 15 January 1847, Chowan Co., N. C.

GRIFFIN, Jesse and Ann Clarey, 18 February 1772, Rowan Co., N. C.

GRIFFIN, John and Zilpa Airs, 26 December 1775, Tyrrell Co., N. C.

GRIFFIN, John and Martha Jones, 27 April 1761, Edgecombe Co., N. C.

GRIFFIN, Lewis and Susanna Davidson, 5 June 1801, Charleston, S. C.

GRIFFIN, Martha and Witfield Jennings, 4 November 1857, Edgefield District, S. C.

GRIFFIN, Sarah and Dennis Smith, 1 June 1858, Laurens Co., S. C.

GRIFFIN, William and Polly Wyley, 19 December 1784, Charleston, S. C.

GRIFFIN, Youkley and Sally Mullicar, 19 January 1796, Rowan Co., N. C.

GRIFFIS, Lewis and Mary Braswell, 28 June 1764, Edgecombe Co., N. C.

GRIFFITH, Ann E. and John W. Brown, 13 January 1753, Mecklenburg Co., N. C.

GRIFFITH, Aurora and Thomas Achison, 17 April 1793, Mecklenburg Co., N. C.

GRIFFITH, Catherine and Joseph Byram, 17 February 1818, Mecklenburg Co., N. C.

GRIFFITH, David and Hannah Middleton, 11 June 1750, Orangeburg Co., S. C.

GRIFFITH, Edward and Martha Miles, 19 November 1767, St. Pauls Parish, S. C.

GRIFFITH, Edward and Elizabeth Sharpe, 1 April 1783, Rowan Co., N. C.

GRIFFITH, Harrison P. and Amanda Lanford, 22 January 1861, Laurens Co., S. C.

GRIFFITH, John and Jane Hardin, 2 November 1785, Rowan Co., N. C.

GRIFFITH, John X. and Ann M. Thewratt, 4 October 1764, Rowan Co., N. C.

GRIFFITH, Rachel and Michael Baker, 13 May 1812, Mecklenburg Co., N. C.

GRIFFITH, Michael and Joseph Rutherford, 5 June 1808, Edgefield District, S. C.

GRIFFITH, Roger and Faithy Wall, 14 February 1765, Edgecombe Co., N. C.

GRIFFITH, Sicily and Elijah Cooper, 20 March 1845, Laurens Co., S. C.

GRIFFITH, Susan P. and William P. Alexander, 3 November 1857, Mecklenburg Co., N. C.

GRIGGS, Clemand and Lydia Jenkins, 8 June 1771, Santee, S. C.

GRIGGS, Henry and Anne Towe, 26 February 1791, Rowan Co., N. C.

GRIGGS, John and Sarah Webb, December 1783, Charleston, S. C.

GRIGGS, Mary and Thomas Spencer, 31 October 1771, Santee, S. C.

GRIM, Susannah (widow) and Joseph Lyons, 4 January 1740, Orangeburg Co., S. C.

GRIMBALL, John and Eliza Berkeley, 25 April 1797, Beaufort Co., S. C.

GRIMBALL, Isaac and Rebecca Sealy, 7 May 1747, Charleston, S. C.

GRIMBALL, Thomas and Mary Prioleau, 10 June 1765, Charleston, S. C.

GRIMES, Bryan and Nancy Grist, 18 August 1815, Avon, N. C.

GRIMES, Bryan and Charlotte E. Bryan, 15 September 1863, Grimesland, N. C.

GRIMES, Demsie and Penelope Cofield, 24 June 1760, Avon, N. C.

GRIMES, William and Ann Bryan, 21 January 1790, Avon, N. C.

GRIMKE, Ann and Charles M. Cosslett, 17 December 1772, Charleston, S. C.

GRIMKE, Elizabeth and John Rutledge, 1 May 1763, Charleston, S. C.

GRIMKE, Mary and Alexander Fraser, 20 March 1755, Charleston, S. C.

GRIMKIE, John F. and Polly Smith, 5 October 1784, Charleston, S. C.

GRIMMER, Peter and Dorothea Huber, 31 January 1738, Orangeburg Co., S. C.

GRINKLIN, William and Elizabeth Smothers, 9 January 1789, Rowan Co., N. C.

GRIST, Nancy and Bryan Grimes, 18 August 1815, Avon, N. C.

GROCEL, John H. and Elizabeth Kaler, 17 June 1793, Rowan Co., N. C.

GROCHAN, John and Adelle De Grasse, 17 February 1801, Charleston, S. C.

GROEF, Abraham and Mary Adam, 3 November 1779, Rowan Co., N. C.

GROSHON, Peter and Elizabeth Williams, 31 November 1784, Chowan Co., N. C.

GROSS, Frederick and Elizabeth Haller, 21 October 1791, Rowan Co., N. C.

GROSS, Simon and Elizabeth Shirmer, 13 February 1770, Rowan Co., N. C.

GROSSMAN, John and Margaret Stephen, 11 October 1753, Orangeburg Co., S. C.

GROVES, Joseph and Margaret Eller, 4 September 1796, Rowan Co., N. C.

GROVES, Richard and Keziah Waff, 8 July 1779, Chowan Co., N. C.

GRUBB, Conrad and Elizabeth Hartman, 26 March 1795, Rowan Co., N. C.

GUERARD, Benjamin and Mary Ann Kennan, 1 April 1786, Charleston, S. C.

GUERARD, David and Judith de St. Julian, 26 October 1767, Charleston, S. C.

GUERARD, David and Martha Barnwell, 23 September 1770, Port Royal, S. C.

GUERARD, Godin and Anne Matthews, 23 August 1769, Charleston, S. C.

GUERIN, Elizabeth and David Cruger, June 1786, Charleston, S. C.

GUERIN, Henrietta and John Turnbull, 18 December 1800, Charleston, S. C.

GUERIN, Mathurin and Mary Peacock, 7 January 1774, Charleston, S. C.

GUERIN, Miss and Thomas Stone, May 1759, Charleston, S. C.

GUERIN, Susanna and John Gibbes, 26 January 1785, Charleston, S. C.

GUERIN, William and Mary Elliott, 24 November 1763, Charleston, S. C.

GUERRARD, Robert and Harriot L. de Treville, 13 January 1801, Beaufort, S. C.

GUERRY, Mary and Jonah Roberts, 3 May 1774, Santee, S. C.

GUERRY, Peter and Judith Croft, 30 July 1778, Santee, S. C.

GUERRY, Stephen and Mary Sanders, 9 September 1769, Santee, S. C.

GUERRY, Stephen and Frances Michean, 3 December 1779, Santee, S. C.

GUFFY, Elizabeth and Samuel Hughes, 16 December 1792, Rowan Co., N. C.

GUIGNARD, Anne and William Richardson, 13 October 1768, Charleston, S. C.

GUIGNARD, Caroline and Robert Gibbes, 20 December 1827, Columbia, S. C.

GUIGNARD, James S. and Carolina Richardson, 14 January 1801, Charleston, S. C.

GUILD, Jacob and Martha Hoovey, 13 February 1786, Orange Co., N. C.

GUINN, John and Sarah Harper, 26 February 1782, Orange Co., N. C.

GUION, Betsy and Solo Murphy, 29 October 1781, Orange Co., N. C.

GULLENT, Nancy and John W. Byram, 4 August 1828, Mecklenburg Co., N. C.

GULLIATT, Avey (Mrs.) and Hardy Pitman, 16 September 1801, St. Pauls Parish, S. C.

GUNTER, Edward and Martha Melachamp, 12 April 1772, Berkeley Co., S. C.

GUNTER, George and Abby Alkins, 3 August 1774, Rowan Co., N. C.

GUNTER, Sarah and Ezekial Goins, 14 July 1779, Rowan Co., N. C.

GURRIN, Frances and Stephen Taylor, 6 June 1845, Granville Co., N. C.

GUSTON, Mabel and John Fitzpatrick, 3 April 1787, Rowan Co., N. C.

GUSTON, Mary (widow) and William Seward, 20 February 1743, Chowan Co., N. C.

GUTHRIDGE, Garland and Bridget Hampton, 26 September 1778, Rowan Co., N. C.

GUY, Rebecca and Richard Godfrey, 22 January 1743, St. Andrews Parish, S. C.

GWINN, Peter and Sarah Taylor, 21 November 1769, Rowan Co., N. C.

GYGER, Hans Jacob and Margaret Shuler (widow), 1740, Orangeburg Co., S. C.

GYGER, Ann Barbara and Antony Ernst, 1740, Orangeburg Co., S. C.

GYLES, Thomas and Rosena Bouysson, 11 January 1800, Charleston, S. C.

H

HAANER, William and Eliza Woodruff, 24 May 1866, Laurens Co., S. C.

HACKETT, Aaron and Tabitha Hambleton, 25 July 1798, Rowan Co., N. C.

HACKETT, James and Mary Woods, 14 October 1773, Rowan Co., N. C.

HACKETT, Michael (Dr.) and Elizabeth White, February 1765, Charleston, S. C.

HACKNEY, William and Martha Weeks, 17 August 1765, Edgecombe Co., N. C.

HADDRELL, Elizabeth and Robert Gibbes, 2 April 1641, St. Andrews Parish, S. C.

HADLOCK, Robert and Elizabeth Coleman, 6 September 1793, Rowan Co., N. C.

HAGAR, George and Elizabeth Fyte, 17 January 1791, Rowan Co., N. C.

HAGAS, Peter and Elizabeth Reynolds, 14 February, 1780, Rowan Co., N. C.

HAGEY, Jacob and Betsy Brookshire, 28 December 1799, Rowan Co., N. C.

HAGIN, Ann Maria and Francis Koonen, 1 September 1748, Orangeburg Co., S. C.

HAGLER, Adam and Mary Crowell, 28 March 1838, Mecklenburg Co., N. C.

HAGLER, John and Margaret Hinson, 14 February 1828, Mecklenburg Co., N. C.

HAGLER, Lucy and David M. Blackwelder, 24 December 1857, Mecklenburg Co., N. C.

HAGLER, Nellie and Isaac W. Blackwelder, 6 September 1856, Mecklenburg Co., N. C.

HAGLEY, John and Polly Love, 21 April 1795, Rowan Co., N. C.

HAGOOD, Alice and Isaac H. Means, 8 March 1854, Fairfield Co., S. C.

HAHNBAUM, Eliza (widow) and Gilbert Davidson, 14 January 1801, Charleston, S. C.

HAHNBAUM, Mary (Mrs.) and John R. Switzer, 14 January 1801, Charleston, S. C.

HAIG, Elizabeth and Peter Leger, (Jr.), 23 November 1760, Charleston, S. C.

HAIG, George (Dr.) and Susanah McKewn, 2 May 1769, St. Pauls Parish, S. C.

HAIG, George and Mary Maham, 17 July 1785, Charleston, S. C.

HAIG, Sarah and William Allan, 18 April 1801, Charleston, S. C.

HAINES, Jane and William Brown, 12 April 1800, Mecklenburg Co., N. C.

HAINEY, Nancy and Reuben Read, 11 August 1837, Mecklenburg Co., N. C.

HAINLINE, Christopher and Elizabeth Cross, 29 August 1786, Rowan Co., N. C.

HAINS, Elizabeth and Robert Miller, 15 September 1720, Charleston, S. C.

HALDE, Joseph and Mary Bailey, 30 November 1789, Rowan Co., N. C.

HALE, Rachel and Solomon Forehand, 24 September 1763, Edgecombe Co., N. C.

HALER, Elizabeth and John H. Grocel, 17 June 1793, Rowan Co., N. C.

HALES, Mary and William Glascock, 4 September 1795, Rowan Co., N. C.

HALEY, Eleanor and Nicholas Fitzpatrick, 1 January 1801, Charleston, S. C.

HALL, Adam and Sarah Freeman, 26 March 1778, Rowan Co., N. C.

HALL, Andrew and Jean Linster, 12 March 1793, Rowan Co., N. C.

HALL, Anna and Thomas Thomson, 26 December 1799, Charleston, S. C.

HALL, Daniel and Susannah Matthews, 21 January 1775, Charleston, S. C.

HALL, Edward and (Mrs.) Martha Norcom, 10 July 1750, Chowan Co., N. C.

HALL, Edward and Rachel Haughton, 30 July 1753, Chowan Co., N. C.
HALL, Edward and Ann Allen, 23 June 1813, Mecklenburg Co., N. C.
HALL, Eliza and Robert Hazlehurst, 1788, Charleston, S. C.
HALL, Eliza M. and Robert D. Lawrence, 19 December 1799, Charleston, S. C.
HALL, Elizabeth and John Harvey, 11 March 1778, Chowan Co., N. C.
HALL, Faithful and Benjamin Graham, 13 November 1782, Rowan Co., N. C.
HALL, George A. and Lois Matthews, 14 February 1764, Charleston, S. C.
HALL, Isabella and James Ramsey, 8 February 1792, Mecklenburg Co., N. C.
HALL, James and Mason Hall, 19 December 1764, Edgecombe Co., N. C.
HALL, James and Surena Dulin, 6 February 1851, Mecklenburg Co., N. C.
HALL, James and Rachel Johnston, 9 January 1792, Rowan Co., N. C.
HALL, James and Elizabeth Orr, 14 August 1740, Mecklenburg Co., N. C.
HALL, John and Mary Ann Dodd, 10 April 1774, Charleston, S. C.
HALL, John and Mary Hare, 10 May 1781, Rowan Co., N. C.
HALL, John and Sarah Anderson, 2 March 1796, Rowan Co., N. C.
HALL, Joseph and Katherine Wilson, 7 August 1788, Rowan Co., N. C.
HALL, Joseph and Margaret Linster, 9 August 1793, Rowan Co., N. C.
HALL, Joseph and Hannah Campbell, 16 March 1796, Rowan Co., N. C.
HALL, Lucretia and A. F. Brown, 13 December 1860, Mecklenburg Co., N. C.
HALL, Margaret and John Graham, 6 September 1791, Rowan Co., N. C.
HALL, Maria and William S. Brisbane, 19 March 1795, Charleston, S. C.
HALL, Mary and Mr. Osmond, 13 April 1732, Charleston, S. C.
HALL, Mary J. and James G. Brown, 4 September 1860, Mecklenburg Co., N. C.
HALL, Mason and James Hall, 19 December 1764, Edgecombe Co., N. C.
HALL, Phebe and Isaac Eaton, 27 November 1768, Rowan Co., N. C.
HALL, Polly and Henry Peronneau, 2 October 1783, Charleston, S. C.
HALL, Robert and Ann Leary, 4 August 1742, Chowan Co., N. C.
HALL, Robert and Mary Wasson, October 1790, Rowan Co., N. C.
HALL, Samuel and Lucretia Rodgers, 21 August 1826, Mecklenburg Co., N. C.
HALL, Sarah and John Cattell, 24 April 1728, Berkeley Co., S. C.
HALL, Susan M. and Peyre Gaillard, 26 December 1799, Charleston, S. C.
HALL, Thomas and Mary Newton, 7 November 1785, Charleston, S. C.
HALL, William and Elizabeth Wilson, 7 January 1783, Rowan Co., N. C.
HALL, William and Polly Murdock, 9 February 1786, Orange Co., N. C.
HALL, William T. and Frances Witherspoon, June 1863, Lancaster Co., S. C.
HALLER, Elizabeth and Frederick Griss, 21 October 1791, Rowan Co., N. C.
HALLER, John and Margaret Len, 16 October 1794, Rowan Co., N. C.
HALLIDAY, Ann and Captain Peterson, 2 January 1801, Charleston, S. C.
HALLIDAY, Mary (Mrs.) and George Thompson, 18 May 1800, Charleston, S. C.
HALLMAN, Anthony and Elizabeth Gingery, 11 July 1774, Rowan Co., N. C.
HALSEY, Ann and Lewis Jones, 18 June 1761, Chowan Co., N. C.
HALSEY, Azenath and Hezekiah Jones, 6 March 1776, Chowan Co., N. C.
HALSEY, Colon and Elizabeth Boyd, 16 December 1785, Chowan Co., N. C.
HALSEY, James and Frances Grant, 12 July 1764, Santee, S. C.
HALSEY, John and Lucy Tiller, 11 April 1811, Edenton, N. C.
HALSEY, Malachi and Esther Copeland, 19 October 1785, Chowan Co., N. C.
HALSEY, Mehitable and John Frazee, 21 April 1778, Chowan Co., N. C.
HALSEY, Samuel and Zilphia Bentley, 12 July 1770 Chowan Co., N. C.
HALSEY, William and Margaret Miller (widow), 27 June 1767, Chowan Co.,
    N. C.

HALTER, Nelly and Robert McCrary, 13 September 1800, Guilford Co., N. C.

HALTON, Mary and Isaac Gardner, 21 January 1764, Tyrrell Co., N. C.

HALY, John (Dr.) and Mary Shaw (widow), 19 January 1763, Charleston, S. C.

HAMBLETON, Tabitha and Aaron Hackett, 25 July 1798, Rowan Co., N. C.

HAMER, Robert P. and Sallie D. McCall, 31 October 1859, Marion, S. C.

HAMES, Ramoth L. and William Jefferies, 3 April 1860, Jonesville, S. C.

HAMILTON, Alexander and Elizabeth Sullivan, 9 June 1774, Chowan Co., N. C.

HAMILTON, Elizabeth and John Ferguson, 25 August 1789, Rowan Co., N. C.

HAMILTON, Esther and William Hart, 2 January 1788, Mecklenburg Co., N. C.

HAMILTON, John and Catherina Myers (widow), 1 July 1741, Orangeburg Co., S. C.

HAMILTON, John and Mary Skellington, 22 February 1791, Mecklenburg Co., N. C.

HAMILTON, Marlboro S. and (Mrs.) Euphenia Miller, 10 January 1795, Charleston, S. C.

HAMILTON, Mary and William McKellton, 24 June 1787, Guilford Co., N. C.

HAMILTON, Sarah and James Hart, 27 December 1788, Mecklenburg Co., N. C.

HAMLETT, Peter A. and Franks Marter, 9 December 1823, Mecklenburg Co., N. C.

HAMLIN, Thomas and Sarah Wingwood, June 1785, Charleston, S. C.

HAMLIN, Thomas and Margaret Jordan, 23 August 1780, Santee, S. C.

HAMMOND, Anthony and Susanna Horner, 23 February 1779, Rowan Co., N. C.

HAMMOND, Samuel G. and Martha D. Meacham, 17 August 1841, Mecklenburg Co., N. C.

HAMMONDS, Rebecca and John DeLong, 21 November 1846, Laurens Co., S. C.

HAMPTON, Bridget and Garland Guthridge, 26 September 1778, Rowan Co., N. C.

HAMPTON, David and Mary Bryan, 18 August 1786, Rowan Co., N. C.

HAMPTON, Ephriam and Elizabeth Enochs, 28 March 1794, Rowan Co., N. C.

HAMPTON, George and Cornelia Henderson, 29 February 1804, Mecklenburg Co., N. C.

HAMPTON, John and Judith Woodson, 9 June 1795, Rowan Co., N. C.

HAMPTON, Nancy and Henry Hora, 12 February 1784, Rowan Co., N. C.

HAMPTON, Wade and Harriet Flud, August 1786, Charleston, S. C.

HAMPTON, Wade and Polly Cantey, July 1801, Santee, S. C.

HANBACK, Silas and Eliza M. Gwin, 6 January 1848, Laurens Co., S. C.

HANCE, Enheina and Thomas B. Crews, 26 October 1856, Laurens Co., S. C.

HANCOCK, Dunham and (Miss) Stellay, 1742, Pitt Co., N. C.

HANCOCK, Fanny and Augustus S. Rope, 12 January 1833, Mecklenburg Co., N. C.

HANCOCK, Mary and James Goelett, 27 February 1743, Charleston, S. C.

HANCOCK, Harmon and Rhody Wetherington, November 1799, Pitt Co., N. C.

HANCOCK, James and Elizabeth Hardy, 1766, Pitt Co., N. C.

HANCOCK, James and Mary Frizzle, 1796, Pitt Co., N. C.

HANCOCK, Josiah and Amy Mills, 1801, Pitt Co., N. C.

HANCOCK, Sarah and Naisby Pettit, 1800, Pitt Co., N. C .

HANCOCK, Sophia A. and Benjamin R. Tillman, 14 May 1823, Edgefield Co., S. C.

HANCOCK, William and Elizabeth Durham, 1715, Pitt Co., N. C.

HANCOCK, William M. and Margaret Clemmer, 1 March 1792, Rowan Co., N. C.

HANDSHY, Mary and Matthias Keller, 1740, Orangeburg Co., S. C.

HANDY, Thomas and Dorothy Gilchrist (widow), 6 August 1799, Charleston, S. C.

HANFIELD, James and Elizabeth Cunningham, 25 July 1832, Mecklenburg Co., N. C.

HANKINS, Mary J. and Benjamin Morrow, 20 April 1847, Mecklenburg Co., N. C.

HANKS, Abraham and Judy Rodin, 12 October 1825, Mecklenburg Co., N. C.

HANKS, Cynthia and Charles M. Baker, 28 June 1836, Mecklenburg Co., N. C.

HANKS, Thomas and Miss Hargroves, 2 March 1789, Mecklenburg Co., N. C.

HANNA, Joseph and Mary Davis, 5 January 1789, Rowan Co., N. C.

HANNAH, Polly and James Riggs, 22 January 1788, Orange Co., N. C.

HANNAHAN, John (Jr.) and Ann Godfrey, 20 November 1800, Charleston, S. C.

HANNAN, Jesse and Casia Stephens, 26 March 1844, Mecklenburg Co., N. C.

HANNER, Jane and Reuben Martin, 24 September 1857, Laurens Co., S. C.

HANNER, Laburn and Epsey Campbell, 25 March 1848, Laurens Co., S. C.

HANNER, Rebecca and William Barnett, 9 December 1865, Laurens Co., S. C.

HANNIGAN, Sarah and John McKibbens, 17 September 1827, Mecklenburg Co., N. C.

HANNON, Thomas A. and Martha Stephens, 15 January 1842, Mecklenburg Co., N. C.

HANSEMAN, William and Mary Black, 9 February 1790, Rowan Co., N. C.

HAPOLDT, John C. and Elizabeth Ernst, 22 May 1795, Charleston, S. C.

HAPPOLDT, John M. (Dr.) and Dorcas H. Foster, 2 March 1837, Mecklenburg Co., N. C.

HAPSEY, Mary and Donnell McDaniel, 23 October 1786, Orange Co., N. C.

HARDEN, Alexander and Ann Bishop, 16 February 1773, Rowan Co., N. C.

HARDEN, Martha and Miles Prescott, 1 December 1836, Edgefield District, S. C.

HARDEN, William and Margaret Nichols, 15 April 1797, Rowan Co., N. C.

HARDIN, Jesse and Rosana Sloan, 29 August 1797, Rowan Co., N. C.

HARDIN, Jane and John Griffith, 2 November 1785, Rowan Co., N. C.

HARDISON, Elizabeth and Ezekiel Moore, 19 December 1766, Tyrrell Co., N. C.

HARDISON, Elizabeth and Thomas Harrison, 1784, Tyrrell Co., N. C.

HARDISON, Jasper and Alse Evans, 3 September 1763, Tyrrell Co., N. C.

HARDISON, Joseph and Mary A. Collins, 13 November 1765, Tyrrell Co., N. C.

HARDISON, Mary and Levi Stubbs, 1781, Tyrrell Co., N. C.

HARDY, Elizabeth and James Hancock, 1766, Pitt Co., N. C.

HARDY, Elizabeth and Henry Bonner, 4 January 1758, Chowan Co., N. C.

HARDY, Elizabeth and Samuel Black, 10 October 1765, Bertie Co., N. C.

HARDY, James and Bettie Gaskins, 30 September 1788, Bertie Co., N. C.

HARDY, Lamb and Winifred Boswell, 23 August 1790, Bertie Co., N. C.

HARDY, Tha and Joseph G. Rutherford, 15 December 1831, Edgefield District, S. C.

HARE, Ann and Richard C. Croom, 1806, New Berne District, N. C.

HARE, Charity and William Haywood, 11 March 1754, Chowan Co., N. C.

HARE, James and Penelope Jackson, December 1779, Chowan Co., N. C.

HARE, Mary and John Streeter, 2 July 1750, Chowan Co., N. C.

HARE, Mary and John Hall, 10 May 1781, Rowan Co., N. C.

HARE, Nancy and Thomas Buckle, 1788, Charleston, S. C.

HARE, Ruth and James Ambrose, 1784, Tyrrell Co., N. C.

HARELL, Susanna and Needham Bryan, 1732, Snowfield, N. C.

HARFORD, Elizabeth and Humphrey Elliot, 25 January 1725, Berkeley Co., S. C.

HARFORD, John and Elizabeth Clark, 8 June 1779, Chowan Co., N. C.

HARGETT, Helen and David Newell, 10 October 1843, Mecklenburg Co., N. C.

HARGETT, James and Diana Johnston, 23 December 1800, Mecklenburg Co., N. C.

HARGRAVE, Frederick and Mary Wagg, 23 January 1790, Rowan Co., N. C.

HARGRAVE, Miss and John Montieth, 10 September 1814, Mecklenburg Co., N. C.

HARGREAVES, Joshua and Elizabeth B. Canty (widow), 10 January 1801, Charleston, S. C.

HARGROVE, Agness and William Robison, 9 October 1804, Mecklenburg Co., N. C.

HARGROVE, Ann and Richard Rankin, 18 May 1825, Mecklenburg Co., N. C.

HARGROVE, Juda and Jacob Bryant, 29 January 1800, Edgecombe Co., N. C.

HARGROVE, —— and Thomas Hanks, 2 March 1789, Mecklenburg Co., N. C.

HARKEY, Elizabeth and Cyrus Black, 31 May 1831, Mecklenburg Co., N. C.

HARKEY, John and Sarah Baker, 1 August 1822, Mecklenburg Co., N. C.

HARKEY, Mathias and Elizabeth Starnes, 17 January 1837, Mecklenburg Co., N. C.

HARKEY, Peter and Peggy Drew, 9 December 1813, Mecklenburg Co., N. C.

HARKEY, Sally and Isaac Robison, 6 February 1821, Mecklenburg Co., N. C.

HARKEY, William F. and A. L. Orr, 10 November 1865, Mecklenburg Co., N. C.

HARKLEY, Reuben and Joana Green, 6 November 1798, Rowan Co., N. C.

HARKNESS, Jemina and Joseph Rea, 15 July 1809, Mecklenburg Co., N. C.

HARLAN, George and Hannah Leslie, 19 January 1803, Mecklenburg Co., N. C.

HARLAN, Jane and James McClure, 15 December 1800, Mecklenburg Co., N. C.

HARLEE, Mary A. and Benjamin H. Covington, 17 June 1847, Richmond Co., N. C.

HARLESTON, John and Elizabeth Lynch, May 1777, Charleston, S. C.

HARLESTON, Margaret and Thomas Corbett, 8 June 1769, Berkeley Co., S. C.

HARLIN, John and Mary Dunn, 5 December 1795, Mecklenburg Co., N. C.

HARLLEE, David Stuart and Harriett Pope Barns, 3 February 1819, Roberson Co., N. C.

HARLLEE, Thomas H. and Margaret McColl, 20 March 1856, Florence Co., S. C.

HARLLEE, Thomas and Elizabeth Stuart, 16 June 1789, Richmond Co., N. C.

HARLLEE, W. W. (Gen.) and Martha Shackleford, 18 September 1837, Charleston Co., S. C.

HARLOE, Martha and Thomas Norcom, 24 August 1744, Chowan Co., N. C.

HARLOE, Sarah and Francis Penrice, 12 April 1744, Chowan Co., N. C.

HARLOW, Mary and John Weir, 11 August 1775, Chowan Co., N. C.

HARMAN, George and Barbra Lopp, 27 December 1795, Rowan Co., N. C.

HARMAN, Godfrey M. and Pauline Boozer, 24 November 1864, Lexington, S. C.

HARMAN, Nicholas and Anne Dunning, 3 November 1802, Bertie Co., N. C.

HARMAN, Stephen and Judy Farmer, 26 October 1790, Bertie Co., N. C.

HARMON, E. M. (Miss) and William M. Black, 11 May 1861, Mecklenburg Co., N. C.

HARMON, Nancy and Hambleton Peason, 29 January 1857, Laurens Co., S. C.

HARNEY, Elizabeth and Peter Butt, 10 July 1782, Santee, S. C.

HARPER, Abner and Massey Howell, 18 December 1763, Edgecombe Co., N. C.

HARPER, Arthur and (Mrs.) Elizabeth Milligan, 10 August 1799, Charleston, S. C.

HARPER, Charlotte and Joshua Clark, 1 January 1801, Charleston, S. C.

HARPER, Elizabeth and Joseph Hopkins, 25 April 1776, Chowan Co., N. C.

HARPER, George and Charlotte McKinzie, 27 December 1809, Charleston, S. C.

HARPER, Lewis F. and Caroline Raynolds, 20 November 1801, Charleston, S. C.

HARPER, Polly and Samuel Felps, 14 October 1791, Rowan Co., N. C.

HARPER, Samuel and Mary Ford, 26 August 1784, Rowan Co., N. C.

HARPER, Sarah and John Guinn, 26 February 1782, Orange Co., N. C.

HARPER, Thomas and Sarah Wilson, 12 February 1789, Rowan Co., N. C.

HARRAMOND, Elizabeth and Peter Bacot, 11 November 1764, Charleston, S. C.

HARRELL, Christian and Thomas Trotman, 27 February 1770, Chowan Co., N. C.

HARRELL, Gring and Elizabeth Kittrell, 23 August 1790, Bertie Co., N. C.

HARRELL, Henry and Annis Davis, 10 March 1788, Bertie Co., N. C.

HARRELL, John and Margaret A. Miller, 9 January 1845, Chowan Co., N. C.

HARRELL, Zackariah and Martha Everit, 10 September 1764, Edgecombe Co., N. C.

HARRESPERGER, John and Elizabeth Frichman, 30 April 1751, Orangeburg Co., S. C.

HARRIES, Peter and Mary Cain, 4 June 1761, Santee, S. C.

HARRIETT, George D. and Dorothy Ann Rutherford, 19 February 1839, Edgefield District, S. C.

HARRIS, Aaron and Jannet Remington, 22 April 1783, Rowan Co., N. C.

HARRIS, Charles and Betsy Christie, 1 January 1773, Charleston, S. C.

HARRIS, Charles and Sally Harris, 8 April 1790, Rowan Co., N. C.

HARRIS, Coleman and Hannah Mabley, 25 April 1839, Mecklenburg Co., N. C.

HARRIS, Eleanor and Ezekial Robinson, 23 March 1812, Mecklenburg Co., N. C.

HARRIS, Elizabeth and Samuel A. Burns, 27 August 1851, Mecklenburg Co., N. C.

HARRIS, Franklin and Martha Neely Carothers, 25 November 1836, York Co., S. C.

HARRIS, George and Elizabeth Finney, 3 July 1800, Mecklenburg Co., N. C.

HARRIS, Hannah and John Ross, 16 June 1798, Mecklenburg Co., N. C.

HARRIS, Harriot C. and Dionisus Alexander, 31 December 1846, Mecklenburg Co., N. C.

HARRIS, Henrietta L. and R. N. Caldwell, 2 September 1857, Mecklenburg Co., N. C.

HARRIS, Hugh and Elizabeth T. Still, 26 February 1825, Mecklenburg Co., N. C.

HARRIS, Hugh and Jane H. Matthews, 1 September 1835, Mecklenburg Co., N. C.

HARRIS, Isham and Anne Campbell, 5 April 1791, Rowan Co., N. C.

HARRIS, James and Sally Harris, 19 November 1794, Mecklenburg Co., N. C.

HARRIS, James and Margaret Davidson, 10 December 1813, Mecklenburg Co., N. C.

HARRIS, Jane E. and L. S. Bigham, 2 February 1849, Mecklenburg Co., N. C.

HARRIS, Jane F. and John M. Alexander, 2 January 1814, Mecklenburg Co., N. C.

HARRIS, Jane M. and Levi Hope, 1 October 1823, Mecklenburg Co., N. C.

HARRIS, John and Elizabeth Waller, June 1687, Berkeley, N. C.

HARRIS, John (of Steel Creek) and Martha Hunter, 31 March 1790, Mecklenburg Co., N. C.

HARRIS, John and Ruth Cowan, 30 July 1795, Rowan Co., N. C.

HARRIS, John and Pamelia Whitlock, 28 November 1843, Edgefield Distrct, S. C.

HARRIS, John H. and Margaret A. Hunter, 13 August 1817, Mecklenburg Co., N. C.

HARRIS, Josiah and Harriet Cristenberry, 21 December 1841, Mecklenburg Co., N. C.

HARRIS, Joshua and Ann Allen, 10 September 1811, Mecklenburg Co., N. C.

HARRIS, Laird H. and Hannah Alexander, 23 June 1840, Mecklenburg Co., N. C.

HARRIS, Margaret and Matthew Henderson, 6 March 1798, Mecklenburg Co., N. C.

HARRIS, Margaret E. and James F. Carothers, 28 July 1847, York Co., S. C.

HARRIS, Martha (Mrs.) and John Polk, 22 October 1803, Mecklenburg Co., N. C.

HARRIS, Molly and James Finley, 29 November 1866, Laurens Co., S. C.

HARRIS, Peggy and John Johnston, 10 January 1817, Mecklenburg Co., N. C.

HARRIS, Parmelia and Thomas Rich, 26 May 1840, Mecklenburg Co., N. C.

HARRIS, Robert and Margaret Robb, 16 January 1793, Mecklenburg Co., N. C.

HARRIS, Robert N. and Mary Stafford, 9 April 1834, Mecklenburg Co., N. C.

HARRIS, Salathiel and Harriet Summerville, 6 April 1839, Mecklenburg Co., N. C.

HARRIS, Sally and Charles Harris, 8 April 1790, Rowan Co., N. C.

HARRIS, Sally and James Harris, 19 November 1794, Mecklenburg Co., N. C.

HARRIS, Samuel and Elizabeth McClure, 21 March 1796, Mecklenburg Co., N. C.

HARRIS, Sarah and Aventon Felps, 21 April 1786, Rowan Co., N. C.

HARRIS, Sarah and Pleasant Bridwell, 1 April 1832, Edgefield District, S. C.

HARRIS, Sarah and Jesse Bryant, 26 January 1836, Edgefield District, S. C.

HARRIS, Sarah F. and William Middleton, 22 March 1800, Guilford Co., N. C.

HARRIS, William and Margaret Sloane, 20 September 1784, Rowan Co., N. C.

HARRIS, William J. and Emeline Wolf, 10 February 1843, Mecklenburg Co., N. C.

HARRIS, Zeplaniah and Tabby Hix, 25 November 1790, Rowan Co., N. C.

HARRISON, Benjamin and Mary Huff, 4 October 1774, Rowan Co., N. C.

HARRISON, Elam and Ellen Flow, 26 August 1847, Mecklenburg Co., N. C.

HARRISON, Elizabeth and William McComb, 25 May 1798, Mecklenburg Co., N. C.

HARRISON, Elizabeth and Samuel L. Earle, 24 December 1840, Greenville, S. C.

HARRISON, Harriet and Samuel Earle, 12 March 1793, Pendleton Co., S. C.

HARRISON, Jane C. and Stewart Rice, 31 December 1847, Mecklenburg Co., N. C.

HARRISON, Margaret N. and W. J. Ross, 18 December 1850, Mecklenburg Co., N. C.

HARRISON, M. L. and David Maxwell, 4 June 1841, Mecklenburg Co., N. C.

HARRISON, Priscilla and Robert Mitchell, 4 November 1859, Guilford Co., N. C.

HARRISON, Reuben and Ann Mitchell, 18 May 1790, Bertie Co., N. C.

HARRISON, Robert and Catherine Wilson, 16 March 1841, Mecklenburg Co., N. C.

HARRISON, Thomas and Elizabeth Hardison, 1784, Tyrrell Co., N. C.

HARRISON, William and Esther Savits, 4 June 1786, Rowan Co., N. C.

HARROD, Elisha and Jenny Rhody, 31 March 1785, Chowan Co., N. C.

HARROD, Joseph and Susannah Sill, 23 February 1795, Rowan Co., N. C.

HARROD, Priscilla and Heine Linart, 9 October 1784, Chowan Co., N. C.

HARRON, Joseph and (Mrs.) Lydia Boyd, 10 April 1742, Chowan Co., N. C.

HARROWOOD, Zachariah and Rachel Croswell, 10 September 1793, Rowan Co., N. C.

HARRY, David and Ann A. Berry, 6 December 1828, Mecklenburg Co., N. C.

HARRY, Mary A. and Green L. Bigham, 11 February 1846, Mecklenburg Co., N. C.

HARRYS, Elizabeth and Samuel Magee, (of Philadelphia), 3 May 1785, Charleston, S. C.

HART, Andrew and Betsy Clendening, 25 January 1800, Mecklenburg Co., N. C.

HART, Ann and James Buzzard, 19 February 1856, Edgefield District, S. C.

HART, Christopher and Elizabeth Graham, 24 December 1784, Charleston, S. C.

HART, David and Peggy Black, 29 May 1789, Rowan Co., N. C.

HART, Eleanor and Samuel McCrum, 2 June 1800, Mecklenburg Co., N. C.

HART, James and Sarah Hamilton, 27 December 1788, Mecklenburg Co., N. C.

HART, James and Ann Lawrence, 19 June 1789, Rowan Co., N. C.

HART, James and Rachel Paul, 13 April 1790, Orange Co., N. C.

HART, James and Hannah Neally, 19 December 1791, Mecklenburg Co., N. C.

HART, James L. and Margaret C. Taylor, 9 July 1830, Mecklenburg Co., N. C.

HART, John and Mary Screven, 17 June 1784, St. Thomas Parish, S. C.

HART, Jane and Thomas Neely, 28 March 1793, Mecklenburg Co., N. C.

HART, Martha P. and David M. Miller, 22 November 1849, Mecklenburg Co., N. C.

HART, Mary J. N. and James B. Neely, 16 December 1828, Mecklenburg Co., N. C.

HART, Matthew and Elizabeth Steele, 24 December 1789, Rowan Co., N. C.

HART, Ritcey and Abraham M. Sexies, 13 November 1777, Charleston, S. C.

HART, Shanky and Abraham Jacobs, 19 October 1785, Charleston, S. C.

HART, William and Esther Hamilton, 2 January 1788, Mecklenburg Co., N. C.

HART, William H. and Susanna Woods, 9 August 1830, Mecklenburg Co., N. C.

HARTGROVE, Clementine and Sinai Alexander, 14 April 1853, Mecklenburg Co., N. C.

HARTGROVE, Dorcas and Sinai Alexander, 6 January 1843, Mecklenburg Co., N. C.

HARTGROVE, Mary P. and Elam E. Alexander, 2 January 1844, Mecklenburg Co., N. C.

HARTGROVE, William and Mary McKinney, 19 June 1811, Mecklenburg Co., N. C.

HARTH, Dovey and Robert Black, 4 April 1808, Mecklenburg Co., N. C.

HARTIS, Charity and John Orr, 3 February 1849, Mecklenburg Co., N. C.

HARTIS, John and Sarah Adams, 14 October 1812, Mecklenburg Co., N. C.

HARTLEY, Ann and Jeremiah Green, Jr., 2 April 1790, Rowan Co., N. C.

HARTLEY, Ann and William Hext, July 1786, Charleston, S. C.

HARTLEY, Charlotte and (Dr.) Thomas Elder, April 1773, Charleston, S. C.

HARTLEY, Clarinda and William Rice, 15 December 1859, Mecklenburg Co., N. C.

HARTLEY, James (Dr.) and (Miss) Perry, March 1785, Charleston, S. C.

HARTLEY, James (Dr.) and Eliza Latson, 1788, Charleston, S. C.

HARTLEY, Margaret and John Farr, 3 October 1784, Charleston, S. C.

HARTLEY, Mary (widow) and Joseph Stanyarne, 9 December 1773, Charleston, S. C.

HARTLEY, Mary and Cornelia Du Pre, 2 December 1784, Charleston, S. C.
HARTLEY, Thomas and Milly Burgess, 9 October 1787, Rowan Co., N. C.
HARTLINE, George and Mary Arnhart, 9 August 1793, Rowan Co., N. C.
HARTMAN, Elizabeth and Conrad Grubb, 26 March 1795, Rowan Co., N. C.
HARTMAN, Jacob and Judah Owen, 4 June 1796, Rowan Co., N. C.
HARTMUS, James H. and Eliza Miller, 23 September 1815, Chowan Co., N. C.
HARTSILE, Jonathan and Mary Beaver, 5 March 1792, Rowan Co., N. C.
HARTSON, Abigail (widow) and John Lloyd, 18 August 1743, Chowan Co., N. C.
HARTT, David and Diana McRee, 16 August 1797, Mecklenburg Co., N. C.
HARVEY, Anne and Alexander Fraser, 6 November 1749, Charleston, S. C.
HARVEY, Benjamin and (Mrs.) Susannah Keeley, 26 January 1795, Charleston, S. C.
HARVEY, Edward and Rebecca Nichols, 8 July 1785, Chowan Co., N. C.
HARVEY, James and Mary Gibbes, 23 March 1769, Ashepoo, S. C.
HARVEY, John and Elizabeth Hall, 11 March 1778, Chowan Co., N. C.
HARVEY, Lewis and Elizabeth Irwin, 26 October 1825, Mecklenburg Co., N. C.
HARVEY, Mary and Thomas Roberts, October 1785, Charleston, S. C.
HARVEY, Polly and William Wilson, 5 January 1772, Charleston, S. C.
HARVEY, Sarah and Lambert Lance, 21 June 1784, Cane Acre, S. C.
HARVEY, Sarah and Joseph N. Warnock, 8 November 1801, Charleston, S. C.
HARVEY, Thomas (Gov.) and Joannah Jenkins, (widow of John Jenkins) 13 April 1682, Perquimans, N. C.
HARVEY, William and Elizabeth Mikel (widow), 6 February 1743, St. Helena, S. C.
HARVIN, Richard and Frances Ragin, 3 August 1775, Sumter District, S. C.
HARWELL, Sylvia and John Hipp, 7 October 1817, Mecklenburg Co., N. C.
HARTWICK, Charity and Richard C. Mason, 23 January 1821, Mecklenburg Co., N. C.
HARTWICK, Conrad and Patsy Stephens, 6 November 1816, Mecklenburg Co., N. C.
HARTWICK, John and Susanna Pitman, 20 October 1806, Mecklenburg Co., N. C.
HARTWICK, Lucy and John Casey, 17 February 1816, Mecklenburg Co., N. C.
HARWOOD, Henry and Martha Bryan, March 1792, Rowan Co., N. C.
HASELL, Andrew and Sarah Wigfall, 28 March 1751, St. Thomas Parish, S. C.
HASELL, Andrew and Mary Milner, 15 October 1778, St. Thomas Parish, S. C.
HASELL, Bentley and Catherine Cruger, 2 April 1828, Charleston, S. C.
HASELL, Elizabeth and William Gibbes, 12 February 1748, St. Andrews Parish, S. C.
HASELL, George P. B. and Penelope Bentley, 20 September 1802, St. Thomas Parish, S. C.
HASELL, Thomas (Rev.) and Elizabeth Ashby, 21 January 1714, Charleston, S. C.
HASELL, Thomas and Alice Merritt, 26 April 1744, Charleston, S. C.
HASELL, Thomas and Margaret Summers, 2 February 1772, Santee, S. C.
HASELWOOD, Edward and Elizabeth Mills, 22 April 1732, Charleston, S. C.
HASFORD, Elizabeth (widow) and Philip Jennings, 7 February 1747, Orangeburg Co., S. C.
HASFORD, Samuel and Mary Pawley, 19 July 1778, Santee, S. C.

HASFORT, Richard and Barbara Diedrick, 3 January 1740, Orangeburg Co., S. C.

HASKELL, Alexander C. (2nd. m) and Rebecca Singleton, 10 September 1861, Richland Co., S. C.

HASKELL, Charles T. and Sophia L. Cheves, 1 December 1830, Charleston, S. C.

HASLETT, John and Mary Wilson, 1 August 1799, Charleston, S. C.

HASSELL, Ann and George Wynne, 7 April 1783, Tyrrell Co., N. C.

HASSELL, Anne and Nicholas Gillird, 1784, Tyrrell Co., N. C.

HASSELL, Benjamin and Ann Snell, 29 October 1765, Tyrrell Co., N. C.

HASSELL, Edward and Ann Massey, 1782, Tyrrell Co., N. C.

HASSELL, Joseph and Elizabeth Tarkinton, 1781, Tyrrell Co., N. C.

HASSELL, Joseph and Mary Mann, 1781, Tyrrell Co., N. C.

HASSELL, Joshua and Elizabeth Lockhart, 3 July 1786, Tyrrell Co., N. C.

HASSELL, Margaret and Friley Jones, 23 September 1763, Tyrrell Co., N. C.

HASSELL, Martha and John Tarkinton, (Jr.), 4 April 1786, Tyrrell Co., N. C.

HASSELL, Mary and William Swain, 1780, Tyrrell Co., N. C.

HASSELL, Nancy and Abram Swain, 1780, Tyrrell Co., N. C.

HASSELL, Priscilla and James Nicholls, 19 January 1767, Tyrrell Co., N. C.

HASSELL, Rachel (widow) and John Wilkins, (Jr.), 10 July 1767, Chowan Co., N. C.

HASSELL, Rachel and Elkanah Davenport, 8 February 1778, Tyrrell Co., N. C.

HASSELL, Rachel and James Edwards, 1781, Tyrrell Co., N. C.

HASSELL, Stephen and Elizabeth Powers, 6 October 1783, Tyrrell Co., N. C.

HASSELL, William and Elizabeth Birtch, 1784, Tyrrell Co., N. C.

HASSELL, Zebedee and Mary Davenport, 15 February 1770, Tyrrell Co., N. C.

HASSETT, Isaac and Rachel S. Tepney, 6 August 1765, Chowan Co., N. C.

HATCH, Edmund and Lucy Richards, 15 March 1742, Chowan Co., N. C.

HATCH, Lucius and George Ann Mays, 30 November 1854, Edgefield District, S. C.

HATCHER, Alfred and Fannie Swearingen, 28 July 1821, Edgefield District, S. C.

HATCHER, B. W. and E. Augustine Long, 8 February 1842, Edgefield District, S. C.

HATCHER, Elizabeth and Amos Landrum, 12 August 1838, Edgefield District, S. C.

HATCHER, Hancock and Margaret Wilkins, 16 August 1763, Edgecombe Co., N. C.

HATCHER, Polly and John Gomillion, 6 July 1820, Edgefield District, S. C.

HATCHER, Rachel and Emanuel Mineor, 27 October 1754, Orangeburg Co., S. C.

HATCHER, Sirrah and John Fuster, 1741, Orangeburg Co., S. C.

HATCHER, William and Martha Vickers, 21 February 1768, Edgecombe Co., N. C.

HATFIELD, John and Sarah Swallow, 6 January 1765, Charleston, S. C.

HATFIELD, Margaret and Simon Kingston, 17 February 1785, Charleston, S. C.

HATH, German and Betsy McKnight, 4 November 1796, Rowan Co., N. C.

HATHAWAY, Maria L. and William P. Clark, 24 July 1816, Mecklenburg Co., N. C.

HATTON, Charles and Jane Chambers, 31 December 1779, Rowan Co., N. C.

HAUGHTON, Ann (widow) and John Kennedy, 19 November 1774, Chowan Co., N. C.

HAUGHTON, Edward and Deborah Gregory, 20 February 1785, Chowan Co., N. C.

HAUGHTON, Elizabeth and Luke Gregory, 29 November 1779, Chowan Co., N. C.

HAUGHTON, Esther and Daniel Garrett, 19 February 1756, Chowan Co., N. C.

HAUGHTON, Jeremiah and Mary Sylvia, 27 January 1756, Chowan Co., N. C.

HAUGHTON, Leah and James Carter, 3 June 1773, Chowan Co., N. C.

HAUGHTON, Margaret and William Flury, 6 May 1752, Chowan Co., N. C.

HAUGHTON, Mary (widow) and Levi Creecy, 1 October 1750, Chowan Co., N. C.

HAUGHTON, Rachel and Edward Hall, 30 July 1753, Chowan Co., N. C.

HAUGHTON, Richard and Jemima Long, 3 August 1774, Tyrrell Co., N. C.

HAUGHTON, William and Mary Ming, 1 April 1748, Chowan Co., N. C.

HAUGHTON, William and Mary Leslie, 16 October 1800, Charleston, S. C.

HAULK, Ofelia and Wade Forgy, 19 October 1865, Laurens Co., S. C.

HAVEY, Nancy and John Matthews, 14 February 1767, Charleston, S. C.

HAWKINS, Abraham and Sarah Dowell, 27 October 1798, Rowan Co., N. C.

HAWKINS, Betsy and William Dennis, 15 September 1800, Guilford Co., N. C.

HAWKINS, John and Polly Goodman, 27 December 1796, Rowan Co., N. C.

HAWKINS, Joshua and Dorothy Beam, 8 April 1780, Rowan Co., N. C.

HAWKINS, Mary and Nathaniel Bullock, 1760, Granville Co., N. C.

HAWKINS, Mary and Joseph Turner, 23 October 1762, Perquimans Co., N. C.

HAWLET, Peter A. and Frank Martin, 9 December 1823, Mecklenburg Co., N. C.

HAWTHORNE, Adam and Ann Holmes, 23 April 1799, Fairfield Co., S. C.

HAWTHORNE, Robert and Priscilla Gibson, 1831, Fairfield Co., S. C.

HAYDEN, Judith and Sergent Hughes, 3 November 1788, Rowan Co., N. C.

HAYDEN, William and Elizabeth Linster, 3 May 1796, Rowan Co., N. C.

HAYES, Cynthia and William M. Neely, 25 May 1813, Mecklenburg Co., N. C.

HAYES, Jane and Robert Algea, 5 January 1811, Mecklenburg Co., N. C.

HAYES, Margaret E. and William A. Alexander, 15 October 1835, Mecklenburg Co., N. C.

HAYES, Martha and Benjamin Johnson, 21 January 1824, Mecklenburg Co., N. C.

HAYES, Widow and James Postell, 23 June 1763, Charleston, S. C.

HAYLER, Evan and Eliza Davis, 24 May 1837, Mecklenburg Co., N. C.

HAYMAN, Jonas and Mary Long, 1 December 1778, Tyrrell Co., N. C.

HAYNE, Elizabeth and Benjamin F. Perry, April 1837, Charleston, S. C.

HAYNE, Eloisa and William E. Martin, 18 May 1837, Colleton, S. C.

HAYNE, Harriet and Edward H. Barnwell, 20 November 1860, Charleston, S. C.

HAYNE, Isaac and Elizabeth Hutson, 18 July 1765, Colleton, S. C.

HAYNE, Isaac and Mary Hopkins, 12 December 1793, Colleton, S. C.

HAYNE, Isaac W. and Alicia Trapier, 1 May 1834, Colleton, S. C.

HAYNE, Sarah and Alexander Taylor, 18 May 1837, Colleton, S. C.

HAYNE, William and Elizabeth Peronneau, April 1786, Charleston, S. C.

HAYNE, William Edward and Eloise Brevard, 28 January 1806, Colleton, S. C.

HAYNER, John George and Eva C. Barrin, 24 August 1755, Orangeburg Co., S. C.

HAYNES, Barth and Sarah Carruth, 30 August 1793, Mecklenburg Co., N. C.

HAYNES, David C. and Harriet Cathcart, 10 November 1835, Mecklenburg Co., N. C.

HAYNES, Eaton and Mary Haynes, 22 January 1804, Edgecombe Co., N. C.
HAYNES, Herbert and Anne Thomson, 6 March 1771, Edgecombe Co., N. C.
HAYNES, John and Margaret Andrew, 29 April 1783, Rowan Co., N. C.
HAYNES, Joseph and Levina Beaty, 25 April 1800, Mecklenburg Co., N. C.
HAYNES, Mary and Eaton Haynes, 22 January 1804, Edgecombe Co., N. C.
HAYNES, Peggy and Joseph Blackwood, 19 April 1824, Mecklenburg Co., N. C.
HAYS, David and Margaret Blue, 10 October 1788, Rowan Co., N. C.
HAYS, John and Penelope Bernard, 8 March 1779, Santee, S. C.
HAYS, Joseph and Mary Van Pelt, 15 August 1811, Mecklenburg Co., N. C.
HAYS, Mary and Isham Watson, 15 February 1810, Marion Co., S. C.
HAYS, William and Jensey Black, 2 April 1805, Mecklenburg Co., N. C.
HAYWARD, Daniel and Elizabeth Simons, 7 September 1771, Charleston, S. C.
HAYWOOD, Thomas and Hester Taylor, 4 June 1719, St. Andrews Parish, S. C.
HAYWOOD, William and Charity Hare, 11 March 1754, Chowan Co., N. C.
HAZARD, John and Martha Watkins (widow), 13 January 1742, Chowan Co., N. C.
HAZELL, John and Mary Shelback, 26 April 1801, Charleston, S. C.
HAZLEHURST, Robert and Eliza Hall, 1788, Charleston, S. C.
HAZZARD, Cornelius and Catherine Roome, 31 March 1815, Mecklenburg Co., N. C.
HAZZARD, Esther and Andrew Matthews, 16 February 1849, Mecklenburg Co., N. C.
HAZZARD, Margaret (Mrs.) and Henry Dolliver, 14 July 1799, Charleston, S. C.
HAZZARD, William and Sarah Screven, 11 January 1798, May River, S. C.
HEADLEY, Martha M. and N. B. Rodden, 15 August 1865, Mecklenburg Co., N. C.
HEADON, Jenny and Joseph Headon, 8 January 1783, Rowan Co., N. C.
HEADON, Joseph and Jenny Headon, 8 January 1783, Rowan Co., N. C.
HEAP, Belinda and Jeremiah Burrows, 30 October 1720, St. Andrews Parish, S. C.
HEARN, Michael and Mary Jones, 24 December 1768, Tyrrell Co., N. C.
HEARN, William and Ruth Skeal, 29 November 1799, Rowan Co., N. C.
HEART, Sarah and William Montgomery, 10 February 1830, Guilford Co., N. C.
HEART, William and Sirrah Young, 3 October 1750, Orangeburg Co., S. C.
HEATLEY, Sophia and Joseph Dulles, February 1785, Charleston, S. C.
HECKLER, Anna Mary and John V. Kranick, 1753, Orangeburg Co., S. C.
HEDGECOCK, Thomas and Elizabeth Wood, 10 July 1783, Rowan Co., N. C.
HEDRICK, Peter and Barbara Myers, 18 February 1797, Rowan Co., N. C.
HEEDSON, Eli and Sarah J. Lane, 14 December 1848, Marion Co., S. C.
HEEKMAN, John and Nancy Patten, 31 October 1785, Rowan Co., N. C.
HEGNIT, Rachel and John Millis, 26 November 1786, Guilford Co., N. C.
HELLAMS, Calvin and Sarah J. Bolt, 22 December 1859, Laurens Co., S. C.
HELLAMS, William and Mary Patten, 21 December 1854, Laurens Co., S. C.
HELLER, John and Esther Ott, 1752, Orangeburg Co., S. C.
HELLINGER, Barbara and Peter Phyte, 11 July 1791, Rowan Co., N. C.
HELM, Peter and Leah Shoults, 5 October 1792, Rowan Co., N. C.
HELMS, Agnes and David Moore, 9 May 1811, Mecklenburg Co., N. C.
HELMS, Gabriel and Rhoda Williams, 23 February 1813, Mecklenburg Co., N. C.
HELMS, Israel and Sarah C. Kaizer, 16 January 1729, Mecklenburg Co., N. C.
HELMS, Margaret E. and H. B. Boyd, 4 October 1865, Mecklenburg Co., N. C.

HELMS, Wiley and Martha Crowell, 3 December 1820, Mecklenburg Co., N. C.

HELTON, Ann and Robert Ormond, 15 September 1864, Mecklenburg Co., N. C.

HEMPHILL, John and Agnes Herrill, 16 July 1783, Rowan Co., N. C.

HENBY, Clarkia and Wilson Horn, December 1819, Wayne Co., N. C.

HENDERSON, Agnes and Robert Matthews, 2 March 1797, Mecklenburg Co., N. C.

HENDERSON, Carnes and Lilly Parks, 24 January 1792, Mecklenburg Co., N. C.

HENDERSON, Caroline and James Knight, 7 February 1848, Laurens Co., S. C.

HENDERSON, Cornelia and George Hampton, 29 February 1804, Mecklenburg Co., N. C.

HENDERSON, David (Capt.) and Hannah Sims, 1765, Ninety Six District, S. C.

HENDERSON, Elizabeth and Allen Baldwin, 3 June 1818, Mecklenburg Co., N. C.

HENDERSON, Elizabeth and Benjamin Newman, 21 November 1858, Laurens Co., S. C.

HENDERSON, Elizabeth M. and Edward H. Rogers, 8 September 1835, Mecklenburg Co., N. C.

HENDERSON, Eugenia and John Davenport, 1 October 1865, Laurens Co., S. C.

HENDERSON, Gerety and James Clardy, 4 April 1844, Laurens Co., S. C.

HENDERSON, Gersette and Hiram Mahaffey, 30 January 1865, Laurens Co., S. C.

HENDERSON, Harriet and John R. Alexander, 14 December 1723, Mecklenburg Co., N. C.

HENDERSON, Harriet A. and John K. Robinson, 2 December 1843, Mecklenburg Co., N. C.

HENDERSON, Isabella M. and James S. Morris, 26 January 1847, Mecklenburg Co., N. C.

HENDERSON, Jane and Adam Miller, 13 April 1804, Mecklenburg Co., N. C.

HENDERSON, Jane and John Boyd, 20 January 1853, Laurens Co., S. C.

HENDERSON, Jane L. and Josiah A. Robinson, 18 May 1843, Mecklenburg Co., N. C.

HENDERSON, John and Rebecca Henderson, 30 January 1798, Mecklenburg Co., N. C.

HENDERSON, John and Ann Sample, 4 April 1804, Mecklenburg Co., N. C.

HENDERSON, John and Priscilla Porter, 9 July 1828, Mecklenburg Co., N. C.

HENDERSON, Leadason and Enna Liza Pinson, 12 October 1865, Laurens Co., S. C.

HENDERSON, Lila A. and J. C. Caldwell, 1 July 1856, Mecklenburg Co., N. C.

HENDERSON, Louisa and Samuel Johnson, 1 March 1813, Mecklenburg Co., N. C.

HENDERSON, Margaret and Robert Robinson, 30 March 1790, Mecklenburg Co., N. C.

HENDERSON, Martha and Francis A. Bradley, 12 August 1836, Mecklenburg Co., N. C.

HENDERSON, Martha H. and E. L. Burney, 1 October 1851, Mecklenburg Co., N. C.

HENDERSON, Mastin and Elizabeth McDaniel, 22 September 1859, Laurens Co., S. C.

HENDERSON, Matthew and Margaret Harris, 6 March 1798, Mecklenburg Co., N. C.

HENDERSON, Nancy and Menoah McPhearson, 4 February 1845, Laurens Co., S. C.

HENDERSON, Narcissa and John Moore, 16 October 1864, Laurens Co., S. C.

HENDERSON, Parmela and Robert Johnston, 11 September 1820, Mecklenburg Co., N. C.

HENDERSON, Rebecca and John Henderson, 30 January 1798, Mecklenburg Co., N. C.

HENDERSON, Rebecca R. and Jeptha Baker, 18 December 1860, Mecklenburg Co., N. C.

HENDERSON, Richard and Isabel Jamison, 8 February 1798, Mecklenburg Co., N. C.

HENDERSON, Richard and Barbary Simpson, 20 February 1851, Laurens Co., N. C.

HENDERSON, Samuel and Sarah Burnett, 8 January 1782, Rowan Co., N. C.

HENDERSON, Sarah (widow) and John P. Fowler, 1 February 1859, Laurens Co., S. C.

HENDERSON, Sasannah and Thomas Ramsey, 4 October 1804, Mecklenburg Co., N. C.

HENDERSON, William Steele and Elizabeth Baldridge, 18 September 1804, Mecklenburg Co., N. C.

HENDREN, Oliver and Arania Ijams, 16 August 1788, Rowan Co., N. C.

HENDRICK, Robert (Dr.) and Polly Daniel, 21 May 1795, Columbia, S. C.

HENDRICKS, Elizabeth and Amos Hendrix, 14 January, 1779, Rowan Co., N. C.

HENDRICKS, Henry and Isabel Luckey, 29 March 1795, Rowan Co., N. C.

HENDRICKS, John and Sarah Lewis, 27 December 1780, Rowan Co., N. C.

HENDRICKS, Joshua and Margaret Wolfskill, 8 April 1779, Rowan Co., N. C.

HENDRICKS, Milly and John Forman, 17 January 1794, Rowan Co., N. C.

HENDRICKS, Thomas and Elizabeth Turner, 2 May 1758, Perquimans Co., N. C.

HENDRICKS, William and Martha Stewart, 22 October 1785, Rowan Co., N. C.

HENDRICKS, William and Margaret Wilkinson, 7 January 1794, Rowan Co., N. C.

HENDRICKSON, John and Elizabeth Berry, 20 December 1784, Rowan Co., N. C.

HENDRIX, Amos and Elizabeth Hendricks, 14 January 1779, Rowan Co., N. C.

HENDRIX, Jacob and Franey Roland, 21 June 1792, Rowan Co., N. C.

HENDRIX, John and Elizabeth Welch, 15 September 1788, Rowan Co., N. C.

HENLEY, Darby and Mary Young, 21 September 1787, Rowan Co., N. C.

HENLEY, William and Jenny Parks, 3 May 1791, Rowan Co., N. C.

HENNEGAN, Eleanor and Andrew Rea, 16 June 1797, Mecklenburg Co., N. C.

HENNINGTON, Betsy and James Strickland, 30 August 1772, Charleston, S. C.

HENOX, Elenor and Nicholas Miller, 21 February 1743, Charleston, S. C.

HENRY, Alexander and Elizabeth Flemming, 5 January 1797, Charleston, S. C.

HENRY, Cyrus and Martha Montgomery, 3 January 1810, Mecklenburg Co., N. C.

HENRY, Dorcas and John Finley, 8 October 1844, Laurens Co., S. C.

HENRY, George R. and Martha Price, 21 December 1809, Mecklenburg Co., N. C.

HENRY, Hugh and Rosanna Robinson, 4 September 1779, Rowan Co., N. C.

HENRY, Isaac and Catherine Barnett, 30 May 1800, Mecklenburg Co., N. C.

HENRY, Jennette and Walter Hill, 20 October 1798, Mecklenburg Co., N. C.

HENRY, Joseph and Elizabeth Porter, 2 January 1800, Mecklenburg Co., N. C.

HENRY, Julien and Mary Coburn, 7 February 1801, Charleston, S. C.

HENRY, Melissa and Harrison Finley, 13 October 1842, Laurens Co., S. C.

HENRY, Susan and Thomas Nickles, 23 December 1845, Laurens Co., S. C.

HEPBURN, Mrs. and Moses Glover, 12 October 1799, Charleston, S. C.

HEPPERDITZEL, Susannah and John Chevillette, 13 January 1745, Orangeburg Co., S. C.

HEPWORTH, Harriet T. and John G. Read, 6 March 1839, Mecklenburg Co., N. C.

HEPWORTH, John and Sally Freeman, 9 June 1818, Mecklenburg Co., N. C.

HEPWORTH, Sarah A. and Thomas Jamieson, 15 March 1848, Mecklenburg Co., N. C.

HERGERSPERGER, Anna B. (widow) and John Julius Tapp, 3 February 1740, Orangeburg Co., S. C.

HERIOT, George and Sally Tucker, February 1775, Charleston, S. C.

HERIOT, Roger and Catherine Booth, 24 March 1801, Charleston, S. C.

HERNDON, Bartlett and Termenia Booth, 27 April 1853, Orange Co., N. C.

HERNDON, Bartlett H. and Martha Cook, 23 December 1858, Orange Co., N. C.

HERNDON, Benjamin and Esther Smith, 15 May 1829, Orange Co., N. C.

HERNDON, Chesley and Tempe Rigsby, 19 October 1824, Orange Co., N. C.

HERNDON, Chesley and Frances Warren, 13 September 1849, Orange Co., N. C.

HERNDON, Chesley and Mary E. George, 3 February 1866, Orange Co., N. C.

HERNDON, Cynthia and Thomas George, 24 March 1842, Orange Co., N. C.

HERNDON, Edmond and Rebecca Rhodes, 14 February 1794, Orange Co., N. C.

HERNDON, Elias and Polly Hopson, 1795, Orange Co., N. C.

HERNDON, Eliza and Alexander Burnett, 5 January 1793, Orange Co., N. C.

HERNDON, Elizabeth and David Alexander Hunt, 19 May 1852, Granville Co., N. C.

HERNDON, Esther and John Barber, 20 March 1790, Orange Co., N. C.

HERNDON, Green E. and Mary Ann Barber, 20 December 1842, Orange Co., N. C.

HERNDON, Harmon and Elizabeth George, 5 April 1837, Orange Co., N. C.

HERNDON, Harmon and Louise Massey, 2 November 1858, Orange Co., N. C.

HERNDON, James and Catherine Collier, 14 June 1802, Orange Co., N. C.

HERNDON, James and Polly Dixon, 3 May 1814, Orange Co., N. C.

HERNDON, Martha and Ezekiel George, 8 June 1831, Orange Co., N. C.

HERNDON, Matilda and William George, 10 June 1826, Orange Co., N. C.

HERNDON, Pomphrett and Polly King, 19 July 1805, Orange Co., N. C.

HERNDON, Pomphrett and Anne Barfield, 28 October 1812, Orange Co., N. C.

HERNDON, Ruben and Frances McCoy, 9 August 1784, Orange Co., N. C.

HERNDON, Sylvinia and David George, 11 December 1837, Orange Co., N. C.

HERNDON, Tapley and Nelly Hutchins, 13 November 1798, Orange Co., N. C.

HERNDON, Thomas S. and Delilah M. Rhodes, 4 October 1856, Orange Co., N.C.

HERNDON, Waller and Eliza Partin, 21 May 1795, Orange Co., N. C.

HERNDON, Westly and America Roberts, 1828, Orange Co., N. C.

HERNDON, William and Hannah Hutchins, 1 January 1795, Orange Co., N. C.

HERNDON, William H. and Elizabeth George, 23 January 1866, Orange Co., N. C.

HERNDON, Zachariah and Milley Rhodes, 28 June 1789, Orange Co., N. C.

HERNDON, Zachariah and Lydia Clifton, 18 March 1824, Orange Co., N. C.

HERON, Benjamin and Mary Marsden, 10 June 1765, Wilmington, N. C.

HERRIES, Mary and Thomas Webb, 31 August 1770, Santee, S. C.

HERRILL, Agnes and John Hemphill, 16 July 1783, Rowan Co., N. C.

HERRING, Margaret and Felix Countz, 15 April 1800, Charleston, S. C.

HERRON, Delilah and James Montgomery, 16 June 1846, Mecklenburg Co., N. C.

HERRON, Jane and Benjamin Brown, 9 June 1809, Mecklenburg Co., N. C.

HERRON, Esther and A. B. Rice, 2 February 1865, Mecklenburg Co., N. C.

HERRON, Isaac and Martha McKee, 25 June 1802, Mecklenburg Co., N. C.

HERRON, Sarah and William Cook, 31 July 1850, Mecklenburg Co., N. C.

HERTZOG, Barnard and Anne Mary Ulmer, 18 February 1755, Orangeburg Co., S. C.

HESS, George and Peggy Bullong, 19 May 1798, Rowan Co., N. C.

HESS, Hans George Henry and Catharina Magdalena Shuler, 12 October 1742, Orangeburg Co., S. C.

HESS, John and Susanna Cryte, 19 April 1790, Rowan Co., N. C.

HESSY, Christian and Jacob Morff, 5 June 1750, Orangeburg Co., S. C.

HESTER, John and Martha Cummings, 28 October 1838, Edgefield District, S. C.

HESTER, Maranda B. and William G. V. White, 6 September 1836, Granville Co., N. C.

HESTER, Nancy and Samuel Allen, 27 August 1782, Orange Co., N. C.

HESTER, Nancy and Joseph Hunt, 1820, Granville Co., N. C.

HESTER, Sarah and Samuel Hunt, 1834, Granville Co., N. C.

HETHERINGTON, John and Mary Miller, 16 August 1763, Berkeley Co., S. C.

HETHERINGTON, Mary (widow) and Brian Cape, 13 May 1770, Charleston, S. C.

HEVIN, Harriet and William P. Brown, 28 April 1846, Mecklenburg Co., N. C.

HEWATT, Andrew and Katherine Elliott (widow), 19 June 1773, Charleston, S. C.

HEWITT, Hill and Martha England, 30 October 1782, Santee, S. C.

HEXT, Alexander and Jane Weaver, 13 December 1743, Colleton Co., S. C.

HEXT, Margaret and Alexander Peronneau, 23 December 1744, Charleston, S. C.

HEXT, Mary (widow) and John Dart, 25 April 1746, Charleston, S. C.

HEXT, William and Ann Hartley, July 1786, Charleston, S. C.

HEYM, Barbara and Christian York, 18 May 1742, Orangeburg Co., S. C.

HEYWARD, Ann (Mrs.) and Nicholas Cruger (Jr.), 2 October 1799, Charleston, S. C.

HEYWARD, Anna and Benjamin W. Taylor, 14 December 1865, Columbia, S. C.

HEYWARD, Edward B. and Lucy Izard, 7 November 1850, Charleston, S. C.

HEYWARD, Joseph and Alice Izard, 6 January 1824, Charleston, S. C.

HEYWARD, Maria and William Brailsford, June 1786, Charleston, S. C.

HEYWARD, Thomas and Elizabeth Matthewes, 20 April 1773, Charleston, S. C.

HEYWARD, Thomas (Jr.) and Susanna Savage, May 1786, Charleston, S. C.

HEYWOOD, John (Jr.) and Mary Barnwell, 1788, Beaufort, S. C.

HIBBEN, Hannah and Arnold Wells, 21 March 1797, Christ Church Parish, S. C.

HIBBETS, James and Nancy Crawford, 28 December 1792, Mecklenburg Co., N. C.

HIBBETTS, James and Agnes Johnson, 1 December 1790, Rowan Co., N. C.

HICKEY, William and Rebecca Gant, 1746, Orangeburg Co., S. C.

HICKLING, Ephriam and Miss Thorp, 19 August 1774, Romney, S. C.

HICKMAN, Elizabeth and Abraham Dew, 2 December 1763, Edgecombe Co., N. C.

HICKMAN, William and Lucretia Stricklin, 19 December 1762, Edgecombe Co., N. C.

HICKS, Joshua and Diana Adams, 19 September 1794, Rowan Co., N. C.

HICKS, Judah and John Hipp, 5 April 1783, Mecklenburg Co., N. C.

HICKS, Mary and Matthew Robinson, 21 January 1794, Mecklenburg Co., N. C.

HICKS, Thomas and Elizabeth Deadman, 29 October 1787, Rowan Co., N. C.

HICKS, William and Mourning Hunt, (widow of John) 27 May 1778, Granville Co., N. C.

HIDE, Benjamin and Mary Ensley, 9 January 1775, Rowan Co., N. C.

HIDE, Benjamin and Margaret Hughey, 25 July 1796, Rowan Co., N. C.

HIGBACK, Ann and John Mayers, 21 February 1761, Santee, S. C.

HIGDEN, Joseph and Margaret Holbrook, 5 April 1786, Rowan Co., N. C.

HIGGINS, Fannie C. and James McIntosh, 25 November 1862, Newberry, S. C.

HIGGINS, George and Elizabeth Colles, 13 February 1769, Charleston, S. C.

HIGGINS, James and Nancy M. Martin, 13 February 1866, Laurens Co., S. C.

HIGGINS, John and Deborah Clemmons, 29 April 1823, Chowan Co., N. C.

HIGGINS, Hany and Jacob Ropp, 27 January 1858, Laurens Co., S. C.

HIGGINS, Martha (widow) and Harman Garrett, 14 December 1843, Laurens Co., S. C.

HIGGINS, Permelia and Preston Fleming, 25 September 1856, Laurens Co., S. C.

HIGGINS, Rachel (widow) and Benjamin Duke, 30 August 1784, Charleston, S. C.

HIGGS, Sally and Edward Vann, 7 February 1788, Bertie Co., N. C.

HIGHS, Charles and Susan Thompson, 13 September 1866, Laurens Co., S. C.

HILBURN, Hugh and Peggy Nobles, 3 April 1825, Edgefield District, S. C.

HILL, Abraham and Kathrine Walton, 7 January 1756, Chowan Co., N. C.

HILL, Abraham and Rachel Scott, 1 May 1761, Chowan Co., N. C.

HILL, Acey (of Boston) and (Mrs.) Jane Thorney, 29 May 1801, Charleston S. C.

HILL, Alice and William Hudgens, 1 February 1866, Laurens Co., S. C.

HILL, Ann and Henry Young, 9 April 1754, Orangeburg Co., S. C.

HILL, Ann and George Denholm, 23 July 1778, Santee, S. C.

HILL, Asa and Mary Alexander, 1784, Tyrrell Co., N. C.

HILL, A. M. (Miss.) and H. N. Beckler, 14 February 1866, Mecklenburg Co., N. C.

HILL, Captain and (Mrs.) Elizabeth Butler, December 1785, Charleston, S. C.

HILL, Caroline and James Chamblen, 7 October 1845, Laurens Co., S. C.

HILL, Carolina and Lycurgus Smith, 15 December 1866, Laurens Co., S. C.

HILL, Charles and Sarah Smith, 7 March 1746, Charleston, S. C.

HILL, Christina and Federick Goodnall, 1 August 1775, Rowan Co., N. C.

HILL, Delilah and James C. Montgomery, 23 February 1825, Rowan Co., N. C.

HILL, Elizabeth and John Croskey, 12 August 1721, St. Andrews Parish, S. C.

HILL, Elizabeth (widow) and (Rev.) Samuel Quincy, 24 April 1747, Charleston, S. C.

HILL, Henry Hampton and (Mrs.) Martha Sarah (Bond) Spann, 19 July 1817, Edgefield District, S. C.

HILL, Isaac and Mary Barnes, 12 January 1788, Rowan Co., N. C.

HILL, James L. and Eliza Holden, 1842, Edgefield District, S. C.

HILL, John and Mary Lynn (widow), 4 January 1780, Rowan Co., N. C.

HILL, Joseph F. and Martha A. Dearmond, 12 November 1825, Mecklenburg Co., N. C.

HILL, John S. and Henrietta Demeese, 5 August 1835, Mecklenburg Co., N. C.

HILL, Juda and Nehemiah Bunch, 14 February 1765, Chowan Co., N. C.

HILL, Martha and John Beaty, 21 August 1798, Mecklenburg Co., N. C.

HILL, Mary and John Beswicke, 16 November 1742, Charleston, S. C.

HILL, Mary and David S. Goodloe, May 1801, Granville Co., N. C.

HILL, Robert and Istal White, 28 December 1815, Mecklenburg Co., N. C.

HILL, Sarah and Daniel Linder, 14 March 1754, Orangeburg Co., S. C.

HILL, Sarah (Mrs.) and William Semple, August 1785, Charleston, S. C.

HILL, Theophilus and Tresa Thomas, 3 September 1762, Edgecombe Co., N. C.

HILL, Theophilus and Susan Richardson, 21 January 1819, Edgefield District, S. C.

HILL, Thomas and Rachel Smith, 6 October 1779, Rowan Co., N. C.

HILL, Thomas (Rev.) and Jane Wells, 28 June 1785, Charleston, S. C.

HILL, Thomas and Susan Boyd, 13 December 1860, Laurens Co., S. C.

HILL, Walter and Jenneatte Henry, 20 October 1798, Mecklenburg Co., N. C.

HILL, Walter A. and Mary N. Montgomery, 27 December 1830, Mecklenburg Co., N. C.

HILL, Whit M. and Mary Sharp, 21 March 1814, Mecklenburg Co., N. C.

HILL, William and Adalade Downs, 19 November 1844, Laurens Co., S. C.

HILLARD, Daniel and Jane Williams, 7 February 1786, Rowan Co., N. C.

HILLARD, George and Catherine Shrock, 29 January 1793, Rowan Co., N. C.

HILLEGAR, Philip and Sarah Mann, 1788, Charleston, S. C.

HILLIARD, Lucy and William E. Walker, 8 May 1856, Nash Co., N. C.

HILLIARD, Mary Williamson and Edmund White, 7 September 1833, Warren Co., N. C.

HILLIARD, Oliver and Ann Crawford, 1 May 1800, Charleston, S. C.

HILLIS, Robert and Sarah McDowell, 1 April 1776, Rowan Co., N. C.

HILTON, Lifas and Milly Moorefield, 5 November 1792, Rowan Co., N. C.

HILTON, Robert and Elizabeth Wasson, 17 April 1787, Rowan Co., N. C.

HIMBY, Eli and Mary Stums, 20 August 1835, Mecklenburg Co., N. C.

HINDESLEY, Joseph and Perthia Gooden, 7 November 1785, Chowan Co., N. C.

HINDS, Deliah and Michael Stealy, 1784, Tyrrell Co., N. C.

HINES, George W. and Rebecca Grant, 6 February 1859, Laurens Co., S. C.

HINES, Jean and Thomas Thurston, 11 April 1782, Santee, S. C.

HINKLE, Charles and Susanna March, 13 May 1797, Rowan Co., N. C.

HINKLE, George and Frances Shaffer, 17 September 1795, Rowan Co., N. C.

HINKLE, John and Mary Rosenbum, 26 February 1790, Rowan Co., N. C.

HINKLE, Michael and Sarah Beecham, 26 November 1787, Rowan Co., N. C.

HINKLE, William and Elender Hunter, 11 December 1793, Rowan Co., N. C.

HINSON, Elenor and David Davidson, 25 March 1788, Bertie Co., N. C.

HINSON, Margaret and John Hagler, 14 February 1828, Mecklenburg Co., N. C.

HINTON, Amos and Susannah Walton, 6 September 1753, Chowan Co., N. C.

HINTON, Christian and Daniel Marshall, 11 June 1773, Chowan Co., N. C.

HINTON, Christian and Richard Freeman, 29 September 1778, Chowan Co., N. C.

HINTON, James and Charlotte Dunscombe, 23 December 1800, Charleston, S. C.

HINTON, Malachi and Sarah Wimberley, 6 June 1764, Edgecombe Co., N. C.

HINTON, Sarah and John Collins, 6 February 1779, Chowan Co., N. C.

HINTON, William and Ann Turner, 7 March 1770, Bertie Co., N. C.

HINTON, William and Margaret Cook, 10 January 1824, Mecklenburg Co., N. C.

HIPP, Amelia R. and Sydney Bryant, 16 August 1860, Mecklenburg Co., N. C.

HIPP, Andrew and Mabel Perry, 24 September 1810, Mecklenburg Co., N. C.

HIPP, Caroline and William Means, 18 December 1838, Mecklenburg Co., N. C.

HIPP, David and Catherine Parish, 22 August 1808, Mecklenburg Co., N. C.
HIPP, Elizabeth and William Johnston, 25 October 1808, Mecklenburg Co., N. C.
HIPP, Harriet C. and David Johnston, 23 July 1838, Mecklenburg Co., N. C.
HIPP, John and Judah Hicks, 5 April 1783, Mecklenburg Co., N. C.
HIPP, John and Polly Rogers, 12 October 1799, Mecklenburg Co., N. C.
HIPP, John and Sylvia Harwell, 7 October 1817, Mecklenburg Co., N. C.
HIPP, Lilly and Ezekial Beaty, 9 June 1847, Mecklenburg Co., N. C.
HIPP, Margaret and James H. Neal, 5 July 1838, Mecklenburg Co., N. C.
HIPP, Margaret and Matthew A. Robison, 2 December 1847, Mecklenburg Co., N. C.
HIPP, Margaret and Jesse Johnson, 8 November 1830, Mecklenburg Co., N. C.
HIPP, Mary and Rueben E. Ross, 3 December 1823, Mecklenburg Co., N. C.
HIPP, Violet A. and David H. McCrea, 15 December 1830, Mecklenburg Co., N. C.
HITCH, Young and Mary Ann Edwards, 19 January 1847, Laurens Co., S. C.
HITCH, Ludy and Margaret Templeton (widow), 28 December 1858, Laurens Co., S. C.
HITCH, Green and Elizabeth Pinson, 24 July 1866, Laurens Co., S. C.
HITCH, Susan and Marion Duvall, 12 January 1860, Laurens Co., S. C.
HIX, Tabby and Zephaniah Harris, 25 November 1790, Rowan Co., N. C.
HOBBIS, Hannah and Aaron Frazey, 24 July 1775, Rowan Co., N. C.
HOBBS, Martha and Artemus Lowe, 2 November 1852, Edgefield District, S. C.
HOBBY, Rodah and Arthur Bryant, 4 January 1766, Edgecombe Co., N. C.
HOBBY, Sarah and John Bryan, 1 July 1766, Edgecombe Co., N. C.
HOBBY, Sarah and John Flewellen, 24 December 1761, Edgecombe Co., N. C.
HOBCRAFT, Amy and James Allan, 13 August 1856, Charleston, S. C.
HOBDAY, Joseph and Abigail Miller, 13 June 1764, Chowan Co., N. C.
HODGE, Elizabeth and John McKee, 23 April 1798, Mecklenburg Co., N. C.
HODGE, Jane and James Johnson, 16 November 1835, Mecklenburg Co., N. C.
HODGE, James and Rebecca Ownley, 30 April 1798, Mecklenburg Co., N. C.
HODGE, Mary and John McClure, 10 February 1795, Mecklenburg Co., N. C.
HODGE, Sarah F. and Daniel Bradham, 13 October 1859, Charendon Co., S. C.
HODGY, P. B. and Sarah E. Cochran, 23 September 1857, Mecklenburg Co., N. C.
HOFF, Richard and Zilpha Everett, 15 July 1769, Tyrrell Co., N. C.
HOGAN, General and Ruth Norfleet, 3 October 1751, South Hampton, N. C.
HOGG, Alexander and Widow Brisbane, 18 July 1773, Charleston, S. C.
HOGG, John and Hannah Painter, 28 December 1721, St. Andrews Parish, S. C.
HOGGIN, Verena and John Nicholas Shuler, 26 September 1752, Orangeburg Co., S. C.
HOGOOD, Johnson and Nancy O'Hear, 8 December 1794, Charleston, S. C.
HOGSTAN, Archibald and Anne Stone, 16 October 1779, Rowan Co., N. C.
HOLBROOK, Margaret and Joseph Higden, 5 April 1786, Rowan Co., N. C.
HOLBROOK, William and Sarah Baker, 14 May 1785, Rowan Co., N. C.
HOLBROOKE, Caleb and Priscilla Baker, 1 April 1780, Rowan Co., N. C.
HOLCOMB, Bradly and Sarah Edwards, 27 January 1848, Laurens Co., S. C.
HOLCOMB, Susan A. and John H. Montgomery, 1857, Spartansburg, S. C.
HOLDBROOK, Theopolis and Margaret A. Horwell, 7 February 1848, Mecklenburg Co., N. C.
HOLDEN, Eliza and James L. Hill, 1842, Edgefield District, S. C.
HOLDEN, James and Mary Rusely, 21 May 1800, Mecklenburg Co., N. C.

HOLDER, Aggie and George Mitchell, 20 December 1830, Bertie Co., N. C.

HOLDER, Levina and Micajah Bunch, 8 April 1791, Bertie Co., N. C.

HOLDER, Shadrack and Minnie Dunning, 4 February 1799, Bertie Co., N. C.

HOLDERFIELD, Valentine and Henny Noland, 13 April 1789, Rowan Co., N. C.

HOLEBAUGH, George and Susannah Savage, 13 June 1787, Rowan Co., N. C.

HOLEMAN, David and Rachel Frost, 8 November 1798, Rowan Co., N. C.

HOLEMAN, Jacob and Liddy Pinchback, 23 November 1795, Rowan Co., N. C.

HOLEMAN, Thomas and Margaret Sutherland, 16 May 1778, Rowan Co., N. C.

HOLEMAN, William and Martha Pinchback, 28 December 1799, Rowan Co., N. C.

HOLIDAY, Jane and Thomas Maris, 17 November 1802, Orange Co., N. C.

HOLLADAY, Asia and William Jones, 23 January 1790, Bertie Co., N. C.

HOLLADAY, Hannah and John Lanier, 6 May 1769, Tyrrell Co., N. C.

HOLLADAY, Mary and Reuben Eason, 24 December 1762, Tyrrell Co., N. C.

HOLLADAY, Samuel and Elizabeth Dugan, 14 November 1763, Tyrrell Co., N. C.

HOLLAND, Abraham and Drury Clark, 8 October 1799, Edgecombe Co., N. C.

HOLLAND, Elizabeth and Alexander Petree, February 1748, Charleston, S. C.

HOLLAND, John and Christina Robinson, 26 August 1783, Rowan Co., N. C.

HOLLAND, John and (Mrs.) Jane Marshall, 1 September 1786, Wilmington, N. C.

HOLLAND, Nancy and William Horn, 26 February 1800, Edgecombe Co., N. C.

HOLLAND, Polly and Daniel Crawford, February 1748, Charleston, S. C.

HOLLAND, Richard and Nina Taylor, 30 November 1775, Rowan Co., N. C.

HOLLAND, Sarah and Tyree Rodes, 25 April 1811, Halifax Co., N. C.

HOLLAND, Thomas and Mary Ross, 17 May 1761, Edgecombe Co., N. C.

HOLLIDAY, James and Mary Ann Goff, 30 April 1855, Edgefield District, S. C.

HOLLIDAY, William E. and Mary S. Barton, 30 April 1845, Mecklenburg Co., N. C.

HOLLINGSWORTH, Margaret A. (widow) and Thomas Thomason, 27 December 1855, Edgefield District, S. C.

HOLLIS, William and Elizabeth Reed, 15 February 1790, Rowan Co., N. C.

HOLLOMAN, Isham and Sarah Wiggins, 29 October 1799, Edgecombe Co., N. C.

HOLLOWAY, John and Mary Ship, 21 October 1761, Edgecombe Co., N. C.

HOLLOWAY, Mary Ann and H. R. Williams, 28 February 1840, Edgefield District, S. C.

HOLLOWAY, Temperance and Caleb Runnells, 30 October 1852, Edgefield District, S. C.

HOLLOWAY, Thomas and Johanna Cain, 5 October 1782, Orange Co., N. C.

HOLLYBUSH, Miss and Plowden Weston, 18 July 1762, Charleston, S. C.

HOLMES, Andrew and Margaret Gray, 22 May 1800, Charleston, S. C.

HOLMES, Ann and John Fitch, 16 January 1748, Orangeburg Co., S. C.

HOLMES, Ann and Adam Hawthorne, 23 April 1799, Fairfield Co., S. C.

HOLMES, Anne and Benjamin Matthews, 5 February 1745, Charleston, S. C.

HOLMES, Elizabeth and Samuel Brailsford, 7 April 1750, Charleston, S. C.

HOLMES, Elizabeth and Thomas Farr (Jr.), 23 November 1760, Charleston, S. C.

HOLMES, Frances (Mrs.) and William Stone, 17 December 1800, James Island, S. C.

HOLMES, Isaac and Elizabeth Perroneau, 19 January 1724, Charleston, S. C.

HOLMES, Isaac and Elizabeth Stanyarne, 11 September 1755, Charleston, S. C.

HOLMES, Isaac and Rebecca Bee, 8 May 1759, Charleston, S. C.

HOLMES, Isaac and Elizabeth Air, 5 January 1779, Charleston, S. C.

HOLMES, John Bee and Elizabeth Edwards, 12 November 1783, Charleston, S. C.

HOLMES, John and Susannah Blackwood, 9 December 1793, Rowan Co., N. C.

HOLMES, John and Harriet Mitchell, 29 July 1830, Edgefield District, S. C.

HOLMES, Matilda and Martin Posey, 23 February 1838, Edgefield District, S. C.

HOLMES, Miss and James Simmons, May 1759, Charleston, S. C.

HOLMES, Rebecca (widow) and John Edwards 30 December 1773, Charleston, S. C.

HOLMES, Richard and Elizabeth McGaughey, 1 January 1781, Rowan Co., N. C.

HOLMES, Sabra and William Williams, 1 January 1835, Edgefield District, S. C.

HOLMES, Sarah and John Raven, 6 November 1750, Charleston, S. C.

HOLMES, Susannah and Thomas Bee, 5 May 1761, Charleston, S. C.

HOLMES, Wyatt L. and Mary E. Elam, 28 November 1754, Edgefield District, S. C.

HOLSENBACK, Eliza and Adam Flemore, 4 September 1841, Edgefield District, S. C.

HOLSENBACK, Sarah and Tillman D. Naper, 22 November 1833, Edgefield District, S. C.

HOLSHOUSE, Andrew and Polly Pool, 21 December 1798, Rowan Co., N. C.

HOLSTEAD, Thomas and Sarah Garrett, 20 July 1762, Tyrrell Co., N. C.

HOLSTEIN, James and Susanna Enex, 14 July 1779, Rowan Co., N. C.

HOLT, Mary and Anthony Thompson, 29 January 1788, Orange Co., N. C.

HOLT, Samuel N. and Martha Wright (widow), 4 August 1785, Charleston, S. C.

HOLTON, Temperance and John Riley, 19 May 1832, Mecklenburg Co., N. C.

HOMEYARD, Alice E. and Philip Prioleau, 30 December 1783, Charleston, S. C.

HOOD, Catherine and Benjamin A. Culp, 23 May 1848, Mecklenburg Co., N. C.

HOOD, Celia A. and John C. O'Brien, 8 February 1846, Mecklenburg Co. N. C.

HOOD, Elizabeth and Robert Maxwell, 7 May 1795, Mecklenburg Co., N. C.

HOOD, Elizabeth and Hugh Bean, 3 November 1809, Mecklenburg Co., N. C.

HOOD, Jane and Samuel Bain, 20 January 1820, Mecklenburg Co., N. C.

HOOD, John H. and Mazy Russell, 10 December 1833, Mecklenburg Co., N. C.

HOOD, Jeremiah and Mary McCroskey, 16 January 1816, Mecklenburg Co., N. C.

HOOD, Lydia and John Black, 25 August 1802, Mecklenburg Co., N. C.

HOOD, Margaret A. and Frederick McCauley, 20 November 1827, Mecklenburg Co., N. C.

HOOD, Mary and William Richards, 13 July 1744, Chowan Co., N. C.

HOOD, Robert and Elizabeth McNevin, 15 May 1797, Mecklenburg Co., N. C.

HOOD, Robert L. and Mary Ann Watt, 8 January 1849, Mecklenburg Co., N. C.

HOOD, Reuben and Mary Neal, 15 December 1825, Mecklenburg Co., N. C.

HOOKER, A. and George Brownrigg, 6 October 1783, Tyrrell Co., N. C.

HOOKER, Mary and Abraham Jennett, 16 December 1767, Tyrrell Co., N. C.

HOOKER, Nathan and Mary Whedbee, 1781, Tyrrell Co., N. C.

HOOKER, Rosannah and Benjamin Spruill, 26 September 1767, Tyrrell Co., N. C.

HOOKER, Stephen and Martha Craddock, 1780, Tyrrell Co., N. C.

HOOKS, Charles and Ann Hunter, 15 November 1796, Bertie Co., N. C.

HOOKS, Elizabeth and Isaac Baker, 15 December 1830, Mecklenburg Co., N. C.

HOOKS, John S. and Susannah J. Biggers, 6 April 1858, Mecklenburg Co., N. C.

HOOKS, Mary and Eli McCall, 22 March 1823, Mecklenburg Co., N. C.

HOOKS, Patsy and James G. Blair, 27 November, 1819, Mecklenburg Co., N. C.

HOOKS, Willoby and Anna Kritz, 23 January 1793, Rowan Co., N. C.

HOOPER, Richard and Anne Forrest, 11 February 1786, Orange Co., N. C.

HOOVER, Adaline and John K. Richardson, 23 April 1849, Mecklenburg Co., N. C.

HOOVER, Adaline and Samuel H. Blakenship, 10 August 1856, Mecklenburg Co., N. C.

HOOVER, Amanda and M. B. Raborn, 14 June 1865, Mecklenburg Co., N. C.

HOOVER, Eliza J. and William R. Rodden, 20 September 1860, Mecklenburg Co., N. C.

HOOVER, George and Margaret Beard, 4 May 1784, Rowan Co., N. C.

HOOVER, Henry and Jane Collins, 28 December 1849, Mecklenburg Co., N. C.

HOOVER, Mary J. and John William Johnson, 28 February 1860, Mecklenburg Co., N. C.

HOOVEY, Martha and Jacob Guild, 13 February 1786, Orange Co., N. C.

HOPE, Levi and Jane M. Harris, 1 October 1823, Mecklenburg Co., N. C.

HOPE, Susan Ann and John R. Long, 20 December 1856, Mecklenburg Co., N. C.

HOPE, Valentine and Jane Watt, 29 November 1787, Rowan Co., N. C.

HOPKINS, Alexander and Moren Brown, 10 February 1796, Bertie Co., N. C.

HOPKINS, Christopher and Ann Cadell, 13 November 1736, Charleston, S. C.

HOPKINS, Daniel and Frances Cobb, 20 November 1793, Bertie Co., N. C.

HOPKINS, Isaac K. and Casandra Bateman, 8 September 1836, Chowan Co., N. C.

HOPKINS, Jane and Philip Massey, 20 January 1733, Charleston, S. C.

HOPKINS, Jehodah and Samuel Hopkins, 1780, Tyrrell Co., N. C.

HOPKINS, John and Janet Stewart, 25 April 1774, Bertie Co., N. C.

HOPKINS, John and Tabitha Cutchens, 16 March 1827, Edgecombe Co., N. C.

HOPKINS, Joseph and Elizabeth Harper, 25 April 1776, Chowan Co., N. C.

HOPKINS, John and Mary King, 10 February 1752, Chowan Co., N. C.

HOPKINS, Mary and Edward Scott, 23 January 1723, Charleston, S. C.

HOPKINS, Mary (widow) and James Luten, 4 March 1754, Chowan Co., N. C.

HOPKINS, Mary and Isaac Hayne, 12 December 1793, Colleton, S. C.

HOPKINS, Philess and Betsy Howett, 1781, Tyrrell Co., N. C.

HOPKINS, Samuel and (Mrs.) Frances Danridge (widow), 21 June 1770, Charleston, S. C.

HOPKINS, Samuel and Jehodah Hopkins, 1780, Tyrrell Co., N. C.

HOPKINS, William and Sally Stancil, 22 October 1799, Edgecombe Co., N. C.

HOPKINS, William and Eliza Welch, 12 August 1770, Charleston, S. C.

HOPKINS, Winnifred and Benjamin Cook, 25 April 1774, Bertie Co., N. C.

HOPPER, John and Lovey Martin, 16 June 1756, Chowan Co., N. C.

HOPPER, Thomas and Nancy Stewart, 16 February 1791, Rowan Co., N. C.

HOPPOLD, John M. and Evelina M. Forester, 14 February 1827, Mecklenburg Co., N. C.

HOPSON, Polly and Elias Herndon, 1795, Orange Co., N. C.

HOPSON, Zachariah and Ruthy George, 22 December 1789, Orange Co., N. C.

HOPTON, Alice and Robert William Powell, 11 January 1774, Charleston, S. C.

HORA, Henry and Nancy Hampton, 12 February 1784, Rowan Co., N. C.

HORAH, Hugh and Mary Moore, 14 January 1788, Rowan Co., N. C.

HORGER, Catharina and Henry Strauman, 1740, Orangeburg Co., S. C.

HORGER, Jacob and Lovisia Shaumloffel, 1740, Orangeburg Co., S. C.

HORGUER, Magdalene and Peter Murer, 2 April 1751, Orangeburg Co., S. C.

HORLBECK, Henry and Eliza Schnierle, May 1838, Charleston, S. C.

HORLBECK, Margaret and John F. Ficken, 30 March 1871, Charleston, S. C.

HORN, Charity and William Battle, 1742, Edgecombe Co., N. C.

HORN, Elias and Sarah Gay, 26 January 1763, Edgecombe Co., N. C.

HORN, Elijah and Susannah Killebrow, 18 August 1799, Edgecombe Co., N. C.

HORN, James and Elizabeth Price, 18 May 1799, Edgecombe Co., N. C.

HORN, Richard and Sarah McKenny, 28 May 1801, Mecklenburg Co., N. C.

HORN, William and Mary Thomas, 20 July 1761, Edgecombe Co., N. C.

HORN, William and Nancy Holland, 26 February 1800, Edgecombe Co., N. C.

HORN, Wilson and Clarkia Henby, December 1819, Wayne Co., N. C.

HORNBY, James and Penelope White, 22 September 1788, Bertie Co., N. C.

HORNE, Peter and Sarah Sellers, 20 May 1771, Colleton Co., S. C.

HORNE, Peter and Mahalah E. Smith, 23 February 1832, Colleton Co., S. C.

HORNER, Susanna and Anthony Hammond, 23 February 1779, Rowan Co., N. C.

HORNY, Ester and Ladoc Mendenhall, 14 November 1817, Guilford Co., N. C.

HORREY, Daniel and Sarah Ford, 20 December 1743, St. James Parish, S. C.

HORRMUTT, Elizabeth and Joseph Huber, 4 September 1753, Orangeburg Co., S. C.

HORRY, Daniel and Harriet Pinckney, 15 February 1768, Charleston, S. C.

HORRY, Daniel and Judith Serri, 9 December 1759, Santee, S. C.

HORRY, Elias (Jr.) and Elizabeth Branford, 15 November 1770, Charleston, S. C.

HORRY, Elias and Margaret Huger, 17 August 1704, Craven Co., S. C.

HORRY, John and Ann Royer, 5 July 1759, Santee, S. C.

HORRY, Thomas and Nancy Branford, 13 June 1772, Charleston, S. C.

HORT, William and Alice Gibbes, 7 January 1772, Charleston, S. C.

HOSKINS, Ann and Samuel Wiggins, 2 June 1770, Chowan Co., N. C.

HOSKINS, Elizabeth and John Coffield, 8 March 1757, Chowan Co., N. C.

HOSKINS, John and Mary Howell, 25 January 1794, Rowan Co., N. C.

HOSKINS, Mary and Edmund Blount, 26 February 1765, Chowan Co., N. C.

HOSKINS, Mary and John Gasser, 29 October 1785, Chowan Co., N. C.

HOSKINS, Nicholas and Mary Allcock, 19 February 1786, Tyrrell Co., N. C.

HOSKINS, Rachel and Job Leary, January 1776, Chowan Co., N. C.

HOSKINS, Sarah and William Jackson, 21 December 1767, Chowan Co., N. C.

HOSKINS, Sarah and Joseph Blount, 15 May 1771, Chowan Co., N. C.

HOSLEY, John and Isabella Avery, 13 February 1801, Charleston, S. C.

HOTTOW, Anna and Peter Grieffous, 25 May 1742, Orangeburg Co., S. C.

HOTTOW, Charles and Ann Tshudy, 1742, Orangeburg Co., S. C.

HOTTOW, Peter and Margaret B. Shuler, 1740, Orangeburg Co., S. C.

HOTTOW, Sirrah and Leonhard Warnedow, 1742, Orangeburg Co., S. C.

HOUGH, Martha Ann and Amos McManus (2nd. m.), 18 December 1849, Lancaster Co., S. C.

HOUGH, Mary (dau. of Richard) and James Bryant, 2 October 1780, Tyrrell Co., N. C.

HOUK, Felix and Catherine Mock, 13 June 1793, Rowan Co., N. C.

HOUSE, Samuel and Betsy Forster, 8 May 1843, Mecklenburg Co., N. C.

HOUSEAL, Bernard (Rev.) and Sibella Margaretta Mayer, 1752, Rotterdam, S. C.

HOUSEAL, William Frederick (Capt.) and Anna Margaretta Geiselhart, 1772, Orangeburg Co., S. C.

HOUSER, John and Amelia Curry, 8 February 1837, Mecklenburg Co., N. C.

HOUSER, Martha M. and Samuel Reed, 15 October 1854, South Edisto River, S. C.

HOUSTON, Ambrose and Eliza B. Lawson, 29 March 1839, Mecklenburg Co., N. C.

HOUSTON, Catherine C. and Ezekial Alexander, 20 December 1836, Mecklenburg Co., N. C.

HOUSTON, David and Eleanor Barkley, 20 March 1788, Mecklenburg Co., N. C.

HOUSTON, David and Anne Patterson, 2 September 1774, Rowan Co., N. C.

HOUSTON, Eliza and Moses H. Cannon, 5 August 1839, Mecklenburg Co., N. C.

HOUSTON, Elizabeth and James A. Bradley, 30 October 1810, Mecklenburg Co., N. C.

HOUSTON, Elizabeth and Jeremiah M. Maxwell, 28 August 1827, Mecklenburg Co., N. C.

HOUSTON, Emily and John Condon, 29 December 1831, Mecklenburg Co., N. C.

HOUSTON, Henry and Martha Houston, 15 October 1791, Mecklenburg Co., N. C.

HOUSTON, James and Cassa Alexander, 1 January 1803, Mecklenburg Co., N. C.

HOUSTON, James N. and Elizabeth Walker, 4 January 1798, Mecklenburg Co., N. C.

HOUSTON, John H. and Clarinda J. Blain, 2 February 1829, Mecklenburg Co., N. C.

HOUSTON, John M. and Jane D. Robinson, 18 March 1834, Mecklenburg Co., N. C.

HOUSTON, Lorina and Robert Caldwell, 27 December 1819, Mecklenburg Co., N. C.

HOUSTON, Margaret and James Osborn, 15 October 1821, Mecklenburg Co., N. C.

HOUSTON, Margaret and William Morrison, 17 December 1821, Mecklenburg Co., N. C.

HOUSTON, Martha and Henry Houston, 15 October 1791, Mecklenburg Co., N. C.

HOUSTON, Martha and John Orr, 28 March 1842, Mecklenburg Co., N. C.

HOUSTON, Mary and Charles Johnson, 10 July 1794, Bladen Co., N. C.

HOUSTON, Mary and Reuben Morris, 1 February 1816, Mecklenburg Co., N. C.

HOUSTON, Mary and Aaron M. Bryan, 14 February 1837, Mecklenburg Co., N. C.

HOUSTON, Peggy and William Andrews, 30 March 1821, Mecklenburg Co., N. C.

HOUSTON, Samuel and Mary Kirk, 30 November 1795, Mecklenburg Co., N. C.

HOUSTON, Thomas and Mary Sample, 6 June 1798, Mecklenburg Co., N. C.

HOVEY, John and Frances Baxter, 22 October 1788, Mecklenburg Co., N. C.

HOW, Mary and Robert Gibbes, 6 February 1855, Columbia, S. C.

HOW, Thomas and Ann Gibbes, 25 June 1829, Charleston, S. C.

HOWARD, Allan and Phoebe Marshall, 1787, Granville Co., N. C.

HOWARD, Amelia E. and John L. Robinson, 24 October 1837, Mecklenburg Co., N. C.

HOWARD, Ann and Benjamin Langstaff, 30 October 1794, Charleston, S. C.

HOWARD, Benjamin and Sarah Middleton, 25 January 1775, Tyrrell Co., N. C.

HOWARD, Charity and Isaac Ellet, 25 August 1798, Rowan Co., N. C.

HOWARD, Edmond and Betsy Wood, 9 March 1791, Rowan Co., N. C.

HOWARD, Francis and (Mrs.) Anne Gear, 11 June 1745, Chowan Co., N. C.

HOWARD, John and Dinah Pinkston, 17 August 1799, Rowan Co., N. C.

HOWARD, John and Margaret Gaither, 26 January 1795, Rowan Co., N. C.

HOWARD, John and Betsy McDarrel, 21 October 1791, Rowan Co., N. C.

HOWARD, Joseph and Sally Enochs, 20 December 1796, Rowan Co., N. C.

HOWARD, Joshua and Elsey Bryon, 7 March 1789, Rowan Co., N. C.

HOWARD, Lucy and Edward Hunt, 4 November 1806, Granville Co., N. C.

HOWARD, Matilda and Jonathan Davis, 14 January 1766, Tyrrell Co., N. C.

HOWARD, Martha and Samuel Ellis, 15 July 1788, Rowan Co., N. C.

HOWARD, Nancy and John M. Ormond, 22 December 1740, Mecklenburg Co., N. C.

HOWARD, Nancy and David M. Johnson, 5 August 1856, Mecklenburg Co., N. C.

HOWARD, Philip and Susannah Gardner, 10 October 1774, Rowan Co., N. C.

HOWARD, Philip and Nancy Dorsey, 20 September 1797, Rowan Co., N. C.

HOWARD, Polly Ann and William Hughs, 3 August 1843, Laurens Co., S. C.

HOWARD, Robert G. and Mary Phifer, 15 April 1838, Mecklenburg Co., N. C.

HOWARD, Sarah and Samuel Hunt, 20 May 1780, Granville Co., N. C.

HOWARD, Sarah and Robert Redding, 19 June 1816, Mecklenburg Co., N. C.

HOWARD, Thomas and Harriet Gaither, 29 October 1799, Rowan Co., N. C.

HOWARD, Tillman and Polly Randall, 26 October 1854, Edgefield District, S. C.

HOWCOTT, Sarah and William Jones (Jr.), 31 August 1772, Chowan Co., N. C.

HOWELL, Adline and Thomas R. Alexander, 30 June 1861, Mecklenburg Co., N. C.

HOWELL, H. W. (Miss) and A. J. Orr, 8 September 1863, Mecklenburg Co., N. C.

HOWELL, James and Susanna Swain, 10 September 1788, Bertie Co., N. C.

HOWELL, John and Mary Ming (widow), 8 September 1753, Chowan Co., N. C.

HOWELL, Jonathan and Mary Fort, 20 May 1766, Edgecombe Co., N. C.

HOWELL, Martha and George W. Morgan, 18 December 1856, Edgefield District, S. C.

HOWELL, Margaret A. and Theophilus Holbrook, 7 February 1848, Mecklenburg Co., N. C.

HOWELL, Mary and John Hoskins, 25 January 1794, Rowan Co., N. C.

HOWELL, Massey and Abner Harper, 18 December 1763, Edgecombe Co., N. C.

HOWELL, Sally and Zadock Braswell, 27 January 1800, Edgecombe Co., N. C.

HOWELL, Sarah and John Bear, 1 December 1865, Mecklenburg Co., N. C.

HOWELL, Sterling P. and Rachel Wyatt, 6 January 1822, Mecklenburg Co., N. C.

HOWELL, William and Ann Mills, 15 June 1776, Tyrrell Co., N. C.

HOWES, James and Nancy Sims, 11 December 1786, Rowan Co., N. C.

HOWETT, Abraham and Judeth Rhodes, 2 September 1775, Tyrrell Co., N. C.

HOWETT, Betsy and Philess Hopkins, 1781, Tyrrell Co., N. C.

HOWEY, William and Mary Gordon, 14 August 1834, Mecklenburg Co., N. C.

HOWEY, Aaron H. and Martha Stitt, 1 June 1835, Mecklenburg Co., N. C.

HOWID, Margaret and John Caldwell, 25 February 1823, Mecklenburg Co., N. C.

HOWIE, Anne and John Houston, 21 December 1797, Mecklenburg Co., N. C.

HOWIE, Robert and Susanna Lesesne, 14 December 1769, Charleston, S. C.

HOWSER, John and (Mrs.) Mary Fleck, January 1786, Charleston, S. C.

HUBBARD, Jane and James Coxe, 21 March 1849, Marlboro Co., S. C.

HUBBARD, Mary and Hardy Boyce, 13 August 1790, Bertie Co., N. C.

HUBBARD, Mrs. and Benjamin Webly, 21 September 1800, Charleston, S. C.

HUBBARD, Wiley A. and Martha Medlock, 24 July 1825, Edgefield District, S. C.

HUBBELL, Walter and Mary Ventures, 22 May 1790, Bertie Co., N. C.

HUBER, Dorothea and Peter Grimmer, 31 January 1738, Orangeburg Co., S. C.

HUBER, John Frederick and Barbara Kreyter, 7 August 1750, Orangeburg Co., S. C.

HUBER, Joseph and Elizabeth Horrmutt, 4 September 1753, Orangeburg Co., S. C.

HUBER, Magdalena and Henry Sally (Jr.), 1748, Orangeburg Co., S. C.

HUCKS, Solomon A. and Mary D. Robards, 5 December 1842, Mecklenburg Co., N. C.

HUDDLESTON, Mary and William Nicholson, 26 August 1822, Mecklenburg Co., N. C.

HUDDLESTON, Ursula and Thomas W. Acock, 23 October 1814, Mecklenburg Co., N. C.

HUDGENS, Elizabeth and (Dr.) John Wolff, 22 July 1857, Laurens Co., S. C.

HUDGENS, John and Mary Chappell, 8 October 1865, Laurens Co., S. C.

HUDGENS, Miss and Dock Blakely, 18 October 1864, Laurens Co., S. C.

HUDGENS, William and Alice Hill, 1 February 1866, Laurens Co., S. C.

HUDGINS, William and Elizabeth Potts, 23 January 1792, Rowan Co., N. C.

HUDNALL, Robert and Lucreasia Kitchen, 2 December 1768, Edgecombe Co., N. C.

HUDNALL, William and Elizabeth Bridgers, 21 February 1766, Edgecombe Co., N. C.

HUDSON, Frances and Aaron Estes, 13 July 1790, Orange Co., N. C.

HUDSON, Joshua H. and Mary Miller, 4 May 1854, Bennettsville, S. C.

HUDSON, Samuel and Margaret Maxwell (widow), July 1746, Orangeburg Co., N. C.

HUDSON, Thomas and Eleanor Johnson, 11 March 1773, Rowan Co., N. C.

HUEY, Agnes and Alexander Craig, 9 March 1804, Mecklenburg Co., N. C.

HUEY, Elizabeth and Hector McCahron, 26 July 1791, Mecklenburg Co., N. C.

HUEY, John and Margaret Craig, 9 March 1804, Mecklenburg Co., N. C.

HUFF, Benjamin and Elizabeth McCain, 10 July 1764, Chowan Co., N. C.

HUFF, Elizabeth and Loveland Bazemore, 13 July 1785, Tyrrell Co., N. C.

HUFF, Jacob and Liddy Maviary, 22 January 1791, Rowan Co., N. C.

HUFF, Sarah (Mrs.) and Broadman Estel, 21 December 1800, Charleston, S. C.

HUFF, Valentine and Jeremiah Hughes, 14 June 1792, Rowan Co., N. C.

HUFFMAN, Daniel and Rachel Parks, 17 January 1781, Rowan Co., N. C.

HUGER, Benjamin and Mary Golightly, 26 July 1767, Charleston, S. C.

HUGER, Benjamin and Polly Kinloch, 1 December 1772, Kensington, S. C.

HUGER, Daniel and Elizabeth Cendron, 25 January 1710, Craven Co., S. C.

HUGER, Daniel E. and Isabel Middleton, 26 November 1800, Ashley River, S. C.

HUGER, Daniel and Mary Cordes, 14 May 1741, Craven Co., S. C.

HUGER, Daniel and Lydia Johnson, 4 December 1747, Craven Co., S. C.

HUGER, Daniel and Anne LeJau, 19 October 1749, Craven Co., S. C.

HUGER, Isaac and Elizabeth Chalmers, 14 March 1762, Craven Co., S. C.

HUGER, John and Charlotte Motte, 15 March 1767, Charleston, S. C.

HUGER, John and Mrs. Cresack, 11 January 1785, Charleston, S. C.

HUGER, Margaret and Elias Horry, 17 August 1704, Craven Co., S. C.

HUGER, William H. and Sabin Lowndes, 10 May 1865, Charleston, S. C.

HUGGENS, Sally and James Downy, 11 February 1858, Laurens Co., S. C.

HUGGINS, Hannah and Paul Severance, 23 February 1797, Charleston, S. C.

HUGGINS, James and Mary Brevard, 21 March 1785, Rowan Co., N. C.

HUGGINS, Robert and Rachel Jetton, 13 February 1787, Rowan Co., N. C.
HUGHES, Edward and Louisa Mathews, 3 January 1797, Charleston, S. C.
HUGHES, Greenburg and Abigail Moncrief, 14 April 1785, Charleston, S. C.
HUGHES, Hudson and Margaret Balfour, 8 September 1796, Rowan Co., N. C.
HUGHES, John and Sarah Winn, 19 May 1792, Columbia, S. C.
HUGHES, John and Martha Burtis, 25 June 1795, Rowan Co., N. C.
HUGHES, John and Bulah Lawton, 28 January 1801, Charleston, S. C.
HUGHES, Jeremiah and Valentine Huff, 14 June 1792, Rowan Co., N. C.
HUGHES, Mary A. and Cicero Adams, 27 May 1856, Edgefield District, S. C.
HUGHES, Meredith and Ann Ford, 9 January 1772, Santee, S. C.
HUGHES, Samuel and Elizabeth Guffy, 16 December 1792, Rowan Co., N. C.
HUGHES, Sergent and Judith Hayden, 3 November 1788, Rowan Co., N. C.
HUGHETT, Hannah and John Foster, 4 November 1782, Rowan Co., N. C.
HUGHEY, Elizabeth and George Eaton, 11 June 1779, Rowan Co., N. C.
HUGHEY, Henry and Mary Cook, 20 March 1773, Rowan Co., N. C.
HUGHEY, Jacob and Margaret Cook, 5 September 1782, Rowan Co., N. C.
HUGHEY, Margaret and Benjamin Hide, 25 July 1796, Rowan Co., N. C.
HUGHEY, Thomas and Mary Bryant, 7 February 1787, Rowan Co., N. C.
HUGHEY, William and Elizabeth Fillips, 3 July 1791, Rowan Co., N. C.
HUGHINS, Mary and Joseph Roox, 24 December 1844, Laurens Co., S. C.
HUGHS, Julia Ann and James Smith, 22 March 1847, Laurens Co., S. C.
HUGHS, Miss and Mancel Garrett, 27 August 1859, Laurens Co., S. C.
HUGHS, Sarah and John Jones, March 1844, Laurens Co., S. C.
HUGHS, William and Polly Ann Howard, 3 August 1843, Laurens Co., S. C.
HUGUENIN, Abraham and Anna M. Gillison, 9 April 1801, St. Lukes Parish, S. C.
HULL, Dawson and Celia Cain, 15 May 1775, Chowan Co., N. C.
HULL, Joseph and Sarah Miller, 29 September 1779, Rowan Co., N. C.
HULL, John and Ann Martin, 12 September 1744, Chowan Co., N. C.
HULL, May and Johnathan Nichol, 8 May 1787, Orange Co., N. C.
HULL, Polly and James Bird, 7 January 1811, Mecklenburg Co., N. C.
HULL, William and Ann Bonney, 1 May 1745, St. Thomas Parish, S. C.
HUME, John and Mary Mazyck, March 1784, Charleston, S. C.
HUME, Susannah (widow) and Roger Pinckney, 26 March 1769, Charleston, S. C.
HUMPHREY, John and Susanna Bradford, 7 January 1793, Rowan Co., N. C.
HUMPHRIES, Richard and Tamer Carothers, 16 December 1785, Chowan Co., N. C.
HUNDGENS, John and Owny Shell, 3 November 1846, Laurens Co., S. C.
HUNDLEY, Mary and John B. Weaver, 26 March 1788, Bertie Co., N. C.
HUNDON, Virginia and Harrison W. Covington, 4 June 1844, Richmond Co., N. C.
HUNT, Abel and Duanna Beard, 17 February 1787, Rowan Co., N. C.
HUNT, Arthur and Jinny Whitaker, 17 September 1791, Rowan Co., N. C.
HUNT, Arthur and Elizabeth Wilson, 10 March 1790, Rowan Co., N. C.
HUNT, Daniel and Betsy Cole, 10 May 1793, Rowan Co., N. C.
HUNT, Daniel and Polly Wiseman, 6 January 1797, Rowan Co., N. C.
HUNT, David Alexander and Elizabeth Herndon, 19 May 1852, Granville Co., N. C.
HUNT, Emma and William Ford, 4 June 1791, Rowan Co., N. C.
HUNT, Edward and Lucy Howard, 4 November 1806, Granville Co., N. C.
HUNT, Enoch and Elizabeth Chaffin, 2 June 1794, Rowan Co., N. C.
HUNT, Frankey and Michael Hunt, 1812, Granville Co., N. C.

HUNT, George and Lucy Woodfork, 15 January 1781, Granville Co., N. C.

HUNT, George Washington and Susan Crews, 25 October 1848, Granville Co., N. C.

HUNT, Hannah and John Green, 16 January 1779, Rowan Co., N. C.

HUNT, Hannah and William Debow, 6 October 1800, Charleston, S. C.

HUNT, James and Ann Satterwhite, 21 July 1785, Granville Co., N. C.

HUNT, James and Ann Thompson, 1814, Granville Co., N. C.

HUNT, James Thomas and Helen George, 22 May 1861, Granville Co., N. C.

HUNT, John and Frances Penn (dau. of Joseph and Mary (Taylor) Penn), 5 August 1771, Granville Co., N. C.

HUNT, John and Betsy Taylor, 17 September 1804, Granville Co., N. C.

HUNT, John Penn and Sally Longmire, 19 December 1811, Granville Co., N. C.

HUNT, Joseph and Martha Gray, May 1772, Charleston, S. C.

HUNT, Joseph and Nancy Hester, 1820, Granville Co., N. C.

HUNT, Malcolm and Elizabeth Love, 12 June 1791, Mecklenburg Co., N. C.

HUNT, Mary and Samuel Bryan, 5 October 1775, Rowan Co., N. C.

HUNT, Mary and Thomas Snipes, 28 December 1793, Granville Co., N. C.

HUNT, Michael and Frankey Hunt, 1812, Granville Co., N. C.

HUNT, Mourning (widow of John) and William Hicks, 27 May 1778, Granville Co., N. C.

HUNT, Robert L. and Narcissa C. White, 2 December 1856, Granville Co., N. C.

HUNT, Samuel and Sarah Howard, 20 May 1780, Granville Co., N. C.

HUNT, Samuel and Sarah Hester, 1834, Granville Co., N. C.

HUNT, Soloman and Elizabeth Sneed, 1817, Granville Co., N. C.

HUNT, Thomas and Mary Jenings, 21 January 1800, Charleston, S. C.

HUNT, William and Mansey Kittrell, 24 January 1780, Granville Co., N. C.

HUNT, William and Elizabeth Taylor, 25 October 1792, Granville Co., N. C.

HUNT, William and Patsy Knott, 22 December 1801, Granville Co., N. C.

HUNTER, Amanda and Jeff Caldwell, 2 January 1866, Mecklenburg Co., N. C.

HUNTER, Ann and Charles Hooks, 15 November 1796, Bertie Co., N. C.

HUNTER, Elenda and William Hinkle, 11 December 1793, Rowan Co., N. C.

HUNTER, Elizabeth and David Graham, 9 January 1770, Santee, S. C.

HUNTER, Esther H. and James H. Richardson, 3 September 1851, Mecklenburg Co., N. C.

HUNTER, David and Abigail Berry, 14 June 1775, Rowan Co., N. C.

HUNTER, Dorcas H. and Stanhope W. Alexander, 24 September 1851, Mecklenburg Co., N. C.

HUNTER, Henry and Asia Blount, 24 March 1783, Tyrrell Co., N. C.

HUNTER, Henry and Caroline Black, 29 August 1810, Mecklenburg Co., N. C.

HUNTER, Henry and Alice Taylor, 10 October 1810, Mecklenburg Co., N. C.

HUNTER, Henry and Martha Clark, 6 October 1840, Mecklenburg Co., N. C.

HUNTER, Hugh M. and Mary Jane Montgomery, 21 August 1850, Mecklenburg Co., N. C.

HUNTER, Humphrey and Margaret Ross, 20 July 1795, Mecklenburg Co., N. C.

HUNTER, James and Mary McClure, 7 July 1800, Mecklenburg Co., N. C.

HUNTER, Jane and Robert Bigham, 23 December 1829, Mecklenburg Co., N. C.

HUNTER, Jane and Ulysses Alexander, 12 January 1831, Mecklenburg Co., N. C.

HUNTER, John and (Mrs.) Mary Watson, 12 June 1801, Charleston, S. C.

HUNTER, Joseph and Rhoda Calthorp, 14 September 1806, Mecklenburg Co., N. C.

HUNTER, Leah and Seth Riddick, 6 January 1772, Chowan Co., N. C.

HUNTER, Liza and Benjamin Young, 24 February 1859, Laurens Co., S. C.

HUNTER, Margaret A. and John H. Harris, 13 August 1817, Mecklenburg Co., N. C.

HUNTER, Margaret H. and William Cooper, 12 June 1823, Mecklenburg Co., N. C.

HUNTER, Martha and John Harris, 31 March 1790, Mecklenburg Co., N. C.

HUNTER, Martha E. and William Neal, 24 January 1843, Mecklenburg Co., N. C.

HUNTER, Mary and Benjamin Sanders, 10 March 1775, Chowan Co., N. C.

HUNTER, Mary M. and James Bigham, 14 February 1831, Mecklenburg Co., N. C.

HUNTER, Nancy J. and David M. Russell, 2 March 1854, Mecklenburg Co., N. C.

HUNTER, Nicholas and Susannah Buchanan, 14 November 1777, Chowan Co., N. C.

HUNTER, Richard and Mary Clerk, 8 June 1786, Rowan Co., N. C.

HUNTER, Robert and Mary Bigham, 14 November 1837, Mecklenburg Co., N. C.

HUNTER, Sarah and James Duckett, 4 June 1845, Laurens Co., S. C.

HUNTER, Sarah A. and Elam B. Boyer, 26 September 1841, Mecklenburg Co., N. C.

HUNTER, Teressa and Thomas Blakly, 8 October 1812, Mecklenburg Co., N. C.

HUNTER, Thomas and Mary Walton (widow), 13 June 1771, Chowan Co., N. C.

HUNTER, Thomas and Anne Sloane, 27 March 1787, Rowan Co., N. C.

HUNTER, Thomas and Peggy H. Walker, 15 October 1810, Mecklenburg Co., N. C.

HUNTER, Thomas and Rosanna A. Walker, 22 February 1832, Mecklenburg Co., N. C.

HUNTER, Timothy and Mary Sumner, 22 October 1774, Chowan Co., N. C.

HUNTER, William and Mary Duckworth, 1816, Mecklenburg Co., N. C.

HURDLE, Henry and Sarah Bush, 14 August 1807, Chowan Co., N. C.

HURST, Elizabeth (widow) and Peter Peyott, September 1783, Charleston, S. C.

HURST, James and Mary Kingman, 7 August 1753, Chowan Co., N. C.

HUSLER, Michael and Jemina Warner, 19 December 1798, Rowan Co., N. C.

HUSON, David and Judy Glover, 11 August 1792, Mecklenburg Co., N. C.

HUSON, Mary and John W. Brown, 5 February 1828, Mecklenburg Co., N. C.

HUSON, Sarah and Robert McComb, 19 August 1817, Mecklenburg Co., N. C.

HUSTON, Archibald and Rosanna Cunningham, 6 October 1784, Rowan Co., N. C.

HUSTON, Catherine and George Rout, 1788, St. Johns Parish, S. C.

HUSTON, Donald and Margaret Monro, 31 December 1779, Rowan Co., N. C.

HUSTON, George and Margaret L. McCoy, 12 January 1825, Mecklenburg Co., N. C.

HUSTON, James and Asenath Brevard, 24 September 1774, Rowan Co., N. C.

HUSTON, John and Anne Howie, 21 December 1797, Mecklenburg Co., N. C.

HUSTON, Joseph and Martha Lucas, 5 March 1783, Rowan Co., N. C.

HUSTON, Thomas and Elizabeth Williams, 20 December 1788, Rowan Co., N. C.

HUTCHINS, Hannah and William Herndon, 1 January 1795, Orange Co., N. C.

HUTCHINS, Nelly and Tapley Herndon, 13 November 1798, Orange Co., N. C.

HUTCHINSON, David and Polly McRee, 22 May 1805, Mecklenburg Co., N. C.

HUTCHINSON, George H. and Mary Hutchinson, May 1786, Ponpon, S. C.

HUTCHINSON, George and Daisy Emerson, 11 June 1799, Mecklenburg Co., N. C.

HUTCHINSON, Hugh and Miss Peyton, 4 October 1800, Charleston, S. C.
HUTCHINSON, John and Esther Perdriau, 7 April 1785, Charleston, S. C.
HUTCHINSON, Louisa and Will M. Auten, 27 December 1860, Mecklenburg Co., N. C.
HUTCHINSON, Mary and George H. Hutchinson, May 1786, Ponpon, S. C.
HUTCHINSON, Mary and J. Dabs, 2 January 1844, Laurens Co., S. C.
HUTCHINSON, Mary C. and R. C. Montgomery, 8 December 1859, Mecklenburg Co., N. C.
HUTCHINSON, Peggy and Armistead Anderson, 14 January 1803, Mecklenburg Co., N. C.
HUTCHINSON, William and Mary Shields, 8 January 1829, Mecklenburg Co., N. C.
HUTSON, Anne and John Barnwell (Jr.), 7 May 1777, Charleston, S. C.
HUTSON, Elizabeth and Isaac Hayne, 18 July 1765, Charleston, S. C.
HUTSON, Mary and Walter Long, 10 December 1744, Chowan Co., N. C.
HUTSON, Mary and Edward Barnwell, 29 July 1790, St. Johns Island, S. C.
HUTSON, Mary and Arthur Peronneau, June 1762, Charleston, S. C.
HUTSON, Sarah S. and John C. Abernathy, 13 May 1843, Mecklenburg Co., N. C.
HUTSON, Seth and Polly Kern, 24 October 1797, Rowan Co., N. C.
HUTSON, William and Maryann Miller, 8 November 1800, Charleston, S. C.
HUTTOW, Mary Catharina and Henry Mell, 24 April 1753, Orangeburg Co., S. C.
HUX, David W. and Mary Kennon, 19 May 1849, Mecklenburg Co., N. C.
HUX, Martha and William Maxwell, 22 November 1832, Mecklenburg Co., N. C.
HYRNE, Henry and Widow Golightly, June 1759, Charleston, S. C.
HYRNE, William A. and Sarah Mitchell, 3 June 1779, Santee, S. C.

I

IJAMS, Arania and Oliver Hendren, 16 August 1788, Rowan Co., N .C.

IMBLER, Elizabeth and Jonah Frisby, 2 November 1794, Rowan Co., N. C.

IMRIE, John and Widow Russell, 7 September 1771, Charleston, S. C.

IMRIE, John and Margaret Esmond (widow), 10 October 1774, Charleston, S. C.

INABINET, Susannah and Hillery Clark, 17 January 1856, Edgefield District, S. C.

INABITNET, Sophronia and Jesse Jennings, 27 December 1855, Edgefield District, S. C.

INGALLS, Peter and Amelia Williamson, 1 September 1861, Mecklenburg Co., N. C.

INGLIS, Alexander and Polly Deas, 28 April 1773, Charleston, S. C.

INGLIS, George and Claudia Elliott, 30 April 1759, Stono, S. C.

INGLISS, Elizabeth and Thomas L. Smith, 29 May 1763, Charleston, S. C.

INGLIT, Jacob and Caroline McDonald, December 1839, Edgefield District, S. C.

INGRAHAM, John and Charity Bell, 1807, Sampson Co., N. C.

INGRAM, Heziah and Nancy Bibb, 22 April 1819, Mecklenburg Co., N. C.

INIS, John and Agnes Campbell, 24 April 1800, Mecklenburg Co., N. C.

INYARD, John and Ann Young, 1 December 1865, Mecklenburg Co., N. C.

I'ON, Mary A. and Samuel Wragg, 19 February 1801, Charleston, S. C.

IRBY, James H. (Jr.) and Orah Lyles , 20 October 1857, Laurens Co., S. C.

IRVIN, Alexander and Margaret Alexander, 14 October 1833, Mecklenburg Co., N. C.

IRVIN, Ann and Captain Swan, August 1785, Charleston, S. C.

IRVIN, Josiah D. and Jane E. Alexander, 31 August 1859, Mecklenburg Co., N. C.

IRVIN, Mary and Cyrus Black, 7 October 1828, Mecklenburg Co., N. C.

IRVIN, Robert and Martha Alexander, 4 August 1838, Mecklenburg Co., N. C.

IRVIN, Robert and Elizabeth Rea, 29 April 1817, Mecklenburg Co., N. C.

IRWIN, Batho and Eleanor R. Barry, 2 December 1833, Mecklenburg Co., N. C.

IRWIN, Batho and Elizabeth C. Flinn, 18 December 1841, Mecklenburg Co., N. C.

IRWIN, Caleb and Sarah Irwin, 29 December 1818, Mecklenburg Co., N. C.

IRWIN, Celia and Thomas O. Black, 2 January 1828, Mecklenburg Co., N. C.

IRWIN, David and Mary Lowry, 29 October 1843, Mecklenburg Co., N. C.

IRWIN, Davis and Mary Flanagan, 7 December 1831, Mecklenburg Co., N. C.

IRWIN, Elizabeth and Lewis Harney, 26 October 1825, Mecklenburg Co., N. C.

IRWIN, Isiah D. and Jane E. Alexander, 25 August 1859, Mecklenburg Co., N. C.

IRWIN, James and Eleanor Davis, 12 December 1845, Mecklenburg Co., N. C.

IRWIN, Jane and Addison P. Bowles, 1 March 1825, Mecklenburg Co., N. C.

IRWIN, Jeremiah and Elizabeth George, 11 December 1766, Edgecombe Co., N. C.

IRWIN, John and Margaret Witherspoon, 11 February 1818, Mecklenburg Co., N. C.

IRWIN, John and Julie Black, 5 October 1820, Mecklenburg Co., N. C.

IRWIN, Joseph H. and Mary A. Ray, 21 February 1850, Mecklenburg Co., N. C.

IRWIN, Margaret S. and Robert M. Clark, 18 December 1838, Mecklenburg Co., N. C.

IRWIN, Martha and John Rogers, 7 April 1827, Mecklenburg Co., N. C.

IRWIN, Mary and William Black, 20 February 1793, Mecklenburg Co., N. C.

IRWIN, Mary A. and Thomas C. Allison, 11 June 1859, Mecklenburg Co., N. C.

IRWIN, Mary Ann and Thomas J. Moore, 20 September 1838, Mecklenburg Co., N. C.

IRWIN, Matthew (Dr.) (of Virginia) and Mary Bulline, August 1783, Charleston, S. C.

IRWIN, Nancy C. and J. L. Banker, 7 October 1844, Mecklenburg Co., N. C.

IRWIN, Octavia C. and Edward P. Jones, 25 November 1849, Mecklenburg Co., N. C.

IRWIN, Peggy and Hugh McDowell, 31 March 1802, Mecklenburg Co., N. C.

IRWIN, Robert and Mary Berry, 26 March 1798, Mecklenburg Co., N. C.

IRWIN, Samuel and Martha Parks, 7 May 1825, Mecklenburg Co., N. C.

IRWIN, Sarah and Thomas Russell, 29 May 1792, Mecklenburg Co., N. C.

IRWIN, Sarah and William Irwin, 7 February 1804, Mecklenburg Co., N. C.

IRWIN, Sarah and John Anderson, 14 September 1811, Mecklenburg Co., N. C.

IRWIN, Sarah and Caleb Irwin, 29 December 1818, Mecklenburg Co., N. C.

IRWIN, Silas and Jenny Sloan, 14 October 1812, Mecklenburg Co., N. C.

IRWIN, William and Mary Cathay, 24 March 1796, Rowan Co., N. C.

IRWIN, William and Rebecca L. Allison, 8 February 1826, Mecklenburg Co., N. C.

IRWIN, William and Sarah Irwin, 7 February 1804, Mecklenburg Co., N. C.

ISAACKS, Esther and Isaac Moses, 2 July 1800, Charleston, S. C.

IVEY, David and Rebecca Jenkins, 15 October 1782, Orange Co., N. C.

IVES, Jeremiah (Captain) and Martha L. Mackey, 2 July 1815, Charleston, S. C.

IVY, Thomas R. and Melinda Scott, 24 August 1812, Mecklenburg Co., N. C.

IZARD, Alice and Joseph Heyward, 6 January 1824, Charleston, S. C.

IZARD, Anna S. and Walter Blake, 16 June 1837, Schevening, S. C.

IZARD, Anne and William Blake, 11 February 1759, Pawlets, S. C.

IZARD, Charles and Mary Izard, 7 October 1742, Berkeley Co., S. C.

IZARD, Charlotte and William L. Smith, 1 May 1786, Charleston, S. C.

IZARD, Elizabeth and Daniel Blake, 21 March 1762, Pawlets, S. C.

IZARD, Elizabeth and Alexander Wright, 6 April 1769, Charleston, S. C.

IZARD, Elizabeth and Thomas Pinckney, 27 December 1803, Charleston, S. C.

IZARD, Esther M. and Charles W. Adams, 3 April 1782, Prince George Parish, S. C.

IZARD, Henry and Margaret Johnson, 26 September 1739, Berkeley Co., S. C.

IZARD, Henry and Anna Middleton, 1 June 1795, Charleston, S. C.

IZARD, Lucy and Edward B. Heyward, 7 November 1850, Charleston, S. C.

IZARD, Margaret and Gabriel Manigault, 6 May 1785, Charleston, S. C.

IZARD, Margaret and (Rev.) Nathan Middleton, 18 January 1832, Charleston, S. C.

IZARD, Mary and William Middleton, 21 April 1730, Crowfield, S. C.

IZARD, Mary and Charles Izard, 7 October 1742, Berkeley Co., S. C.

IZARD, Mary (2nd. m) and Joel Poinsett, 24 October 1833, Charleston, S. C.

IZARD, Mary and Arthur Middleton, 19 August 1764, Ashley River, S. C.

IZARD, Mary (widow) and Thomas Broughton, 5 March 1746, Charleston, S. C.

IZARD, Patience W. B. and (Gen.) Abraham Eustis, 15 May 1823, St. Georges Parish, S. C.

IZARD, Polly and Miles Brewton, 26 May 1759, Charleston, S. C.

IZARD, Ralph and Alice DeLaveey, 1 May 1767, Charleston, S. C.

IZARD, Rebecca and John Wright, 23 January 1797, St. Georges Parish, S. C.

IZARD, Sarah and (Lord) William Campbell, 17 April 1763, St. Georges Parish, S. C.

IZARD, Walter and Mary Turgis, 19 May 1713, St. Georges Parish, S. C.

IZARD, Walter and Elizabeth Gibbs, 20 November 1739, Bulls Island, S. C.

IZARD, Walter and Mary Green, 10 October 1827, Rosehill, S. C.

IZLAR, James and Frances Lovell, 24 February 1859, Orangeburg, S. C.

J

JACKS, Thomas and Nancy Shell, 24 February 1858, Laurens Co., S. C.

JACKSON, Elias and Mary J. Johnston, 18 March 1841, Mecklenburg Co., N. C.

JACKSON, Fanny and William S. Dawes, 18 July 1785, Chowan Co., N. C.

JACKSON, James and Sarah Spruill, 7 April 1766, Tyrrell Co., N. C.

JACKSON, James and Rebecca Weathers, 28 January 1804, Mecklenburg Co., N. C.

JACKSON, John and Laura Johnson, 27 December 1855, Edgefield District, S. C.

JACKSON, Mary and James Millis, 6 December 1785, Guilford Co., N. C.

JACKSON, Miles and Joseph Joyner, 1 January 1741, Orangeburg Co., S. C.

JACKSON, Nancy and David McClure, 24 February 1823, Mecklenburg Co., N. C.

JACKSON, Penelope and James Hare, December 1779, Chowan Co., N. C.

JACKSON, Polly and Robert Bigham, 4 January 1815, Mecklenburg Co., N. C.

JACKSON, Thomas and Elizabeth Duke, 10 June 1784, Charleston, S. C.

JACKSON, William and Fanny Turner, 7 February 1785, Perquimans Co., N. C.

JACKSON, William and Sarah Hoskins, 21 December 1767, Chowan Co., N. C.

JACKSON, William (of N. Y.) and Hetty Brooks (of Norwalk, Conn.), 9 August 1800, Charleston, S. C.

JACKSON, William J. and Elizabeth P. Christenberry, 23 February 1828, Mecklenburg Co., N. C.

JACOBS, Abraham and Shankey Hart, 19 October 1785, Charleston, S. C.

JACOBS, Samuel and Bethiah Cherry, 3 November 1788, Bertie Co., N. C.

JACOBS, William P. and Mary J. Dillard, 20 April 1865, Laurens, S. C.

JAFFRAY, James and Miss Adams, 17 April 1795, Charleston, S. C.

JAMERSON, Elizabeth and Micajah Andrews, 26 January 1763, Edgecombe Co., N. C.

JAMES, Benjamin and Kesiah James, 1 November 1788, Bertie Co., N. C.

JAMES, Charles M. and Margaret J. Kelly, 5 March 1849, Mecklenburg Co., N. C.

JAMES, Elinor and William McKinney, 13 February 1790, Guilford Co., N. C.

JAMES, Emanuel and Patience Gardner, 19 January 1788, Bertie Co., N. C.

JAMES, Kesiah and Benjamin James, 1 November 1788, Bertie Co., N. C.

JAMES, Philip H. and Frances Webb, 20 February 1794, Franklin Co., N. C.

JAMESON, Bond and Teressa Bond, 9 February 1785, Chowan Co., N. C.

JAMESON, Catherine and Samuel Brown, 31 March 1801, Mecklenburg Co., N. C.

JAMESON, E. C. and James L. McClure, 9 June 1847, Mecklenburg Co., N. C.

JAMESON, Harriet and Robert W. Montgomery, 25 February 1875, Mecklenburg Co., N. C.

JAMESON, Isaac and Alice Murphy, 5 March 1825, Mecklenburg Co., N. C.

JAMESON, James and Melinda Long, 28 June 1849, Mecklenburg Co., N. C.

JAMESON, Jean and James Brown, 10 February 1797, Mecklenburg Co., N. C.

JAMESON, Mary and Robert M. Beaty, 7 November 1836, Mecklenburg Co., N. C.

JAMESON, Mary and Benjamin F. Brown, 20 May 1843, Mecklenburg Co., N. C.

JAMESON, Nancy C. and Allen H. Brown, 22 August 1838, Mecklenburg Co., N. C.

JAMESON, Robert and Isabella Johnston, 25 March 1797, Mecklenburg Co., N. C.

JAMESON, R. C. and Catherine Wilson, 9 January 1866, Mecklenburg Co., N. C.

JAMIESON, Eliza J. and Samuel Auton, 25 October 1859, Mecklenburg Co., N. C.

JAMIESON, Isabelle and Richard Henderson, 8 February 1798, Mecklenburg Co., N. C.

JAMIESON, James and Rebecca Simons, 25 May 1773, Charleston, S. C.

JAMIESON, Jane and John M. McKelvey, 31 March 1825, Mecklenburg Co., N. C.

JAMIESON, John R. and Hannah I. Todd, 21 December 1858, Mecklenburg Co., N. C.

JAMIESON, Mary and John H. Barnhill, 20 August 1840, Mecklenburg Co., N. C.

JAMIESON, Mary Ann and William Cross, 7 February 1750, Mecklenburg Co., N. C.

JAMIESON, Nancy and John Barnhill, 28 February 1816, Mecklenburg Co., N. C.

JAMIESON, R. M. and Hannah F. Todd, 25 January 1843, Mecklenburg Co., N. C.

JAMIESON, Sally and Samuel Cox, 10 April 1809, Mecklenburg Co., N. C.

JAMIESON, Thomas and Elizabeth McGinn, 7 July 1819, Mecklenburg Co., N. C.

JAMIESON, Thomas and Jane McClure, 18 April 1844, Mecklenburg Co., N. C.

JAMIESON, Thomas and Rosanna B. McCord, 9 December 1851, Mecklenburg Co., N. C.

JAMIESON, Thomas and Mary Sullivan, 16 September 1789, Mecklenburg Co., N. C.

JAMIESON, William and Polly Johnston, 8 January 1811, Mecklenburg Co., N. C.

JAMIESON, William and Margaret Todd, 6 May 1835, Mecklenburg Co., N. C.

JAMIESON, William J. and Jane E. Brown, 18 March 1844, Mecklenburg Co., N. C.

JAMISON, Andrew and Mary A. Rea, 30 July 1841, Mecklenburg Co., N. C.

JAMISON, Arthur and Mary Simeral, 6 January 1801, Mecklenburg Co., N. C.

JAMISON, Robert and Ann Shuson, 8 November 1817, Mecklenburg Co., N. C.

JAMISON, Robert M. and Sarah L. Todd, 30 September 1862, Mecklenburg Co., N. C.

JAMISON, Thomas and Sarah A. Hepworth, 15 March 1848, Mecklenburg Co., N. C.

JANDON, Paul and Margaret Libray, 21 December 1743, Prince Frederick Parish, S. C.

JANNETT, Ann and Eliakim Swain, October 1783, Tyrrell Co., N. C.

JARNIGAN, Sarah E. and Alexander J. Matheson, 20 April 1780, Marion Co., S. C.

JASEY, Martha and Willis Moore, 3 March 1798, Guilford Co., N. C.

JEANERETTE, Betsy and Joseph Glover, April 1784, Santee, S. C.

JEAUNERET, Margaret and Isaac Rembert, 13 May 1773, Santee, S. C.

JEFFERIES, William and Ramoth L. Hames, 3 April 1860, Jonesville, S. C.

JEFFREYS, William and Mary Gray, 30 July 1773, Edgecombe Co., N. C.

JENKINS, Ann (widow) and Freeman Snellgrove, 26 September 1751, Orangeburg Co., S. C.

JENKINS, Ann and Robert Croft, 24 March 1763, Santee, S. C.

JENKINS, Betsey and Paul Fripp (Jr.), October 1783, Edisto, S. C.

JENKINS, Elias and Hasky Ann Nelson White, 26 November 1830, Granville Co., N. C.

JENKINS, Joannah (widow of John Jenkins) and (Gov.) Thomas Harvey, 13 April 1682, Perquimans Co., N. C.

JENKINS, Lydia and Clemand Griggs, 8 June 1771, Santee, S. C.

JENKINS, Mary and George Walker, 28 April 1757, Chowan Co., N. C.

JENKINS, M. and Thomas Chaley, 13 April 1797, Charleston, S. C.

JENKINS, Rebecca and David Ivey, 15 October 1782, Orange Co., N. C.

JENKINS, Samuel and Mary Penny, 15 December 1788, Bertie Co., N. C.

JENKINS, William and Elinor Parker, 26 October 1809, Mecklenburg Co., N. C.

JENNENS, John and Martha Murrell, 15 January 1767, Santee, S. C.

JENNENS, Mary and Francis Roach, 17 April 1768, Santee, S. C.

JENNER, Elizabeth and Robert Morris, 27 June 1765, Santee, S. C.

JENNESS, Agnes and Moses McWhorter, 26 August 1793, Mecklenburg Co., N. C.

JENNETT, Abraham and Mary Hooker, 16 December 1767, Tyrrell Co., N. C.

JENNETT, Mary and John Smith, 1781, Tyrrell Co., N. C.

JENNETT, Nancy and James Laquer, 28 February 1785, Chowan Co., N. C.

JENNINGS, Adele and Henry J. Brabham, 18 December 1878, Bamberg, S. C.

JENNINGS, Annie Catherine and Curtis Cornelius Faust, 21 December 1860, Orangeburg Co., S. C.

JENNINGS, C. J. and Rachel R. Cook, 14 September 1865, Mecklenburg Co., N. C.

JENNINGS, Elias and (Mrs.) Elizabeth Austen, 21 June 1800, Charleston, S. C.

JENNINGS, George W. and Sarah C. Stanford, 28 October 1858, Mecklenburg Co., N. C.

JENNINGS, Hulda (Mrs.) and James Tompkins, 7 January 1819, Edgefield District, S. C .

JENNINGS, Jesse and Sophronia Inabitnet, 27 December 1855, Edgefield District S. C.

JENNINGS, John and Mary Dutarque, 20 January 1765, Charleston, S. C.

JENNINGS, John and Mary Stroman, 28 February 1807, Orangeburg Co., S. C.

JENNINGS, John and Lucy Smith, 26 December 1818, Mecklenburg Co., N. C.

JENNINGS, John S. and Elizabeth Young, 21 May 1829, Orangeburg, S. C.

JENNINGS, J. H. and Margaret Stanford, 4 January 1859, Mecklenburg Co., N. C.

JENNINGS, Mary and Thomas Hunt, 21 January 1800, Charleston, S. C.

JENNINGS, Millery and John Timmerman, 22 December 1854, Edgefield District, S. C.

JENNINGS, M. C. and W. W. Fulmer, 10 November 1857, Edgefield District, S. C.

JENNINGS, Philip and Elizabeth Hasford (widow), 7 February 1747, Orangeburg Co., S. C.

JENNINGS, Richard and Eliza Carter, 11 August 1825, Mecklenburg Co., N. C.

JENNINGS, Ursetta and Brand Pendarvis, 1748, Orangeburg Co., S. C.

JENNINGS, Whitfield and Martha Griffin, 4 November 1857, Edgefield District, S. C.

JENNINGS, William P. and Mary C. Alexander, 16 July 1836, Mecklenburg Co., N. C.

JENNISON, Elizabeth and Aaron Littell, 27 November 1766, Santee, S. C.

JENNYS, Elizabeth (widow) and John Gibbes, August 1743, Charleston, S. C.

JERARD, Henry and Frances Lassiter, 8 February 1786, Tyrrell Co., N. C.

JERDAN, Elizabeth and John Boone, 19 January 1762, Santee, S. C.

JERNAGAN, Arthur and Mary Bond, 25 February 1790, Bertie Co., N. C.

JESSOP, Elizabeth and James Montgomery, 21 November 1775, Guilford Co., N. C.

JETTON, Abraham and Jane Oliphant, 29 May 1787, Mecklenburg Co., N. C.

JETTON, E. S. (Miss) and J. D. Johnston, 16 March 1853, Mecklenburg Co., N. C.

JETTON, Rachel and Robert Huggins, 13 February 1787, Rowan Co., N. C.

JEWELL, Stephen and Margaret Monteith, 30 July 1792, Mecklenburg Co., N. C.

JINGLES, Elizabeth and Peter R. McAchron, 20 April 1824, Mecklenburg Co., N. C.

JINKES, Edward and Sarah Bare (widow), 11 October 1777, Chowan Co., N. C.

JOHNS, Zeph and Margaret Thorp, 22 December 1824, Mecklenburg Co., N. C.

JOHNSON, Agnes and James Hibbetts, 1 December 1790, Rowan Co., N. C.

JOHNSON, Amelia and Walter Alves, 11 May 1787, Orange Co., N. C.

JOHNSON, Andrew and Sally McKewn, 26 February 1772, Charleston, S. C.

JOHNSON, Andrew and Emmaline Dial, 9 November 1858, Laurens So., S. C.

JOHNSON, Ann and William Wish, 25 May 1797, Charleston, S. C.

JOHNSON, Ann and John Duffus, 2 October 1800, Charleston, S. C.

JOHNSON, Benjamin and Martha Hayes, 21 January 1824, Mecklenburg Co., N. C.

JOHNSON, Charles and Elizabeth Earl, 10 February 1785, Chowan Co., N. C.

JOHNSON, Charles and Mary Houston, 10 July 1794, Bladen Co., N. C.

JOHNSON, Cynthia and James Moore, 13 February 1827, Mecklenburg Co., N. C.

JOHNSON, Daniel and Sallie Wade, 1 September 1820, Edgefield District, S. C.

JOHNSON, David and Sally Vettel, 26 January 1800, Edgecombe Co., N. C.

JOHNSON, David M. and Nancy Howard, 5 August 1856, Mecklenburg Co., N. C.

JOHNSON, Edward and Mary Langley (widow), 25 May 1761, Edgecombe Co., N. C.

JOHNSON, Eleanor and Thomas Hudson, 11 March 1773, Rowan Co., N. C.

JOHNSON, George and Mary Taylor, 3 January 1850, Mecklenburg Co., N. C.

JOHNSON, James and Rebecca Galloway, 14 April 1846, Mecklenburg Co., N. C.

JOHNSON, James and Jane Hodge, 16 November 1835, Mecklenburg Co., N. C.

JOHNSON, James L. and Abigail Dewese, 24 January 1838, Mecklenburg Co., N. C.

JOHNSON, James A. and Sarah A. Tradenick, 23 March 1858, Mecklenburg Co., N. C.

JOHNSON, Jane and John McCready, 1 March 1797, Charleston, S. C.

JOHNSON, Jesse and Margaret Hipp, 8 November 1830, Mecklenburg Co., N. C.

JOHNSON, Jesse B. and Jane Wallace, 6 October 1858, Mecklenburg Co., N. C.

JOHNSON, John and Elizabeth C. Alexander, 18 December 1833, Mecklenburg Co., N. C.

JOHNSON, John C. and Margaret T. Black, 16 April 1833, Mecklenburg Co., N. C.

JOHNSON, John E. and Annie Dewese, 8 January 1836, Mecklenburg Co., N. C.

JOHNSON, John M. and Jane Morrison, 7 January 1861, Mecklenburg Co., N. C.

JOHNSON, John W. and Meriam E. Wallace, 30 April 1863, Mecklenburg Co., N. C.

JOHNSON, John William and Mary J. Hoover, 28 February 1860, Mecklenburg Co., N. C.

JOHNSON, Laura and John Jackson, 27 December 1855, Edgefield District, S. C.

JOHNSON, Lydia and Daniel Huger, 4 December 1747, Craven Co., S. C.

JOHNSON, Malinda and Jefferson Alexander, 29 January 1843, Laurens Co., S. C.

JOHNSON, Margaret and Henry Izard, 26 September 1739, Berkeley Co., S. C.

JOHNSON, Martha A. and Robert E. Kenny, 25 February 1855, Edgefield District S. C.

JOHNSON, Mary and Benjamin Stead, 15 November 1748, Charleston, S. C.

JOHNSON, Mary and Jacob Flowers, 20 November 1765, Edgecombe Co., N. C.

JOHNSON, Mary and Thomas Endless, 9 May 1779, Chowan Co., N. C.

JOHNSON, Meredith and Molly Mathers, 1 January 1763, Edgecombe Co., N. C.

JOHNSON, Nancy P. and George W. Rossich, 3 September 1857, Mecklenburg Co., N. C.

JOHNSON, Polly and Warner Taylor, 9 September 1829, Granville Co., N. C.

JOHNSON, Rachel and James Anderson, 3 December 1778, Tyrrell Co., N. C.

JOHNSON, Reuben and Jenny Curry, 17 September 1816, Mecklenburg Co., N. C.

JOHNSON, Samuel and Louisa Henderson, 1 March 1813, Mecklenburg Co., N. C.

JOHNSON, Sarah and Oliver Cromwell, 30 August 1796, Charleston, S. C.

JOHNSON, Susannah and John Gaither, 17 February 1795, Rowan Co., N. C.

JOHNSON, Thomas A. and (Miss) J. Cox, 21 June 1865, Mecklenburg Co., N. C.

JOHNSON, William and Sarah Nightingale, 15 May 1769, Charleston, S. C.

JOHNSON, William and Rebecca Allen, 11 December 1811, Mecklenburg Co., N. C.

JOHNSTON, Alexander S. and Nancy Norfleet, 29 March 1812, Edgecombe Co., N. C.

JOHNSTON, Andrew and Sarah McCombs, 17 May 1791, Mecklenburg Co., N. C.

JOHNSTON, Andrew D. and Jane Johnston, 20 January 1810, Mecklenburg Co., N. C.

JOHNSTON, Ann and Jonas Clark (Jr.), 15 September 1824, Mecklenburg Co., N. C.

JOHNSTON, Catherine J. G. and William L. D. Alexander, 21 April 1859, Mecklenburg Co., N. C.

JOHNSTON, David and Harriet C. Hipp, 23 July 1838, Mecklenburg Co., N. C.

JOHNSTON, David and Eleanor Clement, 16 December 1800, Charleston, S. C.

JOHNSTON, David and Sarah Overby, 14 May 1849, Mecklenburg Co., N. C.

JOHNSTON, Diana and James Hargett, 23 October 1800, Mecklenburg Co., N. C.

JOHNSTON, D. C. and Robert P. Chapman, 2 August 1865, Mecklenburg Co., N. C.

JOHNSTON, Elizabeth and Samuel W. Beaty, 17 December 1823, Mecklenburg Co., N. C.

JOHNSTON, Elizabeth and James M. Black, 19 November 1836, Mecklenburg Co., N. C.

JOHNSTON, Esther and Samuel A. Greenland, 14 Novmber 1799, Charleston, S. C.

JOHNSTON, Ezekial and Eliza Morris, 10 September 1833, Mecklenburg Co., N. C.

JOHNSTON, Isaac M. and Eleze Finch (or French), 31 December 1844, Mecklenburg Co., N. C.

JOHNSTON, Isaac M. and Sarah A. Cox, 23 February 1854, Mecklenburg Co., N. C.

JOHNSTON, Isabelle and Robert Jamieson, 25 March 1797, Mecklenburg Co., N. C.

JOHNSTON, James and Margaret Craig, 4 March 1788, Orange Co., N. C.

JOHNSTON, James S. and Susanna J. Ruddock, 14 March 1861, Mecklenburg Co., N. C.

JOHNSTON, Jane and Andrew D. Johnston, 20 January 1810, Mecklenburg Co., N. C.

JOHNSTON, Jane C. and John W. Miller, 6 September 1843, Mecklenburg Co., N. C.

JOHNSTON, Jane and William Randall, 27 March 1818, Mecklenburg Co., N. C.

JOHNSTON, John and Peggy Harris, 10 January 1817, Mecklenburg Co., N. C.

JOHNSTON, John T. and Mary Scott, 29 September 1859, Mecklenburg Co., N. C.

JOHNSTON, John and Jane Robinson, 18 November 1829, Mecklenburg Co., N. C.

JOHNSTON, John F. and Sarah L. Campbell, 10 July 1844, Mecklenburg Co., N. C.

JOHNSTON, John H. and Lydia B. Wallace, 3 February 1840, Mecklenburg Co., N. C.

JOHNSTON, John R. and Delia R. Toneva, 17 June 1856, Mecklenburg Co., N. C.

JOHNSTON, Joseph C. and Dorris Orr, 11 October 1815, Mecklenburg Co., N. C.

JOHNSTON, J. D. and (Miss) E. S. Jetton, 16 March 1853, Mecklenburg Co., N. C.

JOHNSTON, Lucy and Reuben Ellis, 20 January 1804, Edgecombe Co., N. C.

JOHNSTON, Margaret and James Morrison, 10 September 1799, Mecklenburg Co., N. C.

JOHNSTON, Martha and R. C. Robinson, 28 July 1847, Mecklenburg Co., N. C.

JOHNSTON, Mary and John Eccles, 1 March 1788, Rowan Co., N. C.

JOHNSTON, Mary and James M. Morrison, 4 December 1830, Mecklenburg Co., N. C.

JOHNSTON, Mary and Marcus F. Alexander, 30 January 1844, Mecklenburg Co., N. C.

JOHNSTON, Mary Ann and William Black, 13 July 1792, Mecklenburg Co., N. C.

JOHNSTON, Mary C. and William A. Johnston, 6 March 1849, Mecklenburg Co., N. C.

JOHNSTON, Mary S. and Elias Jackson, 18 March 1841, Mecklenburg Co., N. C.

JOHNSTON, Mary P. and Joel Battle, 9 April 1801, Edgecombe Co., N. C.

JOHNSTON, M. C. (Miss) and William C. Morris, 4 March 1843, Mecklenburg Co., N. C.

JOHNSTON, M. W. and (Miss) A. H. Bost, 31 October 1859, Mecklenburg Co., N. C.

JOHNSTON, Patrick and Ann Walls, 28 June 1794, Mecklenburg Co., N. C.

JOHNSTON, Patsy and Hugh M. Barnett, 4 January 1819, Mecklenburg Co., N. C.

JOHNSTON, Philip and Rachel Johnston, 23 November 1813, Mecklenburg Co., N. C.

JOHNSTON, Polly and William Jameson, 8 January 1811, Mecklenburg Co., N. C.

JOHNSTON, Rachel and James Hall, 9 January 1792, Rowan Co., N. C.

JOHNSTON, Rachel and Phillip Johnston, 23 November 1813, Mecklenburg Co., N. C.

JOHNSTON, Randolph and Mary Perisho, 1781, Tyrrell Co., N. C.

JOHNSTON, Robert and Mary Davis, 9 January 1806, Mecklenburg Co., N. C.

JOHNSTON, Robert and Pamela Henderson, 11 September 1820, Mecklenburg Co., N. C.

JOHNSTON, Robert and Martha Blair, 29 July 1865, Mecklenburg Co., N. C.

JOHNSTON, Sam and Prudy Moore, 17 July 1811, Mecklenburg Co., N. C.

JOHNSTON, Samuel and Isabella Nuty, 17 January 1810, Mecklenburg Co., N. C.

JOHNSTON, Samuel E. and Rebecca Caldwell, 29 October 1842, Mecklenburg Co., N. C.

JOHNSTON, Samuel N. and Margaret Welch, 13 November 1841, Mecklenburg Co., N. C.

JOHNSTON, S. E. and Cynthia Brem, 19 September 1865, Mecklenburg Co., N. C.

JOHNSTON, Thomas L. and Dorcas E. Lucky, 25 May 1852, Mecklenburg Co., N. C.

JOHNSTON, Thomas J. and Sarah T. Davidson, 9 September 1824, Mecklenburg Co., N. C.

JOHNSTON, Thomas T. and Elizabeth McDonald, 21 July 1814, Mecklenburg Co., N. C.

JOHNSTON, William and Mary Black, 10 October 1807, Mecklenburg Co., N. C.

JOHNSTON, William and Elizabeth Hipp, 25 October 1808, Mecklenburg Co., N. C.

JOHNSTON, William and Rebecca Cunningham, 20 October 1844, Mecklenburg Co., N. C.

JOHNSTON, William and Ann E. Graham, 16 March 1846, Mecklenburg Co., N. C.

JOHNSTON, William A. and Mary C. Johnston, 6 March 1849, Mecklenburg Co., N. C.

JOHNSTON, William C. and Margaret M. McRea, 1 November 1828, Mecklenburg Co., N. C.

JOLLY, James and Priscilla Fort, 15 October 1764, Edgecombe Co., N. C.

JOLLY, Nancy and John McCracken, 27 September 1824, Mecklenburg Co., N. C.

JONES, Albert G. and Nelly Miller, 27 April 1848, Chowan Co., N. C.

JONES, Amanda and T. B. Crooker, 18 December 1856, Edgefield District, S. C.

JONES, Andrew and Rebecca Wilson, 24 October 1821, Mecklenburg Co., N. C.

JONES, Andrew and Abby E. Parks, 3 November, 1829, Mecklenburg Co., N. C.

JONES, Andrew and Jane H. Bain, 5 August 1837, Mecklenburg Co., N. C.

JONES, Ann and Nathan Rhodes, 6 September 1786, Tyrrell Co., N. C.

JONES, Ann and James Carr, 5 March 1776, Chowan Co., N. C.

JONES, Anne and Emanuel Smith, 9 December 1720, St. Andrews Parish, S. C.

JONES, Anne (widow) and John Lloyd, 12 January 1764, Charleston, S. C.

JONES, Bryant and Elizabeth Berry, 10 March 1836, Marion Co., S. C.

JONES, Catherine and Thomas Luten, (Jr.), 14 February 1748, Chowan Co., N. C.

JONES, Deborah and William Webb, 5 February 1721, St. Andrews Parish, S. C.

JONES, Edward H. and Harriet K. Dunlap, 2 November 1843, Mecklenburg Co., N. C.

JONES, Edward P. and Octavia C. Irwin, 25 November 1849, Mecklenburg Co., N. C.

JONES, Elizabeth and Jacob Privitt, 4 July 1751, Chowan Co., N. C.

JONES, Elizabeth (widow) and John Robinson, 8 January 1754, Chowan Co., N. C.

JONES, Elizabeth and Francis Thornton, 1762, Oxford, N. C.

JONES, Elizabeth and William Felps, 20 April 1768, Rowan Co., N. C.

JONES, Elizabeth and Hezekiah Morrow, 5 January 1815, Mecklenburg Co., N. C.

JONES, Elizabeth and Boyd McNary, 3 March 1842, Guilford Co., N. C.

JONES, Elizabeth E. and James Watson, 6 February 1840, Marion Co., S. C.

JONES, Emma and Duff Cary, 19 February 1861, Laurens Co., S. C.

JONES, Esther and James Lewis, 5 September 1751, Orangeburg Co., S. C.

JONES, Francis and Agnes Thompson, 9 January 1789, Orange Co., N. C.

JONES, Friley and Margaret Hassell, 23 September 1763, Tyrrell Co., N. C.

JONES, Harriett and James W. Dillon, 2 April 1851, Marion Co., N. C.

JONES, Hezekiah and Azenath Halsey, 6 March 1776, Chowan Co., N. C.

JONES, Isaac and Nancy Truse, 13 December 1832, Mecklenburg Co., N. C.

JONES, James and Dolly Spell, 4 October 1809, Edgecombe Co., N. C.

JONES, Jesse and Linah Monk, 21 July 1788, Bertie Co., N. C.

JONES, John and Ann Spell, 6 November 1762, Edgecombe Co., N. C.

JONES, John and Anne Smith, 16 June 1788, Edgecombe Co., N. C.

JONES, John and Anne Coffield, 20 December 1766, Edgecombe Co., N. C.

JONES, John and Ann Long, 20 September 1779, Tyrrell Co., N. C.

JONES, John and Sarah Hughs, March 1844, Laurens Co., S. C.

JONES, John and Mary Sharp, 28 December 1769, Charleston, S. C.

JONES, John and Elizabeth Dunning, 23 January 1798, Bertie Co., N. C.

JONES, Johnston and Nancy Ball, 24 August 1790, Orange Co., N. C.

JONES, Joshua and Maria A. Gibbs, 6 November 1800, Charleston, S. C.

JONES, Julius A. and Patsy Walker, 10 July 1821, Mecklenburg Co., N. C.

JONES, Lewis and Merica Barnes, 1764, Edgecombe Co., N. C.

JONES, Lewis and Susannah Ambrose, 6 August 1752, Chowan Co., N. C.

JONES, Lewis and Ann Halsey, 18 June 1761, Chowan Co., N. C.

JONES, Lewis and Rebecca M. Jones, 18 April 1839, Aiken, S. C.

JONES, Lidy and James Robinson, 12 March 1822, Mecklenburg Co., N. C.

JONES, Lloyd and Elizabeth Young, 21 March 1757, Chowan Co., N. C.

JONES, Margaret and Thomas Bonner, 6 May 1767, Chowan Co., N. C.

JONES, Martha and John Griffin, 27 April 1761, Edgecombe Co., N. C.

JONES, Martha and Henry Mitchell, 14 October 1846, Chowan Co., N. C.

JONES, Mary and Michael Hearn, 24 December 1768, Tyrrell Co., N. C.

JONES, Mary and Isaac Waight, 13 November 1719, St. Andrews Parish, S. C.

JONES, Mary (widow) and Ebenezer Simmons, 20 January 1741, Charleston, S. C.

JONES, Mary and James Gaillard, 19 July 1763, Santee, S. C.

JONES, Mary and Jesse Stubbs, 1784, Tyrrell Co., N. C.

JONES, Mary Ann and David W. Ayers, 25 April 1854, Marlboro Co., S. C.

JONES, Millicent and John Colcock, 30 October 1768, Charleston, S. C.

JONES, Miss and Edmund Cossens, April 1774, Charleston, S. C.

JONES, Nancy and John F. Kenney, 29 March 1849, Edgefield District, S. C.

JONES, Nathan and Chordy Bell, 1 January 1763, Edgecombe Co., N. C.

JONES, Nathaniel and (Mrs.) Millerson Blanchard, 17 June 1772, Chowan Co., N. C.

JONES, Penny and Jeremiah Long, 20 November 1777, Tyrrell Co., N. C.

JONES, Rachel and Frederick Luten, 30 September 1772, Chowan Co., N. C.

JONES, Rachel and John Ready, 23 April 1779, Chowan Co., N. C.

JONES, Rebecca M. and Lewis Jones, 18 April 1839, Aiken, S. C.

JONES, Richard and Susan Seymour, 19 October 1835, Mecklenburg Co., N. C.

JONES, Robert and Sarah Poole, 1784, Tyrrell Co., N. C.

JONES, Samuel and Mary Legare, 7 May 1801, Santee, S. C.

JONES, Sarah and James Long, 27 April 1785, Tyrrell Co., N. C.

JONES, Sarah and Peter Baldwin, 25 January 1855, Laurens Co., S. C.

JONES, Sarah and Thomas Waff, 7 April 1779, Chowan Co., N. C.

JONES, Sarah and William Walton, December 1783, Bertie Co., N. C.

JONES, Sarah and Michael Shaver, 18 November 1855, Edgefield District, S. C.

JONES, Sherrard and Margaret Kerr, 23 February 1830, Mecklenburg Co., N. C.

JONES, Stephen and Ann Cockfield, 1831, Darlington Co., N. C.

JONES, Susan and James Evatt, 21 June 1785, Rowan Co., N. C.

JONES, Susan and Josiah Milton, 14 June 1834, Guilford Co., N. C.

JONES, Susannah and (Dr.) James W. Moore, 4 October 1770, Charleston, S. C.

JONES, Thomas and Elizabeth Davis, 19 February 1746, Orangeburg Co., S. C.

JONES, Thomas and (Mrs.) Elizabeth Thompson, 5 May 1749, Chowan Co., N. C.

JONES, Thomas and Miss Townsend, 5 June 1766, Charleston, S. C.

JONES, William and Asia Holladay, 23 January 1790, Bertie Co., N. C.

JONES, William, (Jr.) and Sarah Howcott, 31 August 1772, Chowan Co., N. C.

JONES, William and Anthony Gary, 7 January 1862, Laurens Co., S. C.

JONES, William C. and Margaret Lefaboy, 22 May 1833, Mecklenburg Co., N. C.

JORDAIN, Michael and Eliza Smith, 27 November 1800, Charleston, S. C.

JORDAN, Ananias and Elizabeth A. Spears, 14 July 1856, Mecklenburg Co., N. C.

JORDAN, Daniel and Ann Dubosque, 31 May 1759, Santee, S. C.

JORDAN, Erasmus and Sarah Crump, 13 February 1845, Mecklenburg Co., N. C.

JORDAN, Esther and Jacob Blount, 24 March 1768, Tyrrell Co., N. C.

JORDAN, Hance and Elizabeth Mitchell, 30 March 1859, Chowan Co., N. C.

JORDAN, Henry and Elizabeth L. Furr, 14 October 1858, Mecklenburg Co., N. C.

JORDAN, John and Sarah Stubbs, 2 October 1780, Tyrrell Co., N. C.

JORDAN, John and Mary Gaillard, 19 April 1770, Santee, S. C.

JORDAN, John and Anne Steel, 4 July 1773, Santee, S. C.

JORDAN, Jonathan and Mary Outlaw, 20 September 1775, Chowan Co., N. C.

JoRDAN, Joseph and Elizabeth Ann Clements, 9 December 1845, Chowan Co., N. C.

JORDAN, Keziah and Richard Chappell, 1 May 1779, Chowan Co., N. C.

JORDAN, Margaret and Thomas Hamlin, 23 August 1780, Santee, S. C.

JORDAN, Miriam and James Evans, 19 February 1785, Chowan Co., N. C.

JORDAN, Philip and Christina Cretelow, 30 October 1792, Rowan Co., N. C.

JORDAN, Richard and Martha Cashon, 3 February 1836, Mecklenburg Co., N. C.

JORDAN, Richard and Bailey Christenberry, 25 December 1843, Mecklenburg Co., N. C.

JORDAN, Robert and Martha Murrill, 18 September 1763, Santee, S. C.

JORDAN, Sally and Richard Stubbs, 2 April 1783, Tyrrell Co., N. C.

JORDAN, Samson H. and Jane E. Steele, 25 May 1852, Mecklenburg Co., N. C.

JORDAN, Solomon J. and Delilah D. Ferrell, 1 January 1849, Mecklenburg Co., N. C.

JORDAN, Sophia and Asbury Turner, 9 February 1842, Chowan Co., N. C.

JOURDAN, Mary and Thomas Russell, 27 April 1779, Tyrrell Co., N. C.

JOUDON, Esther and James Barnard, 3 December 1761, Santee, S. C.

JOYCE, Sarah and Joel Mackay, 24 March 1772, Guilford Co., N. C.

JOYNER, Alexander and Elizabeth Laurence, 29 April 1768, Edgecombe Co., N. C.

JOYNER, John and Naomy Bunch, 23 December 1754, Orangeburg Co., S. C.

JOYNER, Joseph and Miles Jackson, 1 January 1741, Orangeburg Co., S. C.

JOYNER, Mary and Martin Kooner, 24 February 1746, Orangeburg Co., S. C.

JOYNER, Sarah O. and John Burton, 15 January 1801, Beaufort, S. C.

JOYNER, Thomas and Faithy Carse, 1740, Orangeburg Co., S. C.
JUDD, John and Eve Catherine Shuler, 1740, Orangeburg Co., S. C.
JUHOAN, Marie and Rene Godard, 7 February 1795, Charleston, S. C.
JULIAN, George and Rebecca McKinna, 9 April 1791, Mecklenburg Co., N. C.
JULIAN, Jacob C. and Catherine E. Moore, 7 July 1853, Mecklenburg Co., N. C.
JULIAN, Mary and Jonas Rogers, 5 January 1798, Mecklenburg Co., N. C.
JULIAN, Peggy and Nathan Orr, 27 January 1802, Mecklenburg Co., N. C.

K

KALE, John and Celia Parker, 8 November 1785, Chowan Co., N. C.

KAHNLE, John H. and (Mrs.) Arabella Booner, 18 September 1794, Charleston, S. C.

KANNADY, John and Mary Godfrey, 29 September 1747, Orangeburg Co., S. C.

KAVANAUGH, Elizabeth and Abe Broom, 13 August 1840, Mecklenburg Co., N. C.

KAWON, Thomas C. and Mary Marion (widow), January 1773, Berkeley Co., S. C.

KEAL, Marian and John Roberson, February 1786, Charleston, S. C.

KEARNEY, Philip and Elizabeth Kinchen, 30 November 1763, Halifax Co., N. C.

KEARNEY, Samuel and Sarah Lindsay, 10 November 1796, Halifax Co., N. C.

KEARNY, Margaret and James P. Adams, 20 January 1852, Mecklenburg Co., N. C.

KEARSEY, E. I. and William C. Tillman, 18 October 1855, Edgefield District, S. C.

KEATER, William and Kediah Wilkinson, 8 July 1789, Bertie Co., N. C.

KEELEY, Susannah (Mrs.) and Benjamin Harvey, 26 January 1795, Charleston, S. C.

KEEN, Ann and John Garnier, July 1786, Georgetown, S. C.

KEEN, Joseph and Anna Crook, 29 July 1779, Santee, S. C.

KEEN, Penelope and William Standley, 25 May 1790, Bertie Co., N. C.

KELIAH, Mary and Jacob Newman, 5 December 1791, Mecklenburg Co., N. C.

KELLER, Matthias and Mary Handshy, 1740, Orangeburg Co., S. C.

KELLER, Willis and Sarah Lamb, 28 August 1851, Laurens Co., S. C.

KELLEY, Ann and William Tetterton, 12 August 1785, Tyrrell Co., N. C.

KELLON, Parthena and John Fee, 23 October 1779, Rowan Co., N. C.

KELLY, Drusilla J. and Joshua J. Caldwell, 6 October 1857, Mecklenburg Co., N. C.

KELLY, Eliza C. and James H. Rogers, 25 March 1839, Mecklenburg Co., N. C.

KELLY, Margaret and James Bilbrowe, 19 February 1766, Edgecombe Co., N. C.

KELLY, Margaret J. and Charles M. James, 5 March 1849, Mecklenburg Co., N. C.

KEMP, William and Melia Ward, 13 November 1764, Tyrrell Co., N. C.

KEMPTON, George and Henrietta Warner, 16 October 1799, Charleston, S. C.

KENDRICK, Margaret and John Randolph, 8 March 1815, Mecklenburg Co., N. C.

KENNAN, Mary Ann and Benjamin Guerard, 1 April 1786, Charleston, S. C.

KENNAN, Mary and David W. Hux, 19 May 1849, Mecklenburg Co., N. C.

KENNEDY, Agnes and Mitchell Fleming, 27 January 1794, Rowan Co., N. C.

KENNEDY, Eleanor and Guion Gibson, 8 December 1773, Pendleton, S. C.

KENNEDY, Elizabeth (Mrs.) and James Thompson, September 1786, Charleston, S. C.

KENNEDY, Hannah and William McCord, 9 September 1794, Mecklenburg Co., N. C.

KENNEDY, James and Nancy Chalmers, 7 December 1784, Charleston, S. C.

KENNEDY, John and Ann Houghton (widow), 19 November 1774, Chowan Co., N. C.

KENNEDY, Margaret and James McCorkle, 14 February 1804, Mecklenburg Co., N. C.

KENNEDY, Rebecca and James Boatwright, 5 March 1857, Edgefield District, S. C.

KENNEDY, William and Elizabeth Turner, 7 August 1722, Berkeley Co., S. C.

KENNEY, Benjamin G. and Vary L. Long, 27 January 1828, Edgefield District, S. C.

KENNEY, Charles H. and Harriet C. Gates, 28 December 1854, Edgefield District, S. C.

KENNEY, Frances E. and Henry T. Wright, 19 November 1844, Edgefield District, S. C.

KENNEY, John F. and Nancy Jones, 29 March 1849, Edgefield District, S. C.

KENNEY, Louisa M. and James R. McCord, 1 September 1853, Edgefield District, S. C.

KENNEY, Martha Y. and Benjamin S. Cogburn, 23 November 1828, Edgefield District, S. C.

KENNEY, Mary C. and William A. Murrell, 5 February 1833, Edgefield District, S. C.

KENNEY, Robert and Mary Gallman, 7 November 1805, Edgefield District, S. C.

KENNEY, Robert E. and Martha A. Johnson, 25 February 1855, Edgefield District, S. C.

KENNEY, Susan and William Cloud, 27 February 1834, Edgefield District, S. C.

KENNON, Mildred and Robert Taylor, 24 April 1816, Granville Co., N. C.

KERN, Polly and Seth Hutson, 24 October 1797, Rowan Co., N. C.

KERNE, Anna M. and Lambert Lance, 21 February 1765, Charleston, S. C.

KERNS, Susanna and John Eller, 5 November 1792, Rowan Co., N. C.

KERR, Agnes and James Graham (Jr.), 27 November 1771, Rowan Co., N. C.

KERR, Alexander W. and Susannah Ross, 28 October 1814, Guilford Co., N. C.

KERR, Ann and David Budd, 11 May 1801, Mecklenburg Co., N. C.

KERR, Catherine L. and John P. Byram, 23 March 1838, Mecklenburg Co., N. C.

KERR, Eliza and Robert Arnold, 13 February 1832, Mecklenburg Co., N. C.

KERR, Elizabeth and Silas Read, 10 December 1827, Mecklenburg Co., N. C.

KERR, Esther and Elihu McCracken, 12 April 1849, Mecklenburg Co., N. C.

KERR, Hannah and Robert Martin, 10 November 1806, Mecklenburg Co., N. C.

KERR, Helena and William Morrison, 11 December 1830, Mecklenburg Co., N. C.

KERR, Isabella and William S. Baker, 3 May 1860, Mecklenburg Co., N. C.

KERR, Jane and Thomas Oliver, 19 February 1821, Mecklenburg Co., N. C.

KERR, Jennett and Francis Gardner, 18 May 1778, Rowan Co., N. C.

KERR, Margaret and John Gillespie, 31 January 1786, Rowan Co., N. C.

KERR, Margaret and Sherrard Jones, 23 February 1830, Mecklenburg Co., N. C.

KERR, Martha and John D. Caldwell, 6 March 1855, Mecklenburg Co., N. C.

KERR, Martha A. S. and Hugh M. Caldwell, 19 October 1857, Mecklenburg Co., N. C.

KERR, Mary C. and James C. Rudesill, 26 November 1825, Mecklenburg Co., N. C.

KERR, Nanica and John M. Brown, 7 April 1832, Mecklenburg Co., N. C.

KERR, Peggy and James Martin, 27 February 1797, Mecklenburg Co., N. C.

KERR, Rachel and John McCauley, 12 September 1795, Mecklenburg Co., N. C.

KERR, Sarah and Ambrose N. Rogers, 9 February 1835, Mecklenburg Co., N. C.

KERRISON, Samuel and (Mrs.) Elizabeth McGivern, 7 November 1801, Charleston, S. C.

KERSHAW, Eli and Mary Cantey, 19 November 1769, Camden, S. C.

KERSHAW, Sarah and Benjamin Perkins, June 1797, Camden, S. C.

KETER, Polly and Ellis Mitchell, 26 January 1848, Guilford Co., N. C.

KEYSER, Eva C. and Jacob Dirr, 22 December 1754, Orangeburg Co., S. C.

KIERMAN, George and Mrs. Montgomery, 28 April 1801, Charleston, S. C.

KILCREASE, William E. and Rode E. Waller, 12 October 1853, Edgefield District, S. C.

KILLEBROW, Susannah and Elijah Horn, 18 August 1799, Edgecombe Co., N. C.

KILPATRICK, Ann and David Foster, 27 January 1795, Rowan Co., N. C.

KIMBALL, Mary and L. Berry Cranshaw, 6 December 1828, Mecklenburg Co., N. C.

KINCHEN, Elizabeth and Philip Kearney, 30 November 1763, Halifax Co., N. C.

KING, Anne and Joseph Speight, 3 March 1752, Chowan Co., N. C.

KING, Anne and Thomas Davis, 25 December 1769, Edgecombe Co., N. C.

KING, Anna D. and Conrad Ehrhardt, 16 February 1851, Barnwell Co., S. C.

KING, Ann H. and John M. Bost, 17 March 1855, Mecklenburg Co., N. C.

KING, Edward and Jerusha Rock, 29 September 1721, St. Andrews Parish, S. C.

KING, Elizabeth and Thomas Exum, 31 July 1800, Edgecombe Co., N. C.

KING, Elizabeth and Thomas Bevans, 18 August 1751, Chowan Co., N. C.

KING, Elizabeth and Joseph M. Roberts, 19 May 1841, Mecklenburg Co., N. C.

KING, Fanny and Joseph M. Robinson, 31 July 1856, Mecklenburg Co., N. C.

KING, Hannah L. and William Lloyd, 16 May 1826, Charleston, S. C.

KING, Harriett and Nathaniel Ramsey, 26 April 1855, Edgefield District, S. C.

KING, Harriet J. and Samuel N. Bishop, 8 January 1821, Charleston, S. C.

KING, Henry and Sarah Worley, 10 February 1789, Bertie Co., N. C.

KING, Jane and William A. L. Owen, 21 March 1848, Mecklenburg Co., N. C.

KING, Martha and Thomas Britt, 2 March 1793, Bertie Co., N. C.

KING, Martha A. and John Williams, 22 April 1855, Edgefield District, S. C.

KING, Mary and John Hopkins, 10 February 1752, Chowan Co., N. C.

KING, Mary (widow) and William Berry, 21 May 1750, Orangeburg Co., S. C.

KING, Mary A. and R. G. Mason, 14 May 1849, Mecklenburg Co., N. C.

KING, Polly and James Read, (Jr.), 13 April 1802, Mecklenburg Co., N. C.

KING, Polly and Pomphrett Herndon, 19 July 1805, Orange Co., N. C.

KING, Sarah and James Mizell, 18 January 1769, Tyrrell Co., N. C.

KING, William and Katherine Cook, 15 June 1774, Chowan Co., N. C.

KINGHAM, Sarah and Jonathan Gibson, 9 September 1775, Chowan Co., N. C.

KINGSTON, John and Ann Camren, 13 January 1743, Charleston, S. C.

KINGSTON, Simon and Margaret Hatfield, 17 February 1785, Charleston, S. C.

KINLOCH, Cleiland and Harriet Simmons, April 1786, Charleston, S. C.

KINLOCH, Francis and Nancy Cleland, 7 February 1751, Charleston, S. C.

KINLOCH, Francis and Martha Rutledge, 8 December 1785, Charleston, S. C.

KINLOCH, Polly and Benjamin Huger, 1 December 1772, Kensington, S. C.

KINNARD, Margaret and John K. Goodwin, 1814, Edgefield, S. C.

KINNERLY, Mary Rall (Mrs.) and Thomas Poindexter, 8 December 1811, Edgefield District, S. C.

KINSE, Kathren and William Turner, 5 March 1793, Berkeley, N. C.

KINSEY, James and Martha Turner, 7 April 1787, Bertie Co., N. C.

KIRK, Agnes and Harris Robinson, 11 May 1795, Mecklenburg Co., N. C.

KIRK, Charles William and Mary N. Roberts, 16 December 1821, Charleston, S. C.

KIRK, Margaret and John Oehler, 21 December 1847, Mecklenburg Co., N. C.

KIRK, Mary and Samuel Houston, 30 November 1795, Mecklenburg Co., N. C.

KIRK, Nancy and Calvin G. Alexander, 27 March 1833, Mecklenburg Co., N. C.

KIRKLAND, Louisa and Aphriam Franklin, 19 December 1838, Edgefield District, S. C.

KIRKLAND, Matilda and Joseph Nobles, 9 May 1838, Edgefield District, S. C.

KIRKPATRICK, Catherine and William Melvin, 30 October 1793, Mecklenburg Co., N. C.

KIRKPATRICK, Isabella and John Boyce, 27 December 1800, Mecklenburg Co., N. C.

KIRKPATRICK, Isabella and William Read, 1 March 1847, Mecklenburg Co., N. C.

KIRKPATRICK, Jane M. and Samuel M. Rogers, 25 February 1823, Mecklenburg Co., N. C.

KIRKPATRICK, M. I. (Miss) and H. C. Read, 10 April 1862, Mecklenburg Co., N. C.

KIRKPATRICK, Mary S. and Charles Brown, 4 September 1848, Mecklenburg Co., N. C.

KISTLER, Mary A. and C. W. Abernathy, 25 September 1856, Mecklenburg Co., N. C.

KITCHEN, Charles and Eugenia Megrew, 1746, Orangeburg Co., S. C.

KITCHEN, John and Barbara Pfund (widow), 1740, Orangeburg Co., S. C.

KITCHEN, Lucreasia and Robert Hudnall, 2 December 1768, Edgecombe Co., N. C.

KITTRELL, Mansey and William Hunt, 24 January 1780, Granville Co., N. C.

KITTRELL, Mary and Alexander Leggett, 2 February 1788, Bertie Co., N. C.

KITTRELL, Rebecca and Thomas P. White, 2 September 1840, Granville Co., N. C.

KLONTZ, Catherine M. and William Brooks, 21 November 1833, Mecklenburg Co., N. C.

KNIGHT, Elford and Sarah Powers, 10 September 1846, Laurens Co., S. C.

KNIGHT, James and Caroline Henderson, 7 February 1848, Laurens Co., S. C.

KNIGHT, Josiah and Mary Thomason, 27 February 1855, Laurens Co., S. C.

KNIGHT, Marion and Martha Knight, 11 February 1855, Laurens Co., S. C.

KNIGHT, Mary and John Meredith, 17 February 1797, Guilford Co., N. C.

KNIGHT, Mary and Berreman Brown, 19 March 1858, Laurens Co., S. C.

KNIGHT, Martha and Marion Knight, 11 February 1855, Laurens Co., S. C.

KNIGHT, Rachel and James Meredith, 23 August 1797, Guilford Co., N. C.

KNIGHT, Robert and Mary Fuller, 10 June 1856, Laurens Co., S. C.

KNIGHT, Samuel (Dr.) and Permealy Miller, 18 May 1859, Laurens Co., S. C.

KNIGHT, Sarah and William Garret, 11 March 1858, Laurens Co., S. C.

KNIGHT, Susan and Benjamin Lanford, 29 October 1857, Laurens Co., S. C.

KNIGHT, Teresay and Drury Goodin, 15 July 1763, Edgecombe Co., N. C.

KNIGHT, William and Sarah Foster, 31 March 1777, Chowan Co., N. C.

KNOBEL, George Frederick and Elizabeth Fichter, 25 March 1753, Orangeburg Co., S. C.

KNOTT, Patsy and William Hunt, 22 December 1801, Granville Co., N. C.

KNOX, Lydia N. and Ezekial Wallace, 19 April 1797, Mecklenburg Co., N. C.

KNOX, Mary and Robert Beard, 15 February 1838, Mecklenburg Co., N. C.

KNOX, Naomi and William Leetch, 1795, Mecklenburg Co., N. C.

KNOX, Robert and Christina Frederick, May 1786, Charleston, S. C.

KNOX, S. E. (Miss) and I. M. S. Rogers, 20 November 1861, Mecklenburg Co., N. C.

KOCH, Regula and Michael Larry, 1740, Orangeburg Co., S. C.

KOLLER, Benedict and Magdalene Spring, 1 January 1740, Orangeburg Co., S. C.

KOONEN, Francis and Ann Maria Hagin, 1 September 1748, Orangeburg Co., S. C.

KOONEN, Jacob and Catharina Negely, 1 September 1748, Orangeburg Co., S. C.

KOONER, Jacob and Anna Tshudy, (widow) 21 July 1752, Orangeburg Co., S. C.

KOONER, Martin and Mary Joyner, 24 February 1746, Orangeburg Co., S. C.

KRANICK, John V. and Anna Mary Heckler, 1753, Orangeburg Co., S. C.

KREPS, Andrew and Ann Pattison, August 1785, Charleston, S. C.

KREUTER, Joseph and Susannah Shuler, 1740, Orangeburg Co., S. C.

KREYTER, Barbara and John Frederick Huber, 7 August 1750, Orangeburg Co., S. C.

KRITZ, Anna and Willoby Hooks, 23 January 1793, Rowan Co., N. C.

KRUM, Polly and Jackson Rodden, 17 February 1810, Mecklenburg Co., N. C.

KUHN, Casper and Anna Barbara Ernst, (widow), 28 June 1750, Orangeburg Co., S. C.

KURNER, George Jacob and Ann Catharina Larrywecht (widow), 12 April 1753, Orangeburg Co., S. C.

L

LA BORDE, Catherine and Andrew Neal (Maj.) 22 January 1854, Edgefield District S. C.

LA BRUCE, Joseph and Hannah Allston, 3 February 1780, Santee, S. C.

LACEY, Samuel and Hannah Hogg, 13 January 1743, Charleston, S. C.

LACY, John and Ann Miller, 2 April 1738, Charleston, S. C.

LACY, Thomas and Ruth Mitchell, 20 November 1800, Charleston, S. C.

LADSON, Eliza and George Taylor (Jr.), 11 December 1794, Charleston, S. C.

LADSON, Jacob and Elizabeth Perry, 18 February 1719, St. Andrews Parish, S. C.

LADSON, Robert and Sally Fleming, 18 March 1773, Charleston, S. C.

LADSON, Thomas and Elizabeth Capers, 24 February 1785, Beaufort, S. C.

LAFITTE, Timothy and Sarah Clayton, 25 September 1741, Chowan Co., N. C.

LAFITTE, Sarah and Samuel Stillwell, 24 March 1742, Chowan Co., N. C.

LAFONT, Francis and Mary Wyatt, 16 July 1778, Chowan Co., N. C.

LADSON, Ann and James Gregory (Jr.), 5 February 1801, Charleston, S. C.

LAIDER, William and Sarah McCaulley, 14 February 1801, Charleston, S. C.

LAKE, Mary Elizabeth and John H. Barus, 19 January 1852, Edgefield District, S. C.

LAMB, William and Delilah Lane, 17 March 1815, Chowan Co., N. C.

LAMB, William G. H. and Evalina Rea, 11 October 1830, Chowan Co., N. C.

LAMB, Sarah and Willis Keller, 28 August 1851, Laurens Co., S. C.

LAMBALL, Polly and (Rev.) John Thomas, 21 February 1768, Charleston, S. C.

LAMBOL, Judith and Richard Miller, 29 December 1724, Charleston, S. C.

LAMBOLL, Thomas and Peggy Edgar, 14 April 1737, Ashley Ferry, S. C.

LAMBTON, Richard and Ann Walters (widow), 27 November 1750, Charleston, S. C.

LAMMON, Robert and Barbara Bronzon (widow), 28 May 1751, Orangeburg Co., S. C.

LAMOTTE, Anthony and Dorcas Ran Randall, 8 March 1767, Charleston, S. C.

LANCASTER, Sarah J. and Thomas Brinkley, 25 June 1861, Mecklenburg Co., N. C.

LANCE, Lambert and Sarah Harvey, 21 June 1784, Cane Acre, S. C.

LANCE, Lambert and Anna M. Kerne, 21 February 1765, Charleston, S. C.

LANCE, Lucy and Jonathan Da Rrazin, 28 September 1763, Charleston, S. C.

LANDELS, James and Damaris Murrell, 23 February 1780, Santee, S. C.

LANDFORD, Martha and Charles Franks, 31 July 1862, Laurens Co., S. C.

LANDFORD, Miss and Willis Curnal, 15 September 1859, Laurens Co., S. C.

LANSFORD, James and Malissa Gining, 10 September 1859, Laurens Co., S. C.

LANDRUM, Amos and Elizabeth Hatcher, 12 August 1838, Edgefield District, S. C.

LANDRUM, Eliza and Collin Rhodes, 17 May 1839, Pottersville, S. C.

LANE, Catherine and William Anderson, 6 November 1733, Charleston, S. C.

LANE, Delilah and William Lamb, 17 March 1815, Chowan Co., N. C.

LANE, Henry and Elizabeth Miller, 9 July 1856, Chowan Co., N. C.

LANE, Hannah and John Gensel, 19 June 1800, Charleston, S. C.

LANE, Lydia and John T. Millar, 8 August 1799, Charleston, S. C.

LANE, Robert and Miss de Berniere, 13 July 1799, Fayetteville, S. C.

LANE, Sarah J. and Eli Heedson, 14 December 1848, Marion Co., S. C.

LANFORD, Amanda and Harrison P. Griffith, 22 January 1861, Laurens Co., S. C.

LANFORD, Benjamin and Susan Knight, 29 October 1857, Laurens Co., S. C.

LANFORD, Mary and Martin Parsons, 2 October 1845, Laurens Co., S. C.

LANGDON, Sarah A. and Samuel A. Weber, 20 November 1861, York Co., S. C.

LANGLEY, Mary (widow) and Edward Johnson, 25 May 1761, Edgecombe Co., N. C.

LANGLEY, Phoebe and John Mehaffey, 6 January 1791, Guilford Co., N. C.

LANGLEY, Thomas and Mary Mitchel, 13 April 1724, Charleston, S. C.

LANGSTON, John (widower) and Sophy Smith, 4 March 1845, Laurens Co.,

LANGSTON, Sarah and Richard Bolton, 1 January 1770, Edgecombe Co., N. C.

LANGSTON, Virginia and John Finley, 7 December 1865, Laurens Co., S. C.

LANIER, Adam and Sarah Bennett, 7 June 1766, Tyrrell Co., N. C.

LANIER, Elizabeth and John Swain, 15 December 1766, Tyrrell Co., N. C.

LANIER, John and Hannah Holladay, 6 May 1769, Tyrrell Co., N. C.

LANING, Biddy and William Moore, August 1833, Mecklenburg Co., Co., N. C.

LANSING, Betsy and Charles Bird, 15 December 1834, Mecklenburg Co., N. C.

LANSING, Patsy and Robert Norton, 14 July 1819, Mecklenburg Co., N. C.

LANGSTAFF, Benjamin and Ann Howard, 30 October 1794, Charleston, S. C.

LAQUER, James and Nancy Jennett, 28 February 1785, Chowan Co., N. C.

LARK, Sarah and S. Joseph Stockdap, 11 February 1830, Edgefield District, S. C.

LARKINS, Margaret and Josiah Evans, 17 February 1755, Orangeburg Co., S. C.

LARRAZIN, Elizabeth and Andrew Reid, 5 May 1765, Charleston, S. C.

LARRY, Margaret and Peter Moorer (Jr.), 1740 Orangeburg Co., S. C.

LARRY, Michael and Regular Koch, 1740, Orangeburg Co., S. C.

LARRYWECHT, Ann Catharina (widow) and George Jacob Kurner, 12 April 1753, Orangeburg Co., S. C.

LASSITER, Aaron and Ruth Smith, 6 January 1785, Chowan Co., N. C.

LASSITER, Christian and Thomas Roberts, 4 May 1785, Chowan Co., N. C.

LASSITER, Frances and Henry Jerard, 8 February 1786, Tyrrell Co., N. C.

LASSITER, Frederick and Sarah Walton (widow), 12 March 1772, Chowan Co., N. C.

LASSITER, John and Mary Elizabeth, 22 April 1790, Bertie Co., N. C.

LASSITER, Lettice and Joseph Everett, 26 November 1775, Tyrrell Co., N. C.

LASSITER, Mary and Jacob Bass, 8 September 1789, Bertie Co., N. C.

LASSITER, Sarah and David Standley, 10 June 1788, Bertie Co., N. C.

LATHAM, Charity and Robert Wilson, 20 November 1800, St. Thomas Parish, S. C.

LATHAM, Eliza and William Pritchard, 1 December 1801, St. Thomas Parish, S. C.

LA TOUR, Miss and Francis Verambaut, 28 July 1767, Charleston, S. C.

LATSON, Eliza and (Dr.) James Hartley, 1788, Charleston, S. C.

LATTA, James and Nancy Allen, 24 August 1790, Orange Co., N. C.

LATTA, James (Rev.) and Sally Wilson, March 1775, Johns Island, S. C.

LAURENCE, Elizabeth and Alexander Joyner, 29 April 1768, Edgecombe Co., N. C.

LAURENS, James and Mary Crawford (widow) 19 August 1761, Charleston, S. C.

LAVINE, Mary and Thomas Thomson, 9 January 1796, Mecklenburg Co., N. C.

LAVIS, Rachel and John Nicholson, 4 February 1796, Mecklenburg Co., N. C.

LAW, Hannah and William Mares, 18 October 1796, Guilford Co., N. C.

LAW, Thomas H. and Anna E. Adger, 16 March 1860, Charleston, S. C.

LAW, William and Abigail Marye, 9 August 1799, Guilford Co., N. C .

LAWING, N. M. and Hugh T. Rhyne, 30 October 1859, Mecklenburg Co., N. C.

LAWING, Samuel and Jane O. Gibson, 23 September 1856, Mecklenburg Co., N. C.

LAWING, Sarah N. and Andrew J. Robinson, 27 September 1855, Mecklenburg Co., .N C.

LAWRENCE, Amelia and John Casswell, 26 December 1785, Tyrrell Co., N. C.

LAWRENCE, Betty and John Evans, 21 January 1782, Rowan Co., N. C.

LAWRENCE, Jenny and John Gracey, 11 February 1784, Rowan Co., N. C.

LAWRENCE, Jonathan and Elizabeth Daniel, May 1777, Charleston, S. C.

LAWRENCE, Margaret and Joseph McLelland, 25 January 1792, Mecklenburg Co., N. C.

LAWRENCE, Obediah and Rachel Fox, 1780, Tyrrell Co., N. C.

LAWRENCE, Robert D. and Eliza M. Hall, 19 December 1799, Charleston, S. C.

LAWRENCE, Samuel and (Mrs.) Elizabeth Givens, 18 January 1801, Beaufort, S. C.

LAWRENCE, Seth and Betsy Britt, 8 February 1796, Bertie Co., N. C.

LAWRENS, Mary and Charles Pinkney, 1788, Charleston, S. C.

LAWRING, Ann and Benjamin Allen, 14 January 1797, Mecklenburg Co., N. C.

LAWRING, Nancy and Cyrus W. Alexander, 23 June 1835, Mecklenburg Co., N. C.

LAWSON, Eliza B. and Ambrose Houston, 29 March 1839, Mecklenburg Co., N. C.

LAWSON, Mary and James White, 1770, Iredell Co., N. C.

LAWSON, Sarah B. and Nelson L. Black, 6 December 1839, Mecklenburg Co., N. C.

LAWTON, Bulah and John Hughes, 28 January 1801, Charleston, S. C.

LAYDEN, Bathsheba and John Fanning, 11 June 1778, Perquimans Co., N. C.

LAYTON, George and Adaline Todd, 1 January 1857, Laurens Co., S. C.

LAYTON, Martha and Simpson Grow, 21 December 1865, Laurens Co., S. C.

LEACROFT, John and Elizabeth Black, 24 October 1784, Beaufort, S. C.

LEAK, William and Mary Willis, 1851, Laurens Co., S. C.

LEANY, Mary A. and James Ormond, 29 May 1832, Mecklenburg Co., N. C.

LEARY, Ann and Robert Hall, 4 August 1742, Chowan Co., N. C.

LEARY, Elizabeth and Thomas Steely, 20 January 1783, Tyrrell Co., N. C.

LEARY, Job and Rachel Hoskins, January 1776, Chowan Co., N. C.

LEARY, Mary and James Luten, 31 January 1755, Chowan Co., N. C.

LEARY, William and Leah Freeman, 24 March 1778, Chowan Co., N. C.

LEATH, Penelope and John Miller, 27 February 1799, Chowan Co., N. C.

LEE, Jane E. and John O. Alexander, 17 February 1857, Mecklenburg Co., N. C.

LEE, Mary A. and John W. Barnett, 18 November 1852, Mecklenburg Co., N. C.

LEE, Sarah and Thomas Denny, 29 October 1769, Santee, S. C.

LEE, Sarah and Clement Crooke, 6 June 1774, Tyrrell Co., N. C.

LEE, Thomas and Ann Long, 13 August 1786, Tyrrell Co., N .C.

LEE, V. and J. Long, 1784, Tyrrell Co., N. C.

LEE, William and Harriet Hrabowski, 16 May 1796, Charleston, S. C.

LEEFE, Benjamin and Harriet S. Bentham, 6 January 1801, Charleston, S. C.

LEEMING, Peter and Martha Lewis, 20 May 1758, Chowan Co., N. C.

LEETCH, William and Naomi Knox, 1795, Mecklenburg Co., N. C.

LEGAR, James and Kezia Stewart, 25 March 1779, Santee, S. C.

LEGARE, Amy and John Baker, 13 October 1767, Charleston, S. C.

LEGARE, Amy and Enos Reeves, 22 December 1784, Charleston, S. C.

LEGARE, Elizabeth and John Webb, 30 March 1786, Charleston, S. C.

LEGARE, Elizabeth and John Ashe, 23 October 1783, Christ Church Parish, S. C.

LEGARE, Elizabeth and William Scott (Jr.), 5 March 1771, Charleston, S. C.

LEGARE, Isaac (Jr.) and Martha White, 30 October 1782, Santee, S. C.

LEGARE, Mary and Thomas Doughty, 11 October 1768, Charleston, S. C.

LEGARE, Mary and Samuel Jones, 7 May 1801, Santee, S. C.

LEGARE, Nathan and Mary Toomer, April 1786, Christ Church Parish, S. C.

LEGARE, Rebecca and Simeon Theus, July 1784, Charleston, S. C.

LEGARE, Sarah and William Somerall, 11 January 1767, Charleston, S. C.

LEGARE, Solomon and Sally Lining, 10 November 1785, Charleston, S. C.

LEGER, Elizabeth and George Croft, 28 January 1765, Charleston, S. C.

LEGER, Peter (Jr.) and Elizabeth Haig, 23 November 1760, Charleston, S. C.

LEIGH, William and Esther Bernard, 27 August 1778, Santee, S. C.

LEIGHTON, Catherine and George Stocker, 31 January 1778, Chowan Co., N. C.

LEGATE, James and Mary Wilkinson, May 1784, St. Pauls Parish, S. C.

LEGGETT, Alexander and Mary Kittrell, 2 February 1788, Bertie Co., N. C.

LEGGETT, Mary and Nathan Rogers, 12 October 1785, Tyrrell Co., N. C.
N. C.

LEMMON, Margaret and Thomas Rutherford, 27 February 1832, Mecklenburg Co.,
N. C.

LEMMOND, Elizabeth and John G. Alexander, 3 April 1811, Mecklenburg Co.,

LEMONS, Nancy M. and John Allison, 28 January 1822, Mecklenburg Co., N. C.

LEMPRIERE, Ann and Lieutenant Prince, 17 November 1763, Christ Church
Parish, S. C.

LEN, Margaret and John Holler, 16 October 1794, Rowan Co., N. C.

LENNOX, Katy and Alexander Moultrie, 21 May 1772, Charleston, S. C.

LENOX, William and Mary Greenage, 6 October 1794, Charleston, S. C.

LENTILE, Jane and William Calhoun, 8 October 1825, Mecklenburg Co., N. C.

LENUD, Henry and Elizabeth Croft, 13 June 1782, Santee, S. C.

LEONARD, Eleanor and Henry Fullinwid, 20 August 1783, Rowan Co., N. C.

LEONARD, Jacob and Eleanor Miller, 16 June 1765, Wilmington, N. C.

LEONORA, Mary and Robert Furgurson, 11 August 1787, Orange Co., N. C.

LEPNER, Caroline and Thomas Cappa, 9 October 1809, Mecklenburg Co., N. C.

LE SERURIER, Marianne and Isaac Mazyck, 14 October 1693, Charleston, S. C.

LESESNE, Anne and Thomas Walter, 26 March 1769, Charleston, S. C.

LESESNE, Susanna and Robert Howie, 14 December 1769, Charleston, S. C.

LESESNE, Thomas and Elizabeth Boyd, December 1785, Charleston, S. C.

LESLEY, William and Mary Stokes (widow), 15 September 1770, Charleston, S. C.

LESLIE, Hannah and George Harlan, 19 January 1803, Mecklenburg Co., N. C.

LESLIE, Mary and William Haughton, 16 October 1800, Charleston, S. C.

LESTER, Frances and Obed Easor, 17 February 1800, Edgecombe Co., N. C.

LESTER, Harriet and (Col.) George Mosely, 1 December 1858, Laurens Co., S. C.

LESTER, Lydia and John Scott, 21 June 1785, Chowan Co., N. C.

LESTER, James and Sarah Dear, 7 March 1778, Chowan Co., N. C.

LEVY, Samuel and Hannah Abrahams, 1 June 1796, Charleston, S. C.

LEWIS, Catherine and Elisha Cain, 6 February 1805, Mecklenburg Co., N. C.

LEWIS, Elias and Mary Logan, 29 July 1761, Santee, S. C.

LEWIS, Heziah and William Robison, 16 January 1812, Mecklenburg Co., N. C.

LEWIS, Isabella and William Miller, 24 October 1797, Mecklenburg Co., N. C.

LEWIS, James and Esther Jones, 5 September 1751, Orangeburg Co., S. C.

LEWIS, John and Mary Champion, 11 March 1754, Chowan Co., N. C.

LEWIS, John (Jr.) and Mary Thompson (widow), 19 November 1755, Chowan Co., N. C.

LEWIS, John and Judith Van Assendelft, 15 December 1799, Charleston, S. C.

LEWIS, Kezia and William Robinson, 16 January 1812, Mecklenburg Co., N. C.

LEWIS, Martha and Peter Leeming, 20 May 1758, Chowan Co., N. C.

LEWIS, Patsey and Edmond Taylor, 24 April 1790, Granville Co., N. C.

LEWIS, Sarah and Keating Simons, 9 June 1774, Charleston, S. C.

LEWIS, Sarah and John Hendricks, 27 December 1780, Rowan Co., N. C.

LEWIS, Sarah and William Cathcart, 7 January 1824, Mecklenburg Co., N. C.

LEWIS, Stephen (Rev.) and Polly Greene, 1 March 1785, Beaufort, S. C.

LEWIS, William and Ann Murrell, 14 May 1767, Santee, S. C.

LEYSATH, John W. and Ursula Giessendanner, 3 October 1752, Orangeburg Co., S. C.

LIGHTWOOD, Edward and Elizabeth Peronneau, 1 January 1770, Charleston, S. C.

LILES, Anne and Aaron Colner, 7 July 1785, Chowan Co., N. C.

LILES, William and Martha Perry, 11 September 1756, Chowan Co., N. C.

LILES, William and Ellen Prescott, 2 March 1837, Edgefield District, S. C.

LILIEN, (or JULIEN) Nancy and Thomas Alexander, 28 January 1845, Mecklenburg Co., N. C.

LILSE, Sarah and John Beasley, 30 September 1752, Chowan Co., N. C.

LIMEHOUSE, Elizabeth and James Oliver, 5 November 1801, Charleston, S. C.

LINART, Heine and Priscilla Harrod, 9 October 1784, Chowan Co., N. C.

LINDER, Daniel and Sarah Hill, 14 March 1754, Orangeburg Co., S. C.

LINDER, Mary and William Young, 2 July 1752, Orangeburg Co., S. C.

LINDREY, Sarah and Joseph Blake, 16 June 1720, Newington, S. C.

LINDSAY, Sarah and Samuel Kearney, 10 November 1796, Halifax Co., N. C.

LING, Mary and Nathaniel Miller, 21 December 1802, Chowan Co., N. C.

LINING, Charles and Mary Rose (widow), 4 November 1784, Charleston, S. C.

LINING, Sally and Solomon Legare, 10 November 1785, Charleston, S. C.

LINSTER, Elizabeth and William Hayden, 3 May 1796, Rowan Co., N. C.

LINSTER, Jean and Andrew Hall, 12 March 1793, Rowan Co., N. C.

LINZY, Dennis and Louisa Styles, 5 April 1843, Laurens Co., S. C.

LIPPINCOTT, Abigail and William Clemens, 25 November 1774, Perquimans Co., N. C.

LITES, Abraham and Jane Atkins, 5 September 1816, Newberry, S. C.

LITTELL, Aaron and Elizabeth Jennison, 27 November 1766, Santee, S. C.

LITTLE, Agnes and William Dancy, 20 August 1765, Edgecombe Co., N. C.

LITTLE, Allen and Susan Berry, 12 December 1839, Edgefield District, S. C.

LITTLE, Anne M. and Jacob Eckle, 5 January 1779, Rowan Co., N. C.

LITTLE, Jane E. and Charles A. Newbold, 17 January 1865, Mecklenburg Co., N. C.

LITTLE, Sally and (Capt.) Barnard Muchmore, 5 March 1795, Charleston, S. C.

LITTLEDALE, Elizabeth S. and John Custis, 11 October 1777, Chowan Co., N. C.

LIVELEY, Catherine and John Furr, 4 August 1783, Rowan Co., N. C.

LIVERMAN, Mary and William Banks, 3 January 1786, Tyrrell Co., N. C.

LIVERMAN, Phebe and Thomas Loverman, 5 February 1777, Tyrrell Co., N. C.

LIVINGSTON, Anne and John Champneys, 3 November 1763, Charleston, S. C.

LIVINGSTON, Hannah and Robert Roulain, 5 November 1799, Charleston, S. C.

LIVINGSTON, Martha and James B. Abney, 21 December 1848, Edgefield Co., S. C.

LIVINGSTON, Mary and Joseph Cooper, 30 March 1791, Mecklenburg Co., N. C.

LIVINGSTON, Polly and John Yerworth, February 1748, Charleston, S. C.

LLOYD, Betsy and John Bradwell, 30 March 1775, Charleston, S. C.

LLOYD, John and Rebecca Boone, 25 November 1752, Charleston, S. C.

LLOYD, John and Anne Jones (widow), 12 January 1764, Charleston, S. C.

LLOYD, Rebecca and William Carson, 16 January 1770, Charleston, S. C.

LLOYD, Susannah and Paul Ravenall, 19 January 1786, Charleston, S. C.

LLOYD, Thomas and Mary Matthews, 24 July 1746, Charleston, S. C.

LLOYD, William and Hannah L. King, 16 May 1826, Charleston, S. C.

LOCK, Mr. and Amanda Gary, 7 May 1857, Laurens Co., S. C.

LOCKE, Elizabeth and John Gibson, 13 January 1775, Rowan Co., N. C.

LOCKHART, Elizabeth and Joshua Hassell, 3 July 1786, Tyrrell Co., N. C.

LOCKHART, Jennison and Elisha Davis, 1784, Tyrrell Co., N. C.

LOCKHEART, Adeline and James Woodruff, 22 January 1851, Laurens Co., S. C.

LOCUST, Ferebee and Jonathan George, 27 January 1802, Orange Co., N. C.

LOFTEN, Rebecca and John Ellis, 11 June 1796, Rowan Co., N. C.

LOFTIS, Martha and John Sheppard, 6 September 1771, Santee, S. C.

LOGAN, John and Rachel Perry, 20 August 1784, Charleston, S. C.

LOGAN, Mary and Elias Lewis, 29 July 1761, Santee, S. C.

LONDON, John and Miss Mauger, July 1796, Wilmington, N. C.

LONG, Ann and John Jones, 20 September 1779, Tyrrell Co., N. C.

LONG, Ann and Thomas Lee, 13 August 1786, Tyrrell Co., N. C.

LONG, Caroline and William A. Taylor, 29 June 1859, Pittsboro, N. C.

LONG, Elizabeth and Benjamin Elston (Sr.), 18 November 1786, Burke Co., N. C.

LONG, E. Augustine and B. W. Hatcher, 8 February 1842, Edgefield District, S. C.

LONG, Hannah and Ebenezer Spruill, 27 October 1770, Tyrrell Co., N. C.

LONG, Isaac and Rodia Wiley, 10 September 1767, Tyrrell Co., N. C.

LONG, Izette and James Murrell, 1 January 1835, Edgefield District, S. C.

LONG, James and Elizabeth Dunning, 12 April 1762, Tyrrell Co., N. C.

LONG, James and Mary Brown, 20 June 1768, Chowan Co., N. C.

LONG, James and Mary Butcher, 15 July 1775, Tyrrell Co., N. C.

LONG, James and Sarah Jones, 27 April 1785, Tyrrell Co., N. C.

LONG, Jemina and Richard Haughton, 3 August 1774, Tyrrell Co., N. C.

LONG, Jeremiah and Penny Jones, 20 November 1777, Tyrrell Co., N. C.

LONG, John and (Mrs.) Joana Blount, 23 December 1766, Tyrrell Co., N. C.

LONG, John R. and Susan Ann Hope, 20 December 1856, Mecklenburg Co., N. C.

LONG, J. and V. Lee, 1784, Tyrrell Co., N. C.

LONG, Kesiah and Jesse Young, 1 June 1767, Tyrrell Co., N. C.

LONG, Lemuel and Celia Copeland, 23 September 1773, Chowan Co., N. C.

LONG, Malinda and James Jamieson, 28 June 1849, Mecklenburg Co., N. C.

LONG, Mary and Jonas Hayman, 1 December 1778, Tyrrell Co., N. C.

LONG, Mary and John Smith, 19 September 1782, Santee, S. C.

LONG, Mary and Bassett Stith, 8 July 1790, Halifax, N. C.

LONG, Penelope and Francis Mills, 29 March 1783, Tyrrell Co., N. C.

LONG, Simeon and Mary Beasley, 4 June 1773, Chowan Co., N. C.

LONG, Vary L. and Benjamin Kenney, 27 January 1828, Edgefield District, S. C.

LONG, Walter and Mary Hutson, 10 December 1744, Chowan Co., N. C.

LONG, William B. and Mary Ann Jane Ayers, 24 March 1840, Marlboro Co., S. C.

LONGMIRE, Sarah and John Penn Hunt, 24 December 1811, Granville Co., N. C.

LONGWORTH, Archibald (of N. J.) and Elizabeth Rich, 20 August 1800, St. Lukes Parish, S. C.

LOONEY, E. J. and Frances L. J. White, 28 January 1847, Granville Co., N. C.

LOPP, Barbra and George Harman, 27 December 1795, Rowan Co., N. C.

LOPP, Elizabeth and Henry Garner, 10 August 1792, Rowan Co., N. C.

LORD, Andrew and Anne Gadson, 15 November 1770, Charleston, S. C.

LORD, John and Margaret Brown, 19 February 1767, Charleston, S. C.

LOTHROP, Seth and (Mrs.) Sarah Weyman, April 1785, Charleston, S. C.

LOTT, Arthur and Sarah Bush, 23 December 1841, Edgefield District, S. C.

LOTT, Eliza and Spencer Elmore, 1 December 1836, Edgefield District, S. C.

LOTT, Sarah and Stephen Whatley, 1 November 1841, Edgefield District, S. C.

LOVE, Charles and Eliza Warner, June 1786, Charleston, S. C.

LOVE, Elizabeth and Malcolm Hunt, 12 June 1791, Mecklenburg Co., N. C.

LOVEDALE, John and Margaret Nearon, August 1783, Charleston, S. C.

LOVELESS, Mary L. and John B. Cartledge, 21 November 1854, Edgefield District, S. C.

LOVELL, Edward and (Mrs.) Mary Mackey, 1742, Chowan Co., N. C.

LOVELL, Frances and James Izlar, 24 February 1859, Orangeburg, S. C.

LOVERMAN, Thomas and Phebe Liverman, 5 February 1777, Tyrrell Co., N. C.

LOWE, Artemus and Martha Hobbs, 2 November 1852, Edgefield District, S. C.

LOWNDES, James and Catherine Osborne, 1 December 1799, Charleston, S. C.

LOWMAN, Jacob W. and Lodusky Rish, 15 September 1858, Lexington Co., S. C.

LOWNDES, Rawlins and Mary Cartwright, 31 December 1751, Charleston, S. C.

LOWNDES, Sarah (widow) and Josiah Perry, 17 December 1772, Charleston, S. C.

LOWNDES, Thomas and Allen Deas, 12 February 1828, Charleston, S. C.

LOWREY, Amina Frances and James T. Ouzts, 13 May 1856, Edgefield District, S. C.

LOWREY, Conrad M. and Amina Hamutal Ganes, 4 February 1815, Edgefield District, S. C.

LOWREY, Sarah M. and Abraham Waight, February 1786, Charleston, S. C.

LOWRY, Lydia M. and Baily Otis, 24 March 1825, Mecklenburg Co., N. C.

LOWRY, Mary and David Irwin, 29 October 1843, Mecklenburg Co., N. C.

LOWRY, Peggy and Thomas Cook, 21 December 1807, Mecklenburg Co., N. C.

LOWRY, Susan Ann and John Webb, 13 December 1855, Edgefield District, S. C.

LOWTHER, William and Barbara Gregory, 22 April 1756, Chowan Co., N. C.

LOYD, James and Manima Martin, 15 June 1843, Laurens Co., S. C.

LOYD, John and (Mrs.) Abigail Hartson, 18 August 1743, Chowan Co., N. C.

LUCAS, Elizabeth and Isaac Cullifer, 1784, Tyrrell Co., N. C.

LUCAS, James J. and Carrie McIver, 21 November 1861, Charleston, S. C.

LUCKEY, Isabel and Henry Hendricks, 29 March 1795, Rowan Co., N. C.

LUCKEY, Mary and Charnal Glascock, 25 October 1794, Rowan Co., N. C.

LUCKEY, Mary and Murrell Brown, 24 July 1840, Mecklenburg Co., N. C.

LUCKY, Mary and David Gillespey, 5 April 1783, Rowan Co., N. C.

LUMPKIN, Mary and Nelson Barnard, 2 February 1851, Surrey Co., N. C.

LUSHINGTON, Richard and Charity Ball (widow), 9 July 1774, Charleston, S. C.

LUTEN, Elizabeth and Nathaniel Mathias, 28 March 1758, Chowan Co., N. C.

LUTEN, Frederick and Rachel Jones, 30 September 1772, Chowan Co., N. C.

LUTEN, James and Mary Pugh, 31 May 1750, Chowan Co., N. C.

LUTEN, James and Mary Leary, 31 January 1755, Chowan Co., N. C.

LUTEN, James and Mary Hopkins (widow), 4 March 1754, Chowan Co., N. C.

LUTEN, John and Sarah Worley, 13 May 1749, Chowan Co., N. C.

LUTEN, Mary (widow) and William Badham, 13 November 1758, Chowan Co., N. C.

LUTEN, Sarah and James Cotton, 5 July 1786, Chowan Co., N. C.

LUTEN, Thomas (Jr.) and Catherine Jones, 14 February 1748, Chowan Co., N. C.

LUTEN, William and Sarah Benbury, 23 December 1756, Chowan Co., N. C.

LUTON, Samuel and Elizabeth Ford, 19 November 1757, Chowan Co., N. C.

LUTON, Sarah and William Wesson, 7 May 1744, Chowan Co., N. C.

LUTON, Sarah and William Bonner, 21 August 1744, Chowan Co., N. C.

LUTZEN, Ann M. and Peter Miller, 11 March 1747, Charleston, S. C.

LYALL, Elizabeth and George Erwin, 8 February 1796, Rowan Co., N. C.

LYALL, Mary and Christopher Ervin, 26 February 1782, Rowan Co., N. C.

LYLES, Orah and James H. Irby (Jr.), 20 October 1857, Laurens Co., S. C.

LYNCH, Elija J. and Stephen S. Crittenden, 17 May 1855, Greenville, S. C.

LYNCH, Elizabeth and John Harleston, May 1777, Charleston, S. C.

LYNCH, Sabina and William Cattell, 8 March 1767, Charleston, S. C.

LYNCH, Thomas and Elizabeth Alston, 5 September 1745, Georgetown, S. C.

LYNCH, Thomas and Hannah Motte, 6 March 1755, Charleston, S. C.

LYNCH, Thomas (Jr.) and Betsy Shubrick, 14 May 1772, Charleston, S. C.

LYNN, Mary (widow) and John Hill, 4 January 1780, Rowan Co., N. C.

LYONS, Joseph and Susannah Grim (widow), 4 January 1740 ,Orangeburg Co., S. C.

LYONS, Joseph and Barbara Gartman (widow), 31 December 1741, Orangeburg Co., S. C.

LYONS, Perneasy and Butler Curry, 3 December 1857, Laurens Co., S. C.

Mc

McACHRON, Peter R. and Elizabeth Jingles, 20 April 1824, Mecklenburg Co., N. C.

McADOO, David and Margaret McClain, 6 March 1786, Guilford Co., N. C.

McADOO, John and Judith Stewart, 27 September 1783, Guilford Co, N. C.

McADOO, John and Mary Dennett, 14 August 1782, Guilford Co., N. C.

McAFEE, Ann and John Glenn, 10 September 1848, Laurens Co., S. C.

McALLISTER, Cornelius and Sarah McGinnis, 4 October 1803, Mecklenburg Co., N. C.

McALLISTER, Elisa and William Read, 18 February 1829, Mecklenburg Co., N. C.

McALLISTER, James and Catherine McClain, 7 December 1779, Guilford Co., N. C.

McALPIN, James and Abigail Pratt, 5 May 1783, Tyrrell Co., N. C.

McAULEY, Daniel and Prudence Alexander, 7 February 1802, Mecklenburg Co., N. C.

McAULEY, Elizabeth and Samuel Black, 26 January 1822, Mecklenburg Co., N. C.

McAULEY, Patrick and Margaret Black, 22 March 1803, Mecklenburg Co., N. C.

McBRIDE, Elizabeth and Thomas McClain, 22 February 1786, Guilford Co., N. C.

McBRIDE, Henry and Clarissa Byram, 26 November 1818, Mecklenburg Co., N. C.

McBRIDE, Jean and William Glover, 4 June 1796, Rowan Co., N. C.

McBRIDE, Margaret and Joseph Magankey, 6 December 1793, Guilford Co., N. C.

McBRIDE, Mary and Thomas Gheen, 17 May 1788, Rowan Co., N. C.

McCAHRON, Hector and Elizabeth Huey, 26 July 1791, Mecklenburg Co., N. C.

McCAIN, Elizabeth and Benjamin Huff, 10 July 1764, Chowan Co., N. C.

McCALL, Ann and John Wodrop, 1 October 1800, Charleston, S. C.

McCALL, Eli and Mary Hooks, 22 March 1823, Mecklenburg Co., N. C.

McCALL, Eliza and James Massey, 25 November 1837, Mecklenburg Co., N. C.

McCALL, Horace and Amanda Moore, 16 February 1836, Mecklenburg Co., N. C.

McCALL, Hext and Elizabeth Pickering, October 1783, Charleston, S. C.

McCALL, Horace and Rachel Stilwell, 27 November 1732, Mecklenburg Co., N. C.

McCALL, James and Anne Dart, 4 May 1777, Charleston, S. C.

McCALL, Jane L. and James J. Orr, 1 March 1852, Mecklenburg Co., N. C.

McCALL, John (Jr.) and Charlotte Glen, 9 November 1767, Charleston, S. C.

McCALL, Josiah and Isabel Blair, 12 March 1833, Mecklenburg Co., N. C.

McCALL, Sallie D. and Robert P. Hamer, 31 October 1859, Marion, S. C.

McCALL, Sarah and Joshua Ward, 22 April 1762, Charleston, S. C.

McCALL, Sarah and Henry McIlveen, 29 November 1810, Darlington Co., S. C.

McCALL, Sarah J. and E. P. Rodgers, 28 September 1865, Mecklenburg Co., N. C.

McCALL, Sylvester and Charlotte Yandle, 8 January 1840, Mecklenburg Co., N. C.

McCALL, Thomas and Elizabeth Black, 8 April 1812, Mecklenburg Co., N. C.

McCALLESTER, James and Eliza Freeman, 8 December 1823, Mecklenburg Co., N. C.

McCALLUM, Edward and Effie McLean, 17 January 1837, Robeson Co., N. C.

McCAMPBELL, Marcus and Martha J. Nelson, 19 February 1852, Mecklenburg Co., N. C.

McCANDLY, James and Sarah Blair, 19 March 1793, Guilford Co., N. C.

McCANN, James and Elender Boyd, 15 October 1799, Mecklenburg Co., N. C.

McCARY, Lucinda and William May, 6 January 1856, Laurens Co., S. C.

McCARY, Nancy and William McCary, 3 November 1833, Edgefield District, S. C.

McCARTNEY, Jean and Elias Elston, 12 November 1796, Rowan Co., N. C.

McCARTNEY, Mary and James W. Alexander, 24 December 1835, Abbeville District, S. C.

McCARTY, Erexly and Benjamin Brown, 7 January 1828, Mecklenburg Co., N. C.

McCAULEY, Amanda E. and Thomas M. Black, 11 March 1858, Mecklenburg Co., N. C.

McCAULEY, E. A. and (Miss) M. S. Alexander, 19 December 1849, Mecklenburg Co., N. C.

McCAULEY, Frederick and Margaret A. Hood, 20 November 1827, Mecklenburg Co., N. C.

McCAULEY, Hugh and Nancy D. Alexander, 13 May 1822, Mecklenburg Co., N. C.

McCAULEY, John and Rachel Kerr, 12 September 1795, Mecklenburg Co., N. C.

McCAULEY, Roderick and Margaret Black, 22 March 1803, Mecklenburg Co., N. C.

McCAULLEY, Sarah and William Laider, 14 February 1801, Charleston, S. C.

McCAY, McKinney and Martha Robinson, 3 August 1788, Mecklenburg Co., N. C.

McCLAIN, Catherine and Josiah Gates, 10 January 1764, Rowan Co., N. C.

McCLAIN, Catherine and James McAllister, 7 December 1779, Guilford Co., N. C.

McCLAIN, John and Mary McGinn, 19 November 1790, Guilford Co., N. C.

McCLAIN, Margaret and David McAdoo, 6 March 1786, Guilford Co., N. C.

McCLAIN, Mary and James Galey, 6 August 1766, Rowan Co., N. C.

McCLAIN, Moses and Susanna Dick, 11 April 1796, Guilford Co., N. C.

McCLAIN, Robert and Nancy Eakin, 6 May 1791, Guilford Co., N. C.

McCLAIN, Thomas and Elizabeth McBride, 22 February 1786, Guilford Co., N. C.

McCLAIN, William and Isabel Aiken, 4 January 1800, Guilford Co., N. C.

McCLAIN, William and Betsy Foster, 11 May 1796, Guilford Co., N. C.

McCLANE, Michael and Mary Tom, 16 July 1792, Guilford Co., N. C.

McCLANE, Thomas and Jane Eakin, 22 December 1800, Guilford Co., N. C.

McCLEARY, Abigail and John Calhoun, 19 September 1803, Mecklenburg Co., N. C.

McCLEARY, Eleanor and Robert Montgomery, 15 November 1804, Mecklenburg Co., N. C.

McCLEARY, William and Susan Campbell, 6 July 1795, Mecklenburg Co., N. C.

McCLEESE, John and Zilpha Alexander, 28 March 1778, Tyrrell Co., N. C.

McCLELLAN, Moses and Hannah Roberts, 5 July 1801, St. Pauls Parish, S. C.

McCLELLAND, Archibald and Ester Des Champs, 3 July 1759, Sante, S. C.

McCLENCHER, Alexander and Mary Falks, 10 January 1782, Santee, S. C.

McCLENDON, Jesse and Aley Melton, 23 February 1830, Edgecombe District, S. C.

McCLINTOCK, William and Lela Weatherby, 16 July 1793, Guilford Co., N. C.

McCLUNG, Jean and James Maxwell, 28 March 1788, Mecklenburg Co., N. C.

McCLURE, Alexander and Esther McGill, 10 October 1798, Mecklenburg Co., N. C.

McCLURE, Charles and Sarah Bill, 15 January 1793, Mecklenburg Co., N. C.

McCLURE, Elizabeth and Samuel Harris, 21 March 1796, Mecklenburg Co., N. C.

McCLURE, Jane and Thomas Jameson, 18 April 1844, Mecklenburg Co., N. C.

McCLURE, James and Jane Harlin, 15 December 1800, Mecklenburg Co., N. C.

McCLURE, James and Mary Sharp, 4 May 1803, Mecklenburg Co., N. C.

McCLURE, James and Jane Sawing, 28 July 1834, Mecklenburg Co., N. C.

McCLURE, James L. and E. C. Jamison, 9 June 1847, Mecklenburg Co., N. C.

McCLURE, John and Sarah Allen, 18 December 1792, Mecklenburg Co., N. C.

McCLURE, John and Mary Todd, 11 December 1799, Mecklenburg Co., N. C.

McCLURE, John and Mary Hodge, 10 February 1795, Mecklenburg Co., N. C.

McCLURE, John and Eleanor Ralston, 5 January 1799, Mecklenburg Co., N. C.

McCLURE, Malinda and Marcus Alexander, 21 August 1811, Mecklenburg Co., N. C.

McCLURE, Margaret and Daniel Rice, 19 February 1852, Mecklenburg Co., N. C.

McCLURE, Mary and James Hunter, 7 July 1800, Mecklenburg Co., N. C.

McCLURE, Mary E. and Samson Beaty, 20 November 1833, Mecklenburg Co., N. C.

McCLURE, Robert and Margaret Wallace, 20 February 1793, Mecklenburg Co., N. C.

McCLURE, Thomas and Jane McCombs, 17 July 1799, Mecklenburg Co., N. C.

McCLURE, William and Sarah Crockett, 13 February 1804, Mecklenburg Co., N. C.

McCOLL, Margaret and Thomas H. Harllee, 20 March 1856, Florence Co., S. C.

McCOLL, W. and Lou A. Dudley, 26 April 1848, Marlboro Co., S. C.

McCOLLOUGH, John and Mary Stocker, August 1783, Charleston, S. C.

McCOMB, Alvia and H. W. Black, 8 October 1841, Mecklenburg Co., N. C.

McCOMB, James and Jane G. Oakes, 22 August 1823, Mecklenburg Co., N. C.

McCOMB, James and Amy Morris, 21 March 1828, Mecklenburg Co., N. C.

McCOMB, Jane and Thomas McClure, 17 July 1799, Mecklenburg Co., N. C.

McCOMB, Jane N. and Green W. Caldwell, 6 December 1832, Mecklenburg Co., N. C.

McCOMB, Margaret and Robert Morrison, 4 March 1797, Mecklenburg Co., N. C.

McCOMB, Margaret E. and Hiram Osborn, 30 December 1859, Mecklenburg Co., N. C.

McCOMB, Minty and Robert J. Morris, 20 January 1825, Mecklenburg Co., N. C.

McCOMB, Rachel and George Rutledge, 18 May 1799, Mecklenburg Co., N. C.

McCOMB, Robert and Sarah Huson, 19 August 1817, Mecklenburg Co., N. C.

McCOMB, Sally and James Black, 12 March 1817, Mecklenburg Co., N. C.

McCOMB, Sarah and Andrew Johnston, 17 May 1791, Mecklenburg Co., N. C.

McCOMBS, William and Mary Phillips, 7 May 1794, Mecklenburg Co., N. C.

McCOMBS, William and Elizabeth Harrison, 25 May 1798, Mecklenburg Co., N. C.

McCONNELL, Amanda and Charles P. Townsend, 1 October 1860, Columbia, S. C.

McCONNELL, Andrew and Jane F. Alexander, 26 February 1822, Mecklenburg Co., N. C.

McCONNELL, Benjamin and Sarah Wilson, 1 October 1789, Mecklenburg Co., N. C.

McCONNELL, James H. and Margaret N. Montgomery, 28 July 1857, Mecklenburg Co., N. C.

McCONNELL, John and Martha Galloway, 15 December 1835, Mecklenburg Co., N. C.

McCORCLE, Alexander and Emily Odell, 9 October 1855, Laurens Co., S. C.

McCORD, Catherine (Mrs.) and Isaac Chanler, 20 December 1800, Charleston, S. C.

McCORD, James R. and Louisa M. Kenney, 1 September 1853, Edgefield District, S. C.

McCORD, Jane C. and James McGinn, 6 August 1823, Mecklenburg Co., N. C.

McCORD, John and Sophinisba Russell, 5 February 1751, Orangeburg Co., S. C.

McCORD, John and Betsy Russell, 16 May 1803, Mecklenburg Co., N. C.

McCORD, John and Mary Means, 10 January 1827, Mecklenburg Co., N. C.

McCORD, Louisa and Augustine Smythe, 27 June 1865, Charleston, S. C.

McCORD, Margaret A. and William Marshall, 5 August 1841, Mecklenburg Co., N. C.

McCORD, Martha K. and Joseph B. McDonald, 24 October 1827, Mecklenburg Co., N. C.

McCORD, Robert C. and Martha Van Pelt, 7 March 1827, Mecklenburg Co., N. C.

McCORD, Rosanna B. and Thomas Jamieson, 9 December 1851, Mecklenburg Co., N. C.

McCORD, Thomas and Rebecca Thompson, 26 January 1819, Mecklenburg Co., N. C.

McCORD, William and Hannah Kennedy, 9 September 1794, Mecklenburg Co., N. C.

McCORD, William and Rachel Campbell, 19 March 1798, Mecklenburg Co., N. C.

McCORD, William and Mary W. Yandell, 24 March 1801, Mecklenburg Co., N. C.

McCORKLE, Hannah and John McNeely, 26 February 1798, Mecklenburg Co., N. C.

McCORKLE, Hannah and Leroy Rea, 8 January 1839, Mecklenburg Co., N. C.

McCORKLE, Hugh P. and Cynthia C. Beaty, 20 February 1843, Mecklenburg Co., N. C.

McCORKLE, Isabella and William Beaty, 21 April 1791, Mecklenburg Co., N. C.

McCORKLE, Jane and Francis Alexander, 5 November 1815, Mecklenburg Co., N. C.

McCORKLE, James and Margaret Kennedy, 14 February 1804, Mecklenburg Co., N. C.

McCORKLE, James and Mary J. Orr, 14 January 1840, Mecklenburg Co., N. C.

McCORKLE, Margaret and Matthew Alexander, 5 October 1824, Mecklenburg Co., N. C.

McCORKLE, Mary and Matthew Ormond, 12 February 1841, Mecklenburg Co., N. C.

McCORKLE, Nelson and Matilda Blount, 28 October 1839, Mecklenburg Co., N. C.

McCORKLE, Patrick and Union Bevins, 15 September 1815, Mecklenburg Co., N. C.

McCORKLE, Sarah M. and James Clark, 15 November 1836, Mecklenburg Co., N. C.

McCORKLE, Thomas and Katherine Evitts, 15 October 1807, Mecklenburg Co., N. C.

McCORKLE, Thomas and Eliza Westmoreland, 21 June 1827, Mecklenburg Co., N. C.

McCORMICK, Charles and Elizabeth Edwards, 13 October 1779, Guilford Co., N. C.

McCORMICK, Daniel C. and Mary McLean, 10 February 1830, Robeson Co., N. C.

McCORMICK, Dougal and Elizabeth Margaret Drake, 29 November 1859, Robeson Co., N. C.

McCORMICK, Nathaniel and Mary Spencer, 28 December 1758, Santee, S. C.

McCORMICK, Rebecca and John McGill, 12 May 1796, Mecklenburg Co., N. C.

McCORMICK, Robert and Adaith Singleton, 8 June 1799, Mecklenburg Co., N. C.

McCOY, Esther and Asahel Boggs, 25 January 1792, Mecklenburg Co., N. C.

McCOY, Frances and Ruben Herndon, 9 August 1784, Orange Co., N. C.

McCOY, Hugh A. and Frances Beaty, 5 September 1838, Mecklenburg Co., N. C.

McCOY, Jennet and John McMurray, 1 February 1804, Mecklenburg Co., N. C.

McCOY, John and Esther Fraser, 16 March 1799, Mecklenburg Co., N. C.

McCOY, John H. and Clarissa C. Beaty, 8 February 1826, Mecklenburg Co., N. C.

McCOY, Lawson H. and Dorris, Berryhill, 3 January 1820, Mecklenburg Co., N. C.

McCOY, Margaret L. and George Houston, 12 January 1825, Mecklenburg Co., N. C.

McCOY, McKinney and Martha Robinson, 3 August 1825, Mecklenburg Co., N. C.

McCOY, William and Sally Cochran, 16 October 1816, Mecklenburg Co., N. C.

McCRACKEN, Barbara M. and James F. Caldwell, 29 December 1852, Mecklenburg Co., N. C.

McCRACKEN, Betsy and Sample Alexander, 21 March 1809, Mecklenburg Co., N. C.

McCRACKEN, Elihu and Esther Kerr, 12 April 1849, Mecklenburg Co., N. C.

McCRACKEN, Jane and David Orr, 14 April 1857, Mecklenburg Co., N. C.

McCRACKEN, John and Nancy Jolly, 27 September 1824, Mecklenburg Co., N. C.

McCRACKEN, Margaret and William Began, 12 September 1791, Mecklenburg Co., N. C.

McCRACKEN, Robert C. and Jane D. McKelvey, 31 July 1845, Mecklenburg Co., N. C.

McCRARY, Elizabeth and Michael Myers, 17 October 1778, Guilford Co., N. C.

McCRARY, Robert and Nelly Halter, 13 September 1800, Guilford Co., N. C.

McCRARY, William and Nancy McCrary, 3 November 1833, Edgefield District, S. C.

McCRARY, James and Elizabeth Nabors, 15 September 1857, Laurens Co., S. C.

McCREA, David H. and Violet A. Hipp, 15 December 1830, Mecklenburg Co., N. C.

McCREADY, John and Jane Johnson, 1 March 1797, Charleston, S. C.

McCREARY, John and Elizabeth Yandell, 27 August 1799, Mecklenburg Co., N. C.

McCREE, Mary and Joseph Gibson, 16 December 1789, Rowan Co., N. C.

McCRORY, William and Therza Neel, 21 July 1828, Mecklenburg Co., N. C.

McCROSKY, Mary and Jeremiah Hood, 16 January 1816, Mecklenburg Co., N. C.

McCUBBINS, James S. and Margaret Bell, 18 October 1860, Statesville, N. C.

McCUE, Margaret and Samuel Dorrah, 26 December 1865, Laurens Co., S. C.

McCUISTION, James and Jean Nicholson, 11 September 1792, Guilford Co., N. C.

McCUISTION, Robert and Isabel Cunningham, 23 November 1792, Guilford Co., N. C.

McCUISTION, Thomas and Mary Nicholson, 19 September 1786, Guilford Co., N. C.

McCULLOCH, Elijah and Jenny Wake, 10 November 1801, Mecklenburg Co., N. C.

McCULLOCH, James and Jenny Potts, 13 January 1807, Mecklenburg Co., N. C.

McCULLOCH, Esther and Drury Morrow, 17 January 1820, Mecklenburg Co., N. C.

McCULLOCH, John and Mary Shanks, 7 December 1797, Mecklenburg Co., N. C.

McCULLOCH, John and D. M. Robinson, 5 June 1829, Mecklenburg Co., N. C.

McCULLOUGH, John J. and Rose E. Mitchell, 17 March 1834, Edgefield District, S. C.

McCULLOUGH, Jenny and David Morrow, 25 November 1802, Mecklenburg Co., N. C.

McCULLOUGH, Polly and Nelson Bird, 21 May 1816, Mecklenburg Co., N. C.

McCUNE, Mary and James Finney, 25 March 1776, Rowan Co., N. C.

McDANIEL, Donnell and Mary Hapsey, 23 October 1786, Orange Co., N. C.

McDANIEL, Elizabeth and Mastin Henderson, 22 September 1859, Laurens Co., S. C.

McDANIEL, Sarah and Joseph Gist, 28 December 1800, Union Co., S. C.

McDARREL, Betsy and John Howard, 21 October 1791, Rowan Co., N. C.

McDOLE, Anderson and Sarah Ball, 10 February 1848, Laurens Co., S. C.

McDONALD, Ann and William Anderson, 2 November 1762, Edgecombe Co., N. C.

McDONALD, Caroline and Jacob Inglit, December 1839, Edgefield District, S. C.

McDONALD, Elizabeth and Thomas T. Johnson, 21 July 1814, Mecklenburg Co., N. C.

McDONALD, George W. and Anne E. Campbell, 6 August 1834, Mecklenburg Co., N. C.

McDONALD, Joseph B. and Martha K. McCord, 24 October 1827, Mecklenburg Co., N. C.

McDONALD, Peggy and Daniel McLeod, 8 June 1809, Mecklenburg Co., N. C.

McDONALD, Thomas and Susan M. Alexander, 20 July 1825, Mecklenburg Co., N. C.

McDONALD, Will and Elizabeth Sadler, 16 September 1789, Mecklenburg Co., N. C.

McDORMAN, John and Judy Bunck, 12 October 1799, Guilford Co., N. C.

McDOUGALL, John and Nancy Stinson, 9 December 1794, Mecklenburg Co., N. C.

McDOUGALL, Mary (Mrs.) and Nicholas Darrell, 9 August 1800, Charleston, S. C.

McDOWELL, Alice J. and Moses Neely, 22 March 1825, Mecklenburg Co., N. C.

McDOWELL, Arabella and Samuel M. Meek, 19 May 1813, Charleston, S. C.

McDOWELL, Dolly and Upton Byram, 13 December 1793, Mecklenburg Co., N. C.

McDOWELL, Hugh and Peggy Irwin, 31 March 1802, Mecklenburg Co., N. C.

McDOWELL, James and Catherine Cochran, 30 June 1799, Charleston, S. C.

McDOWELL, Jane P. and Jonathan Read, 2 January 1822, Mecklenburg Co., N. C.

McDOWELL, John and Rebecca Davis, 2 September 1799, Mecklenburg Co., N. C.

McDOWELL, Sarah and Robert Hillis, 1 April 1776, Rowan Co., N. C.

McDOWELL, Sarah and Thomas Ferguson, 30 March 1776, Rowan Co., N. C.

McDOWELL, Sarah and Washington Mitchell, 14 October 1836, Guilford Co., N. C.

McDOWELL, Savannah and Thomas Timmerman, 14 October 1852, Edgefield District, S. C.

McDUFFIE, John and Mary Douglas, 20 May 1807, Robeson Co., N. C.

McEACHIN, Mary and James McLean, 21 March 1823, Robeson Co., N. C.

McELHENNY, James (Rev.) and Susanna Wilkinson, 13 March 1800, Charleston, S. C.

McELROY, Archibald and Martha Craig, 1799, Pendleton District, S. C.

McELROY, James and Sarah Shreyburg, 13 August 1801, Mecklenburg Co., N. C.

McELROY, William and Martha Brown, 28 January 1801, Mecklenburg Co., N. C.

McEWEN, Duncan and Elizabeth Grier, 5 April 1820, Mecklenburg Co., N. C.

McEWEN, Ellen and James Moore, 12 June 1793, Mecklenburg Co., N. C.

McEWEN, Frances and John Cochran, 3 August 1791, Mecklenburg Co., N. C.

McEWEN, Lena J. and James Rea, 30 July 1857, Mecklenburg Co., N. C.

McEWEN, Margaret and Joseph Rogers, 9 August 1822, Mecklenburg Co., N. C.

McEWEN, Samuel and Sarah Parks, 1 December 1795, Mecklenburg Co., N. C.

McEWEN, Sarah and Ezekial Black, 26 October 1807, Mecklenburg Co., N. C.

McEWEN, Selina and Abner McGinty, 5 August 1816, Mecklenburg Co., N. C.

McFARLAND, Elizabeth and Andrew Ferguson, 11 May 1791, Rowan Co., N. C.

McFARLAND, Jacob and Jane Varner, 14 April 1792, Mecklenburg Co., N. C.

McFARLIN, Benjamin and Elizabeth Nelson, 9 December 1774, Guilford Co., N. C.

McFARUN, Abigail and Abisba Alexander, 23 August 1798, Mecklenburg Co., N. C.

McFATERIDGE, William and Ann Dixon, 1 January 1799, Guilford Co., N. C.

McFERRIN, Robert and Margaret Poterfield, 24 January 1856, Edgefield District, S. C.

McGAHEE, Jane and Thomas Gray, 1 February 1786, Rowan Co., N. C.

McGAUGHEY, Elizabeth and Richard Holmes, 1 January 1781, Rowan Co., N. C.

McGEE, Andrew and Easter McMinn, 20 January 1792, Guilford Co., N. C.

McGEE, Catherine E. and James L. Alexander, 14 December 1854, Mecklenburg Co., N. C.

McGEE, Emily and William Reddy, 6 February 1860, Mecklenburg Co., N. C.

McGEE, John and Hannah Neathery, 2 May 1791, Guilford Co., N. C.

McGEE, John and Agnes Walker, 27 December 1788, Mecklenburg Co., N. C.

McGEE, Lemuel and Sussannah White, 20 September 1822, Granville Co., N. C.

McGEE, Robert and Sarah Capps, 7 April 1831, Mecklenburg Co., N. C.

McGIBBONS, Nancy and Robert Matthews, 11 February 1802, Mecklenburg Co., N. C.

McGIBNEY, Jane P. and Jesse M. Clark, 16 April 1825, Mecklenburg Co., N. C.

McGIBNEY, Patrick and Margaret ———, 16 September 1783, Guilford Co., N. C.

McGILBERY, B. F. and C. Bristow, 23 January 1850, Marlboro Co., S. C.

McGILL, Esther and Alexander McClure, 10 October 1798, Mecklenburg Co., N. C.

McGILL, John and Rebecca McCormick, 12 May 1796, Mecklenburg Co., N. C.

McGINN, Christine and William Rude, 26 September 1806, Mecklenburg Co., N. C.

McGINN, Elizabeth and Thomas Jamieson, 7 July 1819, Mecklenburg Co., N. C.

McGINN, James and Christina Todd, 13 October 1794, Mecklenburg Co., N. C.

McGINN, James and Jane C. McCord, 6 August 1823, Mecklenburg Co., N. C.

McGINN, Mary and John McClain, 19 November 1790, Guilford Co., N. C.

McGINN, John and Rebecca McCormick, 12 May 1896, Mecklenburg Co., N. C.

McGINN, John and Margaret Boal, 3 November 1796, Mecklenburg Co., N. C.

McGINN, Thomas and Ann McKinley, 22 July 1795, Mecklenburg Co., N. C.

McGINN, Thomas and Mary Todd, 16 December 1800, Mecklenburg Co., N. C.

McGINN, William A. and Isabella Dunn, 28 August 1825, Mecklenburg Co., N. C.

McGINNESS, James P. and Jane L. Caldwell, 2 March 1840, Mecklenburg Co., N. C.

McGINNESS, Joseph and Milly Orr, 14 April 1823, Mecklenburg Co., N. C.

McGINNESS, John and Parmelia Park, 6 September 1825, Mecklenburg Co., N. C.

McGINNISS, Martha and James F. Alexander, 16 May 1859, Mecklenburg Co., N. C.

McGINNIS, Sarah and Cornelius McAllister, 4 October 1803, Mecklenburg Co., N. C.

McGINTY, Abner and Selina McEwen, 5 August 1816, Mecklenburg Co., N. C.

McGRATH, Cervas and (Mrs.) Elizabeth Neil, 15 September 1746, Chowan Co., N. C.

McGREGOR, Darnel and Phebe Smith, 25 March 1761, Santee, S. C.

McGREGOR, Daniel and Susan Laurens, 25 February 1768, Santee, S. C.

McGREGOR, Elizabeth and Stephen Sullivan, 23 December 1762, Santee, S. C.

McGREGOR, Mary and William Roach, 15 May 1797, Charleston, S. C.

McGUIRE, John and Sarah Bunch, 10 December 1778, Chowan Co., N. C.

McGUIRE, Mary Ann and Isaac Gillespie, 12 April 1791, Rowan Co., N. C.

McHEATH, James and Ann McHerron, 24 December 1800, Charleston, S. C.

McHENRY, George and Ferebee Butler, 9 March 1764, Tyrrell Co., N. C.

McHENRY, Sarah and Timothy Brogdon, 18 August 1791, Bertie Co., N. C.

McHERRON, Ann and James McHeath, 24 December 1800, Charleston, S. C.

McILVEEN, Elizabeth and Duncan McMillan, 13 March 1849, Darlinton Co., S. C.

McILVEEN, Henry and Sarah McCall, 29 November 1810, Darlington Co., S. C.

McILVEEN, Susannah and John Dougal McNeill, 1853, Sumter Co., S. C.

McINTIRE, Isaac and Betty Thompson, 16 November 1811, Mecklenburg Co., N. C.

McINTIRE, Thomas and Cornelia Cohen, 18 December 1799, Charleston, S. C.

McINTOSH, James and Fannie C. Higgins, 25 November 1862, Newberry, S. C.

McINTOSH, Lachlan and Elizabeth Smith, 17 October 1765, Stono, S. C.

McINTYRE, Sarah C. and Peter E. Ross, 11 March 1830, Mecklenburg Co., N. C.

McIVER, Carrie and James J. Lucas, 21 November 1861, Charleston, S. C.

McIVER, Cornelia and Zimmerman Davis, 10 November 1857, Charleston, S. C.

McIVER, Henry and Caroline H. Powe, 7 June 1849, Cheraw, S. C.

McJUNKIN, Joseph and Annie Thomas, 9 March 1779, Union Co., S. C.

McKAVEN, Adam and Minty Doherty, 9 February 1811, Mecklenburg Co., N. C.

McKEBBINS, Mary and Robert Matthews, 11 February 1802, Mecklenburg Co., N. C.

McKEE, Hannah and John Reynolds, 17 October 1803, Mecklenburg Co., N. C.

McKEE, John and Elizabeth Hodge, 23 April 1798, Mecklenburg Co., N. C.

McKEE, John and Agnes Ramsey, 18 November 1797, Mecklenburg Co., N. C.

McKEE, Mary and Andrew McMekin, 13 April 1792, Mecklenburg Co., N. C.

McKEE, Martha and Isaac Herron, 25 June 1802, Mecklenburg Co., N. C.

McKEE, Ruth and William C. Miller, 14 January 1837, Mecklenburg Co., N. C.

McKEEN, Adam and Elizabeth Oldham, 30 April 1756, Chowan Co., N. C.

McKEEN, Alexander (Jr.) and Mary Doak, 22 December 1795, Guilford Co., N. C.

McKEEN, Hance and Jenny Forbush, 3 October 1787, Guilford Co., N. C.

McKELVEY, Caroline and James McClure, 16 January 1843, Mecklenburg Co., N. C.

McKELVEY, James T. and Nancy Patterson, 8 February 1837, Mecklenburg Co., N. C.

McKELVEY, Jane D. and Robert C. McCracken, 31 July 1845, Mecklenburg Co., N. C.

McKELVEY, John M. and Jane Jameson, 31 March 1825, Mecklenburg Co., N. C.

McKELVEY, William and Betsy Plummer, 3 January 1831, Mecklenburg Co., N. C.

McKELL, Michael and Nancy Small, 13 July 1785, Chowan Co., N. C.

McKELLTON, William and Mary Hamilton, 24 June 1787, Guilford Co., N. C.

McKENNA, Rebecca and George Julian, 9 April 1791, Mecklenburg Co., N. C.

McKENNEY, Mary and Archibald Murphy, 30 March 1798, Mecklenburg Co., N. C.

McKENNEY, Sarah and Richard Horn, 28 May 1801, Mecklenburg Co., N. C.

McKENSEY, James and Susane Thompson, 5 June 1779, Guilford Co., N. C.

McKENZIE, Isabella M. and Joel F. Adams, 9 January 1861, Mecklenburg Co., N. C.

McKEWN, Sally and Andrew Johnson, 26 February 1772, Charleston, S. C.

McKEWN, Susannah and (Dr.) George Haig, 2 May 1769, St. Pauls Parish, S. C.

McKIBBEN, Alexander and Agnes Wiley, 1 June 1796, Mecklenburg Co., N. C.

McKIBBEN, John and Mary Duest, 31 January 1825, Mecklenburg Co., N. C.

McKIBBEN, Margaret and John Matthews, 10 November 1794, Mecklenburg Co., N. C.

McKIBBEN, Rebecca and James Miller, 2 May 1796, Mecklenburg Co., N. C.

McKIBBEN, Robert L. and Jane Blount, 13 July 1840, Mecklenburg Co., N. C.

McKIBBEN, Thomas and Elizabeth Duffey, 1 March 1825, Mecklenburg Co., N. C.

McKIBBENS, John and Sarah Hannigan, 17 September 1827, Mecklenburg Co., N. C.

McKINLEY, Ann and Thomas McGinn, 22 July 1795, Mecklenburg Co., N. C.

McKINLEY, Robert and Peggy Neil, 23 August 1802, Mecklenburg Co., N. C.

McKINLEY, Stephen and Dovey L. Robinson, 4 January 1824, Mecklenburg Co., N. C.

McKINLY, Elizabeth and James Cain, 21 December 1781, Orange Co., N. C.

McKINNEY, Nathaniel and —— Smith, 12 November 1792, Guilford Co., N. C.

McKINNEY, Seth and Jane Merchant, 14 January 1800, Mecklenburg Co., N. C.

McKINNEY, William and Elinor James, 13 February 1790, Guilford Co., N. C.

McKINZIE, Charlotte and George Harper, 27 December 1809, Charleston, S. C.

McKNIGHT, Betsy and German Hath, 4 November 1796, Rowan Co., N. C.

McKNIGHT, Catherine L. and James H. McWorter, 28 September 1826, Mecklenburg Co., N. C.

McKNIGHT, Catherine C. and Joseph Cochran, 8 April 1840, Mecklenburg Co., N. C.

McKNIGHT, Elizabeth, and Etheldred Ellis, 14 July 1795, Rowan Co., N. C.

McKNIGHT, James and Hannah Montgomery, 13 November 1792, Guilford Co., N. C.

McKNIGHT, James and Kezia Addison, May 1784, St. Thomas Parish, S. C.

McKNIGHT, James and Ann Reed, 6 June 1796, Mecklenburg Co., N. C.

McKNIGHT, Nancy and Samuel Bigham, 24 April 1818, Mecklenburg Co., N. C.

McKNIGHT, Robert and Margaret Moore, 27 January 1803, Mecklenburg Co., N. C.

McKNIGHT, Thomas and Margaret Falls, 30 December 1795, Mecklenburg Co., N. C.

McKNIGHT, William and Mary Cumings, 16 January 1802, Guilford Co., N. C.

McKOIN, Thomas and Elizabeth Taylor, 13 May 1779, Chowan Co., N. C.

McKONEY, Nathan and Sarah Bowen, 10 November 1790, Guilford Co., N. C.

McKRUM, Samuel and Eleanor Hart, 2 June 1800, Mecklenburg Co., N. C.

McLAIN, George and Margaret McLain, 28 February 1820, Mecklenburg Co., N. C.

McLARTY, Elizabeth and John Neely, 24 February 1806, Mecklenburg Co., N. C.

McLARTY, Margaret and Edwin Maxwell, 16 June 1832, Mecklenburg Co., N. C.

McLARTY, Polly C. and John F. Morris, 22 July 1830, Mecklenburg Co., N. C.

McLARTY, Samuel W. and Mary Polk, 16 May 1826, Mecklenburg Co., N. C.

McLEAN, Catherine and Neil McLean, October 1819, Robeson Co., N. C.

McLEAN, Christiana and John McLean, 14 October 1813, Robeson Co., N. C.

McLEAN, Daniel H. and Margaret McLean, 17 January 1837, Robeson Co., N. C.

McLEAN, David and Catherine Birney, 5 June 1790, Guilford Co., N. C.

McLEAN, Effie and Edward McCallum, 17 January 1837, Robeson Co., N. C.

McLEAN, James and Mary McEachin, 21 March 1823, Robeson Co., N. C.

McLEAN, John and Mary Pratt (widow), August 1783, Charleston, S. C.

McLEAN, John and Sarah McLean, 14 February 1788, Robeson Co., N. C.

McLEAN, John and Christiana McLean, 14 October 1813, Robeson Co., N. C.

McLEAN, John M. and Elizabeth Dickson, 23 March 1831, Mecklenburg Co., N. C.

McLEAN, Margaret and Daniel H. McLean, 17 January 1837, Robeson Co., N. C.

McLEAN, Margaret and George McLean, 28 February 1820, Mecklenburg Co., N. C.

McLEAN, Martha A. and Samuel River, 14 February 1835, Mecklenburg Co., N. C.

McLEAN, Matilda and James Scott Alexander, 14 December 1814, Mecklenburg Co., N. C.

McLEAN, Hugh and Elizabeth Morris, 24 April 1810, Mecklenburg Co., N. C.

McLEAN, Mary and Daniel C. McCormick, 10 February 1830, Robeson Co., N. C.

McLEAN, Murdoch (Dr.) and Mary W. Pugh, 14 February 1826, Robeson Co., N. C.

McLEAN, Nancy and Alexander McRae, 13 November 1823, Robeson Co., N. C.

McLEAN, Neil and Catherine McLean, October 1819, Robeson Co., N. C.

McLEAN, Patsy and Allen Roach, 27 August 1824, Mecklenburg Co., N. C.

McLEAN, Pruda and Peyton Crane, 10 March 1823, Mecklenburg Co., N. C.

McLEAN, Robert G. and Catherine E. Sandifer, 3 December 1846, Mecklenburg Co., N. C.

McLEAN, Sarah and John McLean, 14 February 1788, Robeson Co., N. C.

McLEAN, Sarah and Alexander Watson, 12 January 1826, Robeson Co., N. C.

McLEAN, William and Mary Davidson, 1792, Gaston Co., N. C.

McLEARY, Isabelle and John W. Auton, 18 May 1847, Mecklenburg Co., N. C.

McLEARY, James and Elizabeth Boyd, 27 February 1822, Mecklenburg Co., N. C.

McLEARY, John and Isabella Dunn, 5 February 1823, Mecklenburg Co., N. C.

McLEARY, Martha and Richard Robinson, 14 June 1790, Mecklenburg Co., N. C.

McLEARY, Melissa and John Rudisill, 27 July 1821, Mecklenburg Co., N. C.

McLEARY, William H. and Eliza Davis, 23 January 1822, Mecklenburg Co., N. C.

McLELLAND, Joseph and Margaret Lawrence, 25 January 1792, Mecklenburg Co., N. C.

McLENDON, Fannie and Gasper Gallman, 6 February 1838, Edgefield District, S. C.

McLENEN, Ann Margaret and John Henry Shilling, 6 August 1754, Orangeburg Co., S. C.

McLEOD, Alexander and Mary Brown, 9 December 1826, Mecklenburg Co., N. C.

McLEOD, Daniel and Peggy McDonald, 8 June 1809, Mecklenburg Co., N. C.

McLEOD, W. A. and M. A. E. Alford, 24 February 1848, Marlboro Co., S. C.

McLIN, Robert L. and Ann Blair, 20 June 1816, Guilford, N. C.

McLURE, David and Nancy Jackson, 24 February 1823, Mecklenburg Co., N. C.

McLURE, James and Caroline McKelvey, 16 January 1843, Mecklenburg Co., N. C.

McLURE, Robert and Eliza Davis, 24 November 1826, Mecklenburg Co., N. C.

McMANUS, Amos, (2nd m) and Martha Ann Hough, 18 December 1849, Lancaster Co., S. C.

McMANUS, Amos and Rebecca J. Roberts, 31 March 1864, Lancaster Co., S. C.

McMATH, Margary and William Boswell, 5 November 1761, Chowan Co., N. C.

McMEKIN, Andrew and Mary McKee, 13 April 1792, Mecklenburg Co., N. C.

McMILLAN, Duncan and Elizabeth McIlveen, 13 March 1849, Darlington Co., S. C.

McMILLAN, Ruth Ann and William Harrison Fisher, 11 April 1861, Sampson Co., N. C.

McMILLAN, Thomas and Louisa R. Ray, 25 February 1830, Camden, S. C.

McMINN, Easter and Andrew McGee, 20 January 1792, Guilford Co., N. C.

McMIRL, Elihu and Jean Donnell, 11 March 1800, Guilford Co., N. C.

McMURRAY, James and Elizabeth Brown, 14 April 1774, Guilford Co., N. C.

McMURRAY, John and Jennet S. McCoy, 1 February 1804, Mecklenburg Co., N. C.

McMURRAY, Margaret and Samuel Mitchell, 19 October 1795, Guilford Co., N. C.

McMURRAY, James and Elizabeth Smith, 21 November 1795, Guilford Co., N. C.

McMURRY, Robert and Mary Scott, 28 December 1791, Guilford Co., N. C.

McNABNEY, Mrs. and (Dr.) William Cleiland, 13 April 1732, Charleston, S. C.

McNARY, Boyd and Elizabeth Jones, 3 March 1842, Guilford Co., N. C.

McNEAL, Thomas and Clarissa Polk, 29 September 1803, Mecklenburg Co., N. C.

McNEEL, William R. and Margaret Porter, 24 February 1831, Mecklenburg Co., N. C.

McNEELY, Agnes and Ebenezer Singletary, 1778 Darlington Co., S. C.

McNEELY, David and Hezra Fincher, 15 May 1798, Mecklenburg Co., N. C.

McNEELY, James and Lavina Scott, 13 November 1828, Guilford Co., N. C.

McNEELY, James and Isabella Mitchell, 25 August 1746, Guilford Co., N. C.

McNEELY, John and Hannah McCorkle, 26 February 1798, Mecklenburg Co., N. C.

McNEIL, Martha (Mrs.) and Ralph McNeil, 28 December 1784, Charleston, S. C.

McNEIL, Ralph and (Mrs.) Martha McNeil, 28 December 1784, Charleston, S. C.

McNEILL, John Dougal and Susannah McIleveen, 1853, Sumter Co., S. C.

McNEVIN, Elizabeth and Robert Hood, 15 May 1797, Mecklenburg Co., N. C.

McNILAGO, Alexander and Margaret Field, September 1784, Charleston, C. C.

McPHEARSON, Menoah and Nancy Henderson, 4 February 1845, Laurens Co., S. C.

McPHEARSON, Sarah and William Graden, 6 December 1855, Laurens Co., S. C.

McPHEETERS, Margaret Ann and John Wilson, 29 January 1841, Milton, N. C.

McPHEETERS, Martha J. and Edward J. Means, 18 April 1860, Fairfield Co., S. C.

McPHERSON, James and Lydia J. Glenn, 10 January 1772, Santee, S. C.

McPHERSON, Matthew and Elizabeth Wilson, 28 September 1797, Iredell Co., N. C.

McPHERSON, Sarah and John Alston, 26 March 1801, Prince William Parish, S. C.

McQUEEN, Alexander and Elizabeth Fuller, 14 January 1774, Berkeley Co., S. C.

McQUEEN, Anne and Thomas Netherclift, 14 February 1767, Charleston, S. C.

McQUESTON, Thomas and Sally Stephens, 11 December 1815, Mecklenburg Co., N. C.

McQUINN, John and Peggy Atchison, 17 November 1827, Mecklenburg Co., N. C.

McQUIRE, Harriet and (Capt,) J. J. Sentell, 17 December 1839, Edgefield District, S. C.

McRACHIN, Esther and John Clancy, 5 November 1822, Mecklenburg Co., N. C.

McRAE, Alexander and Nancy McLean, 13 November 1823, Robeson Co., N. C.

McRAE, Duncan and Mrs. Steward, May 1785, Cheraws, S. C.

McRARY, David and Charlotte Reed, 4 September 1839, Mecklenburg Co., N. C.

McREA, Margaret M. and William C. Johnston, 1 November 1823, Mecklenburg Co., N. C.

McREA, Susanna and Joseph Beaty, 14 August 1798, Mecklenburg Co., N. C.

McREAM, Rachel M. and John Rogers, 17 September 1825, Mecklenburg Co., N. C.

McREAM, Stephen and Mary Ferguson, 3 January 1819, Mecklenburg Co., N. C.

McREE, Andrew and Martha Elliot, 28 May 1791, Mecklenburg Co., N. C.

McREE, David and Sarah Orr, 4 November 1823, Mecklenburg Co., N. C.

McREE, Diana and David Hart, 16 August 1797, Mecklenburg Co., N. C.

McREE, James and Jamina Carothers, 28 March 1825, Mecklenburg Co., N. C.

McREE, Mary and Isaac W. Auten, 1 September 1857, Mecklenburg Co., N. C.

McREE, Polly and David Hutchinson, 22 May 1805, Mecklenburg Co., N. C.

McREE, William and Jane Graham, 23 December 1814, Mecklenburg Co., N. C.

McREE, Winslow J. and Peggy Patterson, 27 June 1808, Mecklenburg Co., N. C.

McREEM, Samuel J. and Sarah H. Rodgers, 2 March 1835, Mecklenburg Co., N. C.

McREEM, Stephen and Matilda P. Rodgers, 8 April 1826, Mecklenburg Co., N. C.

McRONEY, Isaac and Rhody Aydlett, 15 February 1797, Guilford Co., N. C.

McSHEEHEY, Miles and Penelope Stacy, 20 April 1776, Chowan Co., N. C.

McSPAREN, John and Elizabeth Patrick, 9 January 1794, Guilford Co., N. C.

McSPARRON, Margaret and Avery S. Rea, 5 March 1823, Mecklenburg Co., N. C.

McWHANN, William and (Mrs.) Jane Thompson, 3 August 1786, Charleston, S. C.

McWHORTER, James H. and Catherine L. McKnight, 28 September 1826, Mecklenburg Co., N. C.

McWHORTER, Moses and Agnes Jenness, 26 August 1793, Mecklenburg Co., N. C.

McWILLIAMS, Isabel and John Crowell, 2 February 1797, Mecklenburg Co., N. C.

M

MABLEY, Hannah and Coleman Harris, 25 April 1839, Mecklenburg Co., N. C.

MACAY, Elizabeth and Radford Ellis, 6 May 1778, Rowan Co., N. C.

MACKAY, Joel and Sarah Joyce, 24 March 1772, Guilford Co., N. C.

MACKEY, Elizabeth and Simon Theus, 12 February 1754, Orangeburg Co., S. C.

MACKEY, Mary (widow) and Edward Lovell, 1742, Chowan Co., N. C.

MACKEY, Mary and Robert Davidson, 25 February 1776, Tyrrell Co., N. C.

MACKEY, Polly and Arnout Schermerhorn, 26 February 1769, Charleston, S .C.

MACKEY, William and Susanna Walker, 23 January 1779, Tyrrell Co., N. C.

MACKENZIE, John and Sarah Smith, 2 April 1769, Charleston, S. C.

MACKMANUS, Elizabeth and Lewis Bledsoe, 21 February 1850, Edgefield District, S. C.

MACY, Anna and Enoch Macy, October 1763, Guilford, N. C.

MACY, Elizabeth and Uriah Barnard, 21 February 1782, Center, N. C.

MACY, Enoch and Ann Macy, October 1763, Guilford, N. C.

MACY, Joseph and Mary Way, 17 September 1798, Guilford Co., N. C.

MACY, Robert and Elizabeth Gardner, 11 December 1799, Guilford Co., N. C.

MADDEN, Charles and Sarah Carter, 19 December 1865, Laurens Co., S. C.

MADDEN, Moses and Martha Tinsley, 21 December 1852, Laurens Co., S. C.

MADDEN, Sophy and Leander Rodgers, 21 February 1858, Laurens Co., S. C.

MAGAHA, Thomas A. and Eloisa Potts, 14 March 1824, Mecklenburg Co., N. C.

MAGANKEY, Joseph and Margaret McBride, 6 December 1793, Guilford Co., N. C.

MAGAW, Anne and Richard Nicholls, 18 January 1768, Charleston, S. C.

MAGAW, Sarah and (Dr.) Benjamin Willphy, 23 June 1771, Charleston, S. C.

MAGEE, David and Elizabeth Daniel 22 November 1796, Guilford Co., N. C.

MAGEE, John and Ann Shaw, 22 July 1788, Guilford Co., N. C.

MAGEE, Rachel and Lemmy Moore, 21 January 1818, Guilford Co., N. C.

MAGEE, Samuel (of Philadelphia) and Elizabeth Harrys, 3 May 1785, Charleston, S. C.

MAHAFFEY, Hiram and Gersette Henderson, 30 January 1865, Laurens Co., S. C.

MAHAFFEY, Jane and John Power, 20 December 1865, Laurens Co., S. C.

MAHAFFEY, Joseph and Sarah Pharr, 9 March 1826, Mecklenburg Co., N. C.

MAHAFFEY, Sarah and William Clifton, 26 January 1845, Laurens Co., S. C.

MAHAM, Mary and George Haig, 17 July 1785, Charleston, S. C.

MAHON, Curtis and Martha —— 30 December 1826, Mecklenburg Co., N. C.

MAHON, Mary and John Morris, 9 June 1796, Mecklenburg Co., N. C.

MAHON, Nancy and John N. Allen, 1 November 1836, Mecklenburg Co., N. C.

MAIN, Byram and Patsey Cooper, 24 September 1810, Mecklenburg Co., N. C.

MAINE, Isabella and David Crawford, February 1748, Charleston, S. C.

MAIR, John and Ann Graham, 18 November 1800, Beaufort, S. C.

MAIR, Patrick and Martha Bigelow, 17 November 1801, Charleston, S. C.

MAJOR, Giles and Mary Dehart, 2 November 1779, Rowan Co., N. C.

MALLERY, Sarah and Thomas Bythewood, 14 December 1794, Charleston, S. C.

MALONE, Drury and Francis Bentley, 19 July 1788, Bertie Co., N. C.

MALTBY, Elizabeth and William S. Stevens, 23 December 1784, Charleston, S. C.

MANDRING, Andrew and Ann Boltenhamer, 22 March 1789, Guilford Co., N. C.

MANIGAULT, Anne and Thomas Middleton, 8 April 1783, Charleston, S. C.

MANIGAULT, Gabriel and Margaret Izard, 6 May 1785, Charleston, S. C.

MANIGAULT, Joseph and Maria H. Middleton, 1788, Charleston, S. C.

MANIGAULT, Peter and Elizabeth Wragg, 4 June 1755, Charleston, S. C.

MANLOVE, George and Hannah Craner, 17 January 1791, Guilford Co., N. C.

MANN, Ann and Phillip White, 7 February 1797, Granville Co., N. C.

MANN, Dorothy and Samuel Midgett, 6 November 1778, Tyrrell Co., N. C.

MANN, Elizabeth and David Scott, 10 February 1794, Berkeley Co., S. C.

MANN, Esther and Matthew D. Graves, 15 October 1768, Tyrrell Co., N. C.

MANN, Martha and Richard Roughton, 1 August 1778, Tyrrell Co., N. C.

MANN, Mary and Edmund Drake, 3 December 1763, Edgecombe Co., N. C.

MANN, Mary (widow) and Stephen Wescott, 27 February 1771, Tyrrell Co., N. C.

MANN, Mary and Joseph Hassell, 1781, Tyrrell Co., N. C.

MANN, Mary and James Taylor, May 1785, Georgetown, S. C.

MANN, Nancy and Joseph White, 24 October 1799, Granville Co., N. C.

MANN, Sarah and Philip Hillegar, 1788, Charleston, S. C.

MANNING, James and Elizabeth Baker, 7 January 1757, Chowan Co., N. C.

MANNS, Anna E. and Abel Chreitzberg, 26 December 1839, Charleston, S. C.

MANSFIELD, David and Elizabeth Wallis, 25 March 1772, Chowan Co., N. C.

MANSFIELD, Martha and Riddick Miller, 15 November 1832, Bertie Co., N. C.

MANSON, William and Adaline W. Walker, 22 February 1825, Mecklenburg Co., N. C.

MARCH, Susanna and Charles Hinkle, 13 May 1797, Rowan Co., N. C.

MARCKLY, Ann and Hans Eberly, 1748, Orangeburg Co., S. C.

MARES, William and Hannah Law, 18 October 1796, Guilford Co., N. C.

MARIEGU, John and Mary Black, 25 May 1795, Guilford Co., N. C.

MARINER, Ann and James Davenport, 4 April 1778, Tyrrell Co., N. C.

MARION, Catherine and T. Whitehouse, 7 May 1785, Charleston, S. C.

MARION, Charlotte and Anthony Ashby, August 1783 Charleston, S. C.

MARION, General and Mary E. Videau, April 1786, Charleston, S. C.

MARION, Job and Elizabeth Gaillard, 14 December 1762, Santee, S. C.

MARION, Mary (widow) and Thomas C. Kawon, January 1773, Berkeley Co., S. C.

MARION, Theodore S. and Charlotte Ashby, (widow) April 1786, Charleston, S. C.

MARIS, Thomas and Jane Holiday, 17 November 1802, Orange Co., N. C.

MARKERT, Jacob and Jane Gray, 25 November 1827, Mecklenburg Co., N. C.

MARKIS, Joseph and Ann Pickings, 19 July 1750, Orangeburg Co., S. C.

MARKS, Henry and Rebecca A. Cheek, 24 July 1823, Mecklenburg Co., N. C.

MARKS, Mary and Samuel Coombs, 21 August 1812, Mecklenburg Co., N. C.

MARKS, Sarah L. and T. S. Riddle, 11 June 1856, Mecklenburg Co., N. C.

MARKS, Thomas and Nancy H. Robison, 27 June 1854, Mecklenburg Co., N. C.

MARKS, Thomas and Margaret E. Button, 28 April 1832, Mecklenburg Co., N. C.

MARLAN, James C. and Sarah G. Sapp, 16 November 1854, Guilford Co., N. C.

MARLEN, Mary and William Stephens, 22 May 1797, Charleston, S. C.

MARLEN, William C. and Margaret Davis, 18 December 1800, Charleston, S. C.

MARLIN, Edward and (Mrs.) Malinda Strattler, 26 September 1799, Charleston, S. C.

MARR, John and Susannah Baker, 16 July 1833, Mecklenburg Co., N. C.

MARSDEN, Mary and Benjamin Heron, 10 June 1765, Wilmington, N. C.

MARSH, James and Susanna Bisset, (widow), 10 January 1743, Charleston, S. C.

MARSH, Silas and Mary Kinisey, 19 June 1764, Chowan Co., N. C.

MARSH, William and Lydia Pierce, 10 January 1793, Guilford Co., N. C.

MARSHALL, Cornelia and Theodore Gaillard, 3 November 1799, Charleston, S. C.

MARSHALL, Daniel and Christian Hinton, 11 June 1773, Chowan Co., N. C.

MARSHALL, Jesebel and James Gilley, 5 July 1783, Rowan Co., N. C.

MARSHALL, Jane (Mrs.) and John Holland, 1 September 1786, Wilmington, N. C.

MARSHALL, John and Ann Newman, 21 May 1813, Mecklenburg Co., N. C.

MARSHALL, Phoebe and Allan Howard, 1787, Granville Co., N. C.

MARSHALL, Thomas S. and Sarah Hicks Ayers, 27 November 1855, Marlboro Co., S. C.

MARSHALL, William and Margaret A. McCord, 5 August 1841, Mecklenburg Co., N. C.

MARSHALL, William and Cynthia P. Todd, 9 October 1845, Mecklenburg Co., N. C.

MARTERI, James and Elizabeth Walter, 20 December 1785, Chowan Co., N. C.

MARTER, Franks and Peter A. Hamlett, 9 December 1823, Mecklenburg Co., N. C.

MARTIN, Ann and John Hull, 12 September 1744, Chowan Co., N. C.

MARTIN, Bartley and Margaret Morgan, 14 November 1855, Edgefield District.

MARTIN, Catherine and Miles Franks, 13 April 1848, Laurens Co., S. C.

MARTIN, Charles Oden and Africa Garrett, 10 March 1786, Tyrrell Co., N. C.

MARTIN, Edward and Elizabeth Walker, 19 January 1763, Charleston, S. C.

MARTIN, Edward and Elizabeth Trapier, 17 September 1778, Santee, S. C.

MARTIN, Edwin and Mary Westmoreland, 8 January 1829, Mecklenburg Co., N. C.

MARTIN, Eli and Polly Capps, 13 May 1823, Mecklenburg Co., N. C.

MARTIN, Elizabeth and Hugh Gallaher, 26 August 1775, Rowan Co., N. C.

MARTIN, Elizabeth and Herbert Roan, 20 July 1811, Mecklenburg Co., N. C.

MARTIN, Elizabeth (Mrs.) and Sampson Rogers, 1 June 1801, Charleston, S. C.

MARTIN, Emily and John Shocklsy, 29 November 1849, Laurens Co., S. C.

MARTIN, Ephriam R. and Caroline Dewese, 25 December 1839, Mecklenburg Co., N. C.

MARTIN, Fanny and Lanson Owens, 11 February 1851, Laurens Co., S. C.

MARTIN, Henry and Mary Booth, 29 August 1795, Guilford Co., N. C.

MARTIN, Henry and Emily Simpson, 13 July 1837, Mecklenburg Co., N. C.

MARTIN, Henry and Eliza Clark, 17 February 1841, Mecklenburg Co., N. C.

MARTIN, Henry H. and Fanny Garrett, 8 June 1843, Laurens Co., S. C.

MARTIN, Huldy and John Ball, 8 May 1855, Laurens So., S. C.

MARTIN, James and Peggy Kerr, 27 February 1797, Mecklenburg Co., N. C.

MARTIN, James W. and Harriet D. Rea, 21 November 1837, Mecklenburg Co., N. C.

MARTIN, Jenny and Mathew Alexander, 27 September 1810, Mecklenburg Co., N. C.

MARTIN, Joshua and Mary Witty, 22 February 1796, Guilford Co., N. C.

MARTIN, Lewis and Sophy Shell, 15 December 1846, Laurens Co., S. C.

MARTIN, Lewis and Milly Moore, 12 April 1848, Laurens Co., S. C.

MARTIN, Lovey and John Hopper, 16 June 1756, Chowan Co., N. C.

MARTIN, Manima and James Loyd, 15 June 1843, Laurens Co., S. C.

MARTIN, Rebecca and (Dr.) Clayton Cox, 15 September 1857, Laurens Co., S. C.

MARTIN, Reuben and Jane Hanner, 24 September 1857, Laurens Co., S. C.

MARTIN, Robert and Hannah Kerr, 10 November 1806, Mecklenburg Co., N. C.

MARTIN, Robert A. and Sarah S. Bozzle, 4 December 1838, Mecklenburg Co., N. C.

MARTIN, Sophy and Franklin Burns, 21 July 1849, Laurens Co., S. C.

MARTIN, Susanna and Lewis Ogier, 2 October 1783, Charleston, S. C.

MARTIN, Thomas and Charlotte Ogier, September 1786, Charleston, S. C.

MARTIN, Thomas and Ann Blythe, 17 October 1786, Mecklenburg Co., N. C.

MARTIN, Thomas and Elizabeth Riddle, 10 February 1853, Laurens Co., S. C.

MARTIN, William and Eliza Perry, 1 April 1800, Charleston, S. C.

MARTIN, William and Eleanor Booker, 2 November 1808, Mecklenburg Co., N. C.

MARTIN, William and Grace Waring, 8 February 1772, Edgefield District, S. C.

MARTIN, William E. and Eloisa Hayne, 18 May 1837, Colleton, S. C.

MARTINDALE, Justin and Evelina A. Lamb, 24 December 1834, Chowan Co., N. C.

MARYE, Abigail and William Law, 9 August 1799, Guilford Co., N. C.

MASON, Charles and Hannah Clark, 4 November 1814, Mecklenburg Co., N. C.

MASON, Charles C. and Margaret Carothers, 2 October 1835, Mecklenburg Co., N. C.

MASON, Frances and Rufus Berisho, 1 July 1783, Tyrrell Co., N. C.

MASON, Isaac and Mary Montgomery, 22 June 1831, Mecklenburg Co., N. C.

MASON, Richard C. and Charity Hartwick, 23 January 1821, Mecklenburg Co., N. C.

MASON, Richardson and Sarah Phillips, 2 February 1797, Mecklenburg Co., N. C.

MASON, R. G. and Mary A. King, 14 May 1849, Mecklenburg Co., N. C.

MASON, Winfield and Priscilla Miller, 4 May 1808, Mecklenburg Co., N. C.

MASSEY, Adkins and Mary Wynn, 18 February 1765, Tyrrell Co., N. C.

MASSEY, Elizabeth (widow) and John Bedon (Jr.), 29 July 1736, Charleston, S. C.

MASSEY, James and Eliza McCall, 25 November 1837, Mecklenburg Co., N. C.

MASSEY, Joseph and Hannah Mitchell, 1 December 1753, Charleston, S. C.

MASSEY, Louise and Harmon Herndon, 2 November 1858, Orange Co., N. C.

MASSEY, Philip and Jane Hopkins, 20 January 1733, Charleston, S. C.

MASSEY, Pinckney and Frances Archer, 8 October 1839, Guilford Co., N. C.

MASSEY, Thomas P. and Elizabeth Warsham, 24 October 1843, Mecklenburg Co., N. C.

MATHER, James and Jane Still, 25 February 1844, Mecklenburg Co., N. C.

MATHER, William and Nancy Mitchell, 25 August 1787, Guilford Co., N. C.

MATHERS, Molly and Meredith Johnson, 1 January 1763, Edgecombe Co., N. C.

MATHESON, Alexander J. and Sarah E. Jarnigan, 20 April 1780, Marion Co., S. C.

MATHIAS, Mary and John Bond, 27 April 1776, Chowan Co., N. C.

MATHIAS, Nathaniel and Elizabeth Luten, 28 March 1758, Chowan Co., N. C.

MATTHEWES, Elizabeth and Thomas Heyward, 20 April 1773, Charleston, S. C.

MATTHEWES, James and (Mrs.) Charity Cowan, 25 January 1767, Tyrrell Co., N. C.

MATTHEWS, Andrew and Esther Hazzard, 16 February 1849, Mecklenburg Co., N. C.

MATTHEWS, Anne and David Graeme, 21 January 1759, Charleston, S. C.

MATTHEWS, Anne and Gosin Guerard, 23 August 1769, Charleston, S. C.

MATTHEWS, Anne and James J. Morris, 6 June 1822, Mecklenburg Co., N. C.

MATTHEWS, Benjamin and Anne Holmes, 5 February 1745, Charleston, S. C.

MATTHEWS, Charlotte (widow) and James Skirving, 21 March 1769, Charleston, S. C.

MATTHEWS, Edmund (Rev.) and Eliza Ward, 15 January 1801, Charleston, S. C.

MATTHEWS, Elizabeth (widow) and (Dr.) John Moultrie, 6 July 1748, Charleston, S. C.

MATTHEWS, Jane and Robert Bigham, 31 December 1813, Mecklenburg Co., N. C.

MATTHEWS, Jane H. and Hugh Harris, 1 September 1835, Mecklenburg Co., N. C.

MATTHEWS, John and Nancy Havey, 14 February 1767, Charleston, S. C.

MATTHEWS, John and Mary Wragg, 4 December 1766, Colleton Co., S. C.

MATTHEWS, John and Margaret McKibben, 10 November 1794, Mecklenburg Co., N. C.

MATTHEWS, Lois and George A. Hall, 14 February 1764, Charleston, S. C.

MATTHEWS, Louisa and Edward Hughes, 3 January 1797, Charleston, S. C.

MATTHEWS, Margaret and Ephriam Mitchell, 31 August 1825, Mecklenburg Co., N. C.

MATTHEWS, Margaret A. and Samuel W. Orr, 7 November 1836, Mecklenburg Co., N. C.

MATTHEWS, Mary and Thomas Lloyd, 24 July 1746, Charleston, S. C.

MATTHEWS, Nathaniel and Hester Taylor, 10 November 1744, Chowan Co., N. C.

MATTHEWS, Polly and Samuel Allen, 30 January 1821, Mecklenburg Co., N. C.

MATTHEWS, Robert and Agnes Henderson, 2 March 1797, Mecklenburg Co., N. C.

MATTHEWS, Robert and Nancy McGibbins, 11 February 1802, Mecklenburg Co., N. C.

MATTHEWS, Samuel and Mary Rea, 13 November 1809, Mecklenburg Co., N. C.

MATTHEWS, Sarah A. and William A. Robison, 1 February 1842, Mecklenburg Co., N. C.

MATTHEWS, Sarah A. and John P. Ross, 19 November 1839, Mecklenburg Co., N. C.

MATTHEWS, Susannah and Daniel Hall, 21 January 1775, Charleston, S. C.

MATTHEWS, Susan A. and William A. Robinson, 1 February 1842, Mecklenburg Co., N. C.

MATHEWS, William and Esther Sullivan, 25 April 1769, Santee, S. C.

MAVIARY, Liddy and Jacob Huff, 22 January 1791, Rowan Co., N. C.

MAXWELL, Annie M. and Benjamin Sloan, 1 December 1862, Columbia, S. C.

MAXWELL, Catherine and James W. Rogers, 7 February 1856, Mecklenburg Co., N. C.

MAXWELL, David and M. L. Harrison, 4 June 1841, Mecklenburg Co., N. C.

MAXWELL, Edwin and Margaret McLarty, 16 June 1832, Mecklenburg Co., N. C.

MAXWELL, Ellen and Jesse Rogers, 24 February 1820, Mecklenburg Co., N. C.

MAXWELL, Isabella and James Alexander, 14 January 1831, Mecklenburg Co., N. C.

MAXWELL, James and Jean McChung, 28 March 1788, Mecklenburg Co., N. C.

MAXWELL, James J. and Margaret Wallis, 8 February 1823, Mecklenburg Co., N. C.

MAXWELL, John and Elizabeth Black, 19 February 1831, Mecklenburg Co., N. C.

MAXWELL, John G. and Sarah H. Baker, 18 November 1856, Mecklenburg Co., N. C.

MAXWELL, Joseph and Elizabeth Monteith, 10 January 1792, Mecklenburg Co., N. C.

MAXWELL, Jeremiah M. and Elizabeth Houston, 28 August 1827, Mecklenburg Co., N. C.

MAXWELL, Lydia C. and Eli O. Black, 8 March 1830, Mecklenburg Co., N. C.

MAXWELL, Margaret and John Morris, 30 July 1792, Mecklenburg Co., N. C.

MAXWELL, Margaret (widow) and Samuel Hudson, July 1746, Orangeburg Co., S. C.

MAXWELL, Martha and John Brown, 17 December 1792, Mecklenburg Co., N. C.

MAXWELL, Moses and Elizabeth Brown, 1 December 1802, Mecklenburg Co., N. C.

MAXWELL, Robert H. and Ann Rogers, 31 December 1823, Mecklenburg Co., N. C.

MAXWELL, Robert and Elizabeth Hood, 7 May 1795, Mecklenburg Co., N. C.

MAXWELL, Samuel and Mary Garrett, 1 February 1802, Guilford Co., N. C.

MAXWELL, Sarah (widow) and Alexander Chisholm, 10 June 1786, Charleston, S. C.

MAXWELL, Washington and Louisa Rodgers, 26 September 1828, Mecklenburg Co., N. C.

MAXWELL, William and Deborah Andrews, 10 October 1790, Guilford Co., N. C.

MAXWELL, William and Nancy Simpson, 14 July 1804, Mecklenburg Co., N. C.

MAXWELL, William and Martha Hux , 22 November 1832, Mecklenburg Co., N. C.

MAXWELL, William M. and Sarah H. Wilson, 8 June 1824, Mecklenburg Co., N. C.

MAXWELL, William M. and Adeline Wilson, 14 May 1835, Mecklenburg Co., N. C.

MAXWELL, William R. and Nancy A. Morris, 12 November 1836, Mecklenburg Co., N. C.

MAXWELL, William R. and Mary E. Johnston, 21 July 1832, Mecklenburg Co., N. C.

MAY, Lavina and Jesse Montgomery, 22 December 1865, Guilford Co., N. C.

MAY, William and Lucinda McCary, 6 January 1853, Laurens Co., S. C.

MAYBANK, Hester and William Cleiland, 2 June 1785, Christ Church Parish, S. C.

MAYBANKS, Thomas and Miss Peronneau, 22 October 1800, Charleston, S. C.

MAYBERRY, Eliza H. and (Dr.) T. Reilly, 17 December 1801, Charleston, S. C.

MAYER, Sibella Margaretta and (Rev.) Bernard Houseal, 1752, Rotterdam, S. C.

MAYFIELD, Stephen and Margaret Cook, 20 May 1797, Mecklenburg Co., N. C.

MAYNARD, Ann and Samuel Monzen, 17 May 1770, Santee, S. C.

MAYNE, Charles and Miss Michie, 2 October 1755, Charleston, S. C.

MAYRANT, Ann and Henry Gibbes, 15 May 1820, Charleston, S. C.

MAYRANT, John and Anne Stone, 26 September 1753, Charleston, S. C.

MAYRANT, Judith and Stephen Bull, 2 May 1747, Newberry, S. C.

MAYS, George Ann and Lucius Hatch, 30 November 1854, Edgefield District, S. C.

MAZYCK, Alexander and Charlotte Broughton, 15 November 1770, Charleston, S. C.

MAZYCK, Catherine and Stephen Ravenel, 11 December 1800, Charleston, S. C.

MAZYCK, Catherine M. and John Cordes, 1788, St. Johns Parish, S. C.

MAZYCK, Charlotte and Rene Ravenel, 14 February 1788, Pooshwee, S. C.

MAZYCK, Charlotte and Daniel Ravenel (Jr.), 12 February 1759, Charleston, S. C.

MAZYCK, Charlotte and Champion Williamson, 4 July 1765, St. Johns Parish, S. C.

MAZYCK, Isaac and Marianne LeSerurier, 14 October 1793, Charleston, S. C.

MAZYCK, Isaac and Jane M. St. Julian, 17 July 1728, Charleston, S. C.

MAZYCK, Marry and William Mazyck, June 1762, Charleston, S. C.

MAZYCK, Mary and (Dr.) Samuel Wilson, 1788, Charleston, S. C.

MAZYCK, Mary and John Hume, March 1784, Charleston, S. C.

MAZYCK, Mary Anne and Plowden Weston, 26 March 1775, Charleston, S. C.

MAZYCK, Stephen and Ann Wilson, 16 July 1785, Charleston, S. C.

MAZYCK, William and Mary Mazyck, June 1762, Charleston, S. C.

MAZYCK, William and Elizabeth Porcher, 5 July 1764, Charleston, S. C.

MAZYCK, William and Anne Taylor, 20 July 1850, Charleston, S. C.

MAYER, John S. and Charlotte Theus, 1788, Charleston, S. C.

MAYER, Sherwood, and Elizabeth Smith, 25 November 1773, Guilford Co., N. C.

MAYERS, John and Ann Higback, 21 February 1761, Santee, S. C.

MEACHAM, Martha D. and Samuel G. Hammond, 17 August 1841, Mecklenburg Co., N. C.

MEADOW, Manervy and H. R. Shell, 1852, Laurens Co., S. C.

MEADOWS, Frances and Natti O'Brian Cannady, 30 March 1847, Laurens Co., S. C.

MEANS, Catherine and Thomas Backus, 24 October 1786, Chowan Co., N. C.

MEANS, C. T. and Susan S. Robison, 8 December 1841, Mecklenburg Co., N. C.

MEANS, David H. and Frances M. Coalter, 2 January 1817, Fairfield Co., S. C.

MEANS, Edward J. and Martha J. McPheeters, 18 April 1860, Fairfield Co., S. C.

MEANS, Isaac H. and Alice Hagood, 8 March 1854, Fairfield Co., S. C.

MEANS, Mary and John McCord, 10 January, Mecklenburg Co., N. C.

MEANS, Mary H. and Thomas C. Means, 22 December 1853, Fairfield Co., S. C.

MEANS, Thomas C. and Mary H. Means, 22 December 1853, Fairfield Co., S. C.

MEANS, William and Caroline Hipp, 18 December 1838, Mecklenburg Co., N. C.

MEARS, Elijah and Martha Montgomery, 23 May 1811, Guilford Co., N. C.

MEBANE, Robert and Sally Stafford, 18 October 1815, Guilford Co., N. C.

MEBANE, William (Jr.) and Rebecca Burney, 13 December 1794, Guilford Co., N. C.

MECKET, William and Ann Roth, 6 December 1750, Orangeburg Co., S. C.

MEDEARIS, Moses and Selah Bell, 12 August 1800, Guilford Co., N. C.

MEDEL, Jane and John Ruberry (Jr.), 3 March 1797, Charleston, S. C.

MEDLOCK, Martha and Wiley A. Hubbard, 24 July 1825, Edgefield District, S. C.

MEDLOCK, Moses and Mary Ann Mins, 1 June 1826, Edgefield District, S. C.

MEEK, Peggy and John Black, 9 March 1803, Mecklenburg Co., N. C.

MEEK, Rebecca and John A. Conger, 14 December 1822, Mecklenburg Co., N. C.

MEEK, Samuel M. and Arabella McDowell, 19 May 1813, Charleston, S. C.

MEGELY, Catharina and Jacob Koonen, 1 September 1748, Orangeburg Co., S. C.

MEGGETT, Margaret and Benjamin Seabrook, December 1784, Edisto, S. C.

MEGREW, Eugenia and Charles Kitchen, 1746, Orangeburg Co., S. C.

MEGUIRT, David and Rebecca Winchester, 12 November 1833, Mecklenburg Co., N. C.

MEHAFFEY, John and Phebe Langley, 6 January 1791, Guilford Co., N. C.

MELACHAMP, Martha and Edward Gunter, 12 April 1772, Berkeley Co., S. C.

MELL, Henry and Mary Catharina Huttow, 24 April 1753, Orangeburg Co., S. C.

MELL, Mary Ann and Joseph Dubose, 16 October 1800, Santee, S. C.

MELL, Thomas and Mary Boswood, 23 December 1718, St. Andrews Parish, S. C.

MELLICHAMP, Catherine and Thomas Foley, 1 November 1764, Charleston, S. C.

MELTON, Aley and Jesse McClendon, 23 February 1830, Edgefield District, S. C.

MELTON, James and Elizabeth Festerman, 26 February 1833, Mecklenburg Co., N. C.

MELTON, Susan and Gabriel Milton, 23 December 1819, Edgefield District, S. C.

MELVIN, William and Catherine Kirkpatrick, 30 October 1793, Mecklenburg Co., N. C.

MENDENHALL, Richard and Polly Clemmons, 25 July 1799, Guilford Co., N. C.

MENDENHALL, Zadoc and Esther Horny, 14 November 1817, Guilford Co., N. C.

MERCHANT, Eliza and John G. Brown, 2 April 1833, Mecklenburg Co., N. C.

MERCHANT, Elizabeth and William Black, 22 July 1801, Mecklenburg Co., N. C.

MERCHANT, Jane and Seth McKenney, 14 January 1800, Mecklenburg Co., N. C.

MEREDITH, Caroline M. and William S. Saunders, 5 June 1834, Oxford, N. C.

MEREDITH, David and Sarah Browning (widow), 2 June 1773, Chowan Co., N. C.

MEREDITH, Isabella and James H. Walker, 20 April 1831, Oxford, N. C.

MEREDITH, James and Rachel Knight, 23 August 1797, Guilford Co., N. C.

MEREDITH, Jenobia Aurelian and Simon T. Sanders, 15 June 1830, Oxford, N. C.

MEREDITH, John and Frances Gibson, 25 December 1771, Guilford Co., N. C.

MEREDITH, John and Mary Knight, 17 February 1797, Guilford Co., N. C.

MEREDITH, John and Nancy Peoples, 8 July 1842, Guilford Co., N. C.

MEREDITH, Joseph Norfleet and Mary Bastisle, 15 May 1800, Oxford, N. C.

MEREDITH, Mary Ann R. and (Capt.) Armistead Brown, 30 December 1824, Oxford, N. C.

MEREDITH, Salome Baptisle and Albert Gallatin Simms, 26 January 1830, Oxford, N. C.

MERIEGU, John and Hannah Coats, 4 March 1795, Guilford Co., N. C.

MERLIVA, James and Rachel Cook, 27 February 1838, Mecklenburg Co., N. C.

MERRIFIELD, George and Mary Tatum, 6 December 1788, Guilford Co., N .C.

MERRIT, Tabitha and William Goodwin, 8 March 1768, Edgecombe Co., N. C.

MERRITT, Alice and Thomas Hasell, 26 April 1744, Charleston, S. C.

MERRITT, Thomas F. and Jane Weaver, 22 September 1841, Guilford Co., N. C.

MERRYAN, Francis and Solomon Witham, 29 July 1748, Orangeburg Co., S. C.

MESSAN, Jane C (widow) and Joseph Brunet, 15 March 1800, Charleston, S. C.

MESSENGER, John and (Mrs.) Mary Predy, 20 January 1752, Chowan Co., N. C.

MESSENGER, Mary (widow) and Robert Wallace, 1 August 1754, Chowan Co., N. C.

MEYER, Anna Barbara and Elias Schnell, 1738, Orangeburg Co., S. C.

MEYER, Charlotte D. (Mrs.) and (Rev.) Israel Munds, 3 September 1801, Charleston, S. C.

MEYER, John Jacob and Anna Bustrin, 1 January 1740, Orangeburg Co., S. C.

MEYERS, Christian and Rebecca Young, 12 April 1738, Orangeburg Co., S. C.

MICHEAU, Jacob and Esther Cromwell, 11 June 1778, Santee, S. C.

MICHIE, Alexi and Henrietta Carroll, 9 September 1766, Charleston, S. C.

MICHIE, Kenneth and Mary Clap, February 1746, Charleston, S. C.

MICHIE, Miss and Charles Mayne, 2 October 1755, Charleston, S. C.

MICHIE, Widow and David Deas, 12 February 1751, Charleston, S. C.

MICHILL, Flowers and Elizabeth Warren, 1748, Orangeburg Co., S. C.

MIDDLETON, Ann (widow) and Stephen Bull, 25 May 1772, Charleston, S. C.

MIDDLETON, Anna and Henry Izard, 1 June 1795, Charleston, S. C.

MIDDLETON, Anna L. and Daniel Blake, 2 February 1800, Charleston, S. C.

MIDDLETON, Arthur and Mary Izard, 19 August 1764, Ashley River, S. C.

MIDDLETON, Esther and Shadrach Fagan, 1784, Tyrrell Co., N. C.

MIDDLETON, Esther and (Dr.) Charles Drayton, 24 February 1774, Berkeley Co., S. C.

MIDDLETON, Hannah and David Griffith, 11 June 1750, Orangeburg Co., S. C.

MIDDLETON, Henrietta and Edward Rutledge, 1 March 1774, Charleston, S. C.

MIDDLETON, Hester and Charles Drayton, 24 February 1774, Charleston, S. C.

MIDDLETON, Isabel and Daniel E. Huger, 26 November 1800, Ashley River, S. C.

MIDDLETON, John and Mary Dwight, 1782, Tyrrell Co., N. C.

MIDDLETON, John and Sirrah Goodby, 1746, Orangeburg Co., S. C.

MIDDLETON, John I. and Sarah Alston, 28 March 1828, Georgetown Co., S. C.

MIDDLETON, John I. and Eliza Falconet, 11 June 1810, Cedar Grove, S. C.

MIDDLETON, Maria H. and Joseph Manigault, 1788, Charleston, S. C.

MIDDLETON, Mary and Peter Smith, November 1776, Charleston, S. C.

MIDDLETON, Mary J. and Benjamin Read, 16 February 1864, Charleston, S. C.

MIDDLETON, Nathan (Rev.) and Margaret Izard, 18 January 1832, Charleston, S. C.

MIDDLETON, Oliver H. and Susan Chisolm, 5 April 1828, Edisto Island, S. C.

MIDDLETON, Polly and Pierce Butler, 10 January 1771, Charleston, S. C.

MIDDLETON, Sarah and Benjamin Howard, 25 January 1775, Tyrrell Co., N. C.

MIDDLETON, Sarah and Charles C. Pinckney, 28 September 1773, Charleston, S. C.

MIDDLETON, Septima and Henry M. Rutledge, 15 October 1799, Sullivans Island, S. C.

MIDDLETON, Susanna and John Parker, 24 December 1786, Charleston, S. C.

MIDDLETON, Thomas and Mary Gibbes, 17 November 1774, Crowfield, S. C.

MIDDLETON, Thomas and Anne Manigault, 8 April 1783, Charleston, S. C.

MIDDLETON, Thomas and Elizabeth Deas, 22 December 1778, Crowfield, S. C.

MIDDLETON, William and Mary Izard, 21 April 1730, Crowfield, S. C.

MIDDLETON, William and Sarah Wilkinson, 30 July 1747, Suffolk Co., S. C.

MIDDLETON, William and Sarah F. Harris, 22 March 1800, Guilford Co., N. C.

MIDGETT, Samuel and Dorothy Mann, 6 November 1778, Tyrrell Co., N. C.

MIKEL, Elizabeth (widow) and William Harvey, 6 February 1743, St. Helena, S. C.

MILANDER, Lucy and Samuel Simpson, 25 September 1851, Laurens Co., S. C.

MILBURN, Elizabeth and John Blount, 13 January 1790, Bertie Co., N. C.

MILCHAM, Jacob and Mary Burton, 15 September 1795, Guilford Co., N. C.

MILES, Archibald and Patsy Warsham, 25 June 1804, Mecklenburg Co., N. C.

MILES, Augustus N. and Elizabeth Connell, 7 January 1851, Mecklenburg Co., N. C.

MILES, Caroline and Ewel Teague, 20 January 1851, Laurens Co., S. C.

MILES, Elizabeth (widow) and Thomas Fuller, 7 September 1756, Ashley Ferry, S. C.

MILES, Elizabeth (widow) and George Mullins, 17 March 1768, Charleston, S. C.

MILES, Lewis and Ann Simmons, 4 April 1765, Santee, S. C.

MILES, Martha and Edward Griffith, 19 November 1767, St. Pauls Parish, S. C.

MILES, Martha and Ervin Clegg, 3 December 1756, Edgefield District, S. C.

MILES, Mary and Edward Rawlins, 24 April 1710, St. Andrews Parish, S. C.

MILES, Robert and Betsy Smith, October 1772, Stono, S. C.

MILES, Sally and John Boy, 9 November 1784, Ashepoo, S. C.

MILES, Sophia and William Fraser, January 1784, St. Bartholomews Parish, S. C.

MILES, Susannah and James Parsons, 29 May 1753, Charleston, S. C.

MILES, William and Mary Elliott, 26 October 1769, Wappoo, S. C.

MILES, William and Mary A. B. Rose, 8 November 1799, Charleston, S. C.

MILES, William and Sally Farrell, 15 September 1817, Mecklenburg Co., N. C.

MILES, William (Jr.) and Elizabeth North, 20 December 1743, St. Bartholomews Parish, S. C.

MILHADO, Benjamin and Hannah Depass, 20 April 1796, Charleston, S. C.

MILLEGAN, Elizabeth and Mr. Smith (of N. Y.), 8 May 1785, Charleston, S. C.

MILLER, Abigail and Joseph Hobday, 13 June 1764, Chowan Co., N. C.

MILLER, Adam and Jane Henderson, 13 April 1804, Mecklenburg Co., N. C.

MILLER, Andrew and Elizabeth Blount, February 1763, Perquimans Co., N. C.

MILLER, Andrew and Margaret Miller, 28 July 1795, Mecklenburg Co., N. C.

MILLER, Ann and John Lacy, 2 April 1738, Charleston, S. C.

MILLER, Ann and William Demsey, 25 July 1781, Bertie Co., N. C.

MILLER, Anna and Philip Pinyard, 8 February 1743, Charleston, S. C.

MILLER, Augustine and Penelope Smith, 11 September 1855, Chowan Co., N. C.

MILLER, Catherine and Jeremiah Waters, 25 May 1778, Chowan Co., N. C.

MILLER, Christina and Jeremiah Brower, 6 September 1774, Charleston, S. C.

MILLER, Cynthia and James Powland, 25 July 1836, Mecklenburg Co., N. C.

MILLER, Christopher and Angelia Zeigler (widow), 4 November 1753, Orangeburg Co., S. C.

MILLER, David and Hannah Graham, 14 May 1794, Guilford Co., N. C.

MILLER, David and Jane Wilson, 22 May 1815, Mecklenburg Co., N. C.

MILLER, David and (Mrs.) Ann Pell, 3 January 1824, Chowan Co., N. C.

MILLER, David M. and Martha P. Hart, 22 November 1849, Mecklenburg Co., N. C.

MILLER, David W. and Serena Morrison, 8 August 1845, Mecklenburg Co., N. C.

MILLER, Eleanor and Jacob Leonard, 16 June 1785, Wilmington, N. C.

MILLER, Elinor and Joseph Wilcox, 1 September 1743, Charleston, S. C.

MILLER, Eliza and James H. Hartmus, 23 September 1815, Chowan Co., N. C.

MILLER, Eliza and Samuel W. Read, 22 October 1836, Mecklenburg Co., N. C.

MILLER, Eliza and William Nixon, 21 December 1858, Chowan Co., N. C.

MILLER, Elizabeth and Thomas Boulton, 25 July 1724, Charleston, S. C.

MILLER, Elizabeth and James Herron, 9 May 1792, Rowan Co., N. C.

MILLER, Elizabeth and Turner Bynum, 13 August 1799, Charleston, S. C.

MILLER, Elizabeth and Samuel Privett, 17 July 1827, Chowan Co., N. C.

MILLER, Elizabeth and Henry Lane, 9 July 1856, Chowan Co., N. C.

MILLER, Euphame (Mrs.) and Marlborough S. Hamilton, 10 January 1795, Charleston, S. C.

MILLER, Hargrove and Mary Coleman, 22 February 1859, Laurens Co., S. C.

MILLER, Harriet and Alexander W. Myers, 27 January 1857, Chowan Co., N. C.

MILLER, Harriet C. and I. Lafayette M. Rogers, 28 September 1854, Mecklenburg Co., N. C.

MILLER, James and Annie Nandaford, October 1780, Tyrrell Co., N. C.

MILLER, James and May Smith, 30 July 1791, Mecklenburg Co., N. C.

MILLER, James and Rebecca McKibben, 2 May 1796, Mecklenburg Co., N. C.

MILLER, Jane and John Singleton, March 1779, Charleston, S. C.

MILLER, Jenny and Andrew N. Rogers, 21 September 1811, Mecklenburg Co., N. C.

MILLER, John and Mary Ann Smith, 10 January 1794, Mecklenburg Co., N. C.

MILLER, John and Penelope Leath, 27 February 1799, Chowan Co., N. C.

MILLER, John and Rachel Charleton, 22 December 1801, Chowan Co., N. C.

MILLER, John and Penny Ray, 30 January 1821, Bertie Co., N. C.

MILLER, John and Nancy Turner, 3 June 1835, Mecklenburg Co., N. C.

MILLER, John and Jane Viperall, 1 September 1843, Mecklenburg Co., N. C.

MILLER, John B. (Col.) and Mary E. Murrell, 16 July 1808, Statesburg, S. C.

MILLER, John D. and Jane Righton, December 1779, Charleston, S. C.

MILLER, John T. and Lydia Lane, 8 August, 1799, Charleston, S. C.

MILLER, John W. and Jane C. Johnston, 6 September 1843, Mecklenburg Co., N. C.

MILLER, Jonathan and Elizabeth Montgomery, 23 September 1818, Guilford Co., N. C.

MILLER, Jonathan S. and Leah Copeland, 24 January 1850, Chowan Co., N. C.

MILLER, Jonathan and Miley Todd, 26 December 1855, Chowan Co., N. C.

MILLER, Jones and Liza Teague, 18 December 1844, Laurens Co., S. C.

MILLER, Judith and Andrew Ruck, 18 June 1741, Charleston, S. C.

MILLER, Julia and John Craston, 11 October 1742, Charleston, S. C.

MILLER, Julia A. and John B. Miskell, 16 July 1828, Chowan Co., N. C.

MILLER, Lucinda S. and Francis A. Biggers, 22 February 1853, Mecklenburg Co., N. C.

MILLER, Margaret (widow) and Henry Dare, 26 March 1764, Chowan Co., N. C.

MILLER, Margaret (widow) and William Halsey, 27 June 1767, Chowan Co., N. C.

MILLER, Margaret and James Orr, 23 January 1793, Mecklenburg Co., N. C.

MILLER, Margaret and Andrew Miller, 28 July 1795, Mecklenburg Co., N. C.

MILLER, Margaret A. and John Harrell, 9 January 1845, Chowan Co., N. C.

MILLER, Martha and John Bee, 7 June 1731, Charleston, S. C.

MILLER, Martha and William Glen (Jr.), 12 April 1770, St. Thomas Parish, S. C.

MILLER, Martha and Bryant Todd, 4 July 1860, Chowan Co., N. C.

MILLER, Mary and John Hetherington, 16 August 1763, Berkeley Co., S. C.

MILLER, Mary and Joshua H. Hudson, 4 May 1754, Bennettsville, S. C.

MILLER, Mary and Josiah N. Walker, 1845, Barnwell Co., S. C.

MILLER, Maryann and William Hutson, 8 November 1800, Charleston, S. C.

MILLER, Martin and Ann D. Murer, 23 July 1801, Chowan Co., N. C.

MILLER, Matthew and Harriet G. Simmons, 29 October 1844, Mecklenburg Co., N. C.

MILLER, Nancy and Silas Read, 16 February 1812, Mecklenburg Co., N. C.

MILLER, Nancy and Nathaniel Bond, 4 July 1831, Chowan Co., N. C.

MILLER, Nathaniel and Mary Ling, 21 December 1802, Chowan Co., N. C.

MILLER, Nelly and Nathaniel Cullifer, 30 May 1834, Bertie Co., N. C.

MILLER, Nelly and Albert G. Jones, 27 April 1848, Chowan Co., N. C.

MILLER, Nicholas and Elenor Henox, 21 February 1743, Charleston, S. C.

MILLER, Nicholas and Mary Elliott, 19 September 1844, Guilford Co., N. C .

MILLER, Permealy and (Dr.) Samuel Knight, 18 May 1859, Laurens Co., S. C.

MILLER, Peter and Ann M. Lutzen, 11 March 1747, Charleston, S. C.

MILLER, Philip and Martha J. Wilson, 23 June 1853, Lenoir Co., N. C.

MILLER, Priscilla and Winifred Mason, 4 May 1808, Mecklenburg Co., N. C.

MILLER, Reuben and Lavina Coffield, 21 September 1848, Chowan Co., N. C.

MILLER, Richard and Judith Lambol, 29 December 1724, Charleston, S. C.

MILLER, Riddick and Martha Mansfield, 15 November 1832, Bertie Co., N. C.

MILLER, Robert and Elizabeth Hains, 15 September 1720, Charleston, S. C.

MILLER, Robert and Margaret Fluery (widow), 27 June 1772, Chowan Co., N. C.

MILLER, Samuel and Martha Crawford, 10 August 1792, Mecklenburg Co., N. C.

MILLER, Sarah and Joseph Hull, 29 September 1779, Rowan Co., N. C.

MILLER, Smith and Temperance Ward, 22 January 1839, Chowan Co., N. C.

MILLER, Solomon and Sarah Copeland, 16 January 1838, Chowan Co., N. C.

MILLER, Solomon and Thusey Melch, 17 January 1842, Chowan Co., N. C.

MILLER, Susan E. and John H. Furman, 8 May 1853, Sumter Co., S. C.

MILLER, Thomas and Mary Dominque, 28 November 1801, Chowan Co., N. C.

MILLER, Thomas I. and Priscilla Stallings, 27 September 1831, Chowan Co., N. C.

MILLER, William and Isabella Lewis, 24 October 1797, Mecklenburg Co., N. C.

MILLER, William and Mary White, 11 March 1831, Chowan Co., N. C.

MILLER, William and Mary Dail, 31 December 1846, Chowan Co., N. C.

MILLER, William C. and Ruth McKee, 14 January 1837, Mecklenburg Co. N. C.

MILLER, William C. and Nancy Dulin, 16 November 1849, Mecklenburg Co., N. C.

MILLER, Winnie and John Mizell, 9 November 1789, Bertie Co., N. C.

MILLER, Zilla B. and Samuel D. Carothers, 11 February 1836, York Co., S. C.

MILLERSEY, John and Elizabeth Griffin, 22 July 1793, Guilford Co., N. C.

MILLHOUSE, Sarah and James Cook, 15 October 1768, Camden, S. C.

MILLIGAN, Elizabeth (Mrs.) and Arthur Harper, 10 August 1799, Charleston, S. C.

MILLIGAN, Mary and Isaac Parker, 20 July 1800, Charleston, S. C.

MILLIGAN, William and Rebecca Stoll, 4 October 1773, Charleston, S. C.

MILLIS, James and Mary Jackson, 6 December 1785, Guilford Co., N. C.

MILLIS, John and Rachel Hegnit, 26 November 1786, Guilford Co., N. C.

MILLIS, Nicholson and Nancy Snow, 28 May 1799, Guilford Co., N. C.

MILLS, Amy and Josiah Hancock, 1800, Pitt Co., N. C.

MILLS, Ann and William Howell, 15 June 1776, Tyrrell Co., N. C.

MILLS, Eleanor and Robert Shaw, 1 January 1731, Charleston, S. C.

MILLS, Elenor and John Meek, January 1776, Laurens District, S. C.

MILLS, Elizabeth and Edward Haselwood, 22 April 1732, Charleston, S. C.

MILLS, Ezekial (of Va.) and Mary Addison (widow), 5 January 1784, St. Thomas Parish, S. C.

MILLS, Francis and Penelope Long, 29 March 1783, Tyrrell Co., N. C.

MILLS, John and Lewis Underwood, 13 October 1795, Guilford Co., N. C.

MILLS, John and Nancy Mary Patterson, 23 January 1851, Laurens Co., S. C.

MILLS, Jonathan and Hannah Farrington, 8 February 1817, Guilford Co., N. C.

MILLS, William and Grace Parker, September 1732, Charleston, S. C.

MILLS, William H. and Elizabeth Montgomery, 22 July 1769, Santee, S. C.

MILLS, Zebulon and Elizabeth H. Smith, 29 March 1794, Chowan Co., N. C.

MILNER, Job and Mary Bond, May 1759, Charleston, S. C.

MILNER, Mary and Andrew Hasell, 15 October 1778, St. Thomas Parish, S. C.

MILTON, Gabriel and Susan Melton, 23 December 1819, Edgefield District, S. C.

MILTON, Josiah and Susan Jones, 14 June 1834, Guilford Co., N. C.

MINEOR, Emanuel and Rachel Hatcher, 27 October 1754, Orangeburg Co., S. C.

MINER, Richard and Rachel Whelar, 14 July 1793, Guilford Co., N. C.

MING, Annarita and Thomas Collins, 25 January 1742, Chowan Co., N. C.

MING, Mary (widow) and John Howell, 8 September 1753, Chowan Co., N. C.

MING, Mary and William Haughton, 1 April 1748, Chowan Co., N. C.

MING, Sarah and William Wilkins, 18 January 1741, Chowan Co., N. C.

MING, Thomas and Sarah Nixon, (widow) 5 September 1753, Chowan Co., N. C.

MINIS, Frances and (Dr. Levi Myers, 15 February 1794, Georgetown, S. C.

MINOR, Robert and Elizabeth Nicholas, 13 November 1760, Santee, S. C.

MINOT, Amos and Martha Brown, May 1786, Charleston, S. C.

MINOTT, William B. and Jane F. Smith, 12 December 1801, Charleston, S. C.

MINOTT, William and Dorcas Rivers, June 1785, Charleston, S. C.

MINS, Mary Ann and Moses Medlock, 1 June 1826, Edgefield District, S. C.

MINTON, Benjamin and Alice Reed, 15 February 1790, Bertie Co., N. C.

MIOTE, Alexander and Rachel Fitch, 22 December 1763, Santee, S. C.

MISKELL, John B. and Julia A. Miller, 16 July 1828, Chowan Co., N. C.

MITCHELL, Achsa and Elisha Dail, 24 Deccember 1841, Chowan Co., N. C.

MITCHELL, Alexi and Peggy Shoecraft, 13 September 1834, Guilford Co., N. C.

MITCHELL, Alfonso O. and Perlina Williams, 15 August 1860, Guilford Co., N. C.

MITCHELL, Ann and Reuben Harrison, 18 May 1790, Bertie Co., N. C.

MITCHELL, Ann and James Bacchus, 17 October 1811, Chowan Co., N. C.

MITCHELL, Betsy and Thomas Early, 25 September 1821, Bertie Co., N. C.

MITCHELL, Catherine (widow) and John Rombough, 11 May 1747, Chowan Co., N. C.

MITCHELL, Catron and Patrick O'Neil, 23 August 1790, Mecklenburg Co., N. C.

MITCHELL, Charles and Martha Tamilson, 29 June 1743, Charleston, S. C.

MITCHELL, Daniel and Patsy Wiggins, 19 December 1804, Mecklenburg Co., N. C.

MITCHELL, Dickson and Mary Tarkinton, 22 March 1769, Tyrrell Co., N. C.

MITCHELL, Donald G. and Mary Pringle, May 1853, Charleston, S. C.

MITCHELL, Edward and Mary Moore, 9 July 1782, Santee, S. C.

MITCHELL, Edward and Milky Brown, 30 July 1823, Guilford Co., N. C.

MITCHELL, Eliza and Isaac B. Chappell, 19 February 1852, Chowan Co., N. C.

MITCHELL, Elizabeth and James Fleming, 24 January 1784, Rowan Co., N. C.

MITCHELL, Elizabeth and Evan Simpson, 21 January 1812, Chowan Co., N. C.

MITCHELL, Elizabeth and Hance Jordan, 30 March 1859, Chowan Co., N. C.

MITCHELL, Ellis and Polly Keter, 26 January 1848, Guilford Co., N. C.

MITCHELL, Ellis and Mary Curry, 12 February 1857, Guilford Co., N. C.

MITCHELL, Ephriam and Margaret Matthews, 31 August 1825, Mecklenburg Co., N. C.

MITCHELL, George and Aggie Holder, 20 December 1830, Bertie Co., N. C.

MITCHELL, Hannah and Massey, 1 December 1753, Charleston, S. C.

MITCHELL, Hannah and Peter Owen, 20 November 1786, Orange Co., N. C.

MITCHELL, Hannah (Mrs.) and Joseph D. Bell, 18 January 1800, Charleston, S. C.

MITCHELL, Harriet and John Holmes, 29 July 1830, Edgefield District, S. C.

MITCHELL, Henry and Ann Munds, 5 July 1831, Chowan Co., N. C.

MITCHELL, Henry and Martha Jones, 14 October 1846, Chowan Co., N. C.

MITCHELL, Isabella and James Mitchell, 5 December 1832, Guilford Co., N. C.

MITCHELL, Isabella and James McNeely, 25 August 1846, Guilford Co., N. C.

MITCHELL, James and Sarah Bunch, 26 January 1809, Chowan Co., N. C.

MITCHELL, James and Mary Roberts, 25 February 1830, Chowan Co., N. C.

MITCHELL, James and Isabella Mitchell, 5 December 1832, Guilford Co., N. C.

MITCHELL, Jane (widow) and Henry Warner, 13 January 1743, Prince George Parish, S. C.

MITCHELL, Jane and John Allen Orr, 14 January 1811, Mecklenburg Co., N. C.

MITCHELL, Jean and John Mck. Bradley, 13 February 1796, Mecklenburg Co., N. C.

MITCHELL, Jeremiah and Sarah Morris, 4 December 1832, Bertie Co., N. C.

MITCHELL, Jesse and Elizabeth Ashley, 28 September 1802, Chowan Co., N. C.

MITCHELL, John and (Mrs.) Sarah Macpherson, 18 July 1765, Charleston, S. C.

MITCHELL, John and Rebekah Baker, 31 January 1797, Mecklenburg Co., N. C.

MITCHELL, John and Sarah Ashley, 23 December 1797, Chowan Co., N. C.

MITCHELL, John and Rebecca Varner, 17 July 1804, Mecklenburg Co., N. C.

MITCHELL, John and Esther Jarrett, 14 July 1812, Mecklenburg Co., N. C.

MITCHELL, John M. and Elizabeth Banner, 9 July 1850, Guilford Co., N. C.

MITCHELL, Joseph and Sarah Williams, 30 December 1779, Bertie Co., N. C.

MITCHELL, Joseph and Delaney Whittington, 4 January 1837, Guilford Co., N. C.

MITCHELL, Joseph and Franky Reed, 21 August 1848, Guilford Co., N. C.

MITCHELL, Lavinia and Exum Griffin, 22 November 1830, Chowan Co., N. C.

MITCHELL, Lewis and Nancy Ellias, 29 November 1827, Chowan Co., N. C.

MITCHELL, Lewis and Jemina Griffin, 15 January 1847, Chowan Co., N. C.

MITCHELL, Margaret and James Parish, 8 November 1844, Chowan Co., N. C.

MITCHELL, Martha and Solomon Walker, 1779, Granville Co., N. C.

MITCHELL, Martha E. M. and (Lieut.) E. R. Davis, August 1812, Charleston, S. C.

MITCHELL, Martha E. and William W. Mitchell, 15 June 1834, Bertie Co., N. C.

MITCHELL, Mary and David Allen, 14 February 1720, Charleston, S. C.

MITCHELL, Mary and Thomas Langley, 13 April 1724, Charleston, S. C.

MITCHELL, Mary and John Bullock, 12 November 1759, Oxford, N. C.

MITCHELL, Mary and Maurice Simmons, 19 July 1764, Charleston, S. C.

MITCHELL, Mary and Henry Cranshaw, 26 May 1801, Mecklenburg Co., N. C.

MITCHELL, Mary and Isaac Goodwin, 4 January 1821, Chowan Co., N. C.

MITCHELL, Mary and James Todd, 19 June 1828, Bertie Co., N. C.

MITCHELL, Milly and James Overton, 26 November 1788, Bertie Co., N. C.

MITCHELL, Nancy and William Mather, 25 August 1787, Guilford Co., N. C.

MITCHELL, Nancy and William P. White, 18 October 1858, Granville Co., N. C.

MITCHELL, Nathan and Rachel Etheridge, 30 April 1787, Chowan Co., N. C.

MITCHELL, Nathan and Nancy Shields, 9 February 1804, Mecklenburg Co., N. C.

MITCHELL, Penelope and John Castellaw, 30 November 1785, Bertie Co., N. C.

MITCHELL, Randall and Tillitha Wiggin, 14 January 1805, Mecklenburg Co., N. C.

MITCHELL, Rhoda and William Morris, 22 November 1790, Bertie Co., N. C.

MITCHELL, Robert and Jeane Dickson, 16 September 1786, Orange Co., N. C.
MITCHELL, Robert and Isabella Russell, 26 July 1792, Mecklenburg Co., N. C.
MITCHELL, Robert and Elizabeth Rich, 19 March 1822, Guilford Co., N. C.
MITCHELL, Robert and Elizabeth Blumander, 13 November 1839, Guilford Co., N.C.
MITCHELL, Robert H. and Emily J. Freeman, 9 March 1853, Guilford Co., N. C.
MITCHELL, Robert and Minerva Flood, 16 May 1855, Guilford Co., N. C.
MITCHELL, Robert and Priscilla Harrison, 4 November 1859, Guilford Co., N. C.
MITCHELL, Rose E. and John J. McCullough, 17 March 1834, Edgefield District, S. C.
MITCHELL, R. G. and Sarah H. Cheshire, 29 June 1858, Chowan Co., N. C.
MITCHELL, Ruth and Thomas Lacy, 20 November 1800, Charleston, S. C.
MITCHELL, Samuel and Margaret McMurry, 19 October 1795, Guilford Co., N. C.
MITCHELL, Sarah and John Abercrombie, 1777, Charleston, S. C.
MITCHELL, Sarah and William A. Hyrne, 3 June 1779, Santee, S. C.
MITCHELL, Sarah and William Castellaw, 31 March 1784, Bertie Co., N. C.
MITCHELL, Sarah and Julius Dail, 26 November 1824, Chowan Co., N. C.
MITCHELL, Sarah and John Boyce, 4 August 1834, Chowan Co., N. C.
MITCHELL, Susan and Thomas Boyce, 12 January 1838, Chowan Co., N. C.
MITCHELL, Thomas and Anne Rothmabler, 13 August 1778, Santee, S. C.
MITCHELL, Timothy and Ann E. Trotman, 24 April 1855, Chowan Co., N. C.
MITCHELL, Washington and Sarah McDowell, 14 October 1836, Guilford Co., N. C.
MITCHELL, William and Mary Osborn, 28 June 1753, Charleston, S. C.
MITCHELL, William and Nannie Asbell, 22 August 1797, Chowan Co., N. C.
MITCHELL, William and Ruth Thompson, April 1779, Charleston, S. C.
MITCHELL, William and Penelope Deal, 1 December 1819, Chowan Co., N. C.
MITCHELL, William and Elizabeth Blair, 2 December 1828, Guilford, N. C.
MITCHELL, William and Tempy Pettiford, 13 November 1851, Guilford Co., N. C.
MITCHELL, William P. and Elizabeth J. Wagstaff, 10 November 1853, Guilford Co., N. C.
MITCHELL, William W. and Martha Williford, 1 October 1832, Bertie Co., N. C.
MITCHELL, William W. and Martha E. Mitchell, 15 June 1834, Bertie Co., N. C.
MITCHELL, Winney and Nathan Cobb, 9 August 1779, Bertie Co., N. C.
MITCHELL, Winnifred and Amos Weston, 23 September 1780, Bertie Co., N. C.
MITCHELL, Wright and Martha A. Outlaw, 19 December 1827, Bertie Co., N. C.
MITTEN, Rebecca and William Carrigan, 27 December 1793, Mecklenburg Co., N. C.
MIZELL, Charlton and Elizabeth Everitt, 2 August 1764, Tyrrell Co., N. C.
MIZELL, Hannah and John Mizell, 13 November 1768, Tyrrell Co., N. C.
MIZELL, Hezekiah and Nancy Britain, 8 May 1805, Bertie Co., N. C.
MIZELL, James and Sarah King, 18 January 1769, Tyrrell Co., N. C.
MIZELL, John and Hannah Mizell, 13 November 1768, Tyrrell Co., N. C.
MIZELL, John and Winnie Miller, 9 November 1789, Bertie Co., N. C.
MIZZELL, Sarah and Benjamin Richardson, 30 September 1767, Tyrrell Co., N. C.

MOCK, Catherine and Feliz Houk, 13 June 1793, Rowan Co., N. C.

MOFFITT, Charles and Mary Cox, 27 November 1772, Guilford Co., N. C.

MONCRIEF, Abigail and Greenbury Hughes, 14 April 1785, Charleston, S. C.

MONCRIEF, John and Polly Fly, 4 October 1766, Charleston, S. C.

MONCRIEF, Polly and Thomas Wright, 24 February 1751, Charleston, S. C.

MONCRIEF, Polly and John Brailsford, 6 December 1769, Charleston, S. C.

MONCRIEF, Robert and Polly Dewar, 2 April 1755, Charleston, S. C.

MONCRIEF, Susanna Y. and David Dubose, 20 February 1800, Wadnelaw Island, S. C.

MONDAY, Elizabeth and Thomas Moore, 11 September 1797, Guilford Co., N. C.

MONHEIM, Christopher and Catherine Fry, 26 December 1752, Orangeburg Co., S. C.

MONK, John and Magdaline Boineau, 20 October 1767, Santee, S. C.

MONK, Linah and Jesse Jones, 21 July 1788, Bertie Co., N. C.

MONK, Martha and James Calhoun, 5 September 1771, Santee, S. C.

MONK, Thomas and Johannah Broughton, 13 January 1732, Charleston, S. C.

MONK, Thomas and Mary De St. Julien, 11 July 1745, Charleston, S. C.

MONRO, Margaret and Donald Huston, 31 December 1779, Rowan Co., N. C.

MONS, Esther and Matthew Bibbs, 23 March 1818, Mecklenburg Co., N. C.

MONTFORT, Ann and Isaac Speight, 24 July 1764, Chowan Co., N. C.

MONTGOMERY, Alexander and Sarah Cromartie, 18 May 1778, Chowan Co., N. C.

MONTGOMERY, Amanda and Solomon Griffith, 20 January 1880, Mecklenburg Co., N. C.

MONTGOMERY, Anna and James Ross, 5 October 1815, Mecklenburg Co., N. C.

MONTGOMERY, A. F. and (Miss) E. A. Brown, 15 June 1865, Mecklenburg Co., N. C.

MONTGOMERY, Deborah and James G. Barnett, 24 January 1827, Mecklenburg Co., N. C.

MONTGOMERY, Elizabeth and William H. Mills, 22 July 1769, Santee, S. C.

MONTGOMERY, Elizabeth and Joshua Page, 9 October 1787, Bertie Co., N. C.

MONTGOMERY, Elizabeth and Jonathan Miller, 23 September 1818, Guilford Co., N. C.

MONTGOMERY, Elizabeth L. and Robert R. Roberts, 18 May 1840, Mecklenburg Co., N. C.

MONTGOMERY, Esther and Francis Bell, 1773, Guilford Co., N. C.

MONTGOMERY, Hannah and John Ross, 12 June 1816, Mecklenburg Co., N. C.

MONTGOMERY, Hannah and James McKnight, 13 November 1792, Guilford Co., N. C.

MONTGOMERY, James and Elizabeth Jessop, 21 November 1775, Guilford Co., N. C.

MONTGOMERY, James and Rebekah Clark, 8 January 1800, Mecklenburg Co., N. C.

MONTGOMERY, James and Delila Herron, 16 June 1846, Mecklenburg Co., N. C.

MONTGOMERY, James and Leah Ernhardt, 4 August 1851, Rowan Co., N. C.

MONTGOMERY, James A. and Margaret Phifer, 7 December 1841, Rowan Co., N. C.

MONTGOMERY, James C. and Delilah Hill, 23 February 1825, Rowan Co., N. C.

MONTGOMERY, James T. and Martha C. Shaw, 11 February 1857, Guilford Co., N. C.

MONTGOMERY, Jane and William Roberts, 26 September 1832, Mecklenburg Co., N. C.

MONTGOMERY, Jesse and Lavina May, 22 December 1865, Guilford Co., N. C.

MONTGOMERY, John and Elinor Towny, 15 May 1799, Guilford Co., N. C.

MONTGOMERY, John and Mary Clark, 1 August 1795, Mecklenburg Co., N. C.

MONTGOMERY, John and Martha Braley, 16 May 1786, Guilford Co., N. C.

MONTGOMERY, John and Margaret Begett, 26 February 1802, Mecklenburg Co., N. C.

MONTGOMERY, John and Mary Wiley, 14 July 1827, Mecklenburg Co., N. C.

MONTGOMERY, John H. and Susan A. Holcomb, 1857, Spartansburg, S. C.

MONTGOMERY, John H. and Hannah E. Moore, 27 December 1831, Mecklenburg Co., N. C.

MONTGOMERY, Lucinda and William Clark, 27 January 1800, Mecklenburg Co., N. C.

MONTGOMERY, Margaret and Robert Bridger, 2 November 1786, Bertie Co., N. C.

MONTGOMERY, Margaret N. and James H. McConnell, 21 July 1850, Mecklenburg Co., N. C.

MONTGOMERY, Martha and Cyrus Henry, 3 January 1810, Mecklenburg Co., N. C.

MONTGOMERY, Martha and Elikah Mears, 23 May 1811, Guilford Co., N. C.

MONTGOMERY, Martha and Stephen Alexander, 8 September 1819, Mecklenburg Co., N. C.

MONTGOMERY, Martha A. and Nathan F. Orr, 18 September 1851, Mecklenburg Co., N. C.

MONTGOMERY, Mary and Isaac Mason, 22 June 1831, Mecklenburg Co., N. C.

MONTGOMERY, Mary Jane and Hugh M. Hunter, 21 August 1850, Mecklenberg Co., N. C.

MONTGOMERY, Mary N. and Walter A. Hill, 27 December 1830, Mecklenburg Co., N. C.

MONTGOMERY, Melissa N. and Rufus L. Alexander, 22 May 1844, Mecklenburg Co., N. C.

MONTGOMERY, Mrs. and George Kiernan, 28 April 1801, Charleston, S. C.

MONTGOMERY, Nicholas and Jane Phifer, 11 January 1845, Rowan Co., N. C.

MONTGOMERY, Phebe and Samuel Morton, 18 August 1850, Guilford Co., N. C.

MONTGOMERY, Rebekah and David E. Barnett, 7 February 1827, Mecklenburg Co., N. C.

MONTGOMERY, Robert and Elianor McCleary, 15 November 1804, Mecklenburg Co., N. C.

MONTGOMERY, Robert D. and Hannah H. Nelson, 1841, Lancaster, Co., S. C.

MONTGOMERY, R. C. and Margaret B. Wallace, 13 February 1855, Mecklenburg Co., N. C.

MONTGOMERY, R. C. and Mary E. Hutchison, 8 December 1859, Mecklenburg Co., N. C.

MONTGOMERY, R. F. and Eliza Cathay, 17 January 1849, Mecklenburg Co., N. C.

MONTGOMERY, Samuel and Rachel Clark, 28 March 1812, Mecklenburg Co., N. C.

MONTGOMERY, Sarah and Berrisford Bacon, 26 June 1738, Charleston, S. C.

MONTGOMERY, Sarah and Henry Averit, 9 May 1792, Bertie Co., N. C.

MONTGOMERY, Sarah A. and William Morton, 10 November 1855, Rowan Co., N. C.

MONTGOMERY, William and Margaret Forbes, 14 June 1802, Guilford Co., N. C.

MONTGOMERY, William and Sarah Albright, 13 November 1817, Guilford Co., N. C.

MONTGOMERY, William and Sarah Heart, 10 February 1830, Guilford Co., N. C.

MONTGOMERY, Wilson and Mary A. Alexander, 15 April 1846, Mecklenburg Co., N. C.

MONTIER, Lewis and M. Biddys, 1740, Orangeburg Co., S. C.

MONTIETH, Alexi and Elizabeth Walker, 1 December 1790, Mecklenburg Co., N. C.

MONTIETH, Elizabeth and Joseph Maxwell, 10 January 1792, Mecklenburg Co., N. C.

MONTIETH, John and ——— Hargrove, 10 September 1814, Mecklenburg Co., N. C.

MONTIETH, John and Martha Alexander, 29 January 1833, Mecklenburg Co., N. C.

MONTIETH, Lea E. and John G. A. Orr, 30 April 1857, Mecklenburg Co., N. C.

MONTIETH, Margaret and Stephen Jewell, 30 July 1792, Mecklenburg Co., N. C.

MONTIETH, Margaret C. and Daniel A. Blakely, 25 March 1837, Mecklenburg Co., N. C.

MONTIETH, Martha A. and William Brown, 29 October 1839, Mecklenburg Co., N. C.

MONTIETH, Maria A. and James L. V. Orr, 17 January 1861, Mecklenburg Co., N. C.

MONTIETH, William and Susannah Williams, 13 November 1804, Mecklenburg Co., N. C.

MONTIETH, William and Violet Barry, 4 September 1807, Mecklenburg Co., N. C.

MONTIGUE, Thomas and Mary Everett, 17 February 1792, Guilford Co., N. C.

MONZEN, Samuel and Ann Maynard, 17 May 1770, Santee, S. C.

MONZON, Nelly and Joseph Wragg, 23 October 1783, Georgetown, S. C.

MOOER, Daniel and Treacy Strobel, 21 July 1814, Orangeburg Co., S. C.

MOOER, Reubin Ellis and Elizabeth Murray, 7 June 1820, Orangeburg Co., S. C.

MOOER, John and Anna Margaret (Stroman) Brunner, 1792, Orangeburg Co., S. C.

MOONEY, Eliza and Horatio Blease, 23 October 1835, Edgefield District, S. C.

MOOR, Mary and Thomas Eberhard, 1746, Orangeburg Co., S. C.

MOORE, Agnes and Evan Alexander, 2 November 1818, Mecklenburg Co., N. C.

MOORE, Alexander and Dorcas Erwin, 1784, York Co., S. C.

MOORE, Amanda and Horace McCall, 16 February 1836, Mecklenburg Co., N. C.

MOORE, Andrew F. and Arminta B. Christenbury, 20 August 1846, Mecklenburg Co., N. C.

MOORE, Ann M. and Anthony Butler, 15 October 1799, Charleston, S. C.

MOORE, Arminta and John Moore, 22 October 1800, Mecklenburg Co., N. C.

MOORE, Austin and Louisa Power, 3 November 1858, Laurens Co., S. C.

MOORE, Catherine E. and Jacob C. Julian, 7 July 1853, Mecklenburg Co., N. C.

MOORE, Charles and Rebecca Taylor, 1777, Granville Co., N. C.

MOORE, Charles and Elizabeth Creecy, 15 November 1785, Chowan Co., N. C.

MOORE, Charles B. and Catherine Rodden, 19 June 1809, Mecklenburg Co., N. C.

MOORE, David and Jane Porter, 9 September 1780, Guilford Co., N. C.

MOORE, David and Agnes Helms, 9 May 1811, Mecklenburg Co., N. C.

MOORE, David J. and Nancy L. Wilson, 8 October 1845, Mecklenburg Co., N. C.

MOORE, Dunham and Susannah Walker, 1778, Granville Co., N. C.

MOORE, Elam and Eliza Campbell, 18 January 1826, Mecklenburg Co., N. C.

MOORE, Eleanor and Benjamin Bowie, 25 October 1827, Mecklenburg Co., N. C.

MOORE, Ezekiel and Elizabeth Hardison, 19 December 1766, Tyrrell Co., N. C.

MOORE, Fanny S. and Edward A. Osborn, 15 March 1865, Mecklenburg Co., N. C.

MOORE, Frances and Allen Rea, 2 November 1797, Mecklenburg Co., N. C.

MOORE, G. R. and Christine E. Todd, 3 January 1849, Mecklenburg Co., N. C.

MOORE, Hannah E. and John H. Montgomery, 27 December 1831, Mecklenburg Co., N. C.

MOORE, Harriet and Harris Garrett, 20 November 1844, Laurens Co., S. C.

MOORE, Herbert C. and Sarah Peeples, 8 March 1842, Guilford Co., N. C.

MOORE, Hugh and Helena Alexander, 19 March 1824, Mecklenburg Co., N. C.

MOORE, Isaac and Nancy Foard, 5 November 1800, Mecklenburg Co., N. C.

MOORE, Isaac H. and Martha Parks, 22 July 1854, Mecklenburg Co., N. C.

MOORE, Isabella and Hugh Gray, 31 March 1789, Rowan Co., N. C.

MOORE, James and Ellen McEwen, 12 June 1793, Mecklenburg Co., N. C.

MOORE, James W. (Dr.) and Susannah Jones, 4 October 1770, Charleston, S. C.

MOORE, James and Cynthia Johnson, 13 February 1827, Mecklenburg Co., N. C.

MOORE, James H. and Elizabeth Parks, 6 April 1825, Mecklenburg Co., N. C.

MOORE, James W. and Isabella S. G. Davidson, 19 January 1835, Mecklenburg Co., N. C.

MOORE, John and Justina Smith, 22 October 1719, St. Andrews Parish, S. C.

MOORE, John and Comfort Rowan, 20 February 1782, Guilford Co., N. C.

MOORE, John and Arminta Moore, 22 October 1800, Mecklenburg Co., N. C.

MOORE, John and Narcissa Henderson, 16 October 1864, Laurens Co., S. C.

MOORE, Joseph and Priscilla Atkinson, 29 October 1790, Bertie Co., N. C.

MOORE, Joseph S. and Sarah Emberson, 20 December 1826, Mecklenburg Co., N. C.

MOORE, Joshua T. and Locky Abernathy, 6 January 1830, Mecklenburg Co., N. C.

MOORE, Lemmy and Rachel Magee, 21 January 1818, Guilford Co., N. C.

MOORE, Margaret and John Gardner, 25 July 1786, Rowan Co., N. C.

MOORE, Margaret and Samuel Nelson, 14 September 1790, Mecklenburg Co., N. C.

MOORE, Margaret and Robert McKnight, 27 January 1803, Mecklenburg Co., N. C.

MOORE, Margaret and C. L. Alexander, 5 April 1845, Mecklenburg Co., N. C.

MOORE, Margaret C. and James M. Caldwell, 15 January 1851, Mecklenburg Co., N. C.

MOORE, Mary and Edward Mitchell, 9 July 1782, Santee, S. C.

MOORE, Mary and Hugh Horah, 14 January 1788, Rowan Co., N. C.

MORRE, Mary and Thomas Gilbreath, 13 February 1797, Rowan Co., N. C.

MOORE, Mary and Cyrus Morrison, 21 January 1824, Mecklenburg Co., N. C.

MOORE, Mary and Oswald Alexander, 17 October 1826, Mecklenburg Co., N. C.

MOORE, Mary and John Dilliard, 31 March 1762, Edgecombe Co., N. C.

MOORE, Mary and Washington Grant, 25 November 1858, Laurens Co., S. C.

MOORE, Mary Ann and James W. Osborn, 5 April 1842, Mecklenburg Co., N. C.

MOORE, Melissa and James Clark, 24 November 1829, Mecklenburg Co., N. C.

MOORE, Michael and Rebecca Browne, 22 June 1797, Charleston, S. C.

MOORE, Michael and Sally Gibson, 5 April 1820, Edgefield District, S. C.

MOORE, Milly and Lewis Martin, 12 April 1848, Laurens Co., S. C.

MOORE, Miss and Sampson Braswell, 31 May 1762, Edgecombe Co., N. C.

MOORE, Penelope and James Granberry, 18 May 1790, Bertie Co., N. C.

MOORE, Phillip and Peggy Simpson, 12 March 1801, Mecklenburg Co., N. C.

MOORE, Polly Scott and John Cannon, 23 December 1791, Mecklenburg Co., N. C.

MOORE, Potiller and Martha Todd, 16 December 1852, Laurens Co., S. C.

MOORE, Prudy and Sam Johnston, 17 July 1811, Mecklenburg Co., N. C.

MOORE, P. F. and Angelina Drummond, 27 August 1865, Laurens Co., S. C.

MOORE, Rachel and William Allison (Jr.), February 1775, Charleston, S. C.

MOORE, Risdon and Ann Dent, 5 Deccember 1790, Guilford Co., N. C.

MOORE, Robertson and Eliza Todd, 21 November, 1844, Laurens Co., S. C.

MOORE, Samuel and Evaline C. Wallace, 9 March 1830, Mecklenburg Co., N. C.

MOORE, Sarah and Littlebury Abington, 4 May 1790, Bertie Co., N. C.

MOORE, Stephen and Sarah Garrett, 14 August 1845, Laurens Co., S. C.

MOORE, Teenan and Margaret Bowen, 15 June 1797, Guilford Co., N. C.

MOORE, Thomas and Isabella Dunn, 26 February 1793, Mecklenburg Co., N. C.

MOORE, Thomas and Elizabeth Monday, 11 September 1797, Guilford Co., N. C.

MOORE, Thomas and Ann C. Goldsbury, 1 October 1799, Guilford Co., N. C.

MOORE, Thomas J. and Mary Ann Irwin, 20 September 1838, Mecklenburg Co., N. C.

MOORE, William and Susannah Nichols, 1763, Granville Co., N. C.

MOORE, William and Hannah Stanford, 11 November 1800, Mecklenburg Co., N. C.

MOORE, William and Polly Felton, 19 February 1805, Mecklenburg Co., N. C.

MOORE, William and Ann Todd, 7 April 1821, Mecklenburg Co., N. C.

MOORE, William and Biddy Laning, August 1833, Mecklenburg Co., N. C.

MOORE, Willis and Martha Jasey, 3 March 1798, Guilford Co., N. C.

MOOREFIELD, Milly and Lifas Hilton, 5 November 1792, Rowan Co., N. C.

MOORER, Absalom (Dr.) and Dorcas Anne Moorer, 3 March 1842, Orangeburg Co., S. C.

MOORER, David and Anne Bowman, 1789, Orangeburg Co., S. C.

MOORER, Jacob Jenkins and Rebecca Dash, 20 October 1822, Orangeburg Co., S. C.

MOORER, Peter (Jr.) and Margaret Larry, June 1740, Orangeburg Co., S. C.

MOORER, John and Catherine Stroman, 12 November 1776, Orangeburg Co., S. C.

MOORER, Pinckney L. (Dr.) and Martha Harriet Moorer, 1 January 1863, Orangeburg Co., S. C.

MOORER, Pearson and Treacy Anne Moorer, 6 December 1849, Orangeburg Co., S. C.

MOORMAN, Francis and Benjamin H. Covington, 6 March 1780, Anson Co., N. C.

MORANT, John and Isabell Norvill, October 1783, Charleston, S. C.

MORE, Peter J. and Susan Delatour, 14 March 1785, Charleston, S. C.

MORETON, John and Dorothy Dry, 30 July 1747, Charleston, S. C.

MORFF, Barbara (widow) and Henry Wetstine, 24 December 1750, Orangeburg Co., S. C.

MORFF, Jacob and Christina Hessy, 5 June 1750, Orangeburg Co., S. C.

MORGAN, Anne and Thomas Clemens, 28 June 1733, Charleston, S. C.

MORGAN, George and Sarah Valentine, 20 November 1785, Chowan Co., N. C.

MORGAN, George W. and Martha Howell, 18 December 1856, Edgefield District, S. C.

MORGAN, James and Sarah Hubbard, 18 July 1800, Guilford Co., N. C.

MORGAN, John and Naomi Swain, 5 February 1800, Guilford Co., N. C.

MORGAN, Margaret and Bartley Martin, 14 November 1855, Edgefield District, S. C.

MORGAN, Mary and Jacob Flowers, 28 January 1788, Orange Co., N. C.

MORGAN, Nancy and Burwell Branch, 15 October 1788, Bertie Co., N. C.

MORGAN, Nicholson Ross and Mary W. Alexander, 29 November 1820, Mecklenburg Co., N. C.

MORGAN, William and Miss Chandler, 1 January 1770, Charleston, S. C.

MORGAN, William and Sallie Ward, 28 June 1821, Edgefield District, S. C.

MORRALL, Florida and Christopher S. Gadson, 9 May 1861, Charleston, S. C.

MORRIS, Allen and Sally Bond, 30 October 1805, Mecklenburg Co., N. C.

MORRIS, Amy and James McComb, 21 March 1828, Mecklenburg Co., N. C.

MORRIS, Annie and David Biggs, 1781, Camden, N. C.

MORRIS, Edward H. and Martha P. Cochran, 24 October 1854, Edgefield District, S. C.

MORRIS, Elizabeth and Hugh McLean, 24 April 1810, Mecklenburg Co., N. C.

MORRIS, Eliza and Ezekial Johnston, 19 September 1833, Mecklenburg Co., N. C.

MORRIS, Elizabeth and Elijah Rich, 15 August 1834, Mecklenburg Co., N. C.

MORRIS, James and Loving Britt, 7 November 1791, Bertie Co., N. C.

MORRIS, James and Elizabeth Wilson, 16 April 1804, Mecklenburg Co., N. C.

MORRIS, James J. and Anne Matthews, 6 June 1822, Mecklenburg Co., N. C.

MORRIS, James S. and Isabella Henderson, 26 January 1847, Mecklenburg Co., N. C.

MORRIS, John and Margaret Maxwell, 30 July 1792, Mecklenburg Co., N. C.

MORRIS, John and Mary Mahon, 9 June 1796, Mecklenburg Co., N. C.

MORRIS, John F. and Polly C. McLarty, 22 July 1830, Mecklenburg Co., N. C.

MORRIS, John J. and Eliza Young, 12 August 1822, Mecklenburg Co., N. C.

MORRIS, Josiah and Eveline Cannon, 11 August 1842, Mecklenburg Co., N. C.

MORRIS, Mary and Charles Vesey, 26 December 1799, Charleston, S. C.

MORRIS, Mary N. and Dempsey Rich, 7 October 1834, Mecklenburg Co., N. C.

MORRIS, Mikey and Henry Best, 17 January 1789, Bertie Co., N. C.

MORRIS, Nancy and Joseph L. Orr, 7 January 1823, Mecklenburg Co., N. C.

MORRIS, Nancy A. and William R. Maxwell, 12 November 1836, Mecklenburg Co., N. C.

MORRIS, Peggy and William Wood, October 1786, Charleston, S. C.

MORRIS, Philemon and Mary Shaver, 8 April 1794, Mecklenburg Co., N. C.

MORRIS, Reuben and Mary Houston, 1 February 1816, Mecklenburg Co., N. C.

MORRIS, Robert and Elizabeth Jenner, 27 June 1765, Santee, S. C.

MORRIS, Robert and Catherine Conner, 21 December 1811, Mecklenburg Co., N. C.

MORRIS, Robert J. and Minty McCombs, 20 January 1825, Mecklenburg Co., N. C.

MORRIS, Sarah and Jeremiah Mitchell, 4 December 1832, Bertie Co., N. C.

MORRIS, William and Rhoda Mitchell, 22 November 1790, Bertie Co., N. C.

MORRIS, William and Rhoda Weaver, 18 September 1803, Chowan Co., N. C.

MORRIS, William C. and (Miss) Mc Johnston, 4 March 1843, Mecklenburg Co., N. C.

MORRIS, William H. and Lucinda Cochran, 25 January 1844, Mecklenburg Co., N. C.

MORRIS, Winifred and Samuel Todd, 28 November 1789, Bertie Co., N. C.

MORRIS, Zebulon L. and Mary A. Parks, 20 July 1847, Mecklenburg Co., N. C.

MORRISON, Caroline and Isaac Alexander, 8 August 1845, Mecklenburg Co., N. C.

MORRISON, Cynthia and Joel B. Alexander, 16 August 1815, Mecklenburg Co., N. C.

MORRISON, Cyrus and Mary Moore, 21 January 1824, Mecklenburg Co., N. C.

MORRISON, Henry and Jane Porter, 29 December 1823, Mecklenburg Co., N. C.

MORRISON, James and Margaret Johnston, 10 September 1799, Mecklenburg Co., N. C.

MORRISON, James and Mary Simons, 23 February 1819, Mecklenburg Co., N. C.

MORRISON, James M. and Mary Johnston, 4 December 1830, Mecklenburg Co., N. C.

MORRISON, Jane and John M. Johnson, 7 January 1861, Mecklenburg Co., N. C.

MORRISON, John and Jane Bradshaw, 5 April 1791, Mecklenburg Co., N. C.

MORRISON, John and Elizabeth Watson, 11 June 1801, Charleston, S. C.

MORRISON, John and Dolly Rogers, 31 July 1804, Mecklenburg Co., N. C.

MORRISON, Martha and John Foster, 20 March 1768, Rowan Co., N. C.

MORRISON, Nathaniel and Ruth Alexander, 20 January 1827, Mecklenburg Co., N. C.

MORRISON, Robert and Rebecca Spencer, 25 June 1767, Santee, S. C.

MORRISON, Robert and Margaret McComb, 4 March 1797, Mecklenburg Co., N. C.

MORRISON, Samuel F. and Rachel Gingler, 18 April 1818, Mecklenburg Co., N. C.

MORRISON, Serena and David W. Miller, 8 August 1845, Mecklenburg Co., N. C.

MORRISON, Washington and Mary Ann Denkins, 15 October 1825, Mecklenburg Co., N. C.

MORRISON, William and Rosanna Gingler, 9 March 1819, Mecklenburg Co., N. C.

MORRISON, William and Margaret Houston, 17 December 1821, Mecklenburg Co., N. C.

MORRISON, William and Helena Kerr, 11 December 1830, Mecklenburg Co., N. C.

MORROW, Benjamin and Mary J. Hawkins, 20 April 1847, Mecklenburg Co., N. C.

MORROW, David and Jeane McCullogh, 25 November 1802, Mecklenburg Co., N. C.

MORROW, David and Margaret Parks, 20 August 1839, Mecklenburg Co., N. C.

MORROW, Drury and Esther McCullough, 17 January 1820, Mecklenburg Co., N. C.

MORROW, Eli and Mary Cook, 19 December 1838, Mecklenburg Co., N. C.

MORROW, Elizabeth and Isaac Morrow, 14 November 1820, Mecklenburg Co., N. C.

MORROW, Hezekiah and Elizabeth Jones, 5 January 1815, Mecklenburg Co., N. C.

MORROW, Hezekiah and Elizabeth Ray, 25 April 1820, Mecklenburg Co., N. C.

MORROW, Isaac and Sally Powers, 18 July 1811, Mecklenburg Co., N. C.

MORROW, Isaac and Elizabeth Morrow, 14 November 1820, Mecklenburg Co., N. C.

MORROW, Jenny and Adams Brown, 28 April 1801, Mecklenburg Co., N. C.

MORROW, John and Mary Clark, 18 March 1792, Guilford Co., N. C.

MORROW, John White and Patsy Norley, 10 December 1807, Mecklenburg Co., N. C.

MORROW, Margaret H. and Thomas H. Blackley, 20 September 1836, Mecklenburg Co., N. C.

MORROW, Martha and Robert Morrow, 5 March 1812, Mecklenburg Co., N. C.

MORROW, Martha and Stephen W. Morrow, 27 September 1841, Mecklenburg Co., N. C.

MORROW, Martha L. and Joseph Black, 17 August 1837, Mecklenburg Co., N. C.

MORROW, Martha M. and Lewis H. Russell, 23 December 1847, Mecklenburg Co., N. C.

MORROW, Mary and William Busby, 5 March 1812, Mecklenburg Co., N. C.

MORROW, Peggy and James Bonds, 25 November 1802, Mecklenburg Co., N. C.

MORROW, Robert and Martha Morrow, 5 March 1812, Mecklenburg Co., N. C.

MORROW, Robert W. and Sarah Williams, 4 February 1840, Mecklenburg Co., N. C.

MORROW, Stephen W. and Martha Morrow, 27 September 1841, Mecklenburg Co., N. C.

MORROW, William and Margaret Crockett, 17 March 1794, Mecklenburg Co., N. C.

MORSE, John G. and Mary H. ——, 8 January 1822, Mecklenburg Co., N. C.

MORTON, Charles S. and Obedience Osborn, 18 January 1803, Mecklenburg Co., N. C.

MORTON, Dorothy (widow) and John Moultrie (Jr.), 23 April 1753, Charleston, S. C.

MORTON, Samuel and Phebe Montgomery, 18 August 1750, Guilford Co., N. C.

MORTON, William and Sarah A. Montgomery, 10 November 1855, Rowan Co., N. C.

MOSELEY, Edward and Ann Batesman, 16 January 1795, Chowan Co., N. C.

MOSELEY, Cinthia and Thomas Gray, 23 March 1843, Laurens Co., S. C.

MOSELEY, George and Matilda Garrison, 23 December 1851, Laurens Co., S. C.

MOSELEY, George (Col.) and Harriet Lester, 1 December 1858, Laurens Co., S. C.

MOSELEY, Thomas and Tarsy Tolin, 12 December 1850, Laurens Co., S. C.

MOSELY, Elizabeth and James Rose, 12 December 1850, Laurens Co., S. C.

MOSELY, Eveline and James Fleming, 6 March 1848, Laurens Co., S. C.

MOSES, Cherry and Esther Moses, 14 October 1801, Charleston, S. C.

MOSES, Esther and Cherry Moses, 14 October 1801, Charleston, S. C.

MOSES, Isaac and Esther Isaacks, 2 July 1800, Charleston, S. C.

MOSIER, Pheby and James Givens, 19 December 1792, Rowan Co., N. C.

MOSS, C. E. and (Miss) J. S. Alexander, 21 April 1845, Mecklenburg Co., N. C.

MOSS, Jordan D. and Ann Mann White, 5 March 1827, Granville Co., N. C.

MOSS, Richardson and Sarah Turner, 27 September 1783, Perquimans Co., N. C.

MOSS, Ruben J. and Frances Asbury White, 4 October 1839, Granville Co., N. C.

MOSS, William and Elizabeth Burris, 5 November 1851, Edgefield District, S. C.

MOTES, Milford and Francis Abrams, 23 November 1858, Laurens Co., S. C.

MOTES, Permealy and William Garrett, 20 December 1844, Laurens Co., S. C.

MOTES, Sarah and Sidney Finley, 26 January 1858, Laurens Co., S. C.

MOTTE, Hannah and Thomas Lynch, 6 March 1755, Charleston, S. C.

MOTTE, Isaac and Anne Smith, 15 December 1763, Charleston, S. C.

MOTTE, Jacob and Anne Pickering (widow), 19 June 1763, Charleston, S. C.

MOTTE, Sarah and Thomas Shubrick, 8 May 1746, Charleston, S. C.

MOTZ, Catherine and John F. Ellenberger, 28 January 1794, Rowan Co., N. C.

MOULTREE, William and Elizabeth D. St. Julian, 19 December 1749, Charleston, S. C.

MOULTRIE, Alexander and Katy Lennox, 21 May 1772, Charleston, S. C.

MOULTRIE, John (Dr.) and Elizabeth Matthews (widow), 6 July 1748, Charleston, S. C.

MOULTRIE, John (Jr.) and Dorothy Morton (widow), 23 April 1753, Charleston, S. C.

MOUSEY, Thomas J. and Frances J. Covington, 1 March 1849, Richmond Co., N. C.

MOUZON, Elizabeth and John Wells, 16 August 1778, Santee, S. C.

MOW, Alexander and Elizabeth Cleland, 6 January 1763, Chowan Co., N. C.

MOWELL, Peter and Lydia Waff, 8 September 1779, Chowan Co., N. C.

MUCHMORE, Barnard (Capt.) and Sally Little, 5 March 1795, Charleston, S. C.

MUCKENFUSS, Henry and (Mrs.) Frances Postlethwait, 26 April 1797, Charleston, S. C.

MUCKLIN, Hugh and Agnes Anderson, 22 November 1785, Guilford Co., N. C.

MULLEN, Sarah and Benjamin Turner, 10 April 1790, Perquimans Co., N. C.

MULLER, Christina and John Fry, 23 November 1779, Rowan Co., N. C.

MULLER, Sarah and Dempsey Turner, 9 April 1781, Perquimans Co., N. C.

MULLICAR, Sally and Youkley Griffin, 10 January 1796, Rowan Co., N. C.

MULLINS, Clem and Betsy Parker, 4 August 1807, Mecklenburg Co., N. C.

MULLINS, George and Elizabeth Miles (widow), 17 March 1768, Charleston, S. C.

MULLINS, George and Sarah Cattell, 17 June 1773, Berkeley Co., S. C.

MULLINS, Peter and Mary Grier, 19 October 1790, Mecklenburg Co., N. C.

MULIVA, Miles and Sarah Allen, 20 July 1836, Mecklenburg Co., N. C.

MUNCREEF, John and (Mrs.) Sarah C. Schepsler, 26 May 1801, Charleston, S. C.

MUNOS, Ann and Henry Mitchell, 5 July 1831, Chowan Co., N. C.

MUNDS, Israel (Rev.) and (Mrs.) Charlotte D. Meyer, 3 September 1801, Charleston, S. C.

MUNROE, Sarah and John Ryder, 22 February 1800, Charleston, S. C.

MURDOCK, David and Mary Bohannon, 12 August 1788, Orange Co., N. C.

MURDOCK, James and Elizabeth Gray, 10 June 1790, Orange Co., N. C.

MURDOCK, Polly and William Hall, 9 February 1786, Orange Co., N. C.

MURER, Ann D. and Martin Miller, 23 July 1801, Chowan Co., N. C.

MURER, Peter and Magdalene Horguer, 2 April 1751, Orangeburg Co., S. C.

MURPHY, Alice and Isaac Jamieson, 5 March 1825, Mecklenburg Co., N. C.

MURPHY, Archibald and Mary McKenney, 30 March 1798, Mecklenburg Co., N. C.

MURPHY, John and Margaret Carr, 5 November 1786, Guilford Co., N. C.

MURPHY, Joseph and Betty Chadwick, 16 November 1774, Guilford Co., N. C.

MURPHY, Rebecca (widow) and Benjamin Carter, 14 January 1740, Orangeburg Co., S. C.

MURPHY, Solo and Betsy Guion, 29 October 1781, Orange Co., N. C.

MURPHY, Timothy and Milley Ballard, 4 January 1774, Guilford Co., N. C.

MURRAY, Anne and Andrew Bell, 3 December 1767, Charleston, S. C.

MURRAY, Domonick and Millie Sullivan, 7 January 1778, Chowan Co., N. C.

MURRAY, Elizabeth and Alexander Alexander, 1 February 1774, Charleston, S. C.

MURRAY, Isaac and Elizabeth Koger, 1823, Orangeburg Co., S. C.

MURRAY, John (Dr.) and (Lady) Anne Atkins, 16 February 1764, Charleston, S. C.

MURRAY, John Simmons and Mary Caroline Moorer, 24 December 1839, Orangeburg Co., S. C.

MURRAY, Mary and John Creighton, April 1774, Charleston, S. C.

MURRAY, William (Dr.) and Elizabeth Margaret Moorer, 23 June 1835, Orangeburg Co., S. C.

MURRAY, William (Jr.) and Mary Hughes, 23 November 1802, Orangeburg Co., S. C.

MURRAY, William (Sr.) and Martha McQuillan, 1781, Orangeburg Co., S. C.

MURRAY, William (Jr.) and Mary Rhodd, 29 August 1813, Orangeburg Co., S. C.

MURRELL, Ann and William Lewis, 14 May 1767, Santee, S. C.

MURRELL, Damaris and James Landels, 23 February 1780, Santee, S. C.

MURRELL, Elizabeth and John Swearingen, 25 January 1849, Edgefield District, S. C.

MURRELL, James W. and Eliza Sumpter, 19 April 1807, Santee, S. C.

MURRELL, James and Izette Long, 1 January 1835, Edgefield District, S. C.

MURRELL, Martha and John Jennens, 15 January 1767, Santee, S. C.

MURRELL, Mary E. and (Col.) John B. Miller, 16 July 1808, Statesburg, S. C.

MURRILL, Martha and Robert Jordan, 18 September 1763, Santee, S. C.

MURRILL, William and Mary C. Kenney, 5 February 1833, Edgefield District, S. C.

MYER, Hans Jacob and Ann Buser, 1 January 1740, Orangeburg Co., S. C.

MYERS, Alexander W. and Harriet Miller, 27 January 1857, Chowan Co., N. C.

MYERS, Barbara and Peter Hedrick, 18 February 1797, Rowan Co., N. C.

MYERS, Catherina (widow) and John Hamilton, 1 July 1741, Orangeburg Co., S. C.

MYERS, Levi (Dr.) and Frances Minis, 15 February 1794, Georgetown, S. C.

MYERS, Michael and Elizabeth McCrary, 17 October 1778, Guilford Co., N. C.

N

NABORS, Elizabeth and James McCray, 15 September 1857, Laurens Co., S. C.

NANCE, Isabella and Samuel Blythe, 8 January 1822, Mecklenburg Co., N. C.

NANCE, Macilda G. and William J. Bobo, 11 November 1847, Union District, S. C.

NANCE, Martha and John A. Barksdale, 7 October 1852, Newberry, S. C.

NANCE, William and Sarah Alcorn, 18 December 1814, Mecklenburg Co., N. C.

NANDAFORD, Annie and James Miller, October 1780, Tyrrell Co., N. C.

NAPER, Nathan and Pherebe Weatherford, 21 May 1826, Edgefield District, S. C.

NAPER, Tillman D. and Sarah Holsenback, 22 November 1833, Edgefield District, S. C.

NAPIER, Richard and Mary Wills, 1772 Wilmington, N. C.

NEAGLE, Matthew and Ann R. Rudisell, 18 January 1834, Mecklenburg Co., N. C.

NEAL, Alexander G. and Mary A. Price, 9 October 1839, Mecklenburg Co., N. C.

NEAL, Andrew (Major) and Catherine LaBorde, 22 January 1854, Edgefield District, S. C.

NEAL, Elizabeth and James Carson, 7 May 1796, Charleston, S. C.

NEAL, Jenny and Thomas Neal, 19 August 1793, Mecklenburg Co., N. C.

NEAL, Mary and Reuben Hood, 15 December 1825, Mecklenburg Co., N. C.

NEAL, Peggy and Robert McKinley, 23 August 1802, Mecklenburg Co., N. C.

NEAL, Thirza and William McCrory, 21 July 1828, Mecklenburg Co., N. C.

NEAL, Thomas G. and Ann L. Spratt, 24 May 1838, Mecklenburg Co., N. C.

NEAL, William and Mary Poole, 1784, Tyrrell Co., N. C.

NEALE, Philip and Elizabeth Nash Ford, 18 July 1797, Charleston, S. C.

NEARON, Margaret and John Lovedale, August 1783, Charleston, S. C.

NEATHERY, Hannah and John McGee, 2 May 1791, Guilford Co., N. C.

NEEL, Henry and Esther Price, 8 April 1805, Mecklenburg Co., N. C.

NEEL, James H. and Margaret Hipp, 5 July 1838, Mecklenburg Co., N. C.

NEEL, Jesse C. and Sarah Stinson, 30 June 1824, Mecklenburg Co., N. C.

NEEL, John and Sarah Todd, 16 May 1803, Mecklenburg Co., N. C.

NEEL, Samuel J. and Louisa Ross, 29 April 1830, Mecklenburg Co., N. C.

NEEL, Thomas and Jenny Neal, 19 August 1793, Mecklenburg Co., N. C.

NEEL, William and Sarah Calhoun, 13 September 1800, Mecklenburg Co., N. C.

NEEL, William and Hannah Alexander, 23 November 1819, Mecklenburg Co., N. C.

NEEL, William and Martha E. Hunter, 24 January 1843, Mecklenburg Co., N. C.

NEELY, Alexander N. and Martha M. Price, 11 December 1839, Mecklenburg Co., N. C.

NEELY, E. S. (Miss) and D. S. Caldwell, 14 May 1862, Mecklenburg Co., N. C.

NEELY, Hannah and James Hart, 19 December 1791, Mecklenburg Co., N. C.

NEELY, Hannah C. and J. A. Caldwell, 28 June 1841, Mecklenburg Co., N. C.

NEELY, Isabella E. and James Bigham, 4 May 1837, Mecklenburg Co., N. C.

NEELY, James and Elizabeth C. Spratt, 12 November 1812, Mecklenburg Co., N. C.

NEELY, Jenny and John Rodgers, 27 April 1829, Mecklenburg Co., N. C.

NEELY, John and Betsy Todd, 25 October 1804, Mecklenburg Co., N. C.

NEELY, John and Elizabeth McLarty, 24 February 1806, Mecklenburg Co., N. C.

NEELY, John and Betsy Carothers, 3 January 1811, Mecklenburg Co., N. C.

NEELY, John and Anne Simmonds, 29 February 1822, Mecklenburg Co., N. C.

NEELY, John Starr and Margaret H. Carothers, 4 March 1841, York Co., S. C.

NEELY, John and Margaret Swaine, 11 December 1843, Mecklenburg Co., N. C.

NEELY, James B. and Mary J. N. Hart, 16 December 1828, Mecklenburg Co., N. C.

NEELY, Margaret and Matthew Russell, 29 January 1795, Mecklenburg Co., N. C.

NEELY, Margaret Swann and James Carothers, 10 October 1809, Mecklenburg Co., N. C.

NEELY, Moses and Alice J. McDowell, 22 March 1825, Mecklenburg Co., N. C.

NEELY, Robert C. and Margaret P. Reed, 15 September 1830, Mecklenburg Co., N. C.

NEELY, Samuel L. and Rachel L. Whiteside, 1 March 1839, Mecklenburg Co., N. C.

NEELY, Thomas and Jane Hart, 28 March 1793, Mecklenburg Co., N. C.

NEELY, Thomas B. and Ann Reed, 2 October 1832, Mecklenburg Co., N. C.

NEELY, William and Polly Roper, 28 November 1820, Mecklenburg Co., N. C.

NEELY, William M. and Cynthia Hayes, 25 May 1813, Mecklenburg Co., N. C.

NEGLY, Marguaretta and John Inabnet, 30 November 1742, Orangeburg Co., S. C.

NEGRIN, J. J. and Eliza Shroudy (widow), 5 April 1800, Charleston, S. C.

NEIL, Elizabeth (widow) and Cervas McGrath, 15 September 1746, Chowan Co., N. C.

NEIL, Margaret and William Black, 22 September 1801, Mecklenburg Co., N. C.

NEIL, Polly and Stephen Cross, 17 April 1799, Edgecombe Co., N. C.

NEILSON, James and Hester Singletery, 30 January 1774, Charleston, S. C.

NELSON, Elizabeth and Benjamin McFarlin, 9 December 1774, Guilford Co. N. C.

NELSON, Hester and Samuel Rain, 12 December 1801, Charleston, S. C.

NELSON, Hugh and Jane Bigham, 28 August 1794, Mecklenburg Co., N. C.

NELSON, James and Betty Villeponteux, 12 August 1784, Charleston, S. C.

NELSON, Joshia and Nancy Wiley, 8 October 1825, Mecklenburg Co., N. C.

NELSON, Marion and Ellen Brown, 23 November 1865, Laurens Co., S. C.

NELSON, Martha J. and Marcus McCampbell, 19 February 1852, Mecklenburg Co., N. C.

NELSON, Nancy and Charles Pully, 1 November 1865, Laurens Co., S. C.

NELSON, Samuel and Margaret Moore, 14 September 1790, Mecklenburg Co., N. C.

NELSON, Susan and William Pully, 1 November 1865, Laurens Co., S. C.

NELSON, William and Mary D. Cudy, 29 September 1827, Mecklenburg Co., N. C.

NEPHEW, Eliza and Leonard Barton, 31 January 1812, Beaufort, S. C.

NESBIT, Hugh C. and Elizabeth Starner, 16 March 1836, Mecklenburg Co., N. C.

NESSLER, S. I. and Maggie C. Alexander, 28 April 1864, Mecklenburg Co., N. C.

NETHERCLIFT, Thomas and Anne McQueen, 14 February 1767, Charleston, S. C.

NETTLES, George and Mrs. Anderson, 6 August 1797, Charleston, S. C.

NEVIL, Richard and Sarah Reding, 4 December 1746, Chowan Co., N. C.

NEVILL, John and Nathalie Orr, 10 July 1765, Charleston, S. C.

NEWABARY, Charles and Maines Ray, 1782, Tyrrell Co., N. C.

NEWBERRY, John and Joana Swain, 4 July 1786, Tyrrell Co., N. C.

NEWBOLD, Charles H. and Jane E. Little, 19 January 1865, Mecklenburg Co., N. C.

NEWBORN, Thomas and Elizabeth Sparkman, 7 October 1788, Bertie Co., N. C.

NEWBY, John S. and Lucy Bickly, 18 June 1801, Charleston, S. C.

NEWBY, John and Pamela Nicholson, 13 February 1823, Mecklenburg Co., N. C.

NEWCOMBE, George and Hannah Skinner, 9 September 1740, Charleston, S. C.

NEWELL, Boswell and Mary Barker, 11 December 1845, Mecklenburg Co., N. C.

NEWELL, David and Helena Hargett, 10 October 1843, Mecklenburg Co., N. C.

NEWELL, Peter and Polly Simpson, 11 September 1801, Mecklenburg Co., N. C.

NEWELL, Reuben N. and Martha N. Owens, 22 June 1848, Mecklenburg Co., N. C.

NEWELL, Samuel W. and Jane Dobson, 5 December 1843, Mecklenburg Co., N. C.

NEWMAN, Ann and John Marshall, 21 May 1813, Mecklenburg Co., N. C.

NEWMAN, Benjamin and Elizabeth Henderson, 21 November 1858, Laurens Co., S. C.

NEWMAN, Jacob and Mary Keliah, 55 December 1791, Mecklenburg Co., N. C.

NEWTON, Elizabeth and Charles Rivers, September 1785, Charleston, S. C.

NEWTON, Mary and Thomas Hall, 7 November 1785, Charleston, S. C.

NEYLE, Sampson and Martha Gorden, 12 February 1751, Charleston, S. C.

NICHOL, Johnathan and May Hull, 8 May 1787, Orange Co., N. C.

NICHOLAS, Elizabeth and Robert Minor, 13 November 1760, Santee, S. C.

NICHOLAS, Stewart and Betsy Frederick, 1 November 1772, Charleston, S. C.

NICHOLLS, George and Margaret Revel, 17 May 1797, Charleston, S. C.

NICHOLLS, James and Priscilla Hassell, 19 January 1767, Tyrrell Co., N. C.

NICHOLLS, Richard and Anne Magaw, 18 January 1768, Charleston, S. C.

NICHOLLS, Ruth and Stephen Bedon, 11 August 1743, Charleston, S. C.

NICHOLS, Ann (widow) and William Price, 24 May 1772, Charleston, S. C.

NICHOLS, Margaret and William Harden, 15 April 1797, Rowan Co., N. C.

NICHOLS, Mary and John Crickell, 6 June 1744, Chowan Co., N. C.

NICHOLS, Tabitha and Joseph Turner, 26 March 1724, Berkeley Co., S. C.

NICHOLS, Rebecca and Edward Harvey, 8 July 1785, Chowan Co., N. C.

NICHOLSON, Anne and Thomas Whithenberry, June 1785, Charleston, S. C.

NICHOLSON, Jean and James McCuistion, 11 September 1792, Guilford Co., N. C.

NICHOLSON, John and Rachel Lavis, 4 February 1796, Mecklenburg Co., N. C.

NICHOLSON, Joseph C. and Margaret I. Brown, 4 October 1837, Mecklenburg Co., N. C.

NICHOLSON, Mary and Thomas McCuistion, 19 September 1786, Guilford Co., N. C.

NICHOLSON, Parmela and John Newby, 13 February 1823, Mecklenburg Co., N. C.

NICHOLSON, William and Mary Huddleston, 26 August 1822, Mecklenburg Co., N. C.

NICKLES, B. F. and Liza Dicky, 22 January 1846, Laurens Co., S. C.

NICKLES, Thomas and Susan Henry, 23 December 1845, Laurens Co., S. C.

NICOLS, Frances and John Pierce, 24 November 1779, Chowan Co., N. C.

NICOLLS, Sarah and Daniel Davenport, 12 March 1786, Tyrrell Co., N. C.

NIGHTINGALE, Sarah and William Johnson, 15 May 1769, Charleston, S. C.

NISBET, A. S. and (Miss) M. A. Walker, 26 February 1852, Mecklenburg Co., N. C.

NIVEN, Willis and Elizabeth Glover, 27 March 1834, Mecklenburg Co., N. C.

NIXON, John and Elizabeth Bussey, 28 November 1854, Edgefield District, S. C.

NIXON, Sarah (widow) and Thomas Ming, 5 September 1753, Chowan Co., N. C.

NIXON, William and Eliza Miller, 21 December 1858, Chowan Co., N. C.

NOALES, Abraham and Milly Anderson, 30 August 1822, Mecklenburg Co., N. C.

NOAILLE, Rachel and Mathias Brickell, 6 November 1747, N. C.

NOBLE, Jane O. and Warren N. Scoville, 8 December 1858, Orangeburg Co., S. C.

NOBLE, Margaret A. (Mrs.) and Sterling Dixon, 27 September 1801, Abbeville District, S. C.

NOBLE, Ruth and John Cryer, 1 November 1782, Santee, S. C.

NOBLES, Joseph and Matilda Kirkland, 9 May 1838, Edgefield District, S. C.

NOBLES, Peggy and Hugh Hilburn, 3 April 1835, Edgefield District, S. C.

NOLAND, Henny and Valentine Holderfield, 13 April 1789, Rowan Co., N. C.

NOLAND, Mary and Edward Graham, 24 February 1794, Rowan Co., N. C.

NOLES, James and Nancy Phillips, 14 March 1837, Mecklenburg Co., N. C.

NORCOM, John and Ann Bentley, 2 June 1741, Chowan Co., N. C.

NORCOM, Martha (widow) and Edward Hall, 10 July 1750, Chowan Co., N. C.

NORCOM, Thomas and Martha Harloe, 24 August 1744, Chowan Co., N. C.

NORFLEET, James and Sarah Gordon, 1 December 1774, Chowan Co., N. C.

NORFLEET, Nancy and Alexander S. Johnston, 29 March 1812, Edgecombe Co., N. C.

NORFLEET, Ruth and General Hogan, 3 October 1751, South Hampton, N. C.

NORHAM, Sarah A. and James T. Brown, 30 July 1861, Mecklenburg Co., N. C.

NORLEY, Patsy and John W. Morrow, 10 December 1807, Mecklenburg Co., N. C.

NORMAN, James and Esther Davenport, October 1783, Tyrrell Co., N. C.

NORMAN, Jessie and Mary O. Smart, 21 July 1850, Laurens Co., S. C.

NORMAN, Henry and Sarah Bonner, 1784, Tyrrell Co., N. C.

NORMAN, Hezekiah and Sarah Alexander, 3 January 1786, Tyrrell Co., N. C.

NORMAN, Isaac and Joana Phelps, 11 March 1779, Tyrrell Co., N. C.

NORMAN, Martha B. and Richard P. Taylor, 2 May 1838, Granville Co., N. C.

NORMAN, Sarah and William Spruill, 31 January 1786, Tyrrell Co., N. C.

NORMAND, Mary and Daniel Dupree, 8 June 1759, Santee, S. C.

NORMENT, Louise A. and James Blount, 17 May 1826, Mecklenburg Co., N. C.

NORMENT, William S. and Margaret Dow, 12 September 1812, Mecklenburg Co., N. C.

NORRIS, Alfred J. and Mary Fox, 8 February 1863, Edgefield District, S. C.

NORTH, Elizabeth and William Miles (Jr.), 20 December 1743, St. Bartholomews Parish, S. C.

NORTH, Elizabeth and John Stent, 16 December 1800, Charleston, S. C.

NORTH, Thomas and Rose McIver, 4 March 1770, Santee, S. C.

NORTON, George and Elizabeth Conway, 24 October 1720, St. Andrews Parish, S. C.

NORTON, Katherine P. and Daniel Stevens, 6 December 1767, Charleston, S. C.

NORTON, Robert and Patsy Lansing, 14 July 1819, Mecklenburg Co., N. C.

NORVILL, Isabell and John Morant, October 1783, Charleston, S. C.

NORWARD, L. M. and Martha S. F. Williamson, 31 July 1834, Mecklenburg Co., N. C.

NUNN, Elizabeth and Hugh Curry, 22 November 1790, Orange Co., N. C.

NUTY, Isabella and Samuel Johnston, 17 January 1810, Mecklenburg Co., N. C.

O

OAKES, Jane G. and James McComb, 22 August 1823, Mecklenburg Co., N. C.

OATS, Bailey and Lydia M. Lowrie, 24 March 1825, Mecklenburg Co., N. C.

OBERLY, Owen and Jane Sharp, 11 November 1822, Mecklenburg Co., N. C.

OBRIEN, John C. and Celia A. Hood, 8 February 1846, Mecklenburg Co., N. C.

OBRYAN, Mary and Benjamin Fuller, 7 November 1785, Tyrrell Co., N. C.

ODELL, Emily and Alexander McCorcle, 9 October 1855, Laurens Co., S. C.

ODELL, Sarah and (Dr.) Franklin Fuller, 3 April 1845, Laurens Co., S. C.

ODOM, John and Agnes Vinsen, 4 September 1798, Mecklenburg Co., N. C.

O'DRISCOLL, Anna R. and John B. White, 1 October 1819, Charleston, S. C.

OEHLER, George B. and Elizabeth P. Thomson, 5 January 1841, Mecklenburg Co., N. C.

OEHLER, Harriet E. and Thomas F. Brewer, 24 February 1856, Mecklenburg Co., N. C.

OEHLER, John and Margaret Kirk, 21 December 1847, Mecklenburg Co., N. C.

OEHLER, John G. and Jane Shields, 26 August 1837, Mecklenburg Co., N. C.

OFILL, John and Elizabeth Rice, 29 December 1755, Orangeburg Co., S. C.

OGIER, Charlotte and Thomas Martin, September 1786, Charleston, S. C.

OGIER, Lewis and Susanna Martin, 2 October 1783, Charleston, S. C.

O'HARE, James and Nancy Gordon, 10 February 1774, Charleston, S. C.

O'HEAR, Nancy and Johnson Hogood, 8 December 1794, Charleston, S. C.

OLDHAM, Elizabeth and Adam McKeen, 30 April 1756, Chowan Co., N. C.

OLIPHANT, Elizabeth and David Oswald, 18 April 1801, Charleston, S. C.

OLIPHANT, Jane and John A. Walker, 24 February 1774, Berkeley Co., S. C.

OLIPHANT, Jane and Abraham Jetton, 29 May 1787, Mecklenburg Co., N. C.

OLIVER, Alexander and Frances Phelps, 1781, Tyrrell Co., N. C.

OLIVER, Andrew and Jemimah Phelps, 1784, Tyrrell Co., N. C.

OLIVER, Ann and Thomas Smith, 18 December 1786, Tyrrell Co., N. C.

OLIVER, Elizabeth and Sylvester Arms, 22 November 1800, Charleston, S. C.

OLIVER, James and (Mrs.) Alice Clark, 26 June 1800, Charleston, S. C.

OLIVER, James and Elizabeth Limehouse, 5 November 1801, Charleston, S. C.

OLIVER, Jane and Joseph C. Ross, 15 December 1842, Mecklenburg Co., N. C.

OLIVER, John and Harrahan Woodland, 6 April 1785, Tyrrell Co., N. C.

OLIVER, John and Rebecca Davis, 26 March 1783, Tyrrell Co., N. C.

OLIVER, John and Molly Watford, 27 February 1788, Bertie Co., N. C.

OLIVER, Martha A. and Robert E. Bowen, 15 October 1857, Pickens Co., S. C.

OLIVER, Mary and Jeremiah Bateman, 1781, Tyrrell Co., N. C.

OLIVER, Sarah and John P. Ross, 11 January 1859, Mecklenburg Co., N. C.

OLIVER, Thomas and Jane Kerr, 19 February 1821, Mecklenburg Co., N. C.

OLMAN, Joseph and Madame DeVerge, 3 February 1795, Charleston, S. C.

O'NEAL, Gideon and Virginia Forgy, 22 November 1857, Laurens Co., S. C.

O'NEAL, John and Dorcas Battin, 25 September 1778, Tyrrell Co., N. C.

O'NEIL, Patrick and Catron Mitchell, 23 August 1790, Mecklenburg Co., N. C.

ORDE, Elizabeth and William Erwin, 3 March 1766, Rowan Co., N. C.

ORENDALL, Job and Rachel Turner, 6 July 1761, Perquimans Co., N. C.

ORMOND, Frances (widow) and Joseph Chapman, 17 June 1773, Chowan Co., N. C.

ORMOND, Hugh and Eliza Pratt, 10 February 1813, Mecklenburg Co., N. C.

ORMOND, James and Mary A. Leany, 29 May 1832, Mecklenburg Co., N. C.

ORMOND, Jean and Silas Brown, 19 March 1816, Mecklenburg Co., N. C.

ORMOND, John M. and Nancy Howard, 22 December 1840, Mecklenburg Co., N. C.

ORMOND, Matthew and Daisy Emerson, 4 June 1818, Mecklenburg Co., N. C.

ORMOND, Matthew and Mary D. McCorkle, 12 February 1841, Mecklenburg Co., N. C.

ORMOND, Robert and Mary Jane Rea, 12 February 1840, Mecklenburg Co., N. C.

ORMOND, Robert and Ann Helton, 15 September 1864, Mecklenburg Co., N. C.

ORMOND, William and Arabella Faesch, 5 May 1796, Charleston, S. C.

ORR, Abigail and Thomas Boals, 27 February 1799, Mecklenburg Co., N. C.

ORR, Allen and Martha Townsend, 22 November 1814, Mecklenburg Co., N. C.

ORR, Allison and Susanna Pettis, 17 January 1829, Mecklenburg Co., N. C.

ORR, A. J. and (Miss) H. W. Howell, 8 September 1863, Mecklenburg Co., N. C.

ORR, A. L. (Miss) and William F. Harkey, 10 November 1865, Mecklenburg Co., N. C.

ORR, Bunyan and Mary Vizie, 5 January 1797, Mecklenburg Co., N. C.

ORR, David and Jane McCracken, 14 April 1857, Mecklenburg Co., N. C.

ORR, Doris and Joseph C. Johnston, 11 October 1815, Mecklenburg Co., N. C.

ORR, Eliza and John C. Barr, 13 February 1819, Mecklenburg Co., N. C.

ORR, Elizabeth and James Coughorn, 19 January 1798, Mecklenburg Co., N. C.

ORR, Elizabeth and William Voss, 4 April 1799, Mecklenburg Co., N. C.

ORR, Elizabeth and Moses Alexander, 28 January 1800, Mecklenburg Co., N. C.

ORR, Elizabeth and James Hall, 14 August 1840, Mecklenburg Co., N. C.

ORR, Ira A. and Mary Ann Gray, 24 January 1831, Mecklenburg Co., N. C.

ORR, James and Margaret Miller, 23 January 1793, Mecklenburg Co., N. C.

ORR, James H. and Eliza Smith, 26 April 1832, Mecklenburg Co., N. C.

ORR, James J. and Jane L. McCall, 1 March 1852, Mecklenburg Co., N. C.

ORR, James J. and Sophia Alexander, 2 April 1834, Mecklenburg Co., N. C.

ORR, James R. and Nancy B. Cochran, 19 November 1841, Mecklenburg Co., N. C.

ORR, James L. V. and Maria A. Monteith, 17 January 1861, Mecklenburg Co., N. C.

ORR, James I. J. and Amelia S. Alexander, 26 March 1831, Mecklenburg Co., N. C.

ORR, Joaba L. and Eliza Cook, 9 July 1839, Mecklenburg Co., N. C.

ORR, John and Martha Houston, 28 March 1842, Mecklenburg Co., N. C.

ORR, John and Charity Hartis, 3 February 1849, Mecklenburg Co., N. C.

ORR, John Allen and Jane Mitchell, 16 January 1811, Mecklenburg Co., N. C.

ORR, John F. and Elizabeth Byram, 8 October 1835, Mecklenburg Co., N. C.

ORR, John W. and Dorcas C. Starner, 3 December 1857, Mecklenburg Co., N. C.

ORR, John G. A. and Leah E. Monteith, 30 April 1857, Mecklenburg Co., N. C.

ORR, Jonathan and Cynthia Alexander, 18 April 1835, Mecklenburg Co., N. C.

ORR, Joseph L. and Nancy Morris, 7 January 1823, Mecklenburg Co., N. C.

ORR, Louisa and Thomas Orr, 14 September 1865, Mecklenburg Co., N. C.

ORR, Margaret and Eli Alexander, 1 April 1806, Mecklenburg Co., N. C.

ORR, Margaret C. and Laird Blair, 24 July 1833, Mecklenburg Co., N. C.

ORR, Mary J. and James McCorkle, 14 January 1840, Mecklenburg Co., N. C.

ORR, Mildred and Amos Alexander, 23 December 1797, Mecklenburg Co., N. C.

ORR, Milly and Joseph McGinnes, 14 April 1823, Mecklenburg Co., N. C.

ORR, Nancy and William A. Rea, 12 July 1854, Mecklenburg Co., N. C.

ORR, Nancy V. and William A. Roberts, 30 March 1858, Mecklenburg Co., N. C.

ORR, Nathalie and John Nevill, 10 July 1765, Charleston, S. C.

ORR, Nathan and Peggy Julian, 27 January 1802, Mecklenburg Co., N. C.

ORR, Nathan F. and Martha A. Montgomery, 18 September 1851, Mecklenburg Co., N. C.

ORR, Nathan H. and Sarah Young, 21 January 1833, Mecklenburg Co., N. C.

ORR, Samuel W. and Margaret H. Matthews, 7 November 1836, Mecklenburg Co., N. C.

ORR, Sarah and David McRee, 4 November 1823, Mecklenburg Co., N. C.

ORR, Sarah A. and Edward M. Bronson, 6 March 1813, Mecklenburg Co., N. C.

ORR, Thomas and Louisa Orr, 14 September 1865, Mecklenburg Co., N. C.

ORR, Tirza and Robert Cook, 4 August 1814, Mecklenburg Co., N. C.

ORR, William W. and Sarah Rodgers, 19 December 1854, Mecklenburg Co., N. C.

OSBORN, Edward A. and Fanny S. Moore, 15 March 1865, Mecklenburg Co., N. C.

OSBORN, Elizabeth and James Beckett, 30 January 1794, Mecklenburg Co., N. C.

OSBORN, Hiram and Margaret E. McCombs, 30 December 1859, Mecklenburg Co., N. C.

OSBORN, James and Susan Alexander, 28 October 1816, Mecklenburg Co., N. C.

OSBORN, James and Margaret Houston, 15 October 1821, Mecklenburg Co., N. C.

OSBORN, James W. and Mary Ann Moore. 5 April 1842, Mecklenburg Co., N. C.

OSBORN, John and Jemina Sharp, 10 December 1785, Mecklenburg Co., N. C.

OSBORN, L. W. and Darcus Todd, 27 July 1864, Mecklenburg Co., N. C.

OSBORN, Obedience and Charles S. Morton, 18 January 1803, Mecklenburg Co., N. C.

OSBORN, Susanna and Samuel Beckett, 27 July 1801, Mecklenburg Co., N. C.

OSBORN, Thomas and Elizabeth Flanigan, 17 January 1805, Mecklenburg Co., N. C.

OSBORN, William and Ann Rogers, 4 September 1798, Mecklenburg Co., N. C.

OSBORN, William B. and Leora Beard, 7 October 1858, Mecklenburg Co., N. C.

OSBORNE, Agnes and George Black, 25 March 1800, Mecklenburg Co., N. C.

OSBORNE, Jonathan M. and Sarah M. Sharpe, 15 September 1848, Mecklenburg Co., N. C.

OSGOOD, James and M. A. Dudley, 16 October 1865, Mecklenburg Co., N. C.

OSMENT, M. S. and Mary Warren, 12 July 1860, Mecklenburg Co., N. C.

OSMOND, Mr. and Mary Hall, 13 April 1732, Charleston, S. C.

OSWALD, David and Elizabeth Oliphant, 18 April 1801, Charleston, S. C.

OSWALD, Mary and John Witsel, 3 October 1800, St. Bartholomews Parish, S. C.

OTH, Caspar and Mary Stehely, 1752, Orangeburg Co., S. C.

OTT, Esther and John Heller, 1752, Orangeburg Co., S. C.

OTT, Jacob and Margaret Fichtner, 3 December 1754, Orangeburg Co., S. C.

OTT, John Frederick and Magdalene Welchter, 24 June 1750, Orangeburg Co., S. C.

OTT, Melchior and Ann Barbara Zangin, 7 February 1746, Orangeburg Co., S. C.

OTTO, Anna and Peter Grieffous, 25 May 1741, Orangeburg Co., S. C.

OTTERS, Cooney and Mary Stauffer, 6 June 1860, Mecklenburg Co., N. C.

OUTLAW, Jacob and Rachel Garrett, 25 November 1775, Chowan Co., N. C.

OUTLAW, Joshua and Rachel Alexander, 26 March 1805, Bertie Co., N. C.

OUTLAW, Martha A. and Wright Mitchell, 19 December 1827, Bertie Co., N. C.

OUTLAW, Mary and Jonathan Jordan, 20 September 1775, Chowan Co., N. C.

OUTLAW, Sarah and Daniel Britain, 3 May 1803, Bertie Co., N. C.

OUTZS, James T. and Amila Frances Lowrey, 13 May 1856, Edgefield District, S. C.

OUTZS, Mahala and John Shaffer, 4 December 1856, Edgefield District, S. C.

OVERINE, Green and Nelly Shuman, 2 October 1851, Mecklenburg Co., N. C.

OVERMAN, Charles and Ann L. Allison, 6 April 1837, Mecklenburg Co., N. C.

OVERTON, Asa and Patsey Tart, 26 December 1789, Bertie Co., N. C.

OVERTON, Edward and Mary Parsons, 17 April 1783, Tyrrell Co., N. C.

OVERTON, James and Milly Mitchell, 26 November 1788, Bertie Co., N. C.

OWEN, Drady and John Aldrich, 18 August 1822, Edgefield District, S. C.

OWEN, Esther and James Beaty, 25 August 1803, Mecklenburg Co., N. C.

OWEN, Judah and Jacob Hartman, 4 June 1796, Rowan Co., N. C.

OWEN, Peter and Hannah Mitchell, 20 November 1786, Orange Co., N. C.

OWEN, William A. L. and Jane King, 21 March 1848, Mecklenburg Co., N. C.

OWENS, Beline and Nathan Page, 28 July 1798, Bertie Co., N. C.

OWENS, Henry C. and Jane E. Allison, 18 December 1832, Mecklenburg Co., N. C.

OWENS, James and Sarah H. Gray, 14 November 1831, Mecklenburg Co., N. C.

OWENS, Lanson and Fanny Martin, 11 February 1851, Laurens Co., S. C.

OWENS, Martha N. and Reuben N. Newell, 22 June 1848, Mecklenburg Co., N. C.

OWENS, William and Esther Beaty, 25 February 1799, Mecklenburg Co., N. C.

OWENS, William A. and Alice B. Caldwell, 24 November 1857, Mecklenburg Co., N. C.

OWINGS, Catherine and Simeon Putman, 4 January 1844, Laurens Co., S. C.

OWINGS, Raply and Elizabeth Cheshire, 22 December 1842, Laurens Co., S. C.

OWINGS, Reuben and Cassander Garrett, 13 March 1851, Laurens Co., S. C.

OWINGS, Roberson and Charity Garrett, 29 September 1850, Laurens Co., S. C.

OWINS, Young and Martha Brown, 29 October 1865, Laurens Co., S. C.

OWNLEY, Rebecca and James Hodge, 30 April 1798, Mecklenburg Co., N. C.

OZMENT, John A. and Mary L. Collier, 11 December 1855, Mecklenburg Co., N. C.

P

PAGE, George and Catherine Celements, 12 November 1739, Charleston, S. C.

PAGE, Jean and William Bryan, 11 December 1809, Mecklenburg Co., N. C.

PAGE, John S. and Martha Louisa Bass, 10 January 1847, Marlboro Co., S. C.

PAGE, Joshua and Elizabeth Montgomery, 9 October 1787, Bertie Co., N. C.

PAGE, Nathan and Beline Owens, 28 July 1798, Bertie Co., N. C.

PAGE, Solomon and Sarah Hayse, 16 May 1786, Bertie Co., N. C.

PAGETT, Elizabeth and James L. Richards, 3 November 1768, Stono, S. C.

PAGETT, Sarah and Joseph Eelbeck, 2 September 1750, Chowan Co., N. C.

PAINE, Lucinda and (Rev.) William B. Boyd, 22 April 1858, Laurens Co., S. C.

PAINE, Widow and Miles Brewton, March 1743, Charleston, S. C.

PAINTER, Hannah and John Hogg, 28 December 1721, St. Andrews Parish, S. C.

PAINTER, Naomi (Mrs.) and John Strahan, March 1733, Berkeley Co., S. C.

PALMER, Charlotte and Ellison Capers, 24 February 1859, Columbia, S. C.

PALMER, Joseph and Catherine Thomas, 8 November 1759, Santee, S. C.

PARHAM, Sarah and Robert Taylor, 11 July 1809, Granville Co., N. C.

PARISH, Patsy and Daniel Boyd, 15 September 1812, Mecklenburg Co., N. C.

PARISH, Catherine and David Hipp, 22 August 1808, Mecklenburg Co., N. C.

PARISH, James and Margaret Mitchell, 8 November 1844, Chowan Co., N. C.

PARIC, Hannah and Oswald Alexander, 20 March 1809, Mecklenburg Co., N. C.

PARK, Parmela and John McGinness, 6 September 1825, Mecklenburg Co., N. C.

PARKE, Abby E. and Andrew Jones, 3 November 1829, Mecklenburg Co., N. C.

PARKE, William and Margaret Campbell, 3 October 1798, Spartanburg Co., S. C.

PARKER, Abraham and Mary Smith, 9 March 1848, Laurens Co., S. C.

PARKER, Betsy and Clem Mullins, 4 August 1807, Mecklenburg Co., N. C.

PARKER, Celia and John Kale, 8 November 1785, Chowan Co., N. C.

PARKER, Elinor and William Jenkins, 26 October 1809, Mecklenburg Co., N. C.

PARKER, Elisha and Rebecca Warren, 13 November 1752, Chowan Co., N. C.

PARKER, Grace and William Mills, September 1732, Charleston, S. C.

PARKER, Isaac and Mary Milligan, 20 July 1800, Charleston, S. C.

PARKER, John and Susanna Middleton, 24 December 1786, Charleston, S. C.

PARKER, Sarah and James Sweeney, 5 September 1778, Chowan Co., N. C.

PARKER, Sarah and William Holbrook, 14 May 1785, Rowan Co., N. C.

PARKER, Thomas and Teresa Cunningham, 3 October 1779, Chowan Co., N. C.

PARKER, William and Catherine Coward, 4 June 1785, Chowan Co., N. C.

PARKMAN, James and Frances Garner, 27 December 1855, Edgefield District, S. C.

PARKS, Elizabeth and James H. Moore, 6 April 1825, Mecklenburg Co., N. C.

PARKS, James and Jane Barksdale, 28 November 1844, Laurens Co., S. C.

PARKS, Jane and Hugh M. Rogers, 1 May 1824, Mecklenburg Co., N. C.

PARKS, Jenny and William Henley, 3 May 1791, Rowan Co., N. C.

PARKS, Lilly and Carnes Henderson, 24 January 1792, Mecklenburg Co., N. C.

PARKS, Margaret and Leander D. Alexander, 31 July 1843, Mecklenburg Co., N. C.

PARKS, Margaret and David Morrow, 20 August 1839, Mecklenburg Co., N. C.

PARKS, Margaret and David Graham, 3 November 1799, Rowan Co., N. C.

PARKS, Martha and Samuel Irwin, 7 May 1825, Mecklenburg Co., N. C.

PARKS, Martha and Isaac H. Moore, 22 July 1854, Mecklenburg Co., N. C.

PARKS, Mary and Perry Putman, 21 December 1848, Laurens Co., S. C.

PARKS, Mary and James M. Rea, 21 April 1842, Mecklenburg Co., N. C.

PARKS, Mary and Robert Robinson, 9 February 1792, Mecklenburg Co., N. C.

PARKS, Mary A. and Zebulon L. Morris, 20 July 1847, Mecklenburg Co., N. C.

PARKS, Minty and James Caldwell, 12 August 1816, Mecklenburg Co., N. C.

PARKS, M. A. (Mrs.) and Silas Rea (Sr.), 28 February 1856, Mecklenburg Co., N. C.

PARKS, Nathan and Ann Waller, 8 November 1778, Santee, S. C.

PARKS, Rachel and Daniel Huffman, 17 January 1781, Rowan Co., N. C.

PARKS, Rachel and William Reeves, 12 February 1811, Mecklenburg Co., N. C.

PARKS, Sarah and Samuel McEwan, 1 December 1795, Mecklenburg Co., N. C.

PARKS, Sarah and Robert Rogers, 23 September 1822, Mecklenburg Co., N. C.

PARKS, Samuel and Charity Runyan, 6 November 1792, Yadkin, N. C.

PARRISH, Fanny and Solomon Roan, 21 March 1818, Mecklenburg Co., N. C.

PARSONS, James and Susannah Miles, 29 May 1753, Charleston, S. C.

PARSONS, Martin and Mary Lanford, 2 October 1845, Laurens Co., S. C.

PARSONS, Mary and Edward Overton, 17 April 1783, Tyrrell Co., N. C.

PARSONS, William and (Mrs.) Mary Wardrop, May 1785, Charleston, S. C.

PARTIN, Eliza and Waller Herndon, 21 May 1795, Orange Co., N. C.

PARTLIN, Nancy C. and James R. Bailey, 2 January 1842, Mecklenburg Co., N. C.

PARTLOW, Elizabeth and Richard Black, 1 January 1805, Mecklenburg Co., N. C.

PASCHALL, Sarah Jane and Burwell Taylor, 23 September 1844, Granville Co., N. C.

PATERSON, James and Martha Wilks, 7 May 1796, St. Thomas Parish, S. C.

PATON, John and Sarah Dobel, 1 September 1801, Charleston, S. C.

PATRICK, Elizabeth and John McSparen, 9 June 1794, Guilford Co., N. C.

PATRICK, Elizabeth and George Dener, 15 May 1800, Charleston, S. C.

PATRICK, Isaac and Sarah Tarkinton, 20 December 1779, Tyrrell Co., N. C.

PATTEN, Mary and William Hellams, 21 December 1854, Laurens Co., S. C.

PATTEN, Nancy and John Heekman, 31 October 1785, Rowan Co., N. C.

PATTERSON, Anne and David Houston, 2 September 1774, Rowan Co., N. C.

PATTERSON, Frances and John Edwards, August 1796, Rowan Co., N. C.

PATTERSON, Joseph and Nancy Price, 2 February 1834, Edgefield District, S. C.

PATTERSON, Nancy and James T. McKelvey, 8 February 1837, Mecklenburg Co., N. C.

PATTERSON, Nancy Mary and John Mills, 223 January 1851, Laurens Co., S. C.

PATTERSON, Peggy and Winslow J. McRee, 27 June 1808, Mecklenburg Co., N. C.

PATTERSON, Robert and Elizabeth Wellwood, 19 September 1771, Chowan Co., N. C.

PATTERSON, Sarah A. and John C. Brown, 14 December 1854, Mecklenburg Co., N. C.

PATTERSON, William and Rebecca Fleming, 30 October 1756, Laurens Co., S. C.

PATTISON, Ann and Andrew Kreps, August 1785, Charleston, S. C.

PATTON, Harriet and Abel Bullinger, 12 July 1832, Mecklenburg Co., N. C.

PATTON, Isabella and David L. Black, 24 August 1836, Mecklenburg Co., N. C.

PATTON, Margaret (widow) and Alexander Erwin, 21 January 1786, Rowan Co., N. C.

PATTON, N. and Samuel Pickings, 1748, Orangeburg Co., S. C.

PATTON, Nancy H. and William Ross, 27 May 1841, Mecklenburg Co., N. C.

PAUL, Rachel and James Hart, 13 April 1790, Orange Co., N. C.

PAWLEY, Mary and Samuel Hasford, 19 July 1778, Santee, S. C.

PAXTON, Henry W. and Eliza A. Yeadon, 16 December 1801, Charleston, S. C.

PAYNE, Mary and Micajah Bunch, 8 May 1758, Chowan Co., N. C.

PAYNE, Peter and Hannah Slaughter, 8 January 1742, Chowan Co., N. C.

PAYNE, Peter and Mary Bensley, 18 October 1751, Chowan Co., N. C.

PEACE, Joseph and Anne M. Rudhall, 5 July 1796, Charleston, S. C.

PEACOCK, George and Elizabeth Everitt, 17 October 1786, Tyrrell Co., N. C.

PEACOCK, Heaward and Sarah Smith, 27 April 1733, Charleston, S. C.

PEACOCK, Mary and Mathurin Guerin, 7 January 1774, Charleston, S. C.

PEACOCK, —— and Matherin Guerin, 1774, Berkeley Co., S. C.

PEARCE, Hartwell and Dempsey Turner, 23 October 1762, Perquimans Co., N. C.

PEARCE, Kessenhappuck and Reddin Simpson, 18 May 1786, Tyrrell Co., N. C.

PEARCE, Nancy and Benjamin Buford, 1 March 1797, Mecklenburg Co., N. C.

PEARCE, Timothy and Sarah Simpson, 16 April 1786, Tyrrell Co., N. C.

PEARCEY, Elizabeth and John Barton, 9 July 1778, Santee, S. C.

PEARSON, Benjamin and Frances A. Adely, 26 October 1800, Charleston, S. C.

PEARSON, Hambleton and Nancy Harmon, 29 January 1857, Laurens Co., S. C.

PEARSON, James and Judey Ann Bruce, 4 January 1846, Marlboro, S. C.

PEARSON, John and Mary Raiford, 25 April 1742, Orangeburg Co., S. C.

PEARSON, Mandy and Nathaniel Thaxton, 13 December 1849, Laurens Co., S. C.

PEARSON, William and Elizabeth Penrice, 23 March 1772, Chowan Co., N. C.

PEATT, Abigail and Matthew Whiteman, 5 October 1777, Chowan Co., N. C.

PEAY, Austin F. and Mary English, 4 January 1801, Camden, S. C.

PEDRO, Peter and Patsy Graves, 14 April 1800, Charleston, S. C.

PEEPLES, Nancy and John Meredith, 8 July 1842, Guilford Co., N. C.

PEEPLES, Sarah and Herbert C. Moore, 8 March 1842, Guilford Co., N. C.

PELL, Ann (Mrs.) and David Miller, 3 January 1824, Chowan Co., N. C.

PELT, Hannah C. and Jacob Baker, 21 December 1825, Mecklenburg Co., N. C.

PELT, Mary and Michael W. Berryhill, 6 October 1824, Mecklenburg Co., N. C.

PENDARVIS, Alice and Richard B. Screven, 8 March 1800, Charleston, S. C.

PENDARVIS, Ann and John Coburn, 9 October 1800, Charleston, S. C.

PENDARVIS, Brand and Ursetta Jennings, 1748, Orangeburg Co., S. C.

PENDARVIS, James and Catherina Rumph, 3 September 1741, Orangeburg Co., S. C.

PENIX, Susannah and Athenatious Elmore, 5 July 1788, Orange Co., N. C.

PENN, Ann L. and B. C. Bryan, 17 January 1854, Edgefield District, S. C.

PENN, Edmund and Rebecca Cresswill, 9 January 1840, Edgefield District, S. C.

PENN, Elizabeth and West Edwards, 1749, Greene Co., N. C.

PENN, Frances (dau. of Joseph and Mary Penn.) and John Hunt, 5 August 1771, Granville Co., N. C.

PENNY, Mary and Samuel Jenkins, 15 December 1788, Bertie Co., N. C.

PENRICE, Elizabeth and Jacob Butler, 18 December 1755, Chowan Co., N. C.

PENRICE, Elizabeth and William Pearson, 23 March 1772, Chowan Co., N. C.

PENRICE, Francis and Sarah Harloe, 12 April 1744, Chowan Co., N. C.

PEOPLES, Jemima R. and Isaac Auten, 2 January 1741, Mecklenburg Co., N. C.

PEOPLES, Rebecca and Hugh Blakely, 21 December 1843, Mecklenburg Co., N. C.

PERDRIEU, Mary and David Fogartie, 12 June 1763, Santee, S. C.

PERISHO, James and Christian Crank, 16 October 1778, Tyrrell Co., N. C.

PERISHO, Mary and Randolph Johnston, 1781, Tyrrell Co., N. C.

PERISHO, Mille and Robert Combs, 1782, Tyrrell Co., N. C.

PERISHO, Rufus and Frances Mason, 1 July 1783, Tyrrell Co., N. C.

PERKINS, Ann and John Clements, 8 July 1788, Chowan Co., N. C.

PERKINS, Benjamin and Sarah Kershaw, June 1797, Camden, S. C.

PERKINS, Joshua and Frances Pettyjohn, 24 January 1785, Chowan Co., N. C.

PERORIAU, Esther and John Hutchinson, 7 April 1785, Charleston, S. C.

PERMAN, George and Isabella Fell, 15 November 1801, Charleston, S. C.

PERRONEAU, Ann Motte and Jacob Ford, 21 January 1797, Charleston, S. C.

PERRONEAU, Elizabeth and Isaac Holmes, 19 January 1724, Charleston, S. C.

PERONNEAU, Alexi and Margaret Hext, 23 December 1744, Charleston, S. C.

PERONNEAU, Arthur and Mary Hutson, June 1762, Charleston, S. C.

PERONNEAU, Henry and Polly Hall, 2 October 1783, Charleston, S. C.

PERONNEAU, Elizabeth and William Hayne, April 1786, Charleston, S. C.

PERONNEAU, Elizabeth and Edward Lightwood, 1 January 1770, Charleston, S. C.

PERONNEAU, Margaret and (Dr.) Robert Younge, May 1786, Charleston, S. C.

PERONNEAU, Miss and Thomas Maybanks, 22 October 1800, Charleston, S. C.

PERONNEAU, Sarah and John Scott (Jr.), 15 December 1768, Charleston, S. C.

PERREY, Benjamin and Ann M. Werner, 29 March 1800, Charleston, S. C.

PERRY, Benjamin F. and Elizabeth Hayne, April 1837, Charleston, S. C.

PERRY, Eliza (Mrs.) Adrian D. Provaux, 1 May 1795, Charleston, S. C.

PERRY, Eliza and William Martin, 1 April 1800, Charleston, S. C.

PERRY, Elizabeth and Jacob Ladson, 18 February 1719, St. Andrews Parish, S. C.

PERRY, John and Sarah Clift, 8 July 1719, St. Andrews Parish, S. C.

PERRY, Josiah and Sarah Lowndes (widow), 17 December 1772, Charleston, S. C.

PERRY, Linda and Andrew Russell, 30 November 1865, Mecklenburg Co., N. C.

PERRY, Mabel and Andrew Hipp, 24 September 1810, Mecklenburg Co., N. C.

PERRY, Martha and William Liles, 11 September 1756, Chowan Co., N. C.

PERRY, Miss and (Dr.) James Hartley, March 1785, Charleston, S. C.

PERRY, Rachel and John Logan, August 1784, Charleston, S. C.

PERRY, Rebecca and John Drayton, 16 March 1775, St. Pauls Parish, S. C.

PERRY, Susanna and (Rev.) James Tongs, 5 September 1768, St. Pauls Parish, S. C.

PERSON, Betsy and Wyatt Ford, 2 June 1783, Rowan Co., N. C.

PETER, Coffee and Sarah Smith, 1773, Granville Co., N. C.

PETERMAN, Catharina and Christian Reichart, 10 March 1754, Orangeburg Co., S. C.

PETERS, Hannah M. and Thomas Boswell, 23 September 1835, Mecklenburg Co., N. C.

PETERSON, —— and Elizabeth Burnett, 13 November 1854, Edgefield District, S. C.

PETERSON, Ann (widow) and John Vann, 25 February 1752, Chowan Co., N. C.

PETERSON, Captain and Ann Halliday, 2 January 1801, Charleston, S. C.

PETERSON, Caroline and Thomas Burdeth, 27 March 1851, Laurens Co., S. C.

PETREE, Alexi and Elizabeth Holland, February 1748, Charleston, S. C.

PETRIE, Alexander and (Mrs.) Sarah Frederick, January 1785, Charleston, S. C.

PETTIFORD, Tempy and William Mitchell, 13 November 1851, Guilford Co., N. C.

PETTIGREW, Charles and Mary Blount, 28 October 1778, Chowan Co., N. C.

PETTIT, Naisby and Sarah Hancock 1800, Pitt Co., N. C.

PETTY, Charles and Julia D. Davis, 12 April 1859, Spartanburg Co., S. C.

PETTYJOHN, Frances and Joshua Perkins, 24 January 1785, Chowan Co., N. C.

PETTIS, Susan and Allison Orr, 17 January 1829, Mecklenburg Co., N. C.

PEYOTT, Peter and Elizabeth Hurst (widow), September 1783, Charleston, S. C.

PEYTON, John L. and Henrietta C. Washington, 17 December 1855, Vernon, N. C.

PEYTON, Miss and Hugh Hutchinson, 4 October 1800, Charleston, S. C.

PETTON, Richard H. and Anne Stobo, 26 May 1795, Charleston, S. C.

PFUND, Ann and Joseph Deramas, 1742, Orangeburg Co., S. C.

PFUND, Barbara (widow) and John Kitchin, 1740, Orangeburg Co., S. C.

PFUND, Catherina and Thomas Puckridge, 1741, Orangeburg Co., S. C.

PHARR, Sarah and Joseph Mahaffey, 9 March 1826, Mecklenburg Co., N. C.

PHELON, Edward and Susannah F. Barksdale, February 1789, Charleston, S. C.

PHELON, Edward M. and (Mrs.) Mary E. Sigourny, 21 November 1799, Charleston, S. C.

PHELPHS, Deliah and Joshua Powers, 4 April 1786, Tyrrell Co., N. C.

PHELPS, Ann and William Speight, 8 August 1772, Chowan Co., N. C.

PHELPS, Catherine and Martin Dunton, 5 March 1779, Tyrrell Co., N. C.

PHELPS, Enoch and Elizabeth Tarkinton, 6 October 1779, Tyrrell Co., N. C.

PHELPS, Frances and Alexander Oliver, 1781, Tyrrell Co., N. C.

PHELPS, James and Ann Chapman, 17 February 1779, Tyrrell Co., N. C.

PHELPS, Jemimah and Andrew Oliver, 1784, Tyrrell Co., N. C.

PHELPS, Jesse and Rosehannah Daws, 1781, Tyrrell Co., N. C.

PHELPS, Joana and Isaac Norman, 11 March 1779, Tyrrell Co., N. C.

PHELPS, John and May Williams, 12 February 1766, Rowan Co., N. C.

PHELPS, Josiah and Mary Donelson, 6 February 1780, Tyrrell Co., N. C.

PHELPS, Mary and Joseph Godwin, 1781, Tyrrell Co., N. C.

PHELPS, Sarah and Jeremiah Bateman, 28 January 1762, Tyrrell Co., N. C.

PHIFER, Ann B. and John Crawford, 17 October 1816, Lancaster Co., S. C.

PHIFER, Jane and Nicholas Montgomery, 11 January 1845, Rowan Co., N. C.

PHIFER, Margaret and James A. Montgomery, 7 December 1841, Rowan Co., N. C.

PHIFER, Mary and Robert G. Howard, 15 April 1838, Mecklenburg Co., N. C.

PHIFER, Charity and Bailey Barker, 7 September 1839, Mecklenburg Co., N. C.

PHILLIPS, Eleanor (widow) and James Bentham, 5 May 1773, Charleston, S. C.

PHILLIPS, Eleanor G. and James Reid, 10 January 1797, Charleston, S. C.

PHILLIPS, Eliza and Isaac M. Rich, 26 February 1833, Mecklenburg Co., N. C.

PHILLIPS, Elizabeth and Thomas M. Clark, 13 August 1863, Mecklenburg Co., N. C.

PHILLIPS, Mary and William McComb, 7 May 1794, Mecklenburg Co., N. C.

PHILLIPS, Mary and Thomas Barnhill, 18 December 1849, Mecklenburg Co., N. C.

PHILLIPS, Nancy and James Knowles, 14 March 1837, Mecklenburg Co., N. C.

PHILLIPS, Sarah and John Bull, 16 July 1769, Charleston, S. C.

PHILLIPS, Sarah and Mason Richardson, 2 February 1795, Mecklenburg Co., N. C.

PHILLIPS, Sarah and John Roberts, 17 April 1797, Charleston, S. C.

PHYTE, Peter and Barbara Hellinger, 11 July 1791, Rowan Co., N. C.

PICKAM, Margaret (Mrs.) and Archibald Gillen, 10 December 1800, Charleston, S. C.

PICKENS, Maria S. and Matthew C. Butler, 21 February 1858, Edgefield, S. C.

PICKERING, Anne (widow) and Jacob Motte, 19 June 1763, Charleston, S. C.

PICKERING, Elizabeth and Hext McCall, October 1783, Charleston, S. C.

PICKINGS, Ann and Joseph Markis, 19 July 1750, Orangeburg Co., S. C.

PICKINGS, Martha and Jonathan Brimstone, 1748, Orangeburg Co., S. C.

PICKINGS, N. and George Flutt, 1748, Orangeburg Co., S. C.

PICKINGS, Samuel and N. Patton, 1748, Orangeburg Co., S. C.

PICKTON, Charles M. and Elizabeth Byers, 8 May 1800, Charleston, S. C.

PIERCE, John and Frances Nichols, 24 November 1779, Chowan Co., N. C.

PIERCE, Lydia and William Marsh, 10 January 1793, Guilford Co., N. C.

PIERCY, Mary (Mrs.) and Thomas Appleton, 11 December 1801, Charleston, S. C.

PIERCY, Sarah and Paul Taylor, October 1785, Santee, S. C.

PIEREN, Magdalene (widow) and Hans Dorff, 10 December 1740, Orangeburg Co., S. C.

PILLANS, Robert and Ann Clark, April 1785, Charleston, S. C.

PINCHBACK, Liddy and Jacob Holeman, 23 November 1795, Rowan Co., N. C.

PINCHBACK, Martha and William Holeman, 28 December 1799, Rowan Co., N. C.

PINCKNEY, Charles and Frances Brewton, January 1753, Charleston, S. C.

PINCKNEY, Charles C. and Sarah Middleton, 28 September 1773, Charleston, S. C.

PINCKNEY, Elizabeth and William Bellinger, February 1784, Charleston, S. C.

PINCKNEY, Harriet and Daniel Horry, 15 February 1768, Charleston, S. C.

PINCKNEY, Hopson and Elizabeth Quash, 22 November 1772, Charleston, S. C.

PINCKNEY, Mary and Thomas Elliot, 27 October 1785, Charleston, S. C.

PINCKNEY, Miles B. and Lucia Bellinger, 14 June 1796, Charleston, S. C.

PINCKNEY, Roger and Susannah Hume (widow) 26 March 1769, Charleston, S. C.

PINCKNEY, Thomas and Elizabeth Izard, 27 December 1803, Charleston, S. C.

PINKNEY, Charles and Mary Laurens, 1788, Charleston, S. C.

PINKNEY, Rebecca and Benjamin Webb, 16 September 1796, Charleston, S. C.

PINKSTON, Dinah and John Howard, 17 August 1779, Rowan Co., N. C.

PINSON, Ann and Newton Babb, 17 January 1852, Laurens Co., S. C.

PINSON, Enna Liza and Leadson Henderson, 12 October 1865, Laurens Co., S. C.

PINXTON, Mary and James Gheen, 7 March 1788, Rowan Co., N. C.

PINYARD, Philip and Anna Miller, 8 February 1743, Charleston, S. C.

PIPER, Margaret and John Burrows, 3 May 1788, Orange Co., N. C.

PIPPEN, Lucretia and John Bunting, 17 May 1806, Edgecombe Co., N. C.

PITMAN, Abegail and James Robison, 27 August 1816, Mecklenburg Co., N. C.

PITMAN, Abey and John Barron, 5 November 1799, Edgecombe Co., N. C.

PITMAN, Betsy and Jonathan Fincher, 4 January 1797, Rowan Co., N. C.

PITMAN, Elizabeth and Jeptha Baker, 11 March 1797, Mecklenburg Co., N. C.

PITMAN, Hardy and (Mrs.) Avey Guilliatt, 16 September 1801, St. Pauls Parish, S. C.

PITMAN, Katherine and Thomas Allen, 31 March 1813, Mecklenburg Co., N. C.

PITMAN, Levina and Matthew Bryan, 25 July 1810, Mecklenburg Co., N. C.

PITMAN, Rachel and Upton Rodden, 16 May 1806, Mecklenburg Co., N. C.

PITMAN, Sarah and Peter Brown, 29 April 1800, Mecklenburg Co., N. C.

PITMAN, Susanna and John Hartwick, 20 October 1806, Mecklenburg Co., N. C.

PLACIDE, Alexi and Charlotte S. Wrighten, 1 August 1796, Charleston, S. C.

PLATT, Ebenezer and Jane Clark, 22 November 1800, Charleston, S. C.

PLEDGER, Joseph and Christian Alexander, 8 May 1783, Tyrrell Co., N. C.

PLUMMER, Betsy and William McKelvey, 3 January 1831, Mecklenburg Co., N. C.

POAGG, John and Charlotte Wragg, 1 January 1763, Charleston, S. C.

POINDEXTER, Eliza and John Foy, 1 November 1832, Edgefield District, S. C.

POINDEXTER, Thomas and (Mrs.) Mary Rall Kinnerly, 8 December 1811, Edgefield District, S. C.

POINSETT, Joel and Mary Izard (2nd. m) 24 October 1833, Charleston, S. C.

POLK, Clarissa and Thomas McNeal, 29 September 1803, Mecklenburg Co., N. C.

POLK, Elizabeth and Peter Rope, 8 September 1818, Mecklenburg Co., N. C.

POLK, John and (Mrs.) Martha Harris, 22 October 1803, Mecklenburg Co., N. C.

POLK, Matilda and John Campbell, 2 May 1792, Mecklenburg Co., N. C.

POLK, Mary and Daniel Brown, 24 December 1794, Mecklenburg Co., N. C.

POLK, Mary and Samuel W. McLarty, 16 May 1826, Mecklenburg Co., N. C.

POLK, Susan and William H. Rope, 22 October 1832, Mecklenburg Co., N. C.

POLLOCK, Elizabeth and Thomas Williams, 18 June 1785, Chowan Co., N. C.

POOL, Franklin and Mary Fowler, 28 September 1865, Laurens Co., S. C.

POOL, George and Frances Farrow, 7 October 1857, Laurens Co., S. C.

POOL, Margaret J. and William M. Ross, 24 July 1855, Mecklenburg Co., N. C.

POOL, Mary and William Neal, 1784, Tyrrell Co., N. C.

POOL, Polly and Andrew Holshouse, 21 December 1798, Rowan Co., N. C.

POOLE, Sarah and Robert Jones, 1784, Tyrrell Co., N. C.

POPE, George and Sarah Humphrey, 19 June 1739, St. Andrews Parish, S. C.

POPE, Joseph D. and Catherine Scott, 11 December 1845, St. Helena Parish, S. C.

PORCHER, Catherine and George Ancrum, 26 November 1769, Charleston, S. C.

PORCHER, Elizabeth and William Mazyck, 5 July 1764, Charleston, S. C.

PORCHER, Elizabeth and Henry Ravenel, 24 May 1822, Pooshwee, S. C.

PORCHER, Peter and (Mrs.) Elizabeth Wilkinson, January 1786, St. Peters Parish, S. C.

PORCHER, Rachel and William Doughty, 22 February 1770, Charleston, S. C.

PORTER, Catherine and Amos Barnett, 25 December 1819, Mecklenburg Co., N. C.

PORTER, Elizabeth (Mrs.) and James Vinson, 31 December 1799, Charleston, S. C.

PORTER, Elizabeth Clegg and (Rev.) M. Fraser, 31 March 1796, Black River, S. C.

PORTER, Jane and David Moore, 9 September 1780, Guilford Co., N. C.

PORTER, Jane and Henry Morrison, 29 December 1823, Mecklenburg Co., N. C.

PORTER, John M. and Sarah V. V. Prather, 16 November 1847, Mecklenburg Co., N. C.

PORTER, Margaret and James Graham, 6 May 1786, Rowan Co., N. C.

PORTER, Margaret and William R. McNeel, 24 February 1831, Mecklenburg Co., N. C.

PORTER, Margaret A. and John Boatright, 26 May 1832, Mecklenburg Co., N. C.

PORTER, Mary and Samuel W. Boatright, 8 January 1846, Mecklenburg Co., N. C.

PORTER, Melly and Antonio Crispo, 7 August 1828, Mecklenburg Co., N. C.

PORTER, Peggy and Upton Byram, 15 June 1807, Mecklenburg Co., N. C.

PORTER, Priscilla and John Henderson, 9 July 1828, Mecklenburg Co., N. C.

PORTER, Susannah and Samuel Ector, 30 August 1774, Rowan Co., N. C.

PORTER, Susanna and John Ross, 16 May 1799, Mecklenburg Co., N. C.

PORTERFIELD, Margaret and Robert McFerrin, 24 January 1856, Edgefield District, S. C.

PORTEUS, Robert and Ann Wigg, November 1771, Beaufort, S. C.

POSEY, Martin and Matilda Holes, 23 February 1838, Edgefield District, S. C.

POSTELL, Benjamin and Maria Skirving, 15 January 1785, Ponpon, S. C.

POSTELL, James and Widow Hayes, 23 June 1763, Charleston, S. C.

POSTELL, James and Catherine Douxsaint, 30 December 1764, Charleston, S. C.

POSTELL, Jane E. and Richard Singleton, 22 November 1801, Charleston, S. C.

POSTELL, William and Mary Dawson, 29 January 1786, Charleston, S. C.

POSTLETHWAIT, Frances (Mrs.) and Henry Muckenfuss, 26 April 1797, Charleston, S. C.

POTTER, Martha (widow) and James Trotter, 2 December 1743, Chowan Co., N. C.

POTTER, Mary and Tulle Williams, 8 October 1753, Chowan Co., N. C.

POTTER, Mary and James Buchanan, 27 December 1794, Mecklenburg Co., N. C.

POTTS, Eliosa and Thomas A. Magaha, 14 March 1824, Mecklenburg Co., N. C.

POTTS, Elizabeth and William Hudgins, 23 January 1792, Rowan Co., N. C.

POTTS, Jane Levicia and Thomas Milton Carothers, 10 June 1856, Mecklenburg Co., N. C.

POTTS, Jenny and James McCullough, 13 January 1807, Mecklenburg Co., N. C.

POTTS, Lucina and Vincent Barnett, 6 February 1828, Mecklenburg Co., N. C.

POTTS, Peggy and James Robinson, 14 March 1803, Mecklenburg Co., N. C.

POTTS, Rebecca and James Gilpin, 29 April 1789, Rowan Co., N. C.

POWE, Caroline H. and Henry McIver, 7 June 1849, Cheraw, S. C.

POWELL, Elizabeth and Thomas Cryer, 13 July 1752, Orangeburg Co., S. C.

POWELL, James E. and Mary Williams, 16 July 1746, Port Royal, S. C.

POWELL, Martha and Lawrence Quinby, 29 April 1849, Graniteville, S. C.

POWELL, Mary and Akillis Daudy, 13 May 1858, Laurens Co., S. C.

POWELL, Mary B. and (Dr.) Chichester, 11 November 1794, Charleston, S. C.

POWELL, Robert William and Alice Hopton, 11 January 1774, Charleston, S. C.

POWELL, Sally and Charles Augustine Steward, 15 June 1769, Prince George Parish, S. C.

POWER, Isabella and Hosea Garrett, 23 March 1851, Laurens Co., S. C.

POWER, John and Jane Mahaffey, 20 December 1865, Laurens Co., S. C.

POWER, Louisa and Austin Moore, 3 November 1858, Laurens Co., S. C.

POWER, Permealy and Martin Riddle, 19 November 1857, Laurens Co., S. C.

POWER, Sarah and Josiah Carney, 19 August 1789, Bertie Co., N. C.

POWERS, Elizabeth and Stephen Hassell, 6 October 1783, Tyrrell Co., N. C.

POWERS, John and Jane Franks, 17 December 1857, Laurens Co., S. C.

POWERS, Joshua and Deliah Phelphs, 4 April 1786, Tyrrell Co., N. C.

POWERS, Josiah and Mary Cheston, 1780, Tyrrell Co., N. C.

POWERS, Mary and Miles Burk, 10 May 1775, Chowan Co., N. C.

POWERS, Sarah and Elford Knight, 10 September 1846, Laurens Co., S. C.

POWERS, Peter and Mary Burk, 23 June 1778, Chowan Co., N. C.

POWERS, Sally and Isaac Morrow, 18 July 1811, Mecklenburg Co., N. C.

POYAS, James and Ann Frierson, 22 April 1797, Charleston, S. C.

POYAS, John (Dr.) and Catherine Smith, May 1785, Goose Creek, S. C.

POYAS, Louisa and Thomas Gibson, 5 December 1799, Charleston, S. C.

PRATHER, Mary and Mably Roan, 20 May 1820, Mecklenburg Co., N. C.

PRATHER, Sarah V. V. and John M. Porter, 16 November 1847, Mecklenburg Co., N. C.

PRATT, Abigail and James McAlpin, 5 May 1783, Tyrrell Co., N. C.

PRATT, Eliza and Hugh Ormond, 10 February 1813, Mecklenburg Co., N. C.

PRATT, Jeremiah and Penelope Gilbert, 10 March 1772, Chowan Co., N. C.

PRATT, Mary (widow) and John McLean, August 1783, Charleston, S. C.

PREDY, Lawson and Mary Coletrane, 27 June 1745, Chowan Co., N. C.

PREDY, Mary (widow) and John Messenger, 20 January 1752, Chowan Co., N. C.

PRESCOTT, Miles and Martha Harden, 1 December 1836, Edgefield District, S. C.

PRESCOTT, Ellen and William Liles, 2 March 1837, Edgefield District, S. C.

PRESLEY, Betty and Abraham Rock, 18 July 1799, Mecklenburg Co., N. C.

PRESSLY, Elizabeth and Daniel Abbey, 16 February 1843, Edgefield District, S. C.

PRESSLY, Miss and John Woods, 25 November 1853, Laurens Co., S. C.

PRICE, Betty and Joseph Deweese, 22 May 1828, Edgefield District, S. C.

PRICE, Eliza and James S. Reitch, 24 May 1842, Mecklenburg Co., N. C.

PRICE, Elizabeth and James Thompson, 29 July 1773, Chowan Co., N. C.

PRICE, Elizabeth and James Horn, 18 May 1799, Edgecombe Co., N. C.

PRICE, Elizabeth and Enos Anderson, 16 April 1804, Chowan Co., N. C.

PRICE, Elizabeth T. A. and Joseph W. Ross, 10 July 1750, Mecklenburg Co., N. C.

PRICE, Esther and Henry Neal, 8 April 1805, Mecklenburg Co., N. C.

PRICE, Felicia C. and John Davison, 24 March 1757, Chowan Co., N. C.

PRICE, Keziah and Jonathan Coleman, 4 January 1763, Edgecombe Co., N. C.

PRICE, Margaret and Henry Davis, 1795, Rutherford Co., N. C.

PRICE, Martha and George R. Henry, 21 December 1809, Mecklenburg Co., N. C.

PRICE, Martha M. and Alexander N. Neely, 11 December 1839, Mecklenburg Co., N. C.

PRICE, Mary R. and Alexander G. Neal, 9 October 1839, Mecklenburg Co., N. C.

PRICE, Mourning and William Anderson, 21 July 1763, Edgecombe Co., N. C.

PRICE, Nannie R. and Samuel C. Alexander, 25 March 1863, Mecklenburg Co., N. C.

PRICE, Nancy and Joseph Patterson, 2 February 1834, Edgefield District, S. C.

PRICE, Rachel and John Bell, 18 December 1792, Mecklenburg Co., N. C.

PRICE, Rachel and Ezekial Alexander, 25 March 1811, Mecklenburg Co., N. C.

PRICE, Thomas and Susan Chamberlain, 1 November 1857, Edgefield District, S. C.

PRICE, William and Ann Nichols (widow), 24 May 1772, Charleston, S. C.

PRINCE, Anne and William Torrey, 30 May 1800, Charleston, S. C.

PRINCE, Lieutenant and Ann Lempriere, 17 November 1763, Christ Church Parish, S. C.

PRINCE, Sally and William Swallow, 26 October 1771, Charleston, S. C.

PRINGE, John J. and Miss Reed, January 1784, Charleston, S. C.

PRINGLE, Mary and Lawrence Quackenbush, 3 September 1801, Charleston, S. C.

PRINGLE, Mary and Donald C. Mitchell, May 1853, Charleston, S. C.

PRINGLE, Robert and Jane Allen, 18 July 1734, Charleston, S. C.

PRINGLE, Robert and Judith Bull (widow), 16 April 1751, Charleston, S. C.

PRIOLEAU, Catherine and Daniel Revenell, 27 April 1786, Charleston, S. C.

PRIOLEAU, Elizabeth and George Roupell, 7 May 1753, Charleston, S. C.

PRIOLEAU, Hext and Peggy Williams, 9 April 1775, Charleston, S. C.

PRIOLEAU, Mary and Thomas Grimball, 10 June 1765, Charleston, S. C.

PRIOLEAU, Mary M. and Timothy Ford, 18 November 1800, Charleston, S. C.

PRIOLEAU, Philip and Alice E. Homeyard, 30 December 1783, Charleston, S. C.

PRIOLEAU, Sarah (widow) and Jonathan Sarrazin, 22 July 1770, Charleston, S. C.

PRIOLEAU, Samuel (Jr.) and Catherine Cordes, 4 October 1766, Charleston, S. C.

PRITCHARD, Anne and John Purves, February 1775, Charleston, S. C.

PRITCHARD, William and Eliza Latham, 1 December 1801, St. Thomas Parish, S. C.

PRIVITT, Jacob and Elizabeth Jones, 4 July 1751, Chowan Co., N. C.

PRIVETT, Samuel and Elizabeth Miller, 17 July 1827, Chowan Co., N. C.

PRIVOTE, Noah and Penny Evans, 6 September 1790, Bertie Co., N. C.

PROCTOR, John and Eleanor Whatley, 17 March 1839, Edgefield District, S. C.

PROVAUX, Adrian D. and (Mrs.) Eliza Perry, 1 May 1795, Charleston, S. C.

PRUNCEN, Jacob and Barbara Fusters, 26 January 1738, Orangeburg Co., S. C.

PUCKETT, Mary and John Benton, 15 March 1825, Mecklenburg Co., N. C.

PUCKRIDGE, Thomas and Catherina Pfund, 1741, Orangeburg Co., N. C.

PUGH, Mary W. and (Dr.) Murdoch McLean, 14 Febuary 1826, Robeson Co., N. C.

PULLY, Charles and Nancy Nelson, 1 November 1765, Laurens Co., S. C.

PULLY, William and Susan Nelson, 1 November 1865, Laurens Co., S. C.

PURDIE, Joseph and Johanna Besselleu, 6 June 1800, Charleston, S. C.

PURDIE, Joy and Mary Green, 28 August 1765, Chowan Co., N. C.

PURDY, Keziah and John Darby, 14 July 1772, Chowan Co., N. C.

PURRY, Eleanor and John Bull, 29 March 1768, Charleston, S. C.

PURSELL, Sarah (widow) and Samuel Woodard, 2 August 1750, Chowan Co., N. C.

PURVES, John and Anne Pritchard, February 1775, Charleston, S. C.

PURVIANCE, Martha and William D. Crowell, 24 May 1831, Mecklenburg Co., N. C.

PUTMAN, Arinda and Joseph Burdett, 16 January 1851, Laurens Co., S. C.

PUTMAN, Doucinda and William Burdine, 1 August 1859, Laurens Co., S. C.

PUTMAN, Emmaline and Leander Rogers, 28 January 1847, Laurens Co., S. C.

PUTMAN, John and Nancy E. Garrett, 30 December 1847, Laurens Co., S. C.

PUTMAN, Kiziah and Robertson Burns, 7 December 1847, Laurens Co., S. C.

PUTMAN, Manima and Martin Burdine, 12 November 1859, Laurens Co., S. C.

PUTMAN, Minty and Samuel Templeton, 3 May 1855, Laurens Co., S. C.
PUTMAN, Nancy Mary and Y. J. Ball, 30 December 1846, Laurens Co., S. C.
PUTMAN, Perry and Mary Parks, 21 December 1848, Laurens Co., S. C.
PUTMAN, Simeon and Catherine Owings, 4 January 1844, Laurens Co., S. C.
PUTMAN, Zalister and John Cheek, 8 June 1852, Laurens Co., S. C.
PYATT, Mary and William Allston (Dr.), 4 February 1800, Waccamaw, S. C.

Q

QUACKENBUSH, Laurena and Mary Pringle, 3 September 1801, Charleston, S. C.

QUACKENBUSS, Susannah and Jacob Thom, 25 May 1800, Charleston, S. C.

QUARTERMAN, Mary (widow) and William Sanders, 1 February 1774, Berkeley Co., S. C.

QUASH, Elizabeth and Hopson Pinckney, 22 November 1772, Charleston, S. C.

QUAY, Jane A. and Joseph B. Black, 16 December 1842, Mecklenburg Co., N. C.

QUELCH, Harriot and Thomas Blackwood, 23 April 1801, Charleston, S. C.

QUERY, James H. and Isabella C. Reed, 27 March 1850, Mecklenburg Co., N. C.

QUERY, Jane C. and John H. Caldwell, 5 January 1860, Mecklenburg Co., N. C.

QUINCY, Elizabeth and James McRea Berryhill, 2 August 1802, Mecklenburg Co., N. C.

QUINCY, Samuel (Rev.) and Elizabeth Hill (widow), 24 April 1747, Charleston, S. C.

QUIRY, Jane and Abraham Black, 29 June 1818, Mecklenburg Co., N. C.

R

RABORN, M. B. and Amanda Hoover, 14 June 1865, Mecklenburg Co., N. C.

RABEY, Catherine and Owen Cromlies, 18 January 1763, Chowan Co., N. C.

RABY, Adam and Judith Benton, 30 September 1748, Chowan Co., N. C.

RADFORD, Eliza and Stephen Brown, 8 August 1841, Edgefield District, S. C.

RADFORD, Susannah and Simeon Redford, 17 March 1845, Edgefield District, S. C.

RAGIN, Frances and Richard Harvin, 3 August 1775, Sumter District, S. C.

RAIBORN, Mary and Abner Bolton, 14 December 1856, Edgefield District, S. C.

RAIFORD, Mary and John Pearson, 25 April 1742, Orangeburg Co., S. C.

RAILSBACK, Elizabeth and Isaac Ellis, 26 April 1791, Rowan Co., N. C.

RAIN, Samuel and Hester Nelson, 12 December 1801, Charleston, S. C.

RAINS, William and Phebe Risher, 18 November 1779, Santee, S. C.

RAKE, Mary and John Wilson, 14 September 1774, Edisto, S. C.

RALPH, Tamsen and John Addison, May 1784, Charleston, S. C.

RALSTON, Eleanor and John McClure, 5 January 1799, Mecklenburg Co., N. C.

RALTON, Richard and Hepzibah Bedel, 22 February 1722, St. Andrews Parish, S. C.

RAMAGE, Charles and Frances Swallow (widow), 30 June 1774, Charleston, S. C.

RAMBO, Benajah and Mary Ann Dobey, 22 October 1839, Edgefield District, S. C.

RAMSEY, Agnes and John McKee, 18 November 1797, Mecklenburg Co., N. C.

RAMSEY, David (Dr.) and Sabina Ellis, 9 February 1775, Charleston, S. C.

RAMSEY, James and Isabella Hall, 8 February 1792, Mecklenburg Co., N. C.

RAMSEY, John (Dr.) and (Mrs.) Deas, 22 March 1797, Charleston, S. C.

RAMSEY, Nathaniel and Harriett King, 26 April 1855, Edgefield District, S. C.

RAMSEY, Thomas and Susannah Henderson, 4 October 1804, Mecklenburg Co., N. C.

RANDAL, Jackson and Mary Browning, 1 July 1841, Edgefield District, S. C.

RANDALL, C. T. and (Miss) M. Cole, 23 June 1765, Mecklenburg Co., N. C.

RANDALL, Dorcas and Anthony Lamotte, 8 March 1767, Charleston, S. C.

RANDALL, Mary and John H. Bory, 22 July 1778, Chowan Co., N. C.

RANDALL, Polly and Tillman Howard, 26 October 1854, Edgefield District, S. C.

RANDALL, William and Jane Johnston, 27 March 1818, Mecklenburg Co., N. C.

RANDOLPH, Elizabeth and Robert Dunbar, 9 April 1840, Edgefield District, S. C.

RANDOLPH, John D. and Margaret Kendrick, 8 March 1815, Mecklenburg Co., N. C.

RANDOLPH, Margaret and John Bowden, 6 November 1817, Mecklenburg Co., N. C.

RANKHORN, Joseph and Amelia Thomas, 1784, Tyrrell Co., N. C.

RANKIN, John and Sarah Farrar, 21 September 1814, Mecklenburg Co., N. C.

RANKIN, John S. and Elinor Alexander, 28 August 1835, Mecklenburg Co., N. C.

RANKIN, Richard and Elizabeth Doherty, 3 June 1793, Mecklenburg Co., N. C.

RANKIN, Richard and Hargrove, 18 May 1825, Mecklenburg Co., N. C.

RANKIN, Samuel and Mary Doherty, 16 November 1791, Mecklenburg Co., N. C.

RANKIN, Sarah E. and Watson W. Rankin, 22 May 1847, Mecklenburg Co., N. C.

RANKIN, Watson W. and Sarah E. Rankin, 22 May 1847, Mecklenburg Co., N. C.

RASOR, Josiah and Elizabeth Sutton, 27 March 1788, Bertie Co., N. C.

RATCHFORD, James and Esther Carothers, 14 February 1825, Mecklenburg Co., N. C.

RATCHFORD, William and Mary B. Glover, 19 September 1832, Mecklenburg Co., N. C.

RATFORD, Joseph and Eugenia Carse, 1740, Orangeburg Co., S. C.

RATLIFF, Elizabeth and Charles Shepherd, 18 February 1768, Charleston, S. C.

RAVEN, Elizabeth and Arnoldus Vanderhorst, 5 March 1771, Charleston, S. C.

RAVEN, Henrietta (widow), and James Stanyarne, 26 October 1767, Charleston, S. C.

RAVEN, John and Sarah Holmes, 6 November 1750, Charleston, S. C.

RAVEN, Sarah and John Daniel, 23 January 1736, Charleston, S. C.

RAVEN, William and Henrietta Smith, 8 June 1761, Charleston, S. C.

RAVENEL, Daniel (Jr.) and Charlotte Mazyck, 12 February 1759, Charleston, S. C.

RAVENEL, Daniel and Catherine Prioleau, 27 April 1786, Charleston S. C.

RAVENEL, Henry and Mary De St. Julien, 13 September 1750, Hanover, S. C.

RAVENEL, Henry and Catherine Stevens, 17 June 1813, Pooshwee, S. C.

RAVENEL, Henry and Esther Dwight, 19 January 1819, Pooshwee, S. C.

RAVENEL, Henry and Elizabeth Porcher, 24 May 1822, Pooshwee, S. C.

RAVENEL, Paul and Susannah Lloyd, 19 January 1786, Charleston, S. C.

RAVENEL, Stephen and Catherine Mazyck, 11 December 1800, Charleston, S. C.

RAVENEL, Rene and Charlotte St. Julian, 24 October 1687, Pompion Hill, S. C.

RAVENEL, Rene and Charlotte Mazyck, 14 February 1788, Pooshwee, S. C.

RAVENEL, Rene and Isabel de Daux, 26 February 1856, Pooshwee, S. C.

RAVENEL, Thomas P. and Elizabeth M. Wilson, 11 February 1846, Pooshwee, S. C.

RAWORTH, George and Margaret Welch, 5 December 1799, Charleston, S. C.

RAWLINS, Edward and Mary Miles, 24 April 1710, St. Andrews Parish, S. C.

RAWLINS, Ellen and Childermas Croft, 16 August 1781, Santee, S. C.

RAY, Britain and Hannah Cashon, 4 October 1802, Mecklenburg Co., N. C.

RAY, Catherine and Jonathan Bateman, 20 January 1766, Tyrrell Co., N. C.

RAY, Cropley and Mary Evans, 29 April 1765, Tyrrell Co., N. C.

RAY, Elizabeth and Hezikiah Morrow, 25 April 1820, Mecklenburg Co., N. C.

RAY, Jennet and Michael Robinson, 22 November 1788, Orange Co., N. C.

RAY, John and Mary Gray, 22 February 1763, Tyrrell Co., N. C.

RAY, Louisa R. and Thomas McMillan, 25 February 1830, Camden, S. C.

RAY, Maines and Charles Newabary, 1782, Tyrrell Co., N. C.

RAY, Margaret and Henry Fleming, 1 August 1784, Rowan Co., N. C.

RAY, Martha C. and James J. Blair, 5 November 1822, Camden, S. C.

RAY, Nancy and Elisha Dagnell, 27 December 1855, Edgefield District, S. C.

RAY, Muranda E. and James W. Brown, 19 October 1848, Mecklenburg Co., N. C.

RAY, Penny and John Miller, 30 January 1821, Bertie Co., N. C.

RAY, Peter R. and Mary Flint, 1792, Charleston, S. C.

RAY, Sarah and Robert Gordon, 12 August 1769, Tyrrell Co., N. C.

RAYMOND, Franklin and Jennette Sloan, April 1821, Chester District, S. C.

RAYNOLDS, Caroline and Lewis F. Harper, 20 November 1801, Charleston, S. C.

REA, Allan and Frances Moore, 2 November 1797, Mecklenburg Co., N. C.

REA, Andrew and Eleanor Hennegan, 16 June 1797, Mecklenburg Co., N. C.

REA, Avery S. and Margaret McSparron, 5 March 1823, Mecklenburg Co., N. C.

REA, Caroline and William Beaty, 1 April 1841, Mecklenburg Co., N. C.

REA, David N. and Elsy Spears, 29 November 1802, Mecklenburg Co., N. C.

REA, David H. and Charlotte Shepard, 14 November 1836, Mecklenburg Co., N. C.

REA, D. L. and Helen M. Clark, 12 December 1848, Mecklenburg Co., N. C.

REA, Elizabeth and Robert Irvin, 29 April 1817, Mecklenburg Co., N. C.

REA, Evelina and William G. H. Lamb, 11 October 1830, Chowan Co., N. C.

REA, Harriet D. and James W. Martin, 21 November 1837, Mecklenburg Co., N. C.

REA, James and Polly Bozzell, 13 March 1809, Mecklenburg Co., N. C.

REA, James and Mary Walker, 10 March 1814, Mecklenburg Co., N. C.

REA, James and Leanah J. McEwen, 30 July 1857, Mecklenburg Co., N. C.

REA, James M. and Mary Parks, 21 April 1842, Mecklenburg Co., N. C.

REA, Jane and James Biggart, 8 June 1836, Mecklenburg Co., N. C.

REA, John and Elizabeth H. Acock, 1 March 1823, Mecklenburg Co., N. C.

REA, John and Jean Smith, 25 April 1801, Mecklenburg Co., N. C.

REA, John K. and Martha J. Brown, 18 January 1848, Mecklenburg Co., N. C.

REA, John K. and Margaret S. Alexander, 15 March 1860, Mecklenburg Co., N. C.

REA, John L. and Sarah Smith, 29 August 1846, Mecklenburg Co., N. C.

REA, John M. and Sally Rich, 13 March 1821, Mecklenburg Co., N. C.

REA, Joseph and Jemima Harkness, 15 July 1809, Mecklenburg Co., N. C.

REA, Joseph and Sarah Reed, 1 February 1816, Mecklenburg Co., N. C.

REA, Leroy and Hannah McCorkle, 8 January 1839, Mecklenburg Co., N. C.

REA, Margaret E. and Taylor H. Berryhill, 15 May 1832, Mecklenburg Co., N. C.

REA, Martha and Samuel Rea, 5 April 1798, Mecklenburg Co., N. C.

REA, Martha A. and William P. Robinson, 2 February 1854, Mecklenburg Co., N. C.

REA, Martha A. and John W. Abernathy, 11 June 1861, Mecklenburg Co., N. C.

REA, Mary and Samuel Matthews, 13 November 1809, Mecklenburg Co., N. C.

REA, Mary A. and Joseph H. Irwin, 21 February 1850, Mecklenburg Co., N. C.

REA, Mary Jane and Robert Ormond, 12 February 1840, Mecklenburg Co., N. C.

REA, Mary L. and Andrew Jamieson, 30 July 1841, Mecklenburg Co., N. C.

REA, Robert and Mary A. Turner, 23 June 1864, Mecklenburg Co., N. C.

REA, R. R. and Jane R. Flanigan, 18 August 1851, Mecklenburg Co., N. C.

REA, Samuel and Martha Rea, 5 April 1798, Mecklenburg Co., N. C.

REA, Sarah L. and William M. Bigham, 6 June 1844, Mecklenburg Co., N. C.

REA, Silas (Sr.) and (Mrs.) M. A. Parks, 28 February 1856, Mecklenburg Co., N. C.

REA, Terza and Benjamin P. Boyd, 11 November 1839, Mecklenburg Co., N. C.

REA, Thomas M. and Sarah Ressak, 19 March 1829, Mecklenburg Co., N. C.

REA, William and Hannah Berryhill, 23 March 1814, Mecklenburg Co., N. C.

REA, William A. and Nancy Orr, 12 July 1854, Mecklenburg Co., N. C.

REA, William W. and Elizabeth P. Sharpe, 28 August 1854, Mecklenburg Co., N. C.

READ, Ann and James McKnight, 6 June 1796, Mecklenburg Co., N. C.

READ, Ann and Thomas B. Neely, 2 October 1832, Mecklenburg Co., N. C.

READ, Benjamin and Mary J. Middleton, 16 February 1864, Charleston, S. C.

READ, Catherine S. and John Berryhill, 30 March 1836, Mecklenburg Co., N. C.

READ, Charlotte and David McRary, 4 September 1839, Mecklenburg Co., N. C.

READ, Eleanor A. and William A. Cook, 5 September 1848, Mecklenburg Co., N. C.

READ, Isabella C. and James H. Query, 27 March 1850, Mecklenburg Co., N. C.

READ, Jane A. and R. J. Read, 22 March 1847, Mecklenburg Co., N. C.

READ, Jonathan and Sally Glass, 4 June 1816, Mecklenburg Co., N. C.

READ, Margaret A. and William H. Ballard, 2 April 1861, Mecklenburg Co., N. C.

READ, Margaret C. and Robert C. Neely, 15 September 1830, Mecklenburg Co., N. C.

READ, Martha Young and Robert Bigham, 31 December 1799, Mecklenburg Co., N. C.

READ, Mary L. and William R. Berryhill, 11 December 1837, Mecklenburg Co., N. C.

READ, Sarah and Joseph Rea, 1 February 1816, Mecklenburg Co., N. C.

READ, Susanna and Hugh Rose, April 1784, Christ Church Parish, S. C.

READ, Warren and Isabella Rogers, 15 December 1857, Laurens Co., S. C.

READ, William K. and A. H. Alexander, 15 January 1841, Mecklenburg Co., N. C.

READY, John and Euphemi Brown, 5 April 1774, Chowan Co., N. C.

READY, John and Rachel Jones, 23 April 1779, Chowan Co., N. C.

READY, William and Emily McGee, 6 February 1860, Mecklenburg Co., N. C.

READER, Catherine and John Spring, 26 October 1800, Charleston, S. C.

REAP, Peggy and Henry File, 6 December 1797, Rowan Co., N. C.

RECHON, Joana S. and Daniel Bize, 3 November 1799, Charleston, S. C.

REDDICK, John and Elizabeth Rice, 2 January 1764, Tyrrell Co., N. C.

REDDING, Robert and Sarah Howard, 19 June 1816, Mecklenburg Co., N. C.

REDFORD, Francis and Elizabeth Smith, 5 May 1771, Santee, S. C.

REDFORD, Mary and Sherry Covar, 28 September 1831, Edgefield District, S. C.

REDFORD, Simeon and Susannah Radford, 17 March 1845, Edgefield District, S. C.

REDIN, Hanel and Jane Fowler, 10 August 1848, Laurens Co., S. C.

REDING, Sarah and Richard Nevil, 4 December 1746, Chowan Co., N. C.

REDMAN, Samuel and (Mrs.) Sarah Andrews, 25 December 1801, Charleston, S. C.

REED, Andrew J. and Nancy C. Taylor, 20 September 1836, Mecklenburg Co., N. C.

REED, Ann Alice and Clark Columbus Cooper, 16 February 1842, Barnwell District, S. C.

REED, David and Jane Alexander, 7 April 1795, Mecklenburg Co., N. C.

REED, Elizabeth and William Hollis, 15 February 1790, Rowan Co, N. C.

REED, Franky and Joseph Mitchell, 21 August 1848, Guilford Co., N. C.

REED, George and Jemima Davis, 18 August 1743, Chowan Co., N. C.

REED, George Anna and W. W. Culler, 1 February 1849, Barnwell District, S. C.

REED, Hugh and Ann Walker, March 1809, Mecklenburg Co., N. C.

REED, James and Margaret Deweese, 7 January 1841, Mecklenburg Co., N. C.

REED, James B. and Mary B. Grier, 14 March 1837, Mecklenburg Co., N. C.

REED, Jemima (widow) and Arthur Allen, 20 October 1750, Chowan Co., N. C.

REED, John G. and Harriet T. Hepworth, 6 March 1839, Mecklenburg Co., N. C.

REED, John H. and Elizabeth Williams, 9 March 1835, Mecklenburg Co., N. C.

REED, Jonathan and Nancy C. Cooper, 19 January 1850, Mecklenburg Co., N. C.

REED, Joseph and Margaret Franklin, 12 March 1811, Mecklenburg Co., N. C.

REED, Margaret and William A. Brown, 12 October 1847, Mecklenburg Co., N. C.

REED, Martha and William L. Robinson, 17 October 1858, Mecklenburg Co., N. C.

REED, Mary and Charles Warren Tyler, 19 August 1841, Barnwell District, S. C.

REED, Miss and John J. Pringe, January 1784, Charleston, S. C.

REED, Olive and Benjamin Minton, 15 February 1790, Bertie Co., N. C.

REED, Rufus and Elizabeth S. Davidson, 24 January 1835, Mecklenburg Co., N. C.

REED, R. J. and Jane A. Reed, 22 March 1847, Mecklenburg Co., N. C.

REED, Samuel and Elizabeth Boilston, 31 December 1823, Barnwell District, S. C.

REED, Samuel and Mary Todd, 4 April 1836, Mecklenburg Co., N. C.

REED, Samuel J. and Martha N. Houser, 15 October 1854, South Edisto River, S. C.

REED, Silas and Nancy Miller, 16 February 1812, Mecklenburg Co., N. C.

REED, Silas and Elizabeth Kerr, 10 December 1827, Mecklenburg Co., N. C.

REED, Thomas and Louisa Blackburn, 5 February 1830, Mecklenburg Co., N. C.

REED, William and Eliza McAllister, 18 February 1829, Mecklenburg Co., N. C.

REED, William and Isabella Kirkpatrick, 1 March 1847, Mecklenburg Co., N. C.

REEVE, Ambrose (Dr.) and Anne Stanyarne (widow), 16 December 1733, Port Royal, S. C.

REEVE, Ann (widow) and Thomas Wigg, 6 March 1752, Beaufort, S. C.

REEVES, Enos and Amy Legare, 22 December 1784, Charleston, S. C.

REEVES, Henry and Charlotte Elliott, September 1763, Charleston, S. C.

REEVES, William and Rachel Parks, 12 February 1811, Mecklenburg Co., N. C.

REEVES, William and Jane H. Cunningham, 20 July 1824, Mecklenburg Co., N. C.

REEVES, William and Hannah Smith, 14 December 1820, Mecklenburg Co., N. C.

REICHART, Christian and Catharina Peterman, 10 March 1754, Orangeburg Co., N. C.

REID, Andrew and Elizabeth Sarrazin, 5 May 1765, Charleston, S. C.

REID, Elizabeth and William Bull, 26 August 1779, Charleston, S. C.

REID, George F. and Margaret N. Auten, 17 July 1856, Mecklenburg Co., N. C.

REID, H. C. and (Miss) M. S. Caldwell, 10 May 1859, Mecklenburg Co., N. C.

REID, H. C. and (Miss) M. C. Kirpatrick, 9 April 1862, Mecklenburg Co., N. C.

REID, H. R. and Eliza Alexander, 21 November 1865, Mecklenburg Co., N. C.

REID, Isaac and Henrietta Tenapough, 25 June 1853, Mecklenburg Co., N. C.

REID, James and Eleanor G. Phillips, 10 January 1797, Charleston, S. C.

REID, James (Jr.) and Polly King, 13 April 1802, Mecklenburg Co., N. C.

REID, Jane (Mrs.) and William Walker, 10 March 1801, Charleston, S. C.

REID, Jeremiah S. and Mary I. Grier, 6 November 1855, Mecklenburg Co., N. C.

REID, John and (Mrs.) Mary Brinley, 12 October 1799, Charleston, S. C.

REID, John and Margaret E. Bigham, 6 March 1844, Mecklenburg Co., N. C.

REID, John and Martha M. Burns, 4 February 1846, Mecklenburg Co., N. C.

REID, Jonathan and Jane P. McDowell, 2 January 1822, Mecklenburg Co., N. C.

REID, Jonathan and Esther M. Robison, 8 November 1854, Mecklenburg Co., N. C.

REID, Katy and Thomas Burrington, 20 June 1751, Charleston, S. C.

REID, Margaret L. and James W. Alexander, 17 December 1850, Mecklenburg Co., N. C.

REID, Reuben and Nancy Hainey, 11 August 1837, Mecklenburg Co., N. C.
REID, Rufus and Nancy A. Latta, 6 December 1824, Mecklenburg Co., N. C.
REID, R. W. and Mary A. Flanagan, 27 November 1844, Mecklenburg Co., N. C.
REID, Samuel C. and Caroline Boyce, 9 December 1847, Mecklenburg Co., N. C.
REID, Samuel W. and Eliza Miller, 22 October 1836, Mecklenburg Co., N. C.
REID, Sarah and Franklin Caldwell, 21 February 1864, Mecklenburg Co., N. C.
REID, Sarah A. and William J. Alexander, 22 February 1860, Mecklenburg Co.,
    N. C.
REID, William B. W. and Terza Alexander, 22 January 1839, Mecklenburg Co.,
    N. C.
REID, William H. and Sophia Todd, 9 February 1860, Mecklenburg Co., N. C.
REID, William K. and Margaret Berryhill, 3 February 1830, Mecklenburg Co.,
    N. C.
REID, William M. and Sarah Berryhill, 7 March 1854, Mecklenburg Co., N. C.
REILLY, T (Dr.) and Eliza H. Mayberry, 17 December 1801, Charleston, S. C.
REITCH, James S. and Eliza Price, 24 May 1842, Mecklenburg Co., N. C.
REMBERT, Elizabeth and Thomas England, 12 November 1782, Santee, S. C.
REMBERT, Isaac and Elizabeth Varner, 24 May 1770, Santee, S. C.
REMBERT, Isaac and Margaret Jeannert, 13 May 1773, Santee, S. C.
REMBERT, Judith and William Walker, 16 August 1764, Santee, S. C.
REMBERT, Peter and Cecelia Dexter, 25 January 1782, Santee, S. C.
REMBERT, Rachel and Henry Varner, 24 May 1770, Santee, S. C.
REMINGTON, Jennet and Aaron Harris, 22 April 1783, Rowan Co., N. C.
REMINGTON, John (Jr.) and Sally Donovan, 6 April 1774, Charleston, S. C.
REMINGTON, Nancy and Isaac Burton, February 1775, Charleston, S. C.
REMINGTON, William (Dr.) and Anne Eaton, 19 May 1769, Edisto, S. C.
REMINGTON, William (Dr.) and Nancy Watts, April 1785, Charleston, S. C.
RENSHAW, N. F. and (Mrs.) E. Sloan, 1 August 1865, Mecklenburg Co., N. C.
RESIDE, William and (Mrs.) Mary M. Clarkson, 3 August 1800, Charleston,
    S. C.
RESSACK, Sarah and Thomas M. Rea, 19 March 1829, Mecklenburg Co., N. C.
REVEL, Margaret and George Nicholls, 17 May 1797, Charleston, S. C.
REVELLS, Eli B. and Mary Bird, 8 February 1837, Mecklenburg Co., N. C.
REYNOLDS, Elizabeth and Peter Hagas, 14 February 1780, Rowan Co., N. C.
REYNOLDS, John and Penelope Stollard, 10 April 1729, Charleston, S. C.
REYNOLDS, John and Hannah McKee, 17 October 1803, Mecklenburg Co., N. C.
REYNOLDS, Lucretia and J. W. S. Bowen, 13 January 1847, Edgefield District,
    S. C.
RHETT, Mary Jane and William Dry, February 1746, Charleston, S. C.
RHETT, Sarah and Thomas Frankland, 27 May 1743, Charleston, S. C.
RHIND, Abrabella and Isaac M. Dart, 26 January 1800, Charleston, S. C.
RHIND, David and Elizabeth Cleiland, 22 December 1774, Charleston, S. C.
RHINE, A. M. and Sallie A. Colvard, 4 August 1865, Mecklenburg Co., N. C.
RHINEHARDT, Charles B. and Mary E. Rudesill, 28 December 1814, Mecklen-
    burg Co., N. C.
RHODES, Coleman and Harriett Swearingen, 1 November 1840, Edgefield Dis-
    trict, S. C.
RHODES, Collin and Eliza Landrum, 17 May 1839, Pottersville, S. C.
RHODES, Delilah M. and Thomas S. Herndon, 4 October 1856, Orange Co., N. C.
RHODES, Judeth and Abraham Howett, 2 September 1775, Tyrrell Co., N. C.

RHODES, Judeth and Edmond Blount, 30 December 1777, Tyrrell Co., N. C.

RHODES, Martha and Steward Walker, 19 May 1778, Chowan Co., N. C.

RHODES, Milly and Anthony Armistead, 5 December 1758, Chowan Co., N. C.

RHODES, Milles and Zachariah Herndon, 28 June 1789, Orange Co., N. C.

RHODES, Nathan and Ann Jones, 6 September 1786, Tyrrell Co., N. C.

RHODES, Rebecca and Edmond Herndon, 14 February 1794, Orange Co., N. C.

RHODY, Jenny and Elisha Harrod, 31 March 1785, Chowan Co., N. C.

RHYNE, Hugh T. and N. M. Lawing, 30 October 1859, Mecklenburg Co., N. C.

RHYNE, Joseph N. and Mary S. Todd, 26 May 1847, Mecklenburg Co., N. C.

RHYNE, Moses H. and Mary C. Springs, 2 March 1864, Mecklenburg Co., N. C.

RIAL, Margaret A. and J. M. Anderson, 11 August 1841, Mecklenburg Co., N. C.

RICE, A. B. and Esther Herron, 2 February 1865, Mecklenburg Co., N. C.

RICE, Daniel and Margaret McLure, 19 February 1852, Mecklenburg Co., N. C.

RICE, Elizabeth and John Ofill, 29 December 1755, Orangeburg Co., S. C.

RICE, Elizabeth and John Reddick, 2 January 1764, Tyrrell Co., N. C.

RICE, John and Catherine Cook, 30 January 1818, Mecklenburg Co., N. C.

RICE, Medora and William W. Duncan, 19 March 1861, Union, S. C.

RICE, M. W. and Ester Starnes, 7 November 1865, Mecklenburg Co., N. C.

RICE, Owen and Maria R. Vierling, 18 March 1811, Salem, N. C.

RICE, Stewart and Sophia Cornelia Wentz, 2 December 1839, Mecklenburg Co., N. C.

RICE, Stewart and Jane C. Harrison, 31 December 1847, Mecklenburg Co., N. C.

RICE, Valentine W. and Matilda Baker, 15 October 1853, Mecklenburg Co., N. C.

RICE, V. W. and Elizabeth Yandell, 24 March 1856, Mecklenburg Co., N. C.

RICE, William and Elizabeth Barnett, 14 July 1803, Mecklenburg Co., N. C.

RICE, William and Clarinda Hartley, 15 December 1859, Mecklenburg Co., N. C.

RICH, Betsy and John Hamby, 23 August 1843, Mecklenburg Co., N. C.

RICH, Dempsey and Mary N. Morris, 7 October 1834, Mecklenburg Co., N. C.

RICH, Elizabeth and Archibald Longworth (of N. J.), 20 August 1800, St. Lukes Parish, S. C.

RICH, Elizabeth and Robert Mitchell, 19 March 1822, Guilford Co., N. C.

RICH, Elijah and Elizabeth Morris, 15 August 1834, Mecklenburg Co., N. C.

RICH, Isaac M. and Eliza Phillips, 26 February 1833, Mecklenburg Co., N. C.

RICH, Sally and John M. Rea, 13 March 1820, Mecklenburg Co., N. C.

RICH, Sarah and Solomon George, October 1784, Orange Co., N. C.

RICH, Thomas and Parmela Harris, 26 May 1840, Mecklenburg Co., N. C.

RICHARD, Elizabeth and Daniel Shyder, 1748, Orangeburg Co., S. C.

RICHARDS, James L. and Elizabeth Pagett, 3 November 1768, Stono, S. C.

RICHARDS, Lucy and Edmund Hatch, 15 March 1742, Chowan Co., N. C.

RICHARDS, Samuel and Mary Singleton, 6 December 1801, Charleston, S. C.

RICHARDS, Sarah and John Steele, 27 June 1744, Chowan Co., N. C.

RICHARDS, William and Mary Hood, 13 July 1744, Chowan Co., N. C.

RICHARDSON, Benjamin and Sarah Mizzell, 30 September 1767, Tyrrell Co., N. C.

RICHARDSON, Carolina and James S. Guignard, 14 January 1801, Charleston, S. C.

RICHARDSON, Ediph and Edmond Echeson, 14 October 1779, Rowan Co., N. C.

RICHARDSON, Henry (Dr.) and Mary Fraser, 2 November 1801, Charleston, S. C.

RICHARDSON, James and Sally Burd, 11 December 1817, Mecklenburg Co., N. C.

RICHARDSON, James H. and Ester H. Hunter, 3 September 1851, Mecklenburg Co., N. C.

RICHARDSON, John and Amy Welshuysen, 29 March 1768, Charleston, S. C.

RICHARDSON, John K. and Adaline Hooser, 23 April 1849, Mecklenburg Co., N. C.

RICHARDSON, Mary and Samson D. Belk, 3 December 1834, Mecklenburg Co., N. C.

RICHARDSON, Mason and Sarah Philips, 2 February 1795, Mecklenburg Co., N. C.

RICHARDSON, Sukey and John Smyth, 26 April 1772, Charleston, S. C.

RICHARDSON, Susan and Theophilus Hill, 21 January 1819, Edgefield District, S. C.

RICHARDSON, William and Anne Guignard, 13 October 1768, Charleston, S. C.

RICHEY, Edmund and Rachel Cochran, 28 November 1799, Mecklenburg Co., N. C.

RICKENBACKER, Ann (nee Burgin) and Conrad Alder, 1 January 1740, Orangeburg Co., S. C.

RICKENBACHER, Henry and Ann Diel, 1742, Orangeburg Co., S. C.

RICKETTS, Benjamin and Sarah Simpson, 16 August 1746, Chowan Co., N. C.

RIDDICK, Cader and Elizabeth Garrett, 18 December 1771, Chowan Co., N. C.

RIDDICK, Doctor and Elizabeth Sumner, 1 March 1776, Chowan Co., N. C.

RIDDICK, Seth and Leah Hunter, 6 January 1772, Chowan Co., N. C.

RIDDLE, Ann and William Ellis (Jr.), 27 March 1792, Rowan Co., N. C.

RIDDLE, Elizabeth and Thomas Martin, 10 February 1853, Laurens Co., S. C.

RIDDLE, Graden and Gilly Fowler, 10 January 1850, Laurens Co., S. C.

RIDDLE, John and Betsy Wiggins, 19 December 1839, Edgefield District, S. C.

RIDDLE, Martin and Permealy Power, 19 November 1857, Laurens Co., S. C.

RIDDLE, Mary and James Gordon, 12 February 1779, Rowan Co., N. C.

RIDDLE, Nancy and Wiley Fowler, 10 February 1853, Laurens Co., S. C.

RIDDLE, Polly and Trainham Brownlee, 4 February 1847, Laurens Co., S. C.

RIDDLE, Richardson and Liza Babb, 5 October 1865, Laurens Co., S. C.

RIDDLE, T. S. and Sarah L. Marks, 11 June 1856, Mecklenburg Co., N. C.

RIDLEY, Mary R. and John C. Taylor, 31 August 1842, Granville Co., N. C.

RIGGS, James and Polly Hannah, 22 January 1788, Orange Co., N. C.

RIGHTON, Jane and John D. Miller, December 1779, Charleston, S. C.

RIGHTON, McCully and (Mrs.) Mary Cook, 27 December 1794, Charleston, S. C.

RIGLER, Mary E. and Moses G. Allison, 22 December 1853, Mecklenburg Co., N. C.

RIGSBY, Tempe and Chesley Herndon, 19 October 1824, Orange Co., N. C.

RILEY, Eliza C. and Lee C. Riley, 27 February 1831, Mecklenburg Co., N. C.

RILEY, Ezekial A. and Sarah B. Gibson, 28 December 1835, Mecklenburg Co., N. C.

RILEY, Jane and David Bowers, 29 October 1800, Mecklenburg Co., N. C.

RILEY, Jesse and Sally Wake, 22 June 1825, Mecklenburg Co., N. C.

RILEY, John and Temperance Holton, 19 May 1832, Mecklenburg Co., N. C.

RILEY, John and Mary A. Russ, 21 August 1849, Mecklenburg Co., N. C.

RILEY, Lee C. and Eliza C. Riley, 27 February 1831, Mecklenburg Co., N. C.

RILEY, Miles and Elizabeth Weekly (widow), 22 September 1750, Orangeburg Co., S. C.

RILEY, Sally and Levi Ross, 27 September 1821, Mecklenburg Co., N. C.

RILEY, William and Amy Roberts, 2 December 1805, Mecklenburg Co., N. C.

RIMER, John L. and Mary Jane ——, 27 December 1864, Mecklenburg Co., N. C.

RINER, Samuel and Martha A. McLean, 14 February 1835, Mecklenburg Co., N. C.

RIPLEY, Richard and Augusta Autry, 1 February 1827, Edgefield District, S. C.

RISH, Lodusky and Jacob W. Louman, 15 September 1858, Lexington Co., S. C.

RISHEA, Phebe and William Rains, 18 November 1779, Santee, S. C.

RITTERFORD, Nancy and David Braswell, 14 September 1762, Edgecombe Co., N. C.

RIVERS, Betsey and Benjamin Gibbes, December 1785, St. Andrews Parish, S. C.

RIVERS, Charles and Elizabeth Newton, September 1785, Charleston, S. C.

RIVERS, Dorcas and William Minott, June 1785, Charleston, S. C.

RIVERS, Jonathan and Rachel Bee, 2 March 1786, Charleston, S. C.

RIVERS, Mallory and Lois Burchell, 23 December 1800, James Island, S. C.

RIVERS, Mary and Archibald Scott, 3 February 1774, Berkeley Co., S. C.

RIVERS, Mary Ann and George Smith, 20 February 1801, Charleston, S. C.

RIVERS, Polly and John Wilson, 14 December 1769, Charleston, S. C.

RIVERS, Rebecca and Robert Rose, 10 May 1770, St. Andrews Parish, S. C.

RIVERS, Robert and Jane Taylor, 2 June 1785, James Island, S. C.

ROACH, Allen and Patsy McLean, 27 August 1824, Mecklenburg Co., N. C.

ROACH, Francis and Mary Jennens, 17 April 1768, Santee, S. C.

ROACH, Patsy and John Benton, 8 May 1827, Mecklenburg Co., N. C.

ROACH, William and Mary M'Gregor, 15 May 1797, Charleston, S. C.

ROAN, Herbert and Elizabeth Martin, 20 July 1811, Mecklenburg Co., N. C.

ROAN, Hugh and Harriet Calhoun, 26 May 1792, Mecklenburg Co., N. C.

ROAN, Mabley and Mary Prather, 20 May 1820, Mecklenburg Co., N. C.

ROAN, Solomon and Fanny Parrish, 21 March 1818, Mecklenburg Co., N. C.

ROAN, Susanna and Jacob Frank, 4 June 1768, Rowan Co., N. C.

ROAN, William and Elizabeth Bingham, 25 April 1822, Mecklenburg Co., N. C.

ROBARDS, Betsey and James Taylor, 15 October 1797, Granville Co., N. C.

ROBARDS, Mary D. and Solomon A. Hucks, 5 December 1842, Mecklenburg Co., N. C.

ROBARDS, Polly and Edmond Taylor, 10 September 1798, Granville Co., N. C.

ROBASON, Henry and Sarah Collins, 25 June 1783, Tyrrell Co., N. C.

ROBB, Margaret and Robert Harris, 16 January 1793, Mecklenburg Co., N. C.

ROBERSON, John and Marian Keal, February 1786, Charleston, S. C.

ROBERT, Sarah C. and James C. Brooks, 20 November 1843, Edgefield District, S. C.

ROBERTS, America and Westly Herndon, 1828, Orange Co., N. C.

ROBERTS, Amy and William Riley, 2 December 1805, Mecklenburg Co., N. C.

ROBERTS, Brook and Miss Van Braam, 9 January 1785, Charleston, S. C.

ROBERTS, Hannah and Moses McClellan, 5 July 1801, St. Pauls Parish, S. C.

ROBERTS, James and Margaret Denkins, 3 June 1799, Mecklenburg Co., N. C.

ROBERTS, John and Sarah Phillips, 17 April 1797, Charleston, S. C.

ROBERTS, John and Jane Davis, 10 March 1802, Mecklenburg Co., N. C.

ROBERTS, Jonah and Mary Guerry, 3 May 1774, Santee, S. C.

ROBERTS, Joseph M. and Elizabeth King, 19 May 1841, Mecklenburg Co., N. C.

ROBERTS, Mary and James Mitchell, 25 February 1830, Chowan Co., N. C.

ROBERTS, Mary N. and Charles William Kirk, 16 December 1821, Charleston, S. C.

ROBERTS, Rebecca J. and Amos McManus, 31 March 1864, Lancaster Co., S. C.

ROBERTS, Robert R. and Elizabeth L. Montgomery, 18 May 1840, Mecklenburg Co., N. C.

ROBERTS, Ruth and Thomas Weaver, 14 September 1826, Charleston, S. C.

ROBERTS, Thomas and Mary Harvey, October 1785, Charleston, S. C.

ROBERTS, Thomas and Christian Lassiter, 4 May 1785, Chowan Co., N. C.

ROBERTS, Wiley and Polly Blankenship, 27 January 1808, Mecklenburg Co., N. C.

ROBERTS, William and (Mrs.) Elizabeth Bonner, 21 February 1767, Chowan Co., N. C.

ROBERTS, William and Jane Montgomery, 26 September 1832, Mecklenburg Co., N. C.

ROBERTS, William A. and Nancy V. Orr, 30 March 1858, Mecklenburg Co., N. C.

ROBERTSON, Andrew and Helen Crawford, 8 June 1761, Charleston, S. C.

ROBERTSON, John and Ann Trenholm, 13 May 1795, Charleston, S. C.

ROBERTSON, Martha (widow) and William Sibbaldson, 13 May 1773, Chowan Co., N. C.

ROBERTSON, Milly and Reuben Bramlet, 8 November 1842, Laurens Co., S. C.

ROBERTSON, Sarah (widow) and William Gaskins, 11 April 1774, Chowan Co., N. C.

ROBINETTE, Margaret and Samuel Black, 23 October 1810, Mecklenburg Co., N. C.

ROBINSON, Alexi and Janette Cunningham, 15 October 1791, Mecklenburg Co., N. C.

ROBINSON, Anne and Hugh Anderson, 28 March 1745, Charleston, S. C.

ROBINSON, Charlotte and William Allen, 25 September 1834, Mecklenburg Co., N. C.

ROBINSON, Christina and John Holland, 26 August 1783, Rowan Co., N. C.

ROBINSON, Dovey L. and Stephen McKinley, 4 January 1824, Mecklenburg Co., N. C.

ROBINSON, D. M. and John McCulloch, 5 June 1829, Mecklenburg Co., N. C.

ROBINSON, Ezekial and Eleanor Harris, 23 March 1812, Mecklenburg Co., N. C.

ROBINSON, Frances and Moses Barnett, 16 August 1794, Mecklenburg Co., N. C.

ROBINSON, Frances and Elias Earle, 17 September 1782, Charleston, S. C.

ROBINSON, Henry and Elizabeth Cunningham, 15 August 1809, Mecklenburg Co., N. C.

ROBINSON, Harris and Agnes Kirk, 11 May 1795, Mecklenburg Co., N. C.

ROBINSON, James and Lidy Jones, 12 March 1822, Mecklenburg Co., N. C.

ROBINSON, James B. and Mary Still, 13 December 1836, Mecklenburg Co., N. C.

ROBINSON, Jane D. and John M. Houston, 18 March 1834, Mecklenburg Co., N. C.

ROBINSON, John and Isbell Butcher, 1748, Orangeburg Co., S. C.   (

ROBINSON, John and Elizabeth Jones (widow), 8 January 1754, Chowan Co., N. C.

ROBINSON, John and Keziah Elliott, 31 December 1774, Chowan Co., N. C.

ROBINSON, John and Lydia Brinn, 30 March 1778, Chowan Co., N. C.

ROBINSON, John (Rev.) and Margaret C. Baldrun, 9 April 1795, Mecklenburg Co., N. C.

ROBINSON, John M. and Peggy Walton, 27 August 1813, Mecklenburg Co., N. C.

ROBINSON, Martha and Alexi Robinson, 23 July 1818, Mecklenburg Co., N. C.

ROBINSON, Martha and McKinney McCoy, 3 August 1825, Mecklenburg Co., N. C.

ROBINSON, Mary and Thomas Townsend, 4 February 1785, Charleston, S. C.

ROBINSON, Mary N. and Isaac A. Allison, 10 December 1855, Mecklenburg Co., N. C.

ROBINSON, Michael and Jennet Ray, 22 November 1788, Orange Co., N. C.

ROBINSON, Michael and Ester Brown, 5 January 1828, Mecklenburg Co., N. C.

ROBINSON, Nancy and Adley L. Alexander, 1 January 1817, Mecklenburg Co., N. C.

ROBINSON, Rebecca and James Gibson, 10 March 1787, Rowan Co., N. C.

ROBINSON, Richard and Martha McLeary, 14 June 1790, Mecklenburg Co., N. C.

ROBINSON, Robert and Mary Parks, 1 February 1792, Mecklenburg Co., N. C.

ROBINSON, Rosanna and Hugh Henry, 4 September 1779, Rowan Co., N. C.

ROBINSON, Susan S. and C. T. Means, 8 December 1841, Mecklenburg Co., N. C.

ROBINSON, Susannah and William Gilbert, 15 April 1775, Rowan Co., N. C.

ROBINSON, Wallace and Mary Brown, 5 March 1831, Mecklenburg Co., N. C.

ROBINSON, William and Agnes Hargrave, 9 October 1804, Mecklenburg Co., N. C.

ROBINSON, William and Kezia Lewis, 16 January 1812, Mecklenburg Co., N. C.

ROBINSON, Winny and Stephen Bullock, 24 March 1800, Edgecombe Co., N. C.

ROBINSON, W. W. and (Miss) L. C. Cooper, 18 July 1865, Mecklenburg Co., N. C.

ROBISON, Aaron and Jane Dearmond, 6 June 1803, Mecklenburg Co., N. C.

ROBISON, Alexander and Clarisa Alexander, 16 August 1815, Mecklenburg Co., N. C.

ROBISON, Alexander and Martha Robison, 23 July 1818, Mecklenburg Co., N. C.

ROBISON, Alexander and Elizabeth Robison (or Brown), 3 December 1831, Mecklenburg Co., N. C.

ROBISON, Allen and Susan Boyd, 26 August 1830, Mecklenburg Co., N. C.

ROBISON, Andrew and Sarah N. Lawing, 27 September 1855, Mecklenburg Co., N. C.

ROBISON, Archibald and Abigail Barnett, 16 February 1820, Mecklenburg Co., N. C.

ROBISON, Clarisa and Andrew Beaty, 25 April 1842, Mecklenburg Co., N. C.

ROBISON, Cynthia and S. Washington Boatright, 10 April 1834, Mecklenburg Co., N. C.

ROBISON, C. H. and Mary A. Alexander, 11 March 1844, Mecklenburg Co., N. C.

ROBISON, David and Elinor Bowman, 12 January 1813, Mecklenburg Co., N. C.

ROBISON, David C. and Mary C. Bigger, 27 June 1849, Mecklenburg Co., N. C.

ROBISON, David H. and Jane Sloan, 16 December 1845, Mecklenburg Co., N. C.

ROBISON, Elizabeth (or Brown) and Alexander Robison, 3 December 1831, Mecklenburg Co., N. C.

ROBISON, Elizabeth and Almarine Clark, 27 December 1848, Mecklenburg Co., N. C.

ROBISON, Esther M. and Jonathan Reid, 18 November 1854, Mecklenburg Co., N. C.

ROBISON, Harris and Agness Kirk, 11 May 1795, Mecklenburg Co., N. C.

ROBISON, Isaac and Sally Harkey, 6 February 1821, Mecklenburg Co., N. C.

ROBISON, Isabella and Robert Robison, 10 March 1813, Mecklenburg Co., N. C.

ROBISON, James and Peggy Potts, 14 March 1813, Mecklenburg Co., N. C.

ROBISON, James and Sophia Grey, 11 December 1810, Mecklenburg Co., N. C.

ROBISON, James and Abegail Pitman, 27 August 1816, Mecklenburg Co., N. C.

ROBISON, Jane and John Johnston, 18 November 1829, Mecklenburg Co., N. C.

ROBISON, Joseph M. and Fanny King, 31 July 1856, Mecklenburg Co., N. C.

ROBISON, Josiah A. and Jane L. Henderson, 18 May 1843, Mecklenburg Co., N. C.

ROBISON, John and Ester Wiley, 2 June 1795, Mecklenburg Co., N. C.

ROBISON, John and Betsy Sample, 18 April 1804, Mecklenburg Co., N. C.

ROBISON, John and Amy Fisher, 9 December 1820, Mecklenburg Co., N. C.

ROBISON, John K. and Harriet A. Henderson, 2 December 1843, Mecklenburg Co., N. C.

ROBISON, John L. and Amelia E. Howard, 24 October 1837, Mecklenburg Co., N. C.

ROBISON, John P. and Susan E. Rodden, 27 February 1856, Mecklenburg Co., N. C.

ROBISON, Martha and Alexander Robison, 23 July 1818, Mecklenburg Co., N. C.

ROBISON, Mary and James T. Christenberry, 15 March 1828, Mecklenburg Co., N. C.

ROBISON, Mathew and Mary Hicks, 21 January 1794, Mecklenburg Co., N. C.

ROBISON, Mathew A. and Adalin Rodin, 13 April 1842, Mecklenburg Co., N. C.

ROBISON, Matthew A. and Margaret Hipp, 2 December 1847, Mecklenburg Co., N. C.

ROBISON, Matthew A. and Caroline Byrum, 19 January 1848, Mecklenburg Co., N. C.

ROBISON, Michael and Ester Brown, 5 January 1828, Mecklenburg Co., N. C.

ROBISON, Milly L. and John Culp, 27 January 1852, Mecklenburg Co., N. C.

ROBISON, M. W. and Virginia Q. Clark, 12 April 1849, Mecklenburg Co., N. C.

ROBISON, Nancy H. and Thomas Marks, 27 June 1854, Mecklenburg Co., N. C.

ROBISON, Patsey and Ezekiel Alexander, 8 March 1806, Mecklenburg Co., N. C.

ROBISON, Rachel G. and David Bain, 4 April 1841, Mecklenburg Co., N. C.

ROBISON, Rebecca and Robert Bigger, 31 July 1826, Mecklenburg Co., N. C.

ROBISON, Robert and Margaret Henderson, 30 March 1790, Mecklenburg Co., N. C.

ROBISON, Robert and Isabella Robison, 10 March 1813, Mecklenburg Co., N. C.

ROBISON, Robert B. and Margaret Calder, 25 April 1837, Mecklenburg Co., N. C.

ROBISON, Robert M. and Eliza Jane Taylor, 22 December 1840, Mecklenburg Co., N. C.

ROBISON, R. C. and Martha Johnston, 28 July 1847, Mecklenburg Co., N. C.

ROBISON, Sarah A. and James Brian, 6 November 1850, Mecklenburg Co., N. C.

ROBISON, Sarah J. and John W. Clark, 2 February 1858, Mecklenburg Co., N. C.

ROBISON, Susan S. and C. T. Means, 8 December 1841, Mecklenburg Co., N. C.

ROBISON, Watson and Margaret Eagle, 25 June 1850, Mecklenburg Co., N. C.

ROBISON, William and Sally Stuart, 23 February 1819, Mecklenburg Co., N. C.

ROBISON, William A. and Sarah A. Mathews, 1 February 1842, Mecklenburg Co., N. C.

ROBISON, William L. and Martha Reed, 17 October 1850, Mecklenburg Co., N. C.

ROBISON, William P. and Martha A. Rea, 2 February 1854, Mecklenburg Co., N. C.

ROBISON, William R. and Margaret M. Wiley, 11 May 1833, Mecklenburg Co., N. C.

ROCHE, Francis and Anne Simmons, August 1746, Charleston, S. C.

ROCHE, Martha (Mrs.) and Paul Warley, 12 December 1799, St. Johns Parish, S. C.

ROCK, Abraham and Betty Presley, 18 July 1799, Mecklenburg Co., N. C.

ROCK, Jerusha and Edward King, 29 September 1721, St. Andrews Parish, S. C.

ROCKWELL, Harriet S. and N. Allison Clark, 16 May 1857, Mecklenburg Co., N. C.

RODDEN, Adaline and Mathew A. Robinson, 13 September 1842, Mecklenburg Co., N. C.

RODDEN, Andrew and Harriet A. Rodden, 26 January 1835, Mecklenburg Co., N. C.

RODDEN, Benjamin and Elizabeth Baker, 16 September 1829, Mecklenburg Co., N. C.

RODDEN, Benjamin and Betsy Williams, 30 December 1830, Mecklenburg Co., N. C.

RODDEN, Catherine and Charles B. Moore, 19 June 1809, Mecklenburg Co., N. C.

RODDEN, Damson and Jonathan Baker, 16 September 1801, Mecklenburg Co., N. C.

RODDEN, Dicey and John Rodden, 3 October 1827, Mecklenburg Co., N. C.

RODDEN, Elizabeth and Samuel Berryhill, 16 August 1825, Mecklenburg Co., N. C.

RODDEN, Gabriel and Caroline Cook, 18 October 1842, Mecklenburg Co., N. C.

RODDEN, Hannah R. and William Rodden, 18 March 1847, Mecklenburg Co., N. C.

RODDEN, Harriet A. and Andrew Rodden, 26 January 1835, Mecklenburg Co., N. C.

RODDEN, Jackson and Polly Krum, 17 February 1810, Mecklenburg Co., N. C.

RODDEN, Jacob and Jane Griffin, 25 January 1795, Mecklenburg Co., N. C.

RODDEN, James and Margaret E. Berryhill, 28 January 1847, Mecklenburg Co., N. C.

RODDEN, James J. and Jane Rodden, 10 June 1847, Mecklenburg Co., N. C.

RODDEN, Jane and James J. Rodden, 10 June 1847, Mecklenburg Co., N. C.

RODDEN, John and Dicey Rodden, 3 October 1827, Mecklenburg Co., N. C.

RODDEN, John and Milly Beaty, 1 March 1842, Mecklenburg Co., N. C.

RODDEN, Judy and Irwin Bagot, 11 June 1818, Mecklenburg Co., N. C.

RODDEN, Judy and Abraham Hanks, 12 October 1825, Mecklenburg Co., N. C.

RODDEN, Lewis and Hannah W. Williams, 7 September 1802, Mecklenburg Co., N. C.

RODDEN, Margaret and Thomas Barker, 22 November 1846, Mecklenburg Co., N. C.

RODDEN, Mary E. and William A. Berryhill, 13 January 1858, Mecklenburg Co., N. C.

RODDEN, Matilda and Andrew A. Berryhill, 17 December 1833, Mecklenburg Co., N. C.

RODDEN, Matthew and Hannah Warwick, 26 May 1847, Mecklenburg Co., N. C.

RODDEN, Minton H. and David W. Berryhill, 26 September 1839, Mecklenburg Co., N. C.

RODDEN, N. B. ad Martha M. Headly, 15 August 1865, Mecklenburg Co., N. C.

RODDEN, Rosanna and Thomas Blanchette, 8 September 1805, Mecklenburg Co., N. C.

RODDEN, Susan E. and John P. Robison, 27 February 1856, Mecklenburg Co., N. C.

RODDEN, Thomas M. and Salina Beaty, 8 April 1834, Mecklenburg Co., N. C.

RODDEN, Upton and Rachel Pitman, 16 May 1806, Mecklenburg Co., N. C.

RODDEN, William and Polly Williams, 6 November 1805, Mecklenburg Co., N. C.

RODDEN, William and Hannah R. Rodden, 18 March 1847, Mecklenburg Co., N. C.

RODDEN, William R. and Eliza J. Hoover, 20 September 1860, Mecklenburg Co., N. C.

RODECAP, Anne and George Eicholtz, 13 June 1774, Rowan Co., N. C.

RODES, Tyree and Cynthia Holland, 25 April 1811, Rutherford Co., N. C.

RODGERS, Ann and Robert H. Maxwell, 31 December 1823, Mecklenburg Co., N. C.

RODGERS, Edward H. and Elizabeth M. Henderson, 8 September 1835, Mecklenburg Co., N. C.

RODGERS, E. P. and Sarah J. McCall, 28 September 1865, Mecklenburg Co., N. C.

RODGERS, I. M. S. and (Miss) S. E. Knox, 20 November 1861, Mecklenburg Co., N. C.

RODGERS, James W. and Catherine Maxwell, 7 February 1856, Mecklenburg Co., N. C.

RODGERS, John and Martha Irwin, 7 April 1827, Mecklenburg Co., N. C.

RODGERS, John and Jenny Neely, 27 April 1829, Mecklenburg Co., N. C.

RODGERS, John R. and Elizabeth Alexander, 17 February 1859, Mecklenburg Co., N. C.

RODGERS, Jesse and Ellen Maxwell, 24 February 1820, Mecklenburg Co., N. C.

RODGERS, Leander and Sophy Madden, 21 February 1858, Laurens Co., S. C.

RODGERS, Louisa and Washington Maxwell, 26 September 1827, Mecklenburg Co., N. C.

RODGERS, Martha and James Alexander, 14 November 1806, Mecklenburg Co., N. C.

RODGERS, Mary and Elzey Forrest, 18 June 1839, Edgefield District, S. C.

RODGERS, Rodah and Ira Bruton, 9 October 1865, Laurens Co., S. C.

RODGERS, Samuel M. and Jane M. Kirkpatrick, 25 February 1823, Mecklenburg Co., N. C.

RODGERS, Sarah and William W. Orr, 19 December 1854, Mecklenburg Co., N. C.

RODGERS, Thomas P. and Emily Alexander, 26 September 1848, Mecklenburg Co., N. C.

RODIN, Adalin and Mathew A. Robison, 13 April 1842, Mecklenburg Co., N. C.

ROFFE, Elizabeth (widow) and George Blakey, 22 November 1767, Charleston, S. C.

ROGERS, Ambrose N. and Sarah Kerr, 9 February 1835, Mecklenburg Co., N. C.

ROGERS, Andrew N. and Jenny Miller, 21 September 1811, Mecklenburg Co., N. C.

ROGERS, Ann and William Osborn, 4 September 1798, Mecklenburg Co., N. C.

ROGERS, Barnard and Mary Vail (widow), 5 March 1767, Chowan Co., N. C.

ROGERS, Dolly and John Morrison, 31 July 1804, Mecklenburg Co., N. C.

ROGERS, Esther and Thomas Adams, 12 October 1785, Tyrrell Co., N. C.

ROGERS, Hannah and James Rogers, 4 December 1817, Mecklenburg Co., N. C.

ROGERS, Hugh M. and Jane Parks, 1 May 1824, Mecklenburg Co., N. C.

ROGERS, Isabella and Warren Read, 15 December 1857, Laurens Co., S. C.

ROGERS, I. Lafayette and Harriet C. Miller, 28 September 1854, Mecklenburg Co., N. C.

ROGERS, James and Hannah Rogers, 4 December 1817, Mecklenburg Co., N. C.

ROGERS, James H. and Eliza C. Kelly, 25 March 1839, Mecklenburg Co., N. C.

ROGERS, John and Sarah Yates, September 1783, Charleston, S. C.

ROGERS, John and Margaret Russell, 12 May 1789, Mecklenburg Co., N. C.

ROGERS, John and Rachel M. McReim, 17 September 1825, Mecklenburg Co., N. C.

ROGERS, Jonas and Mary Julian, 5 January 1798, Mecklenburg Co., N. C.

ROGERS, Joseph and Margaret McEwen, 9 August 1822, Mecklenburg Co., N. C.

ROGERS, Joseph and Jane Sadler, 6 April 1825, Mecklenburg Co., N. C.

ROGERS, Julius D. and Mary Jane Flanigan, 1 June 1854, Mecklenburg Co., N. C.

ROGERS, Leander and Emmaline Putman, 28 January 1847, Laurens Co., S. C.

ROGERS, Lucretia and Samuel Hall, 21 August 1826, Mecklenburg Co., N. C.

ROGERS, Mary (widow) and David Gillespie, 12 May 1770, Charleston, S. C.

ROGERS, Matilda P. and Stephen McReam, 8 April 1826, Mecklenburg Co., N. C.

ROGERS, Matthew and Rachel Curry, 4 December 1851, Laurens Co., S. C.

ROGERS, Miss and James C. Ross, 16 January 1822, Mecklenburg Co., N. C.

ROGERS, Nathan and Mary Leggett, 12 October 1785, Tyrrell Co., N. C.

ROGERS, Polly and John Hipp, 12 October 1799, Mecklenburg Co., N. C.

ROGERS, Robert and Sarah Parks, 23 September 1822, Mecklenburg Co., N. C.

ROGERS, Samuel and Susannah Baker, 3 July 1794, Charleston, S. C.

ROGERS, Sampson and (Mrs.) Elizabeth Martin, 1 June 1801, Charleston, S. C.

ROGERS, Sarah H. and Samuel J. McReam, 2 March 1835, Mecklenburg Co., N. C.

ROGERS, Thomas P. and Tabitha M. Seerest, 31 January 1834, Mecklenburg Co., N. C.

ROGERS, William and Mary Rhodes, 15 December 1806, Mecklenburg Co., N. C.

ROLAND, Franey and Jacob Hendrix, 21 June 1792, Rowan Co., N. C.

ROMBOUGH, John and (Mrs.) Catherine Mitchell, 11 May 1747, Chowan Co., N. C.

ROMERING, Henry and Martha Adams, 29 December 1800, Charleston, S. C.

ROOME, Catherine and Cornelius Hazzard, 31 March 1815, Mecklenburg Co., N. C.

ROOX, Joseph and Mary Hughins, 24 December 1844, Laurens Co., S. C.

ROPE, Augustus S. and Fanny Hancock, 12 January 1833, Mecklenburg Co., N. C.

ROPE, Peter and Elizabeth Polk, 8 September 1818, Mecklenburg Co., N. C.

ROPE, William H. and Susan Polk, 22 October 1832, Mecklenburg Co., N. C.

ROPER, Anne and Robert Williams (Jr.), 7 February 1771, Charleston, S. C.

ROPER, Betty and James W. Roper, 10 August 1821, Mecklenburg Co., N. C.

ROPER, James W. and Betty Roper, 10 August 1821, Mecklenburg Co., N. C.

ROPER, John and Sarah Fincher, 16 November 1797, Mecklenburg Co., N. C.

ROPER, Martha and Oliver Tillman, 29 December 1857, S. C.

ROPER, Mary A. E. and William F. Durisoe, 7 March 1830, Edgefield District, S. C.

ROPER, Patty and John Somers, 14 June 1772, Charleston, S. C.

ROPER, Peggy and William Neely, 28 November 1820, Mecklenburg Co., N. C.

ROPER, William (Jr.) and Hannah Dart, 5 May 1771, Charleston, S. C.

ROPP, Jacob and Hany Higgins, 27 January 1858, Laurens Co., S. C.

RORKE, Joseph M. and Mary Ann Curley, 24 January 1856, Mecklenburg Co., N. C.

ROSCOE, Peter and Ann Smithwick, 24 June 1788, Bertie Co., N. C.

ROSE, Elizabeth and James Samways, 7 June 1720, St. Andrews Parish, S. C.

ROSE, Hapzibah and James Christie, 15 November 1768, Charleston, S. C.

ROSE, Hetty and Philip Tidyman, 5 October 1772, Charleston, S. C.

ROSE, Hugh and Susanna Read, April 1784, Christ Church Parish, S. C.

ROSE, James and Elizabeth Mosely, 12 December 1850, Laurens Co., S. C.

ROSE, John S. and Eliza Barton, 16 September 1799, Charleston, S. C.

ROSE, Mary (widow) and Charles Lining, 4 November 1784, Charleston, S. C.

ROSE, Mary A. B. and William Miles, 8 November 1799, Charleston, S. C.

ROSE, Robert and Rebecca Rivers, 10 May 1770, St. Andrews Parish, S. C.

ROSE, Susannah and Alexander Thompson, 5 February 1801, Charleston, S. C.

ROSE, Susanna and Hugh Buchanan, 20 December 1803, Mecklenburg Co., N. C.

ROSE, Thomas and Mary A. C. Saunders, 20 May 1770, Charleston, S. C.

ROSE, Thomas and Mary Blake, 13 October 1774, Berkeley Co., S. C.

ROSE, William and Lucy Billinger, 10 December 1743, Charleston, S. C.

ROSENBUM, Mary and John Hinkle, 26 February 1790, Rowan Co., N. C.

ROSS, Agnes and John Bigham, 4 September 1799, Mecklenburg Co., N. C.

ROSS, Deborah and James Ross, 15 December 1809, Mecklenburg Co., N. C.

ROSS, Elizabeth (widow) and Archibald Carson, May 1784, Charleston, S. C.

ROSS, Esther A. and Abijah F. Alexander, 10 September 1851, Mecklenburg Co., N. C.

ROSS, Francis and Mary Ann Elliott, 3 February 1743, Berkeley Co., S. C.

ROSS, Francis M. and Dorcas N. Gilmore, 29 December 1839, Mecklenburg Co., N. C.

ROSS, George and Margaret Gilroy, January 1786, Charleston, S. C.

ROSS, James and Deborah Ross, 15 December 1809, Mecklenburg Co., N. C.

ROSS, James and Ann Montgomery, 5 October 1815, Mecklenburg Co., N. C.

ROSS, James C. and Miss Rogers, 16 January 1822, Mecklenburg Co., N. C.

ROSS, James N. and Mary L. Wilson, 19 November 1845, Mecklenburg Co., N. C.

ROSS, John and Susanna Porter, 16 May 1799, Mecklenburg Co., N. C.

ROSS, John and Hannah Harris, 16 June 1798, Mecklenburg Co., N. C.

ROSS, John and Hannah Montgomery, 12 June 1816, Mecklenburg Co., N. C.

ROSS, John P. and Sarah Oliver, 11 January 1859, Mecklenburg Co., N. C.

ROSS, John P. and Sarah A. Matthews, 19 November 1839, Mecklenburg Co., N. C.

ROSS, Joseph C. and Jane Oliver, 15 December 1842, Mecklenburg Co., N. C.

ROSS, Joseph W. and Sophia C. Springs, 19 February 1822, Mecklenburg Co., N. C.

ROSS, Joseph W. and Elizabeth T. A. Price, 10 July 1850, Mecklenburg Co., N. C.

ROSS, Levi and Sally Riley, 27 September 1821, Mecklenburg Co., N. C.

ROSS, Louisa and Samuel J. Neal, 29 April 1830, Mecklenburg Co., N. C.

ROSS, Margaret and Humphrey Hunter, 20 July 1795, Mecklenburg Co., N. C.

ROSS, Mary and Thomas Holland, 17 May 1761, Edgecombe Co., N. C.

ROSS, Peter E. and Sarah C. McIntyre, 11 March 1830, Mecklenburg Co., N. C.

ROSS, Robert A. and Mary J. Grier, 31 October 1848, Mecklenburg Co., N. C.

ROSS, Reuben E. and Mary Hipp, 3 December 1823, Mecklenburg Co., N. C.

ROSS, Sarah and Daniel Bean, 29 December 1789, Mecklenburg Co., N. C.

ROSS, Susanna and Alexander W. Kerr, 28 October 1814, Guilford Co., N. C.

ROSS, William and Ann Fuller, 9 December 1743, Charleston, S. C.

ROSS, William and Nancy H. Patton, 27 May 1841, Mecklenburg Co., N. C.

ROSS, W. J. and Margaret N. Harrison, 18 December 1850, Mecklenburg Co., N. C.

ROSS, William M. and Margaret J. Pool, 24 July 1855, Mecklenburg Co., N. C.

ROSSICH, George W. and Nancy P. Johnson, 3 September 1857, Mecklenburg Co., N. C.

ROTH, Ann and William Mecket, 6 December 1750, Orangeburg Co., S. C.

ROTH, Jacob and Catharina Ugly (widow), 1741, Orangeburg Co., S. C.

ROTH, Peter and Agnes Giessendanner, 2 February 1752, Orangeburg Co., S. C.

ROTHMAHLER, Anne and Thomas Mitchell, 13 August 1778, Santee, S. C.

ROTHMAHLER, Judith and Samuel Wragg, May 1753, Charleston, S. C.

ROUGHTON, Richard and Martha Mann, 1 August 1778, Tyrrell Co., N. C.

ROULAIN, James and Angelica Varambaut (widow) 17 July 1768, Berkeley Co., S. C.

ROULAIN, Robert and Hannah Livingston, 5 November 1799, Charleston, S. C.

ROUNDTREE, Georgia O. and S. C. Scott, 16 June 1857, Edgefield District, S. C.

ROUNDTREE, Washington and Elizabeth Stevens, 22 May 1856, Edgefield District, S. C.

ROUPELL, George and Elizabeth Prioleau, 7 May 1753, Charleston, S. C.

ROUPLE, Mrs. and John P. Serjeant, 25 April 1797, Charleston, S. C.

ROUT, George and Catherine Huston, 1788, St. Johns Parish, S. C.

ROUX, Albert and Elizabeth Trapier, (widow) December 1784, Georgetown, S. C.

ROW, George D. and Mary Bradley, 8 December 1799, Charleston, S. C.

ROW, Magdaline and John Stecker, 18 November 1800, Charleston, S. C.

ROWAN, Comfort and John Moore, 20 February 1782, Guilford Co., N. C.

ROWAN, William and Margaret Franklin, 6 April 1809, Mecklenburg Co., N. C.

ROWE, Levi and Rachel Davenport, 6 April 1785, Tyrrell Co., N. C.

ROWE, Mary and Andrew Bloom, 22 January 1797, Charleston, S. C.

ROWE, Peter and Betsy Fetterman, 17 June 1852, Mecklenburg Co., N. C.

ROWLAND, Jackson and Sarah Clardy, 14 January 1857, Laurens Co., S. C.

ROWLAND, James and Cynthia Miller, 25 July 1836, Mecklenburg Co., N. C.

ROYER, Ann and John Horry, 5 July 1759, Santee, S. C.

ROYSTER, David and Mary Daniel, 1775, Granville Co., N. C.

ROYSTER, William and Sarah Puryear, 1775, Granville Co., N. C.

RUBERRY, John and Betsy Wilkins, 1 November 1772, Charleston, S. C.

RUBERRY, John (Jr.) and Jane Medel, 3 March 1797, Charleston, S. C.

RUCK, Andrew and Judith Miller, 18 June 1741, Charleston, S. C.

RUDD, Samuel and Jane Walker, 5 April 1821, Mecklenburg Co., N. C.

RUDE, William and Christian McGinn, 26 September 1806, Mecklenburg Co., N. C.

RUDHALL, Anna M. (Mrs.) and Arthur Bryan, 1788, Charleston, S. C.

RUDHALL, Anne M. and Joseph Peace, 5 July 1796, Charleston, S. C.

RUDISILL, Ann R. and Matthew Neagle, 18 January 1834, Mecklenburg Co., N. C.

RUDISILL, James C. and Mary C. Kerr, 26 November 1825, Mecklenburg Co., N. C.

RUDISILL, John and Malissa McLeary, 27 July 1821, Mecklenburg Co., N. C.

RUDISILL, Jonas and Susannah Clarke, 19 September 1793, Mecklenburg Co., N. C.

RUDISILL, Mary E. and Charles B. Rhinehardt, 28 December 1814, Mecklenburg Co., N. C.

RUFFIN, Penelope and Jesse Deloach, 8 March 1768, Edgecombe Co., N. C.

RUGELEY, Rowland and (Miss) Hamilton Dawson, 16 March 1775, Charleston, S. C.

RUGER, Ann E. and John Warner, 20 July 1784, Charleston, S. C.

RUGGE, Eliza (of Philadelphia) and Charles Carrere, 8 July 1797, Charleston, S. C.

RUMLEY, Alida and Enoch Enochs, 30 September 1789, Rowan Co., N. C.

RUMPH, Barbara and John Tanner, 3 May 1737, Charleston, S. C.

RUMPH, Catherina and James Pendarvis, 5 September 1741, Orangeburg Co., S. C.

RUMPH, Elizabeth and Henry Giessendanner, 25 February 1767, Orangeburg Co., S. C.

RUMPH, Jacob and Ann Dattwyler, 19 May 1748, Orangeburg Co., S. C.

RUMPH, Susannah and John Cart, 14 January 1785, Charleston, S. C.

RUNELL, George and Elizabeth Collins, 20 July 1768, Chowan Co., N. C.

RUNNELS, Caleb and Temperance Halloway, 30 October 1852, Edgefield District, S. C.

RUNYAN, Charity and Samuel Parks, 6 November 1792, Yadkin, N. C.

RUPLE, Elizabeth (widow) and J. P. Sargeant, 20 June 1797, Charleston, S. C.

RUSELY, Mary and Janes Holden, 21 May 1800, Mecklenburg Co., N. C.

RUSH, Mary and James Clatworthy, 15 February 1756, Orangeburg Co., S. C.

RUSH, Matthias and Ann Fair, 1 April 1795, Charleston, S. C.

RUSS, Mary A. and John Riley, 21 August 1849, Mecklenburg Co., N. C.

RUSS, William and Amanda Benfield, 2 October 1856, Mecklenburg Co., N. C.

RUSSELL, Andrew and Linda Perry, 30 November 1865, Mecklenburg Co., N. C.

RUSSELL, Betsy and John McCord, 16 May 1803, Mecklenburg Co., N. C.

RUSSELL, Charles and Ann Dargan, 22 August 1754, Orangeburg Co., S. C.

RUSSELL, Daniel and Sarah S. Cross, August 1784, Charleston, S. C.

RUSSELL, David M. and Nancy Jane Hunter, 2 March 1854, Mecklenburg Co., N. C.

RUSSELL, Eugenia and William Thompson, 14 August 1755, Orangeburg Co., S. C.

RUSSELL, Harry T. and (Miss) J. E. Baker, 19 July 1860, Mecklenburg Co., N. C.

RUSSELL, Isabella and Robert Mitchell, 26 July 1792, Mecklenburg Co., N. C.

RUSSELL, James and Catherine Wolf, 10 December 1824, Mecklenburg Co., N. C.

RUSSELL, James S. and Peggy Gingles, 8 February 1809, Mecklenburg Co., N. C.

RUSSELL, Joseph and Margaret Russell, 24 October 1737, Orangeburg Co., S. C.

RUSSELL, Lewis H. and Martha M. Morrow, 23 December 1847, Mecklenburg Co., N. C.

RUSSELL, Margaret and Joseph Russell, 24 October 1737, Orangeburg Co., S. C.

RUSSELL, Margaret and John Rogers, 12 May 1789, Mecklenburg Co., N. C.

RUSSELL, Mary and George Campbell, 24 January 1791, Mecklenburg Co., N. C.

RUSSELL, Matthew and Margaret Neely, 29 January 1795, Mecklenburg Co., N. C.

RUSSELL, Mazy and John H. Hood, 10 December 1833, Mecklenburg Co., N. C.

RUSSELL, Rachel L. and Moses W. Culbertson, 25 August 1828, Mecklenburg Co., N. C.

RUSSELL, Robert W. and Sarah Flow, 27 January 1853, Mecklenburg Co., N. C.

RUSSELL, Sophinisba and John McCord, 5 February 1751, Orangeburg Co., S. C.

RUSSELL, Thomas and Sarah Irwin, 29 May 1792, Mecklenburg Co., N. C.

RUSSELL, Thomas and Mary Jourdan, 27 April 1779, Tyrrell Co., N. C.

RUSSELL, Widow and John Imrie, 7 September 1771, Charleston, S. C.

RUTHERFORD, Ann D. and Andrew Boulnare, 16 July 1835, Edgefield District, S. C.

RUTHERFORD, Dorothy Ann and George D. Harriett, 19 February 1839, Edgefield District, S. C.

RUTHERFORD, Harriet and John Foy, 13 December 1836, Edgefield District, S. C.

RUTHERFORD, James and Martha Foy, 15 December 1835, Edgefield District, S. C.

RUTHERFORD, Joseph and Michael Griffith, 5 June 1808, Edgefield District, S. C.

RUTHERFORD, Joseph G. and Tha Hardy, 15 December 1831, Edgefield District, S. C.

RUTHERFORD, Mary and John Coleman, 12 January 1830, Edgefield District, S. C.

RUTHERFORD, Thomas and Margaret Lemmon, 27 February 1832, Mecklenburg Co., N. C.

RUTLEDGE, Andrew and Elizabeth Gadsden, 29 September 1767, Charleston, S. C.

RUTLEDGE, Charles and Caroline Smith, 24 March 1800, Charleston, S. C.

RUTLEDGE, Edward and Henrietta Middleton, 1 March 1774, Charleston, S. C.

RUTLEDGE, Elijah and Frances Urie, 6 August 1801, Mecklenburg Co., N. C.

RUTLEDGE, George and Rachel McComb, 18 May 1799, Mecklenburg Co., N. C.

RUTLEDGE, Henry M. and Septima Middleton, 15 October 1799, Sullivans Island, S. C.

RUTLEDGE, Hugh and Ann Smith, 8 October 1783, Charleston, S. C.

RUTLEDGE, John and Elizabeth Grimke, 1 May 1763, Charleston, S. C.

RUTLEDGE, Martha and Francis Kinloch, 8 December 1785, Charleston, S. C.

RUTLEDGE, Polly and Roger Smith, 7 April 1768, Charleston, S. C.

RYDER, John and Sarah Munroe, 22 February 1800, Charleston, S. C.

S

ST. JOHN, Mary and Archibald S. Ball, 13 February 1800, Charleston, S. C.

ST. JULIAN, Charlotte and Rene Ravenel, 24 October 1687, Pompion Hill, S. C.

ST. JULIAN, Jane Mary and Isaac Mazyck, 17 July 1728, Charleston, S. C.

ST. JULIAN, Judith de and David Guerard, 26 October 1767, Charleston, S. C.

ST. JULIEN, Elizabeth Damaris and William Moultree, 10 December 1749, Charleston, S. C.

ST. JULIEN, Mary de and Thomas Monk, 11 July 1745, Charleston, S. C.

ST. JULIEN, Mary de and Henry Ravenel, 13 September 1750, Hanover, S. C.

SABB, Deborah and Robert Swainston, 15 February 1767, St. Johns Parish, S. C.

SADDLER, Daniel M. and Elizabeth Swindarsine, 3 April 1800, Charleston, S. C.

SADER, Peter and (Mrs.) Ann B. Chalmers, 17 October 1799, Charleston, S. C.

SADLER, Elizabeth (widow) and William Thompson, 30 August 1743, Chowan Co., N. C.

SADLER, Elizabeth and Will McDonald, 16 September 1789, Mecklenburg Co., N. C.

SADLER, Esther and John Beaty, 24 January 1817, Mecklenburg Co., N. S.

SADLER, Jane and Joseph Rogers, 6 April 1825, Mecklenburg Co., N. C.

SAFFORD, George and Ann Barnett, 22 April 1785, Tyrrell Co., N. C.

SAHLY, Ann Mary and Joseph Cuttier, 27 March 1741, Orangeburg Co., S. C.

SALLEY, Alexander S. and Julia E. Morrowe, 8 April 1845, Orangeburg, S. C.

SALLY, Henry (Jr.) and Magdalena Huber, 1748, Orangeburg Co., S. C.

SALTUS, Jane M. (widow) and Thomas Coachman, 1 June 1797, St. Lukes Parish, S. C.

SAMPLE, Ann and John Henderson, 4 April 1804, Mecklenburg Co., N. C.

SAMPLE, Aramenta S. and William P. Berry, 28 December 1831, Mecklenburg Co., N. C.

SAMPLE, Betsy and John Robison, 18 April 1804, Mecklenburg Co., N. C.

SAMPLE, Jane and James Carrigan, 18 April 1786, Orange Co., N. C.

SAMPLE, Jemina and Andrew Barry, 15 March 1796, Mecklenburg Co., N. C.

SAMPLE, Mary and Thomas Houston, 6 June 1798, Mecklenburg Co., N. C.

SAMPLE, Mary I. and Robert F. Barnett, 9 December 1828, Mecklenburg Co., N. C.

SAMPLE, Peggy and George Stevens, 26 July 1794, Charleston, S. C.

SAMS, Robert and Bridget Barnwell, 18 April 1741, St. Johns Island, S. C.

SAMWAYS, James and Elizabeth Rose, 7 June 1720, St. Andrews Parish, S. C.

SANDERLIN, Robert and Mary Waff, 3 May 1764, Chowan Co., N. C.

SANDERS, Benjamin and Mary Hunter, 10 March 1775, Chowan Co., N. C.

SANDERS, Elizabeth and (Dr.) Lemuel B. Askew, 5 February 1807, Union District, S. C.

SANDERS, Elizabeth and Lewis Adams, 25 May 1834, Mecklenburg Co., N. C.

SANDERS, Minyard and Henrietta Austin, July 1865, Laurens Co., S. C.

SANDERS, Simon T. and Jenobia Aurelian Meredith, 15 June 1830, Oxford, N. C.

SANDERS, William and Mary Quarterman (widow) 1 February 1774, Berkeley Co., S. C.

SANDERS, William S. and Carolina M. Meredith, 5 June 1834, Oxford, N. C.

SANDERSON, Richard and Sarah Ryan, 19 January 1790, Bertie Co., N. C.

SANDFORD, Greenbury and Julia Ann Cirnal, 25 January 1854, Laurens Co., S. C.

SANDFORD, Polly and John Bodkin, 25 September 1828, Mecklenburg Co., N. C.

SANDIFER, Catherine E. and Robert G. McLean, 3 December, 1846, Mecklenburg Co., N. C.

SANDS, James and Hannah Dewick, 6 December 1767, Charleston, S. C.

SANGER, Simon and Barbara Strowmann, 3 November 1737, Orangeburg Co., S. C.

SANKS, Mary and James Bryan, 18 June 1772, Charleston, S. C.

SANSBURY, Mary and William Clements, 11 November 1856, Chowan Co., N. C.

SANSOM, Susanna and John A. Woodle, 9 November 1800, Charleston, S. C.

SAPP, Sarah G. and James C. Marlan, 16 November 1854, Guilford Co., N. C.

SASS, Margaret H. and John E. Shirmer, 11 June 1800, Sullivans Island. S. C.

SARGEANT, Elizabeth (Mrs.) and John Bride, 27 April 1801, Charleston, S. C.

SARGEANT, J. P. and Elizabeth Ruple (widow), 20 June 1797, Charleston, S. C.

SARRAZIN, Jonathan and Lucy Lance, 28 September 1763, Charleston, S. C.

SARRAZIN, Jonathan and Sarah Prioleau (widow), 22 July 1770, Charleston, S. C.

SATTERWHITE, Ann and James Hunt, 21 July 1785, Granville Co., N. C.

SAULTER, L. G. and Eliza Tompson, 8 November 1854, Edgefield District, S. C.

SAUNDERS, Delilah and Ezekial Black, 30 December 1830, Mecklenburg Co., N. C.

SAUNDERS, Joseph H. and Laura L. Baker, 28 April 1833, Warrenton, N. C.

SAUNDERS, Keziah and Thomas Donohoe, 1774, Orange Co., N. C.

SAUNDERS, Romulus M. and Rebecca P. Carter, 1812 Caswell Co., N. C.

SAUNDERS, William and Hannah Sitterzen, 7 January 1798, Edenton, N. C.

SAUNDERS, William and Miss Adams, 1725, Orange Co., N. C.

SAVAGE, C. A. and F. M. F. Flournoy, 15 December 1839, Edgefield District, S. C.

SAVAGE, Elizabeth and William Branford, 24 April 1751, Charleston, S. C.

SAVAGE, John and Widow Allen, 18 April 1749, Charleston, S. C.

SAVAGE, Rachel and William Smith, 23 May 1789, Bertie Co., N. C.

SAVAGE, Susanna and Thomas Heyward (Jr.), May 1786, Charleston, S. C.

SAVAGE, Susannah and George Holebaugh, 13 June 1787, Rowan Co., N. C.

SAVAGE, William (Major) and Martha Holmes, May 1760, Charleston, S. C.

SAVITS, Esther and William Harrison, 4 June 1786, Rowan Co., N. C.

SAWDERS, Mary A. C. and Thomas Rose, 20 May 1770, Charleston, S. C.

SAWING, Jane and James McClure, 28 July 1834, Mecklenburg Co., N. C.

SAWYER, Ezilla and Thomas Weatherly, 10 April 1786, Tyrrell Co., N. C.

SAWYER, Nancy and Robert Stacher, 13 December 1855, Edgefield District, S. C.

SAYLOR, Ann E. (widow) and James Dennison, 2 September 1796, Charleston, S. C.

SAYLOR, Sarah C. and William N. Carothers, 24 April 1849, Mecklenburg Co., N. C.

SCHAUMLOFFEL, Anna M. and John Jacob Straumann, 18 July 1741, Orangeburg Co., S. C.

SCHAUMLOFFEL, Margaret Anna and John Jacob Stroman, 18 July, 1741, Orangeburg Co., S. C.

SCHEPELER, Sarah C. (Mrs.) and John Muncreef, 26 May 1801, Charleston, S. C.

SCHERMERHORN, Armont and Polly Mackey, 26 February 1769, Charleston, S. C.

SCHNELL, Bernhard and N. Shuler, 1746, Orangeburg Co., S. C.

SCHNELL, Elias and Anna Barbara Meyer, 1738, Orangeburg Co., S. C.

SCHWARDTFEGER, John Abraham and Elizabeth Souderecker (widow), 27 December 1745, Orangeburg Co., S. C.

SCHWARTZ, Christian and Elizabeth Fusterin, 19 November 1741, Orangeburg Co., S. C.

SCHWARTZ, Maria and Kilian Abecklin, 12 January 1740, Orangeburg Co., S. C.

SCHWARTZ, Susanna and Edward Gibson, 22 December 1741, Orangeburg Co., S. C.

SCHWARZ, Elizabeth (widow)) and Christopher Stehely, 23 February 1752, Orangeburg Co., S. C.

SCOTT, Archibald and Mary Rivers, 3 February 1774, Berkeley Co., S. C.

SCOTT, Catherine and Joseph D. Pope, 11 December 1845, St. Helena Parish, S. C.

SCOTT, David and Elizabeth Mann, 10 February 1794, Berkeley Co., S. C.

SCOTT, Edward and Mary Hopkins, 23 January 1723, Charleston, S. C.

SCOTT, Elizabeth and James Elder, 23 August 1764, Chowan Co., N. C.

SCOTT, Elizabeth (widow) and Barnard Beekman, 14 December 1769, Charleston, S. C.

SCOTT, Jane and Benjamin Stiles, April 1785, James Island, S. C.

SCOTT, John and Lydia Lester, 21 June 1785, Chowan Co., N. C.

SCOTT, John (Jr.) and Sarah Peronneau, 15 December 1768, Charleston, S. C.

SCOTT, Joseph and Penina Copeland, 12 April 1768, Chowan Co., N. C.

SCOTT, J. W. and Susan R. Wilborn, 1 June 1856, Edgefield District, S. C.

SCOTT, Lavinia and James McNeely, 13 November 1828, Guilford Co., N. C.

SCOTT, Mary and Robert McMurry, 28 December 1791, Guilford Co., N. C.

SCOTT, Mary and John T. Johnston, 29 September 1859, Mecklenburg Co., N. C.

SCOTT, Melinda and Thomas R. Ivy, 24 August 1812, Mecklenburg Co., N. C.

SCOTT, Nancy and William Boyes, 4 October 1833, Mecklenburg Co., N. C.

SCOTT, Rachel and Abraham Hill, 1 May 1761, Chowan Co., N. C.

SCOTT, Sarah and Rev. Fleet Cooper, 1783, Chowan Co., N. C.

SCOTT, Sarah B. and James Fogartie, 2 July 1799, Charleston, S. C.

SCOTT, Susanna and James Stanyarne, 25 June 1772, St. Andrews Parish, S. C.

SCOTT, S. C. and Georgia O. Roundtree, 16 June 1857, Edgefield District, S. C.

SCOTT, Thomas G. and Mary Stevens, 2 November 1800, Charleston, S. C.

SCOTT, William and Frances Daniell, 17 November 1784, Goose Creek, S. C.

SCOTT, William and Sarah Brailsford, October 1765, Charleston, S. C.

SCOTT, William (Jr.) and Elisabeth Legare, 5 March 1771, Charleston, S. C.

SCOVILLE, Warren N. and Jane O. Noble, 8 December 1858, Orangeburg, S. C.

SCREVEN, Eleanor and John C. M. Cox, 22 December 1800, Charleston, S. C.

SCREVEN, Martha and William Baker, 18 July 1763, James Island, S. C.

SCREVEN, Mary and John Hart, 17 June 1784, St. Thomas Parish, S. C.

SCREVEN, Richard B. and Alice Pendarvis, 8 March 1800, Charleston, S. C.

SCREVEN, Sarah and William Hazzard, 11 January 1798, May River, S. C.

SCRIMPSHIRE, Elizabeth and John Wyatt, 17 February 1768, Chowan Co., N. C.

SCRIVENGER, Susannah and Robert Struthers, June 1785, Charleston, S. C.

SCRIVER, Elizabeth and Robert Elliott, 3 February 1720, St. Andrews Parish, S. C.

SCROTER, J. J. and Elizabeth R. Dubbert, 10 November 1800, Charleston, S. C.

SEABROOK, Benjamin and Margaret Meggett, December 1784, Edisto, S. C.

SEABROOK, Susanna and Abraham Bosomworth, 2 November 1749, Ashley Ferry, S. C.

SEAFARD, Lizzie and John Fisher, 13 June 1798, Rowan Co., N. C.

SEALY, Rebecca and Isaac Grimball, 7 May 1747, Charleston, S. C.

SEAY, James and Elizabeth Crank, 26 July 1788, Bertie Co., N. C.

SEDLEY, Mary and Peter Dinks, 17 August 1790, Orange Co., N. C.

SEERS, Franky and William Ember, 15 May 1794, Rowan Co., N. C.

SEGEL, Mary and Josiah Boyd, 4 July 1839, Mecklenburg Co., N. C.

SEIGLER, John and Emeline Ward, 20 November 1833, Edgefield District, S. C.

SELLARS, Sarah and Thomas Dixon, 15 June 1763, Edgecombe Co., N. C.

SEMANS, Frances and Daniel Dubose, 11 November 1766, Santee, S. C.

SEMPLE, William and (Mrs.) Sarah Hill, August 1785, Charleston, S. C.

SENES, Abraham M. and Ritcey Hart, 13 November 1777, Charleston, S. C.

SENTELL, J. J. (Capt.) and Harriet McQuire, 17 December 1839, Edgefield District, S. C.

SERATT, Honour and James Fraser, 6 June 1785, Rowan Co., N. C.

SERJEANT, John P. and Mrs. Rouple, 25 April 1797, Charleston, S. C.

SERRE, Judith and Daniel Horry, Jr., 9 December 1759, Charleston, S. C.

SERRI, Judith and Daniel Horry, 9 December 1759, Santee, S. C.

SEVERANCE, Paul and Hannah Huggins, 23 February 1797, Charleston, S. C.

SEWARD, Celia and William Waff, 17 December 1777, Chowan Co., N. C.

SEWARD, William and (Mrs.) Mary Guston, 20 February 1743, Chowan Co., N. C.

SEYMOUR, Susan and Richard Jones, 19 October 1835, Mecklenburg Co., N. C.

SHACKLEFORD, Martha and (Gen.) W. W. Harllee, 18 September 1837, Charleston, S. C.

SHACKELFORD, Sarah and Joseph Wigfall, 7 January 1779, Santee, S. C.

SHADD, Ann J. and (Rev.) Robert Wilson, 22 April 1862, Charleston, S. C.

SHADRACK, T. N. and Emmie Byrd, 14 April 1857, Edgefield District, S. C.

SHAFFER, Frances and George Hinkle, 17 September 1795, Rowan Co., N. C.

SHAFFER, John and Mahala Outzs, 4 December 1856, Edgefield District, S. C.

SHAKER, Mary and Philemon Morris, 8 April 1794, Mecklenburg Co., N. C.

SHANKS, Elizabeth and James Black, 24 March 1801, Mecklenburg Co., N. C.

SHANKS, Mary and John McCullough, 7 December 1797, Mecklenburg Co., N. C.

SHANN, Elizabeth and John Cousins, 4 January 1722, St. Andrews Parish, S. C.

SHANNON, Abigal and William Smith, 14 April 1741, Orangeburg Co., S. C.

SHARP, Caroline and Robert J. Byram, 3 September 1829, Mecklenburg Co., N. C.

SHARP, Jane and Owen Oberly, 11 November 1822, Mecklenburg Co., N. C.

SHARP, Jemima and John Osborn, 10 December 1785, Mecklenburg Co., N. C.

SHARP, Joseph and Sarah Fields, 22 September 1801, Charleston, S. C.

SHARP, Matilda and William Erwin, May 1788, Rowan Co., N. C.

SHARP, Mary and John Jones, 28 December 1769, Charleston, S. C.

SHARP, Mary and James McClure, 4 May 1803, Mecklenburg Co., N. C.

SHARP, Mary and Whit M. Hill, 21 March 1814, Mecklenburg Co., N. C.

SHARPE, Betsy and John Brown, 22 February 1802, Mecklenburg Co., N. C.

SHARPE, Elizabeth and Edward Griffith, 1 April 1783, Rowan Co., N. C.

SHARPE, Elizabeth C. and John Mason Carlisle, 30 April 1850, Fairfield Co., S. C.

SHARPE, Elizabeth P. and William W. Rea, 28 August 1854, Mecklenburg Co., N. C.

SHARPE, Mary and William Freemster, 29 May 1783, Rowan Co., N. C.

SHARPE, Sarah M. and Jonathan M. Osborn, 15 September 1848, Mecklenburg Co., N. C.

SHARPLEY, Susanna and Samuel Spruill, 21 August 1779, Tyrrell Co., N. C.

SHARPTON, George and Nancy Franklin, 10 January 1833, Edgefield District, S. C.

SHAUMLOFFEL, Ann Margaret and Jacob Hans Strauman, 18 July 1748, Orangeburg Co., S. C.

SHAUMLOFFEL, Mary E. and Henry Felder, 15 December 1747, Orangeburg Co., S. C.

SHAUMLOFFEL, Lovisia and Jacob Horger, 1740, Orangeburg Co., S. C.

SHAVER, Michael and Sarah Jones, 18 November 1855, Edgefield District, S. C.

SHAW, Ann and William Gray, 1748, Orangeburg Co., S. C.

SHAW, Ann and John Magee, 22 July 1788 Guilford Co., N. C.

SHAW, Elizabeth and Edward Ainger, 26 October 1799, Charleston, S. C.

SHAW, Elizabeth and Robert Shaw, 20 May 1779, Guilford Co., N. C.

SHAW, Martha and Thomas Weaver, 8 January 1745, Charleston, S. C.

SHAW, Martha C. and James T. Montgomery, 11 February 1857, Guilford Co., N. C.

SHAW, Mary (widow) and (Dr.) John Haly, 19 January 1763, Charleston, S. C.

SHAW, Robert and Eleanor Mills, 1 January 1731, Charleston, S. C.

SHAW, Robert and Elizabeth Shaw, 20 May 1779, Guilford Co., N. C.

SHAW, Thomas P. and Mary P. Adams, 30 April 1801 Charleston, S. C.

SHEERER, John and (Mrs.) Elizabeth Stall, 29 May 1785, Charleston, S. C.

SHELBACK, Mary and John Hazell, 26 April 1801, Charleston, S. C.

SHELBY, Isabella and Stephen Alexander, 22 November 1797, Mecklenburg Co., N. C.

SHELBY, Susanah and Dan Alexander, 11 June 1800, Mecklenburg Co., N. C.

SHELL, H. R. and Manervy Meadow, 1852, Laurens Co., S. C.

SHELL, Nancy and Thomas Jacks, 24 February 1858, Laurens Co., S. C.

SHELL, Owny and John Hundgens, 3 November 1846, Laurens Co., S. C.

SHELL, Sophy and Lewis Martin, 15 December 1846, Laurens Co., S. C.

SHELL, Washington and Mary Dial, 31 July 1851, Laurens Co., S. C.

SHELLY, Harriet O. and Allison Alexander, 17 December 1823, Mecklenburg Co., N. C.

SHEPARD, Charles and Elizabeth Gibbes, 1 September 1775, Charleston, S. C.

SHEPARD, Charlotte and David H. Rea, 14 November 1836, Mecklenburg Co., N. C.

SHEPARD, Louisa and William Blalock, 6 July 1840, Mecklenburg Co., N. C.

SHEPHERD, Charles and Elizabeth Ratliff, 18 February 1768, Charleston S. C.

SHEPPARD, John and Martha Loftis, 6 September 1771, Santee, S. C.

SHERRILL, Hiram and Sarah Sherrill, 1820, Sherrills Ford, N. C.

SHERRILL, Sarah and Hiram Sherrill, Sherrills Ford, N. C.

SHIBLEY, Mary E. and J. W. Cheatham, 15 November 1855, Edgefield District, S. C.

SHIELDS, Anne and John Coombs, 1 February 1779, Santee, S. C.

SHIELDS, Isabella and Daniel Caldwell, 18 January 1826, Mecklenburg Co., N. C.

SHIELDS, Jane and John G. Oehler, 26 August 1837, Mecklenburg Co., N. C.

SHIELDS, Mary and Robert Caldwell, 20 March 1819, Mecklenburg Co., N. C.

SHIELDS, Mary and William Hutchinson, 8 January 1829, Mecklenburg Co., N. C.

SHIELDS, Nancy and Nathan Mitchell, 9 February 1804, Mecklenburg Co., N. C.

SHILES, Jane and Joseph Graham, 24 February 1796, Rowan Co., N. C.

SHILLEY, Sarah and John Alexander, 15 August 1798, Mecklenburg Co., N. C.

SHILLING, John Henry and Ann Margaret McLenen, 6 August 1754, Orangeburg Co., S. C.

SHIP, Mary and John Holloway, 21 October 1761, Edgecombe Co., N. C.

SHIPES, Elizabeth and Alfred Daniel, 13 November 1825, Edgefield District, S. C.

SHIPP, Mary and John Giles, 3 October 1788, Rowan Co., N. C.

SHIRMER, Elizabeth and Simon Gross, 13 February 1770, Rowan Co., N. C.

SHIRMER, John F. and Margaret H. Sass, 11 June 1800, Sullivans Island, S. C.

SHLAPPY, George Hans and Magdalene Huber, 1748, Orangeburg Co., S. C.

SHNELL, Adam and Margaret Yootzy, 1746, Orangeburg Co., S. C.

SHNELL, Elias and M. Fritchman, 1746, Orangeburg Co., S. C.

SHOCKLSY, John and Emily Martin, 29 November 1849, Laurens Co., S. C.

SHOECRAFT, Peggy and Alexander Mitchell, 13 September 1834, Guilford Co., N. C.

SHOLAR, Easter and Whitmell Whitacre, 26 April 1790, Bertie Co., N. C.

SHOLAR, Nancy and Thomas Sholar, 4 January 1790, Bertie Co., N. C.

SHOLAR, Thomas and Nancy Sholar, 4 January 1790, Bertie Co., N. C.

SHORT, Dinah and Samuel Foster, 28 August 1795, Rowan Co., N. C.

SHOULTS, Leah and Peter Helm, 5 October 1792, Rowan Co., N. C.

SHREWSBURY, Eliza and Isham Williams, June 1786, Charleston, S. C.

SHREYBURG, Sarah and James McElroy, 13 August 1801, Mecklenburg Co., N. C.

SHROCK, Catherine and George Hillard, 29 January 1793, Rowan Co., N. C.

SHROUDY, Eliza (widow) and J. J. Negrin, 5 April 1800, Charleston, S. C.

SHUBRICK, Betsy and Thomas Lynch (Jr.), 14 May 1772, Charleston, S. C.

SHUBRICK, Richard and Susanah Bulline, 3 October 1772, Charleston, S. C.

SHUBRICK, Susanna (widow) and Thomas Bee, May 1786, Charleston, S. C.

SHUBRICK, Thomas and Sarah Motte, 8 May 1746, Charleston, S. C.

SHULER, Ann Elizabeth and Hans Giegelman, 1740, Orangeburg Co., S. C.

SHULER, Appollonia and Jacob Wolf, 1740, Orangeburg Co., S. C.

SHULER, Catharina Magdalena and Hans George Henry Hess, 12 October 1743, Orangeburg Co., S. C.

SHULER, Eve Catherine and John Jubb, 1740, Orangeburg Co., S. C.

SHULER, John Nichlas and Verena Hoggin, 26 September 1752, Orangeburg Co., S. C.

SHULER, Margaret (widow) and Hans Jacob Gyger, 1740, Orangeburg Co., S. C.

SHULER, Margaret B. and Peter Hottow, 1740, Orangeburg Co., S. C.

SHULER, Mary Barbara and John F. Ulmer, 1752, Orangeburg Co., S. C.

SHULER, N. and Bernhard Schnell, 1746, Orangeburg Co., S. C.

SHULER, Susan and Jacob Wannamaker, 1740, Orangeburg Co., S. C.

SHULER, Susannah and Joseph Kreuter, 1740, Orangeburg Co., S. C.

SHUMAN, Ann and William Campbell, 7 July 1841, Mecklenburg Co., N. C.

SHUMAN, Nelly and Green Overin, 2 October 1851, Mecklenburg Co., N. C.

SHUSON, Ann and Robert Jamieson, 8 November 1817, Mecklenburg Co., N. C.

SHYDER, Daniel and Elizabeth Richard, 1748, Orangeburg Co., S. C.

SIBBALDSON, William and Martha Robertson (widow) 13 May 1773, Chowan Co., N. C.

SIGOURNY, Mary E. (Mrs.) and Edward M. Phelon, 21 November 1799, Charleston, S. C.

SILBERG, Nicholas and (Mrs.) Margaret Clark, 26 March 1797, Charleston, S. C.

SILL, Susannah and Joseph Harrod, 23 February 1795, Rowan Co., N. C.

SILVERS, Joana and Landrine Eggers, 16 April 1779, Rowan Co., N. C.

SIMERAL, Mary and Aruthur Jamieson, 6 January 1801, Mecklenburg Co., N. C.

SIMMONDS, Anne and John Neely, 29 February 1822, Mecklenburg Co., N. C.

SIMMONS, Ann and Lewis Miles, 4 April 1765, Santee, S. C.

SIMMONS, Anne and Francis Roche, August 1746, Charleston, S. C.

SIMMONS, Arthur and Elizabeth Axson, December 1783, Charleston, S. C.

SIMMONS, Betsy and Charles Buchanan, 8 May 1821, Mecklenburg Co., N. C.

SIMMONS, B. F. and Mary J. Tyler (widow)) 23 November 1842, Barnwell District, S. C.

SIMMONS, C. and John S. Allen, 9 February 1840, Edgefield District, S. C.

SIMMONS, Ebenezer and Mrs. Mary Jones (widow), 20 January 1741, Charleston, S. C.

SIMMONS, Elizabeth and Peter Des Champs, 2 August 1759, Santee, S. C.

SIMMONS, Harriet and Cleiland Kinloch, April 1786, Charleston, S. C.

SIMMONS, Harriet G. and Matthew Miller, 29 October 1844, Mecklenburg Co., N. C.

SIMMONS, James and Miss Holmes, May 1759, Charleston, S. C.

SIMMONS, John and Catherina Zorn, (widow), 1741, Orangeburg Co., S. C.

SIMMONS, John and Mary Brownlee, 3 December 1844, Laurens Co., S. C.

SIMMONS, Josiah and Jemima Coburn, 1782, Tyrrell Co., N. C.

SIMMONS, Mary and Childermas Croft, 28 May 1767, Santee, S. C.

SIMMONS, Mary and Nathaniel Arthur, 3 December 1772, Santee, S. C.

SIMMONS, Mary A. and Jonathan Collins, 3 January 1743, St. Thomas Parish, S. C.

SIMMONS, Maurice and Mary Mitchell, 19 July 1764, Charleston, S. C.

SIMMONS, Nancy and Thomas Eveleigh, 23 March 1773, Charleston, S. C.

SIMMONS, Patience and George Greenland, 10 December 1770, Santee, S. C.

SIMMONS, Peter and Mary Greenland, 30 December 1770, Santee, S. C.

SIMMONS, Thomas and Amelia Ward, 1 December 1800, Johns Island, S. C.

SIMMONS, William and Sarah Yonge, 3 March 1801, Charleston, S. C.

SIMMS, Albert Gallatin and Solome Baptisle Meredith, 26 January 1830, Oxford, N. C.

SIMMS, Patsy and Reddick Barnes, 20 December 1799, Edgecombe Co., N. C.

SIMONDS, Elizabeth and David Boyd, 1 June 1822, Mecklenburg Co., N. C.

SIMONS, Ann and Henry Calhoun, 5 June 1796, St. Bartholomews Parish, S. C.

SIMONS, Edward and Lydia Ball, 17 October 1771, Charleston, S. C.

SIMONS, Elizabeth and Daniel Hayward, 7 September 1771, Charleston, S. C.

SIMONS, Elizabeth and William Dunbar, 29 December 1799, Charleston, S. C.

SIMONS, James and Sarah Dewar, 8 January 1784, Charleston, S. C.

SIMONS, John and Ann Butler, 5 June 1742, Chowan Co., N. C.

SIMONS, Keating and Sarah Lewis, 9 June 1774, Charleston, S. C.

SIMONS, Mary and James Morrison, 23 February 1819, Mecklenburg Co., N. C.

SIMONS, Rachel and John Bryan, 28 April 1777, Charleston, S. C.

SIMONS, Rachel and William Bibb, 3 December 1818, Mecklenburg Co., N. C.

SIMONS, Rebecca and James Janieson, 25 May 1773, Charleston, S. C.

SIMONS, Robert and Mary White, April 1784, Georgetown, S. C.

SIMONS, Shadrick and Elizabeth Britton(widow), August 1785, Pedee, S. C.

SIMONTON, Mary and William Falls, 13 March 1786, Rowan Co., N. C.

SIMPSON, Barbary and Richard Henderson, 20 February 1851, Laurens Co., S. C.

SIMPSON, Emily and Henry Martin, 13 July 1837, Mecklenburg Co., N. C.

SIMPSON, Evan and Elizabeth Mitchell, 21 January 1812, Chowan Co., N. C.

SIMPSON, Judith and Whitmarsh Fuller, 30 June 1761, Charleston, S. C.

SIMPSON, Mary and Solomon Ward, 27 September 1784, Chowan Co., N. C.

SIMPSON, Mary and John Williamson, 19 November 1785, Chowan Co., N. C.

SIMPSON, Mary and John W. H. Biggers, 13 October 1832, Mecklenburg Co., N. C.

SIMPSON, Nancy and William Maxwell, 14 July 1804, Mecklenburg Co., N. C.

SIMPSON, Peggy and Phillip Moore, 12 March 1801, Mecklenburg Co., N. C.

SIMPSON, Polly and Peter Newell, 11 September 1801, Mecklenburg Co., N. C.

SIMPSON, Reddin and Kessenhappuck Pearce, 18 May 1786, Tyrrell Co., N. C.

SIMPSON, Richard W. and Maria Garlington, 10 February 1863, Anderson Co., S. C.

SIMPSON, Samuel and Mary Swain, 21 September 1764, Tyrrell Co., N. C.

SIMPSON, Samuel and Lucy Milander, 25 September 1851, Laurens Co., S. C.

SIMPSON, Sarah and Benjamin Ricketts, 16 August 1746, Chowan Co., N. C.

SIMPSON, Sarah and Timothy Pearce, 16 April 1786, Tyrrell Co., N. C.

SIMPSON, Sarah and Thomas Bull, 12 May 1771, Charleston, S. C.

SIMS, Hannah and (Capt.) David Henderson, 1765, Ninety Six District, S. C.

SIMS, Nancy and James Howes, 11 December 1786, Rowan Co., N. C.

SINCLAIR, Mary and John L. Gervais, 1773, Charleston, S. C.

SING, Nancy and Thomas B. Clark, 21 December 1836, Mecklenburg Co., N. C.

SINGER, Nancy and Absolom Giles, 21 August 1778, Rowan Co., N. C.

SINGLETARY, Ebenezer and Agnes McNeely, 1778, Darlington Co., S. C.

SINGLETARY, Hannah and Josiah Cockfield, 1807, Darlington Co., S. C.

SINGLETARY, Isaac and Elizabeth Attmore, April 1786, Charleston, S. C.

SINGLETARY, Mary and William Capers, September 1783, St. Thomas Parish, S. C.

SINGLETARY, Thomas and Mary Gillideau, 6 January 1785, Charleston , S. C.

SINGLETERRY, Eliza and John P. Bland, 11 November 1857, Edgefield District, S. C.

SINGLETERY, Hester and James Neilson, 30 January 1774, Charleston, S. C.

SINGLETON, Adaith and Robert McCormick, 8 June 1799, Mecklenburg Co., N. C.

SINGLETON, Elizabeth and William Youngblood, 16 November 1800, Charleston, S. C.

SINGLETON, Hezekiah and (Mrs.) Margaret Ash, 6 March 1745, Chowan Co., N. C.

SINGLETON, John and Rebecca Richardson, 1774, Sumter Co., S. C.

SINGLETON, John and Jane Miller, March 1779, Charleston, S. C.

SINGLETON, Mary and Samuel Richards, 6 December 1801, Charleston, S. C.

SINGLETON, Rebecca and Alexander C. Haskell (2nd. m.) 10 September 1861, Richland Co., S. C.

SINGLETON, Richard and Jane E. Postell, 22 November 1801, Charleston, S. C.

SINKLER, Daniel and Ann Dupree, 20 August 1769, Santee, S. C.

SINKLER, Peter and Polly Walter, 6 October 1784, Charleston, S. C.

SINKLER, Rebecca and Robert A. Darby, 23 October 1800, Charleston, S. C.

SISTRANK, Joel and Mary Mooer Hughes, 8 February 1821, Orangeburg Co., S. C.

SISTRANK, Joel and Susannah Murray, 3 November 1831, Orangeburg Co., S. C.

SITTERZEN, Hannah and William Saunders, 7 January 1798, Edenton, N. C.

SIVELS, Ann and William Basnight, 1781, Tyrrell Co., N. C.

SKEAL, Ruth and William Hearn, 29 November 1799, Rowan Co., N. C.

SKELLINGTON, Mary and John Hamilton, 22 February 1791, Mecklenburg Co., N. C.

SKINNER, Evan and Sarah Swain, 5 April 1779, Tyrrell Co., N. C.

SKINNER, Ferebee and William Acree, 12 March 1791, Bertie Co., N. C.

SKINNER, Hannah and George Newcombe, 9 September 1740, Charleston, S. C.

SKINNER, Margaret and William Bowen, 1 August 1771, Santee, S. C.

SKINNER, Nathan I. and Eliza Wells, 16 January 1855, Edgefield District, S. C.

SKIRVING, Ann and Thomas Rhett Smith, 28 May 1795, Ponpon, S. C.

SKIRVING, James and Sarah Champney (widow), May 1761, Charleston, S. C.

SKIRVING, James and Charlotte Matthews (widow), 21 March 1769, Charleston, S. C.

SKIRVING, Maria and Benjamin Postell, 15 January 1785, Ponpon, S. C.

SKITLETHROPE, John and Bethany Thomas, 10 December 1786, Tyrrell Co., N. C.

SKOTTOWE, Thomas and Lucy Bellinger, 22 December 1766, St. Andrews Parish, S. C.

SKRINE, Jonathan and Elizabeth Gaillard (widow), 26 March 1718, St. Andrews Parish, S. C.

SLADE, Elizabeth and Samuel Smithwick, 10 January 1765, Tyrrell Co., N. C.

SLADE, Joshua and Elizabeth Wardle, 9 December 1769, Tyrrell Co., N. C.

SLANN, Jane (Mrs.) and Daniel Boyle, 10 November 1800, Charleston, S. C.

SLATE, (SLADE?), Samuel and Gracy Dees, 29 December 1822, Edgefield District, S. C.

SLAUGHTER, Abigail and Jasper Charlton, 14 January 1757, Chowan Co., N. C.

SLAUGHTER, Elizabeth and John Wallace, 4 September 1741, Chowan Co., N. C.

SLAUGHTER, Hannah and Peter Payne, 8 January 1742, Chowan Co., N. C.

SLOAN, Benjamin and Annie M. Maxwell, 1 December 1862, Columbia, S. C.

SLOAN, E. (Mrs.) and N. F. Renshaw, 1 August 1865, Mecklenburg Co., N. C.

SLOAN, Elizabeth E. and Cyrus J. Alexander, 17 September 1814, Mecklenburg Co., N. C.

SLOAN, Jenny and Silas Irwin, 14 October 1812, Mecklenburg Co., N. C.

SLOAN, Jane E. and David H. Robison, 16 December 1845, Mecklenburg Co., N. C.

SLOAN, Jennett and Franklin Raymond, April 1821, Chester District, S. C.

SLOAN, Martha J. and Abdon Alexander, 27 August 1860, Mecklenburg Co., N. C.

SLOAN, Rosana and Jesse Hardin, 29 August 1797, Rowan Co., N. C.

SLOAN, Sarah and Thomas Cashon, 18 November 1820, Mecklenburg Co., N. C.

SLOANE, Anne and Thomas Hunter, 27 March 1787, Rowan Co., N. C.

SLOANE, Elizabeth and Samuel Espey, 5 April 1785, Rowan Co., N. C.

SLOANE, Jane and Jacob Fisher, 25 February 1793, Rowan Co., N. C.

SLOANE, Margaret and William Harris, 20 September 1784, Rowan Co., N. C.

SLOCUMB, Ezekial and Mary Hooks, 1778, Wayne Co., N. C.

SLOMAN, John and Rebecca Wilkins, July 1786, Charleston, S. C.

SMALAGA, Mary and William Yeo, 17 June 1770, Santee, S. C.

SMALL, Absallah and William Fallon, 12 May 1785, Chowan Co., N. C.

SMALL, Nancy and Michael McKell, 13 July 1785, Chowan Co., N. C.

SMART, Mary O. and Thomas J. Dillard, 17 January 1833, Laurens Co., S. C.

SMART, Mary O. and John Alfred Dillard, 1 April 1842, Laurens Co., S. C.

SMART, Mary O. and Jessie Norman, 21 July 1850, Laurens Co., S. C.

SMERDON, Elias and Priscilla Coburn, 16 June 1795, Sullivans Island, S. C.

SMISER, Dolly and (Rev.) Hugh Alison, 11 January 1770, Charleston, S. C.

SMITH, Agnes and John Blair, 8 October 1799, Mecklenburg Co., N. C.

SMITH, Altona L. and Joshua D. Boyd, 28 December 1826, Mecklenburg Co., N. C.

SMITH, Ann and Edward Darrell, 15 May 1770, Charleston, S. C.

SMITH, Ann and Hugh Rutledge, 8 October 1783, Charleston, S. C.

SMITH, Ann and Robert B. Gibbes, 30 November 1799, Charleston, S. C.

SMITH, Anne and Isaac Motte, 15 December 1763, Charleston, S. C.

SMITH, Anne and John Jones, 16 June 1788, Edgecombe Co., N. C.

SMITH, Arthur and Rebecca Boone, 1788, Black River, S. C.

SMITH, Barbara and Tobias Forrer, 12 August 1790, Rowan Co., N. C.

SMITH, Barbara and Jonathan Alston, 18 April 1791, Rowan Co., N. C.

SMITH, Benjamin and Katherine Ball, 9 April 1773, St. Johns Parish, S. C.

SMITH, Benjamin (Jr.) and Sarah Dry, 20 November 1777, Charleston, S. C.

SMITH, Betsy and Robert Miles, October 1772, Stono, S. C.

SMITH, Brigitta and Jacob Beck, 19 February 1754, Orangeburg Co., S. C.

SMITH, Caroline and Charles Rutledge, 24 March 1800, Charleston, S. C.

SMITH, Catherine and (Dr.) John Poyas, May 1785, Goose Creek, S. C.

SMITH, Catherine and Abner L. Black, 7 August 1845, Mecklenburg Co., N. C.

SMITH, Catherine M. and Allison H. Biggers, 24 May 1860, Mecklenburg Co., N. C.

SMITH, Christina and George Feaser, 18 August 1787, Rowan Co., N. C.

SMITH, Dennis and Sarah Griffin, 1 June 1858, Laurens Co., S. C.

SMITH, Eliza and Michael Jordain, 27 November 1800, Charleston, S. C.

SMITH, Eliza and James H. Orr, 26 April 1832, Mecklenburg Co., N. C.

SMITH, Elizabeth and William Bryan, 1744, Snowfield, N. C.

SMITH, Elizabeth and Lachlan McIntosh, 17 October 1765, Stono, S. C.

SMITH, Elizabeth and Francis Redford, 5 May 1771, Santee, S. C.

SMITH, Elizabeth and Sherwood Mayer, 25 November 1773, Guilford Co., N. C.

SMITH, Elizabeth and Henry Folts, 17 August 1790, Rowan Co., N. C.

SMITH, Elizabeth and James McMurray, 21 November 1795, Guilford Co., N. C.

SMITH, Elizabeth and Arthur Bowden, 31 March 1832, Mecklenburg Co., N. C.

SMITH, Elizabeth A. and John W. Cameron, 5 October 1741, Chowan Co., N. C.

SMITH, Elizabeth H. and Zebulon Mills, 29 March 1794, Chowan Co., N. C.

SMITH, Elizabeth H. and William Taylor, 8 December 1804, Granville Co., N. C.

SMITH, Elizabeth J. and James Boyd, 10 October 1831, Mecklenburg Co., N. C.

SMITH, Elsy and James Foster, 28 December 1785, Rowan Co., N. C.

SMITH, Emanuel and Anne Jones, 9 December 1720, St. Andrews Parish, S. C.

SMITH, Emanuel and Margaret Elmes, December 1722, St. Andrews Parish, S. C.

SMITH, Esther and Benjamin Herndon, 15 May 1829, Orange Co., N. C.

SMITH, Felix and Elizabeth Autry, 6 January 1842, Edgefield District, S. C.

SMITH, George and Mary Smith, May 1784, St. Bartholomews Parish, S. C.

SMITH, George and Mary Ann Rivers, 20 February 1801, Charleston, S. C.

SMITH, George and Rebecca Blake, 9 March 1717, Plainsfield, S. C.

SMITH, Hannah and William Reeves, 14 December 1820, Mecklenburg Co., N. C.

SMITH, Henrietta and William Raven, 8 June 1761, Charleston, S. C.

SMITH, Henry and Elizabeth Ball, 13 December 1764, Berkeley Co., S. C.

SMITH, Hosea H. and Mary B. Hoke, 1853, Lincolnton, N. C.

SMITH, Jacob and Fanny Spruill, 1781, Tyrrell Co., N. C.

SMITH, James and Julia Ann Hughs, 22 March 1847, Laurens Co., S. C.

SMITH, Jane F. and William B. Minott, 12 December 1801, Charleston, S. C.

SMITH, Jean and John Rea, 25 April 1801, Mecklenburg Co., N. C.

SMITH, John and Mary Jennett, 1781, Tyrrell Co., N. C.

SMITH, John and Elizabeth Bacot, 11 February 1768, Santee, S. C.

SMITH, John and Mary Long, 19 September 1782, Santee, S. C.

SMITH, John and Elizabeth Cameron, 2 October 1794, Charleston, S. C.

SMITH, Joseph and Elizabeth Hardy, 21 July 1779, Chowan Co., N. C.

SMITH, Justina and John Moore, 22 October 1719, St. Andrews Parish, S. C.

SMITH, Lucy and John Jennings, 26 December 1818, Mecklenburg Co., N. C.

SMITH, Lydia and Alfred Brown, 14 November 1865, Mecklenburg Co., N. C.

SMITH, Margaret E. and Henry L. Beaty, 6 October 1857, Mecklenburg Co., N. C.

SMITH, Mary and Capers Boone, 16 July 1767, Santee, S. C.

SMITH, Mary and Robert Gibbs, 1788, Charleston, S. C.

SMITH, Mary and James Miller, 30 July 1791, Mecklenburg Co., N. C.

SMITH, Mary Ann and John Miller, 10 January 1794, Mecklenburg Co., N. C.

SMITH, Mary and David Caldwell, 29 June 1791, Mecklenburg Co., N. C.

SMITH, Mary and Abraham Parker, 9 March 1848, Laurens Co., S. C.

SMITH, Mary and John Taylor, 28 June 1800, Granville Co., N. C.

SMITH, Miriam and Benjamin Wood, 8 November 1785, Chowan Co., N. C.

SMITH, M. Will and H. E. Bass, 10 January 1850, Marlboro Co., S. C.

SMITH, Nancy and Robert Alderson, 20 February 1804, Mecklenburg Co., N. C.

SMITH, Nancy and James Brown, 28 February 1804, Mecklenburg Co., N. C.

SMITH, O'Brien and Miss Webb, March 1785, Charleston, S. C.

SMITH, O. D. and Eliza C. Gable, 24 January 1856, Edgefield District, S. C.

SMITH, Patty and Daniel Bourdeaux, 11 January 1770, Charleston, S. C.

SMITH, Penelope and Augustine Miller, 11 September 1855, Chowan Co., N. C.

SMITH, Peter and Mary Middleton, November 1776, Charleston, S. C.

SMITH, Phebe and Daniel McGregor, 25 March 1761, Santee, S. C.

SMITH, Polly and John F. Grimkie, 5 October 1784, Charleston, S. C.

SMITH, Polly L. and William T. Connell, 4 March 1803, Mecklenburg Co., N. C.

SMITH, Rachel and Thomas Hill, 6 October 1779, Rowan Co., N. C.

SMITH, Robert and Elizabeth Withers, 1788, Charleston, S. C.

SMITH, Roger and Polly Rutledge, 7 April 1768, Charleston, S. C.

SMITH, Ruth and Aaron Lassiter, 6 January 1785, Chowan Co., N. C.

SMITH, Sarah (widow) and Peter Adams, 3 June 1745, Chowan Co., N. C.

SMITH, Sarah and Charles Hill, 7 March 1746, Charleston, S. C.

SMITH, Sarah and John Mackenzie, 2 April 1769, Charleston, S. C.

SMITH, Sarah and John L. Rea, 29 August 1846, Mecklenburg Co., N. C.

SMITH, Sarah A. and Josiah Brown, 4 October 1825, Mecklenburg Co., N. C.

SMITH, Sophy and John Langston (widower), 4 March 1845, Laurens Co., S. C.

SMITH, Thomas and Ann Oliver , 18 December 1786, Tyrrell Co., N. C.

SMITH, Thomas L. and Elizabeth Ingliss, 29 May 1763, Charleston, S. C.

SMITH, Thomas Rhett and Ann Skirving, 28 May 1795, Ponpon, S. C.

SMITH, William (Capt.) and Mrs. Fairchild, 1 August 1785, Charleston, S. C.

SMITH, William and Margaret Van Bibben (widow), 3 December 1785, Charleston S. C.

SMITH, William and Charlotte Izard, 2 May 1786, Charleston, S. C .

SMITH, William and Abigal Shannon, 14 April 1741, Orangeburg Co., S. C.

SMITH, William and Elizabeth Wilkinson, 27 January 1779, Tyrrell Co., N. C.

SMITH, William and Wally Wood, 10 February 1790, Bertie Co., N. C.

SMITH, William and Rachel Savage, 23 May 1789, Bertie Co., N. C.

SMITH, William and Mary Galloway, 1 January 1795, Charleston, S. C.

SMITH, William and Harriet Valk, 14 August 1801, Charleston, S. C.

SMITHWICK, Ann and Peter Roscoe, 24 June 1788, Bertie Co., N. C.

SMITHWICK, Edmondson and Eleanor Bowen, 1 September 1768, Tyrrell Co., N. C.

SMITHWICK, Samuel and Elizabeth Slade, 10 January 1765, Tyrrell Co., N. C.

SMITZER, Elizabeth and Benjamin Spurlock, 12 May 1754, Orangeburg Co., S. C.

SMOTHERS, Elizabeth and William Grinklin, 9 January 1789, Rowan Co., N. C.

SMYLIE, Andrew and (Mrs.) Susannah Bruce, 8 October 1801, Charleston, S. C.

SMYTH, James and Ann Thomas, 18 March 1773, Charleston, S. C.

SMYTH, John and Sukey Richardson, 26 April 1772, Charleston, S. C.

SMYTHE, Augustine and Louisa McCord, 27 June 1865, Charleston, S. C.

SNEED, Elizabeth and Soloman Hunt, 1817, Granville Co., N. C.

SNEED, Susan and (Dr.) Patrick Turner, 22 February 1853, Laurens Co., S. C.

SNELL, Ann and Benjamin Hassell, 29 October 1765, Tyrrell Co., N. C.

SNELL, Elizabeth and John Blair, 26 March 1800, Mecklenburg Co., N. C.

SNELL, James and Mary Spruill, 12 September 1783, Tyrrell Co., N. C.

SNELL, Mary and William B. Biggers, 10 September 1827, Mecklenburg Co., N. C.

SNELL, Mary A. and William Biggers, 16 January 1802, Mecklenburg Co., N. C.

SNELL, Polly and Richard Ellis, 16 May 1785, Charleston, S. C.

SNELL, Sarah and Robert Carlisle, 10 February 1764, Chowan Co., N. C.

SNELL, Sarah and Joseph Biggers, 23 February 1811, Mecklenburg Co., N. C.

SNELLGROVE, Freeman and Ann Jenkins (widow), 26 September 1751, Orangeburg Co., S. C.

SNELLGROVE, N. and John Sullivan, 1746, Orangeburg Co., S. C.

SNELLING, Mary J. and Peter Stevenson, 1 January 1773, Charleston, S. C.

SNIPES, Thomas and Mary Hunt, 28 December 1793, Granville Co., N. C.

SNOW, Miss and Leander Brown, 21 September 1844, Laurens Co., S. C.

SNOW, Nancy and Nicholson Millis, 28 May 1799, Guilford Co., N. C.

SNOWDEN, Sarah and Miles Turner, 30 January 1785, Perquimans Co., N. C.

SNOWDON, Zebulon and Sarah Taylor, 3 August 1765, Chowan Co., N. C.

SOMMERS, Henrietta and John Dart (Jr.), 20 December 1772, Charleston, S. C.

SOMMERS, Mary and David Deas, 18 October 1800, Charleston, S. C.

SOMMERS, John and Patty Roper, 14 June 1772, Charleston, S. C.

SOMERSALL, William and Sarah Legare, 11 January 1767, Charleston, S. C.

SOMERSALL, William and Sarah Crossthwaite (widow), 27 January 1774, Charleston, S. C.

SOMERVILLE, John and Mary Goodloe, 10 August 1779, Granville Co., N. C.

SOPHIA, Mary and John Everhart, 24 August 1788, Rowan Co., N. C.

SOUDERECKER, Elizabeth (widow) and John Abraham Schwardtfeger, 27 December 1745, Orangeburg Co., S. C.

SOWARD, Margaret and Charles Boswell, 7 October 1790, Bertie Co., N. C.

SPANN, Martha Sarah Bond (Mrs.) and Henry Hampton Hill, 19 July 1817, Edgefield District, S. C.

SPANN, Mary Ann and Lovett Gomillon, 3 January 1852, Edgefield District, S. C.

SPARKMAN, Elizabeth and Thomas Newborn, 7 October 1788, Bertie Co., N. C.

SPEAK, Rosanna and Michael Goodman, 9 November 1785, Rowan Co., N. C.

SPEARS, Catherine and Eaton Jones White, 4 January 1826, Granville Co., N. C.

SPEARS, Elizabeth A. and Ananias Jordan, 14 July 1856, Mecklenburg Co., N. C.

SPEARS, Elsy and David N. Rea, 29 November 1802, Mecklenburg Co., N. C.

SPEED, Rosalie and Thomas J. Taylor, 2 October 1843, Granville Co., N. C.

SPEIGHT, Isaac and Ann Montfort, 24 July 1764, Chowan Co., N. C.

SPEIGHT, Joseph and Anne King, 3 March 1752, Chowan Co., N. C.

SPEIGHT, Joseph and Eleanor Bond (widow), 11 January 1775, Chowan Co., N. C.

SPEIGHT, Leah and Everard Garrett, 30 January 1758, Chowan Co., N. C.

SPEIGHT, Lydia and Josiah Coffield, 28 August 1790, Bertie Co., N. C.

SPEIGHT, William and Ann Phelps, 8 August 1772, Chowan Co., N. C.

SPELL, Ann and John Jones, 6 November 1762, Edgecombe Co., N. C.

SPELL, Dolly and James Jones, 4 October 1809, Edgecombe Co., N. C.

SPELL, Selveah and John Booth, 24 December 1799, Edgecombe Co., N. C.

SPENCE, Peter (Dr.) and Fanny Brown, 8 April 1771, Charleston, S. C.

SPENCER, Calvin and Rebecca Ford, 21 August 1782, Santee, S. C.

SPENCER, Mary and Nathaniel McCormick, 28 December 1759, Santee, S. C.

SPENCER, Nancy and John Campbell, 28 July 1823, Mecklenburg Co., N. C.

SPENCER, Rebecca and Robert Morrison, 25 June 1767, Santee, S. C.

SPENCER, Sheppard and Sue Frazier, January 1857, Edgefield District, S. C.

SPENCER, Thomas and Susanna Money, 8 October 1761, Santee, S. C.

SPENCER, Thomas and Mary Griggs, 31 October 1771, Santee, S. C.

SPIER, John (Jr.) and Penelope Conner, 13 March 1764, Tyrrell Co., N. C.

SPIRES, Mary and Samuel Carson, 4 March 1793, Orange Co., N. C.

SPIVEY, Margaret E. and Richard O. Britton, 10 November 1830, Bertie Co., N. C.

SPRATT, Ann L. and Thomas G. Neal, 24 May 1838, Mecklenburg Co., N. C.

SPRATT, Elizabeth C. and James Neely, 12 November 1812, Mecklenburg Co., N. C.

SPRING, John and Catherine Reader, 26 October 1800, Charleston, S. C.

SPRING, Magdalene and Benedict Koller, 1 January 1740, Orangeburg Co., N. C.

SPRINGS, Mary and John H. Caldwell, 3 October 1832, Mecklenburg Co., N. C.

SPRINGS, Mary C. and Moses H. Ryne, 2 March 1864, Mecklenburg Co., N. C.

SPRINGS, Sophia C. and Joseph W. Ross, 19 February 1822, Mecklenburg Co., N. C.

SPRUELL, Jesse and Mary Arnold, 23 December 1785, Tyrrell Co., N. C.

SPRUELL, John and Sarah Casswell, 15 April 1766, Tyrrell Co., N. C.

SPRUILL, Benjamin and Rosannah Hooker, 26 September 1767, Tyrrell Co., N. C.

SPRUILL, Betsey and Joseph Williams, 1780, Tyrrell Co., N. C.

SPRUILL, Ebenezer and Hannah Long, 27 October 1770, Tyrrell Co., N. C.

SPRUILL, Fanny and Jacob Smith, 1781, Tyrrell Co., N. C.

SPRUILL, Godfrey and Mary Alcock, 1780, Tyrrell Co., N. C.

SPRUILL, Mary (widow) and John Alexander, 23 February 1763, Tyrrell Co., N. C.

SPRUILL, Mary and James Snell, 12 September 1783, Tyrrell Co., N. C.

SPRUILL, Miriam and John Anderson, 4 December 1778, Tyrrell Co., N. C.

SPRUILL, Samuel and Susanna Sharpley, 21 August 1779, Tyrrell Co., N. C.

SRRUILL, Sarah and James Jackson, 7 April 1766, Tyrrell Co., N. C.

SPRUILL, William and Sarah Norman, 31 January 1786, Tyrrell Co., N. C.

SPRUILL, William H. and Margaret Tillett, 21 August 1779, Tyrrell Co., N. C.

SPURLOCK, Benjamin and Elizabeth Smitzer, 12 May 1754, Orangeburg Co., S. C.

STACEY, Elizabeth and Malachi Deale, 4 December 1786, Chowan Co., N. C.

STACHER, Robert and Nancy Sawyer, 13 December 1855, Edgefield District, S. C.

STACKPOLE, Grace and George Atkinson, April 1832, Charleston, S. C.

STACY, Penelope and Miles McSheehey, 20 April 1776, Chowan Co., N. C.

STAFFORD, John and Mary Turner, 31 January 1797, Perquimans Co., N. C.

STAFFORD, Mary and Robert N. Harris, 9 April 1834, Mecklenburg Co., N. C.

STAFFORD, Sally and Robert Mebane, 18 October 1815, Guilford Co., N. C.

STAFFORD, Thomas and Mary Turner, 6 January 1786, Perquimans Co., N. C.

STAFFORD, William and Miriam Turner, 30 September 1786, Perquimans Co., N. C.

STALL, Elizabeth (Mrs.) and John Sheerer, 29 May 1785, Charleston, S. C.

STALLINGS, John and Delitha Dunning, 19 September 1789, Bertie Co., N. C.

STALLINGS, Priscilla and Thomas I. Miller, 27 September 1831, Chowan Co., N. C.

STALLINGS, Simeon and Monica Walton, (widow), 24 June 1772, Chowan Co., N. C.

STAMP, Elizabeth and Job Charlton, 20 September 1741, Chowan Co., N. C.

STANCIL, Sally and William Hopkins, 22 October 1799, Edgecombe Co., N. C.

STANDING, Edmund and Amarita Ward, 9 October 1753, Chowan Co., N. C.

STANDING, Mary and Thomas Bonner, February 1752, Chowan Co., N. C.

STANDING, Sarah and John Theach, 27 April 1748, Chowan Co., N. C.

STANDLEY, David and Sarah Lassiter, (widow) 10 June 1788, Bertie Co., N. C.

STANDLEY, Mary and James Thomas, 6 September 1790, Bertie Co., N. C.

STANDLEY, William and Penelope Keen, 25 May 1790, Bertie Co., N. C.

STANFORD, Hannah and William Moore, 11 November 1800, Mecklenburg Co., N. C.

STANFORD, Margaret and J. H. Jennings, 4 January 1859, Mecklenburg Co., N. C.

STANFORD, Sarah C. and George W. Jennings, 28 October 1858, Mecklenburg Co., N. C.

STANTON, Mary and Thomas Turner, July 1786, Perquimans Co., N. C.

STANYARNE, Anne (widow) and (Dr.) Ambrose Reeve, 16 December 1733, Port Royal, S. C.

STANYARNE, Archibald and Sarah Elliott, May 1759, Stono, S. C.

STANYARNE, Elizabeth and Isaac Holmes, 11 September 1755, Charleston, S. C.

STANYARNE, James and Henrietta Raven (widow) 26 October 1767, Charleston, S. C.

STANYARNE, James and Susan Scott, 25 June 1772, St. Andrews Parish, S. C.

STANYARNE, Joseph and Mary Hartley (widow) 9 December 1773, Charleston, S. C.

STANYARNE, Mary and Morton Brailsford, 25 October 1753, Charleston, S. C.

STANYARNE, Sally and James Brisbane, 25 May 1772, Charleston, S. C.

STANYARNE, Thomas and Anne Barnwell, 29 March 1726, Beaufort, S. C.

STAR, Parmela and Jonathan Austin, 14 December 1809, Mecklenburg Co., N. C.

STARK, Robert and Mary Hay, 1902, Columbia, S. C.

STARNER, Dorcas C. and John M. Orr, 3 December 1857, Mecklenburg Co., N. C.

STARNER, Elizabeth and Hugh C. Nesbit, 16 March 1836, Mecklenburg Co., N. C.

STARNES, Elizabeth and Mathias Harkey, 17 January 1837, Mecklenburg Co., N. C.

STARNES, Esther and M. W. Rice, 7 November 1865, Mecklenburg Co., N. C.

STARRETT, Catherine and Moses Christenberry, 15 March 1828, Mecklenburg Co., N. C.

STAUFFER, Mary and Cooney Otters, 6 June 1860, Mecklenburg Co., N. C.

STEAD, Benjamin and Mary Johnson, 15 November 1748, Charleston, S. C.

STEALY, Michael and Deliah Hinds, 1784, Tyrrell Co., N. C.

STECKER, John and Magdaline Row, 18 November 1800, Charleston, S. C.

STEEDMAN, Reliance and Watson Crouch, 11 November 1854, Edgefield District, S. C.

STEEL, Anne and John Jordan, 4 July 1773, Santee, S. C.

STEEL, John and Dorothy Chicken, 30 March 1773, Santee, S. C.

STEEL, Peter and Anne Varner, 15 August 1773, Santee, S. C.

STEELE, Alice L. and William C. Covington, 31 July 1864, Richmond Co., N. C.

STEELE, Anna M. and Robert Wilson Brice, 4 March 1850, Chester Co., S. C.

STEELE, Elizabeth and Matthew Hart, 24 December 1789, Rowan Co., N. C.

STEELE, Jane E. and Samson H. Jordan, 25 May 1852, Mecklenburg Co., N. C.

STEELE, John and Sarah Richards, 27 June 1744, Chowan Co., N. C.

STEELY, Thomas and Elizabeth Leary, 20 January 1783, Tyrrell Co., N. C.

STEHELY, Christopher and Elizabeth Schwartz (widow), 23 February 1752, Orangeburg Co., S. C.

STEHELY, Elizabeth and Lewis Golsen, 19 December 1752, Orangeburg Co., S. C.

STEHELY, Mary and Caspar Oth, 1752, Orangeburg Co., S. C.

STELLEY, Miss and Dunham Hancock, 1742, Pitt Co., N. C.

STENT, John and Elizabeth North, 16 December 1800, Charleston, S. C.

STENT, Martha and Daniel Boyden, 25 May 1797, James Island, S. C.

STEPHEN, Margaret and John Grossman, 11 October 1753, Orangeburg Co., S. C.

STEPHENS, Casia and Jesse Hannan, 26 March 1844, Mecklenburg Co., N. C.

STEPHENS, Elizabeth and Josiah Walker, 1802, Barnwell Co., S. C.

STEPHENS, Hannah and James Davenport, 1784, Tyrrell Co., N. C.

STEPHENS, Martha and Thomas A. Hannon, 15 January 1842, Mecklenburg Co., N. C.

STEPHENS, Martha A. and William H. Baker, 2 February 1842, Mecklenburg Co., N. C.

STEPHENS, Patsy and Conrad Hartwick, 6 November 1816, Mecklenburg Co., N. C.

STEPHENS, Sally and Thomas McQuestion, 11 December 1815, Mecklenburg Co., N. C.

STEPHENS, William and Mary Marlen, 22 May 1797, Charleston, S. C.

STEPHENSON, John and Mary Pacy, 15 October 1782, Santee, S. C.

STEPHENSON, Polly and William Air, 2 August 1770, Charleston, S. C.

STEPHENSON, Susannah and Kader Coleman, 5 April 1764, Edgecombe Co., N. C.

STERNEY, Rachel and Isaac Hassett, 6 August 1765, Chowan Co., N. C.

STERON, Elizabeth and William Davis, 14 November 1778, Chowan Co., N. C.

STEUART, Martha and William Hendricks, 22 October 1785, Rowan Co., N. C.

STEVENS, Asa and Miss Green, 13 November 1854, Edgefield District, S. C.

STEVENS, Catherine and Henry Ravenel, 17 June 1813, Pooshwee, S. C.

STEVENS, Cotton M. and Elizabeth Brett, 28 November 1784, Charleston, S. C.

STEVENS, Daniel and Katherine P. Norton, 6 December 1767, Charleston, S. C.

STEVENS, Elizabeth and Washington Roundtree, 22 May 1856, Edgefield District, S. C.

STEVENS, George and Peggy Sample, 26 July 1794, Charleston, S. C.

STEVENS, Hannah and Thomas Carlock, 26 April 1831, Mecklenburg Co., N. C.

STEVENS, Jarvis H. and Susanna Sullivan (widow), 24 December 1784, Charleston, S. C.

STEVENS, Mary and Thomas G. Scott, 2 November 1800, Charleston, S. C.

STEVENS, Miss and George Cogdell, 11 May 1777, Charleston, S. C.

STEVENS, Sarah and John Calhoun, 5 May 1801, Charleston, S. C.

STEVENS, William S. and Elizabeth Maltby, 23 December 1784, Charleston, S. C.

STEVENSON, Peter and Mary J. Snelling, 1 January 1773, Charleston, S. C.

STEVENSON, Sarah and James Elder, 3 March 1767, Rowan Co., N. C.

STEWARD, Charles Augustus and Sally Powell, 15 June 1769, Prince George Parish, S. C.

STEWARD, Elizabeth and William Arkill, 15 February 1748, Chowan Co., N. C.

STEWART, Ann and Edward Tonge, 1 November 1794, Charleston, S. C.

STEWART, George and Catherine Wilson, 2 November 1778, Chowan Co., N. C.

STEWART, Isabella and Daniel Baxter, 10 February 1807, Mecklenburg Co., N. C.

STEWART, Janet and John Hopkins, 25 April 1774, Bertie Co., N. C.

STEWART, John and Penelope Daly, 21 March 1770, Tyrrell Co., N. C.

STEWART, John and Elizabeth M. Wish, 22 December 1799, Charleston, S. C.

STEWART, Judith and John Beamore, 29 November 1719, St. Andrews Parish, S. C.

STEWART, Judith and John McAdoo, 27 September 1783, Guilford Co., N. C.

STEWART, Kezia and James Legar, 25 March 1779, Santee, S. C.

STEWART, Nancy and Thomas Hopper, 16 February 1791, Rowan Co., N. C.

STILES, Benjamin and Jane Scott, April 1785, James Island, S. C.

STILL, Elizabeth T. and Hugh Harris, 26 February 1825, Mecklenburg Co., N. C.

STILL, Jane and James Mather, 25 February 1844, Mecklenburg Co., N. C.

STILL, Mary and James B. Robinson, 13 December 1836, Mecklenburg Co., N. C.

STILLWELL, Samuel and Sarah Laffitte, 24 March 1742, Chowan Co., N. C.

STILWELL, Rachel and Horace McCall, 27 November 1832, Mecklenburg Co., N. C.

STINSON, Amanda H. E. and John W. Jones, 3 October 1867, Mecklenburg Co., N. C.

STINSON, Elizabeth and Alexander Cooper, 4 March 1824, Mecklenburg Co., N. C.

STINSON, Nancy and John McDougall, 4 December 1794, Mecklenburg Co., N. C.

STINSON, Sarah and Jesse C. Neal, 30 June 1824, Mecklenburg Co., N. C.

STIRLING, James and Jane Wood (widow) November 1747, Port Royal, S. C.

STITH, Bassett and Mary Long, 8 July 1790, Halifax, N. C.

STITT, Martha and Aaron H. Howey, 1 June 1835, Mecklenburg Co., N. C.

STOBBO, Polly and John Fraser, 23 June 1771, Charleston, S. C.

STOBO, Ann and Richard H. Peyton, 26 May 1795, Charleston, S. C.

STOBO, James and Ann Wilkinson, August 1786, St. Pauls Parish, S. C.

STOCKDAP, S. Joseph and Sarah Lark, 11 February 1830, Edgefield District, S. C.

STOCKER, George and Catherine Leighton, 31 January 1778, Chowan Co., N. C.

STOCKER, Henry B. and Jane Fickland, 27 October 1784, Charleston, S. C.

STOCKER, Mary and John McCollough, August 1783, Charleston, S. C.

STOCKS, Anne and Thomas Gibson, 30 January 1720, St. Andrews Parish, S. C.

STOCKS, Mary and David Galloway, 12 September 1719, St. Andrews Parish, S. C.

STOKES, Mary (widow) and William Lesley, 15 September 1770, Charleston, S. C.

STOKES, Mary A. and Laurens W. Youmans, 15 June 1865, Hampton Co., S. C.

STOLL, Rebecca and William Milligan, 4 October 1773, Charleston, S. C.

STOLLARD, Penelope and John Reynolds, 10 April 1729, Charleston, S. C.

STONE, Anne and John Mayrant, 26 September 1753, Charleston, S. C.

STONE, Anne and Archibald Hogstan, 16 October 1779, Rowan Co., N. C.

STONE, Benjamin and Elizabeth Knight, 6 March 1774, Santee, S. C.

STONE, Julia Ann and James Cheek, February 1851, Laurens Co., S. C.

STONE, Mary L. and Thomas Bennett, (Jr.), 19 February 1801, Charleston, S. C.

STONE, Thomas and Miss Guerin, May 1759, Charleston, S. C.

STONE, William and Miss Waldron, 19 January 1754, Charleston, S. C.

STONE, William and (Mrs.))Frances Holmes, 17 December 1800, James Island, S. C.

STONEY, John and Harriet E. Wells, 4 April 1801, Charleston, S. C.

STORY, Sarah (widow) and Robert Coleman, 13 August 1762, Edgecombe Co., N. C.

STOUT, Susan and James L. Coker, 28 March 1860, Hártsville, S. C.

STOUTMIRE, John and Jennet Carr, November 1799, St. Matthews Parish, S. C.

STOW, Elizabeth (widow) and Michael Clinch, 6 February 1718, St. Andrews Parish, S. C.

STOW, Susan and William Buford, 20 December 1803, Mecklenburg Co., N. C.

STRAHAN, John and Mrs. Naomi Painter, March 1733, Berkeley Co., S. C.

STRAIN, Sarah and Richard Barton, 2 June 1801, Mecklenburg Co., N. C.

STRATTLER, Malinda (Mrs.) and Edward Marlin, 16 September 1799, Charleston, S. C.

STRAITS, J. and Ann Brainer, 1784, Tyrrell Co., N. C.

STRAUMAN, Hanry and Catharina Horger, 1740, Orangeburg Co., S. C.

STRAUMAN, Jacob Hans and Ann Margaret Shaumloffel, 18 July 1748, Orangeburg Co., S. C.

STREATOR, Sarah and Nehemiah Bateman, 22 March 1779, Chowan Co., N. C.

STREET, Elizabeth (widow) and John Goodwin, August 1743, Ashley Ferry, S. C.

STREETER, John and Mary Hare, 2 July 1750, Chowan Co., N. C.

STRICKLAND, James and Betsy Hennington, 30 August 1772, Charleston, S. C.

STRICKLAND, Ozy and Jennet Alexander, 7 January 1828, Mecklenburg Co., N. C.

STRICKLIN, Lucretia and William Hickman, 19 December 1762, Edgecombe Co., N. C.

STRINGFELLOW, Elizabeth and James Alexander, 26 May 1834, Mecklenburg Co., N. C.

STROBACKER, Christina and J. G. Werdeman, 5 December 1799, Charleston, S. C.

STROBEL, Daniel and Elizabeth Eberly, 1787, Orangeburg Co., S. C.

STROBEL, Lewis and Jane S. Austen, 15 January 1801, Charleston, S. C.

STROHECKER, Elizabeth and Benjamin Casey, 17 December 1799, Charleston, S. C.

STROHECKER, John and Mary Charles, 22 May 1800, Charleston, S. C.

STROMAN, John Jacob and Anna Margaret Schaumloffel, 18 July 1741, Orangeburg Co., S. C.

STROMAN, Mary and John Jennings, 28 February 1807, Orangeburg Co., S. C.

STROWMANN, Barbara and Simon Sanger, 3 November 1737, Orangeburg Co., S. C.

STRUTHERS, Robert and Susannah Scrivenger, June 1785, Charleston, S. C.

STUART, Clarissa and William Brinkley, 15 January 1828, Mecklenburg Co., N. C.

STUART, Elizabeth and Thomas Harllee, 16 June 1789, Richmond Co., N. C.

STUART, Elizabeth and John Garrett, 18 July 1860, Laurens Co., S. C.

STUART, John and Mary Stuart, 12 September 1865, Laurens Co., S. C.

STUART, Mary and George Gray, 1 July 1769, Rowan Co., N. C.

STUART, Mary and John Stuart, 12 September 1865, Laurens Co., S. C.

STUART, Robert and Mary Dial, May 1855, Laurens Co., S. C.

STUART, Sally and John Graham, 16 July 1767, Charleston, S. C.

STUART, Sally and William Robison, 23 February 1819, Mecklenburg Co., N. C.

STUBBS, Elizabeth and Thomas Carrell, 17 November 1769, Tyrrell Co., N. C.

STUBBS, James and Sally Cannaday, 1780, Tyrrell Co., N. C.

STUBBS, Jesse and Mary Jones, 1784, Tyrrell Co., N. C.

STUBBS, Levi and Mary Hardison, 1781, Tyrrell Co., N. C.

STUBBS, Mary and William Fagan, 29 December 1777, Tyrrell Co., N. C.

STUBBS, Richard and Sally Jordan, 2 April 1783, Tyrrell Co., N. C.

STUBBS, Sarah and John Jordan, 2 October 1780, Tyrrell Co., N. C.

STUBBS, Thomas (Jr.) and Hannah Swinson, 8 December 1774, Tyrrell Co., N. C.

STUMS, Mary and Eli Himby, 20 August 1835, Mecklenburg Co., N. C.

STYLES, Louisa and Dennis Linzy, 5 April 1843, Laurens Co., S. C.

SULLIVAN, Ann and Thomas Bishop, 26 February 1763, Chowan Co., N. C.

SULLIVAN, Catherine and William Anderson, 11 April 1840, Hamburg, S. C.

SULLIVAN, Elizabeth and Alexander Hamilton, 9 June 1774, Chowan Co., N. C.

SULLIVAN, Esther and William Matthews, 25 April 1769, Santee, S. C.

SULLIVAN, Hannah and Jacob Bonhoste, 21 April 1768, Santee, S. C.

SULLIVAN, John and N. Snellgrove, 1746, Orangeburg Co., S. C.

SULLIVAN, Mary and Thomas Jamieson, 16 September 1789, Mecklenburg Co., N. C.

SULLIVAN, Millie and Demonick Murray, 7 January 1778, Chowan Co., N. C.

SULLIVAN, Rebecca and Michael Cochran, 11 January 1759, Santee, S. C.

SULLIVAN, Susanna (widow) and Jarvis H. Stevens, 24 December 1784, Charleston S. C.

SULLIVAN, Stephen and Elizabeth McGregor, 23 December 1762, Santee, S. C.

SULLIVANT, Stephen and Esther Axson, 11 October 1770, Santee, S. C.

SUMMER, John Adam and Miss Jostin, September 1743, Rotterdam, S. C.

SUMMERALL, Elizabeth and William Terry, 27 December 1855, Edgefield District, S. C.

SUMMERALL, Jane and Roland Terry, 30 October 1855, Edgefield District, S. C.

SUMMERS, Margaret and Thomas Hasell, 2 February 1772, Santee, S. C.

SUMMERVILLE, Harriet and Salalthiel Harris, 6 April 1839, Mecklenburg Co., N. C.

SUMMERVILLE, Mary I. and George L. Campbell, 1 January 1845, Mecklenburg Co., N. C.

SUMNER, Christian and William Barksdale, 7 April 1788, Bertie Co., N. C.

SUMNER, Elizabeth and Jetho Ballard, 30 December 1744, Chowan Co., N. C.

SUMNER, Elizabeth and Doctor Reddick, 1 March 1776, Chowan Co., N. C.

SUMNER, Elizabeth and Joseph Sumner, 9 March 1800, Hurtford Co., N. C.

SUMNER, Joseph and Elizabeth Sumner, 9 March 1800, Hurtford Co., N. C.

SUMNER, Mary and Timothy Hunter, 22 October 1774, Chowan Co., N. C.

SUMPTER, Eliza and James W. Murrell, 19 April 1807, Santee, S. C.

SUN, Sarah J. and Samuel C. Brown, 29 August 1859, Mecklenburg Co., N. C.

SUTHERLAND, Margaret and Thomas Holeman, 16 May 1778, Rowan Co., N. C.

SUTTER, Susannah (Mrs.) and Archibald B. Clarke, April 1786, Beaufort, S. C.

SUTTON, Elizabeth and Josiah Rasor, 27 March 1788, Bertie Co., N. C.

SUTTON, Henrietta and Caleb Gollins, 12 March 1786, Tyrrell Co., N. C.

SUTTON, Lurana and James Wiley, 5 September 1785, Tyrrell Co., N. C.

SUTTON, Stephen and Polly Autry, 17 December 1822, Edgefield District, S. C.

SWAIN, Abram and Nancy Hassell, 1780, Tyrrell Co., N. C.

SWAIN, Eliakim and Ann Jannett, October 1783, Tyrrell Co., N. C.

SWAIN, Joana and John Newberry, 4 July 1786, Tyrrell Co., N. C.

SWAIN, John and Elizabeth Lanier, 15 December 1766, Tyrrell Co., N. C.

SWAIN, John and Lydia Blount, 19 February 1780, Tyrrell Co., N. C.

SWAIN, Joshua and Elizabeth Blount, 1 March 1753, Chowan Co., N. C.

SWAIN, Margaret and John Neely, 11 December 1843, Mecklenburg Co., N. C.

SWAIN, Mary and Samuel Simpson, 21 September 1764, Tyrrell Co., N. C.

SWAIN, Mary and Joseph Ainesley, (Jr.), 15 March 1786, Tyrrell Co., N. C.

SWAIN, Naomi and John Morgan, 5 February 1800, Guilford Co., N. C.

SWAIN, Sarah and Evan Skinner, 5 April 1779, Tyrrell Co., N. C.

SWAIN, Susanna and Aaron Dugan, 28 March 1767, Tyrrell Co., N. C.

SWAIN, Susanna and James Howell, 10 September 1788, Bertie Co., N. C.

SWAIN, Susannah and John Watlington, 5 March 1795, Charleston, S. C.

SWAIN, William and Mary Hassell, 1780, Tyrrell Co., N. C.

SWAINSTON, Robert and Deborah Sabb, 15 February 1767, St. Johns Parish, S. C.

SWALLOW, Frances (widow) and Charles Ramage, 30 June 1774, Charleston, S. C.

SWALLOW, Sarah and John Hatfield, 6 January 1765, Charleston, S. C.

SWALLOW, William and Sally Prince, 26 October 1771, Charleston, S. C.

SWAN, Captain and Ann Irwin, August 1785, Charleston, S. C.

SWAN, Margaret and Thomas Wills, 26 August 1779, Chowan Co., N. C.

SWANN, Anne (widow) and Peter Taylor, 21 October 1762, Goose Creek, S. C.

SWANN, Elizabeth and John Vail, 20 September 1748, Chowan Co., N. C.

SWANN, Thomas and Margaret Chisnell, 1 July 1771, Chowan Co., N. C.

SWEARINGEN, Fannie and Alfred Hatcher, 28 July 1821, Edgefield District, S. C.

SWEARINGEN, Harriett and Coleman Rhodes, 1 November 1840, Edgefield District, S. C.

SWEARINGEN, John and Elizabeth Murrell, 25 January 1849, Edgefield District, S. C.

SWEARINGEN, L. G. and Ann Toney, 13 October 1853, Edgefield District, S. C.

SWEARINGEN, Van and Polly Bush, 17 November 1822, Edgefield District, S. C.

SWEENEY, James and Sarah Parker, 5 September 1778, Chowan Co., N. C.

SWIN, Elisa H. and Silas Hanback, 6 January 1848, Laurens Co., S. C.

SWINDERSINE, Elizabeth and Daniel M. Saddler, 3 April 1800, Charleston, S. C.

SWINSON, Hannah and Thomas Stubbs (Jr.), 8 December 1774, Tyrrell Co., N. C.

SWINSON, Richard and Chloe Bevanham, 1782, Tyrrell Co., N. C.

SWINT, Elizabeth and James Badger, September 1786, Charleston, S. C.

SWITZER, John and Elizabeth Glenn, 25 April 1859, Laurens Co., S. C.

SWITZER, John R. and (Mrs.) Mary Hahnbaum, 14 January 1801, Charleston, S. C.

SYLVIA, Mary and Jeremiah Haughton, 27 January 1756, Chowan Co., N. C.

T

TADLOCK, Absalom and Sarah Turner, 19 August 1780, Bertie Co., N. C.

TADLOCK, Martha and Byron Waller, 27 May 1734, Bertie Co., N. C.

TALIAFERRO, Lucy H. and David S. Taylor, September 1826, Pendleton, S. C.

TALIAFERRO, Sarah A. and O. R. Broyles, 20 March 1823, Pendleton, S. C.

TALIFERRO, Elizabeth and William Farr, 1779, Union District, S. C.

TALLIFER, ——— and Eliza Bellinger, 21 March 1769, Charleston, S. C.

TAMILSON, Martha and Charles Mitchell, 29 June 1743, Charleston, S. C.

TANNER, John and Barbara Rumph, 3 May 1737, Charleston, S. C.

TAPP, Ann Barbara (widow) and George Adam Ernst, 1740, Orangeburg Co., S. C.

TAPP, John Julius and Anna B. Hergersperger (widow)) 3 February 1740, Orangeburg Co., S. C.

TARDINE, Antoinette and John You, 8 January 1801, Charleston, S. C.

TARKINGTON, Mary and Dickson Mitchell, 22 March 1769, Tyrrell Co., N. C.

TARKINTON, Elizabeth and Enoch Phelps, 6 October 1779, Tyrrell Co., N. C.

TARKINTON, Elizabeth and Joseph Hassell, 1781, Tyrrell Co., N. C.

TARKINTON, John and Priscilla Tarkinton, 3 October 1786, Tyrrell Co., N. C.

TARKINTON, John (Jr.) and Martha Hassell, 4 April 1786, Tyrrell Co., N. C.

TARKINTON, Joseph and Cenia Tarte, 5 January 1780, Tyrrell Co., N. C.

TARKINTON, Mary and Dickson Mitchell, 22 March 1769, Tyrrell Co., N. C.

TARKINTON, Priscilla and John Tarkinton, 3 October 1786, Tyrrell Co., N. C.

TARKINTON, Sarah and Isaac Patrick, 20 December 1779, Tyrrell Co., N. C.

TARKINTON, Sarah and Richard Davis, 26 March 1783, Tyrrell Co., N. C.

TARKINTON, William and Elizabeth Ainesley, 6 April 1785, Tyrrell Co., N. C.

TARR, Barbara and Frederick Fisher, 30 January 1793, Rowan Co., N. C.

TART, Patsey and Asa Overton, 26 December 1789, Bertie Co., N. C.

TART, Polly and Alexander Chovin, November 1772, Charleston, S. C.

TARTE, Cenia and Joseph Tarkinton, 5 January 1780, Tyrrell Co., N. C.

TATUM, Mary and George Merrifield, 6 December 1788, Guilford Co., N. C.

TATUM, Richard and Mary Bethea, 19 June 1857, Marlboro Co., S. C.

TAVEROON, Stephen and Sarah Turner, 4 November 1724, Charleston, S. C.

TAYLOR, Alexander and Sarah Hayne, 18 May 1837, Colleton, S. C.

TAYLOR, Alice and Henry Hunter, 10 October 1810, Mecklenburg Co., N. C.

TAYLOR, Anderson and Jane Young, 20 December 1790, Granville Co., N. C.

TAYLOR, Anne and William Mazyck, 20 July 1850, Charleston, S. C.

TAYLOR, Benjamin W. and Anna Heyward, 14 December 1865, Columbia, S. C.

TAYLOR, Betsy and John Hunt, 17 September 1804, Granville Co., N. C.

TAYLOR, Barwell and Sarah Jane Paschall, 23 September 1844, Granville Co., N. C.

TAYLOR, David S. and Lucy H. Taliaferro, September 1826, Pendleton, . C.

TAYLOR, Edmond and Patsey Lewis, 24 April 1790, Granville Co., N. C.

TAYLOR, Edmond and Polly Robards, 10 September 1798, Granville Co., N. C.

TAYLOR, Elenor and Edward Walker, 16 April 1763, Tyrrell Co., N. C.

TAYLOR, Eliza Jane and Robert M. Robison, 22 December 1840, Mecklenburg Co., N. C.

TAYLOR, Elizabeth and Thomas McKoin, 13 May 1779, Chowan Co., N. C.

TAYLOR, Elizabeth and William Hunt, 25 October 1792, Granville Co., N. C.

TAYLOR, Elizabeth and Daniel Bythewood, 17 April 1792, Charleston, S. C.

TAYLOR, George (Jr.) and Eliza Ladson, 11 December 1794, Charleston, S. C.

TAYLOR, Helen, and Drayton Madden, 9 October 1866, Laurens Co., S. C.

TAYLOR, Henry T. and Susanna Hargan, 20 March 1785, Charleston, S. C.

TAYLOR, Hester and Thomas Haywood, 4 June 1719, St. Andrews Parish, S. C.

TAYLOR, Hester and Nathaniel Matthews, 10 November 1744, Chowan Co., N. C.

TAYLOR, James and Sallie Eaton, 19 December 1786, Cranville Co., N. C.

TAYLOR, James and Betsey Robards, 15 October 1797, Granville Co., N. C.

TAYLOR, James and Elizabeth Barrie, (widow) 20 August 1754, Orangeburg Co., S. C.

TAYLOR, James and Mary Mann, May 1785, Georgetown, S. C.

TAYLOR, Jane and Robert Rivers, 2 June 1785, James Island, S. C.

TAYLOR, Jane and Benjamin Thorp, 5 January 1800, Granville Co., N. C.

TAYLOR, John and Ann Chopard, 1 October 1770, Charleston, S. C.

TAYLOR, John and Mary Smith, 28 June 1800, Granville Co., N. C.

TAYLOR, John and Lucy A. Boyd, 27 September 1815, Granville Co., N. C.

TAYLOR, John and Susannah Bullock, 16 March 1784, Granville Co., N. C.

TAYLOR, John C. and Mary R. Ridley, 31 August 1842, Granville Co., N. C.

TAYLOR, Liza and Robert Gray, 7 August 1845, Laurens Co., S. C.

TAYLOR, Lucretia and William Clark, 30 August 1845, Mecklenburg Co., N. C.

TAYLOR, Margaret and George Johnson, 3 January 1850, Mecklenburg Co., N. C.

TAYLOR, Margaret C. and James L. Hart, 9 July 1830, Mecklenburg Co., N. C.

TAYLOR, Nancy C. and Andrew J. Read, 20 September 1836, Mecklenburg Co., N. C.

TAYLOR, Nina and Richard Holland, 30 November 1775, Rowan Co., N. C.

TAYLOR, Paul and Sarah Piercy, October 1785, Santee, S. C.

TAYLOR, Peter and Anne Swann, (widow) 21 October 1762, Goose Creek, S. C.

TAYLOR, Rebecca and Charles Moore, 1777, Granville Co., N. C.

TAYLOR, Richard and Lucy Byne, 15 February 1775, Granville Co., N. C.

TAYLOR, Richard P. and Martha B. Norman, 2 May 1838, Granville Co., N. C.

TAYLOR, Robert and Sarah Parham, 11 July 1809, Granville Co., N. C.

TAYLOR, Robert and Mildred Kennon, 24 April 1816, Granville Co., N. C.

TAYLOR, Sarah and Zebulon Snowden, 3 August 1765, Chowan Co., N. C.

TAYLOR, Sarah and Peter Gwinn, 21 November 1769, Rowan Co., N. C.

TAYLOR, Sarah Cornelia and William Neely Carothers, 1 May 1849, Mecklenburg Co., N. C.

TAYLOR, Stephen and Frances Gurrin, 6 June 1845, Granville Co., N. C.

TAYLOR, Thomas J. and Rosalie Speed, 2 October 1843, Granville Co., N. C.

TAYLOR, Warner and Polly Johnson, 9 September 1829, Granville Co., N. C.

TAYLOR, William and Elizabeth H. Smith, 8 December 1804, Granville Co., N. C.

TAYLOR, William and Frances Wilson, 9 March 1836, Granville Co., N. C.

TAYLOR, William L. and Sally M. Gregory, 11 January 1845, Granville Co., N. C.

TEAGUE, Elias and Rachel Atkins, October 1814, Newberry, S. C.

TEAGUE, Elizabeth and Alsey Coleman, 29 October 1846, Laurens Co., S. C.

TEAGUE, Ewel and Caroline Miles, 20 January 1851, Laurens Co., S. C.

TEAGUE, Lavina and James Coleman, 23 December 1852, Laurens Co., S. C.

TEAGUE, Liza and Jones Miller, 18 December 1844, Laurens Co., S. C.

TEAGUE, Ludy and Parthenie U. Williams, 26 October 1858, Laurens Co., S. C.

TEAGUE, Pickney and Elizabeth Felts, 4 January 1866, Laurens Co., S. C.

TEMPLETON, Emma and Daniel S. Bush, 29 December 1855, Edgefield District, S. C.

TEMPLETON, Margaret (widow) and Ludy Hitch, 28 December 1858, Laurens Co., S. C.

TEMPLETON, Samuel and Minty Putman, 3 May 1855, Laurens Co., S. C.

TENAPLOUGH, Henrietta and Isaac Read, 25 June 1853, Mecklenburg Co., N. C.

TENNENT, Charles E. and Mary J. Fripp, 25 July 1844, St. Johns Parish, S. C.

TENNENT, Susanna and Charles Brown, October 1783, Charleston, S. C.

TERRANCE, Ann E. and Edward Caldwell, 11 August 1826, Mecklenburg Co., N. C.

TERRESS, Agnes and Moses McWhorter, 26 August 1793, Mecklenburg Co., N. C.

TERRY, Benjamin and Frances Madden, 11 November 1866, Laurens Co., S. C.

TERRY, Elizabeth and William James Gooding, 4 September 1856, Beaufort District, S. C.

TERRY, Roland and Jane Summerall, 30 October 1855, Edgefield District, S. C.

TERRY, William and Elizabeth Summerall, 27 December 1855, Edgefield District, S. C.

TETTERTON, William and Ann Kelley, 12 August 1785, Tyrrell Co., N. C.

TEW, Malienda and George Cathay, 10 March 1842, Mecklenburg Co., N. C.

THAXTON, Nathaniel and Mandy Pearson, 13 December 1849, Laurens Co., S. C.

THAYER, Caroline and Edwin Gibbes, 30 November 1821, Charleston, S. C.

THEACH, John and Sarah Standing, 27 April 1748, Chowan Co., N. C.

THEUS, Charlotte and John S. Mayer, 1788, Charleston, S. C.

THEUS, James and Mary Theus, August 1783, Charleston, S. C.

THEUS, Mary and James Theus, August 1783, Charleston, S. C.

THEUS, Simeon and Rebecca Legare, July 1784, Charleston, S. C.

THEUS, Simon and Elizabeth Mackey, 12 February 1754, Orangeburg Co., S. C.

THEWRATT, Ann M. and John X. Griffith, 4 October 1764, Rowan Co., N. C.

THOM, Jacob and Susannah Quackenbush, 25 May 1800, Charleston, S. C.

THOMAS, Amelia and Joseph Rankhorn, 1784, Tyrrell Co., N. C.

THOMAS, Ann and James Smyth, 18 March 1773, Charleston, S. C.

THOMAS, Annie and Joseph McJunkin, 9 March 1779, Union Co., S. C.

THOMAS, Bethany and John Skitlethrope, 10 December 1786, Tyrrell Co., N. C.

THOMAS, Catherine and Ezekial Griffin, 27 September 1786, Rowan Co., N. C.

THOMAS, Edward and Anne Gibbes, 27 September 1767, Charleston, S. C.

THOMAS, James and Mary Standley, 6 September 1790, Bertie Co., N. C.

THOMAS, John and Sarah Britt, 26 November 1800, Bertie Co., N. C.

THOMAS, John (Rev.) and Polly Lamball, 21 February 1768, Charleston, S. C.

THOMAS, Mary and William Horn, 20 July 1761, Edgecombe Co., N. C.

THOMAS, Mourning and James Dickenson, 19 November 1770, Edgecombe Co., N. C.

THOMAS, Noah and Catherine Chicken, 5 August 1762, Santee, S. C.

THOMAS, Priscilla and George Crudup, 1761, Edgecombe Co., N. C.

THOMAS, Samuel and Jane Douxsaint, 30 October 1768, Charleston, S. C.

THOMAS, Tresa and Theophilus Hill, 3 September 1762, Edgecombe Co., N. C.

THOMASON, Catherine and James C. Alexander, 24 February 1831, Mecklenburg Co., N. C.

THOMASON, Mary and Josiah Knight, 27 February 1855, Laurens Co., S. C.

THOMASON, Mary E. and D. W. Barnett, 22 September 1859, Mecklenburg Co., N. C.

THOMASON, Thomas and Margaret A. Hollingsworth, 27 December 1855, Edgefield District, S. C.

THOMPSON, Agnes and Francis Jones, 9 January 1789, Orange Co., N. C.

THOMPSON, Alexander and Susannah Rose, 5 February 1801, Charleston, S. C.

THOMPSON, Ann and William Clark, 2 November 1796, Mecklenburg Co., N. C.

THOMPSON, Ann and John Coffield, 20 March 1778, Chowan Co., N. C.

THOMPSON, Anthony and Mary Holt, 29 January 1788, Orange Co., N. C.

THOMPSON, Betsy and Isaac McIntire, 16 November 1811, Mecklenburg Co., N. C.

THOMPSON, Catherine and Robert Biggers, 1 January 1788, Mecklenburg Co., N. C.

THOMPSON, David and Mary Turner, 12 November 1774, Bertie Co., N. C.

THOMPSON, Elisha G. and Nancy A. Carothers, 6 October 1836, York Co., S. C.

THOMPSON, Elizabeth (widow) and Thomas Jones, 5 May 1749, Chowan Co., N. C.

THOMPSON, Gracey and James Drummond, 19 March 1800, Charleston, S. C.

THOMPSON, George and (Mrs.) Mary Halliday, 18 May 1800, Charleston, S. C.

THOMPSON, James and (Mrs.) Elizabeth Kennedy, September 1786, Charleston,. S. C.

THOMPSON, James and Elizabeth Price, 29 July 1773, Chowan Co., N. C.

THOMPSON, James H. and Elizabeth M. Trezevant, 21 January 1775, Charleston, S. C.

THOMPSON, Jane and William Barton, 24 September 1773, Santee, S. C.

THOMPSON, Jane (Mrs.) and William McWhann, 3 August 1786, Charleston, S. C.

THOMPSON, Jeremiah S. and Beatrix Fleming, 21 December 1794, Charleston, S. C.

THOMPSON, John and Mary Fullerton, 4 August 1744, Chowan Co., N. C.

THOMPSON, Mary (widow) and John Lewis (Jr.), 19 November 1755, Chowan Co., N. C.

THOMPSON, Rebecca and Thomas McCord, 26 January 1819, Mecklenburg Co., N. C.

THOMPSON, Ruth and William Mitchell, April 1779, Charleston, S. C.

THOMPSON, Selena and Troy Brown, 6 December 1840, Mecklenburg Co., N. C.

THOMPSON, Susan and Charles Highs, 13 September 1866, Laurens Co., S. C.

THOMPSON, Susane and James McKensey, 5 June 1779, Guilford Co., N. C.

THOMPSON, William and (Mrs.) Elizabeth Sadler, 30 August 1743, Chowan Co., N. C.

THOMPSON, William and Eugenia Russell, 14 August 1755, Orangeburg Co., S. C.

THOMSON, Anne and Herbert Haynes, 6 March 1771, Edgecombe Co., N. C.

THOMSON, Elizabeth P. and George M. Oehler, 5 January 1841, Mecklenburg Co., N. C.

THOMSON, George and Jane Yorston, 13 December 1767, Charleston, S. C.

THOMSON, Thomas and Mary Lavine, 9 January 1796, Mecklenburg Co., N. C.

THOMSON, Thomas and Anna Hall, 26 December 1799, Charleston, S. C.

THOMSON, Thomas (Capt.)) and Eliza Allen, September 1839, Edgefield District, S. C.

THORNEY, Jane (Mrs.) and Acey Hill, of Boston, 29 May 1801, Charleston, S. C.

THORNTON, Catherine and Jonathan Eccles, 1805, Camden, S. C.

THORNTON, Francis and Elizabeth Jones, 1762, Oxford, N. C.

THORP, Benjamin and Jane Taylor, 5 January 1800, Granville Co., N. C.

THORP, Margaret and Zeph Johns, 22 December 1824, Mecklenburg Co., N. C.

THURSTON, Thomas and Jean Hines, 11 April 1782, Santee, S. C.

TIDDIMAN, Mary and John Drayton, 6 November 1794, Charleston, S. C.

TIDYMAN, Philip and Hetty Rose, 5 October 1772, Charleston, S. C.

TILLETT, Margaret and William H. Spruill, 21 August 1779, Tyrrell Co., N. C.

TILLINGHAST, Mary E. and LeRoy F. Youmans, December 1857, Beaufort, S. C.

TILLMAN, Benjamin R. and Sophia A. Hancock, 14 May 1823, Edgefield Co., S. C.

TILLMAN, Iwanowna and (Major) W. A. Wardlaw, 23 May 1840, Abbeville, S. C.

TILLMAN, Oliver and Martha Roper, 29 December 1857, S. C.

TILLMAN, William C. and E. I. Kearsey, 18 October 1855, Edgefield District, S. C.

TIMES, Mary and William Campbell, 2 June 1749, Charleston, S. C.

TIMMERMAN, John and Millery Jennings, 22 December 1854, Edgefield District, S. C.

TIMMERMAN, Thomas and Savannah McDowell, 14 October 1752, Edgefield District, S. C.

TIMMERMAN, Washington and Pauline Asbill, June 1856, Edgefield Co., S. C.

TINSLEY, Martha and Moses Madden, 21 December 1852, Laurens Co., S. C.

TISDALE, Ony and Malachi Barnes, 22 February 1800, Edgecombe Co., N. C.

TOBIAS, Joseph and Rachel Aarons, 2 November 1785, Charleston, S. C.

TODD, Adaline and George Layton, 1 January 1857, Laurens Co., S. C.

TODD, Ann and Joseph Gheen, 4 April 1797, Rowan Co., N. C.

TODD, Ann and William Moore, 7 April 1821, Mecklenburg Co., N. C.

TODD, Ann A. and William H. Clark, 14 October 1852, Mecklenburg Co., N. C.

TODD, Betsy and John Neely, 25 October 1804, Mecklenburg Co., N. C.

TODD, Bryant and Martha J. Miller, 4 July 1860, Chowan Co., N. C.

TODD, Christina and James McGinn, 13 October 1794, Mecklenburg Co., N. C.

TODD, Christina and Robert H. Clark, 23 December 1841, Mecklenburg Co., N. C.

TODD, Christine E. and G. R. Moore, 3 January 1849, Mecklenburg Co., N. C.

TODD, Cynthia M. and Thomas P. Berryhill, 3 March 1821, Mecklenburg Co., N. C.

TODD, Cynthia M. and John M. Alexander, 27 December 1854, Mecklenburg Co., N. C.

TODD, Cynthia P. and William Marshall, 9 October 1845, Mecklenburg Co., N. C.

TODD, Darcus and L. W. Osborn, 27 July 1864, Mecklenburg Co., N. C.

TODD, Eliza and Robertson Moore, 21 November 1844, Laurens Co., S. C.

TODD, Hannah F. and R. M. Jamieson, 25 January 1843, Mecklenburg Co., N. C.

TODD, Hannah I. and John R. Jamieson, 21 December 1858, Mecklenburg Co., N. C.

TODD, Harriet and Joseph J. Berryhill, 15 June 1825, Mecklenburg Co., N. C.

TODD, James and Mary Mitchell, 19 June 1828, Bertie Co., N. C.

TODD, Jane and Hugh Bailey, 11 April 1807, Mecklenburg Co., N. C.

TODD, Jean and Andrew Ellison, 4 September 1786, Rowan Co., N. C.

TODD, Jennet and Robert Barnett, 7 May 1789, Mecklenburg Co., N. C.

TODD, John and Frances Darrell, (widow) 1 January 1786, Charleston, S. C.

TODD, John and Malissa Vice, 7 December 1865, Laurens Co., S. C.

TODD, Margaret and William Jamieson, 6 May 1835, Mecklenburg Co., N. C

TODD, Martha and Potiller Moore, 16 December 1852, Laurens Co., S. C.

TODD, Mary and John McClure, 11 December 1799, Mecklenburg Co., N. C.

TODD, Mary and Samuel Read, 4 April 1836, Mecklenburg Co., N. C.

TODD, Mary and Thomas McGinn, 16 December 1800, Mecklenburg Co., N. C.

TODD, Mary S. and Joseph N. Rhyne, 26 May 1847, Mecklenburg Co., N. C.

TODD, Miley and Jonathan Miller, 26 December 1855, Chowan Co., N. C.

TODD, Patrick (Dr.) and Ann Fuller, 18 October 1857, Laurens Co., S. C.

TODD, R. A. (Miss) and A. W. Clark, 17 January 1866, Mecklenburg Co., N. C.

TODD, Samuel and Winifred Morris, 28 November 1789, Bertie Co., N. C.

TODD, Sarah and John Neal, 16 May 1803, Mecklenburg Co., N. C.

TODD, Sarah L. and R. M. Jamieson, 30 September 1862, Mecklenburg Co., N. C.

TODD, Sophina and William H. Read, 9 February 1860, Mecklenburg Co., N. C.

TODD, Susan and Griffith Baker, 22 May 1819, Mecklenburg Co., N. C.

TOLIN, Tarsy and Thomas Moseley, 12 December 1850, Laurens Co., S. C.

TOM, Mary and Michael McClane, 16 July 1792, Guilford Co., N. C.

TOMLINSON, Elizabeth (widow) and James G. Williams, January 1774, Johns Island, S. C.

TOMMEN, Veronica (widow) and Jacob Wolf, 10 December 1740, Orangeburg Co., S. C.

TOMPKINS, James and (Mrs.) Hulda Jennings, 7 January 1819, Edgefield District, S. C.

TOMPKINS, John Warren and Elizabeth E. Allen, 24 November 1848, Edgefield District, S. C.

TOMPLET, Peter and Isabella Black, 17 April 1732, Berkeley Co., S. C.

TOMPSON, Eliza and L. G. Saulter, 8 November 1854, Edgefield District, S. C.

TONEVA, Delia R. and John R. Johnston, 17 June 1856, Mecklenburg Co., N. C.

TONEY, Anna and L. G. Swearingen, 13 October 1853, Edgefield District, S. C.

TONGE, Edward and Ann Stewart, 1 November 1794, Charleston, S. C.

TONGS, James (Rev.) and Susanna Perry, 5 September 1768, St. Pauls Parish, S. C.

TOOMER, Anthony and Nancy Warham, 4 August 1767, Charleston, S. C.

TOOMER, Eliza B. and Hugh Wilson, 10 November 1830, Charleston, S. C.

TOOMER, Henry and Mary Baker, 23 June 1719, St. Andrews Parish, S. C.

TOOMER, Mary and Nathan Legare, April 1786, Christ Church Parish, S. C.

TORRANS, Eliza and Thomas Cochran (Jr.), 18 December 1799, Charleston, S. C.

TORRENCE, Letitia A. and S. E. Bratton, 7 September 1847, Mecklenburg Co., N. C.

TORREY, William and Anne Prince, 30 May 1800, Charleston, S. C.

TOWE, Anne and Henry Griggs, 26 February 1791, Rowan Co., N. C.

TOWNSEND, Charles P. and Amanda McConnell, 1 October 1860, Columbia, S. C.

TOWNSEND, Daniel A. and Sallie B. Douglas, 4 November 1854, Union, S. C.

TOWNSEND, Martha and Allen Orr, 22 November 1814, Mecklenburg Co., N. C.

TOWNSEND, Miss and Thomas Jones, 5 June 1766, Charleston, S. C.

TOWNSEND, Sarah and Mr. Godwin, 9 April 1785, Charleston, S. C.

TOWNSEND, Thomas and Mary Robinson, 4 February 1785, Charleston, S. C.

TRADENICK, Sarah A. and James A. Johnson, 23 March 1858, Mecklenburg Co., N. C.

TRAPIER, Alicia and Isaac W. Hayne, 1 May 1834, Colleton, S. C.

TRAPIER, Elizabeth (widow) and Albert Roux, December 1784, Georgetown, S. C.

TRAPIER, Elizabeth and Edward Martin, 17 September 1778, Santee, S. C.

TRAPIER, Paul and Elizabeth Foisson, 19 November 1771, Santee, S. C.

TRENHOLM, Ann and John Robertson, 13 May 1795, Charleston, S. C.

TRESCOTT, Edward and Rachel Bouquet, May 1777, Charleston, S. C.

TREZEVANT, Elizabeth M. and James H. Thompson, 21 January 1775, Charleston, S. C.

TREZEVANT, Esther and William Wayne, 7 May 1777, Charleston, S. C.

TRIBBLE, Warren and Frances Copeland, 20 January 1859, Laurens Co., S. C.

TRICE, Betsey and David George, 18 December 1792, Orange Co., N. C.

TROTMAN, Ann E. and Timothy Mitchell, 24 April 1855, Chowan Co., N. C.

TROTMAN, Thomas and Christian Harrell, 27 February 1770, Chowan Co., N. C.

TROTMAN, Thomas and Winnifred Cullen, 3 March 1788, Bertie Co., N. C.

TROTT, John and Mary Endid, 1788, Charleston, S. C.

TROTTER, James and (Mrs.) Martha Potter, 2 December 1743, Chowan Co., N. C.

TROTTER, James and (Mrs.) Mary Ward, 27 February 1745, Chowan Co., N. C.

TROUP, John and Frances Gordon, 30 May 1763, Charleston, S. C.

TRUSE, Nancy and Isaac Jones, 13 December 1832, Mecklenburg Co., N. C.

TSHUDY, Ann and Charles Hottow, 1742, Orangeburg Co., S. C.

TSHUDY, Anna (widow) and Jacob Kooner, 21 July 1752, Orangeburg Co., S. C.

TUCKER, Bethiah and John Charlton, 25 June 1778, Chowan Co., N. C.

TUCKER, Dolly and John Cashin, 1 July 1801, Mecklenburg Co., N. C.

TUCKER, Lydia and Sanders Glover, May 1784, Charleston, S. C.

TUCKER, Sally and George Heriot, February 1775, Charleston, S. C.

TUCKER, Thomas T. (Dr.) and Esther Evans, 7 July 1774, St. Georges Parish, S. C.

TUNNO, Thomas and Harriot Ward, 1 May 1800, Johns Island, S. C.

TUPPER, Tristram and Eliza Yoer, 3 December 1816, Charleston, S. C.

TURGIS, Elizabeth (widow) and Joseph Blake, December 1698, Pawlets, S. C.

TURGIS, Mary and Walter Izard, 19 May 1713, St. Georges Parish, S. C.

TURNBULL, James and Emma Whittaker, 8 November 1800, Charleston, S. C.

TURNBULL, John and Henrietta Guerin, 18 December 1800, Charleston, S. C.

TURNBULL, R. F. and Claudia Gervais, 10 January 1797, Charleston, S. C.

TURNER, Agnes (widow) and George Campbell, 21 January 1769, Chowan Co., N. C.

TURNER, Ann and William Hinton, 7 March 1770, Bertie Co., N. C.

TURNER, Anne and Thomas Dixon, 28 May 1793, Orange Co., N. C.

TURNER, Arthur and Keziah Young, 22 December 1779, Tyrrell Co., N. C.

TURNER, Ashbury and Sophia Jordan, 9 February 1842, Chowan Co., N. C.

TURNER, Benjamin and Sarah Mullen, 10 April 1790, Perquimans Co., N. C.

TURNER, Dempsy and Hartwell Pearce, 23 October 1762, Perquimans Co., N. C.

TURNER, Dempsy and Sarah Muller, 9 April 1781, Perquimans Co., N. C.

TURNER, Elizabeth and William Kennedy, 7 August 1722, Berkeley Co., S. C.

TURNER, Elizabeth and Joseph Williams, 10 January 1749, Berkeley Co., S. C.

TNRNER, Elizabeth and Thomas Hendricks, 2 May 1758, Perquimans Co., N. C.

TURNER, Fanny and William Jackson, 7 February 1785, Perquimans Co., N. C.

TURNER, Hannah and Christopher Clark, 17 January 1773, Bertie Co., N. C.

TURNER, Henry McN. and Eliza A. Peachee, 31 August 1856, Columbus, S. C.

TURNER, Jane and John Fireash, 12 September 1786, Perquimans Co., N. C.

TURNER, Jane and Robert Campbell, 30 March 1791, Mecklenburg Co., N. C.

TURNER, John B. and Amelia Barnes, 29 December 1789, Bertie Co., N. C.

TURNER, Joseph and Tabitha Nichols, 26 March 1724, Berkeley Co., S. C.

TURNER, Joseph and Mary Hawkins, 23 October 1762, Perquimans Co., N. C.

TURNER, Joshua and Polly Colson, 25 September 1794, Perquimans Co., N. C.

TURNER, Martha and John Fort, 30 December 1774, Bertie Co., N. C.

TURNER, Martha and James Kinsey, 7 April 1787, Bertie Co., N. C.

TURNER, Mary and David Thompson, 12 November 1774, Bertie Co., N. C.

TURNER, Mary and Simon Braswell, 25 February 1764, Edgecombe Co., N. C.

TURNER, Mary and Thomas Stafford, 6 January 1786, Perquimans Co., N. C.

TURNER, Mary and John Stafford, 31 January 1797, Perquimans Co., N. C.

TURNER, Mary A. and Robert Rea, 23 June 1864, Mecklenburg Co., N. C.

TURNER, Miles and Sarah Snowden, 30 January 1785, Perquimans Co., N. C.

TURNER, Milly and William Weeks, 7 July 1797, Perquimans Co., N. C.

TURNER, Miriam and Elias Briggs, 14 August 1779, Perquimans Co., N. C.

TURNER, Miriam and William Stafford, 30 September 1786, Perquimans Co., N. C.

TURNER, Nancy and John Miller, 3 June 1835, Mecklenburg Co., N. C.

TURNER, Patrick (Dr.) and Susan Sneed, 22 February 1853, Laurens Co., S. C.

TURNER, Rachel and Job Orendall, 6 July 1761, Perquimans Co., N. C.

TURNER, Sarah and Stephen Taveroon, 4 November 1724, Charleston, S. C.

TNRNER, Sarah and Absalon Tadlock, 19 August 1780, Bertie Co., N. C.

TURNER, Sarah and Richardson Moss, 27 September 1783, Perquimans Co., N. C.

TURNER, Sarah and Gilbert Colson, 13 August 1792, Perquimans Co., N. C.

TURNER, Thomas and Mary Stanton, July 1786, Perquimans Co., N. C.

TURNER, William and Mary Millen, 11 October 1780, Bertie Co., N. C.

TURNER, William and Kathren Kinse, 5 March 1793, Berkeley, N. C.

TURQUAND, Ann and Felex Warley, 16 December 1784, St. Matthews Parish, S. C.

TYLER, Mary J. (widow) and B. F. Simmons, 23 November 1842, Barnwell District, S. C.

TYLER, Warren Charles and Mary Reed, 19 August 1841, Barnwell District, S. C.

U

UGLY, Catharina (widow) and Jacob Roth, 1741, Orangeburg Co., S. C.

ULMER, Anne Mary and Barnard Hertzog, 18 February 1755, Orangeburg Co., S. C.

ULMER, John F. and Mary Barbara Shuler, 1752, Orangeburg Co., S. C.

UNDERHILL, Edward and Elizabeth Branch, 9 April 1755, Chowan Co., N. C.

UNDERWOOD, Levis and John Mills, 13 October 1795, Guilford Co., N. C.

URBALL, Eve and Henry Ernhart, 24 June 1791, Rowan Co., N. C.

URIE, Frances and Elijah Rutledge, 6 August 1801, Mecklenburg Co., N. C.

UTBERT, Patience and John Clement, 11 April 1721, Charleston, S. C.

V

VAIL, John and Elizabeth Swann, 20 September 1748, Chowan Co., N. C.

VAIL, Martha and Miles Gale, 6 August 1745, Chowan Co., N. C.

VAIL, Mary (widow) and Barnard Rogers, 5 March 1767, Chowan Co., N. C.

VALE, John D. and Elizabeth Alexander, 1788, St. Johns Parish, S. C.

VALENTINE, Sarah and George Morgan, 20 November 1785, Chowan Co., N. C.

VALK, Harriet and William Smith, 14 August 1801, Charleston, S. C.

VAN BRAAM, Miss and Brook Roberts, 9 January 1785, Charleston, S. C.

VAN CLEFT, Jane and Squire Boone, 11 July 1765, Rowan Co., N. C.

VANDERHORST, Arnoldus and Elizabeth Raven, 5 March 1771, Charleston, S. C.

VANDERHORST, Elias and Elizabeth Cooper, 12 July 1763, Charleston, S. C.

VANDERHORST, John and Dorothy Waring, 14 April 1785, Charleston, S. C.

VANDER SLICE, John and Margaret Briggs (widow), 17 November 1752, Chowan Co., N. C.

VAN DYKE, James and Mary Walker, 15 October 1779, Tyrrell Co., N. C.

VAN DYCK, John Brevoort and Mary S. Christian, 10 March 1831, Charleston, S. C.

VANN, Azariah and Elizabeth Waddell, 3 April 1769, Tyrrell Co., N. C.

VANN, Edward and Sally Higgs, 7 February 1788, Bertie Co., N. C.

VANN, John and Ann Peterson (widow), 25 February 1752, Chowan Co., N. C.

VAN PELT, Martha and Robert C. McCord, 7 March 1827, Mecklenburg Co., N. C.

VAN PELT, Mary and Joseph Hayes, 15 August 1811, Mecklenburg Co., N. C.

VAN SANT, Matilda and Pickens Denny, 10 January 1856, Edgefield District, S. C.

VAN VANN, Martha and Micajah Exum, 29 December 1800, Edgecombe Co., N. C.

VARAMBANT, Angelica (widow) and James Roulain, 17 July 1768, Berkeley Co., S. C.

VARNER, Anne and Peter Steel, 15 August 1773, Santee, S. C.

VARNER, Elizabeth and Isaac Rembert, 24 May 1770, Santee, S. C.

VARNER, Henry and Rachel RRambert, 24 May 1770, Santee, S. C.

VARNER, Jane and Jacob McFarland, 14 April 1792, Mecklenburg Co., N. C.

VARNER, Rebecca and John Mitchell, 17 July 1804, Mecklenburg Co., N. C.

VAUNE, Lucretia and John Garrison, 12 February 1772, Rowan Co., N. C.

VAUX, Mary and James Gordon, 13 February 1764, Charleston, S. C.

VEITCH, William and Ann G. Brown, 4 December 1800, Charleston, S. C.

VENTURES, Mary and Walter Hubbell, 22 May 1790, Bertie Co., N. C.

VERAMBAUT, Francis and Miss LaTour, 28 July 1767, Charleston, S. C.

VERDIER, John M. and Elizabeth Grayson, 15 December 1785, Beaufort, S. C.

VEREEN, Rebecca and Joseph Bonhost, 25 April 1770, Santee, S. C.

VESEY, Charles and Mary Morris, 26 December 1799, Charleston, S. C.

VETTEL, Sally and David Johnson, 26 January 1800, Edgecombe Co., N. C.

VICE, Malissa and John Todd, 7 December 1865, Laurens Co., S. C.

VICKERS, Martha and William Hatcher, 21 February 1768, Edgecombe Co., N. C.

VIDEAU, Mary E. and General Marion, April 1786, Charleston, S. C.

VIERLING, Maria R. and Owen Rice, 18 March 1811, Salem, N. C.

VILLEPONTEUX, Betty and James Nelson, 12 August 1784, Charleston, S. C.

VINCENT, John M. and Polly White, 20 March 1811, Granville Co., N. C.

VINSON, Agnes and John Odom, 4 September 1798, Mecklenburg Co., N. C.

VINSON, James and (Mrs.) Elizabeth Porter, 31 December 1799, Charleston, S. C.

VINTZ, Margaret and William Byram, 7 December 1797, Mecklenburg Co., N. C.

VIPERALL, Jane and John Miller, 1 September 1843, Mecklenburg Co., N. C.

VIVINE, John and Mary Grant, 7 June 1771, Santee, S. C.

VIZIE, Mary and Bunyan Orr, 5 January 1797, Mecklenburg Co., N. C.

VOSS, William and Elizabeth Orr, 4 April 1799 Mecklenburg Co., N. C.

W

WADDELL, Elizabeth and Robert Davison, 2 June 1770, Tyrrell Co., N. C.

WADDELL, Elizabeth and Azariah Vann, 3 April 1769, Tyrrell Co., N. C.

WADDELL, Esther and Alexander Cathay, 17 February 1804, Mecklenburg Co., N. C.

WADDELL, Jane and Francis Beaty, 3 January 1806, Mecklenburg Co., N. C.

WADE, Eleanor (widow of Richard) and George Cook, 17 July 1777, Charleston, S. C.

WADE, Sallie and Daniel Johnson, 1 September 1820, Edgefield District, S. C.

WADE, Thomas and Mary Duncan, 4 March 1774, Chowan Co., N. C.

WAFF, Keziah and Richard Groves, 8 July 1779, Chowan Co., N. C.

WAFF, Lydia and Peter Mowell, 8 September 1779, Chowan Co., N. C.

WAFF, Mary and Robert Sanderlin, 3 May 1764, Chowan Co., N. C.

WAFF, Thomas and Sarah Jones, 7 April 1779, Chowan Co., N. C.

WAFF, William and Celia Seward, 17 December 1777, Chowan Co., N. C.

WAGG, Mary and Frederick Hargrave, 23 January 1790, Rowan Co., N. C.

WAGSTAFF, Elizabeth J. and William P. Mitchell, 10 November 1853, Guilford Co., N. C.

WALDRON, Miss and William Stone, 19 January 1754, Charleston, S. C.

WAIGHT, Abraham and Sarah M. Lowrey, February 1786, Charleston, S. C.

WAIGHT, Elizabeth and Nathaniel Barnwell, 1 December 1768, St. Johns Island, S. C.

WAIGHT, Isaac and Mary Jones, 13 November 1719, St. Andrews Parish, S. C.

WAKE, Jenny and Elijah McCullough, 10 November 1801, Mecklenburg Co., N. C.

WAKE, Sally and Jesse Riley, 22 June 1825, Mecklenburg Co., N. C.

WAKEFIELD, James and Sally Cannon, 24 November 1771, Charleston, S. C.

WALKER, Adaline M. and William Manson, 22 February 1825, Mecklenburg Co., N. C.

WALKER, Agnes and James Brown, 7 October 1795, Mecklenburg Co., N. C.

WALKER, Agnes and John McGee, 27 December 1788, Mecklenburg Co., N. C.

WALKER, Ann and Hugh Read, March 1809, Mecklenburg Co., N. C.

WALKER, Delilah and James Duncombe, 17 May 1785, Tyrrell Co., N. C.

WALKER, Edward and Elenor Taylor, 16 April 1763, Tyrrell Co., N. C.

WALKER, Elizabeth and Edward Martin, 19 January 1763, Charleston, S. C.

WALKER, Elizabeth and Jesse Cozart, 1786, Granville Co., N. C.

WALKER, Elizabeth and Alexander Montieth, 1 December 1790, Mecklenburg Co., N. C.

WALKER, Elizabeth and James N. Houston, 4 January 1798, Mecklenburg Co., N. C.

WALKER, Elliott and Daniel Dendy, 7 December 1853, Laurens Co., S. C.

WALKER, George and Mary Jenkins, 28 April 1757, Chowan Co., N. C.

WALKER, James H. and Isabella Meredith, 20 April 1831, Oxford, N. C.

WALKER, Jane and Samuel Rudd, 5 April 1821, Mecklenburg Co., N. C.

WALKER, Jeremiah and Hannah Daniel, 1775, Granville Co., N. C.

WALKER, John and Mary A. Williamson, 16 December 1784, Charleston, S. C.

WALKER, John A. and Jane Oliphant, 24 February 1774, Berkeley Co., S. C.

WALKER, Josiah and Elizabeth Stephens, 1802, Barnwell Co., S. C.

WALKER, Josiah N. and Mary Miller, 1845, Barnwell Co., S. C.

WALKER, Kitturah and John R. Fuller, 16 January 1863, Laurens Co., S. C.

WALKER, Louisa and Henry Chandler, 21 August 1856, Laurens Co., S. C.

WALKER, Louvenia and John L. Bolt, 11 August 1859, Laurens Co., S. C.

WALKER, Mary and James Van Dyke, 15 October 1779, Tyrrell Co., N. C.

WALKER, Mary and John Black, 1 September 1790, Mecklenburg Co., N. C.

WALKER, Mary and James Rea, 10 March 1814, Mecklenburg Co., N. C.

WALKER, Martha and James Blakeley, 29 May 1793, Mecklenburg Co., N. C.

WALKER, Nathaniel and Alcy Cain, 1762, Barnwell Co., S. C.

WALKER, Patty and Julius A. Jones, 10 July 1821, Mecklenburg Co., N. C.

WALKER, Peggy H. and Thomas Hunter, 15 October 1810, Mecklenburg Co., N. C.

WALKER, Rosanna A. and Thomas Hunter, 22 February 1832, Mecklenburg Co., N. C.

WALKER, Sarah and James Bigham, 19 July 1803, Mecklenburg Co., N. C.

WALKER, Solomon and Martha Mitchell, 1779, Granville Co., N. C.

WALKER, Steward and Martha Rhodes, 19 May 1778, Chowan Co., N. C.

WALKER, Susanna and William Mackey, 23 January 1779, Tyrrell Co., N. C.

WALKER, Tandy and Dorothy Bailey, 20 March 1856, Laurens Co., S. C.

WALKER, Warren and Letty Fuller, 15 December 1866, Laurens Co., S. C.

WALKER, William and Judith Rembert, 16 August 1764, Santee, S. C.

WALKER, William and (Mrs.) Jane Reid, 10 March 1801, Charleston, S. C.

WALKER, William E. and Lucy Hilliard, 8 May 1856, Nash Co., N. C.

WALKUP, Amelia and William Boyce, 8 January 1852, Mecklenburg Co., N. C.

WALL, Faithy and Roger Griffith, 14 February 1765, Edgecombe Co., N. C.

WALL, Jane and (Gen.) Benjamin H. Covington, 10 June 1802, Richmond Co., N. C.

WALL, Mary and William Covington, 26 July 1750, Anson Co., N. C.

WALL, Phebe and James Alsobrook, 20 March 1764, Edgecombe Co., N. C.

WALL, Sarah and James Watson, 4 May 1797, Charleston, S. C.

WALLACE, Eveline C. and Samuel Moore, 9 March 1830, Mecklenburg Co., N. C.

WALLACE, Ezekial and Lydia N. Knox, 19 April 1797, Mecklenburg Co., N. C.

WALLACE, Robert and Mary Messenger (widow), 1 August 1754, Chowan Co., N. C.

WALLACE, Jane and Jesse B. Johnson, 6 October 1858, Mecklenburg Co., N. C.

WALLACE, John and Elizabeth Slaughter, 4 September 1741, Chowan Co., N. C.

WALLACE, John and Ruth Barlow, 1797, Iredell Co., N. C.

WALLACE, Lydia B. and John H. Johnston, 3 February 1840, Mecklenburg Co., N. C.

WALLACE, Malinda and James Bradford, 12 December 1835, Mecklenburg Co., N. C.

WALLACE, Margaret and Robert McClure, 20 February 1793, Mecklenburg Co., N. C.

WALLACE, Margaret B. and R. C. Montgomery, 13 February 1855, Mecklenburg Co., N. C.

WALLACE, Mary and Jesse Baker, 27 August 1857, Mecklenburg Co., N. C.

WALLACE, Meriam E. and John M. Johnson, 30 April 1863, Mecklenburg Co., N. C.

WALLER, Ann and Nathan Parks, 8 November 1778, Santee, S. C.

WALLER, Byron and Martha Tadlock, 27 May 1834, Bertie Co., N. C.

WALLER, Elizabeth and John Harris, June 1687, Berkeley, N. C.

WALLER, Margaret and Jacobus Callion, 9 July 1769, Santee, S. C.

WALLER, Rode E. and William E. Kilbrease, 12 October 1853, Edgefield District, S. C.

WALLIS, Dinah and Etheldred Andrews, 30 January 1771, Tyrrell Co., N. C.

WALLIS, Elizabeth and David Mansfield, 25 March 1772, Chowan Co., N. C.

WALLIS, Elizabeth and (Major) Thomas Eaton, 27 March 1793, Orange Co., N. C.

WALLIS, Margaret and James J. Maxwell, 8 February, 1823, Mecklenburg Co., N. C.

WALLIS, Mary and (Col.) Allen Burnsides, 21 March 1859, Laurens Co., S. C.

WALLS, Ann and Patrick Johnston, 28 June 1794, Mecklenburg Co., N. C.

WALLS, Mary and George Crawford, 9 December 1856, Edgefield District, S. C.

WALSH, Edward and Emeline Bradfield, 28 December 1852, Edgefield District, S. C.

WALTER, Elizabeth and James Marteri, 20 December 1785, Chowan Co., N. C.

WALTER, John and Jenny Oliphant, 10 February 1774, Charleston, S. C.

WALTER, Polly and Peter Sinkler, 6 October 1784, Charleston, S. C.

WALTER, Thomas and Anne Lesesne, 26 March 1769, Charleston, S. C.

WALTERS, Ann (widow) and Richard Lambton, 27 November 1750, Charleston, S. C.

WALTON, Ann and Jesse Fletcher, 12 August 1793, Perquimans Co., N. C.

WALTON, Katherine and Abraham Hill, 7 January 1756, Chowan Co., N. C.

WALTON, Mary (widow) and Thomas Hunter, 13 June 1771, Chowan Co., N. C.

WALTON, Mary and Jacob Eason, 1 November 1774, Chowan Co., N. C.

WALTON, Monica (widow) and Simeon Stallings, 24 June 1772, Chowan Co., N. C.

WALTON, Peggy and John M. Robinson, 27 August 1813, Mecklenburg Co., N. C.

WALTON, Sarah (widow) and Frederick Lassiter, 12 March 1772, Chowan Co., N. C.

WALTON, Sarah and Jasper Wiseman, 1 August 1772, Chowan Co., N. C.

WALTON, Susannah and Amos Hinton, 6 September 1753, Chowan Co., N. C.

WALTON, William and Sarah Jones, December 1783, Bertie Co., N. C.

WAMER, William and Celia D. Moorer, 17 December 1818, Orangeburg Co., S. C.

WANNAMAKER, Jacob and Susan Shuler, 1740, Orangeburg Co., S. C.

WARD, Amarita and Edmond Standing, 9 October 1753, Chowan Co., N. C.

WARD, Amelia and Thomas Simmons, 1 December 1800, Johns Island, S. C.

WARD, Deborah and Louderick Ward, 19 August 1785, Chowan Co., N. C.

WARD, Elizabeth and (Rev.) Edmund Matthews, 15 January 1801, Charleston, S. C.

WARD, Emeline and John Seigler, 20 November 1833, Edgefield District, S. C.

WARD, Francis and Mary Garrett, 8 April 1779, Tyrrell Co., N. C.

WARD, Harriot and Thomas Tunno, 1 May 1800, Johns Island, S. C.

WARD, John and (Mrs.) Ann Brown, 21 November 1801, Charleston, S. C.

WARD, Joshua and Sarah McCall, 22 April 1762, Charleston, S. C.

WARD, Louderick and Deborah Ward, 19 August 1785, Chowan Co., N. C.

WARD, Mary (widow) and James Trotter, 27 February 1745, Chowan Co., N. C.

WARD, Melia and William Kemp, 13 November 1764, Tyrrell Co., N. C.

WARD, Sallie and William Morgan, 28 June 1821, Edgefield District, S. C.

WARD, Sarah and Thomas Williams, 25 July 1775, Tyrrell Co., N. C.

WARD, Solomon and Mary Simpson, 27 September 1784, Chowan Co., N. C.

WARD, Temperance and Smith Miller, 22 January 1839, Chowan Co., N. C.

WARD, William and Mary Freeman (widow), 29 November 1773, Chowan Co., N. C.

WARDEN, Elizabeth and (Dr.) Lionel Chalmers, 16 August 1766, Charleston, S. C.

WARDLAW, William A. (Major) and Iwanowna Tillman, 23 May 1840, Abbeville, S. C.

WARDLE, Elizabeth and Joshua Slade, 9 December 1769, Tyrrell Co., N. C.

WARDROP, Mary (Mrs.) and William Parsons, May 1785, Charleston, S. C.

WARHAM, Betsey and Oliver Cromwell, 15 July 1773, Charleston, S. C.

WARHAM, Nancy and Anthony Toomer, 4 August 1767, Charleston, S. C.

WARHAM, William C. and Mary Gibbes, 17 July 1784, Charleston, S. C.

WARING, Ann and Thomas Farr, 18 November 1773, Charleston, S. C.

WARING, Dorothy and John Vanderhorst, 14 April 1785, Charleston, S. C.

WARING, Grace and William Martin, 8 February 1772, Edgefield District, S. C.

WARING, John and Charlotte Williamson, 16 September 1770, Charleston, S. C.

WARLEY, Felix and Ann Turquand, 16 December 1784, St. Matthews Parish, S. C.

WARLEY, George and Elizabeth Giles, May 1786, Charleston, S. C.

WARLEY, Paul and (Mrs.) Martha Roche, 12 December 1799, St. Johns Parish, S. C.

WARNEDOW, Leonhard and Sirrah Hottow, 1742, Orangeburg Co., S. C.

WARNER, Eliza and Charles Love, June 1786, Charleston, S. C.

WARNER, Henrietta and George Kempton, 16 October 1799, Charleston, S. C.

WARNER, Henry and Jane Mitchell (widow), 13 January 1743, Prince George Parish, S. C.

WARNER, Jemima and Michael Husler, 19 December 1798, Rowan Co., N. C.

WARNER, John and Ann E. Ruger, 20 July 1784, Charleston, S. C.

WARNER, Magdalene and Conrad Yutzy, 16 July 1754, Orangeburg Co., S. C.

WARNER, Susanna and Thomas Anderson, 9 May 1795, Chowan Co., N. C.

WARNOCK, Joseph N. and Sarah Harvey, 8 November 1801, Charleston, S. C.

WARNOCK, Mary and John S. Bee, 21 May 1796, Charleston, S. C.

WARREN, Elizabeth and Flowers Michill, 1748, Orangeburg Co., S. C.

WARREN, Frances and Chesley Herndon, 13 September 1849, Orange Co., N. C.

WARREN, James and Mary Cherry, 21 June 1788, Bertie Co., N. C.

WARREN, Samuel F. (Rev.) and Lydia Perdriau, October 1784, Charleston, S. C.

WARSHAM, Betsy and Archibald Miles, 25 June 1804, Mecklenburg Co., N. C.

WARSHAM, Elizabeth and Thomas P. Massey, 24 October 1843, Mecklenburg Co., N. C.

WARWICK, Elizabeth J. and James S. Berryhill, 22 March 1866, Mecklenburg Co., N. C.

WARWICK, Hannah and Matthew Rodden, 26 May 1847, Mecklenburg Co., N. C.

WASHINGTON, Jane and James H. Ancrum, 16 November 1801, Sandy Hill, S. C.

WASSON, Barbara and Edeson Foster, 6 June 1798, Rowan Co., N. C.

WASSON, Elizabeth and Robert Hilton, 17 April 1787, Rowan Co., N. C.

WASSON, Mary and Robert Hall, October 1790, Rowan Co., N. C.

WATERIDGE, Margaret (of Virginia) and Job Butler, 29 January 1756, Chowan
Co., N. C.

WATERS, Jeremiah and Catherine Miller, 25 May 1778, Chowan Co., N. C.

WATFORD, Molly and John Oliver, 27 February 1788, Bertie Co., N. C.

WATIES, Thomas and Miss Glover, 19 January 1786, Ponpon, S. C.

WATKINS, Jane and Mattison Daniel, 2 February 1843, Laurens Co., S. C.

WATKINS, Margaret and Hancock Hatcher, 16 August 1763, Edgecombe Co.,
N. C.

WATKINS, Martha (widow) and John Hazard, 13 January 1752, Chowan Co.,
N. C.

WATKINS, Nancy and William Byram, 18 May 1818, Mecklenburg Co., N. C.

WATLINGTON, John and Susannah Swain, 5 March 1795, Charleston, S. C.

WATSON, Alexander and Sarah McLean, 12 January 1826, Robeson Co., N. C.

WATSON, Alice and John Bell, 26 April 1865, Mecklenburg Co., N. C.

WATSON, Elizabeth and John Morrison, 11 June 1801, Charleston, S. C.

WATSON, Hannah and Peter Comett, 8 July 1746, Charleston, S. C.

WATSON, Isham and Mary Hays, 15 February 1810, Marion Co., S. C.

WATSON, James and Sarah Wall, 4 May 1797, Charleston, S. C.

WATSON, James and Elizabeth E. Jones, 6 February 1840, Marion Co., S. C.

WATSON, Lepha and Henry Crouch, 30 May 1771, Charleston, S. C.

WATSON, Lucinda and Robertson Beagles, 17 March 1859, Laurens Co., S. C.

WATSON, Mary (Mrs.) and John Hunter, 12 June 1801, Charleston, S. C.

WATSON, Mary Elizabeth and Jesse Gibson, 17 February 1861, Marion Co., S. C.

WATT, Jane and Valentine Hope, 29 November 1787, Rowan Co., N. C.

WATT, Mary Ann and Robert L. Hood, 8 January 1849, Mecklenburg Co., N. C.

WATTS, Nancy and (Dr.) William Remington, April 1785, Charleston, S. C.

WAY, Mary and Joseph Macy, 17 September 1798, Guilford Co., N. C.

WAYNE, Kitty and George Ford, May 1784, Georgetown, S. C.

WAYNE, Richard and Elizabeth Clifford, 14 September 1769, St. Bartholomews
Parish, S. C.

WAYNE, William and Esther Trezevant, 7 May 1777, Charleston, S. C.

WEANRIGHT, William and Hannah Williams (widow), 1747, Orangeburg Co.,
S. C.

WEATHERBY, Lela and William McClintock, 16 July 1793, Guilford Co., N. C.

WEATHERFORD, Jesse and Mary Grice, 7 August 1845, Edgefield District, S. C.

WEATHERFORD, Pherebe and Nathan Naper, 21 May 1826, Edgefield District,
S. C.

WEATHERLY, Elizabeth and J. Evins, 31 January 1850, Marlboro Co., S. C.

WEATHERLY, E. and F. C. Bristow, 24 January 1850, Marlboro Co., S. C.

WEATHERLY, Thomas and Ezilla Sawyer, 10 April 1786, Tyrrell Co., N. C.

WEATHERS, Nancy and Samuel Boatright, 1 August 1792, Mecklenburg Co., N. C.

WEATHERS, Nancy and Moses Beaty, 1 December 1800, Mecklenburg Co., N. C.

WEATHERS, Rebecca and James Jackson, 28 January 1804, Mecklenburg Co.,
N. C.

WEAVER, Jane and Alexander Hext, 13 December 1743, Colleton Co., S. C.

WEAVER, Jane and Thomas F. Merritt, 22 September 1841, Guilford Co., N. C.

WEAVER, John B. and Mary Hundley, 26 March 1788, Bertie Co., N. C.

WEAVER, Rhoda and William Morris, 18 September 1803, Chowan Co., N. C.

WEAVER, Thomas and Ruth Roberts, 14 September 1726, Charleston, S. C.

WEAVER, Thomas and Martha Shaw, 8 January 1745, Charleston, S. C.

WEBB, Ann R. and Daniel Doyley, January 1784, Charleston, S. C.

WEBB, Anne and Joseph Clendening, 20 February 1787, Orange Co., N. C.

WEBB, Benjamin and Rebecca Pinkney, May 1763, Colleton District, S. C.

WEBB, Benjamin and Sarah Hanna Webb, 15 February 1774, Santee, S. C.

WEBB, Benjamin and Nancy Doyley, 16 March 1775, Ashepoo, S. C.

WEBB, Benjamin and Rebecca Pinckney, 16 September 1796, Charleston, S. C.

WEBB, Elizabeth and Ban. Gaillard, 19 February 1769, Santee, S. C.

WEBB, Elizabeth and Alexander Douglas, 20 November 1777, Chowan Co., N. C.

WEBB, Frances and Philip H. James, 20 February 1794, Franklin Co., N. C.

WEBB, James and Anne A. Huske, 1807, Wilmington, N. C.

WEBB, John and Polly Doughty, 3 January 1769, Charleston, S. C.

WEBB, John and Elizabeth Legare, 30 March 1786, Charleston, S. C.

WEBB, John and Susan Ann Lowry, 13 December 1855, Edgefield District, S. C.

WEBB, Mary and William Earl, 9 September 1779, Chowan Co., N. C.

WEBB, Mary E. and Baxter Davis, 1 October 1801, Granville Co., N. C.

WEBB, Robert and Ann Davenport, 28 April 1767, Tyrrell Co., N. C.

WEBB, Sarah Hanna and Benjamin Webb, 15 February 1774, Santee, S. C.

WEBB, Sarah and John Griggs, December 1783, Charleston, S. C.

WEBB, Thomas and Mary Herries, 31 August 1770, Santee, S. C.

WEBB, William and Deborah Jones, 5 February 1721, St. Andrews Parish, S. C.

WEBER, Samuel A. and Sarah A. Langdon, 20 November 1861, York Co., S. C.

WEBLEY, Edward and Anne Greenhow, 15 September 1763, Charleston, S. C.

WEBLY, Benjamin and Mrs. Hubbard, 21 September 1800, Charleston, S. C.

WEBSTER, Henry and Widow Ford, 18 May 1769, Charleston, S. C.

WEBSTER, Sarah and Jacob Bryan, 10 December 1762, Edgecombe Co., N. C.

WECHMAN, Catherine and Peter Fults, 10 August 1785, Rowan Co., N. C.

WECHTER, Magdalene and John Frederick Ott, 24 June 1750, Orangeburg Co., S. C.

WEDLIN, Anne Mary (widow) and Bernard Zeigler, 1753, Orangeburg Co., S. C.

WEEKLY, Elizabeth (widow) and Miles Riley, 22 September 1750, Orangeburg Co., S. C.

WEEKS, Margaret and Robert C. Barnett, 27 November 1827, Mecklenburg Co., N. C.

WEEKS, Martha and William Hackney, 17 August 1765, Edgecombe Co., N. C.

WEEKS, William and Milly Turner, 7 July 1797, Perquimans Co., N. C.

WEIR, Agnes and John Black, 10 August 1792, Mecklenburg Co., N. C.

WEIR, John and Mary Harlow, 11 August 1775, Chowan Co., N. C.

WELCH, Charity and Mathias Cook, 13 April 1763, Edgecombe Co., N. C.

WELCH, Elizabeth and William Hopkins, 12 August 1770, Charleston, S. C.

WELCH, Elizabeth and John Hendrix, 15 September 1788, Rowan Co., N. C.

WELCH, Margaret and George Raworth, 5 December 1799, Charleston, S. C.

WELCH, Margaret and Samuel N. Johnston, 13 November 1841, Mecklenburg Co., N. C.

WELCH, William and Kissiah Emmons, 7 January 1858, Laurens Co., S. C.

WELLS, Arnold and Hannah Hibben, 21 March 1797, Christ Church Parish, S. C.

WELLS, Eliza and Nathan I. Skinner, 16 January 1855, Edgefield District, S. C.

WELLS, Elizabeth and John Burdeth, 17 June 1852, Laurens Co., S. C.

WELLS, George (Dr.) and Marian Boyd, 3 February 1767, Chowan Co., N. C.

WELLS, Harriet E. and John Stoney, 4 April 1801, Charleston, S. C.

WELLS, Jane and (Rev.) Thomas Hill, 28 June 1785, Charleston, S. C.

WELLS, John and Elizabeth Mouzon, 16 August 1778, Santee, S. C.

WELLS, Martha and James Gordon, 5 August 1784, St. Thomas Parish, S. C.

WELLS, Stephen and Milly Burdett, 23 April 1848, Laurens Co., S. C.

WELLWOOD, Elizabeth and Robert Patterson, 19 September 1771, Chowan Co., N. C.

WELLWOOD, Elliner and Daniel Coleman, 23 May 1753, Chowan Co., N. C.

WELSHUYSEN, Amy and John Richardson, 29 March 1768, Charleston, S. C.

WENTZ, Rachel M. and William L. Black, 22 January 1841, Mecklenburg Co., N. C.

WENTZ, Sophia C. and Stewart Rice, 2 December 1839, Mecklenburg Co., N. C.

WERDEMAN, J. G. and Christina Strohacker, 5 December 1799, Charleston, S. C.

WERNER, Ann M. and Benjamin Perrey, 29 March 1800, Charleston, S. C.

WESCOTT, Stephen and Mary Mann (widow), 27 February 1771, Tyrrell Co., N. C.

WESLEY, Rachel and William Furnas, 1797, Bush River, S. C.

WESSON, William and Sarah Luton, 7 May 1744, Chowan Co., N. C.

WESTMORELAND, Eliza and Thomas McCorkle, 21 June 1827, Mecklenburg Co., N. C.

WESTMORELAND, Mary and Edwin Martin, 8 January 1829, Mecklenburg Co., N. C.

WESTON, Amos and Winnifred Mitchell, 23 September 1780, Bertie Co., N. C.

WESTON, Ann and Francis Butler, 3 December 1764, Chowan Co., N. C.

WESTON, Mary and John Basonan, 17 January 1789, Bertie Co., N. C.

WESTON, Plowden and Miss Holly Bush, 18 July 1762, Charleston, S. C.

WESTON, Plowden and Mary Anne Mazyck, 26 March 1775, Charleston, S. C.

WETHERINGTON, Rhody and Harmon Hancock, November 1799, Pitt Co., N. C.

WETSTINE, Henry and Barbara Morff (widow), 24 December 1750, Orangeburg Co., S. C.

WEYMAN, Polly and John Brewton, 1 January 1771, Charleston, S. C.

WEYMAN, Sarah (Mrs.) and Seth Lothrop, April 1785, Charleston, S. C.

WHATLEY, Eleanor and John Proctor, 17 March 1839, Edgefield District, S. C.

WHATLEY, Stephen and Sarah Lott, 1 November 1841, Edgefield District, S. C.

WHEATLEY, Sarah and William Bennett, 5 September 1766, Tyrrell Co., N. C.

WHEDBEE, Joseph and Thomasine Garrett, 27 July 1771, Chowan Co., N. C.

WHEDBEE, Joseph and Mary Williams, 18 October 1775, Tyrrell Co., N. C.

WHEDBEE, Mary and Nathan Hooker, 1781, Tyrrell Co., N. C.

WHELAR, Rachel and Richard Miner, 14 July 1793, Guilford Co., N. C.

WHETSELL, Joshua M. and Mary A. E. Horne, 19 December 1850, Colleton Co., S. C.

WHITACRE, Whitwell and Easter Sholar, 26 April 1790, Bertie Co., N. C.

WHITAKER, Benjamin and Sarah Godfrey, 20 May 1719, St. Andrews Parish, S. C.

WHITAKER, Jenny and Arthur Hunt, 17 September 1791, Rowan Co., N. C.

WHITE, Abigail and Richard Woodward, 23 January 1752, Chowan Co., N. C.

WHITE, Annie and Thomas Anderson, 25 July 1812, Union District, S. C.

WHITE, Ann Mann and Jordan B. Moss, 5 March 1827, Granville Co., N. C.

WHITE, Anthony and Hanna Barton, 30 August 1770, Santee, S. C.

WHITE, Blakeley and Elizabeth Bowquin, 2 March 1772, Charleston, S. C.

WHITE, Caroline and Robert L. Hunt, 3 December 1856, Granville Co., N. C.

WHITE, Christian and William Floyd, 10 March 1779, Chowan Co., N. C.

WHITE, Coleman Read and Selah Bradford, 13 March 1786, Granville Co., N. C.

WHITE, Coleman Read and Polly Cole, 26 September 1812, Granville Co., N. C.

WHITE, Eaton Jones and Catherine Spears, 4 January 1826, Granville Co., N. C.

WHITE, Edmund and Mary Haygood, 19 December 1821, Warren Co., N. C.

WHITE, Edmund and Mary Williamson Hilliard, 7 September 1833, Warren Co., N. C.

WHITE, Elizabeth and John Gibbes, 6 July 1760, St. Andrews Parish, S. C.

WHITE, Elizabeth and (Dr.) Michael Hackett, February 1765, Charleston, S. C.

WHITE, Frances Asbury and Ruben J. Moss, 4 October 1839, Granville Co., N. C.

WHITE, Frances L. J. and E. J. Looney, 28 January 1847, Granville Co., N. C.

WHITE, Hasky Ann Nelson and Elias Jenkins, 26 November 1830, Granville Co., N. C.

WHITE, Henry and Susan Boone, 5 December 1771, Santee, S. C.

WHITE, Hixey D. and George Winston, October 1819, Granville Co., N. C.

WHITE, Istal and Robert Hill, 28 December 1815, Mecklenburg Co., N. C.

WHITE, James and Mary Lawson, 1770, Iredell Co., N. C.

WHITE, John and Isabella Chappel, 8 June 1772, Santee, S. C.

WHITE, John and Hixey Cole (dau. of John and Susannah Cole), 30 November 1825, Granville Co., N. C.

WHITE, John B. and Anna R. O'Driscoll, 1 October 1819, Charleston, S. C.

WHITE, Joseph and Nancy Mann, 24 October 1799, Granville Co., N. C.

WHITE, Joshua and Rachel Allen, 7 January 1805, Granville Co., N. C.

WHITE, King and Martha Britt, 22 January 1788, Bertie Co., N. C.

WHITE, Margaret and Stephen Ford, 8 July 1779, Santee, S. C.

WHITE, Margaret E. and John M. Beaver, 16 January 1862, Mecklenburg Co., N. C.

WHITE, Martha and Isaac Legare (Jr.), 30 October 1782, Santee, S. C.

WHITE, Martha (Mrs.) and Samuel Dubose, 6 December 1801, Charleston, S. C.

WHITE, Martha and John Anderson, 5 December 1805, Union District, S. C.

WHITE, Mary and Robert Simons, April 1784, Georgetown, S. C.

WHITE, Mary and William Miller, 11 March 1831, Chowan Co., N. C.

WHITE, Mary S. and James Bell Floyd, 2 November 1852, Granville Co., N. C.

WHITE, Narcissa C. and Robert L. Hunt, 2 December 1856, Granville Co., N. C.

WHITE, Penelope and James Hornby, 22 September 1788, Bertie Co., N. C.

WHITE, Phillip and Ann Mann, 7 February 1797, Granville Co., N. C.

WHITE, Polly and John M. Vincent, 20 March 1811, Granville Co., N. C.

WHITE, Ruthy and John Crook, 2 November 1819, Granville Co., N. C.

WHITE, Sally and Isaac Chandler, 9 April 1771, Charleston, S. C.

WHITE, Sally Agnes and (Dr.) W. Coleman White, 19 September 1855, Warren Co., N. C.

WHITE, Sarah L. and William N. Alexander, 29 October 1855, Mecklenburg Co., N. C.

WHITE, Stephen and Patience Britt, 13 February 1795, Bertie Co., N. C.

WHITE, Susannah and Lemuel McGee, 20 September 1822, Granville Co., N. C.

WHITE, Thomas and Charity Gregory, 9 December 1785, Chowan Co., N. C.

WHITE, Thomas P. and Rebecca Kittrell, 2 September 1840, Granville Co., N. C.

WHITE, William G. V. and Maranda B. Hester, 6 September 1836, Granville Co., N. C.

WHITE, William P. and Nancy Mitchell, 18 October 1858, Granville Co., N. C.

WHITE, William R. and Franky Gill, 1830, Granville Co., N. C.

WHITE, William Wallace and Panthia Burwell Boyd, 12 October 1848, Warren Co., N. C.

WHITE, William Coleman (Dr.) and Sally Agnes White, 19 September 1855, Warren Co., N. C.

WHITEFORD, Rachael and Edward Brady, 27 September 1753, Orangeburg Co., S. C.

WHITEHEAD, Chloe and Erasmus Culpepper, 17 August 1765, Edgecombe Co., N. C.

WHITEHOUSE, T. and Catherine Marion, 7 May 1785, Charleston, S. C.

WHITEMAN, John and Mary Clements, 22 September 1814, Chowan Co., N. C.

WHITEMAN, Matthew and Abigail Peatt, 5 October 1777, Chowan Co., N. C.

WHITEMAN, Polly and Jesse Wilson, 26 April 1817, Guilford Co., N. C.

WHITESIDE, Rachel L. and Samuel L. Neely, 15 March 1839, Mecklenburg Co., N. C.

WHITFIELD, Martha (widow) and Isaac Glisson, June 1762, Tyrrell Co., N. C.

WHITFIELD, William and Rachel Bryan, 6 November 1741, Bertie Co., N. C.

WHITHEAD, Rebeckah and Norman Bigelow, 17 January 1787, Orange Co., N. C.

WHITHENBERRY, Thomas and Anne Nicholson, June 1785, Charleston, S. C.

WHITLOCK, Pamelia and John Harris, 28 November 1843, Edgefield District, S. C.

WHITAKER, Emma and James Turnbull, 8 November 1800, Charleston, S. C.

WHITTINGTON, Delaney and Joseph Mitchell, 4 January 1837, Guilford Co., N. C.

WIATT, Mary and Jonathan Elston, 9 August 1793, Rowan Co., N. C.

WIER, Margaret L. and David Allen, 10 January 1826, Mecklenburg Co., N. C.

WIGFALL, Benjamin and Martha Dutarque, 2 August 1771, Berkeley Co., S. C.

WIGFALL, Joseph and Sarah Shackelford, 7 January 1779, Santee, S. C.

WIGFALL, Sarah and Andrew Hasell, 21 March 1751, St. Thomas Parish, S. C.

WIGFALL, Susannah D. and (Dr.) Alexander Garden, 1788, Charleston, S. C.

WIGG, Ann and Robert Porteus, November 1771, Beaufort, S. C.

WIGG, Ann (widow) and (Col.) John Gibbs, 29 August 1760, Beaufort, S. C.

WIGG, Thomas and Ann Reeve (widow), 6 March 1732, Beaufort, S. C.

WIGGIN, Tillitha and Randall Mitchell, 14 January 1805, Mecklenburg Co., N. C.

WIGGINS, Betsy and John Riddle, 19 December 1839, Edgefield District, S. C.

WIGGINS, Patsy and Daniel Mitchell, 19 December 1804, Mecklenburg Co., N. C.

WIGGINS, Sarah and Isham Holloman, 29 October 1799, Edgecombe Co., N. C.

WIGGINS, Samuel and Ann Hoskins, 2 June 1770, Chowan Co., N. C.

WIGGINS, Susan and William Gray, 16 February 1852, Edgefield District, S. C.

WILBORN, Susan R. and J. W. Scott, 1 June 1856, Edgefield District, S. C.

WILCOX, Joseph and Elinor Miller, 1 September 1743, Charleston, S. C.

WILCUT, Susan and Saxton Allison, 26 February 1857, Laurens Co., S. C.

WILD, Martha and James Furse, 1 September 1801, Barnwell District, S. C.

WILDER, Absolem and Ann Britt, 8 July 1779, Bertie Co., N. C.

WILDER, Michael and Prudence Wilson, 29 December 1761, Chowan Co., N. C.

WILEY, Agnes and Alexander McKibben, 1 June 1796, Mecklenburg Co., N. C.

WILEY, Esther and John Robinson, 2 June 1795, Mecklenburg Co., N. C.

WILEY, James and Lurana Sutton, 5 September 1785, Tyrrell Co., N. C.

WILEY, Mary and Elijah Baker, 15 November 1798, Mecklenburg Co., N. C.

WILEY, Margaret M. and William P. Robinson, 11 May 1833, Mecklenburg Co., N. C.

WILEY, Mary and John Montgomery, 14 July 1827, Mecklenburg Co., N. C.

WILEY, Nancy and Joshia Nelson, 8 October 1825, Mecklenburg Co., N. C.

WILEY, Rebecca and Joseph Femey, 16 January 1764, Tyrrell Co., N. C.

WILEY, Rodia and Isaac Long, 10 September 1767, Tyrrell Co., N. C.

WILEY, Zilpah and James Gaylard, 26 February 1771, Tyrrell Co., N. C.

WILKES, Martha and James Patterson, 7 May 1796, St. Thomas Parish, S. C.

WILKIE, Ann E. and Samuel Frickling, 17 November 1801, Charleston, S. C.

WILKINS, Benjamin and Miss Barnes, 6 December 1767, Charleston, S. C.

WILKINS, Betsy and John Ruberry, 1 November 1772, Charleston, S. C.

WILKINS, Elizabeth and John Carruthers, 15 February 1745, Chowan Co., N. C.

WILKINS, John and (Mrs.) Deborah Gray, 3 January 1744, Chowan Co., N. C.

WILKINS, John (Jr.) and (Mrs.) Rachel Hassell, 10 July 1767, Chowan Co., N. C.

WILKINS, John and Mary E. Broughton, 6 January 1801, Prince William Parish, S. C.

WILKINS, Katherine and John C. Bains, 29 March 1757, Chowan Co., N. C.

WILKINS, Martha and Joseph Gladding, 21 March 1801, Charleston, S. C.

WILKINS, Rebecca and John C. Cleland, 10 October 1752, Chowan Co., N. C.

WILKINS, Rebecca and John Sloman, July 1786, Charleston, S. C.

WILKINS, William and Sarah Ming, 18 January 1741, Chowan Co., N. C.

WILKINSON, Ann and James Stobo, August 1786, St. Pauls Parish, S. C.

WILKINSON, Elizabeth and William Smith, 27 January 1779, Tyrrell Co., N. C.

WILKINSON, Elizabeth (Mrs.) and Peter Porcher, January 1786, St. Peters Parish, S. C.

WILKINSON, Francis and Susanna Wilkinson, December 1783, St. Pauls Parish, S. C.

WILKINSON, Kediah and William Keater, 8 July 1789, Bertie Co., N. C.

WILKINSON, Margaret and William Hendricks, 7 January 1794, Rowan Co., N. C.

WILKINSON, Mary and James Legate, May 1784, St. Pauls Parish, S. C.

WILKINSON, Sarah and William Middleton, 30 July 1747, Suffolk Co., S. C.

WILKINSON, Sarah and William Clement, 13 November 1799, Charleston, S. C.

WILKINSON, Susanna and Francis Wilkinson, December 1783, St. Pauls Parish, S. C.

WILKINSON, Susanna and (Rev.) James McElhenny, 13 March 1800, Charleston, S. C.

WILL, Catherine and John Burkhead, August 1784, St. Johns Parish, S. C.

WILLEMAN, Margaret and Angus Bethune, 14 January 1801, Charleston, S. C.

WILLIAMS, Betsy and Benjamin Rodden, 30 December 1830, Mecklenburg Co., N. C.

WILLIAMS, Caroline and B. B. Burton, 7 July 1857, Edgefield District, S. C.

WILLIAMS, Elizabeth and Henry Bonner, 14 June 1779, Chowan Co., N. C.

WILLIAMS, Elizabeth and Peter Groshon, 31 November 1784, Chowan Co., N. C.

WILLIAMS, Elizabeth and Thomas Huston, 20 December 1788, Rowan Co., N. C.

WILLIAMS, Elizabeth and John H. Read, 9 March 1835, Mecklenburg Co., N. C.

WILLIAMS, Esther and Edward Boykin, 2 April 1799, Edgecombe Co., N. C.

WILLIAMS, Fanny (widow) and Jonathan Boulton, 8 April 1773, Chowan Co., N. C.

WILLIAMS, Hannah (widow) and William Weanright, 1747, Orangeburg Co., S. C.

WILLIAMS, Hannah and Abraham Bennett, 24 December 1805, Mecklenburg Co., N. C.

WILLIAMS, Hannah and James Byram, 26 September 1808, Mecklenburg Co., N. C.

WILLIAMS, Hannah W. and Lewis Rodden, 7 September 1802, Mecklenburg Co., N. C.

WILLIAMS, H. R. and Mary Ann Holloway, 28 February 1840, Edgefield District, S. C.

WILLIAMS, Isham and Eliza Shrewsbury, June 1786, Charleston, S. C.

WILLIAMS, James and Jane Hislop, 29 June 1797, Charleston, S. C.

WILLIAMS, James G. and Elizabeth Tomlinson (widow), January 1774, Johns Island, S. C.

WILLIAMS, Jane and Daniel Hillard, 7 February 1786, Rowan Co., N. C.

WILLIAMS, Jean and Laird Burns, 30 January 1801, Mecklenburg Co., N. C.

WILLIAMS, John and Mary Baker, 16 June 1720, St. Andrews Parish, S. C.

WILLIAMS, John and Martha Collins, 19 May 1785, Chowan Co., N. C.

WILLIAMS, John and Mrs. Bonner, January 1786, Charleston, S. C.

WILLIAMS, John and Mary Chapman, 6 March 1801, St. Pauls Parish, S. C.

WILLIAMS, John and Caroline Alton, 8 May 1856, Edgefield District, S. C.

WILLIAMS, John and Martha A. King, 22 April 1855, Edgefield District, S. C.

WILLIAMS, Joseph and Betsey Spruill, 1780, Tyrrell Co., N. C.

WILLIAMS, Joseph and Elizabeth Turner, 10 January 1749, Berkeley Co., S. C.

WILLIAMS, Kate I. and M. W. Robinson, 23 October 1861, Mecklenburg Co., N. C.

WILLIAMS, Kitty and John Frierson, 1788, Charleston, S. C.

WILLIAMS, Margaret and John Davidson, 16 December 1751, Chowan Co., N. C.

WILLIAMS, Martha and Robert Burton, 1775, Granville Co., N. C.

WILLIAMS, Mary and Joseph Whedbee, 18 October 1775, Tyrrell Co., N. C.

WILLIAMS, Mary and James E. Powell, 16 July 1746, Port Royal, S. C.

WILLIAMS, Mary and Nicholas Cullens, 21 October 1757, Chowan Co., N. C.

WILLIAMS, Mary and Samuel Braswell, 30 November 1762, Edgecombe Co., N. C.

WILLIAMS, Mary and Nicholas Bryan, 9 June 1759, Santee, S. C.

WILLIAMS, Mary and Moses Austin, 23 March 1790, Orange Co., N. C.

WILLIAMS, Mary and Oliver W. Barnard, 4 March 1850, Surrey, Co., N. C.

WILLIAMS, Matilda and James Carroll, 11 June 1800, Mecklenburg Co., N. C.

WILLIAMS, May and John Phelps, 12 February 1766, Rowan Co., N. C.

WILLIAMS, Moses and Martha Clardy, 10 November 1842, Laurens Co., S. C.

WILLIAMS, Nancy and John Foster, 1 October 1774, Chowan Co., N. C.

WILLIAMS, Parthenie U. and Ludy Teague, 26 October 1858, Laurens Co., S. C.

WILLIAMS, Peggy and Hext Prioleau, 9 April 1775, Charleston, S. C.

WILLIAMS, Penelope and Thomas Baker, 12 January 1763, Edgecombe Co., N. C.

WILLIAMS, Perlina and Alfonso D. Mitchell, 15 August 1860, Guilford Co., N. C.

WILLIAMS, Polly and William Rodden, 6 November 1805, Mecklenburg Co., N. C.

WILLIAMS, Rhoda and Gabriel Helms, 23 February 1813, Mecklenburg Co., N. C.

WILLIAMS, Rachel and John Giles, 10 January 1782, Rowan Co., N. C.

WILLIAMS, Robert and Widow Gibbes, April 1759, Christ Church Parish, S. C.

WILLIAMS, Robert (Jr.) and Anne Roper, 7 February 1771, Charleston, S. C.

WILLIAMS, Sally and William Barnard, 20 October 1827, Surrey Co., N. C.

WILLIAMS, Sarah and Joseph Mitchell, 30 December 1779, Bertie Co., N. C.

WILLIAMS, Sarah and Robert W. Morrow, 4 February 1840, Mecklenburg Co., N. C.

WILLIAMS, Susanna and William Montieth, 13 November 1804, Mecklenburg Co., N. C.

WILLIAMS, Thomas and Sarah Ward, 25 July 1775, Tyrrell Co., N. C.

WILLIAMS, Thomas and Elizabeth Pollock, 18 June 1785, Chowan Co., N. C.

WILLIAMS, Tulle and Mary Potter, 8 October 1753, Chowan Co., N. C.

WILLIAMS, William and Sabra Holmes, 1 January 1835, Edgefield District, S. C.

WILLIAMSON, Amelia and Peter Ingalls, 1 September 1861, Mecklenburg Co., N. C.

WILLIAMSON, Champ and Charlotte Mazyck, 4 July 1765, St. Johns Parish, S. C.

WILLIAMSON, Charlotte and John Waring, 16 September 1770, Charleston, S. C.

WILLIAMSON, Constant and Joseph Fitch, 5 March 1718, St. Andrews Parish, S. C.

WILLIAMSON, Elizabeth and Charles Goodwin, 1788, Charleston, S. C.

WILLIAMSON, John and Mary Simpson, 19 November 1785, Chowan Co., N. C.

WILLIAMSON, Martha S. F. and L. M. Norwood, 31 July 1834, Mecklenburg Co., N. C.

WILLIAMSON, Mary and Edward Barnwell, 8 June 1783, St. Johns Island, S. C.

WILLIAMSON, Mary A. and John Walker, 16 December 1784, Charleston, S. C.

WILLIAMSON, Sally and Beverly Byram, 13 April 1807, Mecklenburg Co., N. C.

WILLIAMSON, Sarah R. and Hiram T. Capps, 23 March 1840, Mecklenburg Co., N. C.

WILLIAMSON, Sarah A. and Andrew H. Caldwell, Mecklenburg Co., N. C.

WILLIFORD, Martha and William W. Mitchell, 1 October 1832, Bertie Co., N. C.

WILLIS, Achsah and Amer Hiatt, 12 June 1816, New Garden, N. C.

WILLIS, Mary and William Leak, 1851, Laurens Co., S. C.

WILLIS, Mary and Alexander Alexander, 24 September 1851, Laurens Co., S. C.

WILLIS, Melmoth and Fanny Armstrong, 24 September 1850, Laurens Co., S. C.

WILLPLY, Benjamin (Dr.) and Sarah Magaw, 23 June 1771, Charleston, S. C.

WILLS, Mary and Richard Napier, 1772, Wilmington, N. C.

WILLS, Thomas and Margaret Swan, 26 August 1779, Chowan Co., N. C.

WILMER, T. R. and Sarah R. Gibbes, 28 January 1801, Charleston, S. C.

WILSON, Adeline and William M. Maxwell, 14 May 1835, Mecklenburg Co., N. C.

WILSON, Ann and Stephen Mazyck, 16 July 1785, Charleston, S. C.

WILSON, Benjamin and Mary Wilson, 20 September 1817, Mecklenburg Co., N. C.

WILSON, Catherine and George Stewart, 2 November 1778, Chowan Co., N. C.

WILSON, Catherine and Robert Harrison, 16 March 1841, Mecklenburg Co., N. C.

WILSON, Cornelia A. and R. B. Alexander, 19 September 1860, Mecklenburg Co., N. C.

WILSON, Deborah and Archibald Crockett, 12 January 1792, Mecklenburg Co., N. C.

WILSON, Dr. and Nancy Withers, 1788, Charleston, S. C.

WILSON, Elizabeth and Ebenezer Frost, 2 November 1775, Rowan Co., N. C.

WILSON, Elizabeth and Thomas Britain, 1 April 1777, Chowan Co., N. C.

WILSON, Elizabeth and William Hall, 7 January 1783, Rowan Co., N. C.

WILSON, Elizabeth and Arthur Hunt, 10 March 1790, Rowan Co., N. C.

WILSON, Elizabeth and David Enochs, 29 January 1794, Rowan Co., N. C.

WILSON, Elizabeth and John Bean, 7 March 1797, Mecklenburg Co., N. C.

WILSON, Elizabeth and Matthew McPherson, 28 September 1797, Gredell Co., N. C.

WILSON, Elizabeth and James Morris, 16 April 1804, Mecklenburg Co., N. C.

WILSON, Elizabeth M. and Thomas P. Ravenel, 11 February 1846, Pooshwee, S. C.

WILSON, Elvira C. and William J. Alexander, 2 December 1824, Mecklenburg Co., N. C.

WILSON, Frances and William Taylor, 9 March 1836, Granville Co., N. C.

WILSON, Hannah K. and Benjamin F. Alexander, 23 July 1823, Mecklenburg Co., N. C.

WILSON, Hugh and Eliza B. Toomer, 10 November 1830, Charleston, S. C.

WILSON, James W. and Eleanor C. Cook, 23 January 1836, Mecklenburg Co., N. C.

WILSON, Jane and David Miller, 22 May 1815, Mecklenburg Co., S. C.

WILSON, Jesse and Polly Whiteman, 26 April 1718, Guilford Co., N. C.

WILSON, John and Sarah Chalmers, November 1784, Charleston, S. C.

WILSON, John and Polly Rivers, 14 December 1769, Charleston, S. C.

WILSON, John and Mary Rake, 14 September 1774, Edisto, S. C.

WILSON, John and Margaret Ann McPheeters, 29 January 1841, Milton, N. C.

WILSON, John and Eliza Gibbes, 22 January 1811, Charleston, S. C.

WILSON, Katherine and Joseph Hall, 7 August 1788, Rowan Co., N. C.

WILSON, Lemuel and Martha Alston, 29 January 1752, Chowan Co., N. C.

WILSON, Lilly and James Conner, 13 August 1795, Mecklenburg Co., N. C.

WILSON, Lucretia J. and Jackson Adkins, 19 December 1847, Mecklenburg Co., N. C.

WILSON, Margaret and Isom Blaylock, 21 May 1839, Mecklenburg Co., N. C.

WILSON, Margaret E. and C. F. Caldwell, 2 December 1856, Mecklenburg Co., N. C.

WILSON, Margaret J. and Benjamin Brackett, 25 January 1837, Mecklenburg Co., N. C.

WILSON, Martha J. and Philip Miller, 23 June 1853, Lenoir Co., N. C.

WILSON, Mary and George Fritz, 3 January 1780, Rowan Co., N. C.

WILSON, Mary and John Haslett, 1 August 1799, Charleston, S. C.

WILSON, Mary (Mrs.) and Samuel Bowman (Major), 12 July 1801, Mecklenburg Co., N. C.

WILSON, Mary and Benjamin Wilson, 20 September 1817, Mecklenburg Co., N. C.

WILSON, Mary and William H. Gibbes, 21 January 1808, Charleston, S. C.

WILSON, Mary A. and David Blair, 20 August 1828, Mecklenburg Co., N. C.

WILSON, Mary L. and James M. Alexander, 9 July 1844, Mecklenburg Co., N. C.

WILSON, Mary L. and James N. Ross, 19 November 1845, Mecklenburg Co., N. C.

WILSON, Nancy L. and David J. Moore, 8 October 1845, Mecklenburg Co., N. C.

WILSON, Patsey and Enoch Brown, 18 March 1813, Mecklenburg Co., N. C.

WILSON, Polly and John Beaty, 20 May 1806, Mecklenburg Co., N. C.

WILSON, Prudence and Michael Wilder, 29 December 1761, Chowan Co., N. C.

WILSON, Rebecca and Andrew Jones, 24 October 1821, Mecklenburg Co., N. C.

WILSON, Robert and Charity Latham, 20 November 1800, St. Thomas Parish, S. C.

WILSON, Robert and Margaret Alexander, 3 December 1816, Mecklenburg Co., N. C.

WILSON, Robert (Rev.) and Mary S. Gibbes, 22 November 1859, Charleston, S. C.

WILSON, Robert (Rev.) and Ann J. Shadd, 22 April 1862, Charleston, S. C.

WILSON, Samuel (Dr.) and Mary Mazyck, 1788, Charleston, S. C.

WILSON, Sally and Peter Fayssoux, 7 January 1772, Charleston, S. C.

WILSON, Sally and (Rev.) James Latta, March 1775, Johns Island, S. C.

WILSON, Sarah and Thomas Harper, 12 February 1789, Rowan Co., N. C.

WILSON, Sarah and Benjamin McConnell, 1 October 1789, Mecklenburg Co., N. C.

WILSON, Sarah H. and William M. Maxwell, 8 June 1824, Mecklenburg Co., N. C.

WILSON, Sarah R. and (Dr.) Pinckney C. Caldwell, 12 December 1831, Mecklenburg Co., N. C.

WILSON, William and Polly Harvey, 5 January 1772, Charleston, S. C.

WIMBERLEY, Sarah and Malachi Hinton, 6 June 1764, Edgecombe Co., N. C.

WIMBERLEY, Zilpha and Amos Cotton, 23 October 1760, Edgecombe Co., N. C.

WINCHESTER, Ann and William Bradshaw, 8 August 1800, Mecklenburg Co., N. C.

WINCHESTER, Catherine and Samuel Abbott, 11 December 1802, Mecklenburg Co., N. C.

WINCHESTER, Rebecca and David Meguirt, 12 November 1833, Mecklenburg Co., N. C.

WINGWOOD, Sarah and Thomas Hamlin, June 1785, Charleston, S. C.

WINIGUM, Amy and Paul Bunch, 1748, Orangeburg Co., S. C.

WINN, Sarah and John Hughes, 19 May 1792, Columbia, S. C.

WINSTON, George and Hixey D. White, October 1819, Granville Co., N. C.

WISE, Margaret and David Eggender, 18 June 1785, Rowan Co., N. C.

WISEMAN, Jasper and Sarah Walton, 1 August 1772, Chowan Co., N. C.

WISEMAN, Mary and Jeremiah Green 3 October 1773, Rowan Co., N. C.

WISEMAN, Michael and Barbary Eggleston, 11 July 1799, Rowan Co., N. C.

WISEMAN, Polly and Daniel Hunt, 6 January 1797, Rowan Co., N. C.

WISH, Elizabeth M. and John Stewart, 22 December 1799, Charleston, S. C.

WISH, William and Ann Johnston, 25 May 1797, Charleston, S. C.

WITHAM, Solomon and Francis Merryan, 29 July 1748, Orangeburg Co., S. C.

WITHERS, Elizabeth and Robert Smith, 1788, Charleston, S. C.

WITHERS, Frances and Thomas Baker, 13 July 1800, Charleston, S. C.

WITHERS, Mary and Thomas Dunbar, 2 September 1784, Prince George Parish, S. C.

WITHERS, Nancy and Dr. Wilson, 1788, Charleston, S. C.

WITHERS, Richard and (Mrs.) Mary Arthur, April 1786, Christ Church Parish, S. C.

WITHERSPOON, Frances and William T. Hall, June 1863, Lancaster Co., S. C.

WITHERSPOON, Margaret and John Irwin, 11 February 1818, Mecklenburg Co., N. C.

WITHERSTON, John and Martha Peronneau, 11 August 1743, Charleston, S. C.

WITTER, Mary and William Alexander, 30 January 1801, Charleston, S. C.

WITSEL, John and Mary Oswald, 3 October 1800, St. Bartholomews Parish, S. C.

WITTY, Mary and Joshua Martin, 22 February 1796, Guilford Co., N. C.

WODROP, John and Ann McCall, 1 October 1800, Charleston, S. C.

WOLF, Catherine and James Russell, 10 December 1824, Mecklenburg Co., N. C.

WOLF, Elizabeth and John Bullock, 2 February 1789, Orange Co., N. C.

WOLF, Emeline and William J. Harris, 10 February 1843, Mecklenburg Co., N. C.

WOLF, Jacob and Veronica Tommen (widow) 10 December 1740, Orangeburg Co., S. C.

WOLF, Jacob and Appollonia Shuler, 1740, Orangeburg Co., S. C.

WOLFF, John (Dr.) and Elizabeth Hudgens, 22 July 1857, Laurens Co., S. C.

WOLFSKILL, Margaret and Joshua Hendricks, 8 April 1779, Rowan Co., N. C.

WOLPCADE, Mary and Joseph Edswards, 3 May 1785, Rowan Co., N. C.

WOOD, Benjamin and Miriam Smith, 8 November 1785, Chowan Co., N. C.

WOOD, Betsy and Edmond Howard, 9 March 1791, Rowan Co., N. C.

WOOD, Elizabeth and Thomas Hedgecock, 10 July 1783, Rowan Co., N. C.

WOOD, Hezekiah and Sarah Eubanks, 4 December 1856, Edgefield District, S. C.

WOOD, Jane (widow) and James Stirling, November 1747, Port Royal, S. C.

WOOD, Mary and John Cole, 27 May 1767, Chowan Co., N .C.

WOOD, Olivia and Daniel Deruraseux, 14 March 1747, Orangeburg Co., S. C.

WOOD, Priscilla and John Cox, 14 August 1794, St. Georges Parish, S. C.

WOOD, William and Peggy Morris, October 1786, Charleston, S. C.

WOOD, William and Sarah Clements, 4 October 1820, Chowan Co., N. C.

WOOD, Willy and William Smith, 10 February 1790, Bertie Co., N. C.

WOODARD, Samuel and (Mrs.) Sarah Purrell, 2 August 1750, Chowan Co., N. C.

WOODBERRY, John and Sarah Anderson, 26 May 1772, Santee, S. C.

WOODFORK, Lucy and George Hunt, 15 January 1781, Granville Co., N. C.

WOODLAND, Hanrahan and John Oliver, 6 April 1785, Tyrrell Co., N. C.

WOODLE, John A. and Susannah Sansom, 9 November 1800, Charleston, S. C.

WOODRUFF, Edward and Elizabeth Forshaw, 15 February 1800, Charleston, S. C.

WOODRUFF, James and Adeline Lockheart, 22 January 1851, Laurens Co., S. C.

WOODRUFF, Samuel and Jane Farrow, 4 March 1832, Edgefield District, S. C.

WOODS, John and Miss Pressly, 25 November 1853, Laurens Co., S. C.

WOODS, Mary and James Hackett, 14 October 1773, Rowan Co., N. C.

WOODS, Melmoth and Emily Dial, 8 May 1851, Laurens Co., S. C.

WOODS, Rachel and William Erwin, 28 November 1795, Rowan Co., N. C.

WOODS, Susanna and William H. Hart, 9 August 1830, Mecklenburg Co., N. C.

WOODSIDE, Elizabeth and John Farr, 14 January 1773, Rowan Co., N. C.

WOODSON, Judith and John Hampton, 9 June 1795, Rowan Co., N. C.

WOODWARD, Mary and John Gibbs, 25 July 1719, St. Andrews Parish, S. C.

WOODWARD, Mary and Isaac Chardon, 6 November 1735, Charleston, S. C.

WOODWARD, Richard and Abigail White, 23 January 1752, Chowan Co., N. C.

WOODWARD, Samuel and Mary Copeland, 17 September 1754, Chowan Co., N. C.

WORK, Sarah and Nathan Macy, 27 November 1794, Guilford Co., N. C.

WORKMAN, Anne and Ephriam Goss, 23 March 1795, Rowan Co., N. C.

WORLEY, Elizabeth and Richard Collins, 17 November 1769, Tyrrell Co., N. C.

WORLEY, Esther and Henry Bonner, 13 May 1749, Chowan Co., N. C.

WORLEY, Sarah and John Luten, 13 May 1749, Chowan Co., N. C.

WORLEY, Sarah and Henry King, 10 February 1789, Bertie Co., N. C.

WORSHAM, Violet and Wilson Archer, 29 October 1853, Mecklenburg Co., N. C.

WRAGG, Charlotte and John Poagg, 1 January 1763, Charleston, S. C.

WRAGG, Elizabeth and Peter Manigault, 4 June 1755, Charleston, S. C.

WRAGG, Henrietta and William Wragg, 5 February 1769, Charleston, S. C.

WRAGG, Joseph and Nelly Monzon, 23 October 1783, Georgetown, S. C.

WRAGG, Mary and John Matthewes, 4 December 1766, Colleton Co., S. C.

WRAGG, Samuel and Judith Rothmahler, May 1753, Charleston, S. C.

WRAGG, Samuel and Mary A. I'on, 19 February 1801, Charleston, S. C.

WRAGG, William and Henrietta Wragg, 5 February 1769, Charleston, S. C.

WRIGHT, Alexander and Elizabeth Izard, 6 April 1769, Charleston, S. C.

WRIGHT, Helen and Jemmitt Cobley, 30 July 1746, Charleston, S. C.

WRIGHT, Henry T. and Frances E. Kenney, 19 November 1844, Edgefield District, S. C.

WRIGHT, John and Rebecca Izard, 23 January 1797, St. Gorges Parish, S. C.

WRIGHT, Joshua G. and Susan Bradley, 1780, Wilmington, N. C.

WRIGHT, Martha (widow) and Samuel N. Holt, 4 August 1785, Charleston, S. C.

WRIGHT, Thomas and Polly Moncrief, 24 February 1751, Charleston, S. C.

WRIGHTEN, Charlotte S. and Alexander Placide, 1 August 1796, Charleston, S. C.

WROTON, Rebecca and Owen Riley Faust, 13 January 1825, Barnwell Co., S. C.

WYATT, Henrietta and William Akin, 12 November 1801, Charleston, S. C.

WYATT, John and Elizabeth Schimpshire, 17 February 1768, Chowan Co., N. C.

WYATT, Mary and Francis Lafont, 16 July 1778, Chowan Co., N. C.

WYATT, Rachel and Sterling P. Howell, 6 January 1822, Mecklenburg Co., N. C.

WYLEY, Polly and William Griffin, 19 December 1784, Charleston, S. C.

WYMER, John Jacob and Anne Diedrick, 27 January 1756, Orangeburg Co., S. C.

WYNN, Mary and Adkins Massey, 18 February 1765, Tyrrell Co., N. C.

WYNNE, George and Ann Hassell, 7 April 1783, Tyrrell Co., N. C.

WYNNS, William and Zilpha Blanchard, 2 January 1752, Chowan Co., N. C.

Y

YANDEL, Charlotte and Sylvester McCall, 8 January 1840, Mecklenburg Co.,
N. C.

YANDELL, Elizabeth and John McCreary, 27 August 1799, Mecklenburg Co.,
N. C.

YANDELL, Elizabeth and V. W. Rice, 24 March 1856, Mecklenburg Co., N. C.

YANDELL, Mary W. and William McCord, 24 March 1801, Mecklenburg Co.,
N. C.

YATES, Sarah and John Rogers, September 1783, Charleston, S. C.

YEADON, Eliza A. and Henry W. Paxton, 16 December 1801, Charleston, S. C.

YEATS, Timothy and (Mrs.) Rebecca Young, 12 December 1743, Chowan Co.,
N. C.

YEO, William & Mary Smalaga, 17 June 1770, Santee, S. C.

YERWORTH, John and Polly Livingston, February 1748, Charleston, S. C.

YESENHUT, Ann and John Fairy, 5 February 1743, Orangeburg Co., S. C.

YETTON, Isaac and Ermenta Davis, 24 September 1814, Mecklenburg Co., N. C.

YETTON, Sarah S. and G. W. Alexander, 28 February 1855, Mecklenburg Co.,
N. C.

YOER, Eliza and Tristram Tupper, 3 December 1816, Charleston, S. C.

YONGE, Sarah and William Simmons, 3 March 1801, Charleston, S. C.

YOOTZY, Margaret and Adam Shnell, 1746, Orangeburg Co., S. C.

YORK, Christian and Barbara Heym, 18 May 1742, Orangeburg Co., S. C.

YORSTON, Jane and George Thomson, 13 December 1767, Charleston, S. C.

YOU, John and Antoinette Tardine, 8 January 1801, Charleston, S. C.

YOUMANS, Laurens W. and Mary Ann Stokes, 15 June 1865, Hampton Co., S. C.

YOUMANS, LeRoy F. and Mary E. Tillinghast, December 1857, Beaufort, S. C.

YOUNCE, Mary and John Fonts, 31 August 1769, Rowan Co., N. C.

YOUNG, Ann and John Inyard, 1 December 1865, Mecklenburg Co., N. C.

YOUNG, Benjamin and Liza Hunter, 24 February 1859, Laurens Co., S. C.

YOUNG, Eliza and John J. Morris, 12 August 1822, Mecklenburg Co., N. C.

YOUNG, Elizabeth and Lloyd Jones, 21 March 1757, Chowan Co., N. C.

YOUNG, Elizabeth and John S. Jennings, 21 May 1829, Orangeburg Co., S. C.

YOUNG, Henry and Ann Hill, 9 April 1754, Orangeburg Co., S. C.

YOUNG, Jane and Anderson Taylor, 20 December 1790, Granville Co., N. C.

YOUNG, Jesse and Kesiah Long, 1 June 1767, Tyrrell Co., N. C.

YOUNG, Keziah and Arthur Turner, 22 December 1779, Tyrrell Co., N. C.

YOUNG, Margaret and John Erwin, 25 April 1786, Rowan Co., N. C.

YOUNG, Margaret and John Adams, 15 November 1788, Orange Co., N. C.

YOUNG, Margaret and William Beaver, 25 July 1813, Mecklenburg Co., N. C.

YOUNG, Mary and Darby Henley, 21 September 1787, Rowan Co., N. C.

YOUNG, Mary and Samuel G. Hunt, 1855, Granville Co., N. C.

YOUNG, Rebecca and Christian Meyers, 12 April 1738, Orangeburg Co., S. C.

YOUNG, Rebecca (widow) and Timothy Yeats, 12 December 1743, Chowan Co.,
N. C.

YOUNG, Richard H. and Priscilla Gibbs, 11 February 1796, Hyde Co., N. C.

YOUNG, Sarah and Nathan H. Orr, 21 January 1833, Mecklenburg Co., N. C.

YOUNG, Sirrah and William Heart, 3 October 1750, Orangeburg Co., S. C.

YOUNG, William and Mary Linder, 2 July 1752, Orangeburg Co., S. C.

YOUNGBLOOD, William and Elizabeth Singleton, 16 November 1800, Charleston, S. C.

YOUNGE, Robert (Dr.) and Mary Peronneau, May 1786, Charleston, S. C.

YUTZY, Conrad and Magdalene Warner, 16 July 1754, Orangeburg Co., S. C.

Z

ZANGIN, Ann Barbara and Melchior Ott, 7 February 1746, Orangeburg Co., S. C.

ZEIGLER, Angelia (widow) and Christopher Miller, 4 November 1753, Orangeburg Co., S. C.

ZEIGLER, Bernard and Anne Mary Wedlin, (widow) 1753, Orangeburg Co., S. C.

ZELLWEGERIN, Rosina and Samuel Gandy, 14 March 1748, Orangeburg Co., S. C.

ZORN, Catherina (widow) and John Simmons, 1741, Orangeburg Co., S. C.

ZORN, Magdalene and Henry Crummy, 9 June 1752, Orangeburg Co., S. C.